THE
DENEYS REITZ
TRILOGY

*Adrift on
the Open Veld*

The Anglo-Boer War
and its Aftermath

1899 – 1943

THE DENEYS REITZ TRILOGY

Adrift on the Open Veld

The Anglo-Boer War and its Aftermath

1899 – 1943

COMMANDO ◆ TREKKING ON ◆ NO OUTSPAN

BY

DENEYS REITZ

EDITED BY T S EMSLIE

STORMBERG
PUBLISHERS

P O Box 3191 ◆ Cape Town ◆ 8000 ◆ South Africa

1999

Commando was first published by Faber and Faber Ltd in 1929
Trekking On was first published by Faber and Faber Ltd in 1933
No Outspan was first published by Faber and Faber Ltd in 1943

ISBN 0-620-24380-5

COVER DESIGN BY JOY WRENCH
SET BY EILEEN EAGER
PRINTED AND BOUND IN THE REPUBLIC OF SOUTH AFRICA
BY THE RUSTICA PRESS, NDABENI, WESTERN CAPE
D7414

This trilogy is published, a hundred years after the outbreak of the Anglo-Boer War, the Boer War, the South African War, the English War, or the Second War of Independence (Tweede Vryheidsoorlog), whichever you prefer, as a tribute to Deneys Reitz—a brave, adventurous, restless, stubborn, courageous and combative fighter to the bitter end; yet a tolerant, humane, loyal, broad-minded, loving and articulate burgher, son, lawyer, politician, father and conservationist—a South African par excellence.

It is also dedicated to the memory of the men, women and children who suffered and died in concentration camps, and the prisoners of war who returned from across the sea to find they had lost everything.

Editorial Note and Acknowledgements

The text of Deneys Reitz's trilogy has been left as intact as possible, to preserve the flavour of the time when each book was written. Thus Cape Town is 'Capetown' and expressions considered offensive today ('to-day') remain untainted by considerations of political correctness. In certain minor respects, however, the text has been altered to achieve consistency (occasionally also as a concession to my own sensibilities), but the original publications are substantially unaltered.

Marius van Blerck helped me obtain some of the photographs published in this book, and I am very grateful to him for his assistance. At the time of writing, he is busy completing a comprehensive work, *Pillars of Dust*, which he plans to publish in CD-ROM format towards the end of this year. In addition to the trilogy, it will include a translation of the original manuscript written by Deneys Reitz in South African Dutch while exiled after the Anglo-Boer War, telling a more raw, detailed and emotional story than *Commando*. It will also feature the complete diaries of Deneys Reitz after the Anglo-Boer War, through the 1914 rebellion, his extraordinary experience of the First World War, and his political career under General Smuts—with interesting insights into events that shaped the rise of the right wing in South African politics. During the Second World War, Deneys Reitz was in close touch with most of the Allied leaders, and his private comments on the conduct of the war and his anticipation of the iron curtain (which he did not live to see) make fascinating reading. Van Blerck's biography—also entitled *Pillars of Dust*—is included on the CD-ROM. This comprehensive portrait of Deneys Reitz has been researched and written over a period of some eight years, with access to material not previously available. Finally, the CD-ROM will contain much supplementary information on the Anglo-Boer War, the Reitz family and South African historical events during this fascinating period, illustrated by literally hundreds of photographs and maps. Further information is available from the following email address: marius@technologist.com.

Michael Reitz—grandson of Deneys—has kindly made additional photographic and other material available, and it has been a privilege as well as great fun to discuss with him the life and times of Deneys Reitz, and their significance in shaping the landscape of our own lives in South Africa. To Michael, and through him his father Jan, thank you for your open-hearted generosity and support.

I acknowledge the interest and assistance of friends and colleagues to whom I have probably become something of a bore on the subject of Deneys Reitz: John Butler, John Coulton, Archie Henderson, Charles Louw, Ray McClarty, Alasdair Sholto-Douglas, Karen Smalberger, John Watson, Ian Woods and Steve Woods.

Eileen Eagar's typesetting—as well as her longsuffering—are never taken for granted, and Joy Wrench's expertise in the field of design prompts the hope that people often *will* judge a book by its cover.

On a personal level, I hope readers will pardon me for taking this opportunity to pay tribute to some other great South Africans whose support, advice, friendship and influence I cherish: my father, Denis, whose death in 1974 can never erase his memory; the Hon Mr Justice BLS Franklin, Blen, a boyhood hero who also died too young but whose influence lives on; Dr Eric Woods, 'Babe', who always led the Magaliesberg rock-face ascents and whose leadership remains unchallenged; my father-in-law, Dr Jannie Graaff, who has an amazing ability to assume a large presence while at the same time keeping an incredibly low profile; and Colvin Henderson, a wonderful friend whose recent death is keenly felt.

To my wife, Annie, and children, Stephen, Clare, David and James, you make all the difference.

Trevor Emslie

Cape Town
South Africa
June 1999

Contents

Introduction

Adrift on the open veld—these are Deneys Reitz's own words describing the perilous state of his Boer commando invading the Cape Colony two nights before the desperate victory over the 17th Lancers that enabled them to survive. His words, adopted as the title of this publication, seem an apt metaphor for the state of the beloved country, then and subsequently.

Reitz was born in Bloemfontein, capital of the Republic of the Orange Free State, on 2 April 1882. He died in London, South Africa's High Commissioner to Britain, on 19 October 1944. The sixty two years of his life embrace a period as troubled and eventful as any for the people of southern Africa, their allies and adversaries. Deneys Reitz, whom fate seems to have singled out for a life of extraordinary action, adventure and—unlike so many of his peers—survival, gives us an absorbing account of events from the time the storm clouds of the Anglo-Boer War were gathering until the darkest days of the Second World War when he was Deputy Prime Minister of South Africa.

His father, Francis William Reitz, had been first Chief Justice, then President, of the Free State; and on the outbreak of war with Britain in 1899 he was Secretary of State in President Paul Kruger's cabinet in the Transvaal Republic. The seventeen year old Deneys—too young to be signed up for active service at the Field-Cornet's office—explained his frustration to President Kruger, whom he encountered in the company of his father. The old man growled, 'Piet Joubert says the English are three to one—*Sal jij mij drie rooi-nekke lever*?' Deneys answered boldly, 'President, if I get close enough I'm good for three with one shot.' The President took him straight to the Commandant-General's room and there Piet Joubert, head of the Boer army, personally handed the young Reitz a new Mauser carbine and bandolier of ammunition with which to go off to war.

This incident illustrates Deneys Reitz's access—at times—to the very heart of Boer leadership, presenting him with unique story-telling opportunities. Thus, in Pretoria for two days to give evidence in a trial, he walked with his father from the latter's office one morning and met Winston Churchill, a Boer prisoner who had requested an interview. Deneys tells how, at home that evening, his father read to the family from articles handed to him by Churchill with a request that he take them and, if there was nothing wrong with them, send them to the English newspaper for which Churchill was a war correspondent. Reitz senior pronounced the prisoner to be a clever young man, and Deneys—writing in Madagascar in 1903—declared that this was not far off the mark in the light of Churchill's subsequent escape. Such incidents continued throughout the remarkable life of Deneys Reitz.

He relates how, at home in Bloemfontein, scarcely a night passed without a reading from Burns or Scott, so deep was the love of his father—who had studied law there— for Scotland and Scottish literature. Indeed, President Reitz had translated several of the poems of Robbie Burns into Afrikaans (his handwritten translation of *Tam O'Shanter* is in the Burns Museum in Ayr), and the young Reitz tells how, when he was about seven, he thought his father had written the originals and that a fellow named Burns had translated them into very indifferent English! Thus the literary instincts of the young Deneys were nurtured and, by the end of the war, the accomplished guerrilla fighter was able to reflect and write so admirably about the momentous events in which he took part.

The brilliance of Deneys Reitz's story-telling is its simplicity, directness, and understatement. *Commando* is written with a sophisticated detachment remarkable in a twenty one year old *bittereinder* who refused to submit to British rule after the end of the *Tweede Vryheidsoorlog*, but who went on to help suppress the South African rebellion in 1914, command a Scottish regiment by the end of the First World War, and fight fellow-Afrikaner separatists in the 1920's and 30's. Reitz's love of horses; his loyalty to his father, his brothers and comrades; his disdain for theatricality (as on Dingaan's Day 1900—see chapter 15 of *Commando*); his addiction to a life of adventure; his passion to preserve the wild game of South Africa; his devotion to his sons with whom he shared the lore of the bushveld and of fishing in False Bay—all are unravelled in this fascinating story of adventure and struggle.

About a year after Deneys' death, his brother Hjalmar wrote as follows:

'Deneys always was a fighter. I can still vividly remember when he was about nine and I about fifteen, sitting astride on him and pinning his arms to the ground. A very awkward position, especially as I had to keep my face as far from him as possible, to prevent his butting me with his head; I sat on him in this way for at least twenty minutes and when my father ultimately separated us I told him, and it was the truth, that I could not release him as, if I did so, he would have attacked me with any stone or stick he could lay his hands on.

During the Anglo-Boer War he and I served in a German corps under Commandant von Goldeck, an Austrian officer. The men took a delight in egging him on against me, he was such a little bantam.

One day we had a terrific quarrel. He called me a 'bloody Hollander,' probably because I had just come from Holland and, without meaning to, used some or other high-Dutch phrase. There we were at it, hammer and tongs, I about twenty two and he about sixteen. The Germans were much amused, but seeing that it was serious they separated us, fortunately for him as I then thought, but as I later on came to realise, fortunately for me.'

A man's man to his fingertips, Deneys Reitz possessed a curiosity and a universality of vision that enabled him to see events in their broader context even while engaged in the fray. He fought the British, but did not hate them; he engaged in divisive politics, but transcended political divisions; he often found parliamentary debate monotonous, but he never wavered in his support of Smuts, his mentor and his leader.

After Deneys Reitz's death, General Smuts paid tribute to him as follows:

'The passing of Reitz comes as a shattering blow to me. His loss is a national one and will be mourned all over this country which he knew and loved as no other. In him passes one of the greatest South Africans of our generation and he leaves a record of achievement of which South Africa will remain justly proud. But, above all, I remember him as a dear friend and a comrade, the faithful companion through vicissitudes such as few have passed through. He was true, straight, upright, every inch of him, and he leaves a personal memory which I shall treasure all my days.'

Deneys Reitz does not simply write about war, rebellion, politics and adventure—he writes about people, shared hardships and fierce loyalty; and because he writes so entirely without rancour, he draws us in so that we almost feel we were there. His judgments have stood the test of time (his brother Hjalmar said: 'What annoys me so much about Deneys is that he is so often right') and the concluding words of his trilogy are:

> 'I wrote this book because I like setting down things seen and experienced and also because I wished to prove that in spite of our racial and political squabbles, South Africa is a country of good will and good temper, and has the hope and prospect of unity into a single nation in years to come.'

Commando, the international bestseller on the Anglo-Boer War, is the most familiar of Reitz's works, but *Trekking On* and *No Outspan* are equally enthralling, with anecdotal, often amusing accounts of historic events, as well as the private ramblings of a free spirit—adrift on the open veld of Africa. The decision to publish the trilogy in a single volume was motivated by the desire, one hundred years after the cry '*Opsaal kêrels*' first sounded across the veld of the Transvaal and Free State republics, with distant echoes in the Cape and Natal colonies, to recall vividly the story of two small nations' fight for independence and the continuing effect of that freedom struggle in the dramatic years up to the 1940's. The Deneys Reitz trilogy gives an astonishing continuity of insight into what Smuts called the 'wonderful romance of South Africa'.

In 1902 the Boers lost the war, but won peace on favourable terms—by 1907 General Louis Botha was Prime Minister of the Transvaal, a self-governing colony, and by 1910 he was Prime Minister of a united South Africa, including the Cape and Natal. Yet the bitterness of reaction to the suffering and loss of men, women and children in British concentration camps—more than double the total number of fighting men lost on commando—was to leave an indelible mark for decades to come. Who can deny that past brutality gave birth to future oppression, and that the wrongs of the second half of the twentieth century were closely bound up with those of the first?

T S Emslie

Cape Town
South Africa
June 1999

COMMANDO

A BOER JOURNAL
OF THE BOER WAR

BY

DENEYS REITZ

WITH A PREFACE BY

GENERAL THE RIGHT HONOURABLE

J C SMUTS

*'A lamentable tale of things done
long ago—and ill done.'*

THIS BOOK IS DEDICATED
TO MY FATHER

FRANCIS WILLIAM REITZ

THE ONLY LIVING PRESIDENT
OF THE OLD SOUTH AFRICAN REPUBLICS

Victrix causa
Diis placuit
Sed victa Catoni

Contents

Preface

When Colonel Reitz asked me to write a preface to his book of Boer War memories, I at first hesitated, as I feared that I might be introducing a book in which I myself figured in some degree. However, on reading the manuscript, I find that I am only casually mentioned here and there, and have therefore no reason not to comply with his request.

It is a pleasure and a privilege to introduce this book to the reading public. To me it is a wonderful book—wonderful in its simplicity and realism, its calm intensity and absorbing human interest. Here is the book of the Boer War for which I have been waiting for the last twenty-five years and more. Many military books have been written on the Boer War—books full of interest and of valuable material for the future historian; but something else was wanted. The Boer War was other than most wars. It was a vast tragedy in the life of a people, whose human interest far surpassed its military value. A book was wanted which would give us some insight into the human side of this epic struggle between the smallest and the greatest of peoples. Here we have it at last. There is no strategy and little tactics in this plain unvarnished tale. Wars pass, but the human soul endures; the interest is not so much in the war as in the human experience behind it. This book tells the simple straightforward story of what the Boer War meant to one participant in it. Colonel Reitz entered the war as a stripling of seventeen years, fought right through it to the end, and immediately after its conclusion wrote down these memories. Of military adventures there is of course full measure. He passed through as varied a record of exciting experiences as have ever fallen to the lot of a young man. Indeed much of what is written in this book with such boyish simplicity may appear to the reader well-nigh incredible. But it is a true story, and the facts are often understated rather than exaggerated. The exciting incidents, the hairbreadth escapes, the daredevilry are literally true, and the dangers he passed through and courted are such as to make his unvarnished record read like one of pure romance. But there is here more than a record of war adventure. We have not only an unforgettable picture of mobile guerrilla warfare, but also an accurate description of life among the Boer forces. It is given, not in an abstract generalised form, but as the actual experience of one particular individual. As we read, we follow a true personal story, which is often stranger than fiction. The interest of the story deepens as it moves on from the heavy fighting in the Natal campaign under Botha, through the guerrilla warfare under de la Rey in the Western Transvaal, to the climax of marching and privation under me in the Cape Colony. The intimate picture gives us the inner truth of the war. We see how human beings react under the most terrible stresses to the passion of patriotism. We see how, under the influence of an ideal—in this case the ideal of freedom—the most ordinary human material rings true and rises superior to all danger and suffering and privation. And the effect is all the more striking because the story is so simple and unadorned and objective.

This book gives a wonderful personal record. But its wonder does not end with the book. The Boer boy who wrote this book was in the Wordsworthian sense the father of the man of after years. Let me add a few details to bring the account up to date. The boy left the country as an irreconcilable after the conclusion of the Boer War, as he and his family chose not to live under the British flag. He drifted to Madagascar, where these memories were written in the intervals of malaria and transport riding. There a letter from my wife found him, urged him to return and pointed out to him that he was no better than her husband, and if the latter could afford to serve his people under the Union Jack surely his young friend could do the same. The shaft went home; Reitz returned and was nursed back by her to health and peace of mind. He learnt to see Botha's great vision of a united South African people to whom the memories of the Boer War would mean no longer bitterness but only the richness and the inspiration of a spiritual experience. The loyalty of the Boer boy ripened into the broader loyalty of the South African. And I remember a night on the outbreak of the rebellion in 1914, when Reitz once more appeared before me, this time a fugitive, not from the British, but from his own people in the Free State who had gone into rebellion. Such tricks does high fate play upon us poor humans. He did his duty in helping to suppress the rebellion, and thereafter he served on my staff in the German West campaign, just as he had done in the Boer War; in the German East campaign he rose to command a mounted regiment, and in the later stages of the Great War he commanded the First Royal Scots Fusiliers, one of the oldest regiments in the British Army. He was severely wounded early in 1918, but returned to France in time to lead his battalion in the fierce battles that closed the great drama and after the Armistice he led his men to the Rhine.

Since the War, he has taken an active part in the public life of his country. He has been a Cabinet Minister and still is a Member of Parliament in which capacity he is serving under me as loyally as he did in the sterner days of which he writes.

This book is a romance of truth; but behind it is a greater personal romance, and behind that again is the even more wonderful romance of South Africa, to whom much should be forgiven for the splendour of her record during a period as difficult as any young nation has ever passed through.

J C Smuts
Pretoria
16 August 1929

Chapter 1

'Mem'ry's Tower'

We lived in the Orange Free State.

My father was Chief Justice in Sir John Brand's time and subsequently, in 1887, was himself elected President of the Republic.

Our home was at Bloemfontein, the State capital, and here my brothers and I grew up. There were five of us, two older and two younger than myself, and we led a pleasant Tom-Sawyerlike existence such as falls to the lot of few boys nowadays. We learned to ride, shoot, and swim almost as soon as we could walk, and there was a string of hardy Basuto ponies in the stables, on which we were often away for weeks at a time, riding over the game-covered plains by day, and sleeping under the stars at night, hunting, fishing and camping to our heart's content, and clattering home again when we had had our fill.

Sometimes my father took us with him on his long tours into the remoter districts, where there was more hunting and more camping, and great wapenshaws, held by the Boer commandos to do him honour. Our small country was a model one. There were no political parties, nor, until after the Jameson Raid of 1895, was there any bad blood between the Dutch and the English. We had no railways, and the noise of the outside world reached us but faintly, so that in our quiet way we were a contended community, isolated hundreds of miles from the seaboard.

In 1904, when I was twelve years old, we were taken to Europe. It was a wonderful experience for inland-bred boys to journey to the Coast, to cross the ocean in a ship, and to see the great crowds and cities of the old world. We went first of all to England, where we stayed for a while in London, marvelling at the things we saw. Thence to Amsterdam to visit the senior branch of our family, that had remained in Holland when our ancestors emigrated to South Africa long ago. The head of the old stock lived in a house on the Heerengracht; a wealthy man apparently, for he kept many servants and had fine paintings on his walls.

As our republic had taken its name from the House of Orange, my father was well received by the little Queen of the Netherlands, and the Court and people made much of us. Next, we travelled to Paris to meet Casimir-Périer, the newly elected President of the French. He took us to lay a wreath on the grave of Sadi Carnot, his predecessor, lately assassinated by an anarchist at Lyons. From there we went to Brussels to see Monsieur Jesslein, our Consul. His house stood in the rue de la Blanchisserie, and he told us it was the one in which the Duchess of Richmond had given her famous ball on the eve of Waterloo. We were presented to King Leopold, an old man with a hooked nose and a long white beard, who extended only his little finger in greeting, perhaps because we belonged to a republic.

From Belgium we went to Hamburg to take ship across the North Sea to Edinburgh, and from there to visit the Cathcarts at Auchindrayne on the River Doon. My father had studied law in Scotland and my grandfather before him had studied agriculture, and they had both spent much time at Auchindrayne, so that my father wished his sons in turn to carry on the tradition of friendship which for nearly a hundred years linked the two families.

My grandfather first went to Scotland in 1816. He met Sir Walter Scott, to whom he took a lion skin which the poet Thomas Pringle had sent from Capetown, and he became intimate with the great writer. In later days in South Africa, he loved to tell of their meetings and of the banquet at which he was present when Scott for the first time admitted that he was the author of the Waverley Novels. Both my grandfather and my father had returned to South Africa with a deep love of Scotland and Scotch literature, and at our home scarcely a night passed without a reading from Burns or Scott, so that we felt as if we were among our own people.

From Auchindrayne we went to London to meet Sir George Grey, who, as Governor of the Cape, had been a friend of my father many years before. My father used to say that if the English had sent more men like him to South Africa our history would have been a happier one, and although I was only a boy, and Sir George Grey a very old man, he made a deep impression on me—a something of inward beauty not easily described, but which I have not yet forgotten.

From London we sailed for South Africa.

On our return my brothers and I were received by our less fortunate playfellows like pilgrims safely returned from Mecca, so hazardous an undertaking did our journey seem to them in those days.

We took up our old carefree life once more, all unaware of the storm that was brewing between the white races in the Transvaal.

The Jameson Raid had not yet brought matters to a head, but there was trouble in the air. President Kruger and the Commandant-General, Piet Joubert, came frequently to Bloemfontein on official visits to my father, and we eagerly questioned them and listened to their stories of hunting and of the wars against the natives and the British of long ago.

Sir Henry Loch, Governor of the Cape, also visited us, as did Cecil Rhodes, a big florid man who cracked jokes with us boys, but on whose political aims my father looked askance. These two tried to prevent the Free State from entering into an alliance with the Transvaal, but they did not succeed, and a treaty was made with President Kruger wherein we agreed to stand by the Transvaal in case of war with England, a promise which the Free State loyally fulfilled.

My brothers and I did not understand the import of all this coming and going of noted men, and life ran on pleasantly enough, until in 1895 my father's health failed and he had to resign. We went to live at Claremont, a cramped suburb of Capetown, greatly missing our horses and the freedom of our wide Northern uplands.

When my father recovered from his long illness we settled in the Transvaal where he soon became Secretary of State under President Kruger.

My eldest brother, aged nineteen, was now sent to Europe to study law, and after awhile the rest of us were put back to school at Bloemfontein until the middle of 1899.

During our absence at the Cape the ill-fated Jameson Raid had taken place, and we found on our return that feeling was running high between the English and the Dutch; and even in the Free State, where differences of this kind had hitherto been unknown, there was so much ill will that people openly talked of driving the English into the sea, whereas previously we had not given these matters a thought.

By July (1899) the situation had become so serious that my father ordered us up to Pretoria, as war with England seemed inevitable. We said goodbye to Bloemfontein, the town where we had been born and bred and where we had spent such happy days, and journeyed north, leaving behind us the peace of boyhood, to face years of hardship, danger, and ultimate exile.

Chapter 2

On the Brink

When we reached Pretoria, affairs were moving to a climax. Peremptory notes had been exchanged between the Transvaal and the British Governments, and excitement was rising as each cable and its reply was published. Already the Transvaal capital was an armed camp. Batteries of artillery paraded the streets, commandos from the country districts rode through the town almost daily, bound for the Natal border, and the crack of rifles echoed from the surrounding hills where hundreds of men were having target practice. Crowded trains left for the coast with refugees flying from the coming storm, and business was at a standstill.

Looking back, I think that war was inevitable. I have no doubt that the British Government had made up its mind to force the issue, and was the chief culprit, but the Transvaalers were also spoiling for a fight, and, from what I saw in Pretoria during the few weeks that preceded the ultimatum, I feel sure that the Boers would in any case have insisted on a rupture.

I myself had no hatred of the British people; from my father's side I come of Dutch and French Huguenot blood, whilst my mother (dead for many years) was a pure-bred Norwegian from the North Cape, so one race was much like another to me. Yet, as a South African, one had to fight for one's country, and for the rest I did not concern myself overmuch with the merits or demerits of the quarrel. I looked on the prospect of war and adventure with the eyes of youth, seeing only the glamour, but knowing nothing of the horror and the misery.

I was seventeen years old and thus too young to be enrolled as a burgher. President Kruger himself solved this difficulty for me. One morning when I was at the Government buildings, I met him and my father in the corridor and I told the President that the Field-Cornet's office had refused to enrol me for active service. The old man looked me up and down for a moment and growled: 'Piet Joubert says the English are three to one—*Sal jij mij drie rooi-nekke lever?*' (Will you stand me good for three of them?) I answered boldly: 'President, if I get close enough I'm good for three with one shot.' He gave a hoarse chuckle at my youthful conceit and, turning to my father, asked how old I was. When he heard my age he said: 'Well then, Mr State Secretary, the boy must go—I started fighting earlier than that', and he took me straight to the Commandant-General's room close by, where Piet Joubert in person handed me a new Mauser carbine, and a bandolier of ammunition, with which I returned home pleased and proud.

I saw a good deal of the President in these days as I used to go with my father to his house on the outskirts of the town, where they discussed State matters while I sat listening. The President had an uncouth, surly manner, and he was the ugliest man I have ever seen, but he had a strong rugged personality which impressed all with whom he came in contact. He was religious to a degree, and on Sundays he preached in the queer little Dopper church he had built across the street, where I sometimes heard him.

There was Mrs Kruger too, whom I often saw with her pails in the yard, for she kept dairy cows and sold milk to the neighbours. Once she brought us coffee while we were looking at a picture of the statue of her husband that was being set up on Church Square. The President was shown dressed like an elder of the Church in a tophat, and the old lady suggested that the hat should be hollowed out and filled with water, to serve as a drinking-fountain for the birds. My father and I laughed heartily on our way home at her simplicity, but we agreed that it was decent of her to have thought of such a thing.

I also knew Piet Joubert, the Commandant-General, for, apart from his visits to Bloemfontein, his son Jan and I were friends, and I sometimes went home with him to talk about the coming war, and his father was generally there. He was a kindly, well-meaning old man who had done useful service in the smaller campaigns of the past, but he gave me the impression of being bewildered at the heavy responsibility now resting upon him, and I felt that he was unequal to the burden.

One afternoon he showed me a cable which he had received from a Russian society offering to equip an ambulance in case of war, and when I expressed my pleasure I was astonished to hear him say that he had refused the gift. He said: 'You see, my boy, we Boers don't hold with these new-fangled ideas; our herbal remedies (*bossie-middels*) are good enough.' Another time, when describing the festivities at the opening of the Delagoa Bay railway line, which he had attended as Commander-in-Chief, he told me that when the Portuguese paraded a thousand troops in his honour, he had gone down the ranks shaking hands with every one of the soldiers. I liked him very much personally, and to me he was always kind and fatherly, but I felt that he was unfit to lead armies, and it is a great pity that a younger man was not appointed in his place on the outbreak of the war.

And now the days were speeding by and in September of 1899 matters had come to such a pass that British troops were moving up to the western borders of the Transvaal and Free State, and other troops were on the water, while large Boer forces were mobilising on the various fronts. Committees and deputations from the Cape travelled up to make eleventh-hour attempts to avert the catastrophe of war, but it was clear that the die was cast and that neither side was in a mood for further parleying.

My eldest brother (named Hjalmar, after a Norwegian uncle) was away in Europe studying law, and my father had already cabled to him to return. My next brother, Joubert, named after the Commandant-General, was a year older than myself, and although he, too, was ineligible for burgher-rights, he intended volunteering for service, but the two younger ones were put back to school.

Joubert and I had made our preparations long before. Our horses were in good fettle and our saddlebags packed. My brother had a fine upstanding chestnut, and I had a strong little Basuto pony, and we were eager to be off. Many of the country districts had been called up, but thus far no Pretoria men had gone forward. At last, on September 29th, the first batch from the town was ordered to entrain for the Natal border. The moment we heard of this we took our rifles, fetched our horses from the stable, and within ten minutes had saddled up and mounted.

We said goodbye to our stepmother and her children, for my father had remarried years before, and rode up through the town to the Raadzaal to take leave of him. We found him closeted with the President and members of the Executive Council, but we went in and, when we explained why we had come, all rose to shake us by the hand. The old President gave us a solemn blessing, and my father, who had not expected this sudden departure, bade us goodbye in a husky voice and said he knew we would do our best.

From the Government buildings we galloped to the station, where we found a great stir. Hundreds of friends and relatives had come to see the contingent leave, but, in spite of the crowd on the platform and the loading of baggage and batteries, we were able to truck our animals, after which we lent a hand with the stowing of the ammunition and other work.

When all was ready the train pulled out to the sound of the Transvaal National Anthem. There were enthusiastic cheers and the waving of hats and umbrellas by those remaining behind, and we were off to the front in good earnest.

As for my brother and myself, we were not Transvaal burghers, nor had we been called out for service, but we automatically became soldiers of the Boer Army by virtue of having thrown our belongings through a carriage window and clambering aboard, little knowing on how long and difficult a trail this light-hearted enlistment was starting us.

Chapter 3

To the Frontier

Our officer, or Field-Cornet, as he was called, was Mr Zeederberg, a coach contractor, and the rank and file were mostly young fellows from the Civil Service and the legal offices and shops in the town. Few of them had ever seen war, or undergone military training, but they were full of ardour, and in spite of cramped quarters, and rough fare, we were like schoolboys as we clanked along.

After a monotonous journey of three days, often broken by interminable halts, we reached Sandspruit, a small station about ten miles from the Natal border, where we detrained. There were great numbers of burghers from the country districts already encamped on the plain, on either side of the railway line, and the veld on all sides was dotted with tents and wagon-laagers. On the left of the track stood a large marquee over which floated the *vierkleur* flag of the Transvaal, indicating General Joubert's headquarters. Both he and his wife were thus early on the scene, it being her invariable custom to accompany her husband in the field.

When we had detrained our horses, and helped to ground the guns, we moved away to where a halting-ground was assigned us. We off-saddled in the tall grass, and after building fires, and preparing supper, spent our first night in the open. For the next ten days we lay here enjoying the novelty of our surroundings, as if we were on a pleasure jaunt, rather than seriously awaiting the coming of war. One evening my brother and I received a pleasant surprise, for there arrived in camp an old native servant of ours, grinning from ear to ear at having found us. His name was Charley, a grandson of the famous Basuto chief, Moshesh. He had been a family retainer ever since I can remember, first in the Free State, and then in the Transvaal, whither he had followed us. Latterly he had been on a visit to Umbandine, King of the Swazis, but, learning that there was to be a war, he returned at once to Pretoria, and my father sent him on to us. He was more than welcome, for we could now turn over to him our cooking and the care of the horses, duties which we had been performing ourselves up to then; moreover, he had brought me a splendid roan which my father had sent me, as he feared that the Basuto pony would not be up to my weight.

Every morning my brother and I had our horses fetched from the grazing-ground and rode out to visit neighbouring camps and laagers, eager to see all that we could. We saw the stream of fresh contingents arriving daily by rail, or riding in from the adjacent countryside, and watched with never-ending interest the long columns of shaggy men on shaggy horses passing by.

At the end of the week there must have been nearly 15 000 horsemen collected here, ready to invade Natal, and we told ourselves that nothing could stop us from reaching the sea.

Our military organisation was a rough one. Each commando was divided into two or more field-cornetcies, and these again were subdivided into corporalships. A field-cornetcy was supposed to contain 150 to 200 men, and a corporalship nominally consisted of 25, but there was no fixed rule about this, and a popular field-cornet or corporal might have twice as many men as an unpopular one, for a burgher could elect which officer he wished to serve under, and could even choose his own commando, although generally he would belong to one representing the town or district from which he came.

In the Pretoria commando, we divided ourselves into corporalships by a kind of selective process, friends from the same Government department or from the same part of the town pooling their resources in the way of cooking utensils, etc, and in this manner creating separate little groups that in the course of time came to be recognised as military units. One of the number would be elected corporal, to act as the channel through which orders were transmitted from above, and much the same system held in all the other commandos. The commissariat arrangements were equally simple. Our Field-Cornet would know the approximate number of men under his command, and in order to maintain supplies all he needed to do was to send a party to the food depot, stacked beside the railway line, where they would break out as many bags of meal, sugar, and coffee as they considered necessary, load them on a wagon, and dump them in the middle of the camp for each corporalship to satisfy its requirements. The meat supply consisted of an immense herd of cattle on the hoof, from which every commando drew as many animals as it wanted for slaughter purposes. This system, though somewhat wasteful, worked fairly well; the men were plainly but adequately fed on much the same diet as they were accustomed to at home, and there was little grumbling. Officers and men had to supply their own horses, rifles, clothing, and equipment, and nobody received any pay.

Ever since the Jameson Raid the Transvaal Government had been importing large quantities of Mauser rifles from Germany, which were sold to the burghers at a nominal figure, and as great stores of ammunition had likewise been accumulated, the commandos were very efficiently equipped. The two republics had mobilised between 60 000 and 70 000 horsemen, at this moment distributed west and east, ready to invade the Cape Colony and Natal at the given word. This great force, armed with modern weapons, was a formidable fighting machine which, had it been better led, might have made far other history than it did.

How many troops the British had in South Africa I do not know, but they were pouring reinforcements into the country, and I think our leaders underestimated the magnitude of the task on which they were embarked.

So far as our information went in regard to Natal, the nearest British troops lay at the town of Dundee, some fifty miles away. This force we subsequently found to be about 7 000 strong, and still farther south at Ladysmith they had another 6 000 or 7 000 men, but with fresh troops being landed every day it was difficult to say how soon the scales would dip against us.

On the 10th of October a great parade was held in honour of President Kruger's birthday. We mustered what was then probably the largest body of mounted men ever seen in South Africa. It was magnificent to see commando after commando file past the Commandant-General, each man brandishing hat or rifle according to his individual idea of a military salute. After the march-past we formed in a mass, and galloped cheering up the slope, where Piet Joubert sat his horse beneath an embroidered banner. When we came to a halt he addressed us from the saddle. I was jammed among the horsemen, so could not get close enough to hear what he was saying, but soon word was passed that an ultimatum (written and signed by my father) had been sent to the British, giving them twenty-four hours in which to withdraw their troops from the borders of the Republic, failing which there was to be war.

The excitement that followed was immense. The great throng stood in its stirrups and shouted itself hoarse, and it was not until long after the Commandant-General and his retinue had fought their way through the crowd that the commandos began to disperse.

The jubilation continued far into the night, and as we sat around our fires discussing the coming struggle, we heard singing and shouting from the neighbouring camps until cock-crow.

Next day England accepted the challenge and the war began. Once more the excitement was unbounded. Fiery speeches were made, and General Joubert was received with tumultuous cheering as he rode through to address the men. Orders were issued for all commandos to be in readiness, and five days' rations of biltong and meal were issued. Flying columns were to invade Natal, and all transport was to be left behind, so my brother and I were obliged to send our native boy to the central laager, where the wagons were being parked until they could follow later.

My brother and I had joined hands with some friends from our Pretoria suburb of Sunnyside, and after a few days we had become merged in a larger body, of which five brothers, named Malherbe, were the leading spirits. We chose Isaac Malherbe, the eldest of them, to be our Corporal, and a better man I never met. We soon came to be known as 'Isaac Malherbe's Corporalship'. He was about thirty-five years old, dark complexioned, silent and moody, but we looked up to him because of the confidence which he inspired. His brothers were brave men too, but he stood head and shoulders above us all. After his death on the Tugela we found that he was a man of considerable means whose wife and two small daughters were left well provided for.

War was officially declared on October 11th. At dawn on the morning of the 12th, the assembled commandos moved off and we started on our first march.

As far as the eye could see the plain was alive with horsemen, guns, and cattle, all steadily going forward to the frontier. The scene was a stirring one, and I shall never forget riding to war with that great host.

It has all ended in disaster, and I am writing this in a strange country, but the memory of those first days will ever remain.

Chapter 4

We Invade Natal

We reached the border village of Volksrust before noon, and here the entire force was halted for the day, the Pretoria men camping beside the monument erected to commemorate the Battle of Majuba, fought on the mountain nearby in 1881.

The army was now split up to facilitate our passage through the mountainous country lying ahead. The Pretoria commando, about 300 strong, was attached to a larger force of 1 500 men under General Erasmus, nicknamed 'Maroola', with his brother, Commandant Erasmus, nicknamed 'Swart Lawaai' (Black Noise) as second in command. They were tall, swarthy men, clad in black claw-hammer coats, and semi-tophats, trimmed with crêpe, a style of dress and headgear affected by so many Boer officials as virtually to amount to insignia of rank. General Maroola had got his name during a recent native campaign in the Northern Transvaal, in the course of which he was said to have directed operations from behind a maroola tree, while Swart Lawaai's was a tribute to his dark complexion and quarrelsome temper.

Several other forces, more or less equal to ours, were carved out of the main body, and in the afternoon each of these new commandos was assigned its route. We spent an unhappy night in the rain. We had neither tents nor overcoats, so we sat on ant-heaps, or lay in the mud, snatching what sleep we could. It was our first introduction to the real hardships of war, and our martial feelings were considerably damped by the time the downpour ceased at daybreak. When it was light we moved out, shivering and hungry, for it was too wet to build fires.

Our road lay between high mountains, and the rain came down again in torrents. Far away to our right and left we caught an occasional glimpse of other forces marching through the mist, also making slow progress over the heavy country. We did not cross the border, but kept to a parallel road, and by dark we halted at a dismal spot, soon trampled into a quagmire by the multitude of horses. Again it rained all night, and again we could light no fires, and had to appease our hunger by munching biltong from our saddlebags.

It was a severe first test, for, in addition to the rain, a cold wind blew from the great Drakensberg range, cutting through us. Fortunately past troubles are soon forgotten, and when, towards sunrise, the weather lifted and we got under way, we were in good spirits again, with no thought of the unhappy night behind us.

After a long ride we emerged into open country and there, winding across the plain, ran the Buffalo River with the green hills and pleasant valleys of Natal stretching beyond. With one accord the long files of horsemen reined in, and we gazed silently on the land of promise. General Maroola, with a quick eye to the occasion, faced round and made a speech telling us that Natal was a heritage filched from our forefathers, which must now be recovered from the usurper. Amid enthusiastic cries we began to ford the stream. It took nearly an hour for all to cross, and during this time the cheering and singing of the '*Volkslied*' were continuous, and we rode into the smiling land of Natal full of hope and courage.

As soon as we were through the river, we spread out on a front of several miles, and went forward. Far away, on either side we could see the other forces moving abreast of us. There was not a man who did not believe that we were heading straight for the coast, and it was as well that the future was hidden from us, and that we did not know how our strength and enthusiasm were to be frittered away in a meaningless siege, and in the holding of useless positions, when our only salvation lay in rapid advance. The nearest English soldiers were still many miles to the south, so that, beyond sending out vedettes, the men went as they pleased, riding hither and thither to forage for supplies at the farmhouses we passed.

By nightfall we reached the hills near the village of Newcastle, and here we halted, our camp fires glowing far and near like the lights of a great city. Next morning we moved in columns through the streets, such of the inhabitants as sympathised with us waving encouragement, and the rest looking on in sullen resentment, as the long lines of horsemen went by. Beyond the village a halt was called to allow the other forces to come abreast, and then, at dusk, all commandos started on a forced march that lasted throughout the night, except for an occasional halt to rest the horses. By sunrise we had come within fifteen miles of the flat-topped mountain behind which lay the town of Dundee and the nearest English forces.

Contrary to expectation, we halted for the greater part of the day, and again, at sunset, were ordered to prepare for another night march. The commandos had by now closed in, and our Natal army was assembled practically in one body, making a brave show as we rode out. General Joubert had passed among us during the day, and we knew from him that he planned to surround the English troops that night. General Maroola, with the 1 500 men of whom we of the Pretoria Commando formed part, was to occupy the mountain overlooking the enemy's camp at Dundee, while the other forces were to complete the pincers on the flanks and rear. There was much excitement at the prospect of fighting, and even the heavy rain that set in after we started could not depress our spirits. The night was black, and our route seemed to lie chiefly over an open mud-bound plain, varied at times by more broken country in the passage of which there was a good deal of confusion and intermingling between the different commandos, but for all that, steady progress was made, and towards dawn Maroola succeeded in disentangling his commando from the other columns. Soon the frequent lightening revealed the steep side of a mountain, rising like a wall before us, and word was passed to commence the ascent, for this was the mountain from the top of which it was said one could look down on the English encampments on the other side. As there was almost certain to be a strong post holding the summit we climbed up in silence, expecting to be fired on at any moment, but when we reached the wide plateau above we found it deserted. This was so unlooked for that no one seemed to know what to do next, and, as it was still pitch dark, and the rain was coming down in torrents, we waited shivering in the cold for the coming of daybreak. When it grew light the rain ceased, but a mist enshrouded the mountain-top through which everything looked so ghostly and uncertain that we felt more at a loss than ever, and when Maroola was asked for orders he merely stood glowering into the fog without reply. We could not see fifty yards in any direction, but we knew that the English lines were immediately below us, for we could hear muffled shouts and the rumble of wagons, and we expected to be led down the face of the mountain to the attack. But General Maroola and his brother made no sign, and when President Kruger's son Caspar, who was serving with us as a private, and who for once in his life showed a little spirit, went up and implored them to march us to the enemy, Maroola curtly ordered him off.

He must have known what he was about though, for suddenly there came a violent cannonade, bringing us all to our feet as we listened to our first sound of battle.

We could see nothing, but heavy fighting had started close by, for the roar of the guns increased and at times we heard the rattle of small arms and Maxims. None of the fire, however, was directed at us, and so far as we were concerned nothing happened, and we fretted at the thought of standing passively by when others were striking the first blow of the war. After perhaps an hour the sound died down, indicating, although we did not know it at the time, that the English had driven the Vryheid men from Talana Hill with heavy losses. Towards midday the weather cleared somewhat, and while it still continued misty, patches of sunshine began to splash the plain behind us, across which we had approached the mountain overnight. And then, far down, into one of these sunlit spaces rode a troop of English horsemen about 300 strong. This was our first sight of the enemy, and we followed their course with close attention.

How this handful of men came to be right in the rear of the whole Boer Army I never heard, but they were on a desperate errand, for between them and their main body lay nearly 15 000 horsemen, and, now that the fog was lifting, their chance of regaining their base unobserved was gone. Already scattered Boer marksmen were appearing out of the mist, firing from the saddle as they came, and shepherding the soldiers still farther from their own people. Our men were by this time mostly crowding the forward edge of the mountain, hoping to catch sight of the English camp below, so that there were only a few of us who saw the troopers on the plain behind. Among these was our corporal, Isaac Malherbe, my brother and I, and five or six other Pretoria men, and, after watching the squadron below for a few seconds, we mounted our horses and rode down the mountainside as fast as we could go. Arrived at the foot, we raced across the veld in the wake of the English troops, guided by the sound of dropping rifle-shots ahead of us, for we could no longer see our quarry, as they had disappeared for the time being among some low foothills. Following on, we soon came to the scene of action. The English had gone to earth at a small homestead, and we were just in time to see the soldiers jumping from their horses, and running for cover to the walls of a stone cattle kraal, and among the rocks behind the farmhouse. Other burghers were flocking in, and soon the troops were completely surrounded. Across their front ran the dry bed of a spruit, and Isaac led us thither at once. This meant riding towards the enemy over the open, and now, for the first time in my life, I heard the sharp hiss of rifle-bullets about my ears, and for the first time I experienced the thrill of riding into action. My previous ideas of a battle had been different, for there was almost nothing to see here. The soldiers were hidden, and, except for an occasional helmet and the spurts of dust flicked up around us, there was nothing. We reached the spruit we were making for with one man wounded, and leaving him and our horses in the bed below, we climbed the bank and were soon blazing away our first shots in war.

The troops replied vigorously, but they were able to devote comparatively little attention to us, for by now the countryside was buzzing like an angry hive, with men arriving from every direction, and the end was but a question of time. After a few minutes a Creusot gun of the Transvaal Staats Artillery unlimbered and opened fire. The very first shell stampeded all the troop horses. The poor maddened brutes came tearing past us, and we leaped on our horses to head them off, but had to retreat, to avoid being trampled down as they thundered by. I managed to hang on to the skirt of the mob, and, by seizing its flying reins, brought a fine black Waler to a standstill. As I was looking over my prize I saw a white flag go up at the kraal, and another from the farmhouse, so I hastened to be present at the surrender. By the time I got there the soldiers had thrown down their arms and were falling in under their officers. Their leader, Colonel Moller, stood on the stoep looking pretty crestfallen, but the private soldiers seemed to take the turn of events more cheerfully. Officers and men were dressed in drab khaki uniforms, instead of the scarlet I had seen in England, and this somewhat disappointed me as it seemed to detract from the glamour of war; but worse still was the sight of the dead soldiers. These were the first men I had seen killed in anger, and their ashen faces and staring eyeballs came as a great shock, for I had pictured the dignity of death in battle, but I now saw that it was horrible to look upon. I was too elated, however, at having taken part in our first success to be downcast for long, and I enjoyed the novelty of looking at the captured men and talking to such of them as were willing. After a final look round, those of us from Pretoria rode back towards the berg, where we had left the rest of our commando, leaving the wounded to make their way as best they could to the nearest medical assistance.

It fell dark before we reached the foot of the mountain on which our men were, and, heavy rain setting in, we made for a deserted farmhouse, and here we spent a comfortable night, pitying our companions out in such weather.

At dawn the rain stopped, and before long we saw Maroola's force winding down the mountain, so we saddled our horses and made haste to rejoin them as they came down.

The men were cold and wet and hungry, and they looked with envy on our dry clothes and on the trophies in the way of swords and bayonets which we had brought with us. The weather at last was clearing and the sun came shining warmly through, so that all were soon in a more cheerful frame of mind in spite of Maroola's telling us that the encircling movement had failed and that the English forces in Dundee had got away towards Ladysmith. When his brother Swart Lawaai saw the horse I had captured the previous day, he made me hand it over to one of his Field-Cornets whose mount had gone lame, and I was fool enough to comply, for I still had some respect for authority, and that was the last I saw of my booty. This was the more unfortunate because the little Basuto pony that I had been using as a pack-animal had strayed during the night, and my brother and I were left without a led horse to carry our cooking-tins and supplies. We now felt our way round the corner of the mountain into Dundee town. As Maroola was not quite certain that the English evacuation was complete, he sent a patrol of ten men forward to investigate. My brother and I were of the party, and, while we were riding ahead along the base of a kopje, we saw half a dozen English soldiers running up the slope about 500 yards off. We shouted to them to stop, but as they paid no heed, we sprang to the ground and fired, bringing two men down. The others now halted, and, riding up, we found one dead and another badly wounded. The rest told us that they were a signalling party that had lost their way in the rains and mists of the preceding day, and they seemed greatly taken aback when they heard that their troops had evacuated Dundee.

We left the dead man lying where he fell and ordered the prisoners to carry their wounded companion into town, and as we were anxious to be first in, we left them and rode on.

By now Maroola's men were also making for Dundee, galloping hard behind us, but we were well in advance and easily got in before they came. They were not long, however, and soon 1 500 men were whooping through the streets, and behaving in a very undisciplined manner. Officers tried to stem the rush, but we were not to be denied, and we plundered shops and dwelling-houses, and did considerable damage before the Commandants and Field-Cornets were able to restore some semblance of order. It was not for what we got out of it, for we knew that we could carry little or nothing away with us, but the joy of ransacking other people's property is hard to resist, and we gave way to the impulse. My brother and I were hampered by the loss of our pony, but we brought away enough food for a royal feast, and after living on half-cured biltong for all these days, we made up for lost time.

There was not only the town to be looted, but there was a large military camp standing abandoned on the outskirts, and here were entire streets of tents, and great stacks of tinned and other foodstuffs, and, knowing the meagre way in which our men were fed and equipped I was astonished at the numberless things an English army carried with it in the field. There were mountains of luxurious foods, comfortable camp stretchers and sleeping-bags, and there was even a gymnasium, and a profusion of other things too numerous to mention.

The looting of Dundee was the work of General Maroola's men, for the rest of the Boer forces were moving east and west of the town in pursuit of the English garrison that was retreating to Ladysmith.

That afternoon Maroola managed to persuade his men to resume the advance, and he trekked off, but twenty men of our Pretoria commando were picked haphazard by him to remain behind to prevent further looting. I rode by just as he was making his selection and, his eye happening to fall on me, I was included in the party.

The old fellow probably thought he was doing me a good turn, but I was far from pleased, especially as my brother went on with the rest of the commando. After they were gone we searched around for one of the less-damaged houses, as we had no idea how long we might be marooned here and had decided to be comfortable. Towards evening I rode up again to the English camp to have another look at it and, wandering about, I came on the field hospital, flying the Geneva Cross. One of the tents was a large marquee for wounded officers, and here I saw General Penn Symons, the Commander of the English troops. He was mortally wounded and the nurses told me that he could not last out the night. Next morning, as I was again on my way up to the camp, I met a bearer-party carrying his body, wrapped in a blanket, and I accompanied them to where they buried him behind the little English chapel.

Now that the commandos were gone, and we were left in sole charge, we looked like settling down for some time, but that afternoon a dishevelled horseman rode into town with tidings of the disaster that had overtaken the Johannesburg men at Elandslaagte. He was in a state of great excitement and gave us such an exaggerated account of the fight, probably to excuse his presence so far to the rear, that I decided to go off in search of our commando, as I could see that there would be other fighting. The temporary Corporal in charge of us, one Paul de Villiers, forbade me to leave, as our instructions were to stay in Dundee until further orders, but I rode away within the hour.

As it was late when I started, darkness came on before I had got very far, and I spent the night at Glencoe Junction, where I found other fugitives from the Elandslaagte battle, from whom I gathered that it had been a pretty serious affair, in which we had lost two guns and many men killed and wounded, besides some hundreds of prisoners.

At the station, too, I saw the wife of General Kock, who commanded the Johannesburg commando. He had been badly wounded and taken into Ladysmith by the British, and the poor woman was hoping to get through their lines to see him. How she came to be here at all I do not know; probably she had accompanied the forces in the same way as the Commandant-General's wife, but I do not know whether she ever succeeded in reaching her husband, who died a few days later.

I rode on before daylight next morning, the memory of her tear-stained face giving me the first hint of what women suffer in time of war. I went down the Washbank Pass all by myself, and, although I was new to the country, I had no difficulty in finding my way, as the road was trampled and churned by the thousands of horsemen who had gone before.

During the two days while I was in Dundee, General Joubert had moved his whole army southwards, and was at this moment camped about ten miles from Ladysmith, where I rejoined after nightfall. As I approached I saw thousands of fires springing up on the hills, for the commandos were strung out over several miles, and it took me a long time to locate the Pretoria men in the dark. Stumbling about I came on General Maroola squatting by a fire, and, before I could slip away, he saw me, and testily demanded why I had left Dundee without his permission. I said I had come away to help him take Ladysmith, and, grinning sourly at my impudence, he packed me off. When at last I found my corporalship I was told that my brother had been missing since the day before, which troubled me, for we had promised my father to remain together if possible.

Next day our whole line moved forward, and a fine sight it was, as the masses of horsemen breasted the green slopes towards the final hills from which we could look down to Ladysmith. The English were standing on the defensive, for during the morning we had not come in contact with them and we could now see them building forts and redoubts in the low kopjes surrounding the town.

Neither side made any attempt to get to grips that day, but by night our men had occupied Bulwana and Lombaardskop, two prominent heights, and they were also holding a line that stretched around by Pepworth Hill and the ridges lying towards Nicholson's Nek. The following day was spent in preparation for the coming battle, but I was riding from commando to commando in fruitless search for my brother.

A collision with the British was imminent. They had 10 000 to 12 000 men, including those who had retired from Dundee, and we had 14 000 or 15 000, so that something was bound to happen.

That night the Pretoria commando took up a suitable position to the right of Pepworth Hill, where we lay on our arms till morning, expecting an attack at any moment, but sunrise came, and all remained quiet, from which we gathered that another day was to pass before the clash.

Towards eleven in the morning Piet Joubert, the Commandant-General, and his staff rode up to address us. He started by scolding the men for having looted a farm close by, and got so worked up that he forgot to tell us what the real object of his visit had been. We took his wigging in good part, but I am afraid no one treated our Commander-in-Chief very seriously. His staff was jocularly known as the 'Royal Family', mostly relations. There was a story going round of a burgher who saw a man ordering people about. The burgher asked him if he was an officer and the man replied: 'Of course I'm an officer, I am the Commandant-General's nephew.' This tale might have been true, for some of the 'Royal Family' put on airs, and we had no great love for any of them, although in fairness it must be said that none of the Commandant-General's own sons were on his staff, but were serving as ordinary privates. After Piet Joubert had ridden off, Mr Zeederberg, our Field-Cornet, set us to building breastworks in the line of hills forward of our halting-ground, and every man worked hard until sunset, for this was the position we were to hold when the enemy came against us.

Chapter 5

A Battle

When the men returned to the camp that evening after finishing their work, I was left on outpost duty with seven others, at the place where we had been building *schans* during the day.

The hill we were on formed the extreme right of the Boer line. From our station we looked over the plain leading towards Ladysmith, and to our right we looked across a broad valley, running between us and Nicholson's Nek, a flat-topped hill on the far side.

All remained quiet until three in the morning, when out of the darkness there came the sound of shots followed by confused shouting and trampling, but as the noise died down after a while we let things be. Shortly before daybreak, when it was growing light, two large mules came trotting up from below, their head-ropes trailing on the ground, and on bringing the animals to a halt we found that one of them carried on his back the barrel of a mountain gun, and the other a leathern box containing shell ammunition. They had obviously come from the British lines, and we only learned afterwards that a strong force of infantry had marched out of Ladysmith intending to get into our rear under cover of darkness, but that their battery mules had stampeded, throwing the troops into such disorder that, instead of achieving their object, they were obliged to take up a position on our flanks on Nicholson's Nek where, later in the day, I took part in the fighting that led to their capture.

Meanwhile it was sunrise, and we could now make out this force on the level top of Nicholson's Nek across the valley. The soldiers were working like ants, building sangars of stone, and we could see a knot of officers, standing around what looked like an outspread map, while other men were pulling a tarpaulin over a tree for shade.

At this time our commando, as well as the other commandos in the vicinity, was still peacefully at rest some 400 yards to the rear, out of sight behind a low ridge, and no alarm had yet been given, so we fired the first shots of the coming battle.

The range was too great for accurate shooting, but our volley had the effect of dispersing the officers, who hurriedly climbed up to join their troops on the hill-top above, where we could now no longer see any sign of life, as the men who had been working there had taken cover, and the plateau seemed deserted. Our shots had the further effect of arousing the commandos and, before long, horsemen came hurrying from the different camps to occupy the forward crest, and within twenty minutes there were hundreds of riflemen in position, facing the plain that runs to Ladysmith.

As for the English force on Nicholson's Nek, orders were sent to the Free State commandos, coming up from the west, to attack them, and by seven o'clock we heard the popping of rifle shots from that direction, but for the next hour or two we could spare them no thought, for tall pillars of dust were rising from Ladysmith, and soon long columns of infantry debouched into the plain before us. The Transvaal Staats Artillery had dragged a 6-inch Creusot gun ('Long Tom') up Pepworth Hill, a mile to the left, and they had installed several smaller guns there as well, and all these now began to fire on the approaching troops. I expected to see the shells mow great gaps and lanes in the enemy ranks, but instead of this our first shots were spent in finding the range, and by that time the columns had opened out, and, in place of the havoc which I had expected, the firing only caused smoke and local disturbances of earth, while the infantry came steadily on.

And yet a great spectacle was developing.

From where we held the sweep of the hills, we looked down as from an amphitheatre at every movement of the troops on the plain below—infantry hurrying forward in successive waves; guns being galloped up, and all the bustle and activity of a battle shaping before our eyes.

The soldiers, paying little heed to the shells that dropped amongst them, advanced without a halt, although many now fell dead and wounded, while in the rear, battery after battery unlimbered. We saw the horse teams ridden back, and then, to cover the progress of their troops, heavy fire was opened and there came the sound, once heard never forgotten, of shells tearing towards us and exploding around us, and overhead, with deafening concussions.

By now, what with the thunder of the British guns and of our own, the crash of bursting shells and the din of thousands of rifles, there was a volume of sound unheard in South Africa before. I was awed rather than frightened, and, once I had got over my first impression, I felt excited by all I saw and keenly joined in the firing. We were so successful that by the time the foremost infantrymen came within 1 200 yards of us, many fallen dotted the veld, and their advance wavered before the hail of bullets. They did not run away, but we saw them taking cover behind ant-heaps and such other shelter as the ground afforded. From there they directed a heavy fire on us, but their progress was definitely stayed, and our line held for the rest of the day.

Our casualties were not heavy, for we were well protected, but the guns on Pepworth Hill close by were being severely punished. The English batteries concentrated upon silencing our pieces there and we could see that the people were making heavy weather on the hill, for its summit was covered in smoke and flame, and the roar of the bursting shells shook the ground even where we lay.

For the past few days I had been without word of my brother, but now an artilleryman came racing up on horseback with a message from General Maroola to say that most of the guns were out of action. I recognised the man as an old acquaintance, and, when he saw me, he said my brother was at that moment serving as a volunteer with the crew of the big Creusot on Pepworth Hill. Concerned to hear that he was there, I ran back for my horse, which was standing under cover with the rest, and rode for the hill as fast as I could go, through shell and bullet fire. I reached the rear of the hill in safety, and certainly the dispatch-rider had not overstated the case. Six or seven dead artillerymen, some horribly mutilated, were laid out on a square of canvas to which they had been carried from above, and Ferdinand Holz, the German military doctor, was attending to a number of wounded also brought down from the emplacements.

An ambulance-van was standing near by with several of its mule team dead in their traces, and in the distance the native drivers were running wildly to the rear. At the guns above twenty to thirty shells at a time were bursting with terrific noise. I tied my horse to a tree and, after an anxious glance at the dead and wounded, to make sure that my brother was not of their number, I began to work my way up, crawling from stone to stone, and running forward whenever there was a lull in the fire, until I reached the sandbagged ramparts. Here I found my brother, and the surviving artillerymen, crouching behind the wall, unable to serve their guns under the storm that was lashing the position. It was mostly shrapnel, so that none of the guns were actually destroyed, but all were silenced.

More dead lay about and wounded men were sheltering with the rest in the lee of the parapet. I liked the spot so little that I tried to persuade my brother to return with me to our own commando, but, although he was somewhat shaken by this ordeal, he refused to come, and I had to admit that he was right. As there was no object in my remaining I bade him good-bye, and taking advantage of a slackening in the British gun-fire I made my way down. Below I found Dr Holz, lying in a heap, struck dead by a shell while helping the wounded. A fresh ambulance wagon came up just then and I lent a hand at loading the casualties before I sought out my horse, fortunately unscratched, and made haste to get away. I found the Pretoria men still holding the ridge on which I had left them, and on the plain before them the situation had not materially altered. The English troops showed no signs of advancing, and our commandos lay inactive while the guns pounded away, the battle resolving itself into an artillery duel, except that on the right we could hear the continuous crackle of musketry from Nicholson's Nek, where the Freestaters were engaged with the force that had come out of Ladysmith during the night.

Our Corporal, Isaac Malherbe, now suggested to those of us lying near that we should accompany him across the valley to Nicholson's Nek. About a dozen of us followed him to the horses, dodging among the rocks and trees to escape the shrapnel, and we rode down into the broad valley on the opposite side of which rose Nicholson's Nek.

We came under plunging rifle-fire as we moved across the floor of the valley, but we got under cover at the foot of the hill without loss. Here there was a party of Indian doolie-bearers, who had brought down some wounded English soldiers, our unexpected appearance among them causing considerable consternation. Ignoring them, we tethered our horses and started to climb the hill, going warily for fear of blundering into the wrong side of the fighting which we could hear above. The top of Nicholson's Nek is a broad level plateau dotted with outcrops of loose boulders, and, on breasting the rim, we were for a moment or two unable to gauge the situation. Rifles were cracking and bullets were whizzing, but there was no one in sight. Crawling forward, however, we came on small parties of Free State burghers lying behind rocks and other shelter in a rough line across the hill, and when we joined one of these groups they pointed out to us where the English troops lay posted, behind similar cover, thirty or forty yards away.

Both sides were maintaining a vigorous short-range rifle contest, in which the soldiers were being badly worsted, for they were up against real old-fashioned Free State Boers for whom they were no match in sharpshooting of this kind. Time after time I saw soldiers looking over their defences to fire, and time after time I heard the thud of a bullet finding its mark, and could see the unfortunate man fall back out of sight, killed or wounded. We joined in the fight, and for the next hour we slowly but surely pressed the English to the far edge of the hill.

As we gained ground we began to come on their dead and wounded, and realised what heavy losses we were inflicting, for behind almost every rock lay a dead or wounded man, and we knew that we should have possession of the hill before long.

Towards noon, as we were increasingly hustling our opponents, we heard a bugle ring clear above the rifle-fire, and at the same time a white flag went up.

Hundreds of khaki-clad figures rose from among the rocks and walked towards us, their rifles at the trail. We stood up to wait for them. The haul was a good one for there were 1 100 prisoners, mostly Dublin Fusiliers. The commando responsible for this came from the district of Heilbron in the Northern Free State. They were led by

Commandant Mentz, but the man who had chiefly urged on the fight was Field-Cornet Christian de Wet, afterwards the redoubtable guerrilla leader. I saw him here for the first time as he made his way from point to point during the action, and I well remember his fierce eyes and keen determined face.

Shortly after the surrender I was talking to some of the captured officers when I heard one of them exclaim: 'My God; look there!' and turning round we saw the entire British force that had come out against us on the plain that morning in full retreat to Ladysmith. Great clouds of dust billowed over the veld as the troops withdrew, and the manner of their going had every appearance of a rout. There were about 10 000 soldiers, but General Joubert had far more than that number of horsemen ready to his hand, and we fully looked to see him unleash them on the enemy, but to our surprise there was no pursuit. I heard Christian de Wet mutter: '*Los jou ruiters; los jou ruiters*' (loose your horsemen—loose your horsemen), but the Commandant-General allowed this wonderful opportunity to go by, a failure that cost us dear in the days to come.

Judging by the disorderly appearance of the retreat he could have driven the English clean through Ladysmith and out beyond, and he would have lost fewer men in the doing of it than we lost in the subsequent siege, but the English went hurrying back unmolested, save for an occasional shell from Pepworth Hill, where our guns had sprung into life again, and, with the whole Boer Army looking on, no attempt was made to exploit the victory that had been gained.

When we saw the troops falling back, and no chase given, we washed our hands of the business, and began to examine our own immediate surroundings on the hill-top.

Dead and wounded soldiers lay all around, and the cries and groans of agony, and the dreadful sights, haunted me for many a day, for though I had seen death by violence of late, there had been nothing to approach the horrors accumulated here.

Of our party under Isaac Malherbe not one had been hit, but the Free State men had eight or nine dead, and fifteen or twenty wounded. The English casualties were about two hundred killed and as many injured, the disparity being due to the fact that the English soldiers were no match for us in rifle-shooting. Whatever the defects of the commando system may be (and they are many) the Boer superiority in marksmanship was as great now as it had been in 1881. Having looked at the dreadful scenes on the plateau we parted from the Freestaters and, returning down the hill to our horses, rode back through the valley to the Pretoria commando, which we found in the same place in the line where we had left them, the men still holding the ridge, and their horses still under cover behind.

There was on this day, and for long after, much acrimonious discussion regarding the Commandant-General's failure to pursue when the English turned back, and I was told by old Maroola himself, that when officers came up to implore Piet Joubert to follow, he quoted the Dutch saying: 'When God holds out a finger, don't take the whole hand', meaning that the Almighty had sufficiently aided us for one day, and that it did not behove us to presume upon His bounty, a view which Isaac Malherbe said might be sound theology but no good in making war.

With that lack of vision that marred most of our doings in the early stages, we hailed the Ladysmith battle as a great victory, and we acted as if we had a broken and defeated enemy before us. It certainly was a notable success, but in the end it would have been better for us had the British smashed our line that day, for our leaders would then have followed a better plan of campaign than sitting down to a prolonged and ruinous siege.

Had the Boers made for the coast, instead of tying up their horsemen around towns that were of no value to them, the outcome of the war might have been different, but they sacrificed their one great advantage of superior mobility, and allowed splendid guerrilla fighters to stagnate and demoralise in the monotony of siege warfare, at a time when our only salvation lay in pushing to the sea.

Chapter 6

Ups and Downs

We rested on our laurels for a few days, each commando camping immediately behind the position which it had held during the battle.

Ladysmith was soon completely invested; on every hill and kopje lay a force of riflemen, and there must have been nearly ten thousand thus tied down who could have been put to far better use.

The weather remained fine, and we divided our time between watching the beleaguered garrison build forts and breastworks against our ultimate reception, and riding about the rear foraging for supplies.

After awhile we of Pretoria received orders to move forward to occupy a hill named Bell's Kop, facing a murderous-looking English construction that had gone up within the last few days. We rode out before light one morning to take up our new position, which, we were informed, was to be held by us as part of the cordon that was being drawn round the town. When we heard that this was to be our permanent abode, all hands turned to building shelters against the weather, and generally making our camp habitable. Neighbouring farms were laid under tribute and plundered of everything that could be turned to account. My brother rejoined us here. He had had enough of gunnery for the time being, and our native boy Charley also entered appearance, beaming with delight at having tracked us down. He travelled on foot all the way from the Transvaal border, and although several times arrested as a spy, he had talked and argued his way through until he found us. Needless to say, he was received with open arms, as we were once more able to turn over to him our duties of cooking, carrying water, horse-guard, etc, so my brother and I settled down to a life of ease, spending our time in sniping at the English outposts, or in riding to the neighbouring laagers.

Camp life was a pleasant existence. There were no drills or parades and, except for night picket and an occasional fatigue party to the railway depot to fetch supplies, there were no military duties. Our commando received many fresh drafts, and after a while varied from one thousand to fifteen hundred men, but discipline was slack, and there was a continual stream of burghers going home on self-granted leave, so that we never knew from day to day what strength we mustered.

Although we nominally stood under command of General Maroola and his brother, we seldom saw anything of them, for they lived at the head laager miles away, and to all intents and purposes we were a law unto ourselves.

Both Maroola and Swart Lawaai were incompetent leaders, but they were true men nevertheless. They sacrificed all they possessed, and when, later in the war, they were deserted by their men and bereft of all authority, they remained in the field as private soldiers, until the end.

We settled down to a stationary life, and if occasionally time hung heavily on our hands, conditions were otherwise comfortable enough. Our boy Charley proved a capable freebooter, and thanks to his foraging expeditions into the hills among the Zulu kraals where he made play with his descent from Chief Moshesh, our larder flourished and our mess was the envy of the rest of the camp.

After a week or two, tents were served out, and my brother and I shared one with the five good friends of our corporalship with whom we had kept company ever since leaving home. They were Charles Jeppe, a mine-surveyor, Robert Reinecke, Walter de Vos, Frank Roos and Samuel van Zijl, Civil Servants, but they were all killed before long.

So quiet were things around Ladysmith, that, as time went on, many burghers got ox-wagons brought down from their farms, and some even had their wives and families with them, which tended further to increase the spirit of inactivity that was gaining on the commandos. However, reports from all fronts were good, and we deluded ourselves into believing that everything was as it should be and, so far as my brother and I were concerned, we thoroughly enjoyed the business of besieging Ladysmith, and making regular excursions to see the guns fired into the town.

We went once every week to look up a Norwegian uncle or ours, named Theodor Thesen, serving with a Free State commando on the west side of the cordon. He had settled near the Vaal River many years before, and had been commandeered for service very much against the grain, as he held that we were bound to be defeated. I was surprised to see in what good part the burghers took his outspoken comment on their chances, but the real fighting Boer is ever a tolerant, good-natured fellow, and my uncle suffered no inconvenience for his views. Once, while we were chatting to him on a kopje occupied by a portion of the Kroonstad men beyond the Klip River, a considerable English mounted force moved forward to attack, or at any rate to demonstrate, before this position. Their guns unlimbered within range, and opened a cannonade, and their horsemen made as if to come at us. At the first alarm, the Kroonstad men ran from their tents, and directed such a hot fire that the cavalry wheeled round and galloped off; the guns were hooked up, and what looked like the promise of a lively battle fizzled out in a few minutes. Several shells had burst overhead, but as we were well sheltered behind rocks we thought little of it until we found, when the affair was over, that three men had been killed and half a dozen wounded, quite close to us.

On another occasion, while my brother and I were returning from a call on the Commandant-General at the head laager, we were overtaken by darkness, and heavy rain coming on, we tied our horses in the shelter of some trees and, seeing a mule-wagon standing near with a canvas sheet drawn over it and pegged down on either side for a tent, we lifted a flap and crawled into a corner where we slept snug and warm all night. When we woke at daybreak a man on a camp stool with a mug of coffee in his hand was eyeing us appraisingly, so we unrolled ourselves, and went forward to explain our use of his quarters. It was Mr Smuts, the State Attorney, my father's colleague on the Executive Council. He was here on some Government business, and, after a hearty laugh at our impudence, he ordered coffee and breakfast for the pair of us. Afterwards he became a fighting General, and I was to see much hard service under him in the Cape Colony nearly two years later.

I also recovered my little Basuto pony that had been lost near Dundee. I found him tethered to General Joubert's own wagon in the head laager, and I had an angry scuffle with some dispatch-riders, before I was able to undo the head-rope and take him away with me. The Commandant-General was absent and they promised me all sorts of pains and penalties when he returned, but I knew that among the Boers, ownership of a horse is almost sacrosanct, so I carried him off in triumph.

When next I met General Joubert and asked him how he came by my horse, he said that the pony was found straying on the veld by one of his staff, and that he had kept the little animal more as a pet than anything else.

The British now and then shelled our camp, upon which we would take cover at the first sign of trouble, and the damage was generally confined to a riddled tent or two, and perhaps a few horses injured. During one of these squalls our native boy was hit, and for weeks afterwards he walked about proudly displaying a fragment of metal taken from his side.

At this time I was sent for to give evidence in Pretoria against a man who had stolen money and clothing, which my father had given him to take down to my brother and myself. I travelled up by goods train, and the man was put in gaol. I was in Pretoria for only two days. Before returning to Natal I walked with my father from his office in the morning and we touched at the State School where a number of captured British officers were confined, one of whom had asked for an interview. We passed through the sentries into a large classroom where he was playing games with his fellow-prisoners. His name was Winston Churchill, a son of Lord Randolph Churchill, of whom I had often heard. He said he was not a combatant but a war-correspondent, and asked to be released on that account. My father, however, replied that he was carrying a Mauser pistol when taken, and so must remain where he was. Winston Churchill said that all war-correspondents in the Soudan had carried weapons for self-protection, and the comparison annoyed my father, who told him that the Boers were not in the habit of killing non-combatants. In the end the young man asked my father to take with him some articles which he had written for a newspaper in England and if there was nothing wrong with them to send them on via Delagoa Bay. My father read portions of the articles to us at home that evening, and said that Churchill was a clever young man, in which he was not far wrong, for soon after the prisoner climbed over a wall and escaped out of the Transvaal—how, I never heard.

When I got back to Ladysmith all went on as before, and only once during the first month of the siege did we indulge in any military operation. This was a movement against the fort opposite us, the same work that the English had built at the time of our arrival while we stood looking on. It lay eleven hundred yards away, across a level plain, and was known as the Red Fort, and I had spent many moments sniping at it.

Towards the end of November some three hundred men were ordered to attack it at dawn.

Our commando had of late been receiving reinforcements of inferior quality, mostly poor-whites from the burgher-right *erven*, the slum quarters of Pretoria, a poverty-stricken class that had drifted in from the country districts after the great rinderpest epidemic of 1896. They had become debased by town life, and had so little stomach for fighting, that their presence among us was a source of weakness rather than strength. The attacking force was drawn chiefly from these newcomers with Isaac Malherbe's corporalship, and one other of our better corporalships added to stiffen them. We left camp before daybreak, and assembled in a dry watercourse at the foot of Bell's Kop. From there we were to cross the intervening thousand yards of open, and rush the Red Fort at dawn.

Owing to various delays it grew light before we emerged from the spruit, and the soldiers must have observed some movement, for they opened fire before we could make a start. Assistant Field-Cornet de Jager was in charge of the undertaking. He was a poor-white himself, but a stout-hearted old warrior none the less, and seeing that we were discovered, he ordered us to advance, himself leading the way. Isaac Malherbe and his men followed, as did the other corporalship, but the remainder refused to budge from behind the safety of the bank. With de Jager at our head, about fifty of us ran forward, coming under heavy rifle-fire as we went. Visibility was still poor, so that we covered about four hundred yards without loss, until we reached a slight outcrop of rock, where we paused to take breath, and finding that we were not supported, called the attack off. The net result of our efforts was that, having got thus far, we could go neither forward nor backward, as the sun was over the horizon by now, and to advance or retire over the level bullet-swept zone was too risky, so we made the best of it by lying in the blazing sun without food or water for the next ten hours.

The troops in the fort were very wide awake, forcing us to keep our noses glued to the ground to such an extent that we dared scarcely stir without bringing down a hail of bullets about our ears. A man named Anderson was shot through both legs, and Robert Reinecke of our tent pluckily carried him back to the spruit on his shoulders, the English firing all around him, until they realised that he was helping a wounded comrade, after which they left him to go in peace, and were even sporting enough to allow him to return to us without a shot being fired.

We lay sweltering in the heat for the rest of the day, wishing ourselves well out of it, and the moment it began to get dusk we made a bolt, getting back over the plain without further casualties in spite of a hot fusillade. I had a lucky escape, for as we were nearing the dry course I stopped for a moment to see whether anyone had been hit during the retirement, when a bullet grazed my throat, stinging like a hot poker and raising an angry weal. I was more startled than hurt, and quickly followed down into the spruit bed. Here we slaked out thirst from water-holes in the ground, after which we trudged home to find the balance of the assaulting column of that morning comfortably installed in camp, and I got the impression that they rather looked on us as fools for our pains.

The day after this typical piece of bungling I walked across to Surprise Hill, an isolated kopje standing about six hundred yards to the right of our camp. Here the State Artillery had a howitzer gun in position which I often visited, to watch it bombarding the town. On this morning, as I was returning through the bush-covered valley, I saw a man named Mike Hands walking ahead of me leading a horse. As I was going forward to join him I was astonished to see a tall English soldier appear through the trees, his rifle at the ready. The soldier instantly fired at Hands, but hit the horse instead. The animal dropped and Mike fired. The soldier threw out his arms and fell back, and I found him dead with a bullet through his brain. How he came to be behind our lines was a mystery; possibly he had been scouting during the night, and had lost his way in the dark.

I was to know Surprise Hill better before long, but, in the meanwhile, camp life continued uneventfully. The besieged garrison contented themselves with shelling us at intervals, and, as they made no serious attacks, we assumed that they were marking time, for there was great activity on the south bank of the Tugela, twenty miles away, where the English Commander-in-Chief, General Buller, was massing troops to attempt the relief of Ladysmith.

He was reported to have forty thousand men with great numbers of guns, and on our side reinforcements had been brought from the Transvaal and Free State, and there were about fifteen thousand Boers holding the north bank of the river, from a point below Colenso Bridge to Spion Kop, many miles upstream. As for us around Ladysmith, we felt secure in the belief that whatever might happen on the Tugela, the troops in the besieged town at any rate would make no move, so picket and other duties were carried out in a very perfunctory manner.

During the daytime no guards were set at all, as there was always a sufficient number of men on the hill above amusing themselves with sniping to make sure of an alarm being given in case of need, and at night, although we went on outpost so close to the English sentries that we could hear them challenge each other, and sometimes exchanged shouted pleasantries with them, we did not take our watches very seriously.

We used to go on foot after dark in parties of twenty or so, and, on reaching neutral ground on the plain between ourselves and the enemy line, two men at a time would walk forward a short distance. Here they stood or sat on sentry-go while the rest of us pulled off our boots, spread out blankets and went to sleep until it was the turn of the reliefs. At daybreak we collected our belongings, and tramped back to camp in time for morning coffee, and thus far no untoward incident had ever marred these tranquil doings.

But this happy state was disturbed on the night of December 9th, for a detachment of two or three hundred soldiers came out of Ladysmith and, scaling Lombaardskop, destroyed the big Creusot gun ('Long Tom') standing there. The kop lay six or seven miles from our camp, so we heard nothing till next morning, but when we did, it gave us food for reflection, for it looked as if the pleasant immunity of our night duties was a thing of the past.

Our fears were well founded.

The next night Isaac Malherbe was to take out his corporalship to the usual spot on the plain. We mustered only twelve men, the remainder having been sent to the railway for supplies, and, as they did not get back before we had to leave, we started off without them for an eventful night.

Chapter 7

An Affair at Surprise Hill

Two other corporalships went on duty at the same time. One, under Corporal Tossel, a former police detective, was posted at the foot of Surprise Hill and the other a long way to our left. My brother and myself and Samuel van Zijl were the only members of our tent who were present, the other four being absent with the carrying party. As we walked along in the dark behind Isaac Malherbe we discussed the previous night's attack on the Lombaardskop gun, and I remember poor Samuel saying he hoped our turn would not come next. When we reached the usual halting-place two men were sent forward according to custom, and the rest of us turned in. My time to go on duty was 1 am. At about half past twelve I woke, and not thinking it worth while to fall asleep again I lay on my blanket watching the stars.

After awhile I distinctly heard the muffled sound of many footsteps in the direction of Surprise Hill, so I got up and walked forward to the two sentries to consult them. I found that they too had heard the noise, and the three of us listened for a few seconds to what were certainly men climbing the hill. We thought Corporal Tossel's men had taken fright at something, and were withdrawing up the slope towards the howitzer emplacement. This belief was rudely dispelled, for suddenly there broke from the summit of Surprise Hill a crash of musketry followed by wild bursts of cheering, and we realised that English troops were at the gun. As we stood undecidedly watching the hundreds of rifle flashes lighting up the hill-top, a vivid sheet of flame stabbed the darkness, followed by a tremendous roar, and we knew that our howitzer had been blown into the air. The two sentries and I rushed back to where our party were already on their feet. Isaac Malherbe now showed the stuff he was made of. Without a moment's hesitation he went straight for the danger point, the continued cheering of the English soldiery and the volley-firing serving as a guide. His intention was to join hands with Tossel's corporalship if he could find them, and then to prevent or delay the troops from returning to Ladysmith, until the whole of the Pretoria commando could come from camp, and so destroy or capture the intruders.

As it turned out, Tossel's corporalship had bolted when they heard the English coming. They had not only given them a clear field but had fired no warning shot to alarm the unfortunate gunners up above, who were taken unawares and all bayonetted. And as for the remainder of our commando in camp, they stood to arms all night, but Field-Cornet Zeederberg refused to risk the confusion, that he perhaps justly thought would ensue, if he tried to march his men in the dark to an unknown situation. So the twelve of us were left to our own devices.

As we approached we could hear by the firing and shouting that the main body of the attackers were still on the hill, but they had posted a string of pickets at the foot to secure their line of withdrawal back to the town, and before we had gone very far we ran into one of these. Isaac and I were a few yards in advance when a 'Halt! Who goes there?' was shouted at us from a few paces away. We simultaneously fired a shot apiece and ran forward. We came on a dead soldier, a sergeant, as I saw next morning from his badge, but the rest of the picket had run off into the night.

We went forward cautiously and soon we collided once more with another and stronger rearguard party. We were again challenged from close quarters, and, a heavy fire being aimed at us, we took shelter in a dry spruit bed that runs along the base of Surprise Hill. From here we returned the fire, until this outpost too gave us right of way, and we now began to file along the bed in order to seek out a convenient point from which to make a stand against the troops on the hill when they descended.

As we were going, a soldier, lying concealed in the grass on the bank above us, thrust over the muzzle of his rifle, and fired point-blank into us. My tent-mate, Samuel van Zijl, was walking immediately in front of me and I had my hand on his shoulder to steady myself on the uneven path. The bullet struck him full in the throat, and so near was the range that the discharge scorched his face, and set fire to his beard, which flared up for a moment like a fusee. He staggered, and then dropped. He was still alive, but I could hear from his laboured breathing that he was badly wounded, so I made him as comfortable as I could by placing his blanket under his head, before hurrying up the spruit to rejoin the others. By now the troops were descending Surprise Hill, and we could hear them clattering down the slope towards us. Their officers were blowing whistles, and calling out: 'A Company here!' 'This way B Company!' and so on, to collect their men. They seemed unaware that the road was to be disputed, for they made no attempt to conceal their progress, and there was laughter and repeated cries of 'Good old Rifle Brigade', and here and there we caught the gleam of matches being struck and the glow of cigarettes, to show how little they expected opposition.

In the meanwhile Isaac had selected a suitable spot on the bank, our faces towards Surprise Hill, our backs towards Ladysmith, and here we crouched, silently waiting for the oncoming troops.

From the sounds that reached us we judged them to be about three hundred strong and, with no sign of Tossel's men or of help from the commando, it dawned on us that we were in a pretty tight corner.

While the soldiers were still some distance away I ran down to see how Samuel van Zijl was faring. He was only just alive, and he asked me in a faint voice to turn him on his side to ease the pain, but as I did so I felt his body stiffen, and then go limp in my arms, and when I laid him down he was dead. I hurried back, for the laughter and talking were drawing very near. As I made up the course, a huge soldier, or he looked so in the dark, loomed up suddenly on the bank above. He lunged at me with his bayonet, but his insecure footing deflected the thrust and brought him stumbling against me. The man was at my mercy now, for I had my carbine against his side, but there came over me an aversion to shooting him down like a dog, so I ordered him to put up his hands instead, which he did at once, dropping his bayoneted rifle at my feet. I told him to sit down until I called him, a command which he so implicitly obeyed that I found him patiently waiting there next morning with a bullet through his leg from the cross-firing during the subsequent proceedings. This soldier must have come on ahead for when I reached my companions, the main force was just reaching the foot of the hill and approaching us in a body.

Isaac whispered to us to hold our fire and each man peered into the darkness until, about fifteen yards away, we saw a black mass dimly outlined and then, at his word of command, we poured volley after volley into their closely packed ranks, shooting as fast as we could work the bolts of our rifles. When the blast struck them they thought they were being fired at by their own rearguard pickets, for there were cries of 'Rifle Brigade! Rifle Brigade, don't fire!' but, discovering their error, a commanding voice called out 'Bayonets, bayonets', and they came at us like a wall. In spite of our small number we delivered such a volume of fire that the head of the column swerved to the left and slanted across our front to make the spruit lower down, and, although we continued our volleys, we could not prevent their going by.

Several times, however, parties of soldiers who had lost their way in the dark walked in among us, and of these we shot some and took others prisoners.

A Captain named Geo Paley came up to where my brother and I knelt, firing over the edge of the bank, and as he failed to halt when called upon, we both loosed a round and brought him toppling between us. Another time one of our men, Jan Luttig, was seized by some soldiers within a few yards of us, and there was a hand-to-hand scuffle in which he was stabbed with a bayonet and clubbed on the head with a rifle-butt. In the dark we could not make out what was happening, but when we heard his cry for help and ran up, his assailants were gone. A moment later I made out three soldiers in the bed of the spruit behind me and slipped down towards them. One nearly spitted me with a vicious jab of his bayonet, which passed between my arm and body, but before he could repeat the thrust I had him covered and they surrendered. One was an army doctor with a bullet-wound in his foot, and the other two said they were helping him along. I ordered them to remain in the bed of the spruit, where I found them in the morning.

About this time we heard four or five shots in rapid succession, followed by groans, from the direction where the troops were still crossing the spruit twenty or thirty yards off. We did not know the meaning of this, and only at daybreak did we find that we had listened to the death-cry of some of our men who had come from the camp to our assistance.

It was now towards three in the morning, and we had nearly exhausted our ammunition, so we sat quietly watching the tail of the column vanish into the darkness beyond, on its way to Ladysmith.

When daylight came at last, a grim scene met our eyes. Before us, within a radius of less than twenty-five yards, lay over sixty dead and wounded English soldiers, and as we walked forward among them we came on the bodies of three of our men who had not been with us originally. Two were dead and dreadfully hacked with bayonets and the third was at his last gasp.

These had been away to the railway depot with the fatigue party, and on their return had gallantly attempted to make their way to us when they heard the firing. They nearly reached us, but ran into the withdrawing soldiers, and were bayoneted before they could fire more than a few shots. Behind us in the spruit bed lay poor Samuel van Zijl, and close by sat our prisoners, some twenty in number.

Dead, wounded, and prisoners, eleven of us had accounted for more than eighty opponents, an average of seven apiece.

Our work was now done, and shortly after sunrise Mr Zeederberg and a large escort of men came scouting through the bush to see what was left of us, and they were surprised to find so many of us still alive.

We stood among the dead and wounded soldiers, the centre of an admiring crowd, and from now onwards Isaac Malherbe's corporalship was spoken of as the best in the commando.[1]

Chapter 8

A Visit to the Tugela Line—Tragedy of the Red Fort

A few days after our fight at Surprise Hill we woke one morning to the rumble of distant gun-fire from the direction of the Tugela River and there was a buzz of excitement in the camps around Ladysmith when it became known that General Buller was launching his long-expected attempt to break through to the relief of the town. For awhile there was no definite news, and we waited until sunset when word came that the British had been repulsed with heavy losses and that a number of guns had been taken.

Hard on the success at Colenso arrived the news of victories on the other fronts. Piet Cronje had defeated and killed General Wauchope at Magersfontein, and General Gatacre was beaten at Colesberg. These tidings caused universal rejoicing, and there were few of us who did not believe that peace would soon follow, as it had after the battle of Amajuba in 1881.

This time, however, their reverses seemed only to render the British more determined, but, the future being mercifully hidden from us, we confidently awaited the opening of peace negotiations and the surrender of Ladysmith, both of which events were expected to take place at any moment, and meanwhile camp life once more fell into the usual rut.

On Christmas Day another uncle of ours, Jan Mulder, paid us a visit. He was a Hollander by birth and a rolling-stone by nature. After filling varied posts, and taking part in many native campaigns, he was Registrar of the Supreme Court in Swaziland when the war broke out and he enlisted as a private in the Swaziland Police, with which force he was now serving on the Tugela.

---

[1] See Conan Doyle's *History of the Great Boer War*, where he refers to me by name in connexion with this affair. *The Times History of the War* gives the following account:

'The soldiers scrambled down Surprise Hill ... Suddenly a ring of flame blazed forth at their very feet. A party of some twenty Pretorians, mostly young lawyers and business men, had boldly come round the side of the hill and, regardless of the heavy fire, had lain down in a line across the slope to intercept the storming party of whose numbers they probably had no idea.

'Disregarding the misleading orders shouted by the Boers, the men charged in grim silence. The gallant Pretorians emptied their magazines in a vain endeavour to stem the rush, and then the riflemen surged over them, killing or wounding several as they passed. The British casualties were fourteen killed and fifty wounded, not an excessive price to pay for so successful a feat.'

As I was anxious to see the entrenchments there of which we had heard so much, I accompanied him on his return two days later.

We left the Pretoria camp at daybreak and rode round the east side of Ladysmith, touching at the laagers *en route* for a talk or a meal, and reaching the Tugela opposite Colenso by four in the afternoon. The Boer line roughly followed the ragged hills that fringe the north bank of the river, though here and there they were dug-in forward of the hills on the edge of the stream itself, and it was in one of these trench-lengths that we found the Swaziland Police, a small body of about one hundred strong.

The British Army lay across the river where their great tented camps were spread out on the plain. Judging by these and by the large numbers of troops being exercised every day, it was reckoned that there were forty thousand men facing us. I spent an interesting time riding up and down the line, and as things were quiet a party of us even rode through the river one morning to inspect the spot where the British guns had been captured and Lord Robert's son killed in the recent battle. There were only decomposing horses and broken rifles lying about, and as the English gunners presently sent a brace of shrapnel over us we made haste to regain our own side.

Our trench was shelled at intervals by a sixty pound naval gun standing at Chievely, seven miles away, but although some of the huge projectiles fell within a few feet of us, we suffered no damage. This was my first experience of lyddite, a newly invented explosive which went off with an appalling bang, emitting acrid green and yellow fumes that gave one a burning sensation in throat and chest. I had read of its effect on the dervishes at Omdurman, and the English newspapers had predicted equally terrible results for us; but the men made light of it and dubbed the shells 'little niggers' (*klein kafferkies*). Whenever one of them came through the air there was a warning cry: 'Look out—a little nigger', and every one dived for cover behind the sandbags.

I saw the New Year (1900) in with the Swazilanders, who held a sing-song in celebration, and three days later I said good-bye to my uncle, and started home.

This time I rode round the western circle of Ladysmith in order to visit the Free State commandos guarding that side of the cordon, as I had many friends and acquaintances there, and, after spending a pleasant day among them, I timed my journey to reach the Kroonstad camp by sunset, as I wished to put in a night with my Norwegian uncle. I found him making ready to accompany a picket to the plain towards the English lines. His preparations for going on duty were unusual, for he inspanned an American buck-board on which he piled a feather bed, blankets and pillows, and as soon as the rest of the picket moved out after dark he told me to leave my roan horse in camp, and he and I drove in state to the place where we had to do guard for the night. The spot was not more than four hundred yards from the nearest English sentries, but this in no way disturbed my uncle's serenity. He unharnessed his two animals, hitched them to the wheels of the buggy, and giving one of the younger fry half a crown to do his sentry-go, he spread his bedding and was soon comfortably snoring within earshot of the British. I shared his couch, and we both slept soundly until awakened shortly before daybreak in time to harness the horses and get back to camp before it grew light. I spent the day with the Kroonstad people and listened to a council-of-war.

For weeks there had been talk of an attack by the Free State forces against a loose-standing kop called Wagon Hill, considered to be the key of the Ladysmith defences. We had so often heard of the proposed attempt that by now we had ceased to believe in it, but this time it looked as if something was on foot at last, for Commandants and Field Cornets came riding in from neighbouring camps to attend the meeting. Here I learned that it had been decided to storm the hill within the next day or two. It was said that Piet Joubert was growing impatient at the delay of the Ladysmith garrison in surrendering and hoped to help them make up their minds by the capture of this commanding position. I had a good look at Wagon Hill, but I came away somewhat dubious of success, although the Freestaters were eager to have a shot at it.

Next morning I rode through the Klip River and past Nicholson's Nek back to the Pretoria camp, still wondering whether the attack would materialise. When I arrived at our tent I was told that it was in fact due for the very next morning and that four hundred Pretoria men were to create a diversion by falling upon our old friend the Red Fort in order to draw off the enemy's attention from the main objective while the Freestaters attacked Wagon Hill.

Our corporalship was to take part, and Isaac Malherbe had already given the necessary orders.

At 3 am on the morning of January 6th, the whistles blew for the attacking force to assemble, and soon we were marched off on foot, headed by Mr Zeederberg and Assistant Field-Cornet de Jager. We collected in the same dry spruit below Bell's Kop from which we had started on our previous abortive expedition. Our experience on that occasion did not tend to reassure us, for once more there was a strong dilution of burgher-right erven men in our ranks, and we shook our heads when we saw them dejectedly standing behind the bank of the spruit, showing little inclination for the work in hand.

However, nearly half our force were of better calibre, and when, shortly before sunrise, the two Field-Cornets led the way, about two hundred men responded, the rest refusing to follow. There was no time to argue, so, leaving the shirkers behind, we made over the plain towards the enemy work. It was still dark and we went along unobserved until we reached the outcrop of rock halfway across, where some of us had spent such evil hours during the former demonstration six weeks ago. Here the English in the fort observed us, and although the dawn was just breaking, they opened a heavy fire in our direction. This brought us to a standstill, and for a few moments we were uncertain whether to go forward or to fall back. The Field-Cornets seemed equally undecided, but, while they were debating, a man named Willemse intervened. He was a member of President Kruger's bodyguard, a fine tall fellow in police uniform. He was a stranger to us, for he had been on a chance visit to a relative at our camp, and had volunteered when he heard of the attack. He made an eloquent appeal to them to proceed, his words creating such an impression that we started for the fort at a run. The place was built on the brow of a low stony kopje immediately beyond the Harrismith railway line and, except where its earthworks formed an embankment, there was no cover. We had about four hundred yards to go, but the light was still uncertain, so we gained the safety of the ramp with the loss of only one man. This railway causeway proved our undoing, for had it not been there the chances are we should have gone straight on into the fort but the sheltering bank was too tempting, and with one accord the men halted behind it to recover their breath. In the circumstances the delay was fatal, for we lost the original impulse that had carried us thus far and as the light was increasing and with it the fierce volleying, we became disinclined to leave cover, and, instead of resuming our advance, stayed where we were.

We were now close in under the walls of the fort and could plainly see the muzzles of the defenders' rifles as they stuck them through the loopholes to fire at us. Other soldiers were standing by to repel boarders, for above the breastworks their bayonets glinted in the rising sun and gave us still further food for thought.

After awhile, Isaac Malherbe, my brother, and a few more of us crawled along the track and, jumping across the metals, ran up the slope to where fair-sized boulders gave good cover within twenty-five yards of the work. Our intention was to have a quick jumping-off point should the Field-Cornet give the order for a final rush, and from here we lay firing into the loopholes, waiting for the command to advance.

As we were now well ahead of where the rest of our force lay crouching behind the railway embankment, we were out of touch with them, although we kept looking back to see whether there was any sign of their coming on. Just as we were beginning to think that the attack had been called off, we heard a shout, and saw Willemse leap out on to the track with about a dozen or fifteen men at his heels. At this we too sprang up to join in the charge, but almost as we rose, swift destruction overtook the storming party. A single volley flamed along the port-holes, and before we had time to think the attack had withered away. We saw the men go down in a heap, leaving only one man erect. The rest were either dead or wounded or had flung themselves headlong for such cover as they could find.

Those of us with Isaac escaped annihilation because we were out of the direct line of fire and were able to regain protection before the soldiers had time to turn their attention to us, but we did not go quite unharmed, for Frank Roos, my tent-mate, fell dead among us with a bullet through his heart. The man who still faced the enemy was Willemse, and he, undeterred, ran up to the fort and tried to scale the wall. Bayonets were thrust at him which he parried with his rifle until a revolver was fired point-blank into him. He sank below the wall where he sat rocking to and fro, his head resting on his knees as if in great pain, and then another bullet found him, for he suddenly pitched forward on his face. We were so bewildered by the suddenness of everything that before we could collect our thoughts it was all over.

Willemse and six of his band lay dead, the survivors crouching behind cover against the driving bullets. Several of them were wounded, for they lay trying to bandage their injuries without exposing themselves from behind their scant shelter, and it was painful to see their efforts without being able to assist, but it was suicide to venture out under the wall in the teeth of such heavy fire.

We did not know why this piecemeal sally had been made, but after waiting for some time we were satisfied that there was to be no further attempt on the fort, so we recrossed the railway line, one at a time, crawling over until we were all back behind the bank where the rest of the men were gathered. Mr Zeederberg told me that the sortie had been made without his orders. Before he could stop them Willemse and the men were climbing up the slope to the disastrous end which we had witnessed.

There was now nothing else for us to do but to repeat our previous experience by staying where we were until the coming of night would enable us to retire. To renew the attack after what had happened was out of the question, nor was it feasible to withdraw in broad daylight from under the walls of the fort across a thousand yards of open veld.

It was as yet before eight in the morning, but we heard the sound of violent gun- and rifle-fire from Wagon Hill, three or four miles away, where the main battle was being joined. How the Freestaters were prospering we had no means of knowing, but we guessed that heavy fighting was in progress, for the throbbing of the guns increased, and the rattle of thousands of rifles. Our share in the proceedings, however, was over: caught like rats in a trap we had to confine ourselves to loosing an occasional shot, and gazing longingly at the hill far to rearward where the balance of the Pretoria commando looked on comfortably at our plight.

As the hours dragged by, the sun blazed down unbearably, and the wounded moaned and cried for water, of which we had none. By scrambling across the track and crawling from rock to rock we managed to pull most of them into the shelter of the embankment until we had brought in all except a few who were lying too far up. While busy at this I took a hurried glance at the dead. One of them was Assistant Field-Cornet de Jager, the others were men I had seen about camp, but did not know personally. Then I lay reading an old newspaper I had in my pocket, and slept at intervals to pass the time. This brought me subsequent notoriety, for when I unfolded the paper those watching us from the rear thought that it was a white flag, and some busybody rushed down into the laager to spread the news that we were surrendering to the enemy. Before field-glasses could be procured to verify the report it was too late to overtake the rumour, and by nightfall every commando around Ladysmith had heard that we had been marched into the town.

In this manner the day wore through. Occasionally we put a shot into the loopholes above us, but otherwise we lay inactive behind the railway earthwork counting the hours still to elapse before darkness. Through it all we heard the battle on Wagon Hill ebb and flow. At times it flared up and then died away, until some new turn caused a further eruption. The condition of our wounded grew worse and worse as the heat increased, and there was nothing we could do for them. It was bad enough to be thirsty ourselves, but to hear them beg for water and to sit helpless by was terrible, so we averted our eyes and pretended not to hear them.

At length, towards five in the afternoon, when things were getting unbearable, relief came from an unexpected quarter. Almost without warning, black clouds raced across the sky and there broke upon us the most violent storm that I have ever experienced. It leapt at us with a roar, and there fell a deluge which in an instant blotted all from view. The rolling thunder and the drumming of the waters were deafening. For perhaps a minute we waited and then we abandoned our dead and wounded and fled blindly through the hurricane in the direction of our camp, a mile away.

We found the whole place thrown into confusion by the storm. Our tents were down and our belongings were littered a mile or more along the valley, washed away by the flood. As we could neither light a fire nor dry our clothing, we spent a miserable night, made the more unhappy by the knowledge that we had selfishly left our wounded in the dark and rain and, to add to our discomfiture, came the tidings next morning that the Freestaters, despite magnificent courage, had failed to take Wagon Hill, and had lost three hundred men in the attempt.

Later in the day our dead were fetched in by wagon under flag of truce.

We carried poor Frank Roos to our tent, and for the second time in three weeks my companions and I sat by the body of a messmate, wondering whose turn was next.

Chapter 9

The Battle of Spion Kop

About a week later, Mr Zeederberg said I could go to Pretoria for a fortnight, so leaving my brother in charge of my horses, I once again boarded a north-bound goods train and travelled home in a cattle-truck, getting there in three days' time. My father did not know I was coming, and although he gave me a warm welcome, he insisted on my returning at once, as he said the British were on the eve of delivering another great blow on the Tugela, and that my place was in Natal. I told him that the burghers thought there would be no more serious fighting, but he shook his head and said he only wished he could share our optimism.

I was disappointed, as I had been looking forward to the luxury of home life and good food for a little while, but I saw his point and started back on the second day.

I reached our camp at Ladysmith on January 23rd (1900) to find that volunteers were being called for to go to the Tugela, and I now heard that General Buller had moved the English army twenty-five miles upstream from Colenso in preparation for another big-scale attack in the vicinity of Spion Kop, a prominent hill forming part of the Boer line on the north bank of the Tugela. Already they were hammering away at different points, seeking a weak spot at which to thrust; so my father had been right, and, indeed, the situation was so critical that reinforcements were being sent from every commando lying around Ladysmith.

From the Pretoria laager fifty volunteers were asked for, and more than three times that number immediately offered themselves. The Field-Cornet made a selection which included Isaac Malherbe, my brother and myself and our three remaining tent-mates, Charles Jeppe, de Vos and Reinecke, as well as several more of our corporalship.

We set out within an hour of my arrival from Pretoria, and crossed the Klip River after dark, riding all night round by the west until we reached the rear of Spion Kop at daybreak. As we rode, we could hear the sound of heavy gunfire from the forward hills, and it never ceased for any length of time although we were still too far back to be in danger.

After a short halt to rest our horses and cook breakfast, we were ordered to the top of a steep ridge lying about a mile to the right, where we had to dig a reserve trench. A mule-wagon had accompanied us from Ladysmith carrying provisions, ammunition and a supply of pick-axes and shovels, with which unaccustomed tools we started up the slope, horses and all.

When we had dug for some time, Field-Cornet Zeederberg, who was always very kind to me, said that as I was the youngest I need not dig any more and could go down to where the wagon had been left for a rest. Nothing loth, I made haste to reach the halting-place, and, leaving my horse in charge of the mule-drivers, I started out to see what was going on in the front positions, which were out of sight from where we had been digging.

Ever since sunrise there had come the unbroken boom of guns and the rattle of small arms, and now that I was free I decided to walk across the intervening hills to the firing-line. As I went, the gun- and rifle-fire grew louder, and before long I reached a point from which I could see the Boer front strung out along the top of the next rise. Black mushrooms of earth and smoke hung along the course of the positions from the heavy shells flung across the Tugela, and puffs of shrapnel flecked the air above. From the noise I judged that a battle was in full progress and, after some hesitation, I hurried on and reached the line in safety. The spectacle from here was a fine one. Far below on the plain the Tugela wound shining in the sun, and the bank beyond was alive with English foot and horse. From the wooded hills farther back came the flashes of the British guns, and in the din I asked myself more than once why I had been foolish enough to come.

During the preceding days the English had effected a lodgment at numerous points on our side of the river, and their troops were occupying such spurs and ridges running up from the water's edge as they had been able to seize. The Boers, on being pushed back, had reformed along the crest of the height, where they were now holding a series of hastily dug trenches and whatever natural cover they could find, and were stoutly resisting any further encroachments of the enemy, who in places were lying within a few hundred yards of us.

The positions here were held by Free State commandos while downstream lay the Transvaalers. There were probably ten or twelve thousand burghers in all on these hills, with the bastion of Spion Kop standing like a pivot in the centre. For the most part the men made slight reply to the fire in order to husband their ammunition, and our artillery kept silent for the same reason, although it was estimated that there were over two hundred guns firing at us, and I have heard that this was the heaviest concentration of gunfire that has been seen in any war up to the present. The casualties were considerable and I saw some men fearfully mutilated, including a father and son of the Frankfort commando who were torn to pieces by a howitzer shell, their rifles being sent spinning down the incline at the back of us.

It was a day of strain. Not only was there the horror of seeing men killed and maimed, but there was the long-drawn tension and fear of the approaching shells.

This tremendous volume of fire indicated an early attack, and throughout the day we looked to see the storm break at any moment, but, as it turned out, the bombardment was a feint, the real blow being delivered after midnight at a different point.

I was entitled to quit the line as my unit lay in the rear, but I did not like to go, and remained until things died down towards sunset, when I could return without loss of face. I found the Pretoria volunteers where I had left them digging that morning. They must have worked well, for they had completed quite a long trench.

I joined Isaac Malherbe and others sitting round the fires cooking their supper, and, watching the light fade away over the distant Drakensbergen, I chatted for a quiet hour with men who were mostly dead next morning.

Field-Cornet Zeederberg now ordered me down with him to the supply wagon. He said he was going to spend the night there, and, as he might require to send a message up to the trench, I was to come with him for I had good climbing legs.

When we got below, a tent had been pitched for him which I was allowed to share, and I was soon fast asleep. It rained at intervals during the night, and towards three in the morning we were waked by an angry sputter of rifle-fire coming from Spion Kop. We sat up listening, but as there was nothing we could do in the rain and darkness, and as after a while the firing died down, we fell asleep again.

At sunrise loud gun- and rifle-fire broke out along the front on which I had been the day before; but, as it was no worse than it had then been, Mr Zeederberg and I were not unduly perturbed and sat sipping our morning coffee in the lee of the wagon out of the way of the spent bullets that whined over our heads.

As we breakfasted, one of our Pretoria men galloped up with a message from Isaac Malherbe to say that the British had made a night attack and had captured Spion Kop. This was most serious, for if the hill went the entire Tugela line would go with it, and we could hardly bring ourselves to believe the news. The man however assured us that it was true, but he said that a strong force of burghers was assembling below the hill and that Isaac Malherbe had ridden down by a short cut with all the men who were with him, so we shouted to the mule-drivers to saddle our horses, and filling up with ammunition from a box on the wagon, we followed on the heels of our guide.

Heavy shells were lobbing over as we went, but we had not far to go and in less than fifteen minutes reached the bottom of Spion Kop. Here stood hundreds of saddled horses in long rows, and we looked up at an arresting sight.

The Boer counter-attack had started shortly before. Eight or nine hundred riflemen were climbing up the steep side of the hill in face of a close-range fire from the English troops who had established themselves on the flat summit overnight. Many of our men dropped, but already the foremost were within a few yards of the rocky edge which marked the crest, and soldiers were rising from behind their cover to meet the final rush. For a moment or two there was confused hand-to-hand fighting, then the combatants surged over the rim on to the plateau beyond, where we could no longer see them. Spell-bound, we watched until our men passed out of view, and then, recovering ourselves, dismounted, and tying our horses with the rest, hurried up in the wake of the attack.

Dead and dying men lay all along the way, and there was proof that the Pretoria men had gone by for I soon came on the body of John Malherbe, our Corporal's brother, with a bullet between his eyes; a few paces farther lay two more dead men of our commando. Farther on I found my tent-mate, poor Robert Reinecke, shot through the head, and not far off L de Villiers of our corporalship lay dead. Yet higher up was Krige, another of Isaac's men, with a bullet through both lungs, still alive, and beyond him Walter de Vos of my tent shot through the chest, but smiling cheerfully as we passed. Apart from the Pretoria men there were many other dead and wounded, mostly Carolina burghers from the eastern Transvaal, who formed the bulk of the assaulting column. Spion Kop, although steep, is not very high on the northern slope where we went up, and it did not take us long to reach the top. Here we found that the advance had got no farther than the fringe of loose rocks that runs like a girdle around the upper tableland. For the rest of the flat stretch beyond was still wholly in the hands of the British, who lay in a shallow trench behind a long low wall of stone about twenty yards away. From here came a vicious rifle-fire that made further progress impossible. It was marvellous that the Boers had got even thus far, for they had swarmed up the bare hillside in the face of a devastating fire, and they had pushed home the attack with such vigour that the narrow belt of rocks was thickly strewn with their dead.

I met my brother coming down in charge of captured soldiers and did not see him again as he had orders to escort them to Ladysmith, and he took no further part in the battle.

Giving him a hurried handshake, I went forward to the firing-line a few yards farther on. During the short delay I lost touch with Mr Zeederberg, and when I inquired from the men crouching behind the rocks for Isaac Malherbe, I was told by Red Daniel Opperman, the officer in command, that he had sent the Pretorians round to the left a few minutes earlier to rake the English flank. Working my way in that direction, I reached a spot where the outcrop of rocks came to a dead end. From here spread a patch of open ground until the ledge reappeared a hundred yards beyond.

One of the men holding this point told me that the Pretoria men had doubled across the gap shortly before and were now lying among the rocks on the far side, so I decided to follow; but the moment I left cover I drew so hot a fire that I was thankful to dive back for shelter and give up the attempt. Halfway across lay the huddled body of a dead man and now that I had time to look more carefully at him I recognised Charles Jeppe, the last of my tent-mates. His death affected me keenly, for we had been particularly good friends. Outwardly he was a surly man, but he had shown me many a kindness since first we messed together on the Natal border. As I was unable to find my Corporal I now returned to where I had first reached the top and took my place in the firing-line. During my absence about fifty soldiers had run forward to surrender, but otherwise things were going none too well. We were sustaining heavy casualties from the English *schans* immediately in front of us, and the men grew restive under the galling point-blank fire, a thing not to be wondered at, for the moral effect of Lee-Metford volleys at twenty yards must be experienced to be appreciated. The English troops lay so near that one could have tossed a biscuit among them, and whilst the losses which they were causing us were only too evident, we on our side did not know that we were inflicting even greater damage upon them. Our own casualties lay hideously among us, but theirs were screened from view behind the breastwork, so that the comfort of knowing that we were giving worse than we received was denied us.

Fortunately, towards nine o' clock the situation eased, for the Transvaal artillerists got their guns into action on a commanding spur a mile away, and they began to fire over our heads into the troops crowded on the restricted space on the plateau before us. As the guns searched the hill-top the English fire slackened, and from then onward our losses were less. The position, however, remained unsatisfactory. The sun became hotter and hotter, and we had neither food nor water. Around us lay scores of dead and wounded men, a depressing sight, and by midday a feeling of discouragement had gained ground that was only kept in check by Commandant Opperman's forceful personality and vigorous language to any man who seemed to be wavering. Had it not been for him the majority would have gone far sooner than they did, for the belief spread that we were being left in the lurch. We could see large numbers of horsemen collecting at the laagers on the plain behind, but no reinforcements reached us throughout the day. I repeatedly heard old Red Daniel assure the men that help would be forthcoming, but from the way he kept scanning the country below I could see that he was getting uneasy himself.

As the hours dragged on a trickle of men slipped down the hill, and in spite of his watchful eye this gradual wastage so depleted our strength that long before nightfall we were holding the blood-spattered ledge with a mere handful of rifles. I wanted to go too, but the thought of Isaac and my other friends saved me from deserting. No further attempt was made to press forward, and for the rest of this terrible day both sides stubbornly held their ground, and, although the battle remained stationary, the heavy close-range rifle-fire continued hour after hour, and the tale of losses mounted while we lay in the blazing heat.

I saw a strange incident during the morning. Near me was a German named von Brusewitz. He had been an officer in the German army, but the year before he had run a civilian through with his sword during some scuffle in a Berlin café. There was a great outcry over the incident, and to allay popular clamour the German Emperor broke him from his regiment. They say that in Germany the word 'Brusewitzerei' is still used to denote the arrogance of the officer caste. However that may be, von Brusewitz was now on top of Spion Kop, where he seemed bent on getting killed, for, although we warned him not to expose himself too recklessly, he paid no heed, and repeatedly stood out from among the rocks to fire.

As the English soldiers were so close to us this was sheer folly, and after he had tempted Providence several times the inevitable happened. I saw him rise once more, and, lighting a cigarette, puff away careless of the flying bullets until we heard a thud, and he fell dead within a few feet of me, shot through the head. Not long after this something similar happened. An old Kaffir servant came whimpering up among us from below, looking for his master's body. I advised him to be careful, as he went from rock to rock peering over to examine the dead men lying in the open, but he would not listen, and soon he too had a bullet through his brain.

The hours went by; we kept watch, peering over and firing whenever a helmet showed itself, and in reply the soldiers volleyed unremittingly. We were hungry, thirsty and tired; around us were the dead men covered with swarms of flies attracted by the smell of blood. We did not know the cruel losses that the English were suffering, and we believed that they were easily holding their own, so discouragement spread as the shadows lengthened.

Batches of men left the line, openly defying Red Daniel, who was impotent in the face of this wholesale defection, and when at last the sun set I do not think there were sixty men left on the ledge.

Darkness fell swiftly; the firing died away, and there was silence, save for a rare shot and the moans of the wounded. For a long time I remained at my post, staring into the night to where the enemy lay, so close that I could hear the cries of their wounded and the murmur of voices from behind their breastwork.

Afterwards my nerves began to go, and I thought I saw figures with bayonets stealing forward. When I tried to find the men who earlier in the evening had been beside me, they were gone. Almost in panic I left my place and hastened along the fringe of rocks in search of company, and to my immense relief heard a gruff 'Wer da?' It was Commandant Opperman still in his place with about two dozen men. He told me to stay beside him, and we remained here until after ten o' clock, listening to the enemy who were talking and stumbling about in the darkness beyond.

At last Opperman decided to retreat, and we descended the hill by the way which he had climbed up nearly sixteen hours before, our feet striking sickeningly at times against the dead bodies in our path. When we reached the bottom most of the horses were gone, the men who had retired having taken their mounts and ridden away, but our own animals, and those belonging to the dead or wounded, were still standing without food or water where they had been left at daybreak.

The first thing to do was to quench our raging thirst and that of our horses at a spring near by. We then consulted as to our next move. Most of the wounded had been taken off in the course of the day, but we found a few serious cases that would not bear any transport collected in charge of an old man, who, by the dim light of a lantern, was attending to their wants. We could get no coherent information and stood discussing what to do next, for we did not know that the English had also been fought to a standstill, and that they in turn were at that very moment retreating down their own side of Spion Kop. We fully believed that the morning would see them streaming through the breach to the relief of Ladysmith, and the rolling up of all our Tugela line.

While we were talking, Mr Zeederberg came out of the dark. I had lost sight of him during most of the day, but he had been on the hill all the time, and had only come down shortly before us. He had seen nothing of Isaac Malherbe and the rest of our Pretoria men, and had no idea of what had become of them. A few more stragglers joined us and we agreed to lead our horses to the Carolina wagon-laager that, as we knew, lay not far off. We foraged for food in the saddlebags of such horses as were left, and then went off. When we reached the laager we found everything in a state of chaos. The wagons were being hurriedly packed, and the entire Carolina commando was making ready to retire. They had borne the brunt of the day's battle and had fought bravely, but, now that the struggle was over, a reaction had set in and there was panic in the camp. Fortunately, just as the foremost wagons moved away and the horsemen were getting ready to follow, there came the sound of galloping hoofs, and a man rode into our midst who shouted to them to halt. I could not see his face in the dark, but word went round that it was Louis Botha, the new Commandant-General, appointed in place of Piet Joubert who was seriously ill. He addressed the men from the saddle, telling them of the shame that would be theirs if they deserted their posts in this hour of danger; and so eloquent was his appeal that in a few minutes the men were filing off into the dark to reoccupy their positions on either side of the Spion Kop gap. I believe he spent the rest of the night riding from commando to commando exhorting and threatening, until he persuaded the men to return to the line, thus averting a great disaster.

As for Commandant Opperman and our party, now that the Carolina burghers were returning we led our horses back to the foot of Spion Kop, to wait there.

We woke with the falling of the dew and, as the sky lightened, gazed eagerly at the dim outline of the hill above, but could make out no sign of life.

Gradually the dawn came and still there was no movement. Then to our utter surprise we saw two men on the top triumphantly waving their hats and holding their rifles aloft. They were Boers, and their presence there was proof that, almost unbelievably, defeat had turned to victory—the English were gone and the hill was still ours.

Leaving the horses to fend for themselves, we were soon hastening up the slope past the dead until we reached yesterday's bloody ledge. From here we hurried across to the English breastworks, to find them abandoned. On our side of the fighting-line there had been many casualties, but a worse sight met our eyes behind the English *schanses*.

In the shallow trenches where they had fought the soldiers lay dead in swathes, and in places they were piled three deep.

The Boer guns in particular had wrought terrible havoc and some of the bodies were shockingly mutilated. There must have been six hundred dead men on this strip of earth, and there cannot have been many battlefields where there was such an accumulation of horrors within so small a compass.

Shortly after I reached the top, Isaac Malherbe and the remaining Pretoria men came up. They had spent the night somewhere below the kop, and like ourselves had come up the moment they realised that the English were gone. Isaac looked grim and worn, grieved at the death of his brother and of our other companions, but he was full of courage, and so were we all, for from where we stood we could look down on the Tugela River, and we were now able to grasp the full significance of our unexpected success. Long columns of troops and long convoys of transport were recrossing to the south bank, and everywhere the British were in full retreat from the positions which they had captured on this side of the stream, and the clouds of dust rising on the Colenso road told us that General Buller's second great attempt to pierce the Tugela defences had failed. We spent the next hour or two helping the English Red Cross doctors and bearer parties that came up to bury their dead and carry away their wounded. By now hundreds of other burghers had arrived, mostly men who had retreated the day before, but like ourselves had loitered in neighbouring kloofs and gullies to see if they could renew the fight.

Towards midday Isaac Malherbe ordered us to collect our Pretoria dead. We carried them down in blankets, and when the commando wagon came up we placed the bodies on board and escorted them to Ladysmith, whence they were sent to Pretoria for burial. So we rode behind the wagon which carried all that was left of our friends and companions, their horses trotting alongside with empty saddles.

I personally came home to a deserted tent, for within a few weeks four good friends had gone from it to their death, and our fifth messmate, de Vos, was lying dangerously wounded at some laager below Spion Kop. Only my brother and I were left, and he had been sent to Pretoria with the prisoners, so I was all alone, except for our faithful old native retainer, who did what he could to cheer me up.

Chapter 10

The Rest of our Corporalship is Destroyed

For a while the success at Spion Kop went to our heads, and we thought that the English would be sure to make peace, but again the days came and went with no sign.

Indeed, we presently heard that General Buller was back at Colenso collecting an ever larger army to attack again, but we were confident that the Tugela defences would hold and we saw no shadow of the disasters that were soon to overtake us. After a week my brother Joubert returned from Pretoria. He said that he and the escort had been made much of by the townspeople, for, coming straight from the battle on the hill, they were the heroes of the hour, and they were marched down to shake hands with President Kruger, the nearest approach to battle honours that we ever attained.

He arrived in camp with my three remaining brothers. The eldest, Hjalmar, aged twenty, was studying law in Holland when the war broke out, and he had after considerable difficulty succeeded in reaching the Transvaal through Portuguese territory. The other two, Arnt and Jack, aged sixteen and twelve respectively, had been at school up to now, but they had at last persuaded my father to let them come to the war. Jack only remained for a few days, as old Maroola on one of his visits to our laager caught sight of him and ordered him to be sent home, but at any rate from now onward there were four of us in our tent.

About the middle of February, a force of eight hundred mounted men was drawn from different commandos for the purpose of carrying out a raid into Zululand. The exact object of this expedition I never heard, but I think that it was intended to create a diversion, for the British were massing heavily at Colenso. My two newly arrived brothers were absent on a visit to the Tugela, for commando life was a novelty to them, and they spent much of their time riding about, but my brother Joubert and I joined the Zululand column. It assembled at the Commandant-General's headquarters behind Bulwana Hill, and we started the same morning under old Maroola. For several days we travelled due east through lovely mountain country everywhere dotted with picturesque native kraals. The Zulus showed no fear of us and refused to serve as guides, for they sided with the British, as they have always done.

Of English troops we saw no sign, and our journey was a restful interlude after the excitement of the past few weeks. Unfortunately it soon came to an end, for about the fifth day out a messenger came riding post-haste with orders for Maroola to return to Ladysmith at once.

We retraced our steps by forced marches, arriving back at the head laager on about the eighth day after leaving. During the last two days of the journey we heard a constant rumble of gun-fire coming from the direction of Colenso, and, on reaching our Pretoria camp, we were met with the disturbing news that the English had broken into our defences there to the extent of capturing Hlangwane Hill, a commanding position that was considered the key to the Tugela line. Once more volunteers from every commando around the town were called for. My two brothers Hjalmar and Arnt had returned and gone off again on some jaunt, so Joubert and I, with the rest of Isaac

Malherbe's corporalship, handed in our names. There was no difficulty in getting the required fifty men, and at dusk on the day after our return from Zululand we set out on a journey from which few were to come back.

We rode through most of the night in company with other units hurrying to the danger-point. Farther on we fell in with small parties riding in the contrary direction, who made no secret of having quitted the Tugela firing-line, and when we neared the river at daybreak we found a critical situation. Not only had Hlangwane been taken, but every Boer trench on the north bank for a distance of several miles had been evacuated, and, what was far more serious, there was a feeling of discouragement in the air that dismayed us.

Up to now, the prevailing note in Natal had been one of confidence in an early peace, but, almost in a night and without apparent cause, a wave of pessimism had set in and the nearer we came the more evidence was there of growing demoralisation.

Hundreds of men were leaving the new line that had been formed in the hills behind the abandoned trenches. They were dispersing about the back area, some holding meetings, others making for the wagon-laagers in the rear, and from their talk and attitude we snuffed disaster, for, though we knew before starting that Hlangwane had been taken, we did not know that the fighting spirit of the men had gone with it.

Bad as it looked, however, things were not yet quite hopeless, for General Botha had taken up a new line to the rear of the old one and was once more standing on the defensive with eight or nine thousand men. We were met by one of his officers, who allotted different points to the various fresh detachments. We of the Pretoria commando were told to leave our horses in charge of guards and march on foot down a rocky gorge which led towards the Tugela. Heavy lyddite shells crashed against the cliffs on either side as we went down, but we emerged without loss at the lower exit of the canyon, to find ourselves in the bed of a dry spruit which ran across an open plain to where it joined the Tugela River about a mile and a half away. This dry bed skirted along the base of the foothills for some distance before bending away across the plain, and, from the exit of the gorge to the point where it curved away, its bank had been converted into a sector of the new line. We were assigned a position near the top end, not far from where we had come out of the gorge, and we fell to at once, hacking firing steps with pocket-knives and any other implements on which we could lay our hands.

The English infantry were eight hundred yards off, approximately along the line of our former trenches that had been abandoned two days before. From here they were maintaining a continuous rifle-fire, a multitude of bullets whizzing overhead or plugging into the ground in front.

They were also methodically shelling the course of the spruit with many guns, including high-angle howitzers so that we were in a very warm and unpleasant locality.

The casualties were few, owing to the height of the bank, and not one of the Pretoria men was hit, although I got a shell splinter through my hat before I had been there ten minutes, and one or two of our men had scratches from flying earth as the shells exploded in the bed of the spruit below.

The British did not attack on our front, but later in the morning made a determined attempt to our left against some hills known as Pieters Heights, where the Bethal commando was posted.

We saw waves of infantry going forward, but it was too far off for us to participate. At first the soldiers advanced in regular lines, but gradually their progress was stayed, and we could see the survivors crouching behind rocks and stones. They lost heavily, and it was soon evident that the attack had been repulsed.

Nothing further happened that day and by dark all was quiet. We spent an undisturbed night, and next morning (February 26th, 1900) the English sent in under flag of truce to fetch away their dead and wounded, so that there was no firing at all.

Having nothing to do, my brother and I walked down to watch the removal of the fallen soldiers and we spent some hours going over the ground discussing events with the English doctors and stretcher-bearers.

Returning up the spruit on the way to our own quarters we met my Hollander uncle, still serving with the Swaziland Police, a chance encounter which probably saved the lives of both of us. My uncle, seeing us pass, asked us to spend a day or two with him, and, falling in with his suggestion, we went to get our things and to tell Isaac Malherbe where we were going. He made no objection to our visiting the Swazilanders, seeing that they were close by, and he promised to send for us should we be wanted. As we were going off he looked at us with his quiet smile and said: 'Be sure and come quickly should I send word, for how shall I hold this bank without you two boys beside me?' He was referring to the night below Surprise Hill, but we never again saw him alive, nor any of the others.

Carrying our cooking-tins and blankets, we returned to the Swaziland Police. At sunrise next morning the English started in real earnest to bombard the spruit. All day long they shelled us with light and heavy guns, while we hugged the sheltering bank. Shrapnel and lyddite crashed upon us, causing a great many casualties and we suffered a terrible ordeal.

Considering the demoralisation that had set in, the men stood the bombardment well. There were some who retreated up the gorge, but there was no general desertion, and, when at sunset the fire died down, our forces were holding firm after one of the worst days of the war. This heavy shelling was the obvious preparation for an attack next day, so my brother and I, when the fire slackened, went up to find the Pretoria men. In the dusk we made our way along the bed of the spruit, past groups of burghers standing around their dead or wounded and other groups discussing the incidents of the day, but when we came to where we had left our companions the evening before, they were gone, and we were told by those near by that they had marched up the gorge an hour ago for some other point of the line. We could not understand why Isaac had not let us know, but thought that his messenger had missed us in the failing light. We were upset by his departure and decided to follow after at once, so we went back to tell my uncle of our intention. He said he was coming with us too, as he had been thinking of a change for some time, and would like to join the Pretoria commando. Accordingly he told his Field-Cornet of his plans and the three of us set off through the gorge. It was pitch-dark by now, and we had a difficult climb up the boulder-strewn bed, stumbling and groping our way as best we could.

When at last we reached the top entrance, we were so weary with the heavy loads we were carrying, and there was so little chance of finding our corporalship at that time of night, that we flung ourselves down on the first piece of level ground and slept until daybreak. As soon as it was light we made out the tents of the horse-guards, where we found our saddles just as we had left them, and our horses grazing not far away. These guards were here on permanent duty to look after the animals of the burghers in the firing-line, and they told us that Isaac Malherbe and his party had spent the night with them, and had ridden off before dawn to join the Bethal commando at Pieters Heights some miles east of this, so we hurriedly cooked a meal and, saddling our horses, rode after him, following behind the range of hills that formed the Boer line.

As we went along, a bombardment more violent than that of yesterday broke out ahead of us, and, when we came to the rear of Pieters Heights, we saw the ridge on which lay the Bethal men (and our own) going up in smoke and flame. It was an alarming sight. The English batteries were so concentrating on the crest that it was almost invisible under clouds of flying earth and fumes, while the volume of sound was beyond anything that I have ever heard. At intervals the curtain lifted, letting us catch a glimpse of the trenches above, but we could see no sign of movement, nor could we hear whether the men up there were still firing, for the din of the guns drowned all lesser sounds.

We reined in about four hundred yards from the foot of the hill, at a loss what to do. To approach our men through that inferno was to court destruction, while not to try seemed like desertion. For a minute or two we debated and then, suddenly, the gun-fire ceased, and for a space we caught the fierce rattle of Mauser rifles followed by British infantry swarming over the skyline, their bayonets flashing in the sun. Shouts and cries reached us, and we could see men desperately thrusting and clubbing. Then a rout of burghers broke back from the hill, streaming towards us in disorderly flight. The soldiers fired into them, bringing many down as they made blindly past us, not looking to right or left. We went too, for the troops, cheering loudly, came shooting and running down the slope.

Of our Pretoria men who had been on the ridge not one came back. They had been holding an advanced position to the right of the Bethal section, and had been overwhelmed there. They stood their ground until the enemy was on them, and they were bayoneted or taken to the last man. Thus our corporalship was wiped out, with its leader, Isaac Malherbe, the bravest of them all, and their going at this calamitous time was scarcely noticed. For this day marked the beginning of the end in Natal. The British had blasted a gap through which the victorious soldiery came pouring, and wherever we looked Boer horsemen, wagons and guns went streaming to the rear in headlong retreat.

We followed the current, hemmed in by a great throng, all making for the various fords of the Klip River, and it was lucky indeed that the English sent no cavalry in pursuit, for the passages across the river were steep and narrow, and there was frightful confusion of men and wagons struggling to get past.

By nightfall my uncle and my brother and I had managed to cross, and as it started to rain we annexed a deserted tent behind Lombaardskop, picketed and fed our tired horses, and slept there till morning. We now resumed our journey as far as the head laager, where we spent a dismal hour or two watching the tide of defeat roll northward.

We knew that the siege of Ladysmith would have to be raised, and now came the news, while we were halted here, that Kimberley had also been relieved, and that General Cronje had been captured at Paardeberg with four thousand men, so that the whole universe seemed to be toppling about our ears.

From the way in which the commandos were hurrying past, it looked that morning as if the Boer cause was going to pieces before our eyes, and it would have taken a bold man to prophesy that the war had still more than two long years to run.

We hung about the dismantled head laager till midday, after which the three of us rode on gloomily to the Pretoria camp, arriving towards five in the afternoon. Word of the disaster to our men on the Tugela had already preceded us, as is the way with evil tidings, and, as it was not known that my brother and I had escaped, our unexpected appearance caused a sensation, men running up from all sides to hear the truth. My other brothers had returned and their welcome was a warm one.

It was by now clear enough that the siege could no longer be maintained and, indeed, orders had already been received that all commandos were to evacuate their positions around Ladysmith after dark. Our wagons were standing packed, but at the last moment it was found that someone had levanted with the transport mules, so everything had to be burned. It came on to rain heavily by nightfall. Peals of thunder growled across the sky, and, wet to the skin, we stood huddled against the storm in depressed groups, awaiting our final orders. At last, long after dark, Field-Cornet Zeederberg gave the word that we were to move off to Elandslaagte some twenty miles to the rear. It was an inky night, with rain in torrents, through which we had to feel our way, and thus we turned our backs on Ladysmith for good and all.

No march order was attempted; we were simply told to go, and it was left to each man to carry out his own retirement.

At the outset we travelled in company with many others, but, as I knew a short cut threading the hills to the railway depot at Modderspruit, my brothers and I decided to go thither, for we saw no use in floundering about in mud and water, and the four of us, with my uncle and our native boy Charley, branched away by ourselves.

We reached the depot after two hours and found shelter until daybreak, after which we rode on.

The rain now stopped and the sun rose warm and bright, but it looked on a dismal scene. In all directions the plain was covered with a multitude of men, wagons, and guns ploughing across the sodden veld in the greatest disorder. Whenever a spruit or nullah barred the way there arose fierce quarrels between the frightened teamsters, each wanting to cross first, with the result that whole parks of vehicles got their wheels so interlocked that at times it seemed as if the bulk of the transport and artillery would have to be abandoned, for the mounted men pressed steadily on without concerning themselves with the convoys. Had the British fired a single gun at this surging mob everything on wheels would have fallen into their hands, but by great good luck there was no pursuit and towards afternoon the tangle gradually straightened itself out.

Our little family party remained behind with a number of others as a rearguard and we did not reach Elandslaagte until late that night. This place had been the chief supply centre for the Natal forces, and there were still huge quantities of stores that had been left to the enemy. These we burnt lighting a conflagration that must have been visible for fifty miles around.

By now the ruck of the retreat had passed on, and next day we rode along leisurely, climbing up the Washbank valley to Glencoe near Dundee by the following evening. Here were stray remnants of almost every commando that had been in Natal, but things were in such confusion that most of the army had continued straight on, and there was scarcely a man who could tell us what had become of his officers, or what we were supposed to do next.

Mr Zeederberg, however, was at Glencoe when we got there, and during the next few days he succeeded in collecting about three hundred Pretoria men, while more drifted back later on, as did stragglers from the other commandos, until after a week or ten days there was quite a respectable body of men numbering well over five thousand.

During this time my brothers and I with our uncle subsisted on what we could loot from the supply trains at the station, for there were practically no commissariat arrangements, but by raiding the trucks at night we did not do badly.

After a while General Botha reorganised everything, and a new line of defence was established along the forward slopes of the Biggarsbergen, to which all available men were marched. We of the Pretoria commando were assigned a post on the shoulder of the mountain to the right of where the Washbank valley reaches the plain below, and here we lay amongst pleasant scenery, from which we looked regretfully over the wide sweep of country to the south from which we had been driven, but we enjoyed the spell of peace and quiet after the turmoil of the past weeks.

Chapter 11

A Campaign in the Free State

The English Army, having forced the Tugela and relieved Ladysmith, was also resting.

Far down on the plain large camps were springing up, but all through the month of March and half of April they made no move at all and the weeks went by unbroken, except for an occasional patrol when we would leave our horses below some kopje and climb up to watch the troops at exercise in the distance.

While matters went thus easily in Natal, grave rumours reached us as to the situation in the Free State. Reliable information was scarce, but it was freely said that a powerful army under Lord Roberts had crossed the Free State border and was marching on Bloemfontein.

When my brothers and I heard this we felt we ought to go to our own country. We decided to go to Pretoria first and thence south by rail, for since the destruction of our corporalship we considered ourselves free to go where we pleased.

The day before we meant to leave we were ordered to take part in an attack on the English camp lying at Elandslaagte, halfway back to Ladysmith.

This much-criticised affair was to have been carried out by three thousand

Transvaalers in conjunction with an equal force of Freestaters from the Drakensbergen. We assembled after midnight at the exit of the Washbank valley and reached the Elandslaagte hills as it grew light, but we looked in vain for the Free State commandos.

The Free State Commandant-General, Prinsloo (the same who surrendered so ignominiously with three thousand men a few months later), had telegraphed to General Botha at the last moment to say that he and his officers were attending a cattle sale at Harrismith on the day set for the attack, and were therefore unable to be present.

In view of this, General Botha had to change his plans and content himself with a mere demonstration instead of serious business and the whole thing fizzled out in an artillery duel with heavy expenditure of ammunition and very little damage done. To me it was memorable only for the fact that while I was watching one of our Creusot guns being fired, the wind of a shell from the English batteries sent me spinning yards away. It must have passed within a few inches of me and I shall not soon forget being blown head over heels.

We remained before the camps all day, subjected to severe shell-fire at times and after dark we rode back to our stations in the Biggarsbergen, none the better for our outing.

The next day my brothers and I took leave of the Pretoria commando with which we had served for so long. We rode up the valley to the train at Glencoe Junction, and it was months before we saw our old force again.

At the railway station we held up the first north-bound train, loaded our horses in one truck and ourselves in another, and steamed off, leaving Natal behind us for ever.

After the usual three days' journey and the usual delays at halts and stations, we arrived at Pretoria. My uncle, Jan Mulder, was not of our party, for he had remained with the Irish Brigade, a band of two hundred adventurers commanded by an American Colonel named Blake, whose roistering habits and devil-may-care methods suited his own, so that we four brothers and Charley, our boy, formed our party.

My father did not know of our arrival until we came riding up to the front door, but when we told him we were for the Free State he approved. We gathered that the position was very bad, and he himself seemed aged and worn, for he bore great responsibilities upon his shoulders. He had signed the ultimatum to Great Britain, and in a large measure the policy which had led to the war had been his, so the gloomy military situation lay heavily upon his mind, as well as the personal anxiety of having four sons at the front. We spent the next few days in the luxury and comfort of home life, the last we were ever to enjoy.

I even visited Johannesburg for the first time. The city was practically deserted; the shops were boarded up and there was little or no life in the streets, but I remember the visit because that afternoon there came the roar of a great explosion and a column of smoke shot up into the sky a mile high. It was the Begbie foundry, where the Government was manufacturing shells and ammunition, that had gone into the air, by treachery it was said.

About thirty people were killed, but so fierce was the blaze that we could give no assistance and we had to look on helplessly while the fire burnt itself out.

On April 30th (1900) my three brothers and I, with our boy Charley, entrained for the Free State. We knew that the British had occupied Bloemfontein by now and were advancing towards the Transvaal, but no one seemed certain how far they had got, or for how far the railway line to the south was still open. We crossed the Vaal River that night, and, after a slow journey over the rolling plains of the northern Free State, we reached a small station near the banks of the Vet River by eleven o'clock next night. We were now within fifty miles of Bloemfontein and the train was going no farther, as the engine-driver told us that the British advance was at the next station but one down the line. On hearing this, we unshipped our horses and camped beside the track until daybreak, intending then to ride forward in search of the Boer forces that we knew must be somewhere ahead.

As we were preparing to start next morning, another train steamed in from the north, carrying a hundred and fifty men under Commandant Malan, a brother-in-law of the Commandant-General Piet Joubert, who had recently died. Malan had collected a lot of young fellows whom he had formed into a flying column, the 'Africander Cavalry Corps', and they were on their way to the nearest fighting.

They detrained here and we lost no time in enrolling ourselves as members of the 'ACC' as it was called for short. Among them was my old schoolfellow Jan Joubert, the Commandant-General's son, with other friends and acquaintances.

We spent the morning getting ready and that afternoon we trekked off, riding south through the Vet River towards the sound of the distant gun-fire that we could now hear on the wind.

Darkness found us on the wide plain beyond the river, where we met hundreds of horsemen withdrawing, so they told us, to fresh positions, but whom we suspected of being on their way home for good. They said that great swarms of British troops were on the move, and that it was useless to think of fighting them in the open. Nevertheless we rode on until midnight, when we came to where General de la Rey was halted with the Transvaal commandos. We found him squatted by a small fire, a splendid-looking old man with a hawk-like nose and fierce black eyes. Beside him was his brother, nursing an arm shattered by a bullet that afternoon. He gave us a hurried account of the situation, which was very black. The British Army, after capturing Cronje and taking Bloemfontein, was now advancing on the Transvaal and, owing to the demoralised state of the commandos and the lack of defensive cover in this bare region, he saw little or no hope of stopping them. He said he had about four thousand Transvaalers who had escaped the debacle at Paardeberg, but they were discouraged and were making the merest show of opposition. The Free State commandos had disappeared altogether, although he believed that President Steyn and Christian de Wet were trying to reorganise them somewhere in the mountain country to the east, but for the time being they were out of action. The British were within a few miles of us, and would doubtless resume their advance in the morning.

So far as the 'ACC' was concerned, he ordered us to ride forward for half an hour and halt till daybreak, after which we were to fit ourselves into the firing-line and act according to circumstances. We took leave of him and, mounting our horses, rode on for three or four miles. Since we had come south the weather had turned bitterly cold, and we felt the change from the warmer climate of Natal.

For months we were not to spend one really comfortable night until summer came round again, and on this particular night we sat, with our blankets wrapped around our shoulders, shivering till daybreak, for sleep was out of the question with the temperature below zero.

As soon as it grew light we were astir, anxiously scanning the ground before us, and soon we made out dense masses of English infantry on the plain. First came a screen of horsemen, and behind a multitude of infantry, guns and wagons throwing up huge clouds of dust.

We looked in dismay at the advancing host, for there were thirty thousand men approaching, whilst on our meagre front there may have been between three and four thousand Boer horsemen, strung out in a ragged line on the rising ground to right and left of us.

It was plain from the very way in which the men sat their horses that they would not stand, and indeed, on this bare veld and against such heavy odds, the task was manifestly beyond them.

The enemy forces came steadily on until their scouts were close to us. When we fired at these they fell back upon their regiments; the batteries unlimbered and in a few seconds shrapnel was bursting over us.

Our line gave way almost at once. The 'ACC' stayed as long as any, but we recognised the futility of remaining, so we went galloping back with field-gun and pom-pom shells besprinkling us as we rode. We had no casualties, but a number of men from other commandos were killed and wounded before we got clear, and after a hard ride we slowed down at a deserted farmhouse to breathe our winded animals.

The English troops being mainly infantry, their progress was slow, and, although they were quickly at us once more, we were able to retire before them with very little loss for the rest of the day, firing on their scouts when they pressed us too nearly, and moving back in extended order to escape the shell-fire that came in gusts as the guns were brought forward. We were in the saddle until sunset, for we had to exercise ceaseless vigilance to keep the English horse from the wagons that were struggling to get away.

There must have been over a thousand of these, for, in addition to General de la Rey's transport, there were a great many vehicles belonging to the civilian population fleeing before the oncoming invasion.

By dark the English had pushed us right back to the Vet River, a distance of twenty miles or more, and next morning we had scarcely time to prepare a hasty breakfast before we could see the columns again advancing towards us.

General Louis Botha was standing at the drift as we rode through, for he had hurried round by rail from Natal to see for himself what was going on in the Free State.

He and General de la Rey disposed such commandos as were available along the river from the railway bridge to a point about four miles down, with orders to make a stand.

The 'ACC' was allotted the extreme right, so we searched out a suitable spot on the river bank beyond the next furthest commando, and, leaving our horses in the bed below, took up our posts. As we expected trouble, we sent the native boy Charley to the rear with our spare kit loaded on my Basuto pony (which we had brought from Natal as a pack-horse).

The British were by now feeling their way over the plain that ran down to the river, and before long were volleying at us from tall grass in which we could only just see where they lay. Then their guns came forward and started shelling us. Our horses were safe in the river bed behind, but owing to the thorn trees fringing the bank our view was impeded, and we had to crawl to the outside edge of the bush to see the enemy, with the result that we had practically no cover and had casualties almost at once. Several men were killed and wounded close to me, and altogether it was a beastly day. The shelling was not confined to our portion of the line, but ran up and down, like a piano, as far as the bridge and back again, and at times was as heavy as that on the Tugela. It continued until far into the afternoon and it was only at three o'clock that we saw the infantry preparing to charge.

We had six killed and about fifteen wounded by then. The dead had been laid on the sand in the river bed, and the wounded had been placed on their horses and told to get away as best they could, while the rest of us stayed on in such holes and hollows as we had been able to scrabble in the soil. The shell-fire and the casualties had shaken us, and when the British rose to their feet, and from their rear some three hundred cavalry came riding, sword in hand, we rose to fire a few wavering shots, and then broke for the river behind, tumbling down pell-mell to get our horses. Leaving our dead, we rode up the opposite bank and went racing across the open to the hills a mile to rearward. We were heavily fired on, but reached sanctuary with only two or three men down and a few wounded, including my younger brother Arnt with a scalp-wound from a glancing rifle bullet. The English horsemen that had been the chief cause of our flight came no farther than the river, but the infantry were breaking through at several places, and we could see them well on our side of the stream, the rest of the commandos also retreating wildly.

Before long we were again being shelled, and near sunset the soldiers came on to drive us out of the hills to which we had fled. As we were holding the extreme end of the Boer line, we were soon outflanked. We saw a regiment change direction, and before we could stop them they were climbing into the very hills on which we ourselves were at a point about fifteen hundred yards off, from which they began to work their way towards us.

We fronted round to meet them, but the sinking sun was straight in our eyes, making accurate shooting difficult, and, when the soldiers came swarming towards us at short range, another stampede took place. The whole of what remained of the 'ACC' rushed for their horses and made haste to be off. By the time I was in the saddle, the nearest infantrymen were so close that I could see their faces and the brass buttons on their tunics, but they were blown with running and their aim was poor, and although several horses were hit, none of the men were injured. My eldest brother's pony was shot through the body from saddle-flap to saddle-flap, but the plucky little animal carried him a thousand yards before he fell dead. Riderless horses were careering all over the place, and by cornering one of them we succeeded in providing my brother with another mount. Bullets and shells were striking everywhere, so we hurriedly transferred his belongings to the new horse and followed the rout now fast vanishing over the next rise. In the darkness we galloped on to catch up with the press, for all positions along the river had been given up and a wholesale retreat was in progress.

The 'ACC' had over thirty men killed and wounded during the day, and if this was a fair average the total Boer casualties must have been heavy.

We trekked on till after midnight, our only crumb of comfort being our native boy awaiting us beside the road, his voice quavering with emotion at seeing all four of us still alive.

The withdrawal was continued next morning without waiting for the enemy, and we had moved to the rear so rapidly that it was twenty-four hours before we saw the English on the skyline once more. It was towards evening of the next day that they came—a small advance guard of two hundred horsemen with a gun, riding so fast that before we could stand to arms they were on the south bank of the Sand River, and had killed one of the Irishmen preparing to dynamite the bridge. The commandos were some distance back, but the 'ACC' was halted near by, so we ran for our horses and recrossed the river lower down to outflank the intruders. When they saw that they might be cut off, they fired a few shells at us and fell back on their main troops, masses of whom we could now see on the far horizon. We got near enough to use our rifles, bringing down two troopers from their horses. I rode up to have a look at them. They were both Canadians, badly wounded, one of whom told me that many thousands of their people, as well as Australians and other Colonial forces, had volunteered for the war, as if the odds against us were not heavy enough already.

It was getting dark, so we left the wounded men to be fetched by their own side, and for the next two days we were not disturbed, the English apparently resting their men before resuming the advance. On the morning after this, Commandant Malan sent me with a message for General Botha, whom I found, after a fifteen-mile ride, camped beside the railway line. Having delivered my dispatch I started back for the Sand River where I had left the 'ACC', only to find them gone. Men in the neighbourhood told me they had ridden away two hours before, going west on some unknown errand. It was growing dark and bitterly cold, and as it was useless to try and follow, with no idea of where they had gone, I broke enough timber from the pumping station at the railway bridge to make a bonfire, and spent the night in solitary comfort within, my old roan horse snug beside me.

As soon as it grew light next morning, high dust-clouds rising south of the river showed that the English were coming, so I saddled and hastened to fall back to where a force of six hundred burghers was approaching under the personal command of General Louis Botha. He ordered us to open out, and each man stood before his horse awaiting developments. These were not long in coming. Soon the English scouts had crossed the river, and infantry were coming down to the drifts, while the country behind was black with more troops and transport columns. Batteries came into play, and, as the ground was devoid of cover, we mounted and sullenly retired. Now began anew the long-drawn humiliation of retreat. All day we were driven relentlessly; the British herded us like sheep to the incessant shriek of shells and the whizz of bullets, and by evening we were a demoralised rabble fleeing blindly across the veld.

After sunset the pursuit tailed off. I spent a cold night on a kopje with a few other stragglers, and next morning we rode into the town of Kroonstad. Here we found President Steyn addressing a crowd of burghers from a market-table in the square. He had succeeded my father as President of the Free State in 1896, a burly, heavily bearded man, not brilliant, but possessed of dogged courage.

For the moment his words fell on deaf ears, for so universal was the discouragement that few paid any heed to his appeals. His audience consisted mainly of Transvaal burghers, more concerned with getting back home than with forlorn hopes, so there was little response, but I stopped to listen, and was so carried away by what he said that I rode back the way I had come with a dozen more until we reached the scattered hills a few miles south of the town. From here we could see the English columns advancing towards us, and after some time several hundred other men rode up, coming across the plain from various directions. By midday the troops were within range and began to shell us, but made no attempt to push home an attack. In the afternoon my brother Arnt made his appearance from the rear. He brought me bad news of the 'ACC'. He said that after I had left them on the Sand River, they had received orders to go west, to watch the movements of a cavalry force in that direction.

In the neighbourhood of Kopje-Alleen they were ridden down by a regiment of horse. It was a case of every man for himself, and he had escaped by hard riding, but he could not tell whether our remaining two brothers and the native boy had got away.

This was serious news, and when a retreat was called after nightfall we rode back into Kroonstad greatly troubled. The town was in darkness, and we went right on for twenty miles without a halt until we overtook the commandos.

Next day the retreat was continued to the Rhenoster River. In the course of the morning we came on our boy Charley, who had not only escaped but had brought out the Basuto pony as well, thereby saving much of our gear, but he had no word of the other two.

An hour later we saw my eldest brother ambling along in company with the rest of the 'ACC'. They had got off better than we thought, having lost only twelve men in the fight. Of my brother Joubert they could tell us nothing; no one remembered having seen him, and it was a long time before we heard of him again.

The 'ACC' had now lost, in less than a week's fighting, nearly a third of its strength, with very little to show for it, but at any rate we were still a coherent unit, which was more than could be said for most of the other commandos, as the process of disintegration was gaining so rapidly that the major portion of the burghers riding in the retreat were no longer members of any recognised force, but merely individuals on their way home.

At the north bank of the Rhenoster River we lay for nearly a week without sign of the British, during which time the Boer Army melted still further until General Botha had a bare handful of men left.

One morning a dozen of the 'ACC', of whom I was one, were ordered to go back in the direction of Kroonstad to reinforce a small body of Scouts under Captain Daniel Theron, who was keeping touch with the enemy.

We recrossed the river, and after a forty-mile ride south over the plains, we found him and his men on a hill overlooking the English camps that had sprung up around Kroonstad. Captain Theron had gained considerable notice before the war for thrashing Mr Moneypenny, the well-known journalist, and had of late added to his reputation by his daring at the time when Cronje was surrounded at Paardeberg. He was a slight, wiry man of about twenty-six, dark complexioned and short-tempered, and although I never once saw him really affable, his men swore by him for his courage and gift of leadership.

For two days we watched the camps, and then one morning pillars of dust slowly rising and troops marching on every road showed that once more trouble was afoot. We made immediate preparations to depart, for we were only there as an observation-post. Before we started, a companion and I went down to a farmhouse to fill our saddlebags with meal and biltong from a supply stored there, and in returning we rode into a troop of English horse that unexpectedly appeared through the trees. We whipped up and raced away towards where we could see Theron and his men retreating in the distance, but the patrol was hard on our heels, and galloped after us for over a mile, firing about our ears, until at last our men, seeing the danger, came to the rescue. We fell back slowly until dark, and spent the night in view of their camp fires, and next morning, when we reached the north bank of the Rhenoster River, we found it deserted.

A solitary member of the 'ACC', left behind for the purpose, told us that General Botha was summoned to Pretoria and that General de la Rey had taken the remainder of the forces towards the Transvaal border. We were to follow after.

Chapter 12

The British Invade the Transvaal

Travelling on through empty abandoned country, we overtook some sort of a rearguard by next evening at Viljoensdrift, and in their company we crossed over that night into the Transvaal at Vereeniging. Here there were only a few Irishmen of the dynamite squad, who told us that the 'ACC' was camped a few miles on, and that some of de la Rey's men under General Lemmer were ten miles down the river, but that for the rest the Boers had vanished.

Captain Theron asked me to remain with him, but I refused as I wished to rejoin my brothers, so I said goodbye next morning, and went in search of the 'ACC'. This was the last I saw of him, for he was killed a few miles from here; a man who would have made a name for himself had he lived.

The 'ACC' now decided to join General Lemmer's men, and, after a long ride, we came up with them just in time to see a strong body of English cavalry crossing the Vaal River, cheering loudly at setting foot in the Transvaal again, for it was twenty years since a British soldier had trodden its soil.

They had batteries posted on the Free State side, and, as we had ridden too close up, Lemmer lost three men killed and several wounded, with no corresponding advantage to himself. He thereupon drew off into rougher country where we halted for the night, and next morning, seeing the British troops advancing from the Vaal, we retreated in the direction of Johannesburg, thirty miles away.

By noon we found General de la Rey, with nearly a thousand men, holding some low hills within sight of the mine-stacks. I was surprised that he had managed to keep so many with him, considering the way in which things were going to pieces, but he had more control over men than any officer whom I had thus far seen.

At four o'clock the advance was on us again. Armstrong guns were unlimbered, and we were severely handled. The position we held was a strong one, however, and despite casualties we stood our ground until dark, by which time word came through that we must fall back on the Klip River, a small stream on the outskirts of Johannesburg. We groped our way through the night with hundreds of other men all jostling each other on the narrow road, and, having forded the river, we slept till daybreak. We were now practically backed right up against the city, so close that sightseers and even women came out in cabs and on foot to view the proceedings, and soon after dawn the English came pouring over the ground to the south of the Klip River with horse, foot and guns. As we were watching them, Commandant Gravett, of the Boksburg commando, came riding by, asking for volunteers to accompany him to a low ridge just beyond, from which he said we could make a showing against some English cavalry that had crossed the river and were approaching in our direction. The men of the 'ACC' hung in the wind, for they were sulking over some gibe Gravett had flung at us when he elbowed his people off the road the night before, so only a man named Jack Borrius and I went. We rode rapidly forward, reaching the hills just in time to forestall the English horsemen from getting there first. We brought down three, whereupon the rest galloped back through the river, but soon returned reinforced, and they came at us so determinedly that we loosed only a few shots before running for our lives. We came under brisk fire without any casualties, but my roan horse had a piece clipped from his ear by a rifle bullet before I got back to the 'ACC' in the rear.

My two brothers had been absent since earlier in the morning. For several days the younger one had been ailing, and now he was so ill that Hjalmar and our boy Charley had taken him to Johannesburg, one riding on either side to hold him on his horse. We did not know what was wrong with him, but it subsequently turned out to be typhoid fever, from which he barely escaped with his life.

They had not yet returned when I rejoined the 'ACC' and in the meanwhile we were kept busy enough, for the British troops were by now crossing the Klip River in large numbers, deploying on the open ground between us, and before long shelling had commenced. No doubt they knew by now that Johannesburg was theirs for the taking, and they ran no risks with their infantry, confining themselves to most unpleasant gun-fire.

For the first time for many days we too had guns in action, and there were several batteries of Creusots blazing away from close by. The gunners suffered terribly, and I counted seven artillerists killed in less than fifteen minutes during one particularly violent burst. We of the 'ACC' were snugly tucked away in a kopje where the shelter was so good that we did not lose a man or a horse, and we passed most of the day idly watching the scene. Shortly before sunset we saw activity away to our right, and there came line upon line of infantry, with guns roaring. General de la Rey had his Lichtenburg men there, but although they are reputed the best fighting men in the Transvaal, they were overborne by weight of numbers and were soon riding back in full retreat. This was the last effort to defend Johannesburg. When the line gave, all was over, and during the night de la Rey drew off to the west to his own country, where the doughty old warrior was to fight many another battle in days to come.

All semblance of order or resistance now disappeared. Wherever one looked, men were departing wholesale, and the universal cry was: '*Huis-toe*, the war is over'. Several of our 'ACC' men deserted at this juncture, but most of them remained, and we fell back that evening to Langlaagte, a suburb of Johannesburg, where we spent the night. My brother Hjalmar and our boy were waiting for me. They had reached Johannesburg railway station, and had succeeded, in spite of the disorder, in getting Arnt on board a goods train for Pretoria. They said that all trains were crammed with fugitives, but that they had left him in the care of a man who promised to deliver him into my father's hands. With this they had to be satisfied, but they returned towards the firing very worried as to the outcome, for by now he was delirious. Next morning (it must have been about the 1st or 2nd of June) we saw the British feeling their way into Johannesburg, so we followed the drift of retreating men going round by the eastern side of the town. As we passed the gold-mines that lay on our route, there was a small column of cavalry drawn up not far off watching us go by, who made no attempt to interfere with us, probably thinking that we were refugees and not worth bothering about.

When we got to the main road leading to Pretoria, we found it crowded with mounted men, wagons and herds of cattle, and we had to make our way through dreadful confusion. To the right was another British column moving parallel with us, which caused our native Charley to remark, 'Baas, those English people don't know the road to Pretoria, so they are coming along with us to make sure', and indeed I believe that the English could have ridden in amongst us that day without firing a shot, so strong was the conviction that our army was disbanded and the war at an end.

By sunset the 'ACC' worked itself out of the throng and halted at Sixmile Spruit, a rivulet that distance from Pretoria. Commandant Malan intended to wait here until next morning, but my brother and I pushed on as we were anxious to get home and see our father.

We reached Pretoria by ten o'clock, and rode through the deserted streets to our home in the Sunnyside suburb. Here disappointment awaited us, for the place was in darkness and the house was empty. We went to several neighbours to make inquiries. They seemed to think that the enemy was upon them, for it was only after we had tried at several doors that at last a shrinking figure appeared in response to our knocking with rifle-butts, and, seeing who we were, curtly told us that President Kruger and my father had run away, and that Pretoria was to be surrendered to the British in the morning, after which the door was slammed in our faces. We knew the President and my father too well to believe that they had ignominiously run away, and the fact that they had left Pretoria together was proof to us that they had gone to carry on the war, so we returned home, and after stabling and feeding our weary horses, broke open one of the doors and went inside.

We made a roaring fire in the kitchen, at which we cooked a dinner with supplies from the pantry, and then slept in comfortable beds, a change after the freezing nights we had endured of late.

It was nevertheless a dismal homecoming. Our younger brother had been left stranded in a cattle-truck, weak and ill, amid the chaos of a general retreat, our other brother was missing, and for all we knew dead, while my father was gone and our home was deserted.

We only heard later that my stepmother and the younger children had been sent to Delagoa Bay and thence by sea up the East Coast of Africa to Holland, where they still are.

Early next morning we set about making plans for the future. First we saddled our horses and rode uptown to find out what was happening. The streets were swarming with leaderless men, knowing even less of the situation than ourselves. Of the 'ACC' there was no trace, and all was utter confusion, with looting of shops and supply depots, and a great deal of criticism of our leaders.

After commandeering provisions for our future requirements, we returned home. The British by now were shelling the forts outside the town, and an occasional 'over' fell in our vicinity, but we were accustomed to gunfire by now, and remained quietly resting until the afternoon.

Towards three o'clock a gaunt figure appeared before us. It was our missing brother Joubert, whom we had given up for lost. He said that his horse had been killed when the 'ACC' were rushed at Kopje-Alleen a fortnight before, but he had succeeded in escaping on foot. After tramping it for many days, he reached Johannesburg in time to board the last outgoing train, which had just brought him to Pretoria. As burghers now came galloping past, shouting that the English were entering by the road above the railway station, I hurried on horseback to the centre of the town, where I annexed a saddled horse from among several standing before a shop that was being looted, and absconded with this remount for my brother. We now prepared to leave, though as a matter of fact the English only occupied Pretoria the next day, but, as we did not know that the rumour was premature, we thought it safer to get away in good time.

In the circumstances it seemed best to leave our faithful old native boy behind, as we felt that with the increasing difficulty of securing horses and food we could no longer indulge in the luxury of a servant, and besides, we needed his animal as an additional pack-horse. The poor fellow piteously entreated us to keep him, but we had to harden our hearts, and, having no money to give him, we allowed him to take from the house as many blankets and other articles as he could carry, and so parted from him after an affecting scene. Our arrangements were easily made. We loaded what we needed from pantry and wardrobes on to our pack-horses, and after a last look round at our home we rode away on the main road leading east, along which many other fugitives were already hurrying.

By dark we had got as far as the big distillery eight or nine miles distant, where we spent the night. By morning so many other horsemen had arrived that there must have been nearly fifteen hundred, few of whom were under officers, and none of whom seemed to know what to do next. My brothers and I rode about, looking for the 'ACC', but, although we found no trace of them, it did not worry us overmuch, and we agreed to remain on our own until we fell in with them again or until we had made further plans. In going round we met Mr Smuts, the State Attorney, off-saddled under a tree with his brother-in-law, P Krige, who had been one of Isaac Malherbe's men and had been seriously wounded at Spion Kop. I had not seen him since, for he had only just left hospital to avoid being captured in Pretoria by the British.

As Mr Smuts was a member of the Government, we persuaded him to tell us where my father and the President had gone to, and what the general position was. He said that the President and my father were at Machadodorp, a small village on the Pretoria-

Delagoa Bay railway line, at which place they had set up a new capital. So far from making peace, they were determined to carry on the war by means of guerrilla tactics. They hoped to stop the rot that had set in, and Mr Smuts himself was starting immediately for the Western Transvaal to reorganise that area, while similar steps would be taken elsewhere; and in the Free State, President Steyn and Christian de Wet had undertaken to pull things together. The Commandant-General, Louis Botha, was lying not many miles away, collecting as many burghers as he could to form the nucleus of a fresh army, and everyone was to be directed thither. All this was better news than we had heard for a long time, and already we could see, from the animated way in which the men were standing around their fires talking and laughing, that there was a more hopeful feeling in the air.

My eldest brother and I decided that, before joining a commando, we should seek out my father at Machadodorp, partly to find out his news, and partly to hear whether he knew what had become of our younger brother Arnt. My brother Joubert refused to accompany us and rode away to look for General Botha, so that once more we lost sight of him for many days. Machadodorp lay a hundred and seventy miles due east, and Hjalmar and I set out on the long ride without delay. We did the ninety miles to Middelburg in two days, and here we were lucky enough to get a lift by goods train for the rest of the journey, arriving at Machadodorp by the following morning. This village was for the time being the capital of the Transvaal. Long rows of railway coaches constituted the Government Buildings, where such officials as had not preferred surrender made a show of carrying on the public business of the country. In one of these coaches we found my father installed, and his welcome was a warm one, for he had received no news of us since we had left him in April to go south into the Free State. We were greatly relieved to hear that our brother Arnt was at that moment lying in the Russian ambulance at Waterval-onder, in the low country, forty miles down the line. He had arrived delirious some days before, but there was hope of his recovery. My father confirmed what Mr Smuts had told us of the military position, and he said that guerrilla war was better suited to the genius of the Boer people than regular field operations. He spoke of George Washington and Valley Forge, and of other seemingly lost causes that had triumphed in the end, and although we did not altogether share his optimism (for we had the memory of demoralised and flying columns fresh in our minds), yet his faith cheered us tremendously.

When we asked after President Kruger we were told that he too was down at Waterval-onder, for he was an old and feeble man in these days and was unable to stand the bitter cold up here.

Before returning in search of General Botha, Hjalmar and I took train down the mountain to see our sick brother. We found him with many wounded men in a hospital improvised by that very Russian ambulance corps which General Joubert had refused to accept, but which had nevertheless come to our assistance.

He was conscious when we got there, and the Russian nurses said that he had turned the corner, although still in grave danger.

At Waterval-onder we had our last sight of President Kruger. He was seated at a table in a railway saloon, with a large Bible open before him, a lonely, tired man. We stood gazing at him through the window, but as he was bowed in thought, we made no attempt to speak to him. He left for Portuguese territory not long after, and I never saw him again, for he was taken to Holland on a Dutch man-of-war, and he is still an exile.[1]

We now returned up the Berg to Machadodorp, where we said good-bye to my father and travelled back to Middelburg by rail to get our horses, which we had left in charge of one of the townspeople.

Here there was a small contingent of German volunteers, about sixty strong, under an Austrian, Baron von Goldeck, whom we had known in Natal. As we had no idea where the 'ACC' had gone, and as one commando was as good as another, we obtained admission to the 'German Corps', as it was somewhat grandiloquently called. Von Goldeck was preparing to ride his men west to scout for General Botha, so we trekked away the next day, going via Balmoral Station, until in three days' time we gained contact with the British patrols on the outskirts of Pretoria.

Lord Roberts was resting his army around the capital, so we spent the next ten days skirmishing over the uneven country to watch his movements. We had several exciting encounters, in the course of which we lost five Germans, but it was an enjoyable time. We lived on what we could forage, and, what with scouting to within sight of Pretoria and raising alarms in the big camps, there was not a dull moment. Then the country got too hot to hold us and we fell back twenty or thirty miles, to where General Botha was busy collecting as many men as he could get together. We found him halted near the old battlefield of Bronkhorstspruit, where Colonel Anstruther's force was cut up in the war of 1880. He lay by his saddle on the open veld, and save for a few dispatch-riders and some pack-horses, there was nothing to distinguish his headquarters from any of the other groups of burghers dotted about.

He said we had done well and could now take a holiday, so we rode to a deserted farm some distance off, and remained there quietly for some days.

Chapter 13

Farther Afield

It was by now becoming generally known that General Botha was assembling a new army, and the more spirited elements were gradually coming back from their homes and elsewhere, in order to rejoin him.

Already he had three thousand men, and more were riding in daily. Things were therefore shaping better and there was, at any rate, a visible recovery from the deplorable conditions that had held during the retreat through the Free State.

At this stage, remnants of the Natal commandos began to come through. The forces we had left there had been driven out, much as we had been hustled from the Free State, and had endured the same humiliations. Thousands of the weaker men had

---

[1]He died in Switzerland in 1904.

surrendered or gone home, and in many cases entire commandos had melted like snow, whilst those that did remain were mere skeleton formations. The remainder, however, were seasoned fighting men, and nearly two thousand of them joined General Botha here, bringing his total force up to five thousand or more.

One evening I saw a Natal contingent approaching over the hills. When they reached us the men turned out to be the remnant of our old Pretoria commando, now dwindled to about one hundred and fifty, amongst whom were many old friends of the Ladysmith days. The burgher-right men had deserted in a body, and the commando had lost heavily in killed and wounded since we had left them. Mr Zeederberg, the Field-Cornet, had broken down in health, and one Max Theunissen, a young fellow of twenty-five, was in command.

Old General Maroola, they said, and his brother Swart Lawaai, had been deposed, but they had remained in the field and were serving as privates with some other commando.

I had got on well enough with von Goldeck and the Germans, but I decided to return to the Pretoria men. My brother Hjalmar preferred to stay where he was, so I said good-bye, and rode away with my roan horse and the little Basuto pony to join my former unit. The morning after we moved off, going south over the plains for two days and then bending round so as to make for the railway line between Pretoria and Johannesburg, as Max Theunissen was under orders to destroy the English communications. There were, however, so many English soldiers guarding the track that we never got within five miles of it, and for the next fortnight we wandered about searching for an opportunity that did not come. The English troops camped about Pretoria occasionally flung a few long-range shells at us, but otherwise there was nothing of importance.

While we were operating in this quarter I had unexpected word of the 'ACC'. We were taking cover one morning in a hill from the shell-fire of a column that had appeared, when two burghers galloped up to seek shelter. They belonged to the 'ACC', and when I asked after the others they pointed to a farm far out on the plain, where they said Commandant Malan and the rest were off-saddled, so when they rode away I went along with them, partly to see my old companions, and partly to explain to Commandant Malan about my brothers and myself.

To reach the farm we had to ride across the front of the English column, but they let us go in peace, and I was soon shaking hands with Malan and his men. A little later, the English force moved nearer, and began to drop lyddite shells from a howitzer posted on a distant rise. This caused the worst incident I saw in the war. For a time the shells burst harmlessly on open ground, but as the aim grew truer, Commandant Malan ordered us to take cover, and we distributed ourselves behind the garden wall and behind the wall of a small dam that stood near the dwelling-house. By the wall of the dam was a huge willow tree, in the rear of which seven men of the 'ACC' took station. Suddenly a shell hit the bole about two feet from the ground and, passing right through the tree, exploded as it emerged on the other side. The result was terrible, for the seven unfortunate men were blown to pieces which strewed the ground for thirty yards beyond. They were so mangled that, when the English gun ceased firing, their remains had to be collected with a shovel, a most sickening spectacle. And a further trial was in store for the 'ACC'. After the howitzer had gone, Commandant Malan mounted his horse and with a few men rode up towards the English troops to fire the intervening grass. Half an hour later, as I was returning to the Pretoria commando, I saw by the way in which his men were standing that something was wrong, so I galloped up to find him lying with a bullet in his throat, and he died in a few minutes, and any lingering idea I may have had of rejoining the 'ACC' now vanished, for they seemed under an unlucky star. For another week or two the general military situation remained quiet. British columns came from Pretoria now and then, but they were only on the prowl, and there was no serious fighting. This spell of calm was invaluable, for it gave the Boer leaders breathing space in which to reorganise their scattered forces, and it gave the men time to recover from the demoralising effect of the long retreats, with the result that when Lord Roberts resumed operations in the middle of July a far better spirit prevailed.

The British advance started early one morning on a broad front. We of the Pretoria commando took up a position in the nearest kopjes, but before long were so heavily shelled that we withdrew, the other commandos also falling back. The direction in which the English were moving was east along both sides of the Delagoa Bay railway line. Up to now this way to the Portuguese port had been open and the Transvaal Government had been importing supplies on a large scale, but apparently Lord Roberts intended to close this final loophole and cut us off completely from the outer world.

Accordingly great numbers of troops, apparently more than thirty thousand, moved to right and left of the railway, sweeping us easily before them. They were spread fanwise over a distance of fifteen miles, and as the usual curtain of scouts approached, followed by shell-fire from the guns moving up behind, we pursued the same methods that we had employed in the Free State, falling back from hill to hill and rise to rise, firing when opportunity offered, but not really fighting. In this manner we retreated for four or five days, by which time the English had pushed us along the railway line through the town of Middelburg, and right up to Belfast village forty miles beyond. On the night we reached this place there was such a press on the road that in the dark I lost the Pretoria men. By next morning they were nowhere to be seen, but, as I was getting accustomed to quick changes of commando, I joined a body of Boksburgers who happened to be passing. They were part of a larger force under that same Commandant Gravett with whom I had gone down to the river the day before Johannesburg was taken.

Boksburg is a small mining village on the Reef, and the Boksburg men for some reason or other were known as 'Gravett's Guinea Fowls' (*Gravett se tarantaal-koppe*), a title in which they took great pride. Gravett was of English extraction, a fine big man, greatly liked and trusted by all. He was killed a month or two later, and I was with him when he died. In the company of the 'Guinea Fowls' I trekked from Belfast to Dalmanutha, another forty miles up the line. After being marched about for some days over mountainous country, we were allotted a position on the edge of the escarpment near Machadodorp, where General Botha intended making a stand athwart the Delagoa railway.

Along this crest he was going to fight a last pitched battle before taking to guerrilla war. All through the retreat we knew that sooner or later it was planned to break away from before the English advance and scatter in smaller bands, and this knowledge had kept the men in good heart.

Although they had been badly harried, there was no tendency to dissolve as had been the case in the Free State, and when they were called upon to make a final stand they were willing enough. The position General Botha had selected was a natural fortress. Between us and the enemy there stretched a level plain that could be swept by rifle-fire, and immediately behind us the ground fell steeply into a valley, giving excellent cover for men and horses. We were practically on the farthest rim of the high veld, for a few miles back the country drops into the malarial lowlands that lie towards the Portuguese border. The British had come to a temporary halt at Belfast, and for a week there was no sign of them. Towards the end of that time, while I was working on the defences, I saw the Pretoria commando come riding up, and with them were my two elder brothers Hjalmar and Joubert. Needless to say we were all three glad to be together again, and I at once took leave of the Boksburgers in order to join them.

The Pretoria men were given a portion of the line close by, and at sunrise on the next day heavy dust-clouds arose in the distance, and before long masses of British infantry appeared on the skyline.

They were calculated to be thirty-six thousand strong (but it is difficult to count infantry on the march), and within an hour their skirmishers were firing, and their batteries were unlimbering almost within rifle-range of us.

By ten a heavy bombardment was in full swing, although no actual advance was attempted, as they evidently intended first to batter down our works.

This lasted until sunset, but our cover was so good that the casualties were nowhere heavy, and the Pretoria commando went scot-free. By dark it had all died down, and we passed a quiet night lying around our fires. Next day the programme was repeated. We were shelled to such an extent that one dared scarcely look over the edge of the breastworks for the whirring of metal and the whizzing of bullets. Several of our men were wounded, and my brother Hjalmar was shot below the eye. My other brother led him down into the valley, for he was partially blinded, and there placed him on his horse and rode with him for the nearest medical assistance.

This second day of the bombardment was a crowded one. Shortly after my brothers had left there was an earthquake, the first I had ever experienced. It came with a loud rumbling, and the ground rocked beneath us like a ship, while stone fell from the works, causing much alarm, for disturbances of this kind are practically unknown in South Africa. We thus suffered a bombardment from above and an earthquake from below at one and the same time, and this remained a topic for wondering discussion months afterwards. When it was over, a lyddite shell from a howitzer dropped almost on top of me. It was like another earthquake. I was stunned for several minutes, and, after that, lay for a while in a semi-conscious state, hardly knowing whether I was dead or alive.

In the afternoon a detachment of infantry came down a defile on our left. We saw them in time to drive them back, killing and wounding about fifteen, but owing to the cross-fire we could not reach the fallen men until some time after dark, when we groped our way to get their rifles and equipment. The night was so cold that we found only three soldiers alive, some wounded, who might otherwise have survived, having died of exposure. We carried the three men back, and laid them by a fire, where one more died before morning.

As soon as it grew light on the third day, the bombardment recommenced more furiously than ever, but, instead of being spread all over our front, it was concentrated on the section held by the Johannesburg Police, a mile to our right. Tremendous gun-fire was poured on them, and from the massing of the infantry columns we knew that a crisis was at hand. The police behaved splendidly. Twice they threw back the attacks, and hung on doggedly under some of the fiercest pounding of the war. While this was going on the rest of us could do little, and for the most part we sat perched on our *schanses* watching the struggle. By sunset the police were all but annihilated, and in the dusk we saw the English infantry break into their positions. Here and there a hunted man went running down the slope behind, but the majority of the defenders were killed. Our line being broken, we had to give way too, and after dark General Botha ordered a withdrawal. We fetched our horses from the valley below, and fell back for two or three miles before halting for the night.

Next morning we made for Machadodorp, long-range shell-fire accompanying us. We found the village deserted, the movable capital having left the day before for Waterval-onder below the *berg*.

Beyond Machadodorp a single road climbs the last range, and from here one can look down upon the low country. As this was the only avenue of retreat, we soon found ourselves travelling among a medley of burghers, guns, wagons, and a great crowd of civilian refugees fleeing with their flocks and herds and chattels. It was pitiful to see this exodus, for the English brought their guns up with great speed and the road was heavily shelled over at times, as the wagons with women and children came under fire, but on the whole their behaviour was good, and in the end the shelling proved more unpleasant than dangerous.

After a while the Transvaal Artillery managed to get a battery of Creusot guns into action, which held up the advance sufficiently long to enable the non-combatants with their wagons, carts, and animals to get out of range, after which we too moved slowly up the mountain. I had a narrow escape when we halted to rest our horses. I was sitting on an ant-heap reading a book, when someone called to me that my roan horse was in trouble. He was plucking grass some distance off and had got his legs entangled in the reins, so I went to free him. While I was away a shell burst on the ant-heap, blowing holes in my book, and tearing up the mound itself.

We spent the night at Helvetia on the mountain, and next morning rode down the pass to Waterval-onder, a drop of two thousand feet in less than three miles. The British appeared above the *berg* an hour or two later, but did not follow us down, so we wended our way at leisure.

At Waterval-onder the railway comes out of a tunnel from the high country, and here, standing beside the line, were my father and my brother Hjalmar. They had come from Machadodorp by train the day before and were halted to let the engine get up steam, after which they were to be hauled farther down with other officials and a number of wounded. Hjalmar had a bloody bandage over his eye like a pirate, but otherwise he made light of his hurt. Our remaining two brothers were missing, but we were so continuously losing and finding each other nowadays that their absence caused us no undue anxiety, as we felt they would turn up sooner or later.

After a while the engine-driver ran up to say that he was going off, so my father and brother had to climb on board, and I continued down the road behind the retreat which was crowding the long valley that runs towards the Godwan River.

By dark I caught up with the Pretoria commando, and we spent the night pleasantly encamped beside a stream. Since morning we had at one stride descended from the bleak highlands to the warmer climate of the low country, and I for one spent the first comfortable night for many weeks.

Next day the Boer forces retired still farther down the valley to Nooitgedacht, where about two thousand English prisoners were confined in a camp. They were lining the barbed-wire enclosure beside the railway line to watch us go by, and were in high spirits, for they knew that they were to be liberated that day. They exchanged good-natured banter with us as we passed, although one of them, less amiable than the rest, said to me: 'Call this a retreat? — I call it a bl——dy rout!' I must say it looked like it, for by now the English advance was on our heels once more, and the narrow valley road was thronged with horsemen, wagons and cattle, all moving rearward in chaos. With the Boers, however, appearances are often deceptive—what might seem to be a mob of fugitives one day, might well prove to be a formidable fighting force on the next, and the soldier who spoke to me little thought that the men pouring by in disorderly flight were yet to test the endurance and the patience of Great Britain to its utmost.

We now headed down along the banks of the Godwan River for another twenty-five miles, by which time the pursuit had slackened, and for the next three days we lay in peace amid beautiful surroundings of mountain and forest. The English probably thought that General Botha meant to cross over into Portuguese territory for internment, rather than surrender, so they lay on their arms and rested. But General Botha intended far otherwise. One morning my father came up by special train from Nelspruit, where another temporary capital had been established, and he told us that the Commandant-General was going to strike north into the wilds. He would then make for the mountains beyond Lydenburg, where the forces were to be reorganised for the carrying on of guerrilla warfare.

My father had really come up to see how my brothers and I were getting on, but I was the only one there. Hjalmar was at an ambulance recovering from his wound— Joubert had not returned since he had ridden back to the fighting at Dalmanutha, and the youngest was wherever the Russian ambulance wagons had gone, so that at the moment we were a pretty scattered family.

My father remained with me for the day, and then steamed back down the valley. Unfortunately the engine that brought him ran over and killed my poor little Basuto pony. Besides having served me faithfully since the first day of the war, he was an intimate link with our old home life, for he had come with us from the Free State as a foal, and the loss of this loyal companion was a great blow to me. However, there was not much time for repining, as the English resumed their advance early next morning. The commandos fell back at once; some retired down the valley, but others slipped into the mountains. Among the latter was the Pretoria commando, which climbed to a place called Devil's Kantoor, where we arrived that night. The Pretoria men had for some days been discussing the question of doubling back to the high veld. They felt drawn towards their own part of the world, and wished to return to where they might get occasional word of their families left behind in Pretoria: so they now held a meeting and decided to break away along bridle-paths through the mountains. I refused to accompany them, as my father and brothers were ahead, so I said good-bye, and soon they were riding off into the dark. I did not see them again, but they succeeded in making their way back to their own district, where such of them as were not killed or captured remained in the field to the end of the war. I myself joined a party of burghers whom I found on the mountain, and in their company I rode all night, until dawn found us far down on the plain that runs by Barberton towards Kaapmuiden. Beyond this we got into rugged country and, travelling slowly, reached Hectorspruit in three days' time.

This was the last railway station before the Portuguese border, and here lay nearly five thousand horsemen awaiting General Botha's orders. We had shaken off the English army by fifty or sixty miles, and I found all three of my brothers there before me. Hjalmar's wound was better and Arnt had so far recovered that he could sit a horse, while Joubert was none the worse for his wanderings during the retreat. My father was missing, but he arrived two days later. He had abandoned his railway coach owing to a stoppage on the line, and had come across the difficult area above Crocodilepoort on horseback, so our family was united again for the first time after several months.

General Botha now got everything ready. Surplus guns were destroyed or thrown into the Crocodile River, and the sick and wounded were sent over the Portuguese border, while such stores as had been accumulated were distributed among the men or else burnt. Then, on a morning early in September (1900) he led the way into the uncharted bush to begin a new phase of the war.

Chapter 14

New Conditions

Our road ran through the Sabi low country teeming with big game of all descriptions. By day great herds of zebra, wildebeest, and sable, stood fearlessly gazing at us, and at night lions prowled roaring around our camps. Of hunting we had our fill, and to me this journey through a strange and remote region was full of fascination, for we were passing through country as untouched as that upon which the old pioneers had looked when first they came north in the days of the Great Trek.

After long marches we reached the foot of the mighty range that runs north as far as the eye can see. From here General Botha sent the commandos on, with instructions to follow the base of the escarpment to the Murchison Range, two hundred miles away. He himself, escorted by the remnant of the Johannesburg Police and accompanied by the handful of officials who still remained, climbed up by a hunting-path to make for a lost village called Ohrigstad in the Steelpoort Gorge, our way leading by Gras Kop and Pilgrim's Rest amid mountains and forests and gorges more beautiful than any I know of in South Africa.

Now that President Kruger had left the country, the Transvaal Government consisted of my father and Schalk Burger who was the Vice-President, together with a few other heads of departments, and they naturally followed General Botha up the mountain, as did my brothers and I. We remained at Ohrigstad for a week, but when malaria broke out the Government moved to within a few miles of Lydenburg village on higher ground. General Botha now went off to plan guerrilla operations.

He did this so effectively that in a few months' time he had mobile forces in every quarter of the Transvaal harrying and worrying the British far and near, a re-awakening that must have been particularly galling to them considering how close we had been to a general collapse.

All this, however, was still to come, and in the meanwhile my brothers and I lay in the Government laager, fretting at our enforced idleness. We endured it for two weeks, after which we made up our minds to leave. My youngest brother was still so weak from his illness that he had to remain, but the other three of us made ready. My brother Hjalmar, who had a queer bent of his own, preferred to go off by himself, and although we tried to keep him with us he rode away towards the eastern Transvaal. He was subsequently captured and sent to a prison camp in India, and I did not see him again. We had heard from a passing burgher that General Beyers was collecting a force at the Warm Baths, two hundred miles distant, so we agreed to ride thither. Our preparations were soon made, for they were simple enough. We shot a koodoo in the mountain, and made biltong, and we collected a supply of mealies from a neighbouring field. This was all the commissariat we had, for now that we were cut off from the outer world through losing the Delagoa Bay line, we were on Spartan diet, and for the next two years such luxuries as sugar, coffee, tea, bread, and soap were only to be had on rare occasions by capture from the enemy.

We said good-bye to all, and set out.

I did not see my father again for twenty months. He remained in the field until the end of the war with the Government laager, handling his rifle like a private soldier when they came under fire, which was quite often, and doing much to keep up the spirits of the fighting men by his poems and his personal example.

It was a long ride to the Warm Baths. Our way went through bush country, with neither track nor road to guide us, for the region we traversed was untenanted save by native tribes and wild animals. I was on my splendid old roan who had carried me from the start, and my brother rode the horse which we had taken back from our native boy at Pretoria.

On the third day of our journey we had a mournful encounter. We came on Commandant Gravett dying of wounds in the bush. He had been hit by a shell ten days before, and his men had brought him here to prevent his falling into the hands of the British. He knew his end was approaching, but he bore his sufferings without complaint, and spoke of his coming death with resignation. He called us to him a few minutes before the end to tell us of his friendship with my father in former days, and a little while after he lapsed into unconsciousness from which he never recovered. We helped to bury him under a tree, and rode saddened on our way.

For ten days we journeyed, straying far north beyond the Olifants River, misled by natives who told us of a commando in that direction. When we came up with this force, it was only a patrol on their way to Secocoeni's country to inquire into fighting that had broken out between two native tribes. Among the patrol were old General Maroola and his brother Swart Lawaai, now serving in the ranks. They were dressed as in the Natal days, only shabbier from long exposure on the veld, but they greeted us as if nothing had changed since. At length we turned south, and eventually reached Warm Baths, where we found General Beyers with a thousand men. He had been a lawyer before the war, and was now in command of the North-West under General Botha's new scheme of reorganisation. He was a brave man, but I never liked him.

Here we were surprised to find our old 'ACC' commando almost intact. After that unfortunate day, when Commandant Malan and seven men were killed, they had left the high veld and had made straight for these parts. This was why we had never come across them during the retreat to the Portuguese border. They were still about sixty strong, under command of a newcomer, a young officer named Lodi Krause, who invited us to rejoin, which we did at once. We remained in the neighbourhood of the Warm Baths for the better part of a month while General Beyers was raising more men, and the time passed pleasantly enough. We hunted a good deal and several times rode out on patrol to Pienaars River, twenty-five miles towards Pretoria, to watch the doings of a large English camp there. On one of these occasions we had a narrow escape. Six of us were approaching a kopje overlooking the camp, when suddenly a strong body of horsemen tried to cut off our retreat. We turned and made a dash for it, passing so near to some of the troopers that I heard them shouting at us to halt, while their bullets whipped around us as they galloped through the bush. We shook them off, however, without getting a scratch.

Except for these patrols and hunting for the pot, we spent a quiet time. Late in November my younger brother Arnt arrived at the Baths looking fit and well, having ridden hundreds of miles to find us, for he too had found life in the Government laager too slow once he was restored to health. We were very glad to see him, and the three of us built a weatherproof hut and fared well as food was plentiful. Rations were chiefly game and mealie meal, of which last General Beyers had accumulated a large supply from the Waterberg farms. He himself was camped close to us, a dark moody man who lost no opportunity of holding prayer meetings. With him was the Reverend Mr Kriel, a Dutch Reformed parson, equally zealous: so between the two we were continually bidden to religious services, and they even went the length of ordering all the younger men to attend Bible classes. When my brothers and I ignored the order, General Beyers and Mr Kriel rode over in person to expostulate with us, and even threatened to turn us out of the commando, but we stuck to our guns and heard nothing further of it; in fact we rather gained in reputation, for the Boers, although a religious people, are not intolerant in matters of faith.

I did not care for Beyers, but I liked the old *predikant* for all his narrowness, and afterwards in the Cape Colony I grew to admire him as a steadfast man.

On about the 7th of December (1900) we were told to be in readiness to move south next day. My brother Joubert now surprised us by saying he was not coming. He said that he was going to be a gunner with a Creusot gun, one of the few still left, and was leaving us at once with his new unit. He had always wished to be an artilleryman, and his obstinacy defeated our arguments. He rode away that same afternoon and I have not seen him since, for he was captured and sent to Bermuda, where he still is. General Beyers left a few hundred men and his guns behind to oppose the English columns that were preparing to invade the northern Transvaal, and with the rest, about eight hundred strong, he marched off. His purpose was to make south over the

Magaliesbergen to the high veld beyond, in order to carry on guerrilla warfare there.

Our first day's trek brought us to the big native *stad* of a local chief named Koos Mamogali. From here we looked across a valley, twelve miles wide, towards the Magaliesbergen. The mountain range stretches east to west for a hundred miles and more and, in this area, forms the dividing line between the high veld and the bush country from which we were emerging. We crossed the valley that night, and by daybreak reached the foot of a disused pass known as 'the old wagon road'. Here there was evidence that General de la Rey had lately been in the vicinity, for we found a burning convoy of fifty or sixty English supply wagons, and one of his men who came riding by told us that they had ambushed the wagons in a stiff fight and had taken many prisoners.

We looked on this as a good omen after the unbroken run of ill luck that had dogged us for so long, for it showed that General Botha's reorganisation was beginning to take effect.

After a rest we climbed the pass, reaching the top by four that afternoon. From there, southwards, we had a wide view over the grass-covered plains, and far away on the skyline we could even see the smoke-stacks and the gold-mines of the Witwatersrand. The sight raised our spirits, and the men crowded the edge of the cliff animatedly discussing the improved outlook, for we were back from the wilds to within hail of Pretoria and Johannesburg.

Then we came down the south side, and by dark were off-saddled among the gardens and orchards below. We had had no sleep the night before and were looking forward to a good night's rest, but this was not to be. As we were preparing our supper General de la Rey came riding amongst us on his famous little white-faced pony, and word went round that we were to attack an English force camped at the foot of the mountain not far away.

Chapter 15

A Successful Affair, and After

I had last seen General de la Rey during our great retreat through the Free State. Since then he had been busy in the western Transvaal raising fresh commandos, and infusing new spirit into the fighting men by his ceaseless activity, and by the great affection they had for this wonderful old man. Only two days before he had fallen upon and captured the British convoy that we had seen on fire beyond the berg, and now he had crossed over to this side with four hundred men, to strike another blow.

An English commander, General Clements, was camped round a bend of the mountain about nine miles off, with many troops, wagons, and guns, and when Beyers arrived, General de la Rey was quick to sieze the opportunity for combined attack.

A plan of action was soon arranged. De la Rey with his horsemen was to rush the English camp at dawn from the landward side, while we were to return up the pass and make our way along the mountain-top under cover of night, until we could fire down on the enemy from the cliffs.

Having completed his dispositions, de la Rey rode away in the dark to find his own men, and soon the whistles blew for us to saddle our horses. General Beyers led us up the road down which we had come an hour or two before, but when we reached the head of the pass we changed direction, picking our way eastwards along the boulder-strewn crest of the range. We had to lead our animals, for riding was out of the question over the uneven surface and progress was slow.

Towards morning, tired and sleepy, we were halted for an hour, to enable de la Rey's guides who had accompanied us to reconnoitre. When they returned they reported that General Clements's camp stood at the base of the mountain and was held by about five hundred soldiers. On the cliffs above, close to where we now lay, was a force of equal strength entrenched behind sangars and breastworks in case of overhead attack. These men we were to deal with while de la Rey's men fell upon those below.

General Beyers, whatever his faults, was a bold and resourceful leader, and he made immediate preparations for the assault. Ordering all horses to be left behind, he passed word that we were to advance on foot. We knew no drill, so it was difficult to keep alignment in the semi-darkness, but we got ourselves sorted out into some kind of extended order and moved forward in a long ragged front.

We of the 'ACC' were on the extreme right at the edge of the cliff, with a drop of five or six hundred feet below us. Beyers was with us, and to our left walked the Waterbergers, and beyond them the Zoutpansberg men. Before we had gone far, dawn lit the mountain-tops, and with it came a fierce rifle-fire from the enemy *schanses* some distance ahead.

We had gone without sleep for two days and two nights, so that our spirits were low, and our advance came at once to a halt. Our line fell down behind rocks, and whatever shelter was to be had, leaving General Beyers walking alone, his revolver in one hand and a riding-switch in the other, imploring us to go on, but we hugged our cover against the hail of bullets lashing around us.

From where I lay on the tops of the crags, I could look straight down into the English camp hundreds of feet below. I could almost have dropped a pebble upon the running soldiers and the white-tented streets and the long lines of picketed horses.

As I looked down on the plain, from behind a jutting shoulder of the mountain came swinging into view a force of mounted men who galloped hard for the English camp. It was General de la Rey timing his attack to synchronise with our own. They closed in, and for a moment it seemed as if they would overwhelm the British, but then the soldiers rushed to their posts opening heavy fire. The plain became dotted with fallen men and horses, and the attack wavered and broke. The survivors turned towards the shelter of the buttress whence they had come, and in less than ten minutes the assault was over.

The troops facing us on the mountain now made a mistake. Like ourselves, they were able to look down at the attack, and when they saw our men retire in confusion they set up loud shouts of triumph. Stung by their cries our whole force, on some sudden impulse, started to its feet and went pouring forward. There was no stopping us now, and we swept on shouting and yelling, men dropping freely as we went.

Almost before we knew it, we were swarming over the walls, shooting and clubbing in hand-to-hand conflict. It was sharp work. I have a confused recollection of fending bayonet thrusts and firing point-blank into men's faces; then of soldiers running to the rear or putting up their hands, and, as we stood panting and excited within the barricades, we could scarcely realise that the fight was won.

Our losses were severe. On the ground across which we had charged lay a trail of dead and wounded, and yet more by the *schanses*.

In all we had about twenty-five men killed and some seventy wounded, and we shot down nearly a hundred of the English, besides taking as many more prisoners. But it was a heavy price to pay for success, even in this strange affair in which our men who had been cowering disorganised behind the rocks suddenly flung themselves upon a fortified enemy with a furious desire to silence their shouts of triumph.[1]

We had now taken the main defences, but scattered rifle shots were coming from a nest of granite boulders to the rear, and General Beyers ordered Krause, Commandant of the 'ACC', to clear the place. Krause took a dozen of us, and we worked our way forward in short rushes. But he grew impatient and told us to close in more quickly. The result was disastrous, for as we rose a salvo rang out which brought down four of our men. Having fired this parting volley, the soldiers, of whom there were only six, went running towards the mouth of the ravine which led down a cleft to their camp below.

I hit one of them through the thigh, and Krause shot another dead, but the rest escaped. We walked back to see the extent of the damage, and it was bad enough. My old schoolfellow Jan Joubert, son of Piet Joubert the late Commandant-General, had a bad chest-wound, and the other three men were dead. Two of them were young brothers named Koekemoer, about eighteen and nineteen ears old, who had been with the 'ACC' since the Free State days. I also went to see the soldier whom I had shot. He had a nasty wound, but he was bandaging it himself with the first-aid pad which they all carried, and he said he could manage. He was a typical Cockney, and bore me so little ill will that he brought out a portrait of his wife and children, and told me about them. I made him comfortable, and left him cheerfully smoking a cigarette. Jan Joubert was badly hurt, a portion of his rifle-stock having been blown into his lung, so Krause asked me to take a water-bottle from one of the dead soldiers, and go down into the ravine in search of water. I got a flask and went down the slope to the mouth of the gorge. Unknown to us, there was a path to the English camp, along which reinforcements were climbing to dislodge us. I saw twenty or thirty soldiers already near the top, standing in a group not a stone's-throw from me, while many more were coming on behind in single file.

I fired at once and dropped a man, the remainder disappearing amongst the trees. From here they opened fire on me, and I in turn had to take cover, dodging from rock to rock to get back to Krause. On hearing my news he took a number of men, and we ran down just in time to see the path crowded with soldiers. We lost no time in

---

[1] Of this attack *The Times History of the War* gives the following account:

    'In a bold reckless fashion for which there was no precedent since the attack on Wagon Hill a year earlier, and which was a startling novelty to the troops present, the Boers rushed forward on foot, cheering and shouting as they ran. Indifferent to loss, with great skill and dash ... they shot down most of the British officers, rolled up the pickets and, in spite of a stout resistance, mastered the position after killing and wounding ninety-seven officers and men.'

pouring close-range volleys into their midst. In less than a minute only dead and wounded were left; more than twenty men of the Imperial Yeomanry of London lying in the space of a few yards.

This was the final clearing, and we now had the camp below at our mercy, for we were able to fire into it without opposition. Soon we could see the occupants retiring with their guns, and we descended the ravine and entered the camp.

In passing by the intake of the gorge, I found the soldier whom I had killed. I was horrified to see that my bullet had blown half his head away, the explanation being that during one of our patrols near the Warm Baths I had found a few explosive Mauser cartridges at a deserted trading-station, and had taken them for shooting game. I kept them in a separate pocket of my bandolier, but in my excitement had rammed one of them into the magazine of my rifle without noticing it. I was distressed at my mistake, but there is not a great deal of difference between killing a man with an explosive bullet, and smashing him with a lyddite shell, although I would not knowingly have used this type of ammunition. I flung the remainder into the brook that ran by, now red with the blood of dead men lying in the water.

Having sent back for our horses, we hastened down the path into the camp.

On my way down the gorge I found two wounded officers beside the track, one with his thumb shot away and the other with a broken arm. As I came up I heard one of them remark: 'Here comes a typical young Boer for you', and they asked me whether I understood English. I told them 'Yes', and the man with the thumb said: 'Then will you tell me why you fellows are continuing the war, because you are bound to lose?' I replied: 'Oh, well, you see, we're like Mr Micawber, we are waiting for something to turn up.' They burst out laughing and the one said: 'Didn't I tell you this is a funny country, and now here's your typical young Boer quoting Dickens.'

The camp was filled with supplies of all kinds, and such a smashing of cases, and ransacking of tents and wagons, had not been seen since we looted the Dundee camp long before. While we were at this, General Beyers came riding among us in a rage, and ordered us to follow the enemy, but we thought otherwise. We considered that the object of the attack was to capture supplies, and not soldiers, as soldiers would have to be liberated for want of somewhere to keep them, and besides, if we went off, we might return to find the camp already looted during our absence. So we attended to the matter in hand, more especially as de la Rey's horsemen had recovered from their setback earlier in the morning, and could be seen stringing out across the veld towards where Clements and the balance of his troops were withdrawing down the valley in the direction of Pretoria. We told ourselves that we had done our part in the day's work, and that they could do the rest.

My brother brought my roan and his own two riding-horses down the ravine, and we took two more horses from the English lines, where many stood picketed. Searching out saddles and wallets to match, we loaded our caravan with spoil in the shape of tea, coffee, salt, sugar, food, clothing, books and other luxuries of which we had long been deprived. Then we followed the other men who, having taken what they wanted, were riding along the foot of the mountain to the spot below the Old Wagon Pass from which we had started the evening before. Thus ended our share in the fight.

The 'ACC' had lost five men killed and five wounded. Among the latter was our

Commandant Krause with a bullet in his foot, and my Corporal Jan Nagel, with his right shoulder-blade badly shattered. A French gentleman adventurer, Georges de Gourville, who belonged to us, was also badly wounded, but the worst was Jan Joubert, who was carried down to the English camp with the other serious cases, and left there until the British could be asked to send them surgical aid, for we had neither drugs nor doctors.

My brother and I had a glorious feast, and then, having gone without rest for forty-eight hours, we slept the clock round.

Next day, such of the dead as had been carried down the mountain by friends or relations were buried in a single large grave that I helped to dig. General de la Rey was present and he addressed us in eolquent words that moved many to tears, for besides being a fighter he had a fine gift of simple speech.

Here we remained for several days, during which time my brother and I enjoyed high living, after the straight diet of meat and maize on which we had subsisted for so long. We were refitted from head to heel, we carried a Lee-Metford rifle apiece, in lieu of our discarded Mausers, and above all we were well found in horseflesh. My gentle loyal old roan was as flourishing as ever, and I had a fine little chestnut pony, which I had chosen in preference to the larger but less reliable chargers in the English camp. I gave the other horses away in order to reduce our stable to manageable proportions; my brother had the two horses which he had brought with him from the north. One was a toll-free chestnut[1] and the other was the strangest horse I have ever known. My father had purchased him in the Lydenburg district from a homegoing burgher, who omitted to tell us that he was possessed of the devil. He indulged in such extraordinary antics that the police at the Government laager had declared him insane, and christened him 'Malpert' (the mad horse). Sometimes he would allow a single man to walk up and catch him without trouble, but at other times we had to turn out the whole Government from the Vice-President downward to form a cordon around him. He would pretend to be quietly grazing, but as soon as he was completely hemmed in, he would look up in assumed surprise and start to back against the ring, kicking and lashing so furiously that we had to give way, when he would go capering off, heels in air, to crop the grass near by. If another cordon were made he would repeat his performance, until he left the men helpless between cursing and laughing. The only persons for whom he had any respect were my brother Arnt and myself. He was afraid of me because once at the Lydenburg Camp, after he had twice kicked his way through, I leaped at him from a distance of several feet and flung my arms about his neck. He reared and bucked and tried to bite and roll, but I locked my legs around his, so that he could not shake me off, and in the end I bested him. With my brother he was tractable, because he had doctored him for a badly ulcered back, and the 'Malpert' showed his gratitude by obeying him. His reputation had followed him down south, and he was quite an institution among the commandos. Often we would hear a warning cry: 'Look out, here comes the "Malpert",' and the burghers would scatter beyond reach of his heels. Nevertheless, his tricks and pranks were taken good-humouredly,

---

[1]Among the Boers a chestnut horse with white face and four white stockings is called toll-free, there being a tradition that in the old days horses thus marked went through the toll-gates free of charge.

for he had magnificent staying-powers and the men looked upon him with the admiration that born horsemen have for a good animal, and as for Arnt and myself, we had a very soft spot in our hearts for this queer outlaw.

Well mounted as we were, my brother and I felt that we could ride anywhere and be ready for anything, and we looked forward with interest to the next move. General de la Rey, restless as usual, had gone off, leaving us behind with General Beyers. On Dingaansday, December 16th, he and the Reverend Mr Kriel held a religious gathering on a neighbouring hill. They invited all to join in piling a cairn of stones like that raised at PaardeKraal in 1880, during the first English war. My brother and I thought the proceedings somewhat theatrical and kept away, but so far as I know the beacon is still standing in testimony of vain hopes.

On the following day General French, the English cavalry leader, was reported to be moving up the Hekpoort valley from Pretoria, and General Beyers marched out to meet him.

Near Hekpoort the 'ACC' was ordered to take post in a range of hills skirting the valley, to guard our main body against surprise. We spent an uneasy night on a rocky crest overlooking the broad moot, as it is called, and at daybreak next morning we saw an English force of three or four thousand horsemen approaching. We had strict orders from Beyers to keep out of sight, so Krause led us into a gorge to hide our horses, after which we climbed up and peered over the rocks to view the enemy advance. The valley here lies four or five miles broad, and the British scouts were strung across it from side to side, their nearest horsemen passing so close beneath us that we could easily have shot them down. We could see General Beyers's men riding to occupy a line of hills farther up the valley, and before long they were hotly engaged. We had a fine view of the fight, but our interest in the spectacle was damped by the fact that by now the British were between ourselves and our parent body, so that if General Beyers fell back we should be left isolated in the rear.

And as the gun-fire increased and the troops began to mass, we saw our men running for their horses and galloping away. This was not unexpected, considering the heavy odds, but nevertheless there went the commando, pursued hotfoot by the English, and here were we stranded far behind.

Krause decided to recover contact by riding round the left flank of the troops, but we fell foul of so many of their patrols, and were so often shelled by pom-poms and field guns, that we were forced to take refuge in the parallel hills. From here we could make out our men about six miles off, moving west from the valley, white puffs of shrapnel breaking over them as they went, and horsemen hard on their heels.

Krause now led us into the broken country north-west of Johannesburg (Skurwe-bergen), where a small force like ours could lie in hiding for a while, and by dark we were well within the region of its tumbled hills.

Although the rainy season was overdue, we had thus far experienced only sunny days, but now the weather broke, and for the next six days it rained without ceasing. We sought out a lonely farmhouse, and here we lay over, waiting for the deluge to lift. The farm was deserted, but sheep were straying near, and dry fuel was stacked in the barns, so we fared moderately well.

Georges de Gourville, the Frenchman, had insisted on accompanying us in spite of his wound, and he nearly died here, my brother and I nursing him through his fever.

On the evening of the sixth day the clouds thinned, and we decided to set out that night in quest of General Beyers.

We had no idea where he was, but we counted on finding him sooner or later, so we started off immediately after dark. We rode all night, save for short halts, and towards morning came to a farm where a woman told us that General French was camped close by with his columns. She said that the English had given up the chase after Beyers and were on their way back to Pretoria, but had got weather-bound by the rains and were waiting for dry roads before going on.

On hearing this, Commandant Krause in his impetuous way rode off with only two other men to look around, and that was the last we ever saw of them. He and his companions must have ridden straight into the arms of the English, because soon after they left we heard a few distant shots and then silence. We waited until daylight, after which we decided to go on without him.

As a heavy mist hung over the veld, we made our way carefully, and it was as well that we did so, for when my brother and I with another man turned aside to water our horses at a dam lying off the road, four English troopers came riding out of the fog and let their horses drink about a hundred yards away. We gazed at each other suspiciously in the uncertain light, and then one of the soldiers shouted: 'Look out, those men are Boers', and pulling round they galloped away. We dismounted and fired before the mist swallowed them, bring two to the ground. Riding up we found one dead and the other rolling in agony, but both their horses had bolted after the others. Whilst we were trying to help the wounded man the mist lifted somewhat, and a large English camp was outlined close by. We could hear our men splashing over the muddy ground in haste to get away, for they too had caught sight of the camp. Bugles started calling and we caught glimpses of soldiers scurrying for their horses, so we galloped away, guided by the tracks lying clear across the sodden veld.

After a long ride we caught them up, and, when the sun broke through a little later and the fog dissolved, we could see some five hundred English horsemen coming towards us, but had no difficulty in outpacing them, for in spite of our long night's journey their heavy troop horses were no match for our hardier and lighter mounts.

Krause having been captured, we were now leaderless, but with the Boers each man is practically his own commander, so the loss did not weigh heavily upon us and, having shaken off our pursuers, we rode along westward at our leisure, until in two days' time we came on General Beyers and his men camped around the source of the Mooi River in the district of Potchefstroom.

Beyers appointed Corporal Jan Nagel to be our new Commandant, a popular choice, for, although a rough and illiterate man, he was well liked. He was still suffering from the wound received on the *berg*, but had remained in the saddle nevertheless.

We passed Christmas Day undisturbed, but next morning an English column came from the direction of Potchefstroom, and as there was no object in fighting except on ground of our own choosing, General Beyers gave them the satisfaction of thinking that we were running away, and at dark we drew off to spend the night near the village of Ventersdorp. From here we moved about at random, seeking for a chance to strike, but no favourable opening presenting itself, we saw the year 1901 in without further incident.

Chapter 16

From West to East

We now came into the Lichtenburg district, within a day's ride of Mafeking and the Bechuanaland border. This was General de la Rey's military area, but he was farther south at the time, and we only met an occasional roving patrol of his.

Beyers had a mind to raid Mafeking, but before he could do so a messenger arrived from the east with orders from General Botha to bring all his men to the Ermelo district. This meant transferring our force right across the breadth of the Transvaal, a matter of three hundred miles. Fortunately our horses were in good condition, thanks to the abundant rains and consequent good grazing, so we prepared to start at once. We now began our long march, riding eastward until some days later we reached back to the Magaliesberg Valley once more, close to where we had taken General Clements's camp. Since that event the English had apparently decided to garrison this fertile stretch, for we found a strong force a few miles down, busily constructing a fortified camp as though they intended to hold the valley permanently.

We left the camp alone, but for a few hours we lay on a ridge overlooking the troops who sent some shells at us, one of which killed a Waterberg man within a few yards of me. While we were halted here, I rode across the valley to the farmhouse near General Clements's camp to see my friend Jan Joubert, who had been left there with our other seriously wounded, after the fight. Although not yet out of danger, he was on the mend, and he told me that the British were treating them very well. A surgeon came over nearly every day, and medical orderlies were on duty to attend to their wants. They had brought his old mother from Pretoria to be with him, and officers from the camp down the valley often brought them fruit and other luxuries. I did not stay long for fear of a stray English patrol, and rode back after a hurried greeting. I did not hear what happened to him afterwards, but I believe that he made a complete recovery.

We now resumed our march, making for the railway line between Johannesburg and Pretoria. This had to be carefully approached as the track was patrolled night and day by armoured trains.

The 'ACC' was sent ahead to reconnoitre, and after an absence of twelve hours we reported back that the crossing was practicable. On our return journey to rejoin the main commando at the hill called Swart Kop, we found a suspicious-looking native watching our movements, and arrested him for further inquiry. We interrogated him closely, without getting any evidence that he was a spy, but for safety sake we kept him by us during the night, intending to release him next morning. Just before daybreak, however, while I was lying asleep by my saddle, I heard shouts, and looking up, saw the prisoner running as fast as he could go towards Swart Kop Hill. Several of our men were already astir, and as he would not stop when called, they dropped the unfortunate savage dead in his tracks, for which I was sorry, but in the circumstances it could not be helped.

That evening we started off on an all-night march for the Johannesburg railway, which we struck soon after sunrise. The 'ACC' were scouting well in advance, so we were the first to cross the metals. As we were riding over, an English trooper came cantering up to see who we were, and he was considerably taken aback when he found out. We relieved him of his horse, rifle, and equipment, and told him to go off, a command which he obeyed with alacrity, and when we saw him last he was marching steadily for Johannesburg.

On the far side of the line stood a small homestead, out of which several more soldiers came tumbling. They all surrendered, except one man, who made a bid for liberty by running into an orchard, but we shot him dead before he had gone far. At the same moment a trolley came down the line from Kaalfontein Station, and as the crew tried to turn back we fired on them, killing one and wounding a native. The dead man turned out to be a railway-ganger, as were the other four white men with him. They were on their morning round of inspection, so we let the survivors go after telling them that it was their own fault for not halting when challenged.

Our main commando now coming up, some of the burghers foolishly rode along the track towards the station, with the result that they left three men killed and several wounded in the hands of the garrison there. Our whole force now being across the line, we rode to a large farm over the rise to off-saddle.

This crossing of the railway proved a relatively simple matter, but later on in the war, when the English had completed their blockhouse system, it became increasingly difficult, and from all accounts it required something like a pitched battle to negotiate a passage over the Transvaal and Free State lines, though in the Cape Colony I saw none of this.

While we were resting at the farm, patrols were sent out, and in less than an hour one of these came galloping back to say that a strong force of English was approaching from Johannesburg. Scarcely had they returned, when we heard a succession of loud bangs and the roar of shells tearing overhead.

Our horses were out grazing, so that there was a good deal of confusion before we had the frightened animals collected, but we managed to saddle up and get away without loss, our whole force moving in a north-easterly direction with the English following. We could hardly have fought them on such open ground, armed as they were with field-guns, but in any case our object was to effect a junction with the Commandant-General, so we made no pretence of standing. The troops tried to head us off, and an armoured train from Pretoria made a belated appearance, firing heavy lyddite shells, but with our greater mobility we left the soldiers far behind, and by midday were able to come to rest after our long ride.

Next day we trekked to Olifantsfontein, where the seven 'ACC' men had been killed the year before. At this place I suffered a most serious loss, for a young fellow claimed the pony which I had brought from the English camp after the Magaliesberg fight. He brought me and the horse before General Beyers, to whom he proved that it had belonged to his father, who was among those killed that morning during de la Rey's attack. I could not but admit the justice of his case, and handed over the pony, but this left me with only my old roan, a narrow margin of safety in these days when to be horseless meant almost certain capture.

At Olifantsfontein General Botha came up with a small escort. He looked thinner than when I had last seen him in the Lydenburg mountains four months ago, but he was full or energy and confidence. He told us that Lord Roberts had decided to bring the Boers to their knees by a series of drives, in which vast numbers of troops were to sweep across the country like a drag-net. To that end, all through this month of January (1901) they were assembling fifty thousand men along the Johannesburg-Natal railway line, ready to move over the high veld on a front of sixty or seventy miles, with the intention of clearing the Eastern Transvaal, after which the process was to be repeated elsewhere, until every one was dead or taken.

The Boers were as yet mercifully unaware that this new system was to include the burning of farms, the destruction of crops and herds, and the carrying into concentration camps of their wives and children, but they were soon enough to learn that the British had taken the dread decision of laying waste the two republics, regardless of the suffering of the non-combatant population, and ignorant of the fact that these methods, so far from subduing the Boers, would merely serve to stiffen their resistance.

Two days after General Botha had ridden away, the storm broke upon us. As the sun rose, the skyline from west to east was dotted with English horsemen riding in a line that stretched as far as the eye could see, and behind this screen every road was black with columns, guns, and wagons, slowly moving forward on the first great drive of the war.

General Beyers, when he grasped the situation, divided his force in two, and rode away with one half to find the left flank of the enemy, while the rest of us were told to do what we could in front of the advance.

Far away, to our left, parties of General Botha's men were visible from rise to rise, scattered specks before the great host.

All that day we fell back, delaying the enemy horsemen by rifle-fire as far as possible, and breaking away when the gun-fire grew too hot. This went on till sunset without heavy losses on our side, despite the many batteries brought into play from every knoll and kopje. Once I saw my brother disappear from sight as a shrapnel shell burst on him, but he rode out laughing, he and his horse uninjured.

During the course of the morning, pillars of smoke began to rise behind the English advance, and to our astonishment we saw that they were burning the farm-houses as they came. Towards noon word spread that, not only were they destroying all before them, but were actually capturing and sending away the women and children.

At first we could hardly credit this, but when one wild-eyed woman after another galloped by, it was borne in on us that a more terrible chapter of the war was opening.

The intention was to undermine the morale of the fighting men, but the effect was exactly the opposite, from what I saw. Instead of weakening, they became only the more resolved to hold out, and this policy instead of shortening the war, prolonged it by a year of more.[1]

---

[1]The *Times History of the War* says:

'The policy of burning down farmhouses and destroying crops as a measure of intimidation had nothing to recommend it and no other measure aroused such deep and lasting resentment. The Dutch race is not one that can be easily beguiled by threats, and farm-burning as a policy of intimidation totally failed, as anyone acquainted with the Dutch race and the Dutch history could have foreseen. Applying this system against a white race defending their homes with a bravery and resource which has rightly won the admiration of the World was the least happy of Lord Roberts's inspirations and must plainly be set down as a serious error of judgment ...'.

Towards dark the chase slowed down. It rained steadily all night, and we spent a miserable time lying in mud and water on the bare hillsides. At daybreak we were all on the move again, but, owing to the rain and the heavy going, the English could only crawl in our wake, and we had little difficulty in keeping our distance. By now, the news had spread that the English were clearing the country, with the result that the entire civil population from the farms was moving.

The plain was alive with wagons, carts, and vehicles of all descriptions, laden with women and children, while great numbers of horses, cattle, and sheep were being hurried onward by native herdboys, homes and ricks going up in flames behind them.

General Botha directed all non-combatants, wagons, and live-stock to make for Swaziland, and he ordered us to give way before the troops, and let them expend their blow in thin air.

Owing to these measures the drive went to pieces during the next few days. The British could not maintain a continuous front over the increased distances, and the troops were left groping about after the elusive Boer forces, which easily evaded the lumbering columns plodding through the mud far in the rear.

The drive caused an immense amount of material damage to farmhouses and crops, and much live-stock was taken, but so far as its effect on the burghers went it was a complete failure, for it left them more determined than ever to continue the fighting.

As soon as the main pressure of the drive had eased, we of the 'ACC' were deputed to patrol the areas around Bethal and Ermelo, and although we did much hard riding on the flanks of various columns that were trekking along, we had no actual fighting.

I now suffered the loss of my dear old roan horse. One morning he came staggering and swaying up to me from the grazing-ground, and I saw at once from his heaving flanks and glassy eyes that he was stricken with the dreaded horse-sickness, from which scarcely one animal in a hundred recovers. Nosing against me he seemed to appeal for help, but he was beyond hope, and in less than an hour, with a final plunge, he fell dead at my feet. This was a great sorrow, for a close bond had grown up between us in the long months since the war started, during which he had carried me so well.

I had to leave him, for as he fell, English scouts came swarming over the rise. I threw my saddle on a borrowed mount, and galloped away with the rest, and as my brother was absent on patrol with both his horses, I was forced to rely on a succession of loaned animals, but there was no help for it.

On his return a week later he unselfishly made over the 'Malpert' to me, and we now spent some time scouting over the plains in small parties to see what the English were doing, for, although the drive had petered out, large columns were still aimlessly wandering over the country, and our orders were to keep count of them. We had several sharp brushes with their outposts, and one evening were caught by a burst of shrapnel which blew a Carolina man to pieces within arm's-length of me, and wounded his horse so severely that I had to shoot it.

After thoroughly scouring the countryside as far as the Swaziland border, our various 'ACC' patrols re-assembled at a place called Klipstapel, said to be the highest and coldest spot in the Transvaal. That same day instructions came from General Botha that the 'ACC' were to be with him by midnight, as he was going to attack an English force camped near Lake Chrissie.

The attack took place, but we were held in reserve. We heard the sound of heavy firing shortly before dawn, and a rumour passed that the camp was taken. This proved only partly correct, for by sunrise came the trampling of many riderless horses, followed later by galloping riders, who told us that, although they had succeeded in overrunning the camp, the English troop horses had stampeded, creating such confusion in the dark, that our men gave way when success was practically in their grasp.

As it grew light, we could see the English camp lying intact below, and, as the troops turned several guns on us, and on such others as were in sight, we went scurrying away for the shelter of a neighbouring valley, where we found General Botha and most of his men. There was dejection in the air, for our loss overnight had been heavy, about forty killed and many wounded, with nothing to show for it.

But General Botha was not discouraged, for he addressed us, saying there were bound to be ups and downs, and he talked the men into a better frame of mind without any trouble.

After this, he split up his commandos. We had to live by foraging for sheep that were roaming about the veld, and by gathering maize from the unharvested fields, so he hived us off into smaller bodies, for easier provisioning.

As the drive had gone to pieces and there was no immediate need for our further services in the Eastern Transvaal, he ordered Beyers to take his men north to the new storm-centre in the Waterbergen, which the English were now penetrating and from which urgent calls for help had come.

Most of Beyers's men were Waterbergers, so it was only natural to send them up to the threatened parts, but we of the 'ACC' were a mixed community, a sort of Foreign Legion, not hailing from any particular area. As, moreover, we were not over fond of General Beyers, we decided instead to return west and rejoin General de la Rey, especially as messages had come that there, too, another great drive was in progress.

Beyers accordingly started on his long march without us, and we took our leave of General Botha next day. After some days' riding over the plains we got back to the country between Pretoria and Johannesburg, in order to recross the railway line.

This time the track was better guarded, for we found numerous little camps on either side, and the line was closely patrolled by mounted men.

Jan Nagel, our commandant, sent me with another man after dark to find a convenient crossing. We crawled right up to Irene Station, ten miles from Pretoria, passing within a few yards of the tents there, and a thousand yards down we found a suitable spot in a hollow.

We were at this all night, returning to the 'ACC' at a neighbouring farm by daybreak. Here we rested quietly until dark, and my companion and I then led the commando over the railway line without any trouble. We rode on all night, reaching our former haunts near the Swart Kop by morning.

We were now back in the Skurwebergen country near Johannesburg, where we had taken refuge before, and here we rested for seven or eight days, as the British troops rarely visited these broken hills.

This mistake proved our undoing, for the area is notoriously unhealthy for horses during the rainy season, and our animals began to die so rapidly that, by the time we made for higher ground, more than half the 'ACC' were dismounted, but as the

'Malpert' and my brother's toll-free chestnut had escaped the contagion thus far, we were still in the saddle.

Jan Nagel decided that we must reach General de la Rey's commandos in the west, in the hope of getting fresh horses, so we started off, a miserable band, most of the men on foot, carrying their saddles and equipment on their backs, and the rest of us not knowing when we should be doing the same.

Chapter 17

End of the 'ACC'—I Start for the Cape Colony

We struggled along for two days, making west, and losing more horses as we went, until we found our way barred by a body of troops stationed on the height known as Ramagothla, from which they had a wide view over the surrounding country.

Hampered as we were with dismounted men, we could not venture into sight across the open, so we turned north to the friendly refuge of the Magaliesbergen that we could see once more on the far horizon.

By stealing down kloofs and valleys, we made the foot of the mountains unobserved, reaching the very spot where the 'Old Wagon Pass' comes down, the same road along which we had travelled from the Waterbergen, two months before.

On this march the 'Malpert' showed signs of distress, his staring coat and lagging steps telling only too plainly that his course was spent.

A column of English horse was near, so we had to hurry up the pass as it grew dark, and I was obliged to leave him in an orchard below, to give him this slight chance of recovery. Next morning, on looking over the cliffs, I saw him lying dead. He had been game to the end—'*puure paert*' (an 'all-horse')—as the men called him, and my brother and I climbed down to pay a last visit to his poor emaciated carcass.

On our return Nagel discussed the situation. With more horses dying every day, our prospect of safely crossing the open plains and reaching General de la Rey was a poor one, and he suggested that we should return to the hill country from which we had just come. He said that we could wait there until word was got through to General de la Rey, who would doubtless send sufficient fresh horses to enable us to join him.

About half the men agreed to this, but the others refused. They said de la Rey was short of horses himself, and, with winter approaching once more, they preferred making north over the mountain-range for the warmer climate of the bushveld. My brother and I decided to go north too, although for a different reason. I was without a horse, and he might be so at any moment, so we decided to find my father, as we counted on him to fit us out again, after which we would return south.

There was very little discussion and no ill feeling, for Nagel was a sensible man, and that same afternoon all was concluded. He, and those who were accompanying him, said good-bye, and filing down the pass again were soon lost to view. With him went de Gourville the Frenchman, the two sons of our late Commandant Malan, Fred

Hancock, an old Bloemfontein schoolfellow, and many other friends and companions, none of whom I ever saw again.

I think most were hunted down, or shot out, before they could obtain remounts, for, as I was to discover, their hopes of getting horses from General de la Rey were practically nil, as he had none to give.

The men who had chosen for the north now started over the mountains, some on horseback, the majority on foot, and thus ended the 'ACC'.

My brother and I were in no hurry, so we remained resting among the boulders that night.

My father was somewhere in the Lydenburg country, and this was three hundred miles away, no easy journey with a single horse between us, but we reckoned that by riding and walking in turn we should find him in the end, and we hoped that as a member of the Government he would be able to recondition us.

Next day we loaded our gear on the chestnut, and descended the north side of the Magaliesbergen into the great valley which we had crossed with Beyers the night that we found the burning convoy.

We reached the bottom in the afternoon, by which time the 'ACC' men who were travelling the same road had long since disappeared, leaving us seemingly alone in the broad rift. Towards evening, however, we came on an ox-wagon, outspanned in a patch of scrub, and owned by a stout-hearted old Boer lady who told us that she was on her way to the bush country. Her husband was fighting with de la Rey, and as the English were harrying and burning in the west she had thrown her belongings on a wagon, and, leaving the farm to look after itself, she had crossed the Magaliesbergen with her children and a native herdboy. She said she was going north at once, and offered us a lift. As this would save much walking we helped to fetch and yoke the oxen, and started off overjoyed at this timely relief. Before we had gone many yards, however, I remembered that by some oversight I had forgotten my saddlebags where we had halted that morning on our way down the mountain: a slight matter that altered the whole subsequent course of the war for me.

Saddlebags were scarce and valuable, and moreover mine contained a supply of salt that I had been lucky enough to discover at a deserted farm the week before, so it was agreed that my brother would go on with the wagon, while I returned up the pass on his horse to retrieve the missing articles. We thought that I should easily be able to catch up next day, so, leaving the wagon to jolt along, I trotted the chestnut back along the road towards the mountain.

By the time I reached the spot where I had left my wallets it was dark, so I built a fire and spent the night there. At daybreak when I untied the hobbles of the horse he savaged my arm, a sure sign that he was not himself, for ordinarily he was gentle, but I saddled up none the less and rode him down the mountain and half-way across the floor of the valley, by which time the tell-tale flecks of foam at his nostrils showed that the horse-sickness was on him. Seeing an empty farmhouse not far away, I led him there and kept him in the shade (which is said to be the only chance), but in less than an hour he was dead.

I could see up the northern road for ten miles or more, with no sign of the wagon, and, as the sun was blazing down, I decided to rest in the house until it grew cooler, before walking on in search of my brother.

The farmhouse had apparently been used as a place of call for English supply columns, coming and going between Rustenburg and Pretoria, for there was a litter of empty tins and other debris outside and the floors within were strewn with cigarette-ends, matches, and other marks of recent occupation. In going through the rooms looking for a cool spot, I found an unopened packet of newspapers on the floor, and as I had not seen a paper for over nine months I lost no time in reading them. I learned for the first time that Queen Victoria was dead; that there was a war in China; that Lord Roberts had been superseded by Lord Kitchener; and I read of a great many other events that had been passing in the outside world. What interested me most was an account of a Boer commando that was raiding far down into the Cape Colony, and I resolved at once to go south in search of them.

It was not so clear how I was to set about this, for the Cape lay many hundreds of miles away, and I was alone and on foot. But my mind was made up and, abandoning all thought of overtaking my brother, I threw my saddle across my shoulders, and carrying my rifle in one hand, and my cooking-tin in the other, I started back on a journey that was to take me very far indeed.

As I trudged along the road I had come, clouds of dust rising from the direction of Pretoria warned me that an English column or convoy was approaching, so I took to the bush and spent the night there. Starting long before daylight next morning, I reached the foot of the Magaliesbergen once more, at the Old Wagon Pass, and here I found about fifty Rustenberg men who had come in overnight. They were horseless like myself, owing to the ravages of horse-sickness, and, having observed the approach of the English troops, they too had made for the shelter of the *berg*.

By climbing a little distance we could follow the movements of the soldiers, whom we made out to be about three thousand strong, with guns and many wagons, all making in our direction. We fled up the heights to a gorge near the top, where we lay secure, but the weather took a turn for the worse and it rained for eight days and nights without stopping, during which time we had no shelter but overhanging rocks. It was impossible to find dry fuel, so we existed on biltong without a mouthful of anything warm.

We could not descend the mountain, because parties that went down reported that both north and south there was not a dwelling or a barn within reach that was not occupied by weather-bound English troops, who had been driven in from all directions to take cover against the unprecedented downpour. The knowledge that our opponents were comfortably housed merely added to our misery, and every time that the clouds and mist swayed aside we could see smoke cheerfully ascending from every building and shack below.

When the rain ceased, after a dreadful week, we impatiently watched the troops getting under way, and then made haste down the north side of the mountain, to re-occupy some of the farms which they had vacated.

My boots meanwhile had rotted and I had to climb down the sharp slopes on my bare feet, which became so swollen and blistered that I lay for a fortnight in a tobacco shed to which I was carried. The men were kind to me, one old *takhaar* actually walking twenty miles to fetch a piece of leather of which he knew, to make me a pair of rawhide sandals, which served me for many a month to come.

These burghers were Doppers, a religious sect said to be somewhat like the

Quakers. They held strange views on many things, but for all their primitive ways they were brave, unspoilt men.

Among them were some who had been serving with General de la Rey before they lost their horses, and they now began to discuss the possibility of returning to him.

This meant crossing over the Magaliesbergen to the south once more and going thence on foot over the open plains of the high veld, at the mercy of the first mounted enemy patrol that caught sight of us, so that it would not be at all plain sailing.

However, after discussing the pros and cons of the venture, thirteen of us decided to take the risk, in spite of the warnings of those remaining behind.

The prospect of a two-hundred-mile march on foot, burdened with our saddles and other belongings, was not an attractive one, but we began our preparations. While out after game one morning I chanced to pass the derelict English wagon-convoy that had been burnt last year, and looking over the remains I had an inspiration. There was not a single whole wagon, but it seemed to me that by taking an undamaged wheel here and there, and axles and planks from other parts, we might piece together a composite vehicle.

Returning to my companions I put forward this suggestion, which was so well received that they went off in a body to inspect the skeleton convoy, and in two days' time had built a strange-looking but quite trustworthy wagon.

The question of transport animals was just as easily solved. In a deep kloof some miles away ran a large herd of cattle, kept hidden there by General de la Rey's orders, as a reserve supply depot for his commandos in the west. We visited the cattle-guards, and got a dozen good trek oxen from them.

My fellow-travellers were born stockmen, who could tell at a glance which animals were trained to the yoke, and after a trial run they could even tell the exact places at which each ox had previously pulled in the span, so they quickly selected an excellent team, with which we returned to complete our plans by rough-hewing sufficient yokes and curing the necessary straps and riems. In a few days' time all was ready, and loading up our goods we said good-bye to the rest of the Rustenburg men, and with our improvised wagon jolted up the Old Wagon Pass on our journey of discovery.

We climbed over the mountain range in one day, reaching the orchard where poor 'Malpert' had died, in time to see the English still crowning the rise at Ramagothla. The night was black with heavy rain, under cover of which we crawled on to the open plain, hurrying the oxen past the camp until by daylight we were well out of sight in the folds of the hills, cold, drenched, and weary, but pleased with the good progress that we had made. We found ourselves on the scene of recent fighting, for the ground was littered with rotting carcasses of horses and mules, and there were newly made graves.

I heard later that Mr Smuts, the State Attorney, had here besieged a force of Australians, who defended themselves so bravely that they beat off our people with loss.

We now travelled onward for several days through devastated country. The counterpart of the great drive we had witnessed in the east had since rolled over this area, leaving behind it only blackened ruins and trampled fields, so that our course lay through a silent unpeopled waste, across which we navigated our wagon like a lonely ship at sea.

My companions were big heavily bearded men of the old school, who looked on me as something of an alien, for I was town-bred, and they did not always understand my ways, but they were simple kindly souls and we got on well together. The Boers had their full share of laggards, but they had a full share, too, of steadfast yeomen such as these; men whose farms were lying in ruins, whose wives and families were scattered they knew not where, but who, unpaid and unbidden, returned to risk their lives in the fighting that swayed continually backward and forward over the western plains, and I got a truer insight into the fine courage and high qualities of their fighting-men during this journey than at any other time of the war.

On our fourth or fifth day out, a woman came walking towards us with her two small children and a native servant girl. She told us that she had been sheltering for the past ten days in a wooded kloof where her wagon was hidden, but the oxen having strayed into the open had been captured by passing soldiers, so that she was stranded. She said that General de la Rey's wagon-laager was camped at a place called Rietpan, near Tafel Kop, so, ascertaining that she was in no immediate want, we turned south-east, coming in view of the shimmering waters of the pan by noon next day. There was a considerable number of wagons on the shore of the lake, with many horses and cattle out at graze, and we were just congratulating ourselves on having at last found de la Rey when we saw a sudden stir—men began to run for their horses, and oxen were rapidly driven in, and, as we realised that something was amiss, we halted our wagon to await events.

Soon horsemen came riding furiously past, followed after an interval by the wagons and carts, also urged forward in a panic. We managed to stop one rider, who only stayed long enough to say that the English were upon us. We looked in vain for any sign of the enemy, but assuming that they must be near, we turned our tired oxen, and rattled along behind the retreat, which did not slow down until we had covered about six miles. Then horsemen from the rear overtook us with word that the alarm had been a false one.

All concerned had the grace to look ashamed of the stampede, but there was at any rate some excuse for them, as de la Rey had been severely handled early that morning in a surprise attack, in which he had lost over a hundred men. Some of his wounded, galloping up to the wagons, had precipitated a rout among the drivers, cattle-guards, and camp-followers, who formed the bulk of the laager.

In the afternoon General de la Rey himself rode in with his men, and he used withering language.

We now went into laager at Tafel Kop, where de la Rey's commando and the wagons remained for the next few days. There were about a thousand mounted men and perhaps two hundred wagons. A few of these were used to bring maize from the Magaliesberg foothills, but the majority belonged to non-combatant refugees. De la Rey looked with an unfavourable eye on these and their vehicles, and the men said that the old man prayed to the Almighty night and morning for the enemy to relieve him of this incubus.

I saw a good deal of him at this time, as he held a daily levee beside his cart, where all were free to hear his views.

Attached to his person was a prophet, van Rensburg, a strange character, with long flowing beard and wild fanatical eyes, who dreamed dreams, and pretended to be possessed of occult powers. I personally witnessed one of the lucky hits to which he owed his reputation, for one morning while we were congregated around the General's cart, van Rensburg was expounding his latest vision to a hushed audience. It ran of a black bull and a red bull fighting and goring each other, until at length the red bull sank defeated to its knees, which he interpreted to mean that the British would soon be in like case. As he stood before us, his arms outstretched and his eyes ablaze, he suddenly called out: 'See, who comes'; and, looking up, we made out a distant horseman spurring towards us from the east. We waited in silence for the rider. When he came up, travel-stained and weary, he produced a letter from General Botha, hundreds of miles away.

When General de la Rey opened and read it, his face lighted up, and in a voice ringing with emotion he said: 'Men, believe me, the proud enemy is humbled' (*Die trotse vijand se nek is gebuig*). He went on to tell us that the letter contained news that the English had proposed a peace conference. Coming immediately upon the prophecy it was a dramatic moment and I was impressed, even though I suspected that van Rensburg had stage-managed the scene. Of General de la Rey's sincerity there could be no doubt, for he was not a man to stoop to subterfuge, and I knew he firmly believed in the seer's predictions.

These tidings created a great deal of stir and excitement during the next few days, and many of the men thought that the war was as good as over.

A peace conference did in fact take place a little later between General Botha and Lord Kitchener, but it proved abortive, and the only immediate result was to establish van Rensburg's reputation more firmly than ever.

I asked General de la Rey for a horse, but he said I should have to wait until parties he had sent into the Free State had returned, and indeed I could see for myself, from the number of dismounted men with the laager, that he was unable to assist me, so in the meanwhile my companions and I clung to our wagon and team, taking turns at herding the oxen and foraging for maize. Like everyone else, we had to find ourselves in food, excepting meat, which was supplied from a communal drove.

By this time my clothes had fallen from my body, owing to the rains, and my entire wardrobe consisted of a blanket and a pair of sandals, so that, as it was towards the end of March by now, with winter coming on, I felt the cold pretty severely. General de la Rey had noticed my scanty attire, and one morning he walked over to our wagon with a pair of breeches and a coat, a gift I much appreciated, for he could have been none too well supplied himself, but it was of a piece with his natural kindliness and consideration towards all.

From Tafel Kop, after some days, he rode off with the mounted men, and we poor infantrymen and other camp-followers were ordered to a place ten miles away, where there was better grazing for the trek-oxen. Here we remained, my prospects of reaching the Cape Colony looking pretty uncertain, although I was as determined as ever to get through.

On the 3rd of April, or the day we calculated to be that date, the wagon crew and myself were busy preparing a dinner to celebrate my birthday with an ox-tongue and a few odds and ends that we had managed to collect. Suddenly there came the crash of a field-gun, followed by the roar of a shell exploding close by, and almost immediately some of de la Rey's horsemen came riding out of the heavy mist that lay over all the country. They were riding hard to warn us that the English were coming. In a moment there was a wild rush to fetch the oxen, and fortunately the fog was so thick that none of the other shells fell among us and the entire wagon-laager was able to get under way without being seen.

To the sound of small-arm fire where our horsemen were engaged in the mist, the convoy spread out for better speed, each wagon striking out a course of its own, without regard to the others. The fog held, and heavy rain setting in still further decreased the visibility, so that my companions and I got clean away, although at times the English horsemen splashed past so close to us that we could hear them shouting to each other for their bearings.

The bulk of de la Rey's fighting men were not in the vicinity at all, but only some twenty or thirty of them had been approaching the wagon-laager, for a few days' rest, when they unexpectedly stumbled on an English force that was stalking the convoy under cover of the mist. But for this we should have been taken by surprise, and I doubt if a single man would have escaped. As it was, the warning we received enabled us to escape wholesale capture, but it was touch and go, for the boom of the guns, the splutter of rifles through the fog, and the hallooing and galloping, sounded very near. As a matter of fact a number of wagons were taken, although we did not know it at the time. As for our party, we ran beside the team, keeping the oxen at a trot, and as our wagon was light, carrying only our saddles and cooking-tins, we made good progress. The other wagons and carts were almost immediately lost sight of in the mist, but we forged ahead by ourselves, and towards evening reached broken ground to the north, where we were safe enough.

We built a large fire on the banks of a stream and resurrected the remains of my birthday-dinner, which had come along in a leather bag. Afterwards my companions stood in a circle round the blaze, and solemnly sang hymns of thanksgiving for our escape. Then we camped for the night.

Next morning as it grew light, other wagons came crawling over the plain, also making for the safety of the hills, so we yoked our oxen and joined them, heading for a valley in the heart of the rugged tract known as the 'Swart Ruggens', where we found the remnant of our laager assembled.

We could not yet tell how many wagons had fallen into the hands of the enemy. Nearly half were missing, but most of these drifted in during the next day or two, and in the end it was found that less than a dozen had come to grief.

While we were camped in the valley, General de la Rey came up with some of his men to see how the convoy had fared, and, before riding back to the fighting area, he left orders for the wagons to proceed to a spot some thirty miles away, where there were two hundred horses from the Free State, which were to be given out by ballot to the dismounted men of the laager.

Many English columns were moving west at this time in continuance of a drive they were making, but we were able to trek along in comparative safety behind the line of their advance, and in due course reached our destination. Here we found a patrol that had come up from the Free State in charge of the remounts. The animals were mostly unbroken mares, and, as there were over three hundred horseless men, the drawing of lots was followed with keen interest.

I drew a blank, but no less than nine of our original wagon party got a horse apiece. I was cast down at the result, although we were comforted by an assurance that further horses were expected, and those of us who were unsuccessful in the drawings had at least the fun of seeing the winners break in their mounts, a diverting spectacle.

Nearly two hundred horses were bucking and squealing at the same time, their riders biting the dust in all directions, while we sat on the wagon-rails cheering them on. It was wonderful how quickly the men mastered their unruly steeds, so that by the third day practically every animal was broken to the saddle, and the newly mounted force could ride off to war.

With them went the nine men from our wagon, leaving the rest of us to wonder disconsolately when we should sit astride a saddle again, and leaving me to wonder as well whether, at this rate, I should ever see the Cape.

The wagon-laager was now instructed to return to the Swart Ruggens Hills from which we had come, so we lumbered slowly back, halting after some days at the head of a beautiful stream that gushed from the rocks. Here we went into permanent camp, and the place soon became a sort of base depot for de la Rey's fighting commandos. The sick and wounded were brought here, and there was a steady influx of horseless men drifting in from the plains, and of men who had left the firing-line for a rest.

Our numbers varied from two hundred to over four hundred at times, and so securely were we hidden that not once did the British troops come near us, although their columns were ranging far and near over the adjoining open country. Two days after our arrival at the new camp I tried to smash a log for fuel by bringing down a heavy stone on top of it. The stone came back at me like a shot from a catapult, breaking my right tibia halfway between knee and ankle, and for three weeks I lay in great pain and discomfort with splinters of bone working their way out from a suppurating wound.

Luckily there were some Germans here, marooned like the rest of us for want of horses, and one of them had a working knowledge of surgery. Thanks to him and to a healthy constitution, I was at length able to hobble about, so I was doubly fortunate in having his assistance, and in being left in peace by the British while I was incapacitated. By now all but one of our original wagon complement had received horses and ridden away, and all the Germans except two were gone, and it began to look as if I was to become a professional camp-follower, for winter was upon us, and the arrival of more horses from the Free State was very unlikely.

A chance turn, however, brought me relief. One morning, soon after I was able to limp around, a small party of Germans rode into camp under command of a little hunchbacked Field-Cornet named Mayer. At this time there was still in the field a German contingent about thirty strong, with Mayer at its head. In a sense they were the direct descendants of Baron von Goldeck's force, with whom I had served the year before, for although most of the Baron's men had melted away during the retreat to the Portuguese border, some of them had remained, and had collected themselves into a self-contained little commando forming part of General de la Rey's army.

Mayer had heard that there were a few of his compatriots stranded at the wagon-laager, so he had brought some spare horses to remount them. This stood me in good stead, for there were only two horseless Germans left in camp, the others having drawn animals in the lottery and ridden off, and Mayer agreed to let me have a little grey mare on condition that I joined him. The wound in my leg was still far from healed, but as I could not afford to miss the chance I made over my half-share in our wagon and team to the only remaining member of our original company, and with my leg in a splint accompanied the Germans when they set out on their return to de la Rey's forces.

It was a harsh journey. My leg throbbed and ached at every stride, and the winter had set in with great severity. I had not felt the cold so much in the seclusion of the valley where we had been camped up to now, but out in the open it was a different matter. By day clouds of dust and biting winds drove across the bleak plains, and at night we could hear the crackle of ice forming on the pools, as we lay shivering beneath our threadbare blankets. From now onward, indeed, until the end of the cold season, five long months ahead, we endured great hardship and suffering, for never, even in the memory of the oldest man, had there been so prolonged a spell of bitter weather all over South Africa.

For three days we rode on without meeting anyone. Another great drive was in progress with de la Rey's men hanging on to its flanks, the country behind being left wasted and ruined. At length we came on some of his commandos in the ridges near the village of Hartebeestpoort, where they lay in attendance on a large concentration of English troops, said to number twelve thousand. Here we found the balance of Mayer's Germans, with whom we took post in the line that had been established in a half-moon before the enemy columns. For the moment the troops were resting, so we lay watching their camps, guns and convoys, waiting for them to make the first move.

They sent shells over us at times, but were obviously holding their hand until they were ready, an event to which we looked forward with considerable misgiving, as there were only about six hundred burghers present, the rest of de la Rey's men being elsewhere engaged.

But the General himself was with us and, happening to ride past one afternoon while my leg was being dressed by one of the Germans, he sent me off to a kind of field hospital that he had established some miles back. I found it in a ruined farmhouse, with a young Hollander doctor doing what he could for the sick and wounded under his care. It was a cheerless place, with only dried grass to lie on, and in the absence of medicines or bandages there was little enough comfort for the patients. They were mostly lighter cases, as the serious cases were left for the British ambulances to pick up. Amid all the cruelty of farm-burning and the hunting down of the civilian population, there was one redeeming feature, in that the English soldiers, both officers and men, were unfailingly humane. This was so well known that there was never any hesitation in abandoning a wounded man to the mercy of the troops, in the sure knowledge that he would be taken away and carefully nursed, a certainty which went far to soften the asperities of the war.

A few days after I joined the hospital we heard the sound of heavy gun-fire about nine in the morning, and realised that the expected attack had come. I had kept my horse by me all the time, so I saddled and rode back to where I had left the Germans in the firing-line, while the doctor loaded his charges on a mule-wagon and made off to safer quarters. When I reached our men I saw the English attacking away to our left. Under cover of a severe bombardment their cavalry rode cheering towards a spot in our position a mile away, and broke through almost at once.

We of the German contingent were merely spectators, but we were close enough to see the men at the threatened point run for their horses and take to flight. Here and there a man went down, but our casualties were not heavy, as there had been scarcely any resistance in the face of the shell-fire to which we could not reply, and when the burghers on either side of the breach saw what was happening, they too fetched their horses and beat a retreat. Naturally the Germans and I went as fast as the rest, to join the stream that flowed to the rear. We fell back until two in the afternoon, when the English gave up the chase and we were able to come to a halt in a bush-covered hollow, where General de la Rey addressed us in his half-humourous half-serious manner, and soon he had the men laughing and making light of their misfortunes.

We rested our horses here until dark, and then rode west for several hours, as there was word of further columns converging upon us.

There had been a magnificent double-tailed meteor in the sky of late, the two streamers of which looked like the letter 'V', and van Rensburg, the General's prophet, had been giving out that this stood for '*Vrede*' (peace), but on this night as we rode along, I heard a boyish voice from the darkness ahead call out: 'Mijnheer van Rensburg, that letter V up there does not mean *Vrede*, it means *Vlug* (retreat).' There was wry laughter in the ranks at this sally, which the discomfited oracle bore in meek silence, although it did not diminish his output of prophecies, which continued right up to the peace.

We spent a cold night beside a pan, and at daybreak we could make out a large body of English troops in the distance, but we could not tell whether they were our pursuers of yesterday or a fresh column. In any case they were too far away to cause us any immediate anxiety, so we shot some oxen (a number from the larger communal herd having accompanied us) and began to prepare breakfast.

After this General de la Rey divided us into two parties. With half the men he rode south, and before sunset we heard the boom of guns thirty miles away, where the indomitable old man was once more attacking an enemy column.

He left Commandant Jan Kemp in command of the rest of us, with orders to carry out a raid into the territory of Bechuanaland, with a view to capturing a supply train on the Rhodesian railway line. Accordingly, for the next two days, we rode on through barren country, until we reached a point on the Harts River, from which we were to make a night march to our objective.

Mayer asked leave to scout in advance with his men, a request that was granted, so we started two hours ahead of our main body, riding through the Cunana Native Reserve until, at four in the morning, we crossed the British border. The railway ran only a mile or so beyond, and we soon reached the metals. We started tearing up the track, with poles from a neighbouring fence for our only tools. Presently Mayer handed me a pair of pliers, and told me to climb up one of the telegraph standards and cut the wires, no easy task with my sore leg. As I was swarming up, there came a sudden volley from a culvert about fifty yards away. I slid down and in a moment we were on our horses, and away, for now that we were discovered there was no hope of surprising a train.

We rode back to a hill half a mile in the rear, to wait for daylight. When we got there we found a little native village nestling behind it, and went there to get information as to the number of soldiers guarding the line below. It was growing light as we rode through the gateway of the thorn enclosure surrounding the *stad*, and when we entered, two khaki-clad white men rushed out of a hut, rifle in hand, followed by a native also armed. Mayer was off his horse at once, firing almost before he touched the ground. He hit the native through the chest, and the other two men put up their hands. This single shot caused a panic in the village. The natives grabbed their karosses, mats, babies, and whatever else they could lay their hands on, and fled down the slope in the direction of the railway line to seek protection from the British troops, the women setting up a long-drawn wail as they ran.

Mayer ordered me to head off the fugitives, so I galloped round to get in front of them. Unfortunately three or four of the Germans had lagged behind on the way up from the railway line, and, when they saw the rush of natives coming at them in the uncertain light, they opened fire, thinking themselves attacked. Before I could stop the shooting, they killed four and wounded several others, nearly getting me too.

We did what we could for the wounded and had them carried back to the huts, greatly upset at what had happened, for there were two women amongst the dead.

The white men captured in the kraal turned out to be renegades (National Scouts) from Potchefstroom. They were handed over later on to General de la Rey, who had them both executed, I believe.

It had by now grown fully light, and we could see Kemp's men approaching through the bush. They were riding in small parties, making for the railway line, so we sent off a man to warn them that the English were there, but before the messenger got halfway, shells came screeching through the air from a hill beside the line. So far from expecting to be shelled, we had believed this part of the railway to be unguarded, but we could now make out quite a considerable number of tents among the trees and, as the gun kept dropping shells near us, Kemp ordered a withdrawal, and we trekked back into the Transvaal after a profitless venture.

We rode thirty miles that day, reaching Leeuwpan by nightfall, where we found General de la Rey awaiting us. He said there were several English columns halted in a semicircle ahead, and he instructed Kemp to get out of their way that night. Having told us what to do, he rode away with his handful of retainers, and I did not see the doughty old warrior again, for from that night our roads lay far apart.

Chapter 18

The Next Stage

As soon as it was dark enough, Kemp led us off in the direction of the English camps, between which he intended passing. We were skilfully guided, for we slipped through a gap between the two camps, passing so close that we could hear the murmur of voices, and could see the forms of soldiers outlined against their fires. No alarm was raised until we were through, when there was some shouting and firing which did no damage. Once we had put the camps behind us the men were ordered to march on foot to spare their horses, for we had been on the move for over thirty hours, with no rest worth mentioning.

As I still had a limp, I gradually fell behind and, to make matters worse, my poor little mare was delivered of a stillborn foal. With this travail coming upon her she had borne the long treks so unfalteringly, that I had not even known that there was anything wrong with her, but now her strength was gone. After a while she staggered to her feet, and as I could not risk remaining in too close proximity to the English camps, whose fires were still visible in the distance, I led her slowly forward. By this time the rest of our men had long since vanished in the darkness, and I had to plod on alone for an hour or two, dragging my horse behind me, until she could go no farther, when I decided to halt till morning. It was bitterly cold—so cold that earlier in the evening I had heard men say that it was the coldest night they had ever known. As I could find no fuel for a fire, I wrapped my blanket round my shoulders and sat with chattering teeth until sunrise. When it grew light I found myself on a cheerless expanse, with a view that extended for many miles, but there was no sign of the commando.

By a distant thorn tree, however, I found four of my German friends, huddled together against the cold. They said that they had missed me during the night, and, knowing that I was crippled, they had generously remained behind to wait for me.

After collecting what fuel we could in such barren country, we built a small fire to fry some meat, and then set out on the spoor of the commando, making slow progress, for my companions' horses were not in very much better condition than my own. By nine or ten o'clock in the morning, ominous pillars of dust rising in the rear warned us that the English columns of last night were returning in our direction.

The troops were not as yet in sight, but considering the state of our animals, we stood a poor chance of keeping ahead of them once their scouts topped the skyline, so we hurried on as best we could. Just as we were beginning to see an occasional horseman far behind us, we providentially came on the Harts River. It was more of an earth-crack across the plain than a river. No trees stood on its edge, and fifty yards off the banks were invisible, but it was our salvation, for hardly were we and our horses out of sight in the dry bed below, when the troops came swarming towards the river. All went well, however. The English, when they reached the bank, set to digging gradients for their guns and wagons, and, although it was hours before they got their transport through, during which time we anxiously peered over the top in fear of discovery, we had the satisfaction, before dark, of seeing the tail of their convoy vanish over the horizon.

This was good as far as it went, but the question was how to catch up again with our own people, though the fact of being temporarily cut off was not of vital importance, having regard to the fluid nature of guerrilla warfare, and we were not greatly troubled on that score, our worst anxiety being the weak state of our horses.

For the next three or four days we toiled on behind the enemy, who in turn were following our men. We kept some distance to the rear, only moving when the dust-clouds ahead of us showed that the English were advancing too, and in this manner we crawled along on foot, leading our horses by the reins.

One evening a burgher rode up, the first we had seen since the night we dropped behind. He told us that General de la Rey had dispersed his commandos into smaller bands, owing to the pressure from converging British columns. These bands, he said, were by now scattered all over the Western Transvaal, waiting for the end of the drive.

After taking a look at our animals, he said he thought we stood a poor chance of finding Mayer and the other Germans, then he rode off on business of his own, leaving my companions and myself to digest the information received. They were for attempting to work north to the milder climate of the bush-veld, in order to escape the infernal cold of these open plains. They said, as far as Mayer was concerned, we could always find him again once the winter was over, and in any case it mattered little if we didn't.

Seeing that they attached no particular moral value to the necessity of rejoining our unit, I now sprang on them my long-cherished scheme of making for the Cape Colony. They stared at me in surprise when I first broached the subject, but after I had explained my views, and had pictured the Cape to them as a land of beer for the taking at every wayside inn, they became eager converts, and we agreed to start without delay.

The four Germans were a mixture. The eldest, Herman Haase, was a man of about forty-five, in looks the typical sausage-eater of the English comic papers, but, as I found out, a kindly, good-natured gentleman, a Johannesburg merchant, who had been in the field from the beginning. He was the last man one would have suspected of a liking for war, as his talk was all of his wife and family, and the joys of home life.

Next came W Cluver, a clever cynical Berlin student, who told me many interesting things of life in the old world; then there was Pollatchek, also a Berlin student, who had come out to fight for the Boers, as on a crusade. He told me that his initial ardour had long since evaporated, but he liked the life of adventure and so had remained, a pleasant, cheerful fellow whom I grew to like very much.

Lastly, there was a farmhand named Wiese, a clumsy, slow-witted rustic, but brave enough. With these four men my lot was now cast. Wiese and Cluver did not get very far, but with Haase and Pollatchek I was long associated, although they turned back in the end.

Our preparations for going to the Cape were quickly made. We slaughtered a stray sheep, and cut the meat into strips for drying in the wind (as we had no salt), and we ground a quantity of maize into meal in a small coffee-mill that Haase carried on his saddle-tree, and next morning we started.

On the evening of our first day out, we had an exciting interlude. Another of de la Rey's men who, like ourselves, had been left stranded in the rear of the British drive, rode up to see who we were. He said he had been lurking around here for some days, seeking an opportunity to regain the commandos. While stripping mealie cobs in a field that afternoon, he had seen a native ride from a *stad* close by to meet an English patrol. The native had conferred with the officer in command for some minutes, after the patrol went off. As the native was obviously a spy in British pay, the newcomer suggested that we should try to capture him after dark. Accordingly, about nine o'clock that night, we started on foot for the kraal, going quietly so as not to frighten our quarry. When we reached the village, however, we found the headman and all his followers on the *qui vive*. They denied all knowledge of the spy, so our guide cut matters short by seizing the Induna by the throat, threatening to shoot him. On being thus roughly handled, he wrested himself free and shouted loudly, 'Help, help, the Boers are killing me!' In a moment we were surrounded by thirty or forty braves, most of them brandishing assagais and knobkerries in our faces.

They began leaping and dancing about us, uttering fierce yells and menaces, while some tore thatch from the huts, lit it at a fire, and held it aloft instead of torches. From behind the circle of angry savages came the cries of the women, urging them to kill the white men, and things began to look unpleasant. We could have opened fire, but the space inside the stockade was cramped and they were far superior in numbers. Moreover, all through the war the Boers had observed an unwritten law that it was a white man's quarrel, and that the native tribes were to be left alone. For these reasons we did not fire, but closed up, and slowly backed out through the gate-way by which we had entered. Once free of the enclosure we had no trouble in safely reaching our camping-place, much annoyed at the poor figure we had cut. To add to our humiliation, at dawn next morning we saw a native boldly riding from the *stad*, and when we sent a few shots after him, he waved a defiant arm and disappeared over the rise.

Having thoroughly bungled the affair, de la Rey's man took his leave of us, and we continued on our way.

For several days we were unable to travel in a direct line, for we found the countryside alive with British troops moving in all directions, and we calculated that we saw twenty-five thousand of them, before we got clear. It was plain from the way in which they swept forward on an enormous front that they were conducting another of their drives, but as we did not see a single burgher, or the vestige of a commando during all this time, they must have had little to show for their activity. Clearly General de la Rey was resorting to his usual tactics of avoiding these huge concentrations of troops by scattering his men until the blow was spent.

My knowledge of veld-craft brought our party safely through to the Vaal River, for my early experience was of value, and we threaded and twisted successfully between the enemy columns, never having occasion to fire a shot. Once we were held up for half a day while a body of English troops camped within hail of where we lay hidden in a patch of thorn. Another time Cluver and I tried to ambush two officers, but he showed himself too soon and they got away. In the course of these operations we had to jettison Heinrich Wiese. His horse gave in and he himself had blistered feet, so we abandoned him near an English column, where he was sure to be picked up and cared for. My leg was on the mend, but we suffered a great deal from cold at nights. Otherwise we almost grew to enjoy the excitement of dodging the enemy forces and patrols, and the Germans said that it was the best time they had had in the war.

At length, on the fifth or sixth day, we breasted the long rise at Leeuwdoorn, from which the country slopes down to the Vaal River, and we saw the wide plains of the Free State stretching beyond. We slept a night in an unburnt farmhouse on the Transvaal side, and next morning, as we were riding off, we saw a body of English approaching, so we climbed a kopje to see what their plans were.

The soldiers made for the farm we had just vacated, and soon smoke and flames were issuing from door and windows. As we looked on, two old fellows rode up from the direction of the Vaal River, and joined us on the hill. They reminded me of my former commander, General Maroola, and his brother, for they both wore rusty bell-toppers, and the tails of their ancient claw-hammer coats flapped in the breeze as they came. With a curt greeting they dismounted and sat down on the rocks, silently watching the work of destruction below. For a long time neither of them spoke, and it was only when the roof fell in amid a shower of sparks, that the elder of the two sighed and turning to the other said: 'Brother John, there go those teakwood beams I brought from Pretoria after the Jameson Raid.' This was his sole comment on the loss of his home, then the couple remounted their horses to ride back to the river.

As we were also going there, we fetched our animals and overtook them, learning on the way that they were making for a women's laager halted beside the water.

We found that the laager consisted of about thirty wagons, with perhaps three or four times that number of women and children, all under the care of our two worthies. Now that the British were capturing the civil population it had become the practice for the women on the farms, when hostile forces approached, to load what they could on their wagons, and join hands with others similarly situated, in order to form a joint laager. Once the immediate danger was past they returned to what was left of their homes, to subsist as best they could, rather than be taken for internment to the British concentration camps. We rested at the laager for a few hours, while one of the old churchwardens rode out to see what the English were doing. He came galloping back to say that about fifteen hundred English horsemen were on the river bank eight miles higher up. In view of this it was decided that the laager must cross through to the Free State shore, and immediately all was in a bustle. There was a ford of sorts close by, over which we helped the women to get the wagons, but it was pitiful to see them standing waist-deep in the icy water, tugging at the wheels, and urging on the oxen in their anxiety to put the river between themselves and the column. After working hard for nearly two hours, we had the whole laager safely over. We then waded back to the Transvaal bank to fetch our horses, and on our return found the wagons under way, making across the unlimited open country of the Free State that stretches southward for hundreds of miles.

The Germans and I remained resting under the trees to dry our clothes, and slept the night a few miles farther on. In the morning the Englishmen came moving down the river, and by nine o'clock they were fording the stream into the Free State, so we made off, and for the next three days rode leisurely along, following the south bank of the river, and warning the women on the farms as we passed, that the troops were behind.

I took this route as I had decided to make for the neighbourhood of Hoopstad, a village and district that I knew well, for my brothers and I had camped and hunted there as boys.

I counted on finding the herds of semi-wild horses that used to frequent the river, that we might remount ourselves, for there was small chance of the horses we rode being able to last out the bitter winter that was upon us. We found the homesteads along the river bank intact, but as the bulk of the male population of these parts had been captured with old General Cronje at Paardeberg more than a year ago, the farms were for the most part tenanted by women and children. They told us that an occasional British column had marched through during the past six or eight months, but thus far the policy of farm-burning and the removal of the civilian population had not been put into operation here.

This happy condition was now coming to an end, for pillars of smoke were rising far behind us, and at night the sky was reddened with the glare of burning homesteads, to tell the unfortunate inhabitants that their long immunity was over.

The women took the matter bravely, although there were tears and weeping at times, but each family, as soon as they realised the danger, fetched the oxen, inspanned their wagon, and trekked away south across the plains, out of harm's way.

At length we came to Hoopstad town. The place was deserted, the English garrison, for some unexplained reason, having set fire to their stores and marched away two days before. That same afternoon a solitary German trader rode in from the south-east, where he was serving with a small Boer commando. He proved a useful ally, as he showed us a quantity of maize concealed in an underground receptacle, on which we fed our horses for some days, enabling the wretched animals to pick up condition a little.

Our new acquaintance said he must now return to his commando, and he suggested that we should accompany him. He said that the horses running on the veld were so shy that, unless we got assistance, we should never succeed in catching any of them, as all fences were down throughout the district. We agreed to go with him and, travelling over endless rolling plains, within a few days reached the force to which he was attached. This consisted of twenty men under an officer of the now defunct OFS Artillery. They made us welcome, but shook their heads when we mentioned horses, and indeed we found next day that we might as well have tried to catch antelopes. There were lots of horses roaming about, but when the men spread out, the mustangs went racing away, manes and tails in the wind, and, in spite of our endeavours, we failed to capture a single one of them. It appeared that the British troops had been firing on them with machine-guns and rifles, ever since they discovered that General de la Rey was getting remounts from here, which accounted for their bedevilment. In any case they were too fleet for us, and, as there were no wires to stop them, we gave up the business for fear of foundering the horses we had.

We spent a week with our friends. They were a ragged crew carrying a queer assortment of weapons, and what little ammunition they had they reserved for shooting game, which abounded, and they seemed quite happy so long as they could keep out of the hands of the British.

They gave us unfavourable news of the grazing to the south, so I determined to make for the mountain country farther east, where, I was told, the grass would be better, and where we might procure fresh horses, as de la Rey himself had latterly been sending thither in search of remounts.

So, when we had shot enough springbok and blesbok for biltong, the three Germans and I set out once more. On the night after we started, a bitter cold wind drove across the plains. We were halted beside a water-hole without shelter for man or beast, with the result that, towards morning, my little grey mare broke loose, maddened by the pelting earth and pebbles. She fled down the storm, and I never saw her again.

One of our late friends had given Pollatchek a horse, which he made over to me, so the loss of my own, serious as it was, did not prevent my going on. Having ridden out the blizzard without further damage, we pushed on, going roughly east by south. We passed Kopje-Alleen, where my brothers and I had been ridden down with the 'ACC' last year.

It is a curious isolated hill visible for sixty miles around. As a boy I had sat on its summit watching the game-covered plains below, and now, as then, great herds of antelope and troops of wildebeest were grazing at its foot.

I climbed to the top, partly for old times' sake and partly to see whether the land was clear, but there was really no need for anxiety, as we were in empty country.

The farmhouses stood abandoned, the fields lay unploughed, and we saw neither human beings nor domestic animals, even the natives having fled.

We rode through this unpeopled waste until, some days later, we fell in with a party of Freestaters near the Sand River railway bridge. There were nine of them under a Field-Cornet named Botha. They had been trying to derail a train, but the English were building block-houses along here and their attempt had failed, so Botha and his men were returning to their own haunts in the mountain ranges to the east. As we were bound for that region ourselves, we joined them. At eleven o'clock that night we set out to cross the railway line (the main line coming up from Bloemfontein to Johannesburg). The cold was intense and the darkness so thick that those in the front had constantly to shout and whistle to give those behind their bearings. After we had been going for some hours we found that Cluver was missing. We called and whistled and fired shots, but got no reply, so Pollatchek and I rode back to look for him. We retraced our steps for more than a mile, and then, as the directing shouts of the others were growing fainter, we reluctantly rejoined our companions. The trouble was that Cluver was subject to epileptic fits. Three of four times since being with us he had fallen into convulsions, and we supposed one of these attacks had come upon him while he was lagging behind. The night was so freezing that to lie unconscious on the ground meant certain death, but Field-Cornet Botha said it was essential to cross the block-house line before it drew light, and, as we were still a long way from the point at which he intended to slip over, he insisted upon our pushing on, so we continued our journey somewhat heartlessly I admit, but we could not afford to lose the chance of getting through under the guidance of men who knew the lie of the block-houses.

Towards four in the morning we reached a hollow between two fortified posts, and crossed the line without any trouble. We never heard of Cluver again, and I have no doubt that he was dead by morning, for he was not strong enough to have survived that winter night in the open.

By sunrise we were well into the foothills beyond the railway, and now for two days we rode east into increasingly mountainous country, until we reached a lonely farm lying high up amid the crags near Wonder Kop. At this place Botha and his men had their lair. From here they made periodic raids down to the plains, and they must have given a good account of themselves, judging by what they told us, and by their horses, weapons, and equipment, all of which were of British origin. Small private bands like this were common enough in the Free State nowadays, remnants of larger forces that had dwindled away under the misfortunes of war.

Botha told me that he had at one time commanded over three hundred men. Many of them had been killed or captured, others had surrendered, and others again had left him to join larger commandos in the north. He clung to his title of Field-Cornet, and as two of his men called themselves Corporals, the rank and file of his army consisted of but six men. We had reached a very snug haven. The owners of the farm were gone, but there was plenty of good clean straw in the barns to lie on, and in a cave in the cliff overhanging the homestead was a store of wheat, a welcome change from our eternal diet of maize, while in the valleys below half-savage pigs were to be had for the shooting.

Moreover, there was a huge copper cistern, and, as water and fuel were plentiful, we could prepare a hot bath as often as we liked, a rare luxury in this freezing weather.

For ten days the two Germans and I revelled in the unaccustomed joy of good food, cleanliness, and comfortable sleeping quarters, but then I became restless once more. I succeeded in converting Field-Cornet Botha and his followers to my scheme of raiding into the Cape Colony. They were at first disinclined to move so far from their beloved mountains, but eventually I swung them round, and about the end of June (we were vague as to dates and time) we started down the mountains and headed due west, intending to recross the railway line to the plains beyond, and then make a wide detour round Bloemfontein to strike the Orange River somewhere near Fauresmith. On the morning after our departure from the farm, as we were descending the pass near Breslersflat, a young fellow named Jacobus Bosman came riding up. When we told him that we were going to the Cape he said he would come too. As he was one of the Cape rebels who had joined the Boers during their temporary occupation of Colesberg in the beginning of the war, I advised him to stay where he was, for if he were captured on British territory, it would go hard with him. He said he would take the risk, so we enlisted him, but my warning was justified, for he was taken and hanged, as will be seen later on.

After three days of steady progress we were back on the open plains, within sight of the Bloemfontein-Johannesburg railway line, and we scouted round for a suitable crossing. This was becoming more and more difficult to find, now that the English were perfecting their block-house system.

As I spent the rest of the war roving the Cape Colony, I did not experience the full effect of this network, but I have heard that it caused the Free State and Transvaal Commandos great trouble, and in the end contributed largely to the break-up of the Boer resistance.

There were working parties of soldiers dotted along the railway track, engaged in putting up these block-houses, but we had no difficulty in galloping across the metals, despite a fairly heavy rifle-fire, and, having safely negotiated the line, we rode on, passing not far north of Brandfort village. Towards dark we came on a field of maize into which we turned our weary horses, and here we spent the night.

Next morning, just before sunrise, we heard the crack of distant rifle shots, and shortly after two burghers rode by. They pulled up to say that an English column was coming our way, and they advised us to go along with them—they were making for a women's laager not far away, to warn them of the enemy's approach—so we caught our horses and rode off. One of these men, Piet Marais, was an old acquaintance whom I had known as a compositor in a newspaper office at Bloemfontein. He had since inherited money and had bought a farm near by, which he and his companion had been about to visit when they came on the advance-guard of the British force.

As the sun rose we were able to see the column crawling along the road some miles behind. We judged them to be fifteen hundred horsemen, with a string of wagons, and several guns. The women's laager consisted of some fifty wagons and carts, with over two hundred women and children, the collective non-combatant population of the district.

On hearing our news, they began to pack up; the poultry were run to earth, children and household effects were rapidly stowed, and in a very short time the laager was moving off. Women trotted alongside the teams with whips and quirts, while the children peered out anxiously from beneath the hoods at the dust-clouds in the distance, which betokened the approaching enemy. Fortunately the going was easy on these undulating plains, and the wagons made good headway in the direction of the Vet River, lying ten miles north.

By now other men were riding up in twos and threes from various points, until we were about forty strong, and we began to practise our old tactics of galloping across the front of the English advance to fire a few shots, and then falling back to repeat the process farther on, as soon as the shell-fire grew too hot.

This served its purpose sufficiently well to give the laager time to get away, and after a few hours we had no fears for their safety.

Towards three in the afternoon the English halted. We could see them turning out their animals to graze, so we rode up to a kopje near by, where we lay resting under the trees while our horses ready-saddled cropped the grass close by. Before long we heard a clatter, and jumping to our feet, saw a troop of mounted soldiers coming at a gallop. Our look-out had not troubled to keep awake, and the horsemen were within six hundred yards of us before we heard them. As they had two pom-poms with them, we loosed only a single volley, and then ran for our horses.

Rifle bullets were soon spitting about our ears and shells were bursting farther on, but as we were riding wide no one was hit, although once, when we were bunched together at a gap in a fence a shell pitched right among us and killed a led-horse, whose blood was spattered in my face.

We spread out once more, and sprinted for the shelter of the Vet River banks, two or three miles beyond, and here we gave our winded animals time to recover. The British made no further attempt to advance that day, realising perhaps that we had the heels of them. After satisfying ourselves of their intentions, we crossed over the north bank by a bridle-path, to build fires and cook a meal, for we had eaten nothing that day, and after dark we trekked downstream for a few miles, to be in safety. Burghers, who had ridden away earlier to see how the women's laager was getting on, returned to say that all the wagons had escaped, so we spent an easy night under the thorn trees beside the water.

At sunrise yesterday's English approached as far as the river, where they came to rest. Our little party from the mountains thought that we had come far enough out of our course, so we decided to double back behind the column in order to resume our journey southwards. We took our leave of the Freestaters after hearing from them of an insurmountable barrier that we should meet at the Modder River, where, they said, the English had a line of fortified posts that would stop our progress to the south.

Recrossing the Vet River, we rode back along the way we had come the day before, and the soldiers halted along the stream did not even send a shell at us when we skirted round their camp.

We were getting short of ammunition, so during the next two days we followed the road by which the English force had travelled, to pick up Lee-Metford cartridges. The English soldiers were notoriously careless with their ammunition. If a round or two dropped from their bandoliers they would never trouble to dismount, as they knew they could get more, and at their halting-places one could almost always find cartridges lying spilt in the grass. So much was this the case that latterly it had become a regular practice to trail the columns, sometimes for a week on end, to glean these crumbs from the rich man's table, and I doubt if the British ever realised to what an extent the Boers were dependent upon this source of replenishment.

We followed the road back until we came once more in sight of Brandfort village, by which time we had picked up nearly a hundred rounds. Satisfied with this we now turned west, and then south-west, towards the Modder River.

Chapter 19

Farther South

We rode on steadily for three days, making a bend so as to strike the river midway between Bloemfontein and Kimberley. Nothing of interest happened, save for a brush with an English patrol that suddenly bore down on us one morning out of the mist.

The light was so uncertain that both sides drew off, after firing a few shots, for neither party could make out how strong the other was.

We passed the *dorp* of Bultfontein on our way and looked in for what we could find, but the place was gutted. For the rest we rode over interminable plains devoid of human beings. We did not see a single homestead that was not in ruins, and at some places lay hundreds of sheep clubbed to death or bayoneted by the English troops, in pursuance of their scheme of denuding the country of live-stock to starve out the Boers.

In spite of this there was generally an odd sheep or two straying about, and there were plenty of springbok besides, so we did not lack meat. Nevertheless we were leading a pretty hard life. Bread and salt, soap, tobacco and books were things of the past. We had almost forgotten the taste of tea, coffee, sugar and vegetables. If a man was not lucky enough to possess a tinder-box, he had to expend a valuable rifle-cartridge every time he wished to light a fire. It was midwinter, with ice on every pool, and we went in tattered clothing and slept under threadbare blankets at night.

We crossed the Modder River at midnight above Abrahamskraal, and daybreak found us facing the line of military posts we had been told of, that the English had established all the way from Bloemfontein to the Diamond Mine at Koffiefontein, a distance of sixty miles. This cordon was formed to guard thousands of sheep and cattle taken from the farms. Each post consisted of ten or twelve tents, at intervals of perhaps two thousand yards, and as our horses were in too poor a condition to make a dash for it, we turned westward, seeking a convenient spot at which to slink by without attracting attention. We could see patrols of cattle-guards riding about, but they probably took us for their own men, and for a while we went in peace.

Then a heliograph started winking from a kopje, and before long there was activity; soldiers running for their horses, and others galloping in from the plain. Seeing this, we boldly headed between two of the camps for a chain of hills beyond, firing from the saddle and getting well peppered in return, but we gained the cover of the hills before a real pursuit could be organised. A considerable number of horsemen came towards us, and when we opened long-range fire they contented themselves with spattering some volleys against the rocks about us, and then returned to their business of minding the herds. We were now safely across the much-talked-of Modder River barrier, and, continuing our journey, reached the mineral spring near Lotshoek by next day, where we fell in with a small commando of fifty or sixty men under a Field-Cornet named Blignault.

We were now in the Fauresmith district, not more than fifty miles from the Orange River, beyond which lay the Cape Colony, but I was yet to discover that it was farther off than it seemed.

When we told Blignault of our plan of invasion from here, he strongly advised us against the attempt. He said that if we crossed the Orange River here, we should find ourselves in open and arid country, where our horses would surely starve, and where we would be ridden down by the first British force that saw us. On the other hand, if we went east towards the headwaters of the Orange River, a hundred and fifty miles away, and then turned south into the Cape, we should find mountains and good grazing for our horses, and there so small a band as ours would stand some chance of survival. Blignault and his men had much to say of the hardships they had endured when they accompanied General de Wet into the Colony some months previously. Fifteen hundred men had crossed the river, but they were so beset by enemy columns that they had to return to the Free State with the loss of many men and horses. In fact everyone we met in these parts spoke against further raids into British territory.

We were reminded, too, of the disaster that overtook General Hertzog's venture to the south, and of the fate of almost every other party that had crossed the Orange River. It seemed that, like the cave in the fable, many tracks led over the river, but few came back.

This was not encouraging, and Field-Cornet Botha and the rest of my companions were so impressed that they began to waver, but Jacobus Bosman and I talked them into a better frame of mind, and finally persuaded them that, by accepting the advice we had received and going east, we could get into the Cape Colony and hold our own once we were there.

Next day we said good-bye to Blignault's commando and rode away east, coming within sight of Edenburg village the following afternoon. This place lies about forty miles south of Bloemfontein on the main railway, and as we found the line strongly block-housed and saw a big English camp on the outskirts of the village, we lay over for the night, to spy out the land next day.

The night after that we saddled at dark and rode towards the railway track, hoping to get over unobserved at a spot which we had investigated during the day. Just before we started, a sturdy little Shetland pony came wandering up from the English camp, and I took him along with me, which was just as well, as it turned out. After an hour's ride we reached a railway line at what we took to be a point which we had selected, but the night was so dark that we had gone astray, and we ran into a block-house instead. We were met with the usual 'Halt! Who comes there?' followed by rifle shots, so we bore away for a more suitable crossing, and some five hundred yards farther down we made another attempt.

As is the case with most railways in South Africa, a fence ran on either side of the line, composed of thick strands of wire which had to be cut before the horses could be led through. The only implement we possessed was a large file, and with this a young fellow named Verster and I tried to saw the wires, while the others waited a hundred yards back. The file grating across the taut wires made a tremendous noise, and before we had cut even one strand, we were again challenged and fired at by the sentry, who sounded not twenty yards away. We hurriedly mounted to rejoin our companions, but our horses began to plunge and flounder over obstructions staked along the ground. In approaching the railway we had somehow or other missed these entanglements, but now we were in the thick of them, and the tins always attatched to them were clanging and jangling, and increasing the terror of our animals. To this din was added a blaze of musketry from a block-house standing only a few yards away, which in the darkness we had mistaken for a mound of rocks.

Rifle-fire at point-blank range is unpleasant at the best of times, but when one is on a maddened horse staggering amid wire loops, it is infinitely more so, and had there been even a glimmer of light to guide the soldiers we should both have been shot. It was so dark , however, that they were firing at the sounds, and not at us, and Verster managed to wrench his horse free, but mine was shot and I was nearly pinned underneath him. I undid the buckles of the girth, and dragged my saddle from under the prostrate animal and, stumbling over the rest of the obstructions, we got clear away to where the others stood whistling and shouting to us and anxiously watching, not daring to shoot for fear of killing us. I had left the Shetland pony with them when I went forward to the fence, so I now put my saddle on him, and we galloped off, leaving the soldiers firing blindly into the night. We made a half-moon, until we again reached the railway line, intending to have another try, but as soon as I began to use the file, we heard the sound of men running along the track towards us, so we lost no time in decamping, and abandoned all thought of crossing that night. We spent a cold night behind a kopje, and, when it grew light, we were nearer the English camp at Edenburg than we imagined. We had barely time to get our horses saddled before a hundred or more troopers came racing at us, but, riding fast, we got safely into the hills at Boomplaats, my Shetland pony going surprisingly well.

As the English horsemen turned back after a while, we halted by the little cemetery where those English soldiers lie buried who were killed at the battle here between Sir Harry Smith and the Boers, in 1848. This graveyard was of some personal interest to me, because it had almost caused my father the loss of his position as President of the Free State when I was a boy. The British Government many years before had erected headstones over the fallen soldiers inscribed with the words: 'Killed in action against the Rebel Boers'. Many of these stones, in the course of time, fell to pieces, so my father ordered replicas with the original inscription faithfully copied. This gave rise to much ill feeling, for these were indignant patriots who considered the epithet 'Rebel' an insult to the Boers, and my father very nearly lost the next presidential election in consequence. I have another reason for remembering the Boomplaats cemetery, for while we were resting here, Field-Cornet Botha came to me and said that he and the other men had for some days been reconsidering the matter of continuing to the Cape Colony, and he now asked me to give up the plan. Apparently last night's affair and the chase of that morning had put the finishing touch to their indecision, and with the exception of Bosman and myself, they all declared their intention of returning to the Winburg Mountains.

We two said that we had not ridden thus far to turn back now, and we told them that we were going to the Cape even if we had to go alone. We argued and entreated for hours, but in the end Botha and his men, with my two German friends Haase and Pollatchek, saddled their horses and rode off, leaving us behind.

Bosman and I spent the night beside the graveyard, feeling too depressed to light a fire, and the next morning we found our horses had strayed out of sight. It took us the better part of five hours to trail their spoor, and when at last we got back to where we had left our saddles and our other belongings, there was nothing there. This was a serious blow, for saddles were indispensable, and blankets and cooking-tins even more so. We could see from the hoof-marks that there were two mounted thieves, and although we could not say whether they were Boer or British, we decided to follow them. After careful going, on our barebacked horses, for ten miles or more, we saw two men seated beside a fire below a kopje, and stalking them on foot, came close enough to cover them with our rifles before they could stir. They proved to be two Boer boys from a neighbouring outpost, and they had all our missing gear with them. They said that they thought the things belonged to the English scouts, a palpable lie, and we told them plainly what we thought of them, but we did learn from them of a commando under General Hertzog lying in the hills beyond the Riet River forty or fifty miles away, and we decided to go there. For two days we rode on, passing through the deserted mining town of Jagersfontein, and reaching the next village, Fauresmith, by sunset. This place had also been abandoned by its original inhabitants, but we found it occupied by men who were a little better than bandits.

As we went up the main street a number of unkempt individuals rushed at us, rifle in hand, and ordered us to halt. They crowded round threateningly, with shouts of '*Maak dood die verdomde spioene*' ('Kill the cursed spies'), although they must have known that we were nothing of the sort, and only wanted a pretext to rob us. We sat our horses, uncertain what to do with such ugly customers, and it looked as if we were in for serious trouble, for already greedy hands were clutching at our wallets, and trying to pull us from our saddles. Just then two gaunt, famished-looking women rushed from a neighbouring house, and shrilly ordered them off. They had so much influence over the rabble, that they stood aside growlingly and allowed us to accompany our forbidding guardian angels to their home. They were the daughters of a once-wealthy farmer, ruined and killed during the war, and they had taken refuge in an empty house in the village, where they were living in poverty. They told us that the people who had molested us were riff-raff ejected from the fighting commandos, existing on what they could rob and loot. We now heard that General Hertzog's commando had moved west, so we took our leave next morning, and rode for two days in search of them, until we were right on the Griqualand border, where we met a solitary burgher, from whom we learned that we were a long way out of our course and that the commando was back on the Riet River. We turned north-east, and by dark of the following evening we crossed the river by the wagon-bridge which, strange to say, was still intact. On the far bank was a cattle-post in charge of an old man and his two sons. They were looking after the meat supply of General Hertzog's men, lying, we were glad to hear, only ten miles upstream. As it was late, we spent the night with our hosts, an unsavoury trio, who did not belie their looks, for we found next morning that our saddlebags had been rifled. So I stood them in a line while Bosman went through their pockets and recovered our knives, tinderboxes, and other property, after I had grazed the eldest ruffian's arm with a bullet to teach him better manners.

We then rode on, not particularly impressed by the specimens of Fauresmith men whom we had met thus far, for we had been the victims of three attempted robberies in less than a week. These men, however, were only off-scourings, and our subsequent association with the real fighting-men of the district was much happier.

By midday we came on General Hertzog's force, camped on the banks of the river at a place called Bethal. I knew General Hertzog from the old days, a thin high-cheeked man with angry eyes, though his speech was pleasant and I saw that his men held him in great respect. He had been a Judge of the Supreme Court at Bloemfontein before the war, but was now in command of the south-western districts of the Free State. He had with him about three hundred men, the largest commando that I saw on my passage through, and he had other smaller bodies scattered about.

We remained with the commando for ten days, hoping to gain recruits for the Cape, but not a man would come. They said once was enough, and every time we broached the subject we were met with emphatic refusals, and with tales of the privations and losses which they had sustained during the previous expeditions, so it began to look as if Bosman and I would have to go by ourselves after all. During the time we spent with the commando we earned our keep by taking part in a sharp little affair in the hills above the Riet River wagon-bridge.

An English column, a thousand strong, crossed to our side of the river one night, on their way to Kimberley, and we held them up for two days, until at length they fell back over the bridge and returned by the way they had come.

General Hertzog lost only two killed and a few wounded, although the English rifle-fire was very heavy at times, and they had guns as well. On the afternoon of the second day, while two of us were riding down to a dam to water our horses, an English trooper came galloping towards us from round a kopje. He was plucky enough, for when he realised his mistake he fired from the saddle, from so close that, before he could do so again, I was alongside with my rifle in his ribs. He said that he had been scouting and had lost his way, and as my companion was barefooted, we relieved him of his boots, as well as his horse, and we left him gingerly picking his way over the sharp surface towards his own side, a thing I did not envy him, for he had to make a semicircle of several miles to get around our flank, before he could rejoin his companions.

When we found next morning that the English had withdrawn overnight, General Hertzog ordered us to return to our former halting-ground higher up the river, and here Bosman and I had good luck, for, off-saddled close by, was a small party of newcomers, ten in number, amongst whom I recognised several old acquaintances from the Transvaal, and to our great joy they told us that they were on their way into the Cape Colony. This was good news indeed, and we told them of our own plans at once.

As from now onward I was to be intimately associated with this little band, and as so many of them died tragically, I shall give their names.

The leader was Jack Borrius, a short thick-set man of twenty-eight, from

Potchefstroom, whom I had met while serving with Captain Theron's scouts and in the 'ACC'. Next came Benjamin Coetzee, from Pretoria, whose reckless bravery had earned him a reputation as long ago as the Natal days, when I had known him as a member of the Pretoria commando. Then Nicholas Swart and Cornelius Vermaas, both sons of wealthy Transvaal farmers. Vermaas had been wounded and captured by the British six months before, but he had jumped from the train in the mountains near Cape Town while being taken for shipment to Ceylon, and after many trials he had got back on foot to the Transvaal. Next were Percy Wyndall and Edgar Duncker, two English-speaking boys from Johannesburg, and Frits Balogh, a young Austrian from Pretoria.

Then Jan van Zijl, illiterate but witty, and Piet de Ruyt, a Hollander, and lastly young Rittenberg, also from Potchefstroom.

They were all Transvaalers and, with the exception of Borrius, not one was yet twenty years old; and like myself, they had all been taken with the idea of free-lancing it into the Cape Colony.

By way of ironic comment on their tattered clothing and ragged appearance they called themselves the 'Rijk Section' (or 'Dandy Fifth', as Duncker translated it). Of this small band four were to meet their death by execution, and six were wounded or captured, a result that fully justified the many warnings which we had received against entering the Cape Colony.

While we were discussing whether to try the Orange River in this vicinity or to take the advice we had received, and go east towards the headwaters, there arrived another party of horsemen, who decided us for the latter course.

These were Commandant George Brand and a score of followers from the south-eastern districts, come to confer with General Hertzog on military affairs.

He was a son of Sir John Brand, who had preceded my father as President of the Free State. He told me that as soon as he had finished with General Hertzog, he was returning east across the railway line to the area between the Caledon River and Basutoland, and when he heard of our intention to enter the Cape Colony he advised us to accompany him as far as the Caledon River, where the passage would be safer than here.

As we had already received similar advice, and as he assured us that we could get as many horses as we liked in the mountains, we agreed to travel with him.

The very next day, saying good-bye to Hertzog and his men, we set out and made such good progress that by the following afternoon we were back in the same hill overlooking Edenburg village from which we had started with our previous companions on our unsuccessful attempt to cross the railway line.

Now things went better, for we were with men who knew the exact position of every block-house and every sentry along the track, and by midnight we were over without a single casualty, although there was a good deal of firing from block-houses on either side of us as we went through.

The railway is regarded as the dividing line between the Western and Eastern Free State. To the west lie the great plains, while to the east the country grows more and more mountainous as one approaches the Basutoland border.

I knew this region quite well, having hunted here as a boy, so after sunrise we took our leave of Brand and his men, whose course lay in another direction, and we rode on for the next few days in the direction of the upper reaches of the Caledon River.

Only once did we see an English column, to which we passed so close that we heard the bugles sound the alarm and saw the soldiers running for their horses; but after the exchange of a few shots, we went on our way.

Most of the live-stock lay clubbed to death around the burnt farmhouses, and there was no sign of the civilian population, for those who had escaped capture were hiding in caves and gorges.

We did not see many fighting-men either, for they were dispersed in small guerrilla bands among the mountains.

Troops of wild horses were fairly common between Sikonyella's Peak and the Elandsberg, so we searched out a local outpost, and with their help were able to corral sufficient horses to give each of the 'Rijk Section' two fresh mounts, my own share being two spirited mares, a brown and a roan. The horses were entirely untrained, but in a few days we had them broken to bit and rein and our prospects were vastly improved, for the animals we had been riding thus far were in wretched condition. To these we gave their freedom, knowing that when they had picked up flesh they could be recaptured and used by others, and it was pleasant to see them trotting up the mountain-side to a well-earned rest, my little Shetland pony kicking up his heels and whinnying joyously at their head.

It was near the end of August (1901) by now, and the rainy season might be upon us at any moment, when a single freshet might render the Orange River impassable, so, as we were come to within fifteen miles of it, we made ready for our final effort.

Upon the very morning, however, on which we hoped to cross, a large body of horsemen appeared over the shoulder of a distant hill. By their formation and manner of riding we knew them to be Boers, but as there was no commando of that size round here, we waited for them with considerable interest. After an hour the column came abreast of us and we were astonished to see that at its head rode Mr Smuts, the Transvaal State Attorney, now a General, who, after hearty greetings, told us that he was on his way to the Cape Colony with three hundred men.

This was another stroke of luck. Falling in with the 'Rijk Section' had been the first, but to meet with a whole commando making for the river was the greatest fortune of all, far greater than we realised at the time, for our subsequent experiences went to show that a small force like ours would not have lasted a week in the troublesome country beyond.

It was the finest commando with which I ever served. The rank and file were mostly keen young farmers from the Western Transvaal, the pick of de la Rey's fighting men, and in command of them was perhaps the one man in South Africa who could have led us through the perilous days to come.

General Smuts halted his men and ordered them to off saddle. This gave me time to go among them, and I had another pleasant surprise, for I came on my Hollander uncle, Jan Mulder, whom I had not seen since that time in Natal, nearly two years before. I also found the General's brother-in-law, Krige, one of the few survivors of Isaac Malherbe's corporalship, who had been so badly wounded at Spion Kop.

I learned from them of the great hardships and dangers which they had encountered on their way through the Free State. The English had wind of their intention to invade the Cape Colony and strenuous efforts were made to head them off. Large forces were hurried up from all sides, giving them no rest either night or day, and it was only by hard riding and hard fighting that they had escaped, with the loss of many men and horses.

From what I could gather, General Smuts purposed a flying raid into the central districts of the Cape, to test a large-scale invasion later on, in order to relieve the increasing pressure in the north.

Whether this was really his object I do not know, for he was an uncommunicative man, but at any rate here he was, and we were only too eager to go with him, whatever his plans might be. When we went to tell him that the 'Rijk Section' proposed joining his force he said he was very pleased, and he appointed us to be his scouts, a distinction which we accepted gladly, but for which we paid dearly in the long run.

Chapter 20

We Go into the Cape Colony and Meet with a Warm Reception

The adventures of this handful of resolute men led by General Smuts forms one of the most interesting episodes in the whole course of the guerrilla war.—*The Times History*, v, 302.

The place of our meeting with General Smuts and his commando was in sight of the little village of Sastron, about fifteen miles from the Orange River, and his intention was to march nearer that day, and cross during the night. By noon a start was made, and towards five in the evening we could see a dark line in front of us marking the gorge, at the bottom of which runs the river between high mountain walls.

Unfortunately this was not all we saw. Our side of the canyon was held for miles in each direction by a cordon of British troops, stationed there to bar our way. Whenever a footpath led down the cliffs, there stood a tented camp, and the intervening ground was patrolled by strong bodies of mounted men who clearly knew of our coming.

On seeing this, General Smuts led us back into a range of hills, where we waited until next day, whilst men were sent in search of some neighbouring outpost to act as guides.

At dusk a young officer named Louis Wessels arrived with fifty men, a hard-bitten crew, with whom he had been operating for over a year.

He reported enemy columns closing in on us from the rear, and said that unless we were able to effect a crossing that night, we should be trapped. He said, moreover, that the river was everywhere difficult, owing to the depth of the gorge and the perpendicular cliffs, but he had brought with him a veteran of the Basuto wars who knew of a path which might be practicable.

General Smuts decided to start at once, and in the falling dark our force rode out, accompanied by Wessels and his men, who agreed to enter the Colony with us. We travelled on, hour after hour in the dark, over rough ground, and then, towards three in the morning, we caught a glint of white far below, where the Orange River boiled and eddied in its narrow channel. It was yet night when we commenced the final descent, but after toiling down the precipitous path to which our guide had brought us, and along which assuredly no other mounted troops had ever passed, we reached the edge of the water. In single file we began to cross the river, a strong and turbulent mountain torrent, not broad, but so swift that our horses could scarcely maintain their footing, and as dawn lit the cliffs above, the hindmost man was through, and I stood in the Cape Colony at last.

After a short halt we took a path that led to the top of the cliffs opposite, by a deep cleft, up which we tugged our leg-weary animals, until, far above, we emerged on a wide grass-covered tableland, pleasantly dotted with native villages and herds of cattle at pasture.

We were not actually on British territory, but the country here lies in an angle between the Free State, Basutoland, and Cape boundaries, and the region seemed exclusively occupied by Basutos, for there were no European habitations in sight.

As soon as we gained the top, we scattered into small parties, riding from one native village to another, in quest of tobacco and fodder for our horses. Whilst we were thus ranging, a body of mounted Basutos, about three hundred strong, came moving swiftly towards us. Some were armed with rifles, others carried battle-axes, assagais and knobkerries, which they brandished in the air as they approached. We did not know what to make of this, but we thought that they could not be contemplating an unprovoked attack on a white force equal to their own. General Smuts, therefore, contented himself with sending word for the various foraging parties to close in, and the commando continued on its way without paying much attention to the horsemen, who at a shouted word from their leader, came to a halt on a knoll close by, where they sat their horses in silence, watching the Boers pass.

At this stage, my uncle and I with five others whose names I did not know, lagged behind to feed our horses from the grain-baskets to be found in every native village, and as we were not frightened by the Basuto parade, which we put down to curiosity, we allowed the commando to get a considerable way ahead of us. At length, seeing that we were being left too far behind, we mounted and followed our men, the last of whom were just vanishing over the edge of the tableland by a road leading to the plain below.

By the time we could look down, the bulk of the commando was already at the bottom. They were riding along a road flanked on the left by a ledge of overhanging natural rock, part of the footwall of the tableland which they had just quitted, and on the right by a Mission Church and a long rubble fence, separating the road from fields and gardens. A force moving down this enclosed alleyway could be easily ambushed, and we were alarmed to see that the Basutos had left their horses above, and were scrambling down the final shelf of rock overhanging the road, crawling forward to the edge, to look straight down on our men riding unconsciously below. We expected to see them open fire on the crowded ranks at any moment. Indecision, however, came over the natives; they began nudging one another as if each wanted someone else to start shooting, and by the time they had made up their minds the opportunity was gone, for the commando was already debouching from the confined space of the road into the open plain. My fellow stragglers and I were worse off, for although the

Basutos had hesitated to attack the larger force, their intentions were clearly hostile, and we wondered how they would deal with our little band left isolated in the rear.

After hurried consultation we decided to follow on, and attempt to catch up with the commando, so we began to descend the slope. We reached the bottom unmolested, but as we passed the church beside the road we caught sight of many dark faces pressed against the window-panes, and white eyeballs peering at us from within. Then came a deafening crash, as a volley was fired at us point-blank from the building, sending showers of splintered glass about our heads. Fortunately the native is a notoriously bad marksman, for he generally closes his eyes when he pulls the trigger, so not one of us was hit, although the range was under ten yards. When the Basutos lying on the rocky shelf overhanging the road heard the volley, they took courage and also opened fire. The five men with us did the only reasonable thing under the circumstances. They dug their spurs in and rode off as fast as they could, but my uncle with his usual impetuosity loosed his pack animal, swung his horse in behind a massive boulder that had calved from the ledge above, and jumped to the ground. I had to follow suit, relinquishing my own led-horse, and riding in behind the rock, a huge cube that leaned against the parent crag in such a manner as to give us cover against the Basutos overhead as well as from those firing through the shattered windows of the church across the way. We opened fire in turn at the church, but we saw at once that our position was untenable. Immediately above, the natives were excitedly shouting as they fired at our retreating companions, and at such of the rearmost commando men as were still within range.

Already we could hear the voices of several of them craning over to get at us from above. With some of the enemy standing on the roof, as it were, and others shooting from the church not fifteen yards off, we realised that to remain here could have only one ending, and we prepared to mount once more, although our chances of escape seemed desperate.

Looking down the road, we could now see only two of our men, riding for their lives across the fields, for they had succeeded in leaping the dividing wall. The other three men were nowhere to be seen, but two dead horses lay on the road, and a third was galloping riderless in the distance. This looked bad, but no other course was open to us, so we leapt into the saddle and rode out from the sanctuary of the fallen rock. The moment we did so, the natives in the church saw us, and redoubled their fire, while those on the bank above raised blood-curdling yells and also fired.

As we sped past, more natives rose from behind the fence lining the road. Fortunately these last were armed only with assagais and knobkerries, which came whirring about our ears. In this pandemonium we took every moment to be our last, but we ran the gauntlet safely for perhaps sixty yards, when the road fell suddenly into a deep spruit which neither of us had noticed in our excitement. It meant salvation, although at first it looked as if it only meant more danger, for, riding down, we saw some fifteen or twenty natives in a circle, intent upon something that lay on the ground between them. Before they could do more than spring to their feet and strike blindly at us, we were through. Instead of riding up the opposite bank of the spruit, where we should come under fire again, we galloped along the bed under cover of the high banks, until we were able to emerge out of range.

Of the five men who had been with us, the two whom we had seen making across country got clean away, but the other three were either killed on the road, and then dragged into the spruit, or else they were destroyed on reaching there, for we learned long after that their bodies were found on the causeway, dreadfully mutilated by the natives for medicine, in accordance with their barbarous custom. I have little doubt that when my uncle and I rode down amongst them, they were busy at their grisly task of dissection, which we ourselves so narrowly missed.

We were out of danger now, but the prospect was not reassuring. True, we had got off without a scratch, but our pack animals were gone with most of our gear, and looking over our saddle-horses, we were dismayed to find that they were both badly wounded. My brown mare had been hit by a jagged missile that had smashed her lower jaw, and my uncle's horse had a bullet through the crupper and another through the hind leg. I put my poor animal out of her misery at once, but my uncle thought that his might recover (which it did). I shouldered my saddle, and, leading the injured horse, we advanced on foot, dolefully speculating upon our future, for we had only a wounded horse and a handful of cartridges between us in this inhospitable country.

Far away we could see the commando posted on a ridge, to cover the retreat of those who were still in danger, for some of the men had been within range when the firing started on us at the church, and there were several wounded painfully making their way across the plain.

When at last we reached the commando and had time to look around, my uncle and I had a pleasant surprise, for there stood our two led-horses safe and sound, with our blankets and cooking-tins intact. They must have fled straight on when we loosed them on the road, and they had overtaken the commando while we were fighting below the shelf. Now they were contentedly ranged in line with the rest of the horses behind the hill, as if nothing out of the common had happened, so at any rate we still had a riding-horse apiece.

While we were halted here, we saw that another party of ten or twelve men was in difficulties. They, too, had got separated from our main body, while foraging on the tableland earlier in the morning, but no one had missed them until now, when we heard the sound of distant firing and saw them riding into view two miles away, hotly pursued by numbers of mounted Basutos. They were in grave danger, for between them and ourselves ran a deep ravine, towards which they were being shepherded, and as the ravine seemed impassable, it looked for a time as if we should have to stand by helpless and see them killed. In order to do what we could, the whole commando mounted and rode to the edge of the chasm, and here, fortunately, we found a piece of high ground from which we overlooked the scene on the other side, and were able to drop our bullets among the advancing natives with such good effect that they reined in. This gave the cornered men time to search the cliff for a way down, which they succeeded in finding under cover of our fire, and ultimately they rejoined us without casualties.

This final episode reduced my ammunition to four rounds, and indeed many of the rest were no better off, for the long chase to which they had been subjected during their dash through the Free State had depleted their bandoliers to such an extent that the question was becoming a very serious one for a column such as ours, starting to invade a hostile territory.

After this we halted for an hour to give the wounded men a rest, and to enable those whose horses had been killed to get remounted. There were seven men hit, and, as we had no lint, bandages, or medical supplies, there was little that we could do for them.

After a while the injured men were placed in their saddles, and we trekked away, with several bands of natives hovering in our rear, as if they contemplated a further attack, but in the end they retired. After a wearisome ride we got beyond the area of the Native Reserve, and towards afternoon we came across the first European farmhouse, where we left our wounded to be fetched in by the British.

We rested our exhausted animals till dusk, and then, saying good-bye to the wounded men in the house, we rode on for five or six miles before camping.

For months past we had experienced an unbroken spell of fine weather, bitterly cold at night but cloudless sunshine by day. Now, however, there was a change, and it came on to rain heavily, so that we spent the long hours of darkness dismally lying in mud and water. This weather coming on top of the crowded events of the last twenty-four hours, gave us our first taste of what was awaiting us in the Cape Colony, and thus early we began to appreciate the fact that our road was likely to be a thorny one.

Next morning the sky cleared somewhat, although a penetrating drizzle continued for most of the day, through which we rode shivering, our thin clothing being but little protection. My own wardrobe was typical; a ragged coat and worn trousers full of holes, with no shirt or underwear of any kind. On my naked feet were dilapidated rawhide sandals, patched and repatched during eight months of wear, and I had only one frayed blanket to sleep under at night. Few of the men were better off, and we looked with apprehension on the change of weather, for it meant that the rainy season was upon us, with its attendant hardships, the full extent of which we were yet to learn.

Our course during this day took us through more settled parts, and for the first time we looked at farms and homesteads untouched by the hand of war. There were men peacefully working in the fields, and women and children standing unafraid before their doors as we passed, a very different picture from that to which we were accustomed in the devastated republics.

The people were almost exclusively of Dutch origin, so they gave us unselfish hospitality. In the matter of clothing they were hardly able to assist us, on account of the military embargo which prevented them from buying more than certain quantities, but gifts of coffee, sugar, salt and tobacco were ungrudgingly made, and the first slice of bread and butter and the first sip of coffee I had tasted for a year almost made the long journey worth while.

In spite of the bad weather, our first day among a friendly population was a pleasant experience, which put the men in good spirits, and I dare say we posed a little before the womenfolk, laughing and whistling as we rode along.

Our course, later in the afternoon, took us up a mountain-pass, and when we reached the top towards evening, we could see in the distance the comfortable hamlet of Lady Grey nestling to the left, while in a glen below was the old familiar sight of a British column, crawling down the valley. This gave us no anxiety, for being without wheeled transport of any kind, we turned across the heath and easily left the soldiers far behind.

That night it rained again, and a cold wind drove against us from the south. Our commando presented a strange appearance as we wound along; we had no raincoats, so we used our blankets as cloaks against the down-pour, and the long line of draped horsemen looked like a tribe of Red Indians on the warpath.

Long after dark we came to a halt, spending a wretched wet night, and at dawn, cold and miserable, we trekked over bleak country, the biting wind in our faces, until at four in the afternoon we came to rest near a place ominously called Moordenaar's Poort (The Murderer's Way). The rain now ceased, and, a passing herdboy having told us that English troops were camped a few miles off, General Smuts decided to go and see them for himself. He took with him two young Freestaters who had joined him on the way down, and another man named Neethling from Pretoria, an old friend of mine. With these he left, saying that he would be back by dark. At sunset he had not returned, and for hours we anxiously waited for him until, shortly before midnight, he walked in among us on foot and alone. He had been ambushed by a British patrol, who had killed all three of his escort and all the horses, he alone escaping down a nullah. Had he been killed I believe that our expedition into the Cape would have come to a speedy end, for there was no one else who could have kept us together. The commando was divided into two portions commanded by Jacobus van Deventer[1] and Ben Bouwer respectively, both good fighting-men but neither of them possessing the personality or the influence over men that General Smuts had, to save us from going to pieces during the difficult period upon which we were now entering.

We spent the night where we lay, and there was more trouble before daylight, for a porcupine came grunting through our lines, with the result that the horses stampeded in a body. They thundered off in the dark, crashing through fences and undergrowth in blind terror, and at sunrise there was not an animal to be seen.

With an English force in the vicinity this was a serious predicament, for they would make short work of us if we were dismounted, so all hands turned out to hunt for the horses. Luckily a few of the men had hobbled their mounts which prevented them from going as far as the rest, and as these were run to earth in a hollow not far away, they were used to track the others, and after three or four uneasy hours, expecting to see the English appear at any moment, we brought back all the missing horses safe and sound.

We now travelled on for the next three days across windy barrens, heading south-west. The weather grew more and more tempestuous as we went, and we suffered severely from the cold, and from the intermittent rains that accompanied us. Both horses and men began to show signs of distress. The animals looked thin and gaunt, and the men sat on their saddles pinched, shivering, and despondent, for South Africans are peculiarly susceptible to the depressing effects of bad weather. They can stand cold and other hardships as well as anyone, but continued lack of sunshine soon makes them miserable, and for the time being we were a dispirited band, wishing we had never come.

By day we were wet and cold, and the nights were evil dreams. Dry fuel was almost unprocurable, and after a weary day we had to spend the hours of darkness

---

[1]Later Sir Jacobus van Deventer in the Great War.

cowering together to snatch a little sleep on some muddy mountain-side, or in an equally sodden valley.

Soon we were losing horses freely, and not a trek was made without some wretched animals being left behind with tuckered flanks and drooping heads, waiting for the end.

We had three days of this, but our real troubles were only beginning.

Towards sunset one evening we came in sight of the village of Jamestown, and saw a strong English column to our right, so General Smuts moved us on. It grew pitch-dark, and a driving rain smote straight in our faces. The night was so black that it was impossible to see even the man immediately before one, and the cold so bitter that we became stiff and numbed, and it was only with difficulty that we could drag our horses along, for we were ordered to go on foot to husband their strength.

When I was crossing a spruit, my sandals stuck in the heavy pot-clay and came to pieces when I tried to withdraw them, and it was only by cutting corners from my blanket and wrapping one about each foot that I was able to go on at all. Our guide, a young man from a local farm, had lost his bearings, so we had to grope our way through icy rain for five hours, until we could continue no longer, and stood huddled together ankle-deep in mud and water, praying for sunrise.

When it grew light, over thirty horses lay dead from exposure, besides others abandoned overnight, and our spirits, low before, were at zero now.

The rain continued pitilessly until midday, when the sky cleared and the blessed sun shone upon us once more. We moved forward, and not far away saw a large farmhouse and outbuildings containing plenty of fuel. Soon we were warming our numbed bodies, and cooking our first hot meal for days.

The housewife at the farm gave me a pair of old-fashioned elastic-sided boots, and I unearthed an empty grain-bag in which I cut a hole for my head, and one at each corner for my arms, thus providing myself with a serviceable great-coat. My appearance caused much laughter, but I noticed that during the next few days, whenever we passed a barn, grain-bags were in great demand, and soon many of the men were wearing them.

As the people here told us that there was an English force in the neighbourhood, we moved on later in the afternoon, first saying good-bye to Louis Wessels, the young Free State officer and his men, who turned back from here, as they had only come thus far to see our force well launched into the Colony. I believe that they reached their own country again in safety.

We continued for an hour, and then halted in a valley. Whilst we were idly resting in the grass two field-guns banged at us from a hill, and shells came tearing overhead. More followed and, taken by surprise, we leaped into the saddle and made for the cover of a line of hills to the rear. The artillery was poor, and neither man nor horse was hit. Once in safety, we put our animals our of harm's way, and climbed up to see what the English meant to do. We could now see a column of horse coming down towards us, around a spur that had previously hidden them from view. There were about six hundred of them and they had with them two fifteen-pounder Armstrong guns, and several pom-poms which unlimbered and opened fire, while their horsemen cautiously approached us. After a time they quickened pace as though to attack, but, coming under our fire, they took cover behind some farmhouses and kraals. In spite of the shelling, and a lively exchange of rifle-fire, there were apparently no casualties on either side, and the affair terminated after dark. I did not fire a shot on account of the state of my cartridge belts, and the others fired no more than was necessary to stave off the enemy, because, as I said before, the ammunition question was an exceedingly serious one.

When the light went out, we withdrew to a farm close by, hoping for a real rest this time as we had not enjoyed a full night's sleep since we crossed the Orange River, more than a week before.

We did not get that night's rest, for at three o'clock next morning we were ordered up in the dark, and started in a cold drizzle of rain on a record march. Our men were weakened by long privations, our ammunition had dwindled to vanishing point, and our horses were in the last stages of exhaustion, yet during the next six days, beset on all sides, we marched and fought, and in the end successfully got through.

Chapter 21

Horses and Men

When the sun rose and the rain ceased, we found ourselves crossing a high shoulder of land with a wide expanse of mountains to the south of us, and there, in every valley and on every road, stood the white tents of English camps, to bar our progress.

General Smuts surveyed the blocking forces for a while, and then led us due east across the front of the enemy posts. Our road took us through rough country, and he ordered every man to go on foot to spare the horses. The English made no attempt to come after us, their orders apparently being to hold the roads and exits, so we trekked all day, seeking to turn their extreme right flank. Throughout the expedition into the Cape we had no difficulty in getting local sympathisers to act as guides, and on this occasion a young farm-hand volunteered to lead us. He picked his way so unerringly that towards nightfall we had not only succeeded in finding the end of the British line, but had even got round behind them, and could see the town of Dordrecht in the distance. We must have covered nearly thirty miles since getting out that morning, but as we were not yet out of danger of being headed back, we continued after dark, and, hungry and weary but in good cheer, we trudged all through the night, with only an occasional halt, mostly along steep mountain paths, wet and slippery from the rains. When daybreak came our young guide had done his work with such skill that we were well beyond the cordon, and there now lay before us the long mountain chain of the Stormbergen, stretching east to west as far as the eye could see. He told us that we could cross almost anywhere, so he was allowed to return home, and we made for a large farm lying at the foot of the range, where we turned our horses into the fields, and set about preparing a meal, once again hoping to spend the rest of the forenoon in sleep, for we had been on the move for twenty-four hours. But we had

scarcely slaughtered a few sheep and broken our fast, when the well-known cry of
'*Opsaal! Opsaal!*' sent us scurrying to fetch our unfortunate animals, for coming
down the slopes was a long column of English horse making our way. Near by ran a
pass up the mountain, and as it seemed clear of troops, we made for it, and in an hour
stood on the top of the Stormbergen, with the enemy force slewed round and
following us. The summit was a grassy tableland about three miles wide, sloping
gently to where the southern face of the mountain fell abruptly down to the plains
below.

There was no sign of troops up here, but as those in the rear were coming after us,
General Smuts disposed his men to hold them back while we of the 'Rijk Section'
were ordered to ride forward to the far edge of the plateau, to see whether the way in
that direction was clear. We set out in couples, making for different points from which
to look down on the Karroo. My companion was Henry Rittenberg, and when we
reached the rim of the plateau, we saw the narrow ribbon of a railway track winding
across the plain at our feet, with train after train steaming up to a small village station
and disgorging large numbers of soldiers.

The British, having failed to stop us at their first barrier, were now hurrying troops
round by rail to establish a second, and already several mounted columns had
detrained, and were beginning to climb up the mountain. One body was so far
advanced that their scouts were appearing on the tableland itself, so Rittenberg and I
rode nearer to examine their strength. We had not gone half a mile when some two
dozen troopers rode at us from behind a roll in the ground, firing from the saddle as
they came. We whipped round and galloped away, but had not the balance of the 'Rijk
Section' come to our aid we should have been shot or captured, for there was no cover
in which to make a stand, and our horses were in no fit state to compete with the well-
fed English chargers.

We now returned to General Smuts, to report what we had seen, and he looked
grave enough, for, with the original column of that morning closing in behind and all
those fresh troops coming up in front, we were almost invested.

A strong north wind, which had sprung up earlier in the day, had steadily increased
to a violent gale, and most of the men were crouching with their backs to the storm to
escape the flying grit that stung like buckshot.

General Smuts, with Commandants van Deventer and Bouwer, was, however, on
the look-out, standing well forward near the head of the pass up which the commando
had come. While we were explaining the situation, about three hundred soldiers
appeared on foot, having left their horses below. They did not seem to be expecting us
here for, when our men sprang up at a shout from van Deventer, they turned back and
ran.

They were out of sight almost at once, and when we reached the edge we saw
them scrambling down, but the wind in our faces made accurate shooting impossible,
and I do not think any were hit. The soldiers only fired a few shots in reply, and a
young man standing near me, named de la Rey, a nephew of General de la Rey, threw
up his arms and dropped dead with a bullet through his brain. We left him where he
fell, for we had no spade or other implement, nor had we time to bury him, for
looking back we could now see more and more English horsemen emerging on the
tableland, until we were practically encircled, although they were not yet strong

enough to prevent us from moving freely inside the wide ring that they had formed about us.

Nevertheless we could not break out, for soon there were machine-guns at every point of vantage, so commanding the terrain that a burst-through during daylight would have cost us more men than we could afford, and our only course was to try to stave off the pressure until after dark. To that end, with the gale roaring about our ears, General Smuts led us hither and thither all the afternoon, now pushing back one portion of the enemy line, and then another, avoiding the machine-gun fire by using dead ground, and generally preventing them from hustling us too closely. With our tired horses and men the strain was great. Ammunition was at such a low ebb that some had not a round left, and when, towards evening, many more troops had come up our case seemed hopeless.

We and our horses had marched for forty hours on end, and we were all but finished for lack of sleep and rest, while the noose around us had slowly tightened, until by dusk we were at bay around a small farmhouse and kraal, lying somewhat in a hollow, where for the moment we had comparative shelter, but where our speedy capture seemed certain.

When the English troops saw us preparing to make a stand they stayed their advance, in the belief, no doubt, that having cornered us, they could afford to wait for our surrender in the morning.

General Smuts stood before the homestead in whispered consultation with his two lieutenants, while the rest of us leaned on our rifles, too weary to care very much what happened. Then out of the house came a hunchbacked cripple, who said that he would lead us through the English troops to the edge of the tableland, by a way which was unlikely to be watched, for it ran through boggy soil. His offer was eagerly accepted and orders were given to mount at once. Six or seven men had been wounded during the day, two of them so badly that they had to be left behind, but the others chose to accompany us, and in a few minutes we were silently filing off into the darkness, the cripple crouching insecurely on a horse at our head. He took us along a squelching path, that twisted for a mile or two so close to the investing troops that we could hear voices and the champing of bits, but at the end of an anxious hour he had brought us undiscovered to the escarpment. From here the mountain-side fell sharply away into black depths below, how steeply we could not tell, but our guide warned us that it was very steep indeed. Dropping from his horse he plodded off into the night on his crutches, carrying with him our heartfelt thanks, for he had risked his life and goods on our behalf.

We now began to descend what was probably the nearest approach to the vertical attempted by any mounted force during the war. I doubt whether we could have accomplished it by day, but horses are more tractable and surer-footed in the dark, so we pulled them over the edge and went slithering down. At times whole batches of men and horses came glissading past, knocking against all in their course, but luckily the surface was free of rock, and covered with a thick matting of grass which served to break the impact, and after a terrible scramble we got down without serious damage. For the time being we had shaken free of the enemy once more. Our most insistent need now was sleep, but this was still denied us. Somewhere on a plain before us ran the railway line on which we had looked down that morning, and many miles beyond that lay still another track, both of which had to be crossed before sunrise, if we did not wish to have the troop-trains hurrying up more men. So General Smuts implacably ordered us on, and, leading our horses, we tramped obediently but wearily forward, little dreaming that another twenty hours of unbroken marching lay before us, and several days of even greater trials to come.

It was about ten o'clock by now, and the storm that had been raging throughout the day was subsiding, though the aftermath still blew cold, a blessing perhaps, for it served to keep us awake, and it made us step out to keep warm. After an hour we reached the first railway, a branch line from the Indwe Coal Mines. As we approached we saw the lights of a train, but General Smuts would not allow us to pile boulders on the metals nor to fire as the engine thundered by, for fear of killing civilians, so we stood aside, catching a glimpse of officers and others seated in the dining-car, smoking and taking wine, all unaware of the men looking at them from the darkness. General French, the English cavalry leader, told us long after that he was on board that train with his staff, hurrying round by rail to control operations on the *berg* where he imagined us still to be, so unknowingly, we missed a great opportunity.

After crossing the rails, we went on mile after mile, dazed for want of rest. Whenever there was delay at a fence or a ditch, whole rows of men would fall asleep on their hands and knees before their horses like Mohammedans at prayer, and it was necessary to go round shaking them to their feet to prevent them being left behind. Save for occasional halts we continued thus all night, for it was imperative to cross the remaining railway. As we had no guide we travelled by the stars, and the sun was rising before we struck it at a small siding about five miles east of Sterkstroom village, where, from the activity at the station, it was obvious that our escape from the mountain was known. Several trains were unloading troops, and there was no time to be lost. So mounting, we galloped as fast as we could across the rails for fear an armoured train might cut us off.

Commandant van Deventer and a few of us remained behind to search the railway buildings for anything that might come in useful, and while we were busy at this a long goods-train came clanking up, and we brought it to a standstill by switching the points. It was an empty coal train in charge of a driver, stoker, and brakesman, whose faces were a picture when they saw what we were doing. As the train consisted of nothing but incombustible steel trucks, we let them proceed, after extracting a mail-bag from the guard's van. The letters were all private ones, seemingly written under censorship, for not one of them made any reference to the war, but the newspapers were less reticent, and in one of them was unflattering mention of ourselves, for it said that General Smuts had invaded the Cape Colony 'with the riff-raff of the Boer Armies', which caused much merriment when later on I was able to read it to the men.

There was another surprising feature in the mail-bag in the shape of a Proclamation by Lord Kitchener, wherein every burgher under arms after the 15th of September was sentenced to perpetual banishment from South Africa. This was news to us, and seeing that it was the 13th of that month by now, we were left with a bare two days in which to comply. This announcement was received with equal derision, when made known to the commando, and from what I have heard since, it had equally little effect up north in the Republics, where the 'paper-bomb', as it was called, got treated with the scorn it deserved.[1]

After speeding the goods-train on its way, we overtook the commando at the Klaas Smits River, where we halted for about an hour, to give our poor horses a chance to pluck a few mouthfuls of grass, and to prepare a hasty meal for ourselves. Longer than that we were not given, for a column of troops with guns came up, and kept us on the move all day, slowly retiring from hill to hill, half dead with fatigue, but keeping them at arm's length until sunset, when they turned back and left us free to camp at last at a large farm, where we lay like dead men until morning after sixty hours of continuous marching.

This full night's rest was a great relief, but the strain was by no means over, and the worst was yet to come.

Towards nine o'clock next day, an English column appeared from the direction of Sterkstroom, so we saddled up and rode away, skirting the base of some hills running south. The column contented itself with following us slowly, apparently having been sent to keep us under observation, and they dogged our steps until sunset, when it came on to rain and we saw them go into camp. We halted in a patch of thorn trees and, as it poured heavily till dawn, we had another of those wet and miserable nights which had been so frequent since our entry into the Colony.

Daylight saw the troops once more coming after us, and, owing to the shortage of ammunition and the condition of our horses, we had no option but to give way. The going was heavy, and at times the swollen spruits and dongas held us up, but we were in no great danger of being overhauled, for the column had wagons and guns, which impeded them so much that we had miles to spare.

In the afternoon the English camped again, and we halted for the rest of the day at a small farmhouse standing out on the plain. The rain had ceased since morning, but it was cold and threatening; black clouds hung low in the sky, and there was every promise of more dirty weather to come.

We could see smoke curling from the English camp four miles behind, where whole streets of comfortable tents had sprung up, at which we gazed wistfully, for there were warmth and rest, whilst we stood shivering in the biting wind, wondering how it was all to end. The English numbered about a thousand, and it was useless to attempt an attack in our present condition, for we were wet, cold, and in low spirits, and our ammunition was almost finished. So, when darkness fell, General Smuts gave orders for us to saddle up, intending to make for a larger farm where there was said to be ample shelter.

As we started, hard rain came down once more, and the darkness was so intense

---

[1] *The Times History* says of this Proclamation, vol v, 321:

'Lord Kitchener made his first and last attempt to end the war by a minatory proclamation.
It began by giving in a solemn legal preamble an account of the military situation, which must have seemed strangely unconvincing to the Boers, and which, it must be confessed, was replete with unconscious humour. The fourth paragraph in particular where the Boers were informed that they were incapable of carrying on regular warfare was a strange tissue of perverted logic ... The operative part of the Proclamation demanded the surrender of all Boers before September 15th under pain of stringent penalties. The results were not encouraging: Botha, Steyn and de Wet sent defiant replies, and among the burghers at large there was a sullen silence.'

that we could not see a yard ahead. We had not gone three hundred paces before we heard horsemen splashing through the mud in front, and ran into the tail of an English patrol or column, we could not tell which, evidently making for the same farm. Neither side was prepared to risk a fight in the rain and dark. The troopers galloped away, and we sheered off too, but with this difference, that they were able to continue on to the shelter of the farm, whilst we were adrift on the open veld.

The night that followed was the most terrible of all. Our guide lost his way; we went floundering ankle-deep in mud and water, our poor weakened horses stumbling and slipping at every turn; the rain beat down on us, and the cold was awful. Towards midnight it began to sleet. The grain-bag which I wore froze solid on my body, like a coat of mail, and I believe that if we had not kept moving every one of us would have died. We had known two years of war, but we came nearer to despair that night than I care to remember. Hour after hour we groped our way, with men groaning who had never before uttered a word of complaint, as the cold searched their ill-protected bodies. We lost fourteen men that night, and I do not know whether they survived, but we never again had word of them.

We also lost a large number of horses, and I remember stumbling at intervals over their carcasses. We went on till daybreak, dragging ourselves along, and then, providentially, came on a deserted homestead and staggered into shelter, standing huddled together in rooms, stables, and barns until dawn, still shivering, but gradually recovering from the dreadful ordeal. When it grew light, some fifty or sixty horses lay dead outside. My little roan mare was still alive, but both my uncle's horses died here, and he, with thirty or forty more, was now a foot-soldier.[1]

This night's 'Big Rain', as we named it, left such a mark on all of us that later we used to call ourselves 'The "Big Rain" Men' (*Die Groot Reent Kêrels*) to distinguish us from those who had not experienced it, and for my part I passed through no greater test during the war.

The day was cold and wild, but the rain stopped. We broke up the floors and windows, tables and chairs, and everything else that would burn, and made great fires to dry our clothes and blankets, and to warm our chilled limbs. Towards noon, General Smuts ordered us on to another large farm, eight or nine miles away, which had, a native told him, plenty of fodder for the horses.

No attempt was made to send back for the missing men, because we were too exhausted, and they had to be abandoned. We plodded over the water-logged country, a quarter of our number on foot, and the rest soon likely to be, for there was not a fit horse in the commando.

We found this farm also deserted, but there was protection for all, and a good store of oat-sheaves, as well as sheep for slaughter, so that, although the rain came down again, we at last spent a comfortable night.

Although we had managed to avoid the different cordons thrown in our way and had eluded the columns sent in pursuit, we were not yet out of danger, for local natives now told us that southward every road, valley and outlet was blocked by English troops. This meant that they were once more trying to head us back out of the Cape;

---

[1] As practically every man had crossed the Orange River with two horses, the number of dismounted men did not necessarily correspond to the number of horses that were lost.

but, with so many enemies in our rear, our only alternative was to go forward. Next morning we set out on what was to be an eventful day (September 17th, 1901).

Our road ran south down a long valley. The sky was clear, and the sun warm and bright for the first time for weeks, so that the men were cheerful again, although there was little other cause for optimism.

As a fighting force we were on our last legs. In front walked those who still had horses, dragging scarecrows behind them; then came a trail of footmen in twos and threes, their saddles slung across their shoulders, and in the rear rode the wounded in charge of their friends.

However, the sun was shining after the wet and cold and we went hopefully along. After a few miles General Smuts ordered the 'Rijk Section' to scout ahead of the commando, so those of us who still had horses mounted and rode forward as fast as our weakened animals could carry us. When we got to where the valley widened into more open country, a Dutch farmer rushed from a cottage beside the road, and in a voice hoarse with excitement, told us that English cavalry were waiting for us lower down. He said that they had mountain- and machine-guns, and he estimated their strength at two hundred men, with over three hundred horses and mules, all of which proved substantially correct.

Edgar Duncker was sent back to report, and before long he returned with General Smuts, accompanied by Commandant van Deventer and a dozen men. General Smuts immediately decided to attack, and I heard him say that if we did not get those horses and a supply of ammunition we were done for. He ordered van Deventer forward with the men who were with him and the 'Rijk Section', to locate the British force, while he himself waited here to bring up the rest of the commando. We set off at once, and in a few minutes reached the banks of a small river which we crossed. As we were going through the fringe of thorn trees on the other side we rode straight into fifteen or twenty troopers cantering towards us. Most of our men were still among the trees, but four or five of us were in advance, and when we leaped to the ground the soldiers were not more than ten yards away. Opening fire we brought down several, and the rest turned and galloped back along the road. I fired my last two cartridges here, and my first thought was to run to a dead soldier and seize his rifle and bandolier, abandoning my own rusty weapon, then I rushed for my mare and joined in the chase.

The troop-horses were in much better condition than ours, but the soldiers were delayed by a gate, so we got close again, dropping two or three more from the saddle.

At the gate van Deventer himself and half a dozen men turned aside to a kopje for observation, but the rest of us, about twelve in number, followed the retiring patrol to a low stony ridge farther down the road.

They got there several lengths ahead of us and, abandoning their horses, took to the rocks. It was too late for us to retire back across the open plain behind, so we galloped on.

Before we reached their outcrop the soldiers opened fire almost point-blank, and worse still, a mountain-gun unexpectedly fired on us from a point to our left, not thirty yards off, and a machine-gun rattled into action close by. So near was the mountain-gun that smoke from the discharge billowed over us although the shells went wide. It was astonishing that any of us escaped, but owing no doubt to our sudden appearance behind the flying patrol, the firing was wild, and only three men and some horses went down before we reached the rocks in which the soldiers were. Here we, in turn, loosed our horses and ran up, to find ourselves within a few feet of our original quarry and a number of others, who had been posted here before.

Now that we could look over to the far side, we were surprised to see a large English camp less than a stone's throw away, buzzing like a disturbed ant-heap. Officers were shouting orders, and men tumbling out of their tents, some running towards us, others going to the right and left to take their stations.

This placed us in a remarkably tight corner, as we were so far ahead of our main body that they could not help us, for the English, having recovered from their first surprise, were sweeping the plain with gun- and rifle-fire. The result was that our little party was stranded on the very edge of an armed encampment, and practically mixed with the English soldiers. Fortunately General Smuts had hurried the commando on, and in a few minutes they opened fire from a hill in the rear, thus preventing us from being overwhelmed, for our opponents were forced to take cover and could not surround us. Those before us were in rough alignment along the bank of the ledge, so we were able to form a similar front, with a space of two or three yards separating us, while along the perimeter of the camp lay the rest of the troops in a half-moon. A young Transvaaler named Muller and I lay at the end where the rocks ran dead, and from here we could see the mountain-gun close by, busy shelling our commando. The gunners could not open fire on us as they would have to hit their own men, and in any case they did not seem to realise that we were so near, for they were unconcernedly loading and firing at our men on the hill six hundred yards back. Standing behind the gun was a tall man handing shells to the three at the breech. I fired at him, and he spun round and sank in a sitting position against the wheel, where I found him dead when the fight was over. The other three ran for the camp at their backs. I fired at one, and he pitched forward dead, while Muller brought down a third, but the last man got away among the tents. Having disposed of the gun-crew in a matter of seconds we turned to the other work on hand. The place we were fighting in was an outcrop of loose rocks, jutting up like a reef, nowhere much higher than a man, although the rear slope fell somewhat more steeply into the English camp. In this narrow space, where we were facing each other almost at hand-shake, a grim duel began. As the soldiers raised their heads to fire we brought them down, for they were no match for us in the short-range work of this kind, and we killed twelve or thirteen and wounded several more, at a distance of a few yards. We did not suffer a single casualty, except for the three men hit as we rode in. Of these, one was Edgar Duncker with a bullet through his foot, and another a Jew named Cohen, with a smashed ankle. These two had been able to crawl forward to the firing line and were taking part in the attack, but the third man, Raubenheimer (a brother of Vera, Countess of Cathcart), lay out in the open with his thigh broken, and his dead horse pinning him down.

Before he could reach his men, I hit a sergeant who came running up from the camp, a big heavily built man. He doubled up like a knife, and rolled about, shot in the stomach; then he died.

Nicholas Swart by my side shot two other soldiers in quick succession, as they tried to join those in the rocks. There was a young lieutenant a few feet from me. I found out afterwards that his name was Sheridan, and they said he was a cousin of Winston Churchill. Twice he rose to fire at me and missed; at his second attempt I grazed his temple, and he dropped out of sight, but only dazed, for in a moment he was up again, swaying unsteadily on his feet, with his face streaming with blood, but still trying to level his rifle at me. While I was hesitating what to do, Jack Borrius shot him through the brain. Another soldier fired several hasty rounds at me, and I put a bullet into his head, which was protruding from behind the rock near which he was lying. The sudden shock made him leap up, and again Jack Borrius, who was wonderfully quick, shot him dead as he rose.

In this manner the fight went on, until a mile beyond the camp we saw a small force of English troops approaching from the south. There were not many of them, but for all we knew they were the advance-guard of a relief force and, should sufficient reinforcements arrive to drive off our commando, those of us here in the rocks would be marooned, so we decided to clear the rocks by charging. After a whispered consultation from man to man, Jack Borrius gave the signal, and, rising together, we leaped in among the surviving soldiers. There were only ten or fifteen left, and so far as I can remember not a shot was fired on either side. Our sudden onslaught took them unprepared, and they surrendered at once. Without troubling about our prisoners we ran down shouting and cheering into the camp, before the rest of the defenders knew what had happened. When they saw us among the tents in their rear, something like a stampede set in. Soldiers went running in all directions, some making away into the thorn trees, others coming towards us and throwing down their arms. One man rushed to the horselines, and mounting barebacked, flourished a revolver and tried to ride off. I shouted to him to halt, but as he gave no heed I shot him dead. When the commando saw us enter the camp, they came galloping across, and the fight was over.

I took part in a final episode, for William Conradi and I, walking through a patch of trees to disarm some soldiers, came on a stone cattle-kraal, in which a dozen men were holding out. When we looked into the kraal, they were leaning on their rifles on the far wall and firing at some of our commando men moving in the distance. We called out 'Hands up! Hands up!' but they turned instead and blazed a volley into our faces. Only our eyes were showing or we should both have been shot. Conradi killed one man and wounded another with a single bullet, and I wounded one, but even now they did not surrender, for, rushing across the kraal, they ranged themselves against the near wall, which alone separated us, and one of them thrust his rifle so near my face that his shot scorched my cheek and neck with cordite, fragments of which had to be picked out for days afterwards, with the point of a knife. When I seized the muzzle he gave an oath and jerked it back so forcibly that the sharp foresight gashed the ball of my thumb and the palm of my hand, and I had to let go.

The situation was fast becoming dangerous, when, to our relief, we heard the sound of voices through the trees, and a number of our men came running up to see what the firing was about. The soldiers now threw their rifles over the wall, but even this was not the end, for, as I hastened round to the entrance of the kraal to receive the prisoners, I collided with a soldier who came crouching along to get us in the flank. He did not know that the fight was over, and if I had not rammed him when I did, in another moment he would have been round the corner, shooting us down while we were engaged with the men inside. He said I was a 'surprise packet', offered me a cigarette, and came with me to join his captured companions in the kraal with his hand amicably on my shoulder. The whole incident had not lasted five minutes, but it had been sharp enough, and Conradi and I reckoned ourselves well out of it as we hastened back to the camp to take part in the looting. The commando was up and there was a great ransacking of tents and wagons. The small relieving force that had given us cause for alarm turned out to be only a patrol, and it had the doubtful satisfaction of watching us from afar as we turned the camp inside out.

When we had done we were like giants refreshed. We had ridden into action that morning at our last gasp, and we emerged refitted from head to heel. We all had fresh horses, fresh rifles, clothing, saddlery, boots and more ammunition than we could carry away, as well as supplies for every man.

Moreover, we had renewed confidence in our leader and in ourselves, a factor of considerable importance to a body of men in a hostile country.

In the fight we lost only one man, who was killed when we rushed the camp, and six wounded, whereas the enemy had thirty killed, many wounded, and many taken prisoners.

I did not count the number of soldiers opposed to us, but there must have been about two hundred. They belonged to the 17th Lancers, one of the crack regiments of the British Army. Among their wounded was their Commander, Captain Sandeman, and Lord Vivian, whom I found among the rocks where we first rushed them. He it was who told me the fate of the three men killed and mutilated by the Basutos, the day that we crossed the Orange River. He pointed out his little bivouac tent, and said that it would be worth my while to have a look at it. I was not slow to take the hint, with the result that having started that morning with a grain-bag for my chief garment, a foundered horse, an old rifle, and two cartridges, I now appeared in a handsome cavalry tunic, riding-breeches, etc, with a sporting Lee-Metford, full bandoliers and a superb mount, a little grey Arab, which his coloured groom said had been the property of Lieutenant Sheridan. I also selected a strong riding-mule in preference to another horse, for my experience during the past fortnight had taught me that a good mule for long marches and a light nimble pony for use in action, were the ideal combination. After I had completed my equipment, commissariat, and ammunition supply, I walked around the camp.

We considered that the taking of it was chiefly the handiwork of our original storming party, for while we could not have done it without the protection and covering fire of the commando, yet by riding in on the heels of the English troopers and taking post on the very edge of the camp, we had served as the spearhead that made success possible. I also saw the dead gunners and other men whom I had shot, and I looked on them with mixed feelings, for although I have never hated the English, a fight is a fight, and though I was sorry for the men, I was proud of my share in the day's work.

Lastly, I went to see what had become of my roan mare. She was still patiently standing where I had left her at the ledge. On each side of her lay a dead horse, but she had escaped unharmed. The gallant little beast was, however, so exhausted that when I tried to lead her away she could scarcely put one foot before the other, so I unsaddled her, throwing the saddle aside, for it was old and worn with much use since I had taken it from General Clements's camp ten months before. Removing the bridle and halter, I turned her loose in the hope that some neighbouring farmer would look after her, for she too had shown the mettle of her Free State pasture, and the marvellous endurance of the South African horse.

General Smuts now ordered us to set the tents and wagons on fire, and to destroy
the mountain- and machine-guns, as well as such surplus ammunition and other
supplies as could not be removed. Then, leaving the prisoners, mule-drivers and native
servants to shift for themselves, we rode off in triumph.

Chapter 22

Moss-Trooping

Next morning we rode out of the mountain country into the open plains of the
Karroo. In the face of great odds we had broken across the successive barriers placed
in our way, and although we had still many troubles to meet, the English had failed to
turn us back. We now slowly marauded southwards. At the village of Maraisburg, a
large number of troops was waiting for us, but General Smuts skilfully led the
commando through at night without firing a shot, and we continued unmolested.

During this time the 'Rijk Section' came into its own. Our share in the attack on
the 17th Lancers had enhanced our reputation, and in this open country our services as
scouts were in greater demand, so we ranged far ahead, hospitably entertained by the
Dutch-speaking population, and philosophically tolerated by the English farmers with
whom we came in contact.

In our fine khaki tunics, and on our well-found horses, our appearance had
undergone such a transformation that when asked at the English farmhouses who we
were, our stock witticism was to say that we were 'English-killing Dragoons'. We
thoroughly enjoyed it all after the hardships of the past.

The weather had improved, the long winter was over, and cloudless sunny days put
still further heart into us. Then we had another stroke of luck, for we were joined by
Field-Cornet Botha with twenty-five men, the remnant of a band of free-lances that
had been roaming the midlands, until their numbers had so dwindled that they had
been forced into hiding among the mountains. Hearing of our passage they had
hastened to find us, and practically replaced our wastage since coming into the Cape.

But we had to abandon Raubenheimer, whose thigh had been smashed during the
last fight, and a day or two later we had to leave Cohen behind, as his wound became
gangrenous.

Besides being a brave man, Cohen must have been a bit of a wag, for I
subsequently read in an English newspaper that when he was captured and asked by a
British officer why he, a Jew and an Uitlander, was fighting for the Boers, he replied
that he was fighting for the Franchise.

The next loss was heavier for me. My friend Jacobus Bosman, who had so loyally
stood by me when the others turned back in the Free State, was taken ill with some
malignant fever. He gamely tried to keep up but we had to leave him delirious at a
farm. I went off with a heavy heart, for I knew that he was doubly in danger. If the

disease spared him, the English would be waiting with a charge of high treason, and my fears were only too well founded, for about three weeks later I read that he had been sentenced to be hanged as a rebel at Graaff Reinet.

He was the first of our 'Rijk Section' men to meet a humiliating death by execution, but not the last, for three more were destined to stand before a firing party, and also other members of the commando.

Two days after we had left Bosman behind, we reached the foot of a high mountain range, the name of which I have forgotten. There was a road running into a narrow defile called Lily Kloof, into which the 'Rijk Section' was sent scouting. We rode up the gorge for some distance, until we saw an English foraging party going off, each man with sheaves of oats tied to his saddle. Ben Coetzee killed one of them, a local farmer named Brown, who had joined the troops, and the rest of the patrol raced off. A woman ran out of a cottage to warn us that there were English strongly posted at a narrow point farther up, so we turned back to report to General Smuts. Some miles west lies an equally deep ravine, through which we now tried to find a way, but here again we were warned that the route was held. General Smuts said that he was not going to squander men in forcing his way, when there were other means of crossing, so we retraced our steps, and that night, led by a local guide, we picked our way over the range by a bridle-path. It was a long march with no chance of sleep, but dawn found us on the far slopes, in the English-speaking district of Bedford. From here there was a glorious view, across deep mountain valleys and green uplands of one of the loveliest and most fertile parts of South Africa. We had left all serious pursuit so far behind that for the next few days we rode leisurely on our way, while the men scattered about, visiting farmhouses and enjoying themselves.

The inhabitants took our coming in good part, and there was never any sign of ill feeling, although they hoped that we should get rounded up and told us so.

We saw an occasional Defence Force patrol, which, however, gave us no anxiety, for they were local levies merely keeping their eye on us, and there was no trouble until one afternoon when a column of horse showed on a hill and opened long-range fire in our direction. Not wishing to be involved in fighting other than of our own making, we turned up a defile that wound into a mass of rugged mountains before us. These were the Great Winterbergen, and we halted at sunset amid gorgeous forest-covered steeps, where we built huge log-fires, and spend a comfortable night, greatly taken with the fine country we had reached.

Next day our path ran through even more beautiful scenery. Around us was primeval forest, and through an occasional tunnel in the trees we glimpsed green fields and white homesteads in the valleys far below.

The following morning, while halted in a picturesque glade, a woodsman in a log cabin told us of a tavern and trading-station at the foot of a pass leading down close by. The men were all for going to see what was to be had, and towards sunset we reached the bottom, where stood a substantial wayside inn flanked by well-stocked warehouses. So little were we expected in this remote part, that no effort had been made to remove the goods to the protection of the nearest military post, which was generally done when we were approaching, and the owner suffered from our visit, for we were masters by now in the gentle art of commandeering. I would not have mentioned this excursion had it not cost us the life of another member of the 'Rijk

Section'.

There was plenty of beer and spirits at the inn, and although few of the men had tasted liquor for a year or more, there was no drunkenness, but Piet de Ruyt, our Hollander companion, took too much, and when the commando moved away at dusk, he was left asleep unnoticed. Weeks later we learned that he had been discovered in a room, and as, like most of us, he was dressed in a British uniform, the poor fellow was executed, in all probability before his fuddled brain had time to take in what was happening.

Neither then, nor for weeks later, did we know that the death penalty attached to the wearing of khaki, and although after a while rumours reached us through the country people that our men were being executed, these stories left us doubting and perplexed. We could not believe that the English were resorting to the shooting of prisoners, and it was only after many had been executed that we learned of Kitchener's proclamation ordering the death of all Boers caught in khaki.

As far as I know no steps were ever taken by the military to acquaint us with its contents.

From the foot of the Winterbergen we rode on for some hours in the dark, by a footpath winding across a bush-covered plain, and we camped in an open space for the night. At daybreak we made out the little village of Adelaide in the distance, but, as it seemed to be strongly garrisoned, we left it alone, and continued all that day, slowly making south through broken country.

Here again the inhabitants were chiefly English-speaking farmers, who submitted with good grace to our depredations, for we slaughtered what sheep we required, and helped ourselves freely from their larders and orchards. Towards evening a column came following us from Adelaide, halting when we halted, and moving when we moved, and when after dark we went into camp, their fires were soon winking at us five or six miles away. During the afternoon an armed Colonial had ridden up from a farm with a story that he wished to fight the English. He rode a spirited horse and spoke fluent Dutch, and as he seemed genuine he took us in, but now, while we were off-saddling by a pool he suddenly pulled his horse round and galloped away. He was gone before anyone could give chase, and, as he was obviously a spy sent to learn our intentions, we re-saddled and rode on for an hour or two before resting for the night.

Next day we bore away in a somewhat more westerly direction, reaching the Great Fish River by sunset. We crossed at a ford, and a mile or two beyond, at Commadaga Station, we passed over the railway line that comes up from Port Elizabeth through the midlands. As there were no blockhouses we had no difficulty in getting to the other side after dark, and then, as our horses were tired, General Smuts ordered us to camp at a farmhouse five or six hundred yards beyond. We had scarcely turned our animals out to graze, when an armoured train came puffing up, the beams of its powerful searchlight sweeping the veld, but, as we lay in a fold of the ground, the crew could not see us, although they must have suspected our presence, for they sent a number of shells howling into the night, only one of which came within measurable distance of us. It burst harmlessly near by, but we thought that we had been discovered, and ran to find our horses, with the result that there was a good deal of bumping and confusion in the dark before we realised that the English were shooting at random. Then we had a good laugh at ourselves, and spreading our blankets slept in peace till daybreak.

From here we headed south-west, riding at our ease through the district of Somerset, until by sunset we made the foot of the Zuurbergen, the last great escarpment before the country drops away to the sea.

We were by now within fifty miles of Algoa Bay. I do not know what General Smuts's intentions were at any stage of our expedition, for he was a silent man, but I think that at this particular juncture he was contemplating a sudden raid on Port Elizabeth, for next morning, when we saw what looked like over three thousand troops coming after us, he kept us quietly resting at the foot of the mountain, instead of slipping away east or west as he could easily have done. These troops had been brought by rail, and had detrained at Commadaga Station, where we had crossed two nights before, and from their converging front it looked as if they hoped to bring us to bay against the slopes of the range.

We watched them slowly approaching for most of the day, until their scouts were almost within rifle-range, and then General Smuts led the way straight up the steep slope behind us. We spent the night on the crest of the first of the great parallel hogbacks that constitute the Zuurbergen.

From the point where we reached the top, we looked on a world of more mountains, line upon line of high ranges, each separated from the next by deep wooded gorges, and the prospect of being driven into these fastnesses was not inviting. However, with the troops closing in on us from the rear there was no help for it, so we built fires and camped. On the way up Jack Borrius and I had met a native herdboy, who informed us that there was a big troop of horses in a neighbouring kloof. On all our journey through the Cape we had not found a single riding-horse on any of the farms, as the English had cleared the country to prevent us from getting remounts, and the boy said over five hundred horses had been collected by the military within the last few days, on hearing of our approach. Accordingly Jack and I left the commando before daybreak and followed the ridge for some miles, until we found a practicable descent down which to lead our horses into the kloof which the native had pointed out. At the bottom we came on a deserted homestead, with the ground trampled by many hoof marks, but a Red Kaffir, who appeared out of the forest, told us that a patrol had come the day before, and driven all the animals away to the coast. We therefore gave up the idea of finding them and, turning our mounts into a paddock, stretched ourselves under a shady tree and fell asleep.

Some hours later we were waked by a couple of men who had ridden out in search of food. They roused us and told us to listen. Jumping to our feet we heard the sound of distant rifle-fire coming from the quarter where we had left the commando that morning. It was clear that they were fighting, and before long we caught sight of our men on the slope of the next range, crawling like ants up a steep side. They were miles off, but we could see that all was not well with them, for they were strung out in a disorderly line and the firing was coming from an enemy force somewhere out of view.

We caught our horses and led them up the range which the commando was climbing, and on getting above we could see our men hurrying towards us along the top. It took more than an hour for them to come up with us, and then we learned that while they were encamped a number of English had unexpectedly opened fire on them.

After an interchange of shots the commando had fallen back deeper into the mountain, with only one man wounded and a few horses killed. The wounded man was badly injured about the face, but had come on. We were now on the second range. From here we saw many English horsemen riding about on the first crest. They came opposite us, with only the deep kloof, through which we had passed, lying between, and then opened fire upon us with several machine-guns and a field-piece. I do not know how they had succeeded in dragging those up the mountain, but there they were barring the way should we try to break back, while behind us lay mile upon mile of tumbled forest-clad mountains and gorges.

The immediate danger from the troops was not pressing, as we had good cover for ourselves and our horses, but now a fresh complication set in.

Up to now we had found so little difficulty in commandeering supplies from the farms we passed, that no one ever thought about the next day, with the result that when we unexpectedly found ourselves in a wild region without habitations, the men had little or no food with them, and were already beginning to feel hungry. Scattered about stood a strange growth known as 'Hottentot's bread' (*Encephelartos Altensteinii*), a wild fruit not unlike a large pine-apple. It is edible only at certain seasons of the year, but coming from the north, we did not know this, and as one of the men sampled it and found it to his liking, many unfortunately followed suit.

I had not eaten any, and returning to the firing-line, after going to tie up some horses that had broken loose, I was astonished to find more than half our men groaning and retching on the ground in agony, some apparently at their last gasp. General Smuts was worse than the rest, so, with half our number out of action, we were also leaderless, for he was lying comatose.

The horsemen of the strong enemy force before us were even now descending the opposite slope to attack us, while behind were mountain wastes stretching as far as we could see. We had no food, and could not move without abandoning the sick, so our position was critical.

For the moment our most urgent concern was the soldiers advancing towards us. They had by now reached the bottom of the kloof, and some of them, leaving their horses behind, were already swarming up, firing as they came.

Commandant van Deventer was too ill to take charge, but Ben Bouwer, though bad, was able to order every man who could still handle a rifle to extend along the top. It was nearing sunset, and the light was uncertain, so I do not think we did much damage with our shooting, but it served to turn our assailants, for they went back to their horses, and then climbed up the other side, until their camp fires began to shine in the dark, which meant that they were settling down for the night.

Those of us who had been lining the forward crest now had time to look around, and what we saw was not comforting. The sick men were worse than ever. General Smuts was very bad indeed, and van Deventer, his second in command, not much better. From the groans and cries on all sides it was clear that the sufferers could not travel, and there was nothing to do but to wait, although it was urgently necessary to get away before daylight would enable the English to surround us. I shall not soon forget that night. It was dark, and a chill wind blew from seaward. We dared not light a fire, and those of us who were not ill from the poisoned fruit, were starving. We knew that if the men did not recover in time to avoid the pursuing column, our expedition into the Cape would come to a speedy end next morning, and we sat beside the sick men not knowing when we might be fallen upon. However, as the darkness slowly passed, one man after another recovered sufficiently to stagger to his feet, and towards dawn there were not more than twenty unable to stand. General Smuts was still prostrate, but able to take in the position, and he gave orders that the men who could not help themselves were to be tied to their saddles, and that the commando was to march deeper into the mountains. He himself had to be held on his horse, and we started off in the dim light, following a game-track that led down into the next gorge. At the bottom we halted to rest the sick men, and then crawled up the far slope, which was almost as steep as the place we negotiated on the night of our retreat from the Stormbergen.

Bringing up the sick men was a difficult task, made more difficult by the fact that the English troops had actually dragged their gun to the top of the second range where we had spent the night, and opened fire on us as we were climbing. The distance was so great that only a few shells fell among us, their chief effect being to spur the men to greater activity and rouse the invalids, some of whom asked to be lifted to the ground, for they did not relish the idea of being trussed up in the circumstances.

I was one of the last to gain the top, as I had led my horse and mule very slowly, a few yards at a time, to save their legs. But when I got above and chanced to look back, I was surprised to see that General Smuts was still lying below, with three or four men attending him, while down the path above them came a number of English scouts trailing the spoor which the commando had made. At the rate at which the scouts were descending they would soon come on General Smuts and his men, and I realised that there was no time to be lost. I tied my two animals to the nearest tree, and rushed and slid to the bottom unharmed by the bullets of the scouts. When the men with General Smuts heard the firing overhead they lifted him to his horse, and were already starting, a couple on each side to hold him, by the time I got down.

We did not follow the commando, as we should have presented too easy a mark, but kept away to the right where there was a gully up which we could make our way unseen. When we reached the top I fetched my two animals, and we followed on to find the commando waiting for us in a glade.

We were now in the very heart of the mountains, so far from any farms that buffalo were seen, and their tracks and mud-wallows were frequent. Not one of the sick men had died, and most of them were better, perhaps because of the shaking and movement. General Smuts and a few other cases were, however, still in danger, and it was decided to spend the day here, as our scouts reported that the enemy had turned back, and it was thought necessary to give the sick a long rest before continuing. The trouble now was to get food. Parties were sent out in search of native kraals, for smoke had been seen rising from a distant part of the forest, and here, after struggling for hours through dense undergrowth, we found a few poverty-stricken huts whose inhabitants had fled. They belonged to a destitute tribe of Red Kaffirs, but we unearthed a supply of millet, enough to give the commando some sort of a meal.

In the afternoon we moved deeper into the mountains, and, breasting a high grass-covered shoulder, caught a distant view, thirty-five miles away, of white sand-dunes, and of a grey haze, which was the Indian Ocean. We were elated, for we knew that we had now penetrated farther south than any other commando during the war, and that we were the first to come within sight of the coast.

After dark, camped on a height, we could see the lights of Port Elizabeth shining far off, and this strengthened our belief that General Smuts, in spite of his illness, still intended to go there. Next morning we went down into a beautiful valley filled with yellow-wood trees, centuries old, and here we camped for the rest of the day, still subsisting on boiled millet.

One of our men recognised this part, having hunted buffalo and elephant here long before, and he said that he remembered a path running south, by which we could get out of the mountains into the valley of the Sunday River, where we might take the small village of Bayville.

On hearing this a small party, mostly 'Rijk Section', was made up to raid the place. Unluckily both my animals had strayed into the forest, and I had to follow on long after the others had gone. I tracked them until I got clear of the mountains into the wide valley, down whose centre the Sunday River runs to the sea. But the floor of the valley was dense scrub, ten or twelve feet high, in which I got completely bushed, so I had to work my way back with difficulty, reaching the commando at dark, tired and disgusted.

Jack Borrius and his buccaneers had not yet returned, but that night we marched on, as we had exhausted our grain supply.

We led our horses in the dark between high ranges, along a well-beaten path that twisted down a valley, until towards daybreak we reached the Sunday River, at a point still closed in by the mountains, but where, in a clearing, lay a well-stocked barn.

General Smuts remained pale and weak, but he sent for me and thanked me for having come down to warn him two days before.

Some time after sunrise Cornelius Vermaas, Henry Rittenberg and I were ordered to scout up the course of the river, and we set out on what proved to be my companions' last ride. After following the stream and making inquiries from occasional natives, we learned that there were some white men off-saddled close by, and going thither came on Jack Borrius and his detachment, halted under the trees. Jack himself was suffering from terrible wounds. They had entered Bayville unopposed, but on their way back they fell foul of an English patrol, and, in the ensuing encounter, a bullet had entirely blown away his left eye, leaving nothing but a cavity filled with dried blood. In addition his right hand was smashed to pulp, but he had refused to be left behind, and we found him lying in great pain, but determined to remain with the commando. While we were busy with him, General Smuts rode up. He told Ben Coetzee to take over command of the 'Rijk Section', and ordered him to reconnoitre down a lateral valley, to see whether it would bring us out of the mountains, as he intended to enter the lower Sunday River Valley.

Ben Coetzee took with him Rittenberg and myself together with Vermaas and one of van Deventer's men, named van Onselen, who volunteered to come. We five went ahead carefully picking our way, and discovered late in the afternoon that the valley we were in ran to a dead end, against what we took to be the final range of the Zuurbergen.

Coetzee kept van Onselen with him, and told the three of us from the 'Rijk Section' to climb the height ahead, and see what lay on the far side. As we began to lead our horses up the slope, we heard a shout, and van Onselen overtook us, with a message to say that I was to return, as Coetzee thought my horse looked poorly, and that van Onselen was to go in my stead. The fact that my grey pony had a staring coat saved my life, for the three men, on reaching the top, walked straight into the arms of an English force lying in ambush there, and, as they were dressed in khaki uniforms, were executed out of hand. They lie buried where they fell, their graves being the most southerly of any of our republican dead.

We only knew of their actual fate long afterwards. For the moment all we heard was a burst of firing, and looking up we saw large numbers of soldiers on the skyline, so we rode back along the valley full of anxiety.

At dusk we met the commando coming in our direction, and, when we told General Smuts that our progress was barred, he halted us for the night.

At daybreak next morning, while we were saddling our horses, the troops opened fire from above our heads. No one was hit, but we were forced to retire back into the deeper part of the mountains, instead of getting out into the open country to the south. During the retreat we lost three more men. They were looking for their horses when the firing began and, as no one noticed their absence, they were left behind. According to an English newspaper which we saw afterwards, one of them was hanged as a rebel British subject, the sixth man of our force to be executed, not counting the three that had been murdered by the Basutos.

As I have said before, we had not heard of Lord Kitchener's proclamation against the wearing of British uniforms, and I went about wearing Lord Vivian's khaki tunic, with regimental badge and buttons, and the 17th Lancer's skull and cross-bones in my hat, not a little proud of my well-earned trophies, and never dreaming that I was under sentence of death. We made a long trek through the kloofs of this wild region until, after midday, we found a disused pass, made, I was told, by Sir Harry Smith in the 'fifties during the native wars.

This pass ran up a dark ravine, flanked with dense timber, and heavily overgrown with brushwood, but otherwise in good preservation. Its chief drawback was that it led northwards over the mountains back to the plains of the Karroo, from which we had come, whereas our endeavour had been to break seawards, but with the English column of that morning pressing steadily in our rear, we had to go wherever there was an opening. We started to ascend the pass, not knowing if another force was waiting for us above. If so we should have been trapped, but luckily this particular loophole had not been closed, and we found the top clear. Edgar Duncker and I, who were scouting in advance, saw a human skeleton beside the road, a relic of some past tragedy, and we placed the grinning skull on a log as a warning to our pursuers.

Not far from the top was a space of level ground with the ruins of an old building, and the remains of walled gardens and orchards, and as we could see the English troops halted in a glade far below, General Smuts stopped too, for he and others were still very ill. The sick and wounded, with poor Jack Borrius, withdrew to a distance, while the rest of us turned our horses out to graze and lolled about at our ease, admiring the grand forest scenery and enjoying the luxury of our beautiful surroundings. Then some half-savage cattle came out of the woods and we shot several, and had the added satisfaction of eating our fill around big fires. Afterwards, most of the men stretched themselves under the trees, at peace in this pleasant place.

But towards five in the afternoon we began to bestir ourselves. Ben Coetzee,

Nicholas Swart and I sat basking in the sunshine on a wall not far from where the pass came out. Suddenly, while we were talking, we saw the foremost ranks of a body of horsemen appear—at the head of the gorge, not a hundred yards away. Shouting an alarm, we seized our rifles and ran down, followed by the men who had been lying close by. The English must have been under the impression that we had gone straight on over the berg, for they were riding in a compact body of thirty or more, with no advance-guards, and evidently our presence here was as great a surprise to them as their sudden appearance was to us, but we were the first to recover ourselves, and started to fire as we ran.

The English could not deploy on the narrow road, so they pulled around, and made back as fast as they could, for the ground above and below was so steep that they had to keep to the causeway, down which they poured in disorder. They seemed to be boring and pushing each other frantically under our fire, horses and men toppling over the edge of the road, and crashing into the timber beneath. The road became obstructed with dead and wounded horses, for we were firing into the brown, and we could hear angry shouts, as those behind tried to pass. Only a few men reached the bottom, where I caught a glimpse of them lashing their horses, as they rode through a clearing below. The rest abandoned their animals, and took cover in the forest, directing at us so hot a fire that we dared not climb down to get at the ammunition of the dead and wounded, nor at the holsters or wallets of the fallen horses. The main English column, that had been halted at the foot of the pass, now moved nearer, and when their fire was added we withdrew to the top to avoid casualties, and escaped without any.

After dark we went down the far side of the mountains, still following Sir Harry Smith's road, and daylight found us back in the Somerset district. We had now left the mountains on the same side on which we had entered them five days before, and, although we had failed to break out to the south, we were all heartily pleased to be clear at last of this appropriately named range.

As soon as it was light we halted at a farm for a few hours, and here General Smuts called us together. He said that we had reached a turning-point in the expedition, and he told us that from now onward he was going to make for the Atlantic seaboard, and the old-established districts of the South-Western Cape. After thanking the men for the way in which they had borne themselves, he told us that he was dividing our force, partly to mislead the English columns, and partly for easier provisioning, as the inhabitants of the districts through which we had passed had complained that so large a force as ours was too severe a tax upon them. Accordingly he proposed to send Commandant van Deventer off with approximately half the commando, while he himself would take command of the rest. Both units were to advance independently of each other, and ultimately reunite in the far west.

He still looked pale and ill, but his spirit was undaunted, and at midday he ordered those of us who were remaining with him to saddle our horses, and we rode away amid cheers and farewells from van Deventer's men, who were to start later. We went on until sundown, then halted for the night in a thorn-covered hollow. Next morning we struck across a wide plain, with alternating patches of bush and open country, over which we continued till noon, when we came to rest in a wide tree-covered bottom.

Percy Wyndall and Frits Balogh, of the 'Rijk Section', were sent to a neighbouring rise on outpost-duty, and from where we lay we could see them beneath a tree evidently enjoying a quiet chat, their horses cropping the grass behind. Before long a dozen English trooper's rode out of the thicket in the rear and surrounded them before our eyes.

The distance between us was perhaps half a mile, and when we realised what had happened, we of the 'Rijk Section' (now reduced to six) rushed for our horses, and followed by a few others who happened to have their horses at hand, galloped up the slope. The soldiers were so intent upon their prisoners that they did not see us until we were close by, when they loosed a ragged volley, and leaping into their saddles, abandoned the two captives, and made off.

Shouting to the rescued men to follow, we rode straight after the patrol, and got to within thirty or forty yards of them, bringing three to the ground. Two more, whose horses were hit, surrendered, but the rest scattered in the bush.

A friend of mine, Jack Baxter, one of Bouwer's men, was riding next to me, and he and I singled out one of the flying soldiers. We got near enough to order him to halt, but he rode on, not heeding our shouts. We fired at him but missed, for shooting from the saddle is trick-work, and he might have escaped had he not been brought up by a wire fence across his path. He jumped to the ground, and leaving his horse, climbed through the fence and disappeared into a patch of scrub. Almost at once his bullets were singing about our ears. Fortunately for us his marksmanship was poorer than his courage, and Baxter and I had time to dash our horses out of sight into a thicket. We dismounted, and, tying our animals, started to stalk him down. Crawling through the fence, we wormed our way from tree to tree, until we located him. As we could take no risks with such a resourceful opponent, we emptied our magazines at the spot where we had seen movement. Silence followed, and after a few more shots to make sure, we went up to find him lying face down, riddled with bullets, but still clutching his rifle. We smashed his weapon, and shared the contents of his ammunition-belts, after which we returned to fetch our horses and his, and rode back, feeling almost regretful at the way in which we had hunted down so brave a man.

The rest of our storming party were collected around the soldiers who had been killed. The prisoners and wounded were there, too, and after depriving the living and the dead of their boots (an unpleasant but necessary task, for there was continual shortage of footwear amongst our men), we rode back to rejoin the commando.

In the course of our return journey Ben Coetzee and Edgar Duncker branched away on their own, and soon after, hearing shots, we galloped in their direction. When we came up we found them sitting their horses in considerable agitation, while on the ground lay an officer and a trooper, both dead. It appeared that shortly after leaving us, as they rounded a piece of thorn bush, they ran into a small English patrol. So unexpected was the encounter that they were alongside before they could think, and Duncker, on the spur of the moment, called out, 'Don't fire, we are the 17th Lancers!' The officer in charge, a Captain Watson, said, 'I don't believe you; all Smuts's men are dressed in khaki. Put up your hands.' Then Coetzee and Duncker, both of whom carried Webley revolvers, fired simultaneously, killing Captain Watson and one of his men, and seriously wounding another, who, however, got away with the rest.

This was a very unlucky incident, for the wearing of British uniforms had without doubt been the proximate cause of the death of these two men, and although we knew nothing as yet of Lord Kitchener's proclamation, General Smuts pulled a long face when he was told of the business. Indeed, long afterwards, when we met Lord Kitchener himself, he cited this very case in defence of the execution of so many of our men for wearing khaki.

Well, the harm was done, and I can only say that none of us ever wore captured uniforms with the deliberate intention of decoying the enemy, but only out of sheer necessity.

We met no more soldiers that day, and towards afternoon the commando moved to a camping-place ten miles farther on. Next morning, while scouting ahead, I met a British ambulance-wagon with a doctor and several stretcher-bearers, on their way to fetch in the wounded of the day before. The Medical Officer already knew the manner of Captain Watson's death, for he spoke heatedly of murder, and abuse of military uniforms, although he made no mention of the proclamation, perhaps thinking that we knew about it. After this we went steadily west for some days without anything happening of importance, except that one evening we came in sight of a tiny hamlet called Hobsonville, where there was a small garrison of a dozen men, with whom the 'Rijk Section' and two or three more had a sharp brush, one of Bouwer's men being shot through the thigh. To avoid further damage we galloped in among the houses, in time to see the defenders rush for their horses, and make good their escape, as they had seen the commando coming on behind.

There were two well-stocked shops, and a quantity of military stores, so we did quite well out of the place, and spent the night feasting on tinned food and other luxuries.

In this manner we journeyed slowly on, until at length we reached the Port Elizabeth-Graaff Reinet railway line, which we crossed at night, an armoured train sending a few shells to speed us on our way. Next day we saw the town of Aberdeen, lying seven or eight miles distant, and as there was a large camp on the outskirts, we did not need the local farmers to tell us that there was trouble ahead.

We put the strength of the troops at about fifteen hundred, so we rode up to a large farm, to keep them under observation. They were not yet ready, but by the activity in their lines, we knew that they would soon be after us, especially as their patrols kept hanging about in the offing most of the day.

That afternoon we moved on, bearing slightly north for the Camdeboo Mountains, ten or fifteen miles away. We reached the foot next day, by which time a long English column was marching on our tracks, while various smaller bodies were skirting round the base of the range, in an encircling movement. General Smuts did not wish to get involved in a fight against heavy odds, so we started up the mountain by a gorge, and at sunset reached a high saddle, over which we passed.

Unfortunately the fine weather which we had enjoyed of late now changed. It turned bitterly cold, and a biting rain set in, and when darkness overtook us we had to halt on the rear slope for fear of falling over precipices. The icy water came down in torrents all night and there was no hope of a fire, so we sat before our horses until dawn, cold and drenched. Commandant Bouwer and two others were so benumbed, that when it grew light we had to carry them down in blankets to a valley, where we at last succeeded in getting fires alight, while General Smuts, Jack Borrius, and the rest of the sick and wounded must have endured agony that night.

It was still raining when we marched over a bleak upland, apparently uninhabited. To the north lay a world of barren-looking peaks and heights draped in heavy clouds, a sight that made our hearts sink, for, with an English column in our rear, it seemed as if we were in for another spell of cold and hungry mountaineering.

By midday the rain had stopped, and the sun showed through, and after plodding for hours over sodden turf, we came upon a farm with fuel to dry our clothes, and a flock of sheep for supplies.

A picket had been left behind at the neck which we had crossed the night before, and these men rode in after a time to say that the English column was nearing the top.

General Smuts sent the 'Rijk Section' and other patrols to look for a way down the south face of the mountain, for he liked the idea of being forced higher up as little as we did. We rode to what seemed a likely kloof, but when we got to the edge and peered down, an enemy force lay waiting for us below. The other parties brought similar reports—all the exits from the tableland were guarded, and our position unpleasantly resembled that on the Stormbergen. However, things shaped better this time, for here again the owner of the farm where we had halted (and whose sheep we had freely slaughtered), volunteered to lead us to a bridle-path, and after five or six miles brought us out on another high saddle, over which a faint goat-track led to the bottom. As soon as it was dark, we took our horses along the easy gradient, and got down in an hour or two without trouble. In order to shake off the columns more effectively, and to get clear of the terrible cactus-belt that girdles the foot of the mountains, we trekked on till daybreak.

This cactus (prickly pear) was brought from Central America about fifty years ago, and found the Karroo such congenial soil that there are now vast tracts rendered valueless by it. Our way now ran through a veritable forest of this vile growth, standing twenty feet high in places.

Soon after sunrise we reached the Kareega River, which rises in the mountains which we had just left, and runs due south across the plains.

We camped for the day on its wooded banks, seeing no sign of the English. In the course of the morning the 'Rijk Section', with the exception of my uncle and myself (and Jack Borrius), rode off to forage. I could not go, because General Smuts ordered me to ride through the river to a rise beyond, to watch the country towards Aberdeen. Before leaving I asked my uncle to look after my riding-mule during my absence, and that was the last I ever saw of either of them. It was well that I went off on my Arab pony, for his fleet legs were to be my salvation that day. I kept watch on the hill for many hours without seeing anything of note, but when General Smuts sent a messenger up in the afternoon to say that I was to remain until half an hour before sunset, I sent back a warning that I could not tell what might be going on at the river, as the heavily timbered banks made it impossible to see along its course.

When I judged from the height of the sun that my time was over, I rode down to the river, on my way back to where the commando was camped on the opposite side. Near the ford in a clearing stood a farmhouse, and, being thirsty after my long spell in the hot sun, I touched there to ask for a cup of coffee. The old lady inside was eager to grant my wish, but, as the kettle was not boiling, she asked me to sit down while she piled more wood on the fire. I knew that the commando was moving at sunset, so I decided not to wait, and, bidding her good-bye, rode off.

I had not gone thirty yards when I heard the trample of many horses, and, glancing over my shoulder, saw a swarm of English troopers gallop into the glade and surround the house.

Had I still been seated there, I should have been caught in full khaki, and that would have been the end of me, but out here in the open my English tunic saved me, for the soldiers took me for one of their own men, and let me ride away. Seeing this, I went slowly until I was out of sight among the trees, and then rode all out to rouse the commando.

I crossed the ford, and, as I breasted the other bank, looked back to see that the English had discovered their mistake and were streaming behind me like hounds on a hot scent. My grey pony was equal to the occasion and I was able to keep well ahead of my pursuers, firing alarm shots as I went, for I knew that if all these troops came on our commando unprepared and off-saddled among the trees, with their horses out at graze, there might be a serious disaster. I had still about six hundred yards to go, and when I rode in among our men I was relieved to find that they were rushing about the thorn trees bringing in their horses.

There was not a moment to lose, for, at the rate at which the English were approaching, they would be there long before the horses could be brought in and saddled. About fifteen or sixteen men, however, were mounted, having had their animals by them, and General Smuts called to them to ride forward and delay the oncoming enemy until the rest were ready.

With Commandant Bouwer at our head we galloped back, but, before we had gone far, a hundred or more English horsemen came charging at us. We jumped to the ground and fired, upon which the troopers opened out and also dismounted, giving rapid fire and obliging us to fall back behind the wall of a small dam, that very opportunely stood close by.

From here we were in a more favourable position to rake them, which we did so effectively that the men withdrew into denser bush, from which they fired heavily, but we kept our heads well down and had no casualties.

Thus far we had satisfactorily carried out our orders to hold up the enemy until the commando was collected, but we could see parties of English horsemen filtering round us through the bush in constantly increasing numbers, and, to make matters worse, they were unlimbering a field-gun on rising ground to our left. In a few moments shells were bursting overhead, against which the wall offered little or no protection, so Bouwer, boldly riding on to the crest of the dam, scanned the country to the rear, until he saw the commando move from the clearing where we had left them, which meant that our task was accomplished. When he called out that the commando was making fast down the river to the south, we retreated at once. As soon as the English saw us go, they came in hot pursuit. The sun was setting and the short twilight giving way to darkness, otherwise it would have gone harder with us than it did. The troops were on our heels, yelling and firing as they pounded behind, and, had there been more daylight, I think we should all have been captured.

My khaki uniform saved me for the second time that day, for a batch of troopers rode by in the dusk, and, mistaking me for one of their men, shouted that I was to hurry, but passed on without taking further notice.

Owing to the bush, both English and Boers got separated into smaller groups, and single horsemen and parties of twos and threes were galloping about. It was soon quite dark, and, to avoid being further accosted, as there were soldiers in front and behind me, I halted in a copse to let them through. I waited for a long time, until the hue and cry had died down and I could see camp fires springing up ahead, which showed that the English were halting for the night.

I could not tell how my companions had fared, but my own position was sufficiently difficult, for I was alone with the enemy across my path and the commando gone. When I thought that the soldiers had settled down, I cautiously rode on, picking my way with difficulty through the bush, for it was a dark night. After an hour or two I had skirted round their camp, and was following the course of the river once more.

At length I saw the gleam of a lighted window, and, stealing up, peered in to see five of our rearguard party of that afternoon standing in conversation with the inmates of the house.

I joined them at once, eager to hear news of the rest of our band, but they knew nothing, nor did they know what had become of the commando. As it was useless trying to pick up the spoor on so dark a night, and as our horses were tired, we got some food, and went a little distance to sleep amongst the trees, confidently expecting to overhaul our men next day. Shortly before sunrise we saddled up and crossed the river towards a conical hill lying on the other side, from which we should be able to see over the plains. As we rode on, we found two more of our men, who had escaped from last night's affair, and had also taken to the thickets on the banks. There were now eight of us, and, when we got to the foot of the hill, we left our horses and climbed up. As we reached the top the sun was rising, and, like sailors adrift in a boat, we anxiously scanned the horizon for a sign of the commando, but the country to the south lay open before us without a horseman in view.

General Smuts must have ridden all night, for although we could see for half a day's journey, he and his men had vanished, and difficult weeks were to elapse before we found them again.

Chapter 23

A Long Trail

For a long time we remained on the top, still hoping to see our men, but at last yesterday's English column came down the opposite bank of the river, so we made haste to get down to our horses and reach safer quarters. Searching out a less conspicuous hill, we left our animals to graze in a neighbouring hollow, while we lay amongst the boulders watching the progress of the enemy. Instead of trekking on, as we expected them to do, they went into camp at a farm three miles away. This was a misfortune, as our chief desire was to make a start towards picking up the trail, but, with the English halted by the river and their patrols scouring the plain in all directions, we dared not venture out into the open, and were obliged to let the valuable hours go by while our commando was getting farther and farther away.

They kept us until sunset before moving off, and then went south, from which we inferred that they were starting on a night march after General Smuts. So we only waited until the last horseman was riding away before we went down to the farm to get information.

It was dark before we reached there, and the owner, a well-to-do Dutch farmer, named le Roux, quickly told us such news as he had gleaned from the officers and soldiers during the day.

In the first place he said that three or four of our delaying party had been captured, and that one of them, my friend Jack Baxter, had been executed that morning at an adjoining farm for wearing khaki.

We were thunderstruck. The inhabitants of the districts through which we had passed could not have known of the death penalty or they would surely have mentioned it to us, and it was only when le Roux produced a recent newspaper, containing Lord Kitchener's proclamation, that we understood the position. We learned, too, for the first time, that other men of ours had been shot for the same reason, although it was only later, as more newspapers came into our hands, that we found out their names.

From what I could make out, the executions had been kept quiet, but now, for some reason or other, perhaps the killing of Captain Watson, the military authorities were giving them publicity. From a farm labourer who came in, we had details of Baxter's shooting, which brought home to me how narrowly I had on several occasions missed a similar fate, so I lost no time in changing the tunic I wore for a coat which I borrowed from our host, who also supplied such of my companions as were in khaki with whatever he had in the way of civilian dress.

As to the commando, le Roux said that General Smuts was believed to be heading for the Swartbergen, a great range whose peaks we had seen during the day, looming fifty or sixty miles to the south. We said good-bye and rode on all night, and for the next three days made our way across the plains that lie towards the mountains.

The local inhabitants gave us word that General Smuts had passed by, but there were several English columns moving between, and their patrols were so active that we had to go warily. Once at dawn we were hotly chased for many miles, so our progress was slow, and our chance of speedily overtaking the commando grew perceptibly less.

William Conradi, who was with me at the Kraal during the 17th Lancers fight, as the oldest and most experienced of our party, took charge. The others were: Albert von Rooyen, Albert Pienaar, Cornelius Brink, W Pypers, W van der Merwe and a boy named Michael du Preez, all Transvaalers, except Conradi, who came from the Western Cape, and all good, brave fellows. On the afternoon of the third day I was ahead to watch the doings of a small English force, when I saw a horseman detach himself from them, and come riding up the road in my direction. I lay in wait for him behind some trees, and, as he passed, I leaped out and knocked him from the saddle with the butt of my rifle. He turned out on closer inspection to be a Hottentot soldier, such as the English employed as scouts and dispatch-bearers. He was more terrified than hurt, and, when on the off chance I ordered him to hand over the message which I thought he might be carrying, he did actually produce one from his boot. When my companions came up we carefully studied this document, which was addressed to a Colonel Scobell, informing him that General Smuts had crossed the Swartbergen into the district of Oudtshoorn the night before. It added that he had been reinforced by nearly a hundred men, which was a mystery to us, but we found afterwards that a roving band of fifty men had joined him the day before. They were the remnant of a commando that had long been operating in these parts under Commandant Scheepers, who had recently been executed for train-wrecking. All was therefore well with the commando, and we were still on the right track, so we divested our prisoner of his horse, rifle and ammunition, and told him to clear off, a command he obeyed with a cheerful '*Dag, mij baasies*', as he trotted up the road.

We were by now within fifteen or twenty miles of the Swartbergen, but a ragged tract of foothills had to be crossed before we could reach the bottom of the range itself, and it took us the whole of the ensuing night to get there, for the going was dreadfully rough. Towards morning we came to a beaten highway, which, from information previously received, we knew to be the approach to Meiring's Poort, a pass leading over the mountains near here. The pass was not for us, because it was held by a garrison, but we decided to make use of the road for a while, as preferable to the boulder-strewn country across which we had been toiling. This landed us in a mess, for we ran into a body of English horsemen. It was too dark to make out their strength, and we were so mixed up with them that no one could shoot. For a few seconds we were milling about, neither side quite certain whether we were dealing with friend or foe, and no one uttered a word for fear of precipitating trouble. Then we heard William Conradi shout to us in English to break away, so we disengaged ourselves and turned back into the rough, while the English clattered away along the road without a shot having been fired.

After this we went more carefully, and sunrise found us leading our horses up the street of a tiny village standing at the bottom of the pass. Dogs began to bark, and windows to open, and we saw soldiers running to a large building, so we mounted and rode hastily out.

Before us rose the Swartbergen, steep as a house, but we climbed it all day, dragging our leg-weary horses, until we reached the top at dusk.

From here we could look south over more mountains and deep valleys, and far beyond lay a grey haze, which we took to be the sea.

Our ascent during the day had not been unreasonably difficult, for the north face, up which we had come, though steep, was grass-covered and devoid of krantzes, but the slope down which we had now to go was fringed with high crags, so, with darkness coming on, we were obliged to halt for the night.

We had eaten nothing for twenty hours, as the presence of the troops the day before had prevented us from foraging, so we sat cold and hungry, looking down into the black depths below.

After a while there was a faint twinkle of a light, evidently a farmhouse in some valley, and, as Michael du Preez and I were the youngest and hungriest of the party, we prevailed on the others to let us go down the mountain. It was a bad climb, for we had to feel our way in the dark by cracks and crevices, to the bottom of the cliffs, and it took us the rest of the night to do the remainder. So it was not till well after sunrise that we reached the farm whose light we had seen in the evening. The owner, an Englishman named Holm, gave us a generous meal, including an omelette made from ostrich egg, to which we did full justice. After getting from him a further supply of food for our companions, and eliciting the information that General Smuts had passed down the valley the day before with enemy troops hanging on behind, Michael and I started up the mountain once more. We were desperately tired, having had no sleep for two nights running, so it took us seven hours to drag ourselves to where the others were waiting. They had, in the meanwhile, succeeded in finding a practicable way down the cliff for the horses, and we found them considerably below the spot at which we had left them the night before. They were so famished that they had begun to look over the horses with a view to shooting the worst of them for food, but our arrival, each with a bag containing an ostrich egg, meat, and bread, made this unnecessary, and they fell to cooking a huge meal instead. When all had finished, Conradi ordered an immediate start, for we had told him that General Smuts was in the valley, and he was for not losing a moment in going after him, so Michael and I had to go along once more.

Climbing down was difficult, and in places we had to roll boulders into the torrent that rushed down the gorge we were descending, to form a bridge for the horses. Half-way down, we came on a cattle-path, which made progress easier, and we reached the foot of the mountain by ten or eleven that night. We halted in an orchard, and I was asleep almost as soon as I had the saddle off my horse.

We were now in the great valley that runs parallel to the Swartbergen towards the town of Oudtshoorn, and I well remember how oppressed we felt in this region of mountains, for we were accustomed to the open country and wide horizons of the north.

As we made our way down the valley all that day, we were comforted with the news of General Smuts at every farmhouse, and we were hopeful of coming up with him at any moment, for the commando tracks lay plain before us on the road. By nightfall we were so hot on the trail that we passed a homestead where our men had halted that afternoon, and a little farther on we were told that Edgar Duncker and Nicolas Swart had gone by on foot only an hour before. Their horses had been killed during the retreat at the Kareega River, and, like ourselves, they had been following the commando ever since.

We hurried on, intending to catch up before halting, but after dark we lost the tracks owing to stony soil, and could find no farmhouse at which to make enquiries, so we camped in a gully for the night, feeling sure that we should see the commando the first thing in the morning.

We were up at sunrise, eagerly gazing down the valley. Sure enough there rose a cloud of dust, and we could make out horsemen riding among the trees, and we saddled in haste, congratulating ourselves that our search was over.

But disappointment was in store, for, as we hurried down the road, a woman ran from a field with outstretched arms, to warn us that those men were English troops who had come into the valley overnight, and indeed, before long, so many of them came riding from farm to farm in our direction that we had to go up one of the smaller lateral valleys to escape their attentions. We did not know what had become of our men, but from what the woman told us, General Smuts had evidently got wind of the

English movements and had escaped under cover of darkness, but in which direction we were unable to discover—a sad blow, after having so nearly rejoined the commando.

We continued up the smaller valley, then climbed over a height and descended into another of the broad valleys that abound in these parts.

I had never been here before, but our family clan is a large one, some of whose branches have spread far from the older settlements around Table Bay, so I was not surprised that afternoon to come on a connection of mine named Rex, a lineal descendant of George Rex, the morganatic son of King George III by Hannah Lightfoot, the Quakeress. George Rex had been sent out to South Africa in 1775, and given a large tract of land at the Knysna, on condition that he did not again trouble his august parent. His descendants still live there, and one of them had married my mother's brother.

Rex and I spent an hour discussing family ties, and before I left he insisted upon giving me a pair of new boots, as mine were considerably the worse for wear. For this he was fined and imprisoned by the military, and I read in a newspaper that he was convicted of 'comforting the King's enemies', which amused me greatly, although I was sorry that I had landed him in trouble.

Soon after this the ubiquitous English patrols were once more in evidence, on a house-to-house visitation, so a local farmer accompanied us to where a path led into a narrow kloof, and, having put us on our way, slipped home again. This path ran between high crags, that sometimes almost met overhead, until at length it reached the side of a mountain up which it ran. We followed to the top, and got there long after sunset. We could not see the country beyond, but through the darkness shone a light from a farmhouse, and, as we were anxious to pick up the lost trail of the commando, Pypers and I went down to make inquiries. The slope was steep, but clear of rocks, and by midnight we were hammering at the door of a large homestead. It belonged to an Englishman named Guest, who, when he opened the door and saw who we were, exclaimed, 'My God! First come the Boers this morning and slaughter my sheep; then come the British, who kill more sheep instead of catching the Boers; and now I am hauled out of bed at this time of night by more Boers!' We spoke to him pleasantly, and the old fellow cooled down enough to explain that General Smuts had camped on his farm at eleven that morning, and was followed by a pursuing English force that had also halted here and made free of his live-stock, so he not unnaturally looked upon our arrival as the last straw in a distressful day. Becoming more affable, he roused the servants and gave us a good supper, during which he told us that Duncker and Nicolas Swart had caught up the commando here. Having eaten well, and obtained as much information as we could, we persuaded our host to give us enough food for our friends, and started back.

As we went off he doubtless heaved a sigh of relief at having got rid of us, but, had he known it, his troubles were only beginning.

Pypers and I reached the others shortly before daybreak, and as Conradi was not one to let the grass grow under his feet, he started us off at once. At the first dawn of what turned out to be a lively day, we began leading our horses down the mountain, and towards eight o'clock were nearing Guest's house, when there swung into view, round a bend of the valley, some two hundred English horsemen, riding hard for the farm. Our presence there during the night must have been reported to them, for they were riding like men with a set purpose, and on nearing the homestead they divided to right and left, to surround the buildings and orchards. Luckily we were able to hustle ourselves and our animals into a gully, without being seen, and from our hiding-place we watched the activities of the soldiers with considerable interest. When they drew a blank at the farm, they deployed along the foot of the slope on which we were, and, splitting into parties, began a systematic search. Soon on every knoll and hillock men stood scanning the mountainside, as if they knew that we were somewhere about, but, although some of the troopers came within a hundred yards of us, we were not discovered. We did not fire, for we knew that if we did it would all be over with us, so we lay hidden, meaning only to shoot when there was no other alternative. A man on a white-faced Argentine came trotting up to within twenty yards of us. He dismounted to examine the path for hoof marks, and was so close to us, that had one of our horses jingled a bit, he must have heard it. We held our breath until he got into the saddle again and rode away, little thinking on what a thread his life had hung, for we had him covered, and, had he seen us, he would have been a dead man, but we had no wish to precipitate a general battle against impossible odds, and we let him go.

After what seemed an age, the hunt died down and the soldiers gradually drifted back to the farmhouse, where they camped for two hours, during which we could not move. We saw the men flinging oat-sheaves from a loft, and chasing poultry, and I could not help feeling sorry for Mr Guest, who was once more being put under the harrow, and not for the last time either, as it proved.

When the troops at length saddled and rode away, we waited barely long enough for the last man to be off the premises before we hurried to the house.

When Mr Guest saw us appear, with the soldiers only just going through the garden beyond, he looked as if he had just seen an apparition, and when we laid him under further contribution he seemed to be on the verge of a fit. However, he complied with our demands, grumbling and complaining at first, and then laughing at his ill luck. Having satisfied our requirements, we rode up the valley a little distance, to where there was a pleasant orchard and a large cultivated field hedged round with high branches of thorn, in the manner customary in this area. This was the one error of judgment we made throughout our trip, for instead of making for the wider country lower down, we had entered a cul-de-sac.

We thought that the English were finally gone, and prepared a meal, after which I made a second mistake, for, while the others kept their horses by them, I turned my little Arab, all saddled as he was, into the field, and, thoroughly weary from having been up all night, sought out a shady spot in the lee of the thorn fence and, without telling the others where I was, fell sound asleep.

I was awakened, I do not know how long after, by the crash of rifle-fire near by, and, starting to my feet half dazed, saw a number of English soldiers standing before their horses and blazing away at my seven companions, who were riding down the valley for their lives. I had only myself to blame for being left behind, as they did not know where I was, and were in any case unable to wait. My chief hope of escape was my horse, but he was standing inside the field in full view of the firing soldiers. They had not yet noticed me, as I was screened by the fence, so I parted some of the branches to see what chance there was of getting at my pony. By great good luck he was standing on the other side within a few yards of me. The firing had alarmed him, for he was restlessly tossing his head and snuffing the air, and I could see that in another moment he would bolt, so I called to quiet him, and, worming my way through a weak spot in the fence, ran up to where he stood quivering with excitement. Jumping into the saddle, I rode for a small gateway in the far corner, which was the only outlet. The soldiers saw me at once and turned their fire upon me, in spite of which I managed to get through the opening, but, just as I was gathering speed beyond, a bullet brought my poor horse headlong to the ground, and flung me yards over his head. Picking up my rifle I ran towards the homestead, thinking that my party might be making a stand there. The soldiers beyond the field kept firing at me as I appeared and disappeared amongst the trees, but I got within hail of the house unharmed. At the corner of a barn stood six or seven men, whom in my haste I took to be my friends, and I made straight for them. But as I came within thirty yards of them, one stepped forward, and, leveling his rifle, called on me to halt.

They were English soldiers, and not the only ones, for more came rushing round from the stables, and out of the dwelling-house. Escape seemed impossible, but I made a bid for it. To my right was a small grove of poplars, and, swerving aside, I dashed for this cover before they could send more than a bullet or two after me.

Volleys came crashing through the trees as I ran, but I emerged safely on the other side into hummocky ground, where I twisted and turned to such good effect that, although the men came hurrying round to cut off my retreat, I got into a broken stretch with no more serious damage than a gash from a bullet, which ripped up the sole of my boot and made running difficult.

Breasting a knoll I glanced back. The soldiers near the field had mounted their horses, and were coming after me. Of those around the homestead, some were running in my direction, and others were in the yard throwing saddles on their animals, and I had a final glimpse of Mr Guest in his shirtsleeves on the stoep, wildly gesticulating, but whether he was urging on the men to my capture or protesting against the crowning disaster of a battle on his doorstep, there was no time to consider, for I was in a very tight corner.

There was no sign of my companions. The sharp ground was cutting my foot, the horsemen were close behind me, and already I could hear the men yelling at me to stop, and I was just deciding that I had better do so, when I came upon a deep nullah running down the mountain-side. Here it flashed on me that if my pursuers saw me disappear over the bank, they would naturally think that I was making down its bed to the centre of the valley, or up towards the mountain. Looking aslant my shoulder, to make sure that they saw what I was doing, I went over the bank, but instead of trying to escape up or down the water-course, as they would expect, I found a spot on the opposite side, where the rains had washed out a shallow runnel, and, crawling up this, went flat on my face into the bushes beyond, which stood just high enough to conceal a prostrate man. Having left the nullah unperceived, I worked myself forward another fifty yards to a slightly denser patch, and stopped there.

The soldiers, seeing me jump into the spruit, did exactly what I anticipated. On reaching the spot where they had seen me vanish, they separated into two parties, one of which galloped up the mountain-side, and the other down towards the valley. I had a clear view of the search from where I lay, and after a while I could see, from the undecided way in which they were riding about, that they were completely nonplussed.

In the end they must have concluded that I had got away on the upper side, for they spread out along the mountain slope like beaters at a shoot, moving farther and farther from my hiding-place. I knew now that I was comparatively safe, for the sun was setting, and before long I heard them clattering back to the farm, where presently their camp fires shone out, indicating that Mr Guest was once more to be an unwilling host.

I felt proud of my successful ruse, but there was little else pleasant to contemplate. I lay in the bracken like a hunted rabbit; my foot throbbed painfully; my companions were gone, and so was the commando; my horse was dead and my saddle and belongings were in the hands of the enemy.

As thinking did not mend matters, I rose at length, and limped off in the dark.

After about an hour, I heard the sound of a hymn and the wheeze of a harmonium, such as stands in almost every Dutch farmhouse, and knew that I was nearing friends. When I knocked at the door there was a hush at first, for in these disturbed times a visit late at night meant military requisition, but then I heard a shuffle of feet and the door opened.

A whole family was peering from within. When I told them who I was, they almost dragged me into the house, so eager were they to help. I must have looked very dishevelled, for the women wept with pity while removing the boot from my sore foot, and during the more painful process of extracting a thorn, nearly an inch long, that had run into the palm of my hand when I was thrown from my horse that afternoon. They fetched hot water and tore up clean linen for bandages; a meal was laid, with coffee, and the kindly people almost quarrelled for the right to serve me, so keen was their sympathy, although they knew that it might mean for them fines and imprisonment. Having attended to my wants, they took further counsel. It was agreed that I could not remain here, for even if the continuous patrols did not ferret me out for themselves, my presence was certain to be reported by the coloured farm labourers, who all over the Cape sided with the British. As I assured them that I was well able to walk, it was decided that I must continue westward on the off chance of coming up with General Smuts, who might be held up somewhere. It seemed a forlorn hope, but as there was the risk of an enemy detachment coming by at any moment, I made ready to start as soon as my boot had been sufficiently repaired.

The head of the family, a patriarch of seventy, insisted on acting as my guide during the first stage of the journey and firmly refused to waive the right in favour of his sons, who offered themselves. A grain-bag was packed with food, and after an affecting leave-taking, the old man and I set out. We trudged along, hour after hour, until his strength gave out and I made him turn back, his voice shaking with emotion as he wished me God-speed. My foot scarcely hindered me, and now that I was alone I made good speed on the well-marked wagon-road upon which he had set me, until, towards three in the morning, it dipped down into a ravine. By the time I reached the bottom the moon was clear, and by its light I saw several fresh hoof marks on the ground. On examining these, I recognised the slightly malformed marks of Michael du Preez's pony, and closer investigation showed me the footprints of men which I knew at once as those of some, if not all, of my seven missing companions, who had crossed the road here on their way down the ravine. This providential discovery cheered me immensely, for I had known all along that my hopes of overtaking the commando by myself were slim, but it was pretty certain that I could catch up with the men who had passed here so recently, and I lost no time in following their spoor.

After some miles they had branched off into a smaller kloof, and I followed along this without difficulty, for the tracks lay clear in the dusty cattle-path. At last, as day was breaking, I heard the whicker of a horse and, going forward carefully, found all seven men asleep beneath the trees. They were astonished to see me, as they had made certain that I was either dead or taken. They themselves had been hard put to make their escape from the farm, and although not one of them had received a scratch, yet out of the nine horses we had possessed between us, no less than six had been killed, and, what was almost as serious, we had lost the bulk of our saddles, cooking-tins, and blankets. We agreed that the first thing to do was to replenish our equipment, so we continued along the gully, until a long march brought us into the thickly populated valley of the Caminassi River, where we heard many rumours about our commando, but no certain news, beyond the fact that General Smuts was making west with a strong force of cavalry closely pressing him. The people willingly supplied our wants, and, for the next three days, we slowly felt our way down the broad valley. Far ahead were tall pillars of dust, made, they told us, by General French with thousands of horsemen, engaged in a great drive behind our commando, and occasionally we heard the distant boom of guns. As five of us were on foot, we had to proceed with great caution, and repeatedly we had to hide for hours at a time, to avoid bodies of horsemen passing from the rear to joint their advance-columns ahead.

The more we saw of the valley, crowded with columns on the march, the less we liked it. William Conradi, after watching for some time, said that he had a better plan. Instead of following the commando any longer, he proposed to turn north across the Swartbergen, back into the Karroo country from which we had come. He said that General Smuts was almost certainly heading for the Western Cape, and, if we got that mountain range between ourselves and the troops, we could travel unmolested and perhaps join him when the chase had died down. We agreed, and set off at once. For two days we worked our way through the intervening country, towards where the Swartbergen stood like a wall on the northern horizon. At a village called Armoed we had trouble, for a party of soldiers rode at us as we were leaving it, and only the falling dusk and our brisk reply to their firing enabled us to escape through the river, into the bush on the other side.

My foot gave me no pain, and we got along safely, thanks to the local farmers, who kept us well informed.

On the morning of the third day we reached the foot of the mountain chain, just east of the Seven Weeks Gorge. Into this poort ran the main road to the open Karroo, but the pass was garrisoned, and our only course lay up the flank of the range. As there were English patrols riding about we began the ascent without delay, toiling upward steadily, until we made the summit by evening. These were the same mountains which we had crossed coming in the opposite direction days before. At that crossing the Swartbergen had consisted of a single clear-cut barrier, but here it forked out into numerous sierras, that looked like giving us much trouble.

As it was getting dark, and heavy rain began to fall, we dropped some distance over the crest to seek shelter for the night. It was too cold to sleep and too damp to light a fire, so we sat shivering until dawn, when we started to grope our way down the mountain-side enveloped in a dense mist. Towards four in the afternoon we were below the clouds, and could see a long narrow canyon lying at our feet, its sides closed in by perpendicular cliffs. On the floor of the chasm, a thousand feet below, we made out a cluster of huts, and, thinking to find natives there to guide us, we went down in a body to investigate, leaving the horses in a ravine to look after themselves. We climbed through a fissure in the crags, and reached the bottom soon after sunset. As we approached the huts, a shaggy giant in goatskins appeared and spoke to us in strange outlandish Dutch. He was a white man named Cordier, who lived here with his wife and a brood of half-wild children, in complete isolation from the outside world. He knew all about us, for one of his sons had been up the mountain that morning, and, hearing the sound of men and horses in the mist, had stalked us and carefully noted our number and the language we spoke, after which he had vanished over the edge of the cliffs to warn his father.

We were received with uncouth but sincere hospitality, and we applied ourselves gratefully to the goats' meat, milk, and wild honey that were placed before us. Cordier told us that no British troops had ever penetrated this fastness and that we were the first Boers to do so. He had heard vaguely of the war, but his knowledge of the events of the last two years was scanty.

We spent that night and the next day with this curious Swiss Family Robinson, and in the evening toiled up the cliffs again, accompanied by our host and some of his colts, who stayed with us around our camp fires, and led us the following morning across rugged mountains, until by dark we looked down at last upon the northern plains. Our intention now was to descend to the open country and, keeping the mountains well on our left, to strike west towards the districts of the Cape lying along the Atlantic seaboard two hundred miles away, where we hoped ultimately to get news of General Smuts.

We spent another night on the heights, and, parting from our guides at daybreak, climbed down the slopes to level ground and headed across the plains. We were now in the 'Gough' Karroo, as the Hottentots call it, an arid, waterless region, sparsely occupied by wandering herdsmen. By next day we crossed the railway line that runs from Cape Town to the north. There were no block-houses, as in the Transvaal and Free State, so we had no difficulty, although we saw the double-tiered watch-towers at either end of the bridge over the Dwyka River.

On the far side of the line lay country even less inhabited, and we suffered severely from thirst and hunger, for water was to be had only by digging in the dry gravel-courses with our bare hands, and for food we had to subsist on what we had brought with us.

About a week after passing the railway line, always going due west, a patrol of English soldiers appeared on the baking plain. They opened fire at us, and, when we replied, they made off, doubtless to report to some larger force in the neighbourhood.

The day after that we reached a prosperous-looking farmhouse, the first we had seen since crossing the Swartbergen. At this place we had a miniature battle, for while we were talking to the owner and his wife, twelve or fifteen troopers suddenly rode on to a ridge and fired on us. We told our friends to go indoors, and ran down into a spruit, from which we worked forward, thinking to get near enough to our opponents to dislodge them and capture their horses, but by the time we got within a hundred yards of the troopers they were pinning us down with such accurate shooting that we had to hug the earth, and were only too glad to crawl back out of harm's way after dark, and retrieve our three horses and belongings at the farm.

For the next two days we travelled slowly on, gradually approaching the more thickly settled district that lies towards Calvinia.

At every house at which we touched we made inquiries for General Smuts, but no word of him was known. However, a pleasant surprise was awaiting us. Early one morning, as we sat by our fire, we saw a diminutive cart come over the rise, drawn by two donkeys. On the seat was a grey-bearded old Dutch farmer of the poorer class and, beside him, a smart English sergeant. When we stopped this queerly assorted couple, we were astonished to learn that they had quitted General Smuts and his commando only an hour or two before. The soldier said that he had been captured the previous day while scouting, and after spending the night with our men, had been released that morning.

We were so delighted with this unexpected good news that we insisted on shaking hands with our informant, who could not at first understand our elation. When we explained, he said that for his part he had less cause for congratulation because, having been deprived of his horse, and having no mind to walk ninety-odd miles to the nearest military post, he had ordered his fellow-traveller in the King's name to provide him with transport.

As the only available conveyance was the one we saw, he was not looking forward to the journey, particularly as relations were strained with the driver. The farmer was glum and angry at having to drive a *verdomde rooi-nek* (as he called him) on a journey that would take him from home for the better part of a fortnight, and would subject him to the jeers of all his neighbours on his return, while the sergeant was no better pleased with his companion, who, he said, did not understand a word of English and only grunted when spoken to. We did not waste much time on the incongruous pair, and, after wishing them a pleasant journey, hurried on.

Tramping forward for seven or eight miles, we breasted a rise, and there, on the banks of a river below, was the welcome sight of many horses at graze and smoke rising from among the trees to show that our long quest was at an end. A mounted sentry rose out to see who we were, and, after shaking hands, galloped back to spread the news of our arrival. Soon the entire commando was running to meet us, and we were surrounded by a laughing, cheering crowd, all anxious to show their pleasure at our safe return. General Smuts was among the foremost to greet us. He said he had long given us up for lost, and warmly praised the way in which we had come through without losing a man.

Great indeed was our joy at getting back, but for me there was a fly in the ointment, for I found that the 'Rijk Section' was practically wiped out. First, there was Jack Borrius minus an eye, and still suffering from a swollen, festering hand; then there lay Ben Coetzee with a bullet in his leg; Nicolas Swart, with a shattered arm, the result of a revolver shot at close quarters; and Edgar Duncker, with a bullet through his thigh and three fingers of his right hand blown to pieces. In addition, my uncle Jan Mulder (he was really my step-uncle) and our inconspicuous but loyal companion, Jan van Zijl, had been captured, so that there was very little left of the old unit, Wyndell,

Frits Balogh, and I being the only foundation members not incapacitated.

The total loss to the commando during our absence, apart from a dozen wounded who had come along, was not more than seven or eight men, in spite of heavy fighting on the way.

In the meanwhile, the other half of our force under van Deventer was not yet accounted for, but General Smuts fully expected that, under so experienced a leader, they would eventually turn up.

Chapter 24

Calmer Waters

From now onward, the circumstances of our expedition into the Cape radically altered for the better. Here in the far west there were no railways, and the country was so difficult for large bodies of troops that we had reached comparative sanctuary. North, stretching towards the Orange River hundreds of miles away, lay a great territory practically free of the enemy, save for rare columns passing by, and a few garrisons scattered long distances apart, so that we had the country almost to ourselves.

Small bands of local rebels had long been carrying on desultory warfare of their own, between here and the coast, and General Smuts told us that he was going to reorganise these into larger commandos until he was strong enough to undertake big-scale operations, which he thought might ease the pressure in the two Republics. Thus we looked forward with fresh interest to the new stage of the war opening before us.

That same evening we moved off, still going west, our wounded now comfortably driven in carts, while those of us who had returned without horses were provided with temporary mounts, a welcome change after our long tramp. In a few days' time we reached Elandsvlei, an oasis with waving palms and running water, and here we halted for two whole days. This was the first time since crossing the Orange River into the Cape that we had stayed in one place for even a day and a night, and, needless to say, both man and beast revelled in the unaccustomed holiday. In the hills near by ran a troop of mules, and some friends and I managed to catch half a dozen of them, mine being a powerful black, who squealed and bit and threw me several times before I mastered him. Then he was quite gentle and I rode him for many hundreds of miles during the next few months.

From Elandsvlei we went north-west via Biddow to a place called Kobbee, a deep valley that reminded me of Dreadful Hollow in *Robbery under Arms*, and here again we lay over for several days, feeding our animals on the plentiful crops. Thence we crossed intervening mountains to the great plain that runs towards the Atlantic, sixty miles away. At the foot of these mountains lies the village of van Rijnsdorp. It had been recently garrisoned by the British, but Commandant Maritz had swooped down and captured it. This Maritz was a policeman from Johannesburg, who, after many adventures, had established himself in these parts as a leader of various rebel bands.

He was a short, dark man, of enormous physical strength, cruel and ruthless in his methods, but a splendid guerrilla leader, and according to his lights an ardent patriot, of whom I was to see more later on.[1]

He had sacked the village and disappeared with his retainers, and we found the original civil population in peaceful occupation, the English having apparently abandoned the place for good.

As the 'Rijk Section' was now practically defunct, General Smuts ordered William Conradi and me to join his staff. This was in recognition of our late exploit, and was tantamount to military promotion. The rest of the 'Rijk Section' was absorbed into Commandant Bouwer's commando, with the exception of Ben Coetzee, who rode away, his leg still in splints, in search of Maritz, for they were old friends. This, then, was the end of that small company with whom I had come into the Cape. Like Isaac Malherbe's Corporalship and the 'ACC', it, too, had been destroyed, but I am glad to have served with three such bodies of men.

I was now what might correspond to a staff officer in a regular army, although none of us on General Smuts's headquarters bore any distinguishing title, beyond the fact that the rest of the men in friendly derision referred to us as 'Kripvreters'—a 'Kripvreter' being a stall-fed horse, as distinguished from one having to scratch for its own living on the veld.

On assuming my duties, however, I soon found that, so far from being stall-fed, the members of the staff, in addition to having to fight and forage for themselves like the rest, were employed as dispatch-riders, and during the next few weeks our life was one continual round of weary rides in search of one portion or another of the commando, for General Smuts had now divided his force into smaller groups, often stationed days apart, to provide more easily for grazing and food.

In December (1901) he left the commando scattered along the banks of the Olifants River near van Rijnsdorp, and, with his staff, moved up the mountains to a spot called Willems River, where he began his work of collecting the various rebel bands into organised commandos. A large number of men from this area had either joined Maritz or were riding about on their own, sniping at British columns or waylaying convoys, and, in order to get into touch with these irregulars, we 'Klipvreters' were sent during the next few weeks on long rides, in the course of which we travelled unnumbered miles from south of the Olifants River to far beyond Calvinia and back, until we knew every inch of the country.

The inhabitants sympathised with us, and looked upon us as their champions, so we were welcomed wherever we went, and, despite the long gruelling journeys on mule-back, I enjoyed myself, for I was not above feeling a pleasant glow when the womenfolk waved from before the farmhouses, and the men shouted greetings from the road-side.

On Christmas Day, returning from a hundred-mile errand beyond Calvinia, I saw mounted men camped in the distance, and making thither, found them to be Commandant van Deventer's missing column. My unexpected appearance amongst

---

[1]See page 171 for Maritz's description of Deneys Reitz—Ed.

them was hailed with joy, for this was their first word of us since we had parted below the Zuurbergen, and for a long time I was busy telling them how we had fared and listening to their experiences. They had only just arrived here, having been driven out of their course for several weeks, but they had done well, for they had captured several convoys and many prisoners, and they had more horses, rifles, and ammunition than they could use.

After a pleasant evening's talk around the camp fires, I remained there for the night, and took the road south again next day, getting back by the 28th to General Smuts, who was greatly pleased at my news.

My mule had unflinchingly trotted the better part of two hundred miles in five days, and the following morning I was off again in search of Maritz, whom I found eighty miles away in the neighbourhood of Tontelbos. This place was an important grain-growing centre, at which the British had posted a force of men, to prevent the crops from being carried away. Maritz attacked the garrison the day before I arrived, but was repulsed with heavy loss, he himself being severely wounded. I found him seated on a chair in a farmhouse with two of his men dressing his wound, a terrible gash below the right armpit, exposing the lung, an injury that would have killed most men, but he was like a bull and seemed little the worse for it.

I saw the year 1902 in with them, and then started back, catching up General Smuts three days later at Nieuwoudsville on the escarpment. During all this time our main commando under Commandant Bouwer was lying down on the plains to the south, having occasional brushes with the English, but on the whole passing a quiet time. Some of our patrols went beyond Porterville, to within sight of Table Mountain, and my old companion Krige (the General's brother-in-law), with whom I had served in Isaac Malherbe's Corporalship, and who had been so badly wounded at Spion Kop, even penetrated as far as Malmesbury, and brought back a large sum of money for the use of the commando from General Smuts's father, who lived there.

During a visit which I paid at this time to our men along the Olifants River, I met my old Ladysmith tent-mate, Walter de Vos, who had likewise been wounded on Spion Kop, and whom I had last seen lying on the slope of that hill, on the day of the big fight two years before. He had latterly been in command of one of the local rebel bands, and we spent the morning talking over old times; but he was killed an hour after my going, in an outpost affair near by.

Early in January General Smuts decided to go north to the Orange River, to organise the numerous rebel patrols that were under arms there. Our company consisted of himself and his staff only. It was a three-hundred-mile ride through desert country, and we went first of all to Tontelbos, now evacuated, as the crops were in. Maritz was here on a pallet of straw in an empty dwelling-house, but he made light of his wound and was well on the mend.

From Tontelbos we moved north through country thinly occupied by Nomad Boers (Trek Boers), who spend their lives going from one well to another with their flocks, like the old peoples in the Bible. They are a primitive patriarchal folk, knowing little of the outside world, but of a brave and sturdy stock, and many of them were under arms.

We travelled mostly at night to avoid the blazing heat of day, and at length reached Kakamas, a small irrigation colony founded by the Dutch Church on the south bank of the Orange River. The settlement was still in its infancy, and the inhabitants lived in rude huts and shelters made of grass and reeds, but they had built a canal from the river, and had established fields and orchards so successfully that the place had become a supply depot for the surrounding districts. We spent a pleasant fortnight here, eating fruit and swimming in the river every day. As soon as General Smuts had completed his arrangements with the guerrilla bands, many of whom rode in from the desert to meet him, we returned south, reaching Tontelbos again towards the second week in February. Maritz was no longer here, but, as the grazing was good in the cropped wheat-lands, we lay over a few days to rest our animals and ourselves.

General Smuts then decided to go eastwards in search of Commandant van Deventer. We did not know exactly where his commando was, but we travelled up along the Fish River, and after a day or two got word that he was thirty or forty miles away. We rode thither all that night, and towards daylight heard the sound of gun-fire and small-arms, and saw a red glare in the sky. Quickening our pace we reached a farmhouse called Middelpost at dawn, and found two or three men here in charge of a dozen wounded.

They told us that van Deventer was fighting close by with an English column on its way to Calvinia, so, after a few hurried questions, we rode to where we could see his men, lining the crest of some small kopjes, their horses tethered below. On higher ground away to the left were small parties of English troops, and a single field-piece stood in full view, but out of rifle-range. The men at the farmhouse warned us to ride for it, as they said that the gunners had the distance to a yard, so we set off at a gallop. They were right, for when we had got about halfway, there was a flash at the gun, and a shell came tearing at us.

A local schoolmaster named Hugo, who had joined a few weeks before, was riding beside me. The shell burst on us with a roar, but although I was nearer the gun, neither my mule nor I received a scratch. But when the smoke cleared I saw that my companion was badly hit. He was swaying in his saddle with blood streaming from his chest. His rifle dropped to the ground, and he fell forward on the neck of his animal. Then he recovered himself and said he was not going to give the gunners the satisfaction of knowing that they had hit anyone, so raising himself he rode for cover of the hill. Other shells came after, but no one else was hit, and, having retrieved the fallen rifle, I rode on and found that Hugo had fainted and fallen from his horse, and that General Smuts and the others were trying to stanch his wound. It was at the base of his left lung, and I fished out the twisted buckle of his braces, and a cartridge clip with five rounds of ammunition, all of which had been driven into the cavity, in addition to the shell-fragment which I could not recover. I thought that he had not ten minutes to live, but two months later he was in the saddle once more. We made him comfortable, and climbed up to where Commandant van Deventer and his men were holding the ridge above. This was the first time that General Smuts had come among them since the parting in Somerset East, and there were cheers and shouts of greeting when they saw him. Van Deventer himself hastened forward to welcome us, and in a few seconds we were in the firing-line. Looking down the forward side of the hill, we saw an interesting sight.

Immediately below, on the level ground by the banks of a spruit, stood some hundred and twenty English convoy-wagons, most of them burning fiercely to the crackle of exploding rifle ammunition, for every wagon seemed to carry several cases.

Scattered among the blazing vehicles lay dead men and horses, and there were a large number of live troop-horses and mules, that had stampeded during the night, but had drifted back into the burning camp, where, in spite of the smoke and flames and the bursting cartridges, they were feeding on the seed oats and other fodder that our men had flung from the wagons during their hasty search for loot, before setting them on fire.

Van Deventer gave us a brief account of what had happened. A long convoy had approached the evening before, accompanied by a mounted column. He had disputed their way, whereupon the English troops parked their wagons beside the spruit, and took up covering positions, but during the night he and his men broke through the line on foot, and, entering the camp, set it on fire. In the dark the troops were unable effectively to hinder the work of destruction, and the position when we arrived was that van Deventer, having fired the wagons, had withdrawn before daylight, and the two sides were now facing one another with the convoy burning between them, neither side permitting the other to approach it. The bulk of the English soldiers had taken post at a farmhouse surrounded by a walled garden, about nine hundred yards away, from which they were maintaining a hot rifle-fire.

To the left, four hundred yards off, lay more of them on a stony hill, with their field-gun on a rise behind, and on the right in another kopje was an isolated detachment, so placed that they had anyone under short range who tried to enter the camp. Van Deventer told General Smuts that he was anxious to recover the animals feeding amongst the wagons, to which end he had a few minutes previously sent Field-Cornet Van der Berg with twenty-five men to clear the kopje overlooking the camp by a surprise attack from the rear. He had ordered them to ride round behind some other kopjes that screened the view.

I had now ridden my mule for upwards of a thousand miles. He was a willing animal, but with his shambling gait and long stride a mule at best makes a tiring mount, and I yearned for the easier seat of a horse. Another man on the staff, Martin Brink, had also been on a mule for months past, and was equally anxious for a change, so we decided to overtake the attacking party in the hope of getting a troop-horse or two. We ran down, and, mounting, followed the tracks made by Van der Berg's men as fast as we could go. He had led them with skill, for nowhere was their route visible from the kopje, and when, after a breathless gallop, we raced round the corner of a ridge into the open, we found that he had taken the soldiers by surprise and that he and his men had reached the foot, and were climbing up under a ragged rifle-fire, without having sustained any visible loss. By the time we joined them the affair was as good as over. A shot or two was loosed, but in a few seconds the last of the soldiers stood up to surrender. It had, however, been an expensive little fight. Alouin Weber, an ex-Transvaal artillery officer, and two more men lay dead, and Field-Cornet Van der Berg and another were badly wounded, while several soldiers were killed and three or four wounded, out of the dozen or so who had been holding the post.

In any case, now that the kopje was in our hands, it was possible to make our way down to the spruit, on the opposite bank of which stood the burning wagons, so, leaving their friends to attend to the wounded, the rest of us lost no time in descending the slope and jumping into the spruit. We ran along the sandy bottom until we could peer over at the camp, a stone's throw away. Then we climbed out and rushed for the horses that were nosing the fodder-strewn ground. When the troops from the distant farmhouse saw us running amongst the wagons, they opened fire, but we were not to be denied. My first effort was to insure myself against further mule-riding, and in three successive raids I brought away three good horses with saddles and holsters complete. I hurried each into the shelter of the spruit, and ran out again for the next. The other men were just as busy, and luckily no one was hit. As soon as I had secured my horses, I went back for other portable property, for several of the wagons and their loads were only half burnt, while some were scarcely damaged at all, and there was much useful loot still to be had. In dodging among the smouldering wagons I came on a fully laden scotch-cart that had been overlooked in the dark. It was quite intact, and, as the firing from the farmhouse was increasing, I seized a large portmanteau and shovelled into it all that I could find in the way of books, papers, boots and clothing, including some Bank of England notes, and then dragged it over the ground to the spruit.

I found that most of it belonged to Colonel Dorran, who had commanded the convoy, and that amongst his papers were the records of the Court Martial of Commandant Scheepers, at which he had presided. We had heard already that this well-known guerrilla leader had been captured and executed in the Midlands some months before for alleged train-wrecking.

After a hurried inspection of my new property, I distributed my haul evenly on my three horses and my mule, and rode back to General Smuts very pleased with the morning's work, for, no longer a ragged muleteer, I was now better horsed, shod, and equipped than at any time of the war.

Soon after this the English troops sent off their gun and began to retire southward, abandoning a large number of horses and mules that had broken away, and were roaming about the veld.

General Smuts and Commandant van Deventer decided not to pursue the retreating column, for, even if we captured them, we should only have to let them go again, and we had done so well in horseflesh that it did not seem worthwhile to go after them. We were now free to revisit the camp unmolested, and, in addition to hundreds of animals, the men recovered a considerable quantity of ammunition, saddlery, etc, and, most valuable of all, many cases of horse shoes and nails. Five or six soldiers lay dead in the camp, and, when some of us rode up to the farmhouse where their main body had been, we found twenty or thirty wounded who had been left there in charge of a military doctor, several of them very badly injured. At the request of the Medical Officer I rode round to shoot the wounded horses and mules standing about the house, some with broken legs, others with blood dripping from their flanks, for, with no one to look after them, it was best to put them out of their misery. One of the horses I had taken from the camp was a beautiful little dark-grey Arab mare with a coat like velvet and nimble as a goat. I was mounted on her when I rode to the farmhouse, and here her former owner, a wounded officer named Chapman, lying on a stretcher outside, recognised her, and offered to buy her back from me for £65. He said her name was 'Jinny' and that she was the best horse in the country. As money was of no use to me, and I knew a good horse when I saw one, I refused to sell, but I promised to look after her and treat her well.

The commando spent the night at the other little farmhouse, where we had first found van Deventer's wounded, and here we buried our dead at sunrise next day. The bodies had been placed ready on a wagon, and, not knowing this, I spent the night under it, and, waking in the morning, found myself clotted with blood that had oozed through the planking overhead.

At the funeral General Smuts made a moving speech. He pointed out that among the dead were a Transvaaler, a Freestater, and a Colonial, all parts of South Africa being thus represented in the common sacrifice for liberty. When the ceremony was over I was ordered to ride to the place twenty miles away to which our wounded had been taken, to see that all was well. I found most of the men fairly comfortable, although there were several bad cases. One was a Colonial who had been shot through the stomach, and the woman of the house asked me to have a look at him as his side was inflamed. While she and I were examining the wound, he gave a deep groan and died without speaking. A wagon-driver helped me to bury him. We dug a hole beside the threshing-floor, and as we knew no funeral service, we simply carried him by the shoulders and knees, laid him in the grave, covered him with earth, and left him. While I was at this farm we saw forty or fifty strange horsemen approaching from the north, and there was some alarm at first amongst the wounded, as we could not make out who they were. I fetched my horse and rifle and rode in their direction, until I was close enough to see that they were not British. They proved to be the survivors of a portion of the commando that General Smuts had left behind on his way through the Free State the year before, because their horses were too worn out to go on. He had placed Field-Cornet Dreyer in charge, with orders to follow later, when the condition of their animals permitted, and the faithful band had carried out these instructions to the letter. As soon as possible they started south in our tracks, and, after many trials and dangers, this remnant had come through. Among them was the Reverend Mr Kriel, with whom my brothers and I had quarrelled at Warm Baths in December, 1900.

In spite of his religious bigotry, he was a stout-hearted old man, whom I learned to respect. When they heard that General Smuts was in the district, they were so anxious to see him that they wanted to go off at once, but I told them to wait, as I knew that the General was coming our way, and he arrived that evening with van Deventer and his commando and there was great rejoicing on both sides.

Ever since General Smuts had gone to Kakamas in December, Commandant Bouwer with his commando had remained down on the plains near the Olifants River beyond van Rijnsdorp, and I was now sent to find them. I gave away my mule, but took all three of my newly acquired horses, loaded with my loot from the camp. I reached van Rijnsdorp in three days, going via Nieuwoudsville, and thence down the mountain pass to the country below. I found Bouwer in van Rijnsdorp, and most of his men camped along the True-true River not far off. They were the more pleased when I told them of van Deventer's success, because they had suffered an unpleasant reverse the previous morning.

A week before a Colonial named Lemuel Colaine had turned up amongst them with a tale that the English had put him in prison at Clan-William on a false charge of high treason. He said that he had escaped over the wall one night and had come in revenge to take up arms. Believing his story, they gave him a rifle and he joined the commando.

Colaine, however, was a spy in British pay, and, after collecting what information he could, he disappeared. No particular notice was taken of his absence, as the men were constantly riding off to visit farms, or look up friends at distant outposts, and it was thought that he had done the same; but the commando had a rude awakening when a body of English horse, with Colaine riding at their head, fell upon them at dawn, killing and wounding seventeen men, including my young friend Michael du Preez.

The attacking force took our men so completely by surprise that the troopers rode through the camp using their swords, and got away safely on the other side before our men could recover their wits. All were fierce in their denunciation of Colaine's treachery, and hoped that he would fall into their hands. And later Nemesis ran the right man to earth for once.

Meanwhile Bouwer was smarting under this setback, for not only had he lost good men, but the British were following up their success by an advance in force, with the object of retaking van Rijnsdorp, which we had come to regard as our headquarters, for it was the only town in South Africa still in Boer hands.

I remained with Bouwer overnight in the threatened village, and, as his scouts reported next morning that a strong column of English horsemen was pushing forward, he decided to retire northwards to the mountains until reinforcements could reach him.

I went out to watch the enemy movements with a party, among them being my old friends Nicolas Swart and Edgar Duncker, the former with his arm still in a sling, while the latter had his shattered hand in splints, and a pillow strapped to his saddle to ease his wounded thigh, for the sound of rifle-fire was an irresistible attraction to these two, and they refused to remain behind when they heard shots beyond the town. After going forward for a mile or two, we saw a long column of horsemen coming up from the direction of the Olifants River, their scouts thrown forward on a wide front, and we were soon engaged in a running fight, which continued until they pressed us back through the streets into the open country, where we took to our heels, to catch up with Bouwer's main body making for the mountains. In the course of one of these skirmishes, Duncker, riding beside me, was shot through the chest. We plugged the bullet holes with pieces of his shirt, and he rode on with us for the fifteen-odd miles that we had to go before we overtook the commando. He was then sent to a farm among the foothills, and completely recovered in a few weeks. The English contented themselves with reoccupying our little Capital and came no farther, so Bouwer did not retire up the mountains after all, but, determined to recover his lost ground, he sent me hurrying up the pass to ask General Smuts for help.

After riding hard for two days I came up with him near Calvinia, sixty miles off, and, when he heard that the troops were back in van Rijnsdorp, he ordered the commando to gather. He sent word to van Deventer to bring his men to the head of the pass at Nieuwoudsville, where he would wait for him, while another messenger was sent to Bouwer, bidding him keep his men below until assistance came.

The various smaller local patrols were also ordered in, and General Smuts and his staff made for the appointed rendezvous at the edge of the *berg*.

The arrangements worked perfectly. In three days van Deventer arrived with his fighting-men, and we descended the mountains to Urion's Kraal on the plains, where Bouwer was eagerly awaiting us. This was the first time that our entire original commando had been reunited since parting under the Zuurbergen, and there was great cheering and handshaking when we rode up. That night our whole force marched out, intending to attack van Rijnsdorp at daybreak, but when it grew light we found that the English troops had been withdrawn to a place called Windhoek, ten miles back, which was being turned into a fortified camp, so we lay over in the recovered village until dark. General Smuts had decided to attack Windhoek at dawn the next morning, but I missed the fight, for I was not told of what was pending, and was sent off at sunset with a message to a post stationed towards the Olifants. I arrived after midnight, and spent the night with the picket. At dawn I was in the saddle on the return journey, and, as I rode towards van Rijnsdorp, I heard distant rifle-fire, and hurried towards it.

As I approached, the firing grew heavier for a while, and then died down altogether, so that I knew one side had been worsted. Then I came on Commandant van Deventer huddled on the ground before his horse, badly wounded and in great pain. Blood was pouring from a bullet-wound in his throat, and his tongue was so lacerated that he could not speak. Two men with him told me that the fight was over, and that the English camp at Windhoek had been captured. I galloped on, and met about a hundred disarmed soldiers, marching across the veld without their boots. They said our men had ordered them to find their way back to Clan-William, fifty miles away.

In a few seconds I reached the scene of the action. General Smuts had surrounded the camp at daybreak, and, after a sharp fight, had overwhelmed it, killing and wounding many, and capturing the rest, about two hundred in number. He had not come off lightly either, having lost five men killed and sixteen wounded, but he had taken wagons, horses, arms and ammunition, and he had re-established his hold on these parts. As I rode through the camp I found Nicolas Swart lying on the ground apparently dead. A bullet had struck him in the chest and had traversed the length of his body, emerging at his left thigh, showing that he must have been bending forward when he was hit. His face was so pale that I thought him dead, so I went to one of the wagons in search of something to throw over his body, but when I came back his eyes were open, and he asked me in a whisper for a drink of water, which I gave him from my bottle. We carried him into the shade of a wagon, and roughly bandaged his wounds. As we could do nothing further for the moment, I left him, in order to look around the rest of the captured convoy now being ransacked by the men. It was parked around the dwelling-house in which the troops had made their last stand, and, seeing Wyndell of the 'Rijk Section', I went to tell him about Nicolas. He had shared in the attack, but did not know that Nick was wounded, and he said we must search the house for pillow-slips or sheeting for better bandages. As we went through the rooms, strewn with upturned chairs, etc, in the hand-to-hand fighting, we saw a man in civilian clothing crouched under the arched fireplace in the kitchen. I thought it was the owner of the farm, not yet recovered from his fright, but when I drew Wyndell's attention to him he exclaimed, 'By God! It's Colaine!' I did not know Colaine, but Wyndell dragged him from the house, shouting to the men outside to come and see who was here, and soon dozens of angry men were muttering threats and curses at the wretched spy. He was a man of about forty-five, in appearance a typical back-veld Boer, with flowing beard and corduroys. He was brave enough now, for when the men fiercely assured him of his certain fate he shrugged his shoulders, and showed no sign of fear. Commandant Bouwer came up while we were crowding round, and ordered two men to guard him until General Smuts was notified.

Wyndell and I, having found some linen, went back to look for Nicolas, but found him gone, and were told that he had been loaded on a mule-wagon with other casualties, for removal to another farm.

As I was well found in horses and equipment since the Middelpost affair, the present convoy did not much interest me, but I collected some newspapers and books, and, leaving the men at their looting, I prepared to ride down to the farm known as Aties, belonging to old Isaac van Zijl, the local member of Parliament, where General Smuts was said to be. But first I went to see who were killed, and was sad to find among them young Martin Wessels, a school-friend who had spent many of his holidays with my brothers and myself in the old Bloemfontein days. I had met him two days before, for the first time during the war, having come on him with one of the small rebel bands in the neighbourhood. He had been wounded and captured by the British a year ago, but with Cornelius Vermaas, now also dead, he had leaped the train in the Hex River Mountains to rejoin the commandos. When I entered the homestead at Aties, General Smuts was in the dining-room talking to the owner, Isaac van Zijl, whose wife and daughters were there too, and before long Colaine, the spy, was ushered in by his guards, who wanted to know what to do with their prisoner. General Smuts had heard the whole story of Colaine's treachery, and, after questioning the escort to make sure of the man's identity, he sentenced him to death without further formality. When the General said to the guards, 'Take him out and shoot him!' Colaine's nerve failed him, and, falling on his knees, he begged for mercy, while the women fled from the room in tears. General Smuts repeated his order, but as the condemned man was being led out, the Reverend Mr Kriel came in, and asked leave to pray for the soul of this poor sinner. So Colaine was taken to a little smithy behind the dwelling-house, and, when I looked in a little later, I saw him and the clergyman kneeling side by side against a plough-tail, deep in prayer. After a while Andries de Wet of our staff was told to collect a firing party, and, as he disliked the job, he asked me to accompany him. We sent some Hottentot servants to dig a grave out of sight of the house, to spare the feelings of its inmates, and, ordering three men who were off-saddled in the garden to fetch their rifles, we went to the workshop door. Catching Mr Kriel's eye, de Wet pointed to the prisoner, and the clergyman touched the kneeling man on the shoulder and said, 'Brother, be a man, your time has come.' Colaine took the news calmly; he rose from his knees, shook the parson by the hand, and bidding good-bye to the guards, said that he was ready. We led him to where the grave was being dug. On the way he spoke to us. He said he knew he deserved to die, but he was a poor man, and had taken blood-money to keep his wife and children from starving. The Hottentots were just completing the grave when we came up, and the unfortunate man blanched when he looked into the shallow pit. Perhaps he had still hoped for a reprieve, until he saw it. Even now he tried to gain time, by appealing to us to send for Mr Kriel, to say a final prayer with him. Then he turned to me, and asked me to fetch General Smuts, but we felt that the sooner it was over the better, so de Wet blindfolded him, and placed him at the head of the grave. Realising that this was the end, Colaine held up his hands, and in a low tone recited the Lord's Prayer, while the firing party silently ranged themselves. As he came to the final 'Amen', they fired.

With a convulsive jerk he pitched backward into the grave, and the frightened Hottentots quickly covered him with earth.

When we returned, we found that the wounded had been brought down from Windhoek, and were being placed in the main dwelling-house. Nicolas Swart was still alive, in fact the jolting seemed to have improved his condition, for he was conscious and able to speak. He was put in a room by himself, whilst the rest were laid on mattresses or on straw, wherever the mistress of the house and her daughter could find room for them. Nicolas was taken with a sick man's fancy that I should remain by his side. When I tried to leave him, he seized my hand and would not let me go, so General Smuts said I was to stay, and I sat by his side all that afternoon and all through the following night. At intervals I renewed the wad of damp cloth over the wound in his chest, doing this for close on twenty hours, and soon after daybreak he fell into an easy sleep. From then onward he began slowly to mend, and within a month was well again. Of the other wounded only one man died, the rest all making good progress, thanks to the care of the women and the wonderful climate.

The camp at Windhoek had cost us more men than it was worth, but the English were discouraged from further attempts to dislodge us, and from the Olifants northwards we were left in possession of an area that we were beginning to regard as our peculiar property. So much was this the case that General Smuts once more broke up the commandos, and distributed the men in small patrols until he should need them for a fresh effort. This entailed much work for the members of the staff, who were kept riding backwards and forwards from one detachment to another, in order to maintain contact.

I, however, stayed behind at the farm, as Nicolas Swart would not hear of my leaving.

While I was here I had time to read the English newspapers that I had found in the Windhoek camp. I gathered from certain letters and articles that there were many people in England who thought the war unfair. I cut out one poem and have kept it ever since. It ran:

PEACE ON EARTH, GOODWILL TO MAN
Christmas Day, 1901

The story is too old: no more it thrills.
Pity is dead; peace is a paltry art.
How can a glory on Judaean hills
Make glad my heart?

The mighty splendours of our state shall show
A worthier creed than decalogue or love,
Let death and vengeance, launched on every foe,
Our greatness prove.

Why mock us with the thoughts of Bethlehem
And glory humbled, and exalting grace?
Celestial music fits not with our theme,
Our pride of race.

Dear God, forgive! Let other hearts be stone;
Christ's natal message shakes me like a reed.
Nor pride nor power nor country can condone,
The wild beast's creed!

At the end of ten days Nicolas was so much better that I was able to get away in search of General Smuts, whom I found on the banks of the Olifants River down towards the mouth. The sea lay only twenty-five miles from here, and the day after my return he sent word to the units quartered within reach, that all who had never seen it were to be sent to him. Some sixty or seventy men arrived within the next forty-eight hours, and with these we set off for a small inlet on the coast called Fishwater. We rode via the Ebenezer Mission Station, and towards afternoon caught a glint of the sea through a gap in the dunes. It was amusing to watch the expression on the men's faces as the great expanse of ocean burst on their view, for few of them had seen anything bigger than the dam on their parents' farms, and, as we topped the last sandhills, they looked in amazement on water that stretched beyond the horizon. With one accord they reined in their horses in silence, and then, like the Greek soldiers, rushed forward in a body, crying, 'The sea! The sea!' each wanting to be first on the beach.

Soon they were throwing off their clothes, and our trouble was, not to get them to enter the waves, but to prevent them from venturing in too deep, for they were pitching down their saddles, and, riding barebacked into the surf, shouting and laughing whenever a rider and his mount were thrown headlong by the breakers.

After a while General Smuts ordered three of us to ride along the shore towards some huts in the distance, to inquire whether any troops had been here of late. In doing so we had an amusing encounter with a Hottentot fisherman. He stared open-mouthed at the sight of armed Boers patrolling the water-line, and, seeing his surprise, I halted my horse, and ordered him in a peremptory tone to show me where the road went through. He said, 'What road, Baas?' Pretending to be angry, I replied, 'The road to England, you fool, and show me the way at once, for we are crossing tonight to capture London.' He looked at me for a moment, and then exclaimed, 'My God, Baas, don't do it; the water is over your head here, and you will all be drowned.'

When I next met Maritz and told him this story, he said that two of his men had recently ridden on to the beach at Lambert's Bay, where an English cruiser lay at anchor close in-shore. Dismounting they opened fire. Their bullets pattered harmlessly against the armoured side of the warship, and when the crew turned a gun on them they made haste to disappear into the sandhills, but, on their return to the commando, they boasted that they had fought the only naval action of the war!

That night we camped in the dunes, sitting around great fires of driftwood, the men discussing what they had seen until far into the night, and telling each other of the things they would have to recount when they got home again.

We spent two more days here, boating on the estuary, and helping the local fishermen to drag their nets. Then we returned along the Olifants River to our starting-place, proud of having our horses into the sea.

Chapter 25

The Last Phase

General Smuts now made further plans.

To the north, one hundred and fifty miles away, lay the important copper-mining centre of O'Okiep, with its subsidiary villages of Springbok and Concordia. These places were held by British garrisons, and he decided to look them up. So far as I could gather, his intention was not so much to capture the towns, as to lure a relief expedition thither, for he calculated that, if he threatened them, the British would be compelled to hurry a force round by the sea to their assistance. He would then break away south, and make for the old settled districts around the Cape. This at any rate was the rumour current among us, and the men were enthusiastic at the thought of raiding down towards Table Bay. They even talked of taking Cape Town itself, and we on the staff were cheered, as we rode to tell the outlying patrols and corporalships that they were to gather once more.

After a few days the whole commando was assembled, and we faced north on a long journey through the barren rugged country of Namaqualand.

Owing to difficulties of food-supply and water, we were presently split into smaller parties, each with instructions to make for a point in the Kamiesbergen. General Smuts and his staff travelled by a separate route to the Leliefontein Mission Station, which we reached in six days.

We found the place sacked and gutted, and, among the rocks beyond the burned houses, lay twenty or thirty dead Hottentots, still clutching their antiquated muzzle-loaders. This was Maritz's handiwork. He had ridden into the station with a few men, to interview the European missionaries, when he was set upon by armed Hottentots, he and his escort narrowly escaping with their lives. To avenge the insult, he returned next morning with a stronger force and wiped out the settlement, which seemed to many of us a ruthless and unjustifiable act. General Smuts said nothing, but I saw him walk past the boulders where the dead lay, and on his return he was moody and curt, as was his custom when displeased.[1]

We lived in an atmosphere of rotting corpses for some days, for we had to wait here for news that our forces had arrived within striking distance of the copper-mines; then we moved nearer. At Silverfountains we found Bouwer with his men, as well as Maritz and a considerable number of local rebels, but, as van Deventer's commando was still absent, I was sent in search of him.

I started at daybreak one morning on what was the longest unbroken spell of riding and fighting that I had during the war, for I did not rest or sleep for eighty hours. I rode all that day, continually changing horses (I had my two spare mounts alongside), and making inquiries from farmers and shepherds. With the help of a guide I located

---

[1]Maritz responds to this criticism in his book *My Lewe en Strewe*, asserting that he and his men had to fight hard for their lives and that had the Hottentots gained the upper hand, they would have been mercilessly killed. Shortly before, he says, the Hottentots had murdered two burghers by suffocating them with sand in their mouths. —Ed.

van Deventer by midnight, and on receipt of my message he took the road at once. I had to travel back with him through that night and for most of the next day until, towards sunset, we reached General Smuts and the rest of our force at Silverfountains. Having now been in the saddle for thirty-six hours, I hoped for a rest, but at dusk the whistles blew, and the commando started off for the village of Springbok, thirty miles away. Our course ran at first among rough hills, through which we made slow progress, and then across more open country, until, by four in the morning, we closed in on the village, the different sections moving round to prearranged posts, under the guidance of local farmers, who had volunteered to lead them.

Springbok lies about three miles from O'Okiep, which is the same distance from Concordia, and all three were helped by mixed garrisons of British troops and Hottentot levies. Each place was to be attacked in turn, and Springbok came first. Its defenders only numbered about one hundred and twenty, but they occupied three well-built forts on high ground, whose loopholes commanded all approaches, so that the disproportion of fighting strength (we had about four hundred men) was not so great as it seemed, particularly as we had to detach nearly half our men to watch Concordia and O'Okiep, in case of a sortie.

Whenever there was any fighting, the staff were re-absorbed into the ranks as ordinary privates, so I was now under Commandant Bouwer, with a detached party, whose instructions were to occupy a low neck over which the main road from O'Okiep crosses into Springbok.

Each contingent filed off quietly in the dark to its allotted post, our orders being to invest the place, but to make no frontal attack, as it was expected that the forts would surrender when they found themselves to be isolated.

No 1 Fort, which we were to deal with, was a large round-house, standing on the slag-heap of a mine-shaft. It was heavily loopholed, and the approaches were obstructed by barbed-wire entanglements, so that although less than three dozen men were holding it, they had a clear sweep in all directions, and its capture would be by no means easy without our losing a number of men.

No 2 Fort lay some hundreds of yards farther away on a low hill, and No 3 was built on rock overlooking the streets and houses at the far side of the village.

Our party of about forty strong made its way to the neck under a guide, and halted to consult. The night was black, and, as none of us knew exactly where our fort lay, although the guide said it was close by, we decided to send a small patrol to investigate. There were two Irishmen with us, Lang and Gallagher, members of Bouwer's commando, and, with the Irish love of explosives, they had ferreted out a quantity of dynamite and fuses from some outlying mine the day before, with which they had made half a dozen hand-grenades. They were eager to try these, and volunteered to go forward with Edgar Duncker and myself. Leaving the rest behind the neck, we groped our way on until we could make out the dim outline of a wall, whereupon the Irishmen drew the blanket they had brought over their heads, and ignited the fuses of two of the bombs.

The moment the fuses took, the blanket was flung aside and the projectiles went sizzling through the air, while we hugged the ground to await the result. The bombs blew up simultaneously, with a crash, and we rushed forward to find that they had exploded harmlessly in an empty cattle-kraal.

The noise, however, brought the enemy to life, for we heard a hoarse 'Halt! Who comes there?' out of the darkness ahead, followed by a crash of musketry, by the light of which we saw the fort, fifteen or twenty yards away, with every port-hole belching fire. One bullet struck the top of the kraal wall as I was looking over, and the fragments of lead and nickel splashed into my face. I thought at first that I was blinded, but I got off lightly, the punctures being only skin-deep, and I had the pieces of metal removed next day with a knife.

In the meanwhile, as the fire was heavy, we remained crouching under cover of the kraal, loosing an occasional shot, but making no attempt to advance on the fort, as we were already nearer than we liked. By now there was also fierce rifle-fire from the other forts, showing that there, too, our men had stirred up hornets' nests, and, when there was a slight lull on our front, we bolted back for the shelter of the neck behind which the others were halted.

General Smuts rode up out of the dark as we were discussing our next move, and, as it was nearing dawn, he ordered us to stay here and see that no one entered or left the fort during the coming day. Having given his instructions, he went off to visit the other posts, and our men distributed themselves amongst the rocks to watch for daylight, while I carried out a small operation of my own. Taking advantage of the still uncertain light, I slipped away, and crawled to a rise at the back of the fort. Here I searched out a convenient stone within forty yards of the enemy, and lay down to wait until the visibility was good enough for shooting. As soon as the sun was well up, I began putting bullets into the loopholes, until I had almost emptied my bandoliers.

The soldiers in the round-house tried hard to locate me, but there was a shrub screening my hiding-place, and, although an occasional bullet flattened itself close by, I lay undetected. When I had nearly finished my ammunition, I wormed my way from rock to rock until I was safe behind the slope and able to rejoin my companions, satisfied that I had given the occupants of the fort an unpleasant time. This was my birthday, the third I had spent in the war, and we passed the rest of the day making more hand-grenades, as we were determined to try again that night.

General Smuts paid us another visit, and, after watching our efforts, told us to send dynamite round to our men at the other two places, which he thought should also be bombed. As soon as it was dark we made ready. Commandant Bouwer came up with some more men, and it was arranged that a smaller party should again go forward to throw the dynamite, after which the others would make a dash at the fort.

Commandant Bouwer, the two Irishmen, and Duncker and I formed the advance-guard. Carrying our boots in our hands for greater silence, we felt our way to the foot of the mound on which the fort stood. Quietly scaling the slope, we reached the outer circle of wire entanglements, without an alarm being raised, and, as we could get no farther, we crouched below the rim, and each lit and threw a bomb. Nearly all of them burst on the roof, and there followed a second or two of dead silence, which we took to mean that the men inside were dead or stunned, but, as we were preparing to climb the wires, a roll of fire flashed along the loopholes and sent us tumbling pell-mell down for cover. The moment the explosions had taken place the balance of our party had rushed through the dark, in order to push home the attack, and they were scrambling up just as we came down, so that there was a collision, which brought us to the bottom in a heap, where we lay laughing helplessly, before we could disentangle ourselves. Despite the stream of bullets, General Smuts now came to us, and, after having climbed the embankment to look at the fort, told Bouwer to remain where he was, without making a direct assault, as the soldiers were bound to surrender sooner or later. Of this, however, there was no immediate sign, for, so far from surrendering, they were shouting strongly flavoured remarks at us, as an accompaniment to their rifle-fire, so we sat down below the rubble-heap to await developments.

During all this time there was firing from the other two forts, and after a while we heard a dull explosion at No 2, followed by cheers from our men. Soon word was shouted that Albert van Rooyen, of our staff, had breached it with a single bomb that brought about the surrender of the defenders. From what we had seen of No 3 in daylight, we judged it to be the most difficult of all, for it stood on a high rock, like a castle on the Rhine, and we had not much hope that it would be easily overcome. Before long, however, a bomb went off there too, and we heard the voice of Ben Coetzee calling out to the soldiers to give in. After a short interval there was more cheering, and No 3 had also surrendered. We shouted to tell the men in No 1 Fort, but they replied by jeers and volleys. We flung our remaining bombs at them, without apparent effect, and although, as we found afterwards, the steel girders of the roof were buckled, yet they braved it out.

As our stock of grenades was exhausted, General Smuts told me to make my way round the outside of the village to No 3, to bring back dynamite from Maritz, who must have plenty left. I slipped away into the dark, escaping the bullets, but, instead of going wide, I ran as fast as I could through the streets, past the darkened houses.

When I reached No 3, I saw light shining through the loopholes above, so I climbed the narrow sandbagged stairway, and got through the steel trap-door that gave access to the inside, and here I found Maritz and some of his men sorting out ammunition and firearms by lantern light.

The English had hit on the same idea as ourselves for making hand-grenades, and there were several dozen home-made bombs very similar to ours, only smaller.

Filling a bag with as many as I could carry, I accompanied Maritz to where his prisoners were collected at an hotel near by. There were about thirty, including the officer in command of the village. I asked him to give me a letter to No 1 garrison advising them to lay down their arms. This he refused to do. He told me that he had been obliged to surrender his own fort because part of it was built jutting over on wooden beams, and some of our men had got underneath it and were placing dynamite, so that resistance was useless, but he said that, if the men in No 1 were able to hold out, then good luck to them.

The most I was able to get from him was a pencilled note, scribbled on the bar counter, and addressed to a Mr Stewart, who was in command there, to say that 2 and 3 had been taken, and that he must act according to circumstances.

With this and the bombs, I returned once more through the streets and reached No 1 mound in safety. When I told General Smuts that I had a note for Mr Stewart, he said I was to climb up and give it to him. This was more easily said that done, for, when I reached the top, the wire entanglements stopped me, and the soldiers, moreover, were still firing. However, I stood up, and called out, 'Mr Stewart, Mr Stewart, here's a letter for you.' At this there was silence, followed by a murmur of voices consulting within, and then a gruff voice asked what I wanted with Mr Stewart.

I said I wanted him to surrender, whereupon I was told to go to hell, and there was a renewed burst of firing, which I only escaped by leaping down.

As a matter of fact, although we did not know it, Mr Stewart had been lying dead inside the round-house for many hours, and his men were holding out by themselves.

General Smuts, finding them resolute, ordered us to fling the bombs which I had brought. We did this, but they were too light, and only produced more sarcastic remarks and more firing, so he ordered Commandant Bouwer to withdraw his men to the neck, as thirst and hunger would subdue the garrison in the end. When the men slipped back I made off into the town again, for on my return journey through the streets I had heard the stamping of horses in a stable, and had decided to fetch them out. After groping about the main street for some time, I found the stable, and, striking a match, saw two fine animals at a manger. While I was bringing them away I heard a horseman approaching in the dark. As he passed I seized his reins, and brought him to a standstill, at the same time digging the muzzle of my rifle into his side. He proved to be a British officer, a Lieutenant McIntyre, who told me, when he had got over his surprise, that he had been away on a long patrol towards the Orange River for over a week.

He had heard the sound of firing as he neared Springbok, but did not know that the place had been surrounded. I relieved him of his horse, a sporting Lee-Metford, and a Webley revolver (a weapon which I had long coveted), and, as the hotel at which Maritz and his men were celebrating was brilliantly lit up, I directed my prisoner thither, for I did not wish to be bothered with him. He pretended to go there, but I discovered afterwards that he had pluckily doubled back, and made his way past our men to O'Okiep, where I had word of him a few days later, when I went in to demand its surrender.

As for the rest of his patrol, I could hear by the jingling of bits and trampling of hoofs that they were waiting for their officer close by in the dark, so I yelled at them in Dutch and fired several shots, which sent them galloping back, and at sunrise our men rounded them up in a kopje a mile or two away, their horses being too done up to go farther.

I led my three captured horses along and as I went I stumbled on Edgar Duncker looking for a shop to loot. We joined hands and going along the street saw an open lighted doorway. Here we found a room full of soldiers, with their rifles still in their hands. When we appeared some stood to attention, and one of them said that they were the defenders of No 1 Fort, that had so stubbornly denied us. They had held out for as long as they could, but their water-supply had long since given out, and they had been forced by thirst to vacate the block-house. Finding that our men had gone from below, they had marched silently into the town, hoping to find a dwelling-house provided with water-tanks where they could carry on the fight. When we appeared, they realised how forlorn was their hope of further resistance, and, after Duncker and I had helped them to find some drinking-water in a yard behind, we took them to join their fellows at the hotel. We were anxious to see the inside of No 1 Fort, so we got a lantern, and, taking one of the soldiers to lead the way, went to inspect it. The entrance was a zig-zag passage, built high with sandbags, and the doorway was so low that we had to crawl inside. From floor to roof stood a huge iron water-cistern, occupying most of the cramped space. It had been pierced by so many bullets that the water had run out, and in the end the men had been obliged to leave. On a sort of firing-platform lay several dead men. One was Mr Stewart, and another was a young local volunteer named van Couvorden, son of a doctor from Holland. Both had been shot through the head, and our guide said that they had been killed by a sniper from a rock, which he pointed out to me, when it grew light. It was the very rock from which I had fired the morning before, and this left little doubt in my mind that these two men had fallen to my rifle.

The whole village was now in our hands. Certainly we had far outnumbered the soldiers, but nevertheless it was good work done, for we had captured over a hundred prisoners, and a large stock of rifles, ammunition, and supplies, without the loss of a single man killed or wounded, and this against fortified works. General Smuts took up his quarters after daybreak in a large dwelling-house, and we members of the staff busied ourselves with collecting foodstuffs and stores for the use of our mess.[1]

As I had gone for three full days and nights without sleep or rest, I now sought out a bed and turned in without removing my boots. I slept for twenty-four hours, and did not wake until the morning of the next day, when I found my friend Nicolas Swart sitting on the bed beside me. He was almost recovered from his wounds, and had just arrived from the south. He said that General Smuts had taken van Deventer's and Bouwer's men against the neighbouring town of Concordia, but had left special instructions that I was not to be disturbed, so they had gone away without me. Nicolas promised to take care of my spare horses and other belongings, so I saddled my mare Jinny, and rode after them.

When I reached Concordia, five miles away, it had just surrendered. About one hundred and fifty prisoners were taken, a motley collection of volunteers and Hottentot levies, with many rifles, and an abundance of clothing and other supplies.

In view of this success, General Smuts sent P Mullar and myself to O'Okiep, the largest of the three mining places, with a letter demanding its surrender.

We set off at a gallop with a white cloth on a whipstick, and as the place lay only four miles away, we were soon approaching it. I saw at once that here was a harder nut to crack, for a ring of block-houses and wire entanglements stood all around the town, and inside the circle was a large central fort, flanked by a strong redoubt on a conical hill. As we rode to the nearest block-house on the plain, half a dozen soldiers ran forward, and when I told them that we had a letter from our General demanding their surrender, one of them slapped the stock of his rifle and said, 'Surrender! Surrender be damned; we're Brummagem boys, we're waiting for ye,' which also seemed unpromising. As we sat our horses, an infuriated officer rushed up from the next block-house, and violently abused us. He was an officer, but no gentleman, for he blustered and swore, and at the point of his revolver ordered us to put up our hands, while he went through our pockets. When I protested that we were under the flag of

---

[1]In his book *My Lewe en Strewe*, Maritz says the following:

'Die môre vroeg, voor sonop, kom ek om 'n hoek, en daar sit Deneys Reitz plat in die winkel se deur, met 'n blik konfyt, besig om dit met sy mes te eet. Ek vra hom of dit lekker was, en hy sê „lekker lê hier". Toe was hy nog Deneys Reitz „van hier". Deneys was so'n „traak my nie" maar dapper.'
('That morning early, before sunrise, I came around a corner and there sat Deneys Reitz plumb in the doorway of a shop, with a tin of jam, eating it with his knife. I asked him if it was nice, and he said: "Simply the best". He was then still "our" Deneys Reitz. Deneys was a real devil-may-care character, but he was brave.')—Ed.

truce, he violently told me to hold my tongue, and, blindfolding us, marched us into town on foot, to a running fire of angry comment at our effrontery in daring to demand their surrender. I answered him at intervals, until he clapped his revolver to my forehead, and threatened to blow my brains out if I uttered another word, when I began to suspect that we had to do with a madman, and held my tongue.

The climax came when his eyes fell on my horse, being led behind us. I had taken the saddle from Lieutenant McIntyre, whose name was marked on the holsters, and the fact that I had come into their lines on a British saddle, and a horse marked with the British broad-arrow, threw him into a fresh paroxysm, and, bawling obscene oaths, he hustled and jostled us along as if we were common malefactors. He was the most disagreeable, in fact the only disagreeable, Englishman whom I met in the war, for, with this one exception, I had no unpleasant word from officer or private in all the time that we were out against them. At length we reached some sort of a camp, to judge by the sounds around us, and here we were left sulkily standing for about an hour, still subject to abuse. Then a different stamp of man rode up, a superior officer, at whose approach our tormentor faded away, not to reappear. The newcomer was furious when he heard of our treatment, and he at once led us into a tent, and gave us each a cigar and a cooling drink. When, after some time, a reply arrived from Colonel Shelton, the officer in command of O'Okiep, our host personally helped us to mount our horses (for we were still blindfolded), and accompanied us to a point beyond the outer defences. There he uncovered our eyes and bade us a friendly good-bye.

The reply we brought from Colonel Shelton was couched in more elegant language than that received earlier in the morning from the Brummagem boys, but it was to much the same effect, for it said that he had plenty of men and munitions in the town, and that we could do as we liked.

When we handed this answer to General Smuts, he decided on a blockade. He said he did not very much care whether he took O'Okiep or not, as he had all the arms, ammunition, and horses that he wanted, but he was going to make a show of beseiging the place, until a relief force arrived, after which he would decide what to do next.

In order to judge for himself how the land lay, he took a patrol out within half an hour of our return. We rode forward until we reached a line of hills overlooking the town. From here we could see troops paraded on an open space close to the main fort, and it seemed that they were being addressed by an officer. This was probably Colonel Shelton, for heliograph messages from him to the relief force, intercepted later, showed that he was given to oratory, and high-flown phrases about England's far-flung Empire and the upholding of the flag.

We opened fire at fifteen hundred yards, and, although we could not see that we had hit anyone, we cleared the parade ground in a few seconds, the soldiers running to their stations, and returning our fire from the blockhouses. If we did no damage below, I drew blood nearer at hand. A large flock of goats was coming up the slope of the hill from the direction of the town, in charge of a Hottentot herdboy. When the firing started, he turned the animals back towards the English lines, so I ran down to within shouting distance, and beckoned him to drive the goats up our way, but, instead of obeying me he, bravely enough, urged them back the faster. As it would have been foolish to allow so valuable a meat-supply to escape, I was obliged to shoot, but I aimed low, and brought him to earth with a bullet through his leg. Then I chased the flock to our side of the hill, with shots from the town spattering about. The wounded herdboy crawled down to the block-house fence, and was fetched in on a stretcher, and I daresay he recovered. As a result of his inspection, General Smuts decided that it would be worth his while to bomb some of the defences. He said that by pressing we should force the authorities to send reliefs round by sea from Cape Town. Already there was a heliograph winking away towards Port Nolloth on the coast, no doubt asking for help, and his forecast ultimately proved correct in every particular, for in a few days we had word that ships were arriving with a considerable force.

We now returned to our headquarters at Concordia, and, as there was a supply of dynamite and fuses at the copper-mine, we once more set about making bombs.

That night a party of Maritz's men was sent against two block-houses that had been marked down during the day. One of them was the redoubt on a high sugar-loaf kopje, the other was to the right on a somewhat lower ridge.

The assaulting party consisted of twenty men, and as they were under Ben Coetzee, my old friend, I joined them when they met after dark. We started from Concordia, and, when we reached the spot from which we had watched the town that afternoon, we left our horses behind, and worked our way on foot over broken ground to the ridge on which the smaller block-house was situated. We crawled stealthily upward until we were challenged by a sentry, 'Halt! Who goes there?' Ben immediately lit and flung a bomb, timing it so well that it brought down a section of the block-house wall, out of which the garrison of ten men came tumbling. They belonged to the Warwickshire Regiment, and, although none of them were killed, all were shaken and dazed. We sent the prisoners, rifles and ammunition to the rear under escort, and then set out to look for the second work on the hill. It was so dark that we lost our bearings and presently found ourselves in the town cemetery.

After yet more floundering we were challenged and fired at from Fort Shelton, the main stronghold of O'Okiep, situated in the village. We retreated, intending to make back for our horses, but as we went we were halted for the third time, a voice calling to us from somewhere high above our heads. Rifle shots followed, in the glare of which we made out the block-house for which we were looking. Ben Coetzee said we must climb up to it, and we did so unharmed, for the shooting was wild. As soon as we got under cover of the rock-capped summit, we lobbed our remaining bombs on to the roof and against the loopholed wall without making any visible impression, the soldiers within continuing to fire.

Then we wormed our way down to our horses, and home to Concordia by midnight.

When General Smuts got our report in the morning, he ordered another raid against the same block-house for the next night. This time Commandant Bouwer supplied the bombers, and I went with them. We left our horses at the same place after dark, and again climbed up. We threw more than a dozen bombs, but in vain; the men within maintained an unceasing fire; the dynamite seemed ineffective, and we had to return empty-handed. Our efforts must have been anxiously followed by the rest of the O'Okiep garrison, for, as we scrambled down, there came a hail through the darkness, 'No 4 Block-house, how are you lads?' to which a voice replied, 'No 4 Block-house a-a-all right,' and there was much cheering in the town below.

Next morning General Smuts said that the block-house was of no value to us, but that, as we had committed ourselves to taking it, we must carry the work, and he ordered Maritz to go in person. With him went the Marquis de Kersauson, a young French adventurer who had been his constant associate since the war began. I went too, and, as before, we were challenged, but reached the ledge in safety. The first thing Maritz did was to stand on another man's shoulders in order to calculate the throwing distance. He then climbed down and fastened three bombs together, weighing about twenty pounds.[1] No other man could have hoped to throw so heavy a missile that length, but standing precariously on the shoulders of one of his men, he lit the fuse and hurled the triple grenade right on the roof. The fuse flared and sizzled for a second or two, lighting up the scene for many yards around, and then there was a tremendous roar, and stones and sandbags went flying in all directions. Silence followed, and realising that the defenders were dead or stunned, we helped each other on to the rocky platform and, crawling over and under the wire entanglements, rushed the entrance passage. From within we heard groans and a muffled voice, 'Stop throwing; stop throwing,' so we crowded in. Striking matches, we saw that the roof was blown down upon the soldiers. A few were dead, and the rest lay on the ground stunned. About half were Warwicks and the rest Hottentot levies. The sergeant in command, on recovering, told us they were the original garrison who had been there since our first attack, having specially asked to remain, and certainly they had acquitted themselves well. The dead and injured men were removed, also the arms and ammunition, and then we placed the remaining sticks of dynamite in the loopholes, and blew No 4 Block-house into still further ruin before we returned to Concordia.

As the other works and block-houses around O'Okiep could only be approached over level ground bare of cover, General Smuts forbade any further bombing expeditions, and contented himself with investing the town, until such time as the relief force arrived. We had captured some two hundred prisoners in the other two villages and a large stock of supplies, so we could afford to rest for the present, and the next two weeks were spent quietly. I thoroughly enjoyed the lull, and commandeered a small cottage in Concordia to set up housekeeping with Duncker and Nicolas Swart, who was not yet completely recovered from his wounds and required attention. We pressed several Hottentot prisoners into our service as grooms and cookboys, and as there was plenty of food in the military and mining depots, and sheep and goats in the hills to be had for the fetching, we lived well. General Smuts and the rest of the staff took another building in the village, while Bouwer and Maritz, with their men, lay camped in small parties in the hills around O'Okiep, and van Deventer's commando was posted twenty miles west astride the railway line that comes up from Port Nolloth, to watch the progress of the relief expedition which was now assembling. And so we waited quietly for the order to break away south, on what would have been the most dramatic stroke of the war.

---

[1] In his book *My Lewe en Strewe*, Maritz denies that the bombs were this heavy and states that they weighed about one pound each. The difficulty, he says, was to time the throwing of the bombs so that they exploded before falling off the roof of the fort.—Ed.

Chapter 26

The Lost Cause

On the surface things looked prosperous. Five months ago we had come into this western country hunted like outlaws, and to-day we practically held the whole area from the Olifants to the Orange River four hundred miles away, save for small garrison towns here and there, whose occupants could not show themselves beyond the range of their forts without the risk of instant capture at the hands of the rebel patrols told off to watch them, while we roamed all the territory at will. We had enjoyed a number of successes which the British probably regarded as minor incidents, but which our men looked upon as important victories, and all this had greatly raised their spirits. Unfortunately, while matters stood thus well with us, the situation in the two Republics up north was far otherwise. Lord Kitchener's relentless policy of attrition was slowly breaking the hearts of the commandos. We had been out of touch with them for so long that we did not realise the desperate straits to which they had come, and our men judged the position from our own more favourable circumstances. Personally, I was not quite so sanguine, for, from such English newspapers as had come my way, I had learned something of the true state of affairs, but I hoped that all would yet be well and I kept my thoughts to myself.

Towards the end of April (1902) I rode out one afternoon with Duncker and Nicolas Swart to snipe at the English posts on the other side of O'Okiep, and, as we were returning to our horses, we saw a cart coming along the road from the south with a white flag waving over the hood. Galloping up, we found two British officers inside, who said that they were the bearers of a dispatch from Lord Kitchener.

We took them to Concordia, our pickets amongst the hills riding down from all sides to hear what it was about, but the officers professed ignorance of the contents of their message, although I had an uneasy suspicion of the truth.

When we reached Concordia, General Smuts took them inside his house and remained closeted with them for some time, after which he came out and walked away into the veld by himself in deep thought. We knew then that there was grave news.

That evening he showed me the dispatch. It was a communication from Lord Kitchener to say that a meeting between the English and Boer leaders was to be held at Vereeniging, on the banks of the Vaal River, with a view to discussing peace terms, and he was summoned to attend. A safe-conduct was enclosed, under which he was to proceed through the English lines to Port Nolloth, whence he would be taken by sea to Cape Town, and from there by rail to the Transvaal.

All this was ominous, and he spoke forebodingly of the future, but, in spite of the shadow that hung over us, one item almost made me forget the darker side, for the safe conduct provided for a Secretary and an orderly, and he said that I was to go with him as one of these. I was so delighted at the prospect of going on a journey like this that for the time being I gave thought to little else.

The men were the real tragedy. They had endured against great odds, facing years of peril and hardship without pay or reward, and they still had so much faith in the cause for which they were fighting that, when the news trickled through next day that General Smuts was to go to a peace conference, they were convinced that the British were suing for terms and were ready to restore our country.

It was pitiful to listen to their talk, and to see their faces light up when they spoke of having won through at last, and I, for one, had not the heart to disillusion them, or even to hint at a result other than favourable, so steadfast was their trust.

General Smuts set to work at once. Next morning a messenger was sent into O'Okiep, to advise the garrison that both sides were to refrain from active military operations while the Congress lasted, and the two British officers went on ahead to Steinkopf, to warn the relief force collecting there that we were shortly passing through their pickets.

The day after that the commando came in from the outlying posts to say good-bye to their leader. The men paraded before the Court House, each man sitting his horse, rifle at thigh, while General Smuts addressed them. He briefly told them of the object of his going, and asked them to be prepared for disappointment if need be, but there were only cheers and shouts of courage, as they pressed from all sides to wish him farewell.

I steered through the throng to shake hands with such as I could reach, waving to others beyond, and in this way I saw the last of many good friends and companions.

We set off next day, escorted by a small patrol. I left my spare horses, rifle, and gear with Nicolas Swart and Edgar Duncker, my best friends, whom I have not met again. We reached van Deventer's commando that afternoon, where they were watching the troops that had come up from the sea, and for the last time we spent a night around camp fires. In the morning we made ready to pass into the English lines. As we started, General Smuts told me that his brother-in-law, Krige, was the other man to accompany him, and he said we were to arrange amongst ourselves which was to be Secretary and which Orderly, so I chose to be Orderly, as I thought it meant an aide-de-camp, and left my companion to be Secretary. Soon after that we saddled our horses, said goodbye to van Deventer and his men, and rode down the valley towards the English lines. Far down we were met by Colonel Collins, who commanded the relief expedition. Here our escort took over our horses, and, after singing our Commando Hymn, and firing a farewell volley into the air, they wheeled round and galloped cheering away towards their own side, to the manifest interest of the English officers and troopers lined up beside the road. With them went the last of our free life and all that it had meant to us.

A cart was brought, in which General Smuts, Krige and I were driven to a large camp standing beside the railway line, where a guard of honour was drawn up to receive us, behind which crowds of soldiers had gathered to see the Boer Emissaries. I now discovered that I had made a mistake, and that an Orderly was an officer's batman, whereas a Secretaryship carried commissioned rank. Krige was invited into Colonel Collins's tent with General Smuts, while I was led to the servants' mess, and when, an hour later, a train stood ready to take us to Port Nolloth, he and General Smuts were ceremoniously ushered into a first-class compartment, whilst I was put aboard an open cattle-truck with the luggage. However, being in an enemy camp and travelling by rail for the first time for nearly two years was so exciting that it made no difference to me where I was, and Krige and I appreciated the humorous side of our respective positions. Whenever he looked out of the carriage window and saw me sitting in the truck behind, he roared with laughter, and so did I, at his having become an officer, and I a servant.

When the train drew up at the next station there was another guard of honour for General Smuts and his Secretary, who were taken in to a grand luncheon, whilst I foregathered with the batmen in the kitchen behind. At the next halting place I underwent record promotion. There was an officer of the Hussars, Captain Barclay, who had been deputed to accompany us to the coast, and having seen me standing about, he asked General Smuts who I was. The General explained that on commando there were no social distinctions, but that he had brought me along because he thought my father might be at the Conference. Captain Barclay telephoned up the line to Colonel Collins, to say that a son of the Transvaal State Secretary was of the party as an Orderly, and he presently came to me and said, 'Young man, you are Chief-of-Staff to General Smuts; come along and join us.' He jokingly assured me that the promotion from batman to field rank in the course of one morning was the quickest known in any army.

Towards evening we reached Port Nolloth, a dreary little seaport, where many troopships lay at anchor. One of these, the *Lake Erie*, was under steam, and even as the train ran into the station, a boat set out to fetch us.

This was the end of our long roving. We stood on the quayside, silently looking back on the way we had come, each busy with his own thoughts. I do not know what was in the minds of my companions, but perhaps they, too, were thinking of the long road we had travelled, of camp-fires on mountains and plains, and of the good men and splendid horses that were dead.

With heavy hearts we got into the boat that was to take us to the ship, and the moment we were on board they weighed anchor, and we sailed southward.

In spite of our mission, the voyage was one of great pleasure to me. After years of rough fare and hard living, we had luxurious cabins, with soft beds to lie on; a steward with coffee in the morning, a bath ready prepared and food such as I had almost forgotten the existence of. All this seemed like a dream, and I enjoyed every moment of it.

We reached Capetown in five days, and were transshipped to Simonstown on board the battleship *Monarch*, under Captain Parkes, and here again we spent a week in comfort, for officers and men vied with each other in their efforts to welcome us. The British, with all their faults, are a generous nation, and not only on the man-of-war, but throughout the time that we were amongst them, there was no word said that could hurt our feelings or offend our pride, although they knew that we were on an errand of defeat.

At length orders came for us to go north. We were rowed ashore after dark to a landing-stage below the Simonstown railway station, and taken to a train that was standing ready. We were hurried through the suburbs of Capetown and then switched on to the main line at Salt River Junction, to find ourselves at Matjiesfontein in the Karroo next day. Here General French came to see us, a squat, ill-tempered man, whom we did not like, although he tried to be friendly. He sat talking to us for an hour or more trying to draw General Smuts, who had no difficulty in parrying his clumsy questions. When he made no headway, he became more natural and spoke of his experiences during the war, in the course of which he told us how narrowly we had missed capturing him that night below the Stormbergen.

From Matjiesfontein we continued our journey, travelling at night only, an armoured train puffing ahead all the way, its searchlight sweeping the veld. Each day we were side-tracked at some lonely spot till dark, and thus made slow progress. I have been told that we were purposely delayed lest, coming from the Cape where the outlook was brighter, we might persuade the Transvaalers that things were not so bad as they seemed. For this reason Lord Kitchener did not wish us to appear amongst them until matters had gone too far for them to turn back. However that may be, it took us the better part of a week to reach Kroonstad in the Northern Free State, where Lord Kitchener was to meet us. Soon after our arrival he rode up to the station on a magnificent black charger, followed by a numerous suite, including turbaned Pathans, in Eastern costume with gold-mounted scimitars.

His retinue waited outside while he came into our compartment to talk. He was anxious to bring the war to a close, for he referred again and again to the hopelessness of our struggle, telling us that he had four hundred thousand troops in South Africa against our eighteen thousand. He said that he was prepared to let the burghers retain their horses and saddles in recognition of the fight that they had made, and that the British Government would help to rebuild the destroyed farmhouses, the burning of which he defended on military grounds.

General Smuts taxed him with having unfairly executed our men in the Cape, and this, too, he justified, on the plea that we had used khaki uniforms to decoy his soldiers.

Before going he told us that we were to proceed to the Eastern Transvaal, to find General Botha, and that the Conference at Vereeniging would only take place after that. Accordingly, from Kroonstad, still escorted by an armoured train, we crossed the Vaal River into the Transvaal. We went through Johannesburg at night, and here they turned us east on to the Natal line, until we came to the town of Standerton, where we left the train and travelled by cart along a block-house line that ran straight over the high veld. At intervals there were small English camps, at each of which the troops turned out and treated us with courtesy. We journeyed for a day and a half, until we reached a point where a party of horsemen sent by General Botha was awaiting us. They had brought spare horses, so we left the cart with the troopers, and, striking across country, travelled for two days over bare and deserted plains, to the place where the Commandant-General was expecting us. Here about three hundred men were assembled. They were delegates from every commando in the Eastern Transvaal, come to elect representatives to the Peace Congress to be held at Vereeniging, and nothing could have proved more clearly how nearly the Boer cause was spent than these starving, ragged men, clad in skins or sacking, their bodies covered with sores, from lack of salt and food, and their appearance was a great shock to us, who came from the better-conditioned forces in the Cape. Their spirit was undaunted, but they had reached the limit of physical endurance, and we realised that, if these haggard, emaciated men were the pick of the Transvaal commandos, then the war must be irretrievably lost.

Food was so scarce that General Botha himself had only a few strips of leathery biltong to offer us, and he said that, but for the lucky chance of having raided a small herd of cattle from the British a fortnight before, he would have been unable to hold the meeting at all.

I inquired at once for news of my father and my three brothers. General Botha gave me word of my father. He told me that he was with one of the northern commandos, and would in all probability be at the coming Conference. He could tell me nothing of my brothers, but by asking among the men, I learned that my eldest brother, Hjalmar, had been captured by the Australians more than a year before, and that my second brother, Joubert, was taken prisoner whilst lying ill of malarial fever in the low country, apparently not long after I had last seen him at the Warm Baths, towards the end of 1900. I could find out nothing about my youngest brother Arnt.

Next day the elections were held. Even in adversity the Boer instinct for speeches and wordy wrangling asserted itself, and the time was passed in oratory, and with nominations and re-nominations of candidates, but by evening the complicated balloting was finished, and some thirty delegates elected.

Next morning the gathering dispersed, the men riding off on their hungry-looking horses to rejoin their distant units, while General Botha and the successful deputies started back for the English block-house line.

We arrived here by the following evening. The troops supplied us with food, for we were famishing, and we now returned along the block-houses to Standerton, the soldiers everywhere standing respectfully to attention as our tattered cavalcade went by. At Standerton we entrained for Vereeniging. This is a small mining village on the banks of the Vaal River, where, nearly two years before, I had watched the Irishmen burning the railway stores during the retreat from the south.

The British had prepared a large tented camp for our reception, and almost the first man I saw as we entered was my father, shaggy and unkempt, but strong and well, and our greeting after so long a parting was deep and heartfelt.

And now the delegates came in from the rest of the Transvaal and from the Free State. Every leader of note was there. General de la Rey, Christian de Wet, President Steyn, Beyers, Kemp, and many others, the best of the Boer fighting-men. We learned from General de Wet that my younger brother had been serving under him for more than a year, and that he was still safe and sound, so we were all accounted for. Although two were prisoners of war, we had been luckier than the majority of families, most of whom were mourning their dead, whereas all five of us were still alive.

I know little of the actual Peace Conference as I was not a delegate, but the outcome was a foregone conclusion. Every representative had the same disastrous tale to tell of starvation, lack of ammunition, horses, and clothing, and of how the great block-house system was strangling their efforts to carry on the war. Added to this was the heavy death-roll among the women and children, of whom twenty-five thousand had already died in the concentration camps, and the universal ruin that had overtaken the country. Every homestead was burned, all crops and live-stock destroyed, and there was nothing left but to bow to the inevitable.

After prolonged debates the Conference suspended its sittings for a day, whilst General Botha, my father, General de la Rey and others, went to Pretoria to conclude the final treaty with Lord Kitchener and Lord Milner.

On their return peace was an accomplished fact.

Of the sting of defeat I shall not speak, but there was no whining or irresponsible talk. All present accepted the verdict stoically, and the delegates returned quietly to their respective commandos, to make known the terms of surrender. I was spared the ordeal of returning to break the news to our men in the Cape, for my father insisted upon my remaining with him when General Smuts went south. When he came to take leave of me, he said that he dreaded the task of telling the men, and our hearts were heavy at the thought of the disappointment awaiting them. We shook hands for the last time, and then he, too, was gone.

My father was sent into the low country, to arrange for the bringing in of the commando with which he had been serving. We travelled by rail to Balmoral Station on the Delagoa Bay line, and from there on horseback into the wild country, through which my brother and I had ridden in search of General Beyers, earlier in the war. After two days' hard going we found the camp, and my father had the unpleasant duty of telling the men that all was over. Most of them took it calmly, but some cursed and vowed that they would never surrender. My father, although he had himself voted against peace at the Conference, pointed out to them that they should either submit to what had been done, or leave the country, as he intended doing. This quieted the more turbulent, and we started back next day for Balmoral, where the men were to hand in their rifles. This depressing ceremony was presided over by an English officer, seated at a table beneath the trees, with a regiment of troops in reserve close by. Despite his protests, our men fired away their ammunition into the air, smashed their rifle-butts and sullenly flung the broken weapons down, before putting their names to the undertaking which each man was called upon to sign, that he would abide by the peace terms.

When my father's turn came, he handed over his rifle to the officer in charge, but refused to sign. He said that although he was one of the signatories to the Peace Treaty, he had told Lord Milner at the time that he was setting his hand to the document in his official capacity as State Secretary of the Transvaal and not as a private individual, and Lord Milner had accepted his signature on that basis.

The officer pointed out that he would not be allowed to remain in the country, and my father agreed.

I had no very strong convictions on the subject, but I had to stand by him, so I also refused to sign, and was told that I would be put across the border, which troubled me little, as I was eager to see more of the world.

When all was over, the men rode off on their different ways, to search for what remained of their families and ruined homes.

My father and I went to Balmoral Station, where a message had been received from Lord Milner confirming the order that we were to be deported, but qualifying it to the extent of allowing my father a fortnight in which to settle his affairs in Pretoria. And so we returned, after more than two years of wandering. We found our home in the possession of a British General with sentries outside who forbade approach. Our household goods had disappeared, and had it not been for the hospitality of a friend we should have gone roofless. During this time my younger brother came riding in from the Free State, six inches taller than when I last saw him, and none the worse for his long adventure. He, too, decided to go, and so, towards the end of June, we went into self-imposed exile.

As we were waiting on the border at Komati Poort, before passing into Portuguese territory, my father wrote on a piece of paper a verse which he gave me.

It ran:

SOUTH AFRICA

Whatever foreign shores my feet must tread,
My hopes for thee are not yet dead.
Thy freedom's sun may for awhile be set,
But not for ever, God does not forget.

and he said that until liberty came to his country he would not return.

He is now in America and my brother and I are under the French Flag in Madagascar.

We have heard of my other two brothers. The eldest has reached Holland from his prison camp in India, and the other is still in Bermuda awaiting release.

Maritz and Robert de Kersauson are with us in Madagascar. We have been on an expedition far down into the Sakalave country, to see whether we could settle there.

General Gallieni provided us with riding-mules and a contingent of Senegalese soldiers, as those parts are still in a state of unrest. It was like going to war again, but all went quietly, and we saw much that was of interest—lakes and forests; swamps teeming with crocodiles, and great open plains grazed by herds of wild cattle. But for all its beauty the island repels one in some intangible manner, and in the end we shall not stay.

At present we are eking out a living convoying goods by ox-transport between Mahatsara on the East Coast and Antananarive, hard work in dank fever-stricken forests, and across mountains sodden with eternal rain; and in my spare time I have written this book.

Antananarive
Madagascar
1903

F W Reitz senior, grandfather of Deneys Reitz, probably in the early 1870's.

The extended Reitz family at Klip River, Swellendam, in the Cape Colony. This was the birthplace of Deneys Reitz, and home of the Reitz family for a long period. F W Reitz, father of Deneys Reitz, is standing on the far right, holding baby Hjalmar Reitz. On his right is his wife Blanca (née Thesen), who died in 1887. F W Reitz senior, with the flowing white beard, and his wife Cornelia are seated in the centre of the group.

The Reitz brothers in 1886. Deneys Reitz is seated in the centre.

President F W Reitz and his family in 1893. Taken outside the *Presidensie*,
the President's residence in Bloemfontein. Deneys Reitz is on the left. His
stepmother Cornelia sits on the right, and standing in the centre is her brother, Jan Mulder.

On holiday in Plettenberg Bay. The writing is that of Deneys Reitz.

Deneys Reitz, right, in 1899, with his father and brother Arnt
(also called Atie and Arend) outside their Pretoria home.

PHOTOGRAPH: COURTESY OF THE REITZ FAMILY.

Isaac (Izak) Malherbe with some of the Pretoria Dorp men at Ladysmith, December 1899.
Malherbe is marked 3, Deneys Reitz is marked 1, and Polly Burger is marked 4.

PHOTOGRAPH: A T B BOEKH—COURTESY OF THE REITZ FAMILY.

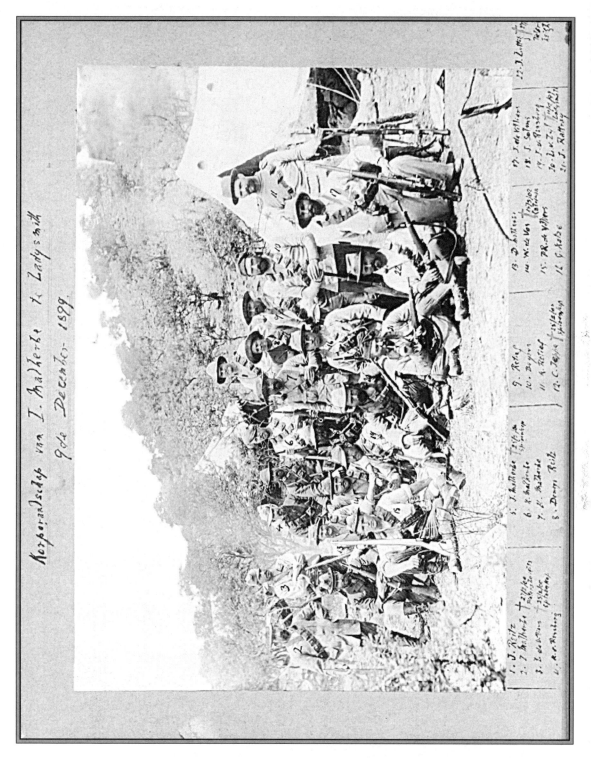

The Corporalship of Isaac (Izak) Malherbe at Ladysmith, December 1899. Deneys Reitz is marked 8, and his brother Joubert is immediately above him, marked 1. Corporal Isaac Malherbe is on the extreme left, marked 2. The writing is that of Deneys Reitz.

The rocky outcrop at the farm *Modderfontein*, near Tarkastad, where
Deneys Reitz and his comrades took part in the close combat that resulted in the
surrender of the 17th Lancers on 17 September 1900.

PHOTOGRAPH: MARIUS VAN BLERCK.

Deneys Reitz (crouching, left) with General Smuts and other comrades-in-arms at Concordia,
northern Cape Colony, in the closing stages of the Anglo-Boer War in 1902.

PHOTOGRAPH: COURTESY OF THE REITZ FAMILY.

Transport riding in Madagascar.

PHOTOGRAPH: COURTESY OF THE REITZ FAMILY.

Deneys Reitz's own map of Madagascar.

COURTESY OF THE REITZ FAMILY.

Deneys Reitz, marked 1, Manie Maritz, marked 2, and others in Madagascar.

PHOTOGRAPH: COURTESY OF THE REITZ FAMILY.

Deneys Reitz, left, and his eldest brother, Hjalmar,
after the former's return to South Africa from Madagascar.

PHOTOGRAPH: COURTESY OF THE REITZ FAMILY.

Deneys Reitz, marked 1, leading a commando into a Free State town,
probably Heilbron, at the time of the 1914 rebellion.

PHOTOGRAPH: COURTESY OF THE REITZ FAMILY.

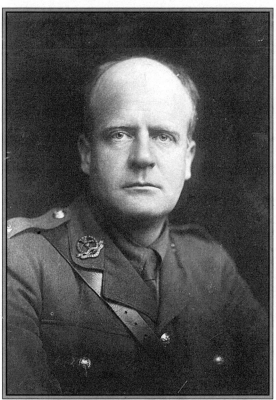

The reverse side of this photograph reads: 'My father as a major of the Royal Scots Fusiliers.'

Deneys Reitz discussing his book *Trekking On* with the Officer Commanding, Royal Scots Fusiliers, in Pietermaritzburg in 1942.

Deneys Reitz, 'adrift on the open sea',
sometime in the 1930's.

PHOTOGRAPH: COURTESY OF THE REITZ FAMILY.

Deneys Reitz, 2nd from left, during
a trip to Kenya.

PHOTOGRAPH: COURTESY OF THE REITZ FAMILY.

Deneys Reitz, then High Commissioner in London, and his wife Leila, meeting Field Marshall
Jan Smuts at an English aerodrome on 5 October 1943, Smuts having flown from South Africa.
Accompanying the welcome party is General Wavell.

PHOTOGRAPH: COURTESY OF THE REITZ FAMILY.

The reverse side of this photograph reads:
'My father at home—he didn't know this picture was being taken—I like it best of all.'

The reverse side of this photograph reads: 'My father—three days before he died.'

TREKKING ON

by

DENEYS REITZ

With a preface by

GENERAL THE RIGHT HONOURABLE

J C SMUTS

Contents

Preface

The writer of this book, as a boy of seventeen, served under me during the days when he and I raided British camps and convoys and outposts during the Boer War in South Africa.

Of those doings he has written a stirring account in a previous work, and now he carries on the story from the time he went into exile rather than submit to British rule. He describes his trials and adventures in Madagascar and he tells of how, at length, at my wife's request, he was induced to return to South Africa to take part in the reconstruction period that followed the Peace Treaty of Vereeniging.

He goes on to tell at first hand of the troubled rebuilding of our country and of a rebellion wherein so many of us found ourselves in the same position as those Southerners who stood by the Union during the American Civil War, and how, like theirs, our road was a thorny one.

Thereafter he soldiered under me in the wilds of Africa, and his is the first connected narrative that I have seen of those strange half-forgotten campaigns that were conducted by General Botha and myself against the far-off German colonies.

He concludes his tale with a vivid description of his experiences in France during the Great War, and he lived to lead a British battalion to the Rhine.

Since then he has taken an active part in the public life of his country and he is, at the time of writing, a member of the present South African Government.

For nearly thirty-five years he and I have been closely associated in peace and war, and it gives me great pleasure to introduce this work to what I trust will be a very wide public.

J C Smuts

Capetown
South Africa
June, 1933

Chapter 1

Exile

On the 31st of May, 1902, the war in South Africa came to an end after three adventurous years.

Of our family, my two elder brothers, Hjalmar and Joubert, had been captured by the British troops, but my father, my younger brother Arend and I served in the field until peace was made.

My father was Secretary of State for the Transvaal Republic under President Kruger at the beginning of the war, but later, when things went badly for the Boer cause, he carried a musket like the rest of us. At the conclusion of the peace treaty of Vereeniging he refused to accept its terms, and my brother Arend and I followed his example. Consequently Sir Alfred Milner, the British High Commissioner, ordered us to be deported.

He allowed us, however, a short period of grace, that my father might settle his affairs in Pretoria, and for a fortnight we were back in the town that had been our home.

We found our house occupied by a British general, and we could not go near it because sentries were posted in the grounds. But my father managed to realise some other properties he owned for what seemed to us a large sum of money, and, our time having expired, we were placed on board a railway train and escorted to Ressano Garcia, the first Portuguese village across the Eastern Transvaal border.

From here we travelled to the coast to Lourenço Marques. We tramped its sandy streets until we found cheap lodgings, and then sat down to consider the future. My father favoured the idea of going to the United States where, he said, one might live a free man under a republican flag, but I did not want to go there.

Nearly two years before, Georges de Gourville, a wounded Frenchman whom I had helped to nurse, told me about Madagascar, a French possession off the east coast of Africa. He said that if we lost the war we could take refuge there, and through the rest of the campaign Madagascar had lain at the back of my thoughts.

Now that we had the world before us, I argued and pleaded with my father until at last he gave in. He agreed that after all the main point was a republic, and as Madagascar belonged to one, my brother and I could go there on condition that we first accompanied him to France to make enquiries.

We were glad enough to compromise, for it meant a longer voyage and more countries to see; and when, a few days later, a German ship stood into the river, we went on board, and as she sailed out we paced the deck taking farewell forever, so we thought, of South Africa, our country.

The ship, though German, was carrying a battalion of Gurkha troops from India for some native war on the Somaliland frontier, and the day after we started there was a strange incident.

There were live cattle on board, and I saw the ship's cook and his assistants lead out an ox. Drawing down his head with block and tackle, they quickly killed him.

When the Indian soldiers realised what had happened, the cook and his companions were attacked by an infuriated mob. They defended themselves with knives and choppers, but were quickly overborne, and all I could see was a squirming mass struggling on the deck.

Whistles blew and trumpets sounded the alarm, bringing European officers to the rescue, but it was only by picking each Gurkha separately from the heap that we succeeded in extricating the three men, almost at their last gasp. Several of the Indians were badly slashed about, and when the affair was over I heard a British officer angrily tell the Captain of the ship that if more cattle were slaughtered he would not be answerable for the consequences.

The ship stopped at every port, no matter how small, to load ivory and rubber, so our progress was slow.

At the island of Zanzibar we again had trouble. There were two German emigrants on board, quiet, well-behaved men with whom I had struck up an acquaintance, as I spoke their language. The younger of them, Muller, fell foul of one of the sailors, a bullying German-American, and while we lay at anchor, the quarrel turned into tragedy. My father and I were standing outside our cabin waiting to go ashore, when the little German came from between decks. His tormentor happened to be close by, and, for no reason that we could see, slapped his face. Quick as lightening the smaller man whipped out a revolver and shot the sailor through the head, the bullet plugging into the planks between my father and me. The fellow dropped dead in his tracks, while the German flung the revolver down, crying '*Ich kann es nicht hilfen; ich kann es nicht hilfen,*' as he gazed down on his handiwork, a picture of despair. Officers and men came to arrest him, and he was manacled, and brought down the ladder into the boat that was awaiting us.

We took our seats, and before we pushed off the body of his victim, wrapped in a shroud, was lowered beside us. The unfortunate prisoner liked it very little and his face blenched every time he looked at the grim package. When later we returned from land we found the German back before us, as the British Consul had refused to hear the case. He said the murder was committed on a German bottom, and should be tried in a German court.

Next day we returned to Dâr-es-Salaam, and here again the Governor refused to act, so Muller was once more with us. I saw the leave-taking between him and his friend before he was finally put into a cell. It was a pathetic scene. Both men were in tears, and I heard the older man say: 'Comrade, no matter what happens, if it be twenty years hence, come to me. With me you shall always have a home,' and so they were parted; one man to go into the interior of Africa, the other to stand his trial in Germany. Nearly all on board sympathised with the poor fellow, and for the rest of the voyage we used to let down bottles of beer and packets of cigarettes for him to take through the grated porthole. A petition was drawn up in which we said that the dead man had started the quarrel. This paper was handed to the Captain for the court in Germany, but I never heard what happened or whether it was of any avail.

At Mombasa we landed the Indian troops, and then sailed slowly up the coast of Africa, touching at many places for cargo, and so worked our way to Aden, and thence through the Red Sea and the Suez Canal to Port Said.

Here a party of Egyptians came to see us. They said their country too was oppressed by the British, and they had come to offer us their fraternal sympathy. In South Africa we had always taken it for granted that aboriginals should be governed by whites, and our colour prejudices are so deep-rooted that we did not relish being claimed as fellow patriots in distress by natives, so the incident helped to open our eyes on a great problem.

From Port Said we crossed the Mediterranean, passing between Sicily and the mainland, and after a five weeks' voyage reached Naples, our port of disembarkment.

My father and brother went ashore first, leaving me to see to the baggage. He had brought with him a dozen rolls of Boer twist, but as there was a heavy import duty on all tobacco landed in Italy, he had asked the Captain to take the parcel on to Amsterdam for him.

Whilst waiting for the rowing boat, I decided that I would at any rate carry one roll with me, as I knew my father would miss his favourite brand. I broke the tobacco into strips and filled my pockets, with the result that the moment I stepped on land I was arrested by two gendarmes who took me to a large prison building. After a long delay, during which I had anxious visions of being lost to sight in an Italian dungeon, I was led before an officer who sat at a table, with a sheathed sword across his knees. My pockets were searched, and with an accusing pile of contraband steadily mounting before them, the magistrate and the police eyed me pretty sternly.

I was unable to follow the proceedings, but I knew I was up for smuggling, and at last I was marched off on my way to the cells.

Luckily an Italian passenger who had been on the ship stopped to enquire what was amiss, and as he spoke English, I was able to tell him. He told my two guards to return me to the courtroom, where he explained that I was a young Boer newly come from the war in South Africa.

The effect was surprising. Throughout the war the continental nations were strongly 'pro-Boer' (as it was called), or at any rate strongly anti-British, and I was released at once with smiles and handshakes, and some of the impounded tobacco was even thrust back on me, while a policeman went to fetch me a cab.

We now journeyed via Rome and Florence to Geneva, where we stopped a few days, revelling in all we saw; then to Holland to meet my stepmother and her children. They had been refugees at the Hague ever since the British occupation of Pretoria more than two years before, and very hearty was our reunion.

During our short stay in the Hague, President Kruger arrived from Switzerland. My father attended a banquet in his honour, and the visit created a stir. Huge crowds gathered in the streets to see the President go by, but so dense was the throng that my brother and I failed to get even a glimpse of him, though we received a minor ovation ourselves, for the people around us saw that we were South Africans.

From the Hague we went to Paris. My brother and I walked the streets, enjoying the sights, while my father did the rounds of various government offices to collect information about Madagascar, for he was a good French scholar. One of the cabinet ministers, (Conseiller d'Etat) M Louis Herbette, called several times to see us, and his well-meant efforts on our behalf were to cause embarrassing complications later on. We had other visitors too, including Miss Maud Gonne and Major McBride, both Irish revolutionaries. Miss Gonne had been concerned in various agitations, and was forbidden her native country, so she was living here in exile. McBride I had met during the siege of Ladysmith, as second in command of the Irish Brigade. He had left the Transvaal after the fall of Pretoria in June 1900, and was also in exile.[1]

Miss Gonne was a beautiful woman nearly six foot tall, while McBride was a brave but ugly, red-headed little man, and their mutual hatred of England was so close a bond between them that they were married soon after.

At the end of an interesting week my father had collected a sufficient supply of literature about Madagascar, from which he copied such items as he thought would prove useful, and we prepared to start. He had never been a good business man, and now, when he began to reckon up the outlay since leaving South Africa, he found that he could only squeeze enough money for two second-class fares to Madagascar and twenty-five pounds in cash, between my brother and me. We bought a cheap rifle and a few cooking utensils, for we planned, on getting there, to march inland on foot, subsisting on the game we could find, and we looked forward to a life of adventure and the exploring of foreign parts.

Therefore, in August 1902, we said good-bye to my father and set out on our journey, while he left for America.

At Marseilles we boarded the *Djemnah*, a French steamer. In crossing the Mediterranean we ran into a violent storm, during which passengers and troops were battened under hatches, for great waves pounded the decks overhead, and it felt as if the ship might capsize at any moment. It was the worst storm that had raged on these waters for many years. Nearly six hundred people were drowned by a tidal wave along the Italian coast, and a number of vessels were sunk, so we were fortunate in escaping.

Soon after re-entering the Red Sea, we passed a squadron of Japanese men-of-war on their way home from King Edward's coronation. As we came abreast, a sailor fell overboard from the ship nearest us. Our crew manned a boat, but before they had swung from the davits, the Japanese were already on the water, rowing hard for the man who was swimming far astern, and in a very short time they fished him out.

I had not even known that Japan possessed a navy, so that their efficiency, and the sight of great ironclads owned by a coloured race, gave me further food for thought.

At Aden we had a surprise of a different kind.

The latest cables were brought on board for posting in the saloon, and one of them referred to us. It said '*les deux Messieurs Reitz*', sons of the former State Secretary of the Transvaal, were on their way to Madagascar, whither ten thousand Boers, fleeing from British tyranny, would shortly follow them. Ample funds were provided by sympathisers on the Continent, and France welcomed these valiant descendants of the Huguenots seeking liberty under the tricolour.

This was the work of our friend M Herbette in Paris. Up to now my brother and I had been unobtrusive second-class passengers whom no one bothered about, but before the anchor was in the Captain was pointing out '*les deux Messieurs Reitz*' to the passengers and their wives, and they, not unnaturally, seemed astonished at our youthful appearance and our shabby clothes.

I had learned sufficient French by now to understand the drift of their remarks, and I caught such expressions as '*des garçons comme ça*', '*mais c'est ridicule*', etc, which

---

[1]McBride was executed in Dublin in 1916 for taking part in the Easter rising.

was embarrassing enough, but our worst fear was that, if similar publicity awaited us in Madagascar, it might defeat our intention of slipping ashore, and marching unnoticed into the interior. As it turned out, our apprehensions on this score were only too well grounded.

Meanwhile the ship continued on its way, and, save for the curiosity of the passengers in regard to us, we enjoyed the long voyage.

We went to Djibout, and thence coasted down Africa, once again touching at many queer little ports. At length we headed across the open sea for the Seychelles, a group of lovely islands lying some days north of the northernmost point of Madagascar.

We stopped at Mahé, and the Captain brought me a French newspaper containing an article in which the number of our adherents had grown to fifteen thousand. It concluded on a high note:

> 'Madagascar is thus destined to be colonised by the Boers, who rightly prefer the rule of France, so just and so liberal, to the tyranny of Great Britain, so harsh and so brutal. As between the Union Jack and the tricolour, the Boers have chosen the latter. Under it they will become French citizens, breathing liberty, under the other they would be crushed by British rapacity. For the Boers to become British subjects is absurd and abominable, for them to become French citizens is in the natural order of things [*dans l'ordre des choses*].'

We gathered, further, that elaborate preparations were being made for our reception in Madagascar, and that our arrival was to be in the nature of a state entry. All this made us still more uneasy, for the knowledge that our Boer followers were a myth, and that we had less than twenty pounds in our joint pockets, lay heavily on our minds.

A few days later we entered the harbour of Diëgo Suarez, the first port of call on the Madagascar coast. There was a French cruiser lying near by, and ashore we could see forts and barracks, for this was an important garrison station. Soon after we anchored, when my brother and I were below, a steward rushed down to say that we were wanted on deck. We came up to find the officer in command of Diëgo Suarez awaiting us with his staff. His name was Colonel Joffre, and he had come to give us an official welcome on behalf of the French Republic. He and his officers appeared to be mystified when they saw two beardless striplings in dingy slops appear before them, but the French are a courteous race. Swallowing their obvious concern, they shook hands with us, and the Colonel made a little speech, which was translated into German for me by a young Alsatian lieutenant. The speaker told us of his admiration for the Boers, and of his joy that so many of them were coming to settle in Madagascar. Passengers and crew stood around during the ceremony, and, to add to our discomfort, the Colonel informed us that we were to be his guests at a banquet on shore that night.

Lastly, I was handed a letter from M Gaston Doumerge, Minister for Colonies in Paris, instructing officers, officials, and residents to lend us every assistance on our travels. With this, the party returned over the side of the ship, leaving us behind in a very perturbed condition, uneasily wondering what was coming next.

However, we had to see the matter through, and as it was getting towards evening, we went down to unpack our Sunday best. Shortly after dark a skiff with two officers came to fetch us off. They took us to the Mess at the barracks, where we were welcomed afresh by Colonel Joffre and twenty or thirty other officers, all sprucely clad in white uniforms plentifully decorated with medals, a great contrast to our ready-made suits.

But we put a good face on it, as we were led round to be introduced to all present. Before the banquet started I told the Alsatian officer that I wished to have a word in private with his chief, so we went into a side room and I there explained the position to the Colonel, telling him that we knew nothing about thousands of Boers, and generally setting out our circumstances. He looked astonished at first, then he lay back and roared with laughter. He said instructions had come from Paris to fête the two Boer leaders on their arrival, and as garrison life was monotonous, they had been looking forward for the last ten days to this opportunity to make merry (*pour faire la noce*). He seemed to consider the matter an excellent joke, and amid chuckles and pleasantries advised me to say nothing more until I had seen General Gallieni, the Governor of the island, whom we were to meet further south.

The banquet was a great success, for the officers were a jolly lot, and there was plenty of good wine. The Colonel made a speech in which he spoke of the bravery of the Boers and of their love of freedom. He was loudly applauded and I then stumbled through a few sentences in French, ending with '*Vive la France!*' which was well received too, and towards midnight we were escorted to the beach by a laughing troop of officers, and rowed to the ship.

Next morning a naval officer came in a boat to take us on board the *Catinat*, the cruiser lying in the bay, and, dressed once more in our pepper-and-salt clothing, we went to inspect her. When we stepped on deck we found ourselves in the presence of the Captain and his officers, and about two hundred marines drawn up as a guard of honour.

At the word of command the men grounded arms, and we replied by respectfully raising our hats. We were then led to see the guns and other weapons, and were given refreshments in the wardroom, after which we were ferried across to our own ship, whose rails were lined with passengers watching the return of the Boer plenipotentiaries.

We sailed again that afternoon, but just before starting I received a telegram in English from Tamatave, the port for which we were making down the coast. It read: 'Whishing you hartly wellcome shall be at your arrival on bort considering you as our gests. Rosseger.'

We did not know who Rosseger was, but we were glad enough to hear that we were to be entertained free of charge, for with our dwindling resources we would not long be in a condition to sustain the onerous role of distinguished visitors.

For some days we followed down the east coast of Madagascar, always within sight of its palm-fringed shores, and we gazed with interest at the country that we thought was to be our new home.

We had taken in a number of local officials at Diëgo Suarez. They spoke mainly of heat, mosquitoes, fever, how many grains of quinine to a dose, *sacré pays, sacrés indigènes*, and *sacré* pretty well everything connected with the island, none of which was calculated to raise our spirits.

At length we reached Tamatave. The anchor was scarcely down before a dignitary in gold lace was calling for *les deux Messieurs Reitz* as he came up the ladder. He was M Dubosc-Taret, the Mayor of the town, and he too seemed staggered when he saw us. Quickly recovering himself, he greeted us cordially, and handed me a large sealed envelope containing a letter from General Gallieni, who bade us welcome to Madagascar in the name of France, and invited us to visit him at Antananarivo, the capital, lying some two hundred miles inland. The letter said, further, that arrangements for our transport were in train, details whereof would be notified us later.

Whatever lingering hopes we may still have cherished of an unobtrusive landing were now finally dispelled, for in addition to the Governor's letter, there was a double row of soldiers and citizens awaiting us at the jetty. With the Mayor by our side we marched between the onlookers, who greeted us with cheers and loud shouts of '*Vivent les Boers!*' The Mayor made a speech before some sort of public building and we were then carried in palanquins to a large hotel, the owner of which turned out to be the author of the telegraphic invitation which we had received.

Rosseger was an Austrian who had served as an artilleryman in the earlier part of the Boer War; and I suspect that his offer to us was based on the belief that we would prove a good draw for his hostelry. In any event, whatever his motives, he treated us with lavish hospitality and we found in him a good friend.

We confided our affairs to him and asked what we should do. He said at once that our idea of going into the interior on foot was impracticable, for there were great swamps and impenetrable jungles, in which we would surely perish from hunger, if we did not die of fever, and he advised us to fall in with the Governor's suggestion and go to Antananarivo. He thought we were lucky to have received the invitation and, indeed, we began to think so too.

Three days later, our instructions having arrived, we said good-bye to him, and at sunrise took the little Decauville train that runs for about fifteen miles to a native town called Ivondrona. Here we boarded a flat-bottomed sternwheeler for the first stage of our journey, through the swamps or 'pangellanes' that lie parallel to the coast.

All that day we sailed through the narrow channels that twisted and turned in every direction amid high walls of vegetation, and we frequently ran aground on sandbanks, from which we were pushed off by the native crew. Now and again a crocodile showed above the water, but otherwise there was no sign of wild life, for Madagascar is a country strangely devoid of game. The swamps, rivers and forests, and the grasslands of the interior seem ideally suited to support animal life of all kinds, but during the time I was there I saw neither antelope nor beast of prey, and except for the little ringtailed apes there appears to be no fauna, so our dream of living by hunting also went by the board.

We tied up after dark at Mahatsara. From here our journey was to be overland by the great military route which the French had recently constructed to Antananarivo, a road I was to retravel many times in days to come, but under less opulent circumstances.

The usual method of European transport in Madagascar is by way of a pole-chair carried by natives, but more luxurious provision had been made for us. General Gallieni had introduced a system of light mule-wagons for conveying the mails to the capital. On special occasions high functionaries were permitted to go in them, and we found that we had been singled out for this honour.

Early next morning we went ashore to where the post-chaise stood ready in charge of a Senegalese soldier, and we moved off under the admiring glances of the few whites and the many natives who had come to see us start.

We sped on all day, halting only at intervals for a change of driver and mules at the relay stations. Our course ran through low hills intersected by numerous streams, but we did not see many people.

By sunset we reached a place near the margin of the great forest belt that lies between the coast and the inland plateaux. Here we spent the night in one of the bamboo resthouses (*gîtes d'étapes*) erected for the convenience of travellers. At dawn we were on the move once more, and the road now entered primeval forest, where the view was shut out much of the time, though we caught glimpses of high timber-clad mountains and very beautiful scenery. In the frequent clearings stood picturesque villages surrounded by cassava fields. It was magnificent, but all so strange and different from our own country that we felt bewildered and lost. The deeper we penetrated into the forest, the more we seemed to be cutting adrift from old familiar things, and we sat most of the time in depressed silence, as the wagon hurried along. That night we halted at another relay post in the forest. We built a fire, and were preparing supper, when a French officer came out of the dark and greeted us with a '*Bon soir, mais òu donc sont les deux Messieurs Reitz?*' Here again came the fleeting look of surprise at finding the two Boer emissaries, whose approach had been heralded by telegraph, squatted by a fire and cooking their own food. He explained that the driver had made a mistake, as a mile further on was a small garrison at a blockhouse, who had been expecting us. We had already helped to stable the mules and laid out our sleeping-bags, so he agreed that it was not worth our while to pack up again, and he left us after a short chat in broken English. Next morning we passed his little fort with the soldiers standing smartly to attention, and we stopped to greet them. All that day and the next we still travelled through the forest, the road now gradually rising towards higher country. On the fourth day of our journey we crossed a height known as the '*col de frais air*', from which there is a distant view of Antananarivo and the ex-Queen's palace, standing on a high hill in the centre.

When we had come to within twenty miles of the capital, we saw a cloud of dust rapidly approaching along the road, and out of it there soon emerged an automobile containing an officer and his lady. They were General and Madame Gallieni come to meet us. He spoke fluent English, and, after a few words of greeting, invited us to change over from the post-wagon, as he wished us to drive in with him.

This was the first time in our lives that we had been in a motor car, so the novelty of travelling in one of these new inventions was an added experience. As we sped along, the only car in the island, with the Governor-General inside, was met on all sides by respectful salutes from the natives on the road.

In little more than an hour we were entering the streets of Antananarivo, and we brought up before the Governor's residency where a guard of honour was in attendance. We were taken into a large hall to be introduced to Gallieni's daughter and several officers, and when I told the General that I wished to have a confidential talk he made an appointment for us to lunch with him next day. We were then driven to the chief hotel, where the proprietor and his whole establishment stood ready to usher in such important guests.

Soon after, a sergeant of the Foreign Legion presented himself. He was a young

Hollander named Nicolas Wolf, and he said he had been ordered to attach himself to us as interpreter and general adviser. He turned out to be a capital fellow and we became great friends in time, though at the moment he seemed a dubious blessing, for it looked as if we would have to keep him as well as ourselves at the most expensive hotel in the place.

When we told him of the state of our finances, and that our Boer followers were a delusion, his face fell, for he had hoped to escape through us from the drudgery of barrack life, and now his own job looked like coming to an untimely end. However, he took the matter philosophically and, as it turned out, his ambitions were not wholly disappointed.

The following day we attended a function at the Residency, and I explained to General Gallieni how M Herbette's mistaken zeal had placed us in a false position. I told him that my brother and I were in Madagascar solely on our own account, and that what we wanted to do was to earn a living until we could advise our father whether to bring out the rest of his family or not.

General Gallieni replied that the Colonel at Dïego Suarez had already reported the gist of what I had told him on the night of the banquet, and he said he was glad that I had cleared the matter up at once. He said half seriously, half jokingly, that the French were very sensitive to ridicule, and that if the English press were to put it about that two Boer youths had hoaxed the authorities, there would be political repercussions in Paris. He added laughingly that a cabinet crisis might even be precipitated.

With regard to our earning a living, he said that need not be thought of for the moment, as he had arranged for us to go on a long journey into the south, to judge for ourselves how we liked the country. He would provide us with riding mules, and since the territory down there was still somewhat unsettled, a company of Senegalese soldiers would go with us.

Arend and I were delighted at this turn of events. We were not cold-shouldered, and what we had told the General made no difference to him; we were to explore unknown parts after all, and under more favourable auspices than if we had been able to put our original plans into operation.

Our pleasure was even greater when he said that he had given orders for Nicolas Wolf to go too. We hurried off as soon as we decently could to tell him the good news, and he fairly hugged us for joy.

In a few days all was ready and we woke one morning to find a dozen Senegalese infantry paraded before the hotel, with Wolf on a mule at their head. There were two other mules for us, as well as a number of porters carrying supplies, for General Gallieni had even provisioned us for the journey.

In a few minutes we were moving through the streets, attended as far as the river by a crowd of Hova natives, who seemed more interested in the mules than in us, for a mule was still a rarity in Madagascar. The natives call him '*Rà-mulet*', that is to say 'Mr Mule', and I was told that for a long time after the landing of the French army of occupation the inhabitants lifted their hats whenever they passed one on the road.

We had a glorious time. We made first for Lake Itassy, travelling mostly by bridle paths over the tumbled hills. We crossed the rivers by swimming. The Senegalese would fearlessly plunge into the water to scare the crocodiles, while we worked the mules and baggage to the other side.

We camped at Lake Itassy for over a week. It is a pretty large sheet of water teeming with wildfowl, and at sunset hundreds of crocodiles lie floating on the surface. We commandeered a pirogue and crew from a native village, so were able to examine the shore line and make short expeditions on foot into the surrounding country. As duck, fish, and eels were plentiful, we fared well. This area holds craters and vents that looked as if they had been recently blown out, although we saw no smoke or steam issuing from the ground.

From Lake Itassy we travelled slowly southward via Antsirabé and Ambositea to Fianarantsoa, a distance of about two hundred miles over open grassy country varied by difficult hill-climbing. This was pacified country, for there were small military posts and blockhouses and occasional French officials, and at Fianarantsoa there was a European garrison with barracks, hospital, and a church. The commanding officer was, I believe, the same man who later became the famous Marshal Lyautey. He entertained us at his quarters for two days, and replenished our supplies of rice from his military stores.

From here we trekked west for some days, until we reached a desert-like region, and then we took a more northerly direction to skirt these arid parts. There was no game to be had except waterfowl, but we saw troops of wild cattle on the uplands, descendants of domestic stock that had escaped to the prairies. I could see no difference in appearance between them and ordinary tame cattle, but they were difficult to approach, and they have to be shot at long range like big game. We were now heading towards the Sakalava tribes, who were still restless and unsubdued, and as we came among the natives bordering on the disturbed area, we found them living in a state of perpetual alarm, for the Sakalava not only objected to the French but constantly raided their neighbours for wives and cattle.

The villages along here were heavily stockaded, and often surrounded by deep moats, and it was a sight at evening to watch the tribesmen bringing in the herds of cattle from the grazing grounds.

At these places, we camped inside the enclosures at night, and let the villagers stand guard. Their method was to post a circle of men, and in the dark these sentries called out a long-drawn watchword every few minutes, each man passing it on to the next, so that by the time it came round again they could tell whether there was anyone missing. As this went on all night, it made for restless slumber, but we grew accustomed to it in the end.

On the Tshirivikina River lived a Sakalava chief who looked like giving trouble, but we went carefully, the three of us on mule-back scouting ahead of our little army, while at night we formed a hollow square with the soldiers posted, and our loaded weapons by our sides. This chief made an incursion in our direction to lift cattle and there was great stir amongst the villages.

Armed bands went hurrying off to meet the invaders, but I do not know how it ended, for the raiding party did not come within sight of us. Nicolas Wolf said he doubted whether General Gallieni had intended us to go as far as this, and he might get into trouble for risking the mules and the soldiers, but we prevailed on him to continue, and crossed the river into the Sakalava country. They soon realised that we meant them no harm, for after a while their headmen began to come to our camp, and there was no unpleasantness at all.

At the river we turned, and made our way back by easy stages to Antananarivo, after an absence of about three months, which Nicolas said was the best time he had had in his life. My brother and I had also enjoyed it very much.

We reached the capital in January 1903, and waited upon the Governor to thank him for his great kindness. Then we hired two rooms and began to look around. The future seemed none too clear. We had crossed countless square miles of good grazing ground and many broad rivers, but they were in remote parts where we would have to live like a Swiss Family Robinson, exiled far from civilisation. And here at Antananarivo the prospects were equally difficult. All agriculture and nearly all trade were carried on by the Hova natives themselves, who are a highly developed race, and there was little scope for us. My brother and I accordingly wrote a long letter to my father telling him what we had seen, and then set about to earn a living while we waited for a reply. We had only about twelve pounds left, so we did our own housekeeping, and food was so cheap that we managed on eight sous a day. My brother found odd jobs, and I joined an Algerian, with whom I went on long tours on foot through the densely populated Imerina highlands, buying cattle from the natives. He paid me ten francs a week. The cattle were shipped to South Africa, as the British Government was in the market to make up for the losses of the Boer War.

We paid thirty shillings to two pounds a head, and I sometimes looked with envy at the oxen, wishing that I were going along with them, for I was homesick at intervals. It was hard work tramping over the hills in the rain and heat, chaffering with the native herd-owners, and sleeping in their villages at night, but it kept me employed, and this was the first money I had earned in my life. I soon picked up the Hova language, and on the whole did not dislike my work. Whenever I was back in town, I stayed with my brother at the rooms we shared. We did our cooking in the yard, which caused some talk among the French people, but they accepted our ways, and some of them used to come in to exchange courtesies. Nicolas Wolf fetched us when he was off duty to spend the evening at some wine shop playing draughts or dominoes with his soldier friends. The legionaries were a tough-looking lot but we met some very decent fellows among them. I had read of their stern discipline and harsh existence, but Wolf was contented enough, and told me that he intended to remain all his life. He was the son of an Amsterdam merchant. He had studied art in Venice where he must have got into some sort of trouble, the details of which he would never discuss, so he shipped over to Algiers to join the Legion.

My brother and I also made friends with two English merchants named Wilson, and sometimes went up to see them. Nicolas could not understand this, considering that we had come to Madagascar to be quit of the British, but the fact of the matter was that in our country we had lived side by side with them for so long that to meet an English family out here brought back to us something of our old life, and we liked going there.

One morning in town, I received a letter written in French and accompanied by a bunch of flowers. It began: '*Cher aimé ami*. Humbly prostrated at the foot of the eternal throne, I take the liberty of expressing to you how much I thank the Most High for granting me a pure heart enabling me to admire the sacred patriotism of your people,' and it went on for several closely written pages to say how much the writer admired the Boers. I was called '*un fils légitime de la liberté*' and it ended up with 'every letter of the word Transvaal vibrates in my soul like a love sublime and I conclude by proudly offering you in honour and in memory of your noble country this bouquet of flowers culled in the splendid capital of this isle set in the bosom of the sea. *Totus tuus in Xto, Benoit du cordon Séraphique.*'

I thought the writer was probably some Catholic priest I had met when tramping, so I sent a note to say that I would be glad to see him. In reply, an hour or two later, there came, not a priest, but a tall young Hova native with the usual white lamba-mantle draped over well-fitting European clothes. His name was Benoit Adrianomanana, and in spite of my inborn colour prejudice we became great friends. He proved to be a man of liberal education who knew much more than I did. He gave me books to read by good French authors, and in the months that followed I learned a great deal from one who would in South Africa have been denied the elementary rights of citizenship.

In March 1903, I happened to be in town after one of my trips into the Imerina district, and I went up to read the overseas cables that were posted before the Residency once a week. They were mostly about '*l'affaire Humbert*' and the celebrated '*coffre-fort*', a sensational fraud that was causing great excitement in France at the time, but there was also an announcement that the Boer general, Maritz, was shortly expected in Antananarivo from Paris. This was my old acquaintance Commandant Maritz with whom I had seen service in South Africa, and my brother and I looked forward with keen interest to his arrival. He reached the capital by the middle of the month, accompanied by a Hollander named Jan van Brummelen, who had fought under him during the war.

Maritz came well provided with money, and he did things handsomely. He took a double-storied villa near the market place, where he lived on a lavish scale. He had brought with him from France two motor cycles, the first I had ever seen, several gramophones, and many other expensive articles, and he kept such open house that the advent of the wealthy Boer officer created quite a stir.

I asked Maritz what had brought him to Madagascar, and how he came by all this cash. He said when peace was made in South Africa, he and van Brummelen had fled north through the desert into German territory. After many trials they reached a seaport and embarked for Europe. In Paris he was lucky enough to fall in with Jacques Lebaudy, a French millionaire, who had sent him to Madagascar to buy up tracts of land. Afterwards he was to proceed to Central Africa to buy more land, over all of which Lebaudy at a later stage was to assume rulership.

From what Maritz told me, and from what I subsequently saw for myself from his letters, Lebaudy was a bit mad.[1] In one letter to Maritz he said that however much the French people might laugh at him, they would live to see in him their Cecil Rhodes, for he meant to build them a great colonial empire in their own despite (*malgré eux*).

Maritz said he intended remaining in Antananarivo for the present, so I returned to my work out in the country with my Algerian employer.

After a few days, a native runner brought me a message to say that General

---

[1] Jacques Lebaudy some years later fitted out a filibustering expedition to North Africa, where he proclaimed himself Emperor of the Sahara. He was ultimately murdered in New York.

Gallieni had arranged for Maritz to go on a journey like the last one, and that my brother and I were to be of the party.

Telling the Algerian I would rejoin him when I got back, I hurried to town as fast as I could. When I got there everything was ready. Mules were once again provided, as well as an escort of Senegalese, and to Wolf's delight he too was included.

We travelled over much the same ground as before to Lake Itassy. Maritz was so taken with the lake that at first he refused to go any further. He said this was the place for him. He would acquire the surrounding country for Lebaudy, and would build himself a house on the high foreland jutting into the water. He was so full of new schemes, and made so many plans, that we could not get him away for a long time. When at last we persuaded him to move on we found that our delay at the lake was to cost us dear, for some days after leaving its shores every one of us went down with malaria. Our expedition now came to an abrupt standstill at a native village perched on a hill, and here we lay for the next fortnight in various stages of the disease. Maritz's previous enthusiasm evaporated, and he spent most of his time cursing Madagascar and all its works. When he was sufficiently recovered to get about, he said he had had enough, and was returning to Antananarivo. Most of us were so weak that we could scarcely sit our saddles, but we made our way slowly back, a miserable crew, and by the end of April were home once more.

Chapter 2

Hard Times

We found several new companions awaiting our arrival. Robert de Kersauson, a young French marquis who had soldiered with Maritz through the Boer War, was here, and a South African named Jan van Zyl had come up to the capital with his wife and infant daughter from the coast, where he had been growing rice. De Kersauson, on reaching France after the peace of Vereeniging, was conscripted into the French Army, and knowing that Maritz was in Madagascar, obtained permission to be stationed there.

Maritz was illiterate and cruel, but he had so much power over men that during the war he had been blindly obeyed even by men as undisciplined as are we South African Dutch, and now here were van Brummelen, a Hollander, and de Kersauson, a French aristocrat, both come to the ends of the earth in order to be with this ex-Boer policeman. He was a short, dark-complexioned man of about thirty. His physical strength was enormous, and he was difficult to get on with. The slightest opposition brought him raging to his feet, and since we knew that he had killed one of his followers in the war with a single blow of his fist, we did not often cross him.

After our return from the south, he settled down to spend his money, for he was an extravagant man who must buy everything he saw, and I returned to purchasing cattle.

I had recurrent attacks of malaria, but was well enough to get about. The state of my brother's health, however, was alarming. He grew so thin and worn that I was anxious about him, and determined to get him out of the country before it was too late. We had just heard from my father. He was in Texas and he wrote to say that, in view of what we had reported to him, we should leave the island, and endeavour to make our way to the States. He was troubled at having no money to send us, and seemed much affected at the thought of our being stranded penniless on the far side of the world.

I felt that as there was not enough cash on hand for both of us to leave, my brother must take what there was and depart. He would not hear of it, but as he was too weak to argue, I hired a push-push and packed him into it with his few belongings, and sent him to the coast. I gave the two natives who relayed him instructions to see him safely on the pangellane boat at Mahatsara, and I wired to Rosseger at Tamatave to meet him. He reached there in a serious condition, but managed later on to ship steerage to Mauritius, and he wrote to me from there. His money was finished, but he was at work, and I heard no more until I returned to South Africa long after. Once he was gone, I continued with the Algerian. I felt lonely without my brother, but my time was fully occupied with our travels among the hills, and I worked at night on a journal of the Boer War that I had begun.[1]

One morning, while returning to Antananarivo, I had a fresh idea. I passed a sort of country estate, and noticed thirty or forty ox-carts abandoned in an enclosure. On making enquiries, I was told that they were the property of two Port Louis creoles, who had tried to run a transport service to the coast. The venture had failed and the carts were laid up where I saw them. I had often watched the long files of native porters coming up with loads from Mahatsara, and had wondered why vehicles were not used instead, but was told that several transport concerns had tried it unsuccessfully, as ox-drawn traffic could not compete with low-paid native labour.

But I thought I knew better. It seemed to me that the previous failures were due to lack of experience in handling oxen, and I got Maritz's Hollander, Jan van Brummelen, to support me.

We searched out the creoles, and suggested that they should restart their convoy with us as overseers. In the end, the two old fellows said they had lost so much money over the business already that they might as well risk some more, and they agreed to equip about thirty carts with the necessary trek oxen and gear. They were to pay us fifty centimes a kilo for all goods brought up from the sea, so we signed a contract, and after I had taken leave of my Algerian friend, we set about our preparations.

Our first task was to collect the necessary animals. Trained draught oxen were unprocurable and the creoles only had a few left from their former experiment, so we had to break in the requisite number from a large herd owned by them. It was hard work. For six weeks we toiled day after day in the blazing heat, varied by rains that brought on bouts of fever, but at last we had some thirty pairs in trim, after which we had to shoe them all. Maritz took a lion's share in the work, for he had nothing to do with his time. He came out each day, and his immense strength was of great assistance. Malagache oxen are on the small side, but so savage and untamed that we had to carry heavy cudgels to fend off their rushes, and we did not always go

---

[1] *Commando: A Boer Journal of the Boer War*, by Deneys Reitz.

unscathed. On one occasion an ox gored Maritz. He felled the animal with his bludgeon, and it never moved again. Another time when he was charged, he flew into one of his ungovernable furies, and seizing the ox below the belly, lifted him bodily from the ground and hurled him yards away. The sight of this feat and of his towering rage was too much for the natives who were helping us. With one accord they threw down ropes or whatever else they had in their hands, and fled for the bush, shouting '*vaza abdalla—vaza abdalla*,' the white man is mad—the white man is mad, and we had considerable difficulty in getting them to return to their work.

The oxen being ready, we had to enlist native drivers, and as I spoke the Hova language, this became my work, a fact which involved me in serious trouble later on. As headman or '*commandeur*' I appointed a Hova named Ramamoens. My first acquaintance with him was due to a letter which he had written me in English some time before. It was headed '*Privet,* I only', and then:

> 'Sir, I have heard your design to establish in Madagascar, and that has urged me to bring you some old men well known in mineral and metal matters. A little after, which will not linger, I will show you a concession rich and auriferous. I have also heard that you have been west of the lac Itassy and I am ready with others living there, who are chiefly respectable, to say can you possibly get a permission from the governor to hunt cattles in this region. In means of enriching this is in the second class. I can assure you more than 1 000 men to furnish the hunt, and in three months will have gains (over the spent) 1 000 bisons or 1 100.
>
> Ramamoens. Agent of the Chiefs.'

He followed up this epistle by a personal visit, bringing large pieces of rock-crystal, which he said were diamonds, and ore samples which he said were heavy with gold from the rich and auriferous concession. He was such a plausible rogue and his efforts at selling me a 'gold-brick' were so transparent and so cheerfully made, that I set him to work collecting a crew of drivers for me. We enlisted chiefly Sakalava bourjanes, as they are excellent cattlemen. They are good-natured, but terribly lazy, and they hold strange beliefs about ghosts and spirits that make it hard to understand their ways.

At long last we were ready. As a trial, we inspanned the whole convoy and rehearsed it around the big square below Antananarivo, and hundreds of natives flocked to see what we were doing.

Next day we loaded a cargo of rice for the coast, and started off on difficult times.

We had twenty-eight transport carts, and a twenty-ninth, somewhat larger than the rest, for sleeping quarters. The road from Antananarivo to Mahatsara is a good one, but it was built for infantry columns and not for ox transport. Throughout its length of two hundred miles it is forever climbing up steep mountain slopes, or dropping down sharp gradients, which require ceaseless vigilance when dealing with clumsy natives and half-wild oxen.

As a rule, we did the journey to Mahatsara and back in about sixteen days. At Mahatsara we loaded wine and meal for the French troops, and downward we carried rice. It rained with tropical violence every other day, so both Jan and I went down with fever regularly once or twice a week. Much of the way led through dank and gloomy forests, our food was rice and brêdi (a shrub growing in the glades), with a rare piece of meat purchased at some native village. The work was gruelling, for the oxen were eternally getting out of hand, upsetting the carts, or breaking their tackle, and we had to walk up and down the convoy all day to supervise.

We travelled in the heat of the day, as the Sakalava resolutely refused to budge after dark, for fear of ghosts. If we happened to be on the road at nightfall, they would squat down at once, refusing even to unyoke the oxen, and no amount of persuasion had any effect on them, so great was their terror of the unseen.

I do not remember how many trips we made to the coast and back, for I kept few notes, but these were months of bitter hardship. Yet with it all there was a fascination about the life, and I grew almost to like the long road and forest-clad mountains, and the great rivers. At such times as we were at Antananarivo, awaiting loads or refitting, Jan and I took turn and turn about in staying with Maritz, one of us remaining to look after the convoy while the other had a rest at his villa.

Maritz never learned a word of French or of Hova while he was on the island, and he retained all the prejudices with which he had arrived. Once when I was at his house my friend Benoit Adrianomanana called. He and I frequently met, but knowing that Maritz classed African negroes, Hovas, Japanese, Indians and all coloured races as 'niggers', I had thus far succeeded in keeping the two apart, though Benoit had several times expressed a desire to pay his respects to '*M le Général*'. On this occasion there came a knock at the front door and Benoit walked in. Maritz bridled at once, and said roughly: 'Ask the bl——y nigger what he wants.' I manoeuvred Benoit into a chair before he tried to shake hands, as I knew that this would cause an explosion. Benoit then said he had intended to bring his wife to call on the General, but as she was ailing he would bring her another time. Maritz's face was a picture when I translated this to him, but at my whispered request he contained himself. I told Benoit that *M le Général* was very glad to see him. He replied that I was to tell the General he hoped some day to make a pilgrimage to visit the sacred battlefields of the Transvaal. I thought this at any rate would please Maritz, but he growled angrily: 'Tell the d——d Kaffir if he sets foot in the Transvaal he will have to carry a pass.' I suitably toned this down, but Benoit realised that all was not well, for he took his leave and did not come to the house again, although he visited me at the convoy whenever I was up.

On our second coastward journey, we had an alarming experience. Some of the larger rivers are provided with '*bacs*' or pontoons, on which goods are ferried across. At the Mangoro River Jan van Brummelen and I decided to swim the oxen through to save their passage money. The French soldier in charge warned us that the river was full of crocodiles, but we thought they would be too scared to come near the pontoon, so, after manhandling the carts over the ferry, we drove the oxen into the water and they were soon making for the far side. One of the animals, however, was blind, and kept swimming against the current. Fearing he would tire and drown, I swam out and, seizing one of his horns, headed him after the rest, who by now were streaming for the opposite bank. As I turned back I heard a bellow of terror and, looking round, saw the blind ox disappear in a swirl of foam, pulled under by a crocodile within a few yards of me.

On this trip I had unexpected news of my elder brother Joubert, who had been captured by the British in South Africa three years before. I knew that he had been sent to Bermuda as a prisoner of war, but I did not know how he had fared since then. One night van Brummelen and I were cooking our supper in the forest, when a man came clattering down in the dark through the trees. He reached the road and without stopping to see who we were, scattered our fire with a vigorous kick that sent pot and kettle flying. He was a French colon, and when I protested furiously, he said he thought we were natives using up the bundles of firewood which he had stacked for the Antananarivo market. After helping to rebuild our fire, he sat down to talk, and when he heard my name, said he had recently met a brother of mine on a plantation at Grande Terre, on the west coast of Madagascar. I thought my brother Arend had somehow or other gone there, but found on further questioning that it was my brother Joubert, and I could not understand how he came to be on the island. I only learned years later that on his release from Bermuda he had made his way to Europe, and hearing that my younger brother and I were in Madagascar, had worked his passage thither in the hope of finding us. Through lack of money and fever he was forced to leave his ship at Majunga, and he was still living on a plantation long after I had gone.

As time went on, we found that things were not running quite smoothly with Maritz up at the capital. Jacques Lebaudy's remittances had grown irregular, and at times ceased altogether. During these periods of dearth Maritz was hard pressed for money, while at other times he entertained all comers, for he had no idea of economy. I have known him buy an expensive suite of mahogany furniture one day and borrow five francs from me the next, and I have been at his house when he had a chef and a troop of native servants, and also when he and I did our own cooking in our shirt-sleeves on the kitchen stove.

Meanwhile our relations with the two creoles were unsatisfactory. We were bringing up heavy loads from the coast each trip, for which substantial payments were due to us, but we could never get a settlement, and were fobbed off with excuses. Instead of being paid in full we received only sufficient money to buy food for ourselves and to keep the natives quiet, but never enough to bring their wages or our own up to date. The result was that the boys were growing restive and it was only because Ramamoens and I knew how to handle them that they remained with us at all. However, we lived in hopes, for the two partners always promised us that on our next return we would receive full pay, and as we scarcely had any alternative, we continued on the road.

We had several accidents. On one journey we lost two carts and loads in one of the mountain passes. Both drivers went too near the edge, and the vehicles toppled over. Luckily the trek ropes broke and the oxen were saved, but carts and cargo went crashing down the slopes, and what was left at the bottom was not worth salvaging. Another time, I got into trouble with the authorities. At a place called Moramanga, Jan and I spent the evening with a *sous-officier* at the blockhouse, and Ramamoens thought I was away for the night. Returning unexpectedly, I found him rolled up in my sleeping-bag in our cart, and here was my fine gentleman reading a Hova newspaper by lantern light. I hauled him out and gave him a sound thrashing. He reported me next morning, and I had to appear before M Compérat, the *Administrateur*, who fined me ten francs, and what rankled even more, he read me a letter on how to treat natives. In addition I was ordered to reinstate Ramamoens as headman, which I was only too pleased to do, as he was indispensable to us.

On this same trip a terrific cyclone struck us at Mahatsara. It raged for several hours, and it blew the whole village away. While it lasted, the safest place was between the wheels of our carts, for we had heavy loads weighing them down, but all else went flying on the blast, and the air was thick with bamboo huts and fowls·and uprooted trees. One or two of our drivers were slightly injured, but eight of the villagers hiding by the river bank were killed or drowned, and many more were seriously hurt. I suffered an after-effect of the disturbance. We had an ox so vicious that I had to handle him myself, for the natives were afraid of him. The cyclone seemed to make him fiercer than ever, and when I tried to yoke him after the storm, he made a rush and tossed me several yards away. I do not know whether any ribs were broken, but it felt like it, and for ten days we had to lie up at a native village that had escaped the hurricane.

Retribution speedily overtook the poor brute, for soon after my recovery, while we were halted for the night on a mountain, he suddenly broke away and sprang over the edge of the road. We heard his body rolling down the incline until it landed with a splash far below. Not even Ramamoens would go down to investigate, but a Sakalava named Ringbar, a cheery giant who drove our living-cart, volunteered to accompany us. He said: 'Vaza, I *know* there are devils down there, but if you white men go, I will go too.' He was a brave fellow, for he firmly believed there were spooks, and his teeth chattered as we slithered down in the rain. We found the ox lying in a stream, with a broken spine. He had reached the limit of his rebellion and in the gleam of the lantern he looked at us so piteously, that I climbed up for my rifle to put him out of his misery. When we reached the capital this time, our trouble with the two creoles was coming to a head. Wages were heavily in arrear and the drivers were mutinous. They said the time of the annual *impôt* was on hand, and they would be arrested if they did not pay the tax. When I referred them to the creoles they replied truly enough that I had hired them, and that they looked to me for a settlement. I went to have it out with our employers, and I felt rather sorry for the two old men, for they were in financial straits themselves. But they assured me that they would do their best to arrange matters on our return from the coast, and we managed to placate the bourjanes, who grumblingly agreed to start on another trip.

Before leaving on what turned out to be our last journey with the convoy, I saw the last of my good friend Benoit. Early one morning, as I lay asleep beneath our cart on the outskirts of Antananarivo, I was waked by a small native boy with a letter:

> 'Cher Ami. Notre Dieu si doux vient de poser une lourde croix sur mon épaule si faible, en m'enlevant ma fidèle et adorée femme Marie Magloire, qui est morte ce matin à 6 heures 52 minutes en odeur da sanctité. Le Divin Créateur l'a reglé ainsi de toute éternité, je préfère de souffrir plutôt de murmurer contre sa Providence à jamais bienfaisante. Je vous invite de venir la voir pour la dernière fois et de prier pour son âme.
>
> Totus tuus in Xto et in Sto P Francisco.
>
> Benoit Adrianomanana.'

Not wishing to hurt Benoit's feelings by a refusal, I followed the errand boy to his house. There were already several hundred natives collected outside, and as soon as I arrived Benoit came to meet me. Taking me by the hand, he led me into a room where the dead woman lay on a bed covered with flowers and surrounded by votive candles. He asked me to kneel by the bedside. I was embarrassed, but did as he wished, and was about to mumble some sort of a prayer when I heard a click, and looking round, saw a native photographer with his camera on a tripod, and Benoit was assisting him to get a proper focus of the scene. I made an excuse to take my leave as soon as I could, in case they wanted me for further obsequies, and I did not meet Benoit again, although he continued to write to me for years afterwards.

We now loaded the convoy with the usual cargo of rice for the trip to the coast, and van Brummelen and I set off. We travelled in heavy rain most of the time, and both suffered severely from fever, which indeed had seldom left us during the past months. We reached Mahatsara in due course, where a heavy consignment of meal and wine was waiting. In order to have more room, we loaded up our living-cart as well. This was the largest vehicle of the convoy, and because of its extra size was drawn by six oxen. Of these, the wheelers were a cream-coloured pair that I had grown very fond of for their tameness and their gentle ways. They used to eat rice from my hand and sometimes, if I lay reading under a tree, one or other of them would come and with a soft low and a nudge invite me to scratch its flanks.

Ringbar, the huge Sakalava who was in charge of the living-cart, was a good-natured fellow and he paid special attention to my favourites. We started on the homeward journey to Antananarivo. All went well until we reached the Pont d'Ampasimboul, a high trestle bridge spanning a gorge in which the river ran, more than a hundred feet below.

Our living-cart always brought up the rear of the column. The other carts crossed the bridge safely, but just as the big cart was halfway, I heard the planking creak, and one of the wheels went through. I was marching at the tail, and as the wheel sank into the flooring, I jammed on the brake but it was too late. There was a crash and a whole section of the bridge gave way. I leaped clear in the nick of time, but cart, team and driver went headlong into the depths. Of the six oxen, the two remained on the far side of the gap, for their trek rope broke, but my cream-coloured wheelers and the rest went hurtling down in a tangled mass, to fall with a sickening thud on the rocks below.

The bridge length on which I had been standing was rocking dangerously, so I scrambled back to land. Then I climbed down the cliff to where the wreckage lay. The cart had been dashed to pieces with its contents, and the poor oxen were dead, their bodies frightfully mangled by the jagged boulders upon which they had fallen beside the stream. Ringbar, miraculously enough, was alive. He had come down on the tented hood of the cart which broke his fall, but his legs were fractured and he was unconscious. As I was cut off from the convoy by the gap in the bridge, and the river was too deep to ford, I made my way upstream to where some Italian labourers were at work on a steel bridge, which was to replace the wooden structure. They were kindly men, for they came down in a body and carried Ringbar to a native village near by. I did not see him again, but Benoit wrote me later that he made a complete recovery in a military hospital to which he was taken, and that he was now looked upon with reverence by his companions, for they considered that he had had a supernatural escape from death.

The Italians ferried me across the river to rejoin the convoy on the other side, and we moved forward without our living-cart and minus my beloved creams. We reached Antananarivo some days later after nightfall, and camped, as we always did, a short distance out of town. Here the crowning disaster befell us. At daybreak the chief *huissier* (sheriff) came with a dozen gendarmes to demand possession of the convoy in the name of the law.

The creoles had gone insolvent during our absence, and everything was laid under attachment by their creditors. To make matters worse, our bourjanes got wind of the position, and when Jan and I started off for the *Palais de Justice* to make enquiries, they came along with us. It was an unpleasant procession, for the sight of two white men surrounded by the angry Sakalava brought a crowd of onlookers, who followed us through the streets. At the Court House matters were even worse. So far from getting our back pay from the creoles, the Commissaire produced the contract which we had signed long ago, and had since forgotten about. One clause required us to make good all losses sustained in regard to livestock and equipment, and he said it had been reported to him that we were short of a number of cattle, several carts, and a quantity of merchandise, totalling over five thousand francs, for which the creditors held us responsible. As if this were not enough, our natives stood outside demanding their wages. Jan and I evaded them by a back door, and we hurried down to find General Gallieni, but he was away on a distant tour. We went to M le Nègre, the *Secrétaire d'Etat*, to whom we stated out case. He gave us little comfort, for he said that while the claim for loss and breakages was a civil one, the claim against me personally by the natives was an offence under the criminal code. It was the settled policy of the French strictly to safeguard native rights in their dealings with Europeans, and as I had engaged our drivers, the consequences would be serious were they to charge me with withholding their money. Thoroughly anxious, we went to seek the creoles at their office. Only the elder partner was there, despondently sitting before his desk. When we told him of our plight, he said he was in worse case himself and could do nothing for us. At this van Brummelen lost his temper, and thrusting the old man aside, began to open the bureau drawers. I assisted him, and our search yielded just over a hundred francs, a high-handed proceeding that would have landed us in still further trouble, had it become known. From here we went to look for Maritz. With all his faults he was a generous man, but we met him at the wrong season, for Lebaudy's remittance was once again overdue, and so far from being able to help us he was in difficulties himself. As a last resort we tried Jan van Zyl, who was employed by the Antananarivo municipality. We found him down with black-water fever, and his wife said she had barely enough money on hand to buy food and medicines. Everything seemed to conspire against us, for Nicolas Wolf and de Kersauson were on outpost duty in the south, and Benoit was away looking for a new wife. Meanwhile the natives were demanding their money. I went to consult André Constans, the lawyer. He agreed with M le Nègre that the claim for dead oxen and broken carts was a civil one, but that if the Sakalava laid a charge against me I would go to gaol. This was too much, so I decided to levant that very night. I wrote a letter to General Gallieni to thank him for his past kindness, and I explained the reason for my unceremonious exit. I also wrote farewell letters to Nicolas Wolf and to Benoit. Then I made a parcel of my Boer War journal and other papers and posted them to Tamatave, and I packed a few necessaries in an empty paraffin tin, to which I fixed a wire handle. Van Brummelen stayed behind with Maritz. He was in no danger of criminal proceedings, as he had not hired the natives, and he said he would remain until Lebaudy sent some money. As soon as it was dark I slung my sleeping-bag across my shoulders, and with my paraffin tin in my hand, threaded the streets of Antananarivo for the last time, until I reached the beginning of the *grande route*, and started for the coast. I was weakened by long-continued fever, but I did not linger on the road. So far as my memory serves me, I did the two hundred miles to Mahatsari in little more than a week, in spite of the rain that fell all the time. I walked mostly at night to avoid attention, fearing arrest every time I passed a block-house or a soldier. As a matter of fact, I was never in danger at all, for Benoit wrote long after to say that M le Nègre had interviewed our two creoles, and it was decided not to prosecute. But I did not know this, and I dared not meet anyone. When at length I reached the pangellanes at Mahatsara I was so wretchedly ill that I could scarcely drag myself on board the paddle-wheeler. For a few francs I got a steerage passage through the swamps, and then by Decauville to Tamatave. The first thing I did was to hire a rowing boat to the ships anchored offshore, and on one of these, a French steamer, I persuaded the Captain to take me as a fireman. Having secured my lines of communication, I recovered my parcel at the post office, went to say goodbye to Rosseger, and returned to the ship, where I went straight down with the worst attack of fever I ever had. I was delirious for several days, and when I came to we were at sea, and strange to say, Maritz and Jan van Brummelen were also on board. A timely draft from Lebaudy had arrived, and they had started by rickshaw for the coast without delay.

This was the last of Madagascar for me. I remember but little of the voyage. I lay in a bunk in the forecastle until we reached Zanzibar, and was there put ashore, too ill to proceed. I was carried to a tavern, but by the time I was on my feet again my money was gone and the proprietor ordered me to leave. A kindly clerk in a German shipping office looked after me until I was well enough to get about.

Maritz, so far as I could gather, had continued on to Europe, and the next time I heard of him we were under arms in opposite camps. I never saw van Brummelen again. I had no definite plans for the future except to rejoin my father in America, but at the back of my head was an insistent longing to return to my own country. At Antananarivo I had received a letter from Mrs Smuts, wife of my old leader, urging me to come back, and other friends had written that the British were dealing fairly by South Africa. I had felt all along that we had made a mistake in exiling ourselves, but I was not yet ready to admit it, so, with the help of my young German friend, I shipped on a Woermann cargo boat bound for Hamburg, once more before the mast. I was miserably ill, but I polished the brass fittings, and did such odd jobs as I could. The food was coarse, chiefly potatoes, rye bread, and tinned beef, and the sleeping accommodation was dirty and verminous, but the Captain and officers were good to me, for they saw that I was ill. The crew, however, were rough ill-natured fellows, who spoke a German *patois* I scarcely understood. There was an old carpenter among them, and whenever we collected in the galley for our meals, he dipped his bread in my coffee to save his own. I took no notice at first, but in the end I pulled him up. This started a fight, for the crew took his part, and one of them attacked me with a skewer, which he unhooked from the kitchen wall. I knocked him down with a bench, but the rest bore me to the floor amid oaths and the drawing of knives. Luckily one of the mates came running to my assistance, before I was much the worse, but after this I berthed with men who showed me hostility at every turn, and my life was an unpleasant one. We travelled slowly up the coast of Africa, and then into the Red Sea. Afterwards we anchored at Hodeida off Arabia, to land pilgrims for Mecca. Here there was another German tramp loading donkeys for South Africa, and the sight of a ship going homeward, coupled with the fact that I was ill and at odds with my messmates, decided me. I consulted the Captain, who accompanied me in a boat to the other ship and arranged a transfer, with the result that by next morning I was in new quarters on another ship, heading south once more.

As on former occasions, we nosed down the African littoral, touching at Mombasa, Tanga, Dâr-es-Salaam and other ports, and in due course reached Zanzibar again. At Zanzibar we took in more goods, and I paid a visit to my German friend; he put me up for a day or two, after which we continued our southward journey. At last we reached Delagoa Bay, from which I had started for Madagascar long ago. I intended landing there, but discovered to my dismay that the Portuguese laws allowed no man to come ashore unless he had a passport and twenty-five pounds in his pocket. This was the first I heard of a passport, and instead of twenty-five pounds I had less than twenty-five pence.

The Portuguese officer at the gangway refused to allow me ashore, and the Captain grumblingly complained that he was saddled with me for good. It looked like it, and I spent an unhappy night on board, tantalised by the thought of being so near my country, and yet so far away.

The following morning, shortly before we were due to sail, help came from an unexpected quarter. A man climbed up the side of the ship, on some business with the Captain. I saw by his appearance that he was a South African, and accosting him, unburdened my troubles. His way of showing sympathy was to count me twenty-five golden sovereigns from his purse, although he did not know me from Adam. He was a Cape rebel named Theron, who had fled to Portuguese territory to escape the proscriptions that followed the Boer War, and he was now living here, hoping that some day the ban would be raised. Having deposited this money with the immigration officer, I was allowed to land, on condition that I obtained a permit to the Transvaal within ten days. This was not as easy as it looked, for when I waited on the British Consul he bluntly told me that I could not enter the Transvaal, as I had refused to submit to the peace terms of Vereeniging.

I lodged with Theron on the waterfront, he paying my board, and for the next five days I importuned the consular office. But I also telegraphed to the Transvaal Chief Justice and others whom I knew in Pretoria, and at last the Consul handed me a passport through the wicket. He said he was glad to be rid of me.

My next difficulty was my train fare, and here again Theron was the man. But I made the mistake of underestimating the cost, and took only thirty shillings from him. As he had left on a journey into the interior, it was too late to borrow more, when I found at the railway station that this sum would not take me to Pretoria. I worked it out, and booked passage as far as Belfast, a village lying well within the Transvaal.

At last the train was off, and after a few hours' run we crossed the Transvaal border at Komatipoort, and, British rule or no British rule, I was delighted to see my own country again. We reached Belfast on a bitter winter's night, and the sudden change of altitude on these bleak plains brought on another severe attack of malaria. The station lay two miles from the village, and I dragged myself down the road in the dark until I reached the main street, where I saw a public house all lit up. There I collapsed unconscious on the floor.

Next morning I found myself in a comfortable bed in a pleasant room. An ex-Republican officer whom I had known in the war (and had thought little of at the time), was my Samaritan, and for the next week he was constantly in and out, seeing to my wants. A British garrison was in occupation of the village, and one evening he came in elated, to say that he had procured me the post of billiard marker at the Officers' Mess, as soon as I was well enough. He thought me ungrateful when I refused the offer, but he lent me sufficient money to take train to Pretoria, and in a day or two I was able to start. I reached Pretoria at sunrise with a fresh bout of fever upon me, which left me so weak that I had only strength to crawl to the Burgher Park, where I lay in a stupor for some hours. Later on I found myself back on the platform of the railway station with a knot of people gathered around me. Then a man recognised me. He must have set to work at once, for soon a Cape cart drove up, into which I was lifted, and I woke to find myself in bed, in the home of my former chief, General Smuts.

Chapter 3

Transition

For nearly three years General Smuts and his wife kept me by them, nursing me back to health of mind and body. During that time I slowly shook free of malaria, and entered an office to study law. Our family seemed in a bad way. My father lay ill far off in America, and his wife and seven small children were in straitened circumstances. My eldest brother, Hjalmar, having returned from his prison, was now in Holland, struggling in poverty to complete his studies, and my brother Joubert was on a fever-stricken plantation on the west coast of Madagascar. My younger brother Arend had after many vicissitudes reached Table Bay, where he was working as a dock hand. Thus, in common with thousands of others, we experienced the aftermath of war.

Nevertheless, things began slowly to improve. The British conferred Responsible Government on the two former republics, and South Africa settled down to rebuild its shattered fortunes. In a measure, I saw one phase of the rebuilding, for Louis Botha, the Commandant-General, came frequently to the house, and I listened to him and General Smuts planning the political future of the country.

I had returned from exile, not hating the British, but resenting the enforced rule of any other nation. These two men showed me that only on a basis of burying past quarrels and creating a united people out of the Dutch and English sections of the population, was there any hope for white men in South Africa. I became their devoted follower, and my acceptance of their creed was profoundly to influence my life in the years to come.

In 1908 I convinced General Smuts that I could at last fend for myself again, so I said goodbye to him and to his wife, the two people to whom I owe most in the world, and with a few law books and the political idealisms which he and General Botha had taught me for my chief possessions, I set out to earn a living.

After many wanderings I reached the little town of Heilbron on the northern Free State plains, and there cast anchor. The place had under fifteen hundred inhabitants, but it was the centre of a sturdy Boer peasantry who had fought bravely during the war, in the course of which they had suffered great losses. Their grim jest, 'my wife and children died in the concentration camps, my home is burnt down and my cattle gone, but otherwise there is nothing to complain of', was a fair illustration of what many of them had suffered, and of their unbroken spirit. Now they were back on their ruined farms, patiently at work, and among them I lived for the next five years.

There were difficult days at first, and I was often hard put to keep afloat, but gradually my legal practice grew. In the course of time I was able to build a small home of my own, to collect books, and to look around me, freed from the cramping effects of financial cares.

In the meanwhile South Africa was moving towards great political changes. In 1910 the Act of Union was passed, merging the two British colonies and the two former republics into one country, and General Botha became our first Prime Minister. He and General Smuts established the South African Party, and there was material progress and peace.

Our family prospects were mending too. My father recovered his health, and realising that under the new order he could return to South Africa without humiliation, he came back from America. He was soon elected President of the Union Senate, and once more held a prominent and respected position among his fellow citizens. My other brothers had also drifted in from their wanderings.

Living as I did, far from the centre of things, I took little part in the political developments that were pending, though I keenly followed the thread of events, and no one rejoiced more sincerely than I did at the goodwill that reigned. But this happy state did not last. The Boers are an intensely race-conscious people, and before long they began to say that General Botha's policy would lead to their being swamped by the British element.

Opposition spread, and General Hertzog seceded from us with his followers. He formed the Nationalist Party, with the object of keeping the Dutch apart as a separate entity, as against General Botha's ideal of merging us all into one nation.

These differences rent South Africa, and the struggle became an exceedingly bitter one. There was scarcely a Dutch-speaking family in the country that was not divided on the issue, and even in my placid district, tempers were beginning to rise. The Free State Boers stood behind General Hertzog almost to a man. They thought he aimed at secession from the British Empire, and the re-establishment of the republics, and to them General Botha's policy looked like a betrayal of their cause. In the Heilbron district, I found myself standing well nigh alone, for the farmers went over in a body to the Nationalist Party. I understood their attitude, but to me General Botha's vision was the only one to follow, and so, haltingly at first, and then with growing assurance, I threw myself into a struggle in which I was to be involved for many years, and which, indeed, is not settled at this day. My countrymen, for all their solid qualities, are inveterate politicians. Everywhere the clamour of party rivalries and personal animosities filled the air, and our district was no exception. The Heilbron men had been dogged fighters during the war, and they were equally obstinate in their political beliefs. They began to look on me, striving to uphold the new faith, as an apostate. My standpoint, and the standpoint of those who thought as I did, was akin to that of the Southerners who stood by the Union during the American Civil War, and like theirs, our lot was an unpleasant one.

President Steyn and Christian de Wet, the two men who had led our little state so brilliantly during the Boer War, joined General Hertzog's crusade, and there was scarcely a Free State leader of any note who was not of the new party. In the Transvaal and in the Cape Colony, the strife waxed equally hot, although opinion was more evenly divided, while Natal was unanimous for General Botha.

My father, whose word had been law to us all our lives, joined the Nationalists, as did my eldest brother, and our family too was a house divided against itself.

There now came to Heilbron a clever young lawyer, named Rocco de Villiers, a champion of the Nationalist cause, and there was instant war between us. In oratory I was not his match, and I fought many a losing battle against him. I vainly advocated the ideal of a united nation, regardless of sectional distinctions, but my hearers would have none of it, and de Villiers would not either. At many an angry meeting I was howled down, and sometimes rough handled, while he was carried shoulder high. In this manner I made many enemies and lost many friends.

It was a depressing experience to find myself branded as a renegade by men of my own race, at whose side I had fought in the war, and whom I respected for their courage, but who now looked at me askance, and as often as not turned the other way when I passed. However, holding the convictions I did, there was no other course and I stood my ground.

Similar dissension was going on all over South Africa, and it led in the end to a civil war, but we were unable to foresee this, and I found the turmoil a relief from the boredom of village life, for, apart from battles with my opponents, there was little enough of interest. We held weekly rifle competitions which, after politics, are the chief recreation of the Boers, and at *Nagmaal* (Communion) they came into town with their ox-wagons and their families to attend the quarterly religious services.

For the rest, I saw to the unexacting details of a country practice, varied by an occasional springbok hunt or fishing expedition out in the district, and we ended the year with the annual Dingaans Day festival, to celebrate the victory over the Zulus in 1836. These were dull gatherings at which the speakers gloated over a long-vanquished enemy, and made speeches extolling our race. We held these meetings at Vegkop where the Zulus had been defeated in a local battle, and on one occasion at any rate there was a touch of humour. We decided to erect a memorial to the unknown dead who had fallen there, long ago. A committee was appointed to collect funds and supervise the construction of the monument. When at last the unveiling ceremony took place there was an inscription in Dutch on the base:

'IN MEMORY OF THE BRAVE MEN WHO DIED HERE, THIS PILLAR HAS BEEN ERECTED BY THE FOLLOWING MEMBERS OF THE BUILDING COMMITTEE'

and then came the names, deeply carved, of the fifteen or sixteen worthies of the committee who had thus perpetuated themselves at our expense.

The quarrel between the Nationalists and the South African Party continued unabated. General Botha was still firmly in power, but he was losing ground in the country districts, and as far as the Free State was concerned, we of his party were in a hopeless minority, only a few stalwarts holding out in every centre.

Things went on in this way for a year or two, the rival sections of the Dutch growing more embittered against each other; for, like the Irish, if we have no external enemy we fight amongst ourselves, and this has been our custom for more than a century.

In 1913 there was a general strike at Johannesburg and Louis Botha called out thirty thousand Boer horsemen to maintain order along the Reef.

Our Heilbron commando was among those for service, and I now realised how deeply our political feuds had bitten. I found that our men looked with suspicion upon instructions emanating from General Botha, and as we rode towards the Vaal River on our way to Johannesburg, there was a great deal of mutinous talk in the ranks. When we reached the south bank, they refused to cross over into the Transvaal. As usual, meetings were held and speeches were made, and some of the orators said that instead of fighting the strikers, we should ride through the river to fight Botha's men. Our commanding officer was David van Coller, a brave soldier but a narrow man and a strong supporter of the Nationalist Party. Nevertheless he did his best to talk reason into his followers, and after two days of haranguing, the bulk of the men pocketed their political scruples, and we forded the river.

We found Johannesburg in a state of siege. The mines were idle and the railways at a standstill, but with so strong an opposing force on the spot, the workers were impotent, and there was no fighting.

We of the Heilbron commando were stationed at Germiston, a mining town eight miles from Johannesburg. Whilst we were lying here, General Beyers came to address us. I had served under him when we took the British camp below the Magaliesbergen in December 1990, but I had never liked him. He had recently been appointed Commander-in-Chief of all the military forces in South Africa, and he rode up in full uniform with befeathered helmet and sword.

I sat my horse directly in front of him, so I heard every word he said. His speech was a scarcely veiled attack on the Government and on Botha and Smuts. He ended by saying that these English townspeople had forgotten what a Boer commando looked like, and that it was time we refreshed their memories. He then ordered us to follow him through the streets of Germiston, a curious performance, I thought, for the head of our army.

Next day he told us to ride through the town again, and to arrest every man who looked as if he were a striker. We galloped along beside the houses, rounding up everyone, and by the time we were finished, we had captured a member of Parliament, two Wesleyan ministers, and several town councillors, as well as many other perfectly innocent citizens. There were curses and complaints, and fainting women, and the incident aroused a great deal of resentment against General Botha, who had nothing to do with it.

There were thirty thousand Boers under arms, many of them Nationalists, and with political feeling running high, there were strange rumours in the air.

Our men said openly that Beyers should utilise the commandos on the Reef to overthrow Botha's Government, and I heard talk of his intending to proclaim a republic. Indeed, Red Daniel Opperman, by whose side I had fought in the Battle of Spion Kop, came riding past one morning, and knowing that I was a Botha man, called me aside, and told me that Beyers had asked him the day before whether the burghers would support him in case he arrested Botha and Smuts. We talked it over and we came to the conclusion that Beyers had only been joking, but in the light of subsequent events, I am not so sure.

The strike now collapsed. At the end of January 1914 we were sent home, and I rode back into the Free State in the company of men against most of whom I was to be in the field before the year was out.

Chapter 4

The 1914 Rebellion

For the next six months the political situation went from bad to worse—until half the population was not on speaking terms with the other half. Like everyone else I carried on a wordy warfare with my local opponents, in the course of which many hard things were said on either side.

In June I camped out in the district, for a rest, about the last rest I have had since then. On the evening of my return to town, I was sitting in our little village hall, when a message was thrown upon the screen to say that the Archduke of Austria had been murdered at a place called Serajevo, in the Balkans. The news did not interest us overmuch, for we were vague as to who he was, and we had never heard of Serajevo.

For the next six weeks South Africa forgot its internal squabbles in the face of vast battles in Europe, and before long we read of German victories, of British and French armies in retreat, and of the invaders sweeping all before them.

The Boer population had no particular love for Germany. They have tenacious memories, and they still bore the Kaiser a grudge for his refusal to meet President Kruger in 1902, and because he had boasted of having advised Queen Victoria how to overcome our two republics. On the other hand they saw no reason why they should side with Britain in a European war, and it was only natural that they began to ask themselves how we would stand if England were defeated.

Then, on the 9th of September, General Botha made his announcement in Parliament at Capetown that the British Government had asked him to equip an expedition of South African troops to invade the German territory lying on our borders, and that he intended to comply with the request. General Hertzog, the leader of the Nationalists, replied that it was folly to antagonise a powerful nation like the Germans. He said we would lose the flower of our men in the sands of the desert, and that it was better to await the issue in Europe. If Germany was defeated, the South-West territory would fall into our laps like a ripe apple, and if she was victorious, South Africa would pay dearly for having sided against her. These utterances reflected the views of the two political parties, and the Nationalists voted unanimously against the expedition.

General Botha's proposal, however, was carried, and preparations for the campaign were immediately taken in hand.

The report of the proceedings in Parliament and the decision to attack the Germans created a sensation, but there was no sign of trouble at first, for in South Africa we had never looked with a kindly eye on their annexation of a territory which we regarded as part and parcel of our own country. Nevertheless, our political opponents took full advantage of the position. Their leaders and their press conducted a violent campaign against the Government, and on the 15th of September, to add to our troubles, came the shooting of General de la Rey, the famous guerrilla leader of the Boer War. A gang of desperadoes had committed a series of murders and robberies along the Reef, and, during the police attempts to capture them, de la Rey was accidentally killed, as he and General Beyers were travelling by car through the suburbs of Johannesburg. It was later established that General Beyers was on his way to start a rebellion in the Western Transvaal and that General de la Rey was accompanying him. If General de la Rey knew of the plot, then his consent was obtained by playing upon his religious beliefs. I had met him only a few days before his death and I saw that his mind was affected, for his talk was of Christian Science, spiritualism, and the dreams of van Rensburg, his tame prophet; and once, when he had gazed at me in a strange manner, I asked him why, and he said that he was testing our souls to bring them *en rapport*, a phrase he must have picked up at a séance.

We all regretted his tragic end, for he was universally loved and esteemed, but now the manner of his death was used against us.

General Beyers, in the Transvaal, and General de Wet, in the Free State, began to make speeches in which they accused the Botha Government of having deliberately murdered de la Rey because he was opposed to the South-West expedition. Beyers was the Commander-in-Chief of all our forces, and de Wet was a member of the Union War Council. With these two levelling charges of such a nature, and with a war against the Germans on our hands, the prospects of the campaign seemed none too promising.

But Botha and Smuts were determined men. They called for volunteers, recruits were enrolled at various centres, and plans for the occupation of South-West were pushed forward.

I volunteered, but I did not like the look of things. In Heilbron, the Boer farmers stood sullenly debating events at the street corners, and when I passed, they turned their backs on me, and I gathered that the rest of the Province was in a similar state of unrest.

A few days after de la Rey's funeral, General de Wet drove through our village. When he saw me, he stopped the car and called me to him. He angrily declared that Botha and Smuts had murdered de la Rey, and he berated me for supporting them.

I had too much respect for him to bandy words, and merely answered that I was doing what I thought was right, whereat he drove off in a temper. Within the next few days I found that he was holding meetings in the district, at which he advocated the use of armed resistance to the Government. This was a very serious matter, for de Wet had immense influence in the Free State. He stood high in the opinion of his countrymen for his record during the Boer War, and whatever attitude he adopted was likely to be followed by thousands of his old fighting men.

This being the case, I went to Pretoria to consult General Botha. I met him and General Smuts in the Government Buildings, and we had a long conference. They said that reports from the Free State were not reassuring, and they feared that Beyers was planning mischief in the Western Transvaal. He had resigned his position as Commandant-General and was moving along the country districts in a suspicious manner.

In spite of these ominous signs, they still hoped that the various agitations were the work of politicians trying to make party capital, but they asked me to keep a strict lookout, and to let them know in good time should there be danger in the south.

Before I left Pretoria, General Botha invited me to his home at Sunnyside. When we arrived, I was astonished to see General Beyers waiting for him at the door. He looked ill at ease, and I wondered what had brought him there, for he was supposed to be raising adherents in the rural areas. I heard him ask for a private interview, so I went off, but I have many times wondered what passed between these two men, once companions in arms, at this last meeting before one of them died a violent death.

A day or two after my return to Heilbron I saw a crowd collected at the Court House, so I walked across to enquire. There was an official announcement posted on the board outside:

> 'October 12th, 1914. Whereas Lieut-Colonel Maritz, with a number of his officers and portion of the forces placed under his command, has shamefully and treacherously gone over to the Germans and is now in open rebellion against the Government and the people of the Union, and is, in conjunction with the forces of the enemy, invading the northern portions of the Cape Province, and whereas there is grave reason to think that the Government of German South-West has communicated with and corrupted other citizens of the Union under the false and treacherous pretext of establishing a republic in South Africa, and whereas the Government considers it necessary to defend the Union against attacks from within and without, now therefore I do hereby declare that all districts of the Union are placed under Martial Law until further notice.
> J C Smuts
> Minister of Defence.'

This Maritz was my old Madagascar associate, whom I had last seen at Zanzibar, years before.

On his return from Europe he had settled in South-West, where he served with the German Army against the Hereros. Latterly he had re-entered the Union, and Beyers had appointed him to the military command of those districts of the Cape Province that lie adjacent to the German border, and here was the result. The moment war broke out, Maritz had opened negotiations with the German military authorities in the South-West territory, and on a given date he arranged for their troops and batteries to surround the fifteen hundred recruits he had in camp. He then addressed his men, telling them of his intention of going over to the enemy who had promised to help him to establish a republic in South Africa. He gave the men the option of following him or of being handed to the Germans as prisoners of war.

A few agreed to join him, but most of them, including my brother Joubert, preferred internment, and they spent the next ten months in a prison camp.

In South Africa, the news of Maritz's action was received with indignation by those who were loyal to the Government, and with unconcealed satisfaction by many of our political enemies.

As far as our district was concerned, things moved swiftly to a head.

On the morning of the 23rd October, a man came into my office, and locking the door behind him, whispered in my ear that David van Coller, the District Commandant, was coming with a strong force that night to take the town on General de Wet's behalf, and that I was to be shot in my back-yard. Having delivered himself of this at a gulp, he unlocked the door and quickly vanished.

I telephoned the information to General Smuts in Pretoria, and I suggested that I should collect volunteers to defend the place. He gave me peremptory orders to do nothing of the kind. He said that if van Coller came in, and we fired on his men, the Nationalists would raise a cry throughout the country, and would say that we had started the trouble. He said he did not like leaving me in the lurch, but they were expecting outbreaks at other centres, so I was to look after myself.

In view of this, I saw no reason why I should tamely remain to be captured by my political opponents. I did not believe that I would be shot, for the Boers are not given to assassination, but in the heat of our long quarrels I had made many enemies, and the least that would happen to me would be arrest and indignities.

I decided therefore to make my escape. I was able to ascertain that already, out of sight, there were rebel pickets on every road leading from the town, so a daylight attempt was out of the question, and my only hope was a getaway after dark.

In the meanwhile, I pretended to be ignorant of what was afoot, and I attended to my affairs until four in the afternoon, when I went home to prepare for flight, and I ordered my native boy, Ruiter, to get our horses ready. Ruiter had been with me for years. He was a bandy-legged, diminutive Hottentot, the ugliest and loyalest servant a man ever had. My horse was a thoroughbred named Bismarck, one of the best in the country, and Ruiter had a fast Basuto pony. When I explained matters to him, he said we had the legs of any animals in the district.

As we were waiting, ready saddled, for darkness to fall, two young farmers, Daniel Malherbe and Fritz Weilbach, came galloping to my house. They were Government men, and they had both taken a prominent stand in the political war, so they had decided that the town was the best place for them. They said that all the countryside had risen, that mounted bands were patrolling in every direction, and that it was only by hard riding that they had got through. When I told them of the orders received from General Smuts, they agreed to join my attempt to bolt.

By now, standing in my yard, we could see rebel horsemen dotting the skyline, so there was no time to lose, and the moment it was dark enough we set off and, slinking by the gaol and the municipal pound, slipped quietly out of the town.

We left not a moment too soon, for we found afterwards that, within twenty minutes of our passing, every exit was occupied by pickets, which must even then have been closing silently in as we went.

Once clear of the streets we proceeded cautiously, our rifles at the ready, for we expected trouble, but we reached the railway crossing four miles away without being challenged, and beyond that we halted in a hollow, in order to take stock. We had no definite plans. Our first impulse had been to escape from the more immediate danger in the town, and now that we had accomplished this, the question arose what we should do next. The whole district, and, for all we knew, the whole country, was in revolt, and as far as we could tell, wherever we went we should still be among enemies, so we decided to remain where we were for the night, and see what the morrow would bring.

At dawn, we told Ruiter to fetch our horses from the paddock into which they had been turned, and I crawled up the slope with my rifle to see whether the coast was clear. Carefully peering over the edge, I found myself looking down on about seventy armed men almost within a stone's throw of me. The majority of them were sitting on the ground before their horses, their heads bowed down, as if wearied by an all-night vigil. This, I learned long afterwards, was a contingent posted here by van Coller, for the especial purpose of intercepting me. He had been told that I intended to escape in this direction after dark, and he had sent these men to watch the railway crossing. They had spent the night there, little knowing that we were lying so close by.

I took a good look at the party, among whom I recognised some of my best clients, and then seeing another outpost on a hill beyond, I wormed my way back to where Malherbe and Weilbach were awaiting me with our horses. Ruiter was still running about, trying to bring in his pony. By now, more men were riding down from the hill, waving and shouting to those out of sight near the crossing, and as I knew that they would not harm him if he were captured, I told him to hide himself in the grass since we could not wait for him, and we galloped off, bearing west, the only direction that seemed open to us.

The instant we rode out of the little hollow the men at the railway saw us, and leaping on to their horses, they gave chase. My horse Bismarck could outdistance any animal which the rebel band behind us was likely to have, and both Daniel and Fritz were noted for the qualify of the horses they bred, so our chief danger was that we might be brought down by a bullet, or that we might be shepherded into the arms of some other rebel force coming our way. Fortunately neither of these things happened. We soon drew out of range, and as van Coller, in his anxiety to make sure of the town, had concentrated most of this men around it during the night, we had the district to ourselves.

Although we were better mounted than our pursuers, they pounded stubbornly behind, and we saw other stray horsemen in the distance, but none came near enough to intercept us, and when we had gone five or six miles we dropped into an easier place, our rebel friends also slowing down. After a while we heard galloping in our rear, and looking round, saw my boy Ruiter, riding hard. He had lain low while the rebels were streaming past, but after they had gone, the plucky fellow had caught his pony, and cutting cross-country to avoid the hunt, had actually overtaken us.

We went on and occasionally met cartloads of womenfolk, driving towards Heilbron. They told us with smiles of triumph that the town was taken by van Coller and 'General' Rocco de Villiers, who had blossomed into field rank overnight.

Our original pursuers were still coming on far behind, but we had no fear of being overtaken by them, and we trotted steadily along. My two companions were inclined to be depressed, for they had left their wives and property to the mercy of their enemies. Their wives were safe enough, for no Boer, rebel or otherwise, would molest a woman, but they knew it would go hard with their flocks and herds, and they were men of substance. I rode along in a more cheerful frame of mind. I had long been tired of the humdrum existence that I had been leading, and now that the whole world was at war, the highway stretching before us seemed to lead to a wider life and, indeed, I have been far afield since that morning.

Towards three in the afternoon we approached Wolvehoek Station, on the railway line that comes up through the Free State to Johannesburg and Pretoria. We had ridden twenty-five miles by then, and most of the rebels had dropped out. About a dozen of them, however, better mounted, or more determined than the rest, made a final bid to get within range before we reached the cover of the station buildings, and they came hurrying towards us in a cloud of dust. We were not certain whether the station was held by rebels or not, but we were relieved, as we rode, to see the mail train steaming in from the south. It was the last train to get through before the line was broken up, and passengers leaned from every window, to view what must have seemed to them like a cinema performance, three armed men and a native boy riding for their lives, and something like a sheriff's posse coming on behind.

The arrival of the mail was an equal surprise to the gentlemen in our rear, for on seeing it they reined in their horses, and presently rode back along the way they had come. There was great excitement. Everyone fired questions at us, and we in turn were eager for news. So far as we could piece matters together, Maritz was invading the Cape Province at the head of German troops, Beyers was in revolt, and the Northern and Western Transvaal were up in arms against General Botha, while much of the Free State had risen at de Wet's behest.

The railway line to Johannesburg and Pretoria was still open, but beyond that all was doubt and uncertainty.

My two friends and I held a hurried consultation, and we agreed to board the train for the Transvaal. I was anxious to see General Smuts, and there was no particular object in remaining here to be picked up by the rebels.

As the mail train consisted of passenger coaches only, we could not load our horses. The Transvaal was still thirty-five miles away, but when I asked Ruiter whether he would ride for Vereeniging on the north bank of the Vaal River that night, he cheerfully undertook the risky mission, and as the train pulled out, we saw his stock figure already in the saddle, our three led horses trotting beside him.

By dark we crossed the Vaal River Bridge, reaching Johannesburg two hours later. Malherbe and Weilbach remained there, while I went on to Pretoria to find General Smuts.

I arrived at 11 o'clock that night, and immediately made for Defence Headquarters. General Smuts was sitting at his desk, working at high pressure. Orderlies rushed in and out, telephone bells rang, and the building hummed with a cheering activity. He gave me a hurried account of the situation. The rumours we had heard that afternoon were true in the main, but somewhat exaggerated.

Beyers was at the head of the Transvaal outbreak, and was at this moment moving about the Pretoria district with a strong rebel force. General Smuts spoke bitterly of his conduct, but he said General Botha had marched out that afternoon to attack him, and he had little fear of the result.

Taking a piece of paper, he scribbled a note appointing me to the command of the Heilbron military district, and with this rapid promotion in my pocket, I took my leave, having likewise blossomed into field rank overnight.

I had spent a long and exciting day, so I walked to the nearest hotel with my rifle and cartridge belts as my only luggage, and having booked a room, was soon fast asleep.

Before daybreak I secured a car and started back for Vereeniging on the Vaal River. In passing through Johannesburg, I picked up Malherbe and Weilbach, and by 10 o'clock in the morning we reached Vereeniging, and across the river lay the Heilbron district. At the police station stood trusty Ruiter, grinning a welcome, our horses safe and sound. He had ridden all night, keeping clear of the roads, and so had come through unharmed.

I now sent the car back to Pretoria, and after fording the Vaal River we were in our own district once more. Coming across the plain were about thirty mounted men, whom, scouting nearer, we recognised as Government supporters making for the Transvaal. Amongst them was Antony Peeters, an old school friend, and there were others from our area, so that when I produced my appointment as Commandant, they agreed at once to serve under me. With this nucleus of a commando I decided to raid deeper in. We went carefully, seeing only a few distant rebel patrols, and by 3 o'clock were at Wolvehoek Station. I had left there as a fugitive the afternoon before, and I was back within twenty-four hours at the head of an armed force, which was pretty quick work, I thought.

The stationmaster told me that van Coller had visited the place during the night with four hundred men. They had looted the shops and torn up the railway line, after which they rode off without even cutting the telephone lines to the north. The stationmaster advised me to be cautious. Van Coller had said in his hearing that if I ventured to return to the district, he was going to make short work of me. I felt none too easy myself, outnumbered as we were, but we rode out as far as the Clydesdale colliery ten miles away, to reconnoitre.

I discovered that van Coller was lurking in the neighbourhood, and I knew him to be a pretty resolute customer. So we waited at the mine until dark. Just as we were preparing to leave the shadow of the pithead, we saw about fifty rebel horsemen riding past. I told the men not to fire. An open fight was one thing, but I was reluctant to shoot down unsuspecting men of my own district, so we sat on our horses and waited for them to go by. One man turned aside, and before he realised it, he was in among us. He was a cousin of Fritz Weilbach's, and Fritz himself steered his horse alongside, and whispered fiercely: 'Neef Wilhelm, if you utter a sound you are a dead man.' The young fellow took it calmly. He said he was glad we were Government men, for he had been pressed into service against his will, and would sooner be with us than on the other side. In any case he remained contentedly with me until the end of the rebellion.

As soon as the rebel column had disappeared, we made for higher ground and camped for the night, but next morning we returned to Wolvehoek Station, whose sheds and stone buildings seemed to me a good defensive position.

It was well that we did so, for in less than half an hour van Coller's force showed on the skyline, a solid mass of horsemen. They halted, and a messenger came galloping towards us, bearing a white flag and a letter addressed to me. It was an ambiguous document, for I was van Coller's 'dear friend', and he requested the meaning of my presence with armed men in a district of which he was in command. I wrote him a reply on the booking counter. I said the meaning of my presence was that I was now in command of the district, and not he, and that I intended to fight him. After sending off this boastful message, I went to the telephone office, and in a few minutes got through to General Smuts at Pretoria. I told him what I was doing and that I thought we could hold our own at the station, but hoped he would be able to send a relief force in a day or two.

Here again he gave me emphatic orders that there was to be no fighting. He said President Steyn was in touch with the rebel leaders in the Free State with a view to preventing bloodshed, and I was on no account to do anything that might imperil the negotiations. Looking through the window of the little office where I stood, I could see the rebel commando still on the rise, but smaller groups of horsemen were detaching from the main body and riding down in our direction. I told General Smuts this and asked him how I was to avoid a fight under these circumstances. He told me to withdraw my men towards the Vaal River immediately. This was across thirty-five miles of open plain, but his instructions were too explicit to be disregarded, so I called the men from their different posts, and we mounted our horses, and rode slowly away. Thereupon the rebel parties came galloping straight for us.

I was riding some distance behind with a few companions as a rearguard, and as I knew that General Smuts would not expect passive resistance, I jumped to the ground and fired at the foremost rebel. The man flung up his arms, and tumbled headlong from his horse, and a brisk little battle ensued. Bullets whistled about our ears, but as the rebels were firing from the saddle, not one of us was hit, and after a few minutes they withdrew, leaving several of their number on the ground.

To show van Coller that I was not afraid of him, we off-saddled at a farm in full view of his commando, and through my glasses I could see them gesticulating and pointing in our direction, as if arguing whether to come after us or to leave us alone. Then van Coller's brother Piet came riding under a white flag with another letter. There was nothing ambiguous about it this time. He said the blood that had been spilt was upon my head; my punishment was being prepared, and I would rue the day I was born. I sent him back a curt reply, and after giving our horses sufficient rest, we rode on, leaving our opponents still given over to debate.

As we went, an Irishman from a neighbouring farm rode up. He had heard the sound of firing and had hurried to ascertain the cause of it. When I told him, he asked me whether this was a war between the British and the Dutch, or between Botha and Hertzog, or between myself and David van Coller. I told him it was a mixture of all three, whereupon he said that, being an Irishman, he had to take part, and as I had helped him one night when he had got into trouble at Heilbron, he might as well join me, which he did there and then, for he had come fully armed. It was like the story that went the rounds in these days of the old Boer who was questioned as to what side he was on. He replied that he was neutral. Asked what he meant by 'neutral', he said he meant he was going to join whichever commando on either side was the first to reach his farm.

We now continued unmolested on our way, and crossed the Vaal River to Vereeniging after dark. I had left here the previous afternoon to recapture my district, and I had been chased out of it in little over twenty-four hours, which was quick work too, I thought.

Next morning we were cheered by the sight of many Government men entering the town. From them we obtained a rough idea of current events. General Botha had defeated Beyers, who was however still at large with many followers; and all over the Transvaal there was confused fighting going on between rebel bands and bodies of Government sympathisers. Along the Orange River, Maritz at the head of German troops had invaded the Cape Province, and in the Free State Christian de Wet and Rocco de Villiers were raising strong rebel commandos, so that, generally, wide areas of South Africa were in a state of disaffection. General Botha and General Smuts boldly faced these many dangers. Troops were being despatched to every threatened point and as de Wet's activities were looked on as likely to involve the entire Free State in the revolt, General Botha had ordered the assembly of commandos at Vereeniging, in order to prepare for an invasion under his personal command. He was still in the west, and for the moment old Coen Brits was in charge. I reported to him, and he greeted me with a slash of his rawhide sjambok, which was his idea of a military salute. He was an amusing character. He stood six foot six inches, did not know a word of English, drank enormous quantities of alcohol without turning a hair, and was celebrated throughout the Transvaal for his racy wit and Rabelaisian stories. But he was a good soldier. He had fought with skill and courage on the Republican side during the Boer War, and General Botha was the only man who had any influence over him. When Botha wired him to mobilise his men for the South-West expedition, he wired back to say he was ready, but wanted to know whether he had to fight the Germans or the British. He was quite prepared to do either, for he worshipped Botha, and obeyed him blindly.

We lay at Vereeniging for several days, during which time a considerable number of Government supporters from the Heilbron district escaped through the Vaal River to join me, and I soon had about two hundred and fifty men.

We now heard that General de Wet was in the central Free State with five thousand men, and that more were joining him daily. When General Botha arrived to take command, we were over six thousand horsemen with several guns, and we set out at once to look for de Wet. After a journey of two hundred miles we found him at Mushroom Valley, with his men strongly posted in the hills.

My commando was attached to Coen Brits's larger force, and we were told to take up a position in the rear, to cut off the rebel retreat. A pretty fierce battle now took place. De Wet was angered at the death of his son, killed in a skirmish, and his fighting spirit was aroused.

After preliminary shell-fire, General Botha attacked, and there were heavy casualties on both sides. Then the rebels broke, and came streaming up the valley in our direction, with de Wet on a white horse at their head. We gave chase and drove him into the mountains towards McQuathlingsnek, but he was too old a guerrilla to be caught, although we took a number of his stragglers, who dropped behind with wounds or foundered horses.

We crossed McQuathlingsnek, a beautiful pass high among the rugged mountains, where lie the graves of British dead killed here in the old war, but by dark de Wet had given us the slip. He next broke cover, and leaving the mountains, went west across the Free State plains, our forces tearing after him.

My place in the drive ran via Bloemfontein, and then down the Modder River, for a distance of one hundred and fifty miles, but neither I nor any other of old Coen's men came in sight of the quarry, for de Wet had changed direction and was now heading north-west for the Kalahari Desert. His course lay so far out of our road that we were ordered to halt at Paardeberg, where Cronje was captured by Lord Roberts in 1900. Here Brits collected his men.

There was a Scotchman with me who owned a set of bagpipes, which he played around our camp fires at night, and old Coen apparently took this to be a Scottish religious observance. One morning a Dutch Reformed clergyman wrote for permission to address the men. Coen, who was somewhat of a pagan, replied that he didn't want any preaching in his camp, and turning to me, said that as he had forbidden the predikant to come, he must be fair as between the sects, and I was to stop that damned Scotchman of mine from playing the bagpipes!

And now word came that strong rebel commandos were reforming in the north-eastern Free State. Coen Brits was ordered to continue after de Wet, but General Botha instructed me to hasten along a route of my own towards the scene of the fresh trouble, and there await his arrival with his troops.

This meant journeying two hundred miles across the width of the Province. Our objective was the little town of Reitz, named after my father, where the rebel concentration was gathering. I went via Kroonstad and Lindley, and thence into our own district of Heilbron. I found that David van Coller had brought his men back from the Mushroom Valley disaster, and they were now dispersed in small bands, making their way to Reitz.

At the headwaters of the Rhenoster River an old friend of mine, named Doris Botha, tried to oppose my passage with some rebels he was commanding. I was riding ahead when he came into view, and he waved his hat at me before dismounting to fire. I got Bismarck behind some rocks, and replied, whereupon he gave me another salute and made off. He and his men then opened a brisk fire, but I turned their flank, and crossed the river higher up, capturing Doris and about twenty others. They all shook hands in the most friendly manner, and later in the afternoon we picked up a dozen more, equally friendly, as they handed over their rifles. They told us a commando of Transvaalers had relieved Heilbron a few days before, so our little hamlet was free again, but we regretted that its taking had not been left to us.

Next morning we rode in. Less than a month before I had fled the place in the night. Now I was returning with a commando and prisoners, so I enjoyed the ovation we received as we filed through the streets to a banquet which the ladies had prepared for us.

I found my house pillaged, but no wanton damage had been done, and, needless to say, every shop and warehouse had been cleared by the rebels. In South Africa, however, the commandeering of supplies in time of trouble is part and parcel of our military system, and the Heilbron insurgents had at any rate shown a sense of humour, for most of their requisition notes were endorsed: 'Payable to bearer by the winning side'.

The Transvaal men who had liberated the town had gone off in the direction of the rebel gathering in the east, and next day we took the same road. As we moved, there was a steady flow of local rebel horsemen going forward in small parties. They kept out of range most of the time, but on several occasions we exchanged long-distance shots, and once I personally captured four men as they were watering their horses at a trough. They were rebels from our district, and they too shook hands smilingly, when I relieved them of their weapons. To them, as to all the rebels I ever met, the rising was but a more acute phase of our original political differences, and I never came across one man who thought that he had committed an offence in taking up arms against the Government of his country.

In spite of the rains that now descended, the heaviest in thirty-five years, it was said, we groped our way across the sodden country, until we came to the neighbourhood of Reitz, where we found the Wilge River in flood, and barring our way. On the far side stood several rebel camps and laagers, and many mounted men were moving about.

By the time the rains had ceased, General Botha was approaching with his force of nearly three thousand men, and we began to close in. One band of rebels, about three hundred strong, tried to break back under cover of an early morning mist but I headed them off, and chased them for over two hours until we cornered them in a bend of the river. After a short fight they put up the white flag, and we were surprised to find that we had captured the major portion of David van Coller's Heilbron commando, from our own district, though he himself was elsewhere with the balance of his men. Nearly three hundred surrendered, with over four hundred horses, and every one of the captured men was an acquaintance, a client, or a friend.

After resting our horses, we went on, and presently fell in with one of Botha's patrols, who told us that he had occupied Reitz that morning. So we went there to hand over our charges. We reached the village by dusk, and as our cavalcade clattered through the streets with the long column of prisoners and led horses, it aroused a good deal of attention from the troops and townspeople who came crowding up.

This little '*dorp*' that bears our family name was strongly rebel in sympathy. One of the Transvaal men told me that when they entered the town, some of the inhabitants expected to see Khaki-clad British soldiers, for they believed that General Botha was fighting them with an auxiliary army from overseas, whereas his men were chiefly old-fashioned Boers from the Eastern Transvaal. Thus it happened that when the advance guard rode in, an ancient rebel dame rushed into the street, and seeing only shaggy burghers, thought they were her own people and called out in Dutch: 'But men, where are the bloody English?' (*Waar is die verdomde Engelse?*) to which a young Boer scout replied in the same language: 'Old lady, we *are* the bloody English.'

The following morning I visited General Botha at his quarters beside the railway station. He looked fit and well, but he was a saddened man. He did his duty in opposing the rebellion, but I know what sorrow it caused him. He explained the situation to me. Beyers had fled across the Vaal River, making for German territory. De Wet, with a mere handful of men, had escaped into the Kalahari Desert, and Coen Brits was still on his trail, while Maritz lay on the Cape border with a mixed contingent of rebels and Germans. In the rest of the country the rebellion was being stamped out by the effective measures which he and General Smuts had taken.

Locally, David van Coller and two other leaders named Wessel-Wessels and Serfontein, were in the field with several thousand retainers. They were more or less hemmed in, and they were disheartened, for General Botha showed me a letter received from them proposing to negotiate. He had replied demanding an unconditional surrender.

That afternoon, when I was again at Headquarters, a telegram came to say that old Coen Brits had captured de Wet. He had collected a number of motor cars, and with these wore down de Wet's horses, until they could go no further. When I heard how the obstinate old guerrilla leader had been run to earth by the help of mechanical contrivances I was almost sorry, for it spelt the end of our picturesque South African commando system. With these new engines of war it would no longer be possible for mounted men to play hide-and-seek across the veld, and the good old days were gone for ever.

General Botha now received another letter signed by the three rebel leaders:

'*6th Dec 1914*

To General Louis Botha

We desire to impress upon you that it was to maintain a cause dear to us beyond every-thing that we resolved upon hostilities. Also, we are pledged to our other commandos in the field, so we cannot surrender without consulting them. Therefore, we tell you the only way is to send General de Wet here. Also, let Beyers and Maritz be present.'

This letter, like the previous one, was in Dutch, and General Botha wrote a reply at once. He told me the three leaders were said to be in a cave that had been used to store grain and ammunition during the Boer War, and as I knew the lie of it, I was to deliver the despatch.

At daybreak Malherbe, Weilbach and I set out. We met numerous rebel horsemen, apparently on their way home, and it was clear that the movement was collapsing. When we reached the cave, there was no sign of anyone. We crawled and stumbled about the dark passages by candlelight, but we had come on a bootless errand, and when we got back that evening it was to learn that van Coller and his fellow leaders had agreed to surrender.

Next morning, what was left of the rebel commandos rode in to lay down their arms. So many had slipped away during the past few days that there were only about fifteen hundred left, and we sat our horses beside the road to watch them pass. First came van Coller at the head of his men, and he glowered fiercely at me as he rode by. Then came Wessel-Wessels and Serfontein, each with their followers at their heels. It was mournful to see the long files of sullen dejected men ride past, many of them old friends, all of them our countrymen.

General Botha now ordered me to take the prisoners from my district back to Heilbron, and to release them there. Having beaten his opponents, he showed no rancour. Even towards men who had betrayed his personal friendship he cherished no ill will, and in all the years I knew him he was the same large-hearted generous man.

After saying goodbye to him and to my two younger brothers, Arend and Jack, who were serving under him, I started off. We formed an imposing array as we trekked through the countryside, with hundreds of prisoners and hundreds of captured horses being driven along. As we passed, the rebel women and children came running from the farmhouses to stare at us, and to call greetings to their menfolk under guard.

In two days' time we reached Heilbron, and once again received a rousing welcome from the citizens. Van Coller and Rocco de Villiers were ordered to stand their trial, and were each sentenced to a term of imprisonment, and I did not see them again. But the rest of the prisoners were returned to their homes.

In our district there were still a few roving parties in the broken country along the Rhenoster River. I ordered them to come in, but as they paid no attention, I collected my men and went after them. We chased these recalcitrants for nearly three weeks, in the course of which we had several sharp encounters. I had a few men wounded and we killed and wounded several of our opponents, but by the end of January they were rounded up, and the district was clear.

By this time, too, General Beyers had met his death in the Vaal River, while attempting to escape through the swollen stream, and Maritz had been disposed of. Jacobus van Deventer, my old Boer War companion, defeated him in a pitched battle at Upington on the Orange River. Maritz, though wounded, escaped into German territory, as he had done in 1902, and eventually made his way to Spain, where he found sanctuary on neutral ground.

My final contact with the rebellion savoured of comedy. Early in February 1915, when everyone was settling down peacefully, I received a telegram from the Commandant of the adjoining district to say that a desperate character named Josiah du Toit was at large in my area, and I was requested to effect his capture. The wire concluded with the statement that this should be facilitated by the fact that his horses were in poor condition.

I knew du Toit and his ways, and I knew him to be a decent fellow, so instead of hunting him, I sent him a message to come in. Two days later I heard a clatter before my office, and looking out, saw Josiah on his horse, fully armed and with two led horses alongside. He dismounted, hitched his animals to the post, and walked in, rifle in hand. He greeted me like a long-lost brother; but drawing myself up, I said: 'Josiah, I'm sorry, but you have to go to gaol.' He answered smilingly: 'Man, don't talk nonsense. How can you put an old friend like me in prison now that the thing is over?'

I conceded this point, but demanded his rifle. Here again he was obdurate. He said: 'You can't have my rifle. I have lost my crops and all my sheep while I was away, and I shall have to live by shooting springbok, so my rifle I keep.' I tried another tack, and told him I required two of his three horses for government purposes. He would have none of this either. He had bred the animals himself; it was through fear of losing them that he had remained out so long; and he would like to see the man who would take them from him.

Brushing this talk aside, he asked me how I had known of his presence in the district, and I showed him the telegram I had received. He spelt it out slowly until he came to the disparaging reference to his horses. Then he angrily flung down the wire and cried: 'How dare they accuse Josiah du Toit of having poor horses! Everyone knows I breed the best in the Free State. This insult I will not endure; you are my lawyer, now you sit down and demand from that officer heavy damages for defamation of my character.'

That he had been concerned in a seditious rising and had remained under arms long after everyone else had surrendered, was to him a mere detail, but being charged with owning third-rate horseflesh was an insult not to be borne, and I had the greatest trouble in smoothing his ruffled feelings. In the end, he compromised by borrowing half-a-crown from me and rode off, horses, rifle and all, with the injured air of one who had received rather less than his just dues.

The rebellion was over. With a great conflict raging in Europe, it passed almost unnoticed in the outside world, but in South Africa the aftermath is with us yet, and the motives and origins are still the subject of fierce controversy.

I personally have not the slightest doubt that it was a direct outcome of our preceding political warfare. That it was essentially a party quarrel is proved by the fact that every member of the South African Party stood by General Botha, and while not every Nationalist was a rebel, it is literally true that every rebel, without a single exception, was a Nationalist.

Furthermore, the rebellion was a domestic dispute among the Boers themselves, and hostility towards the British had comparatively little part in it. Of the thirty thousand men who helped to quell the revolt, twenty-one thousand were Boers, and of the nine hundred casualties we suffered on the Government side, nearly seven hundred were of Dutch descent. The rising was crushed by Boer commandos under Boer officers, and to this day the ill feeling that was engendered lies not between Dutch and British, but between the two sections of the Boer people in South Africa.

Chapter 5

An excursion into German West

During all the time that General Botha and General Smuts were grappling with the rebellion, they had kept steadily in view their intention to conquer German West, and now that the outbreak was crushed, they did not delay.

While I was still busy clearing up my district, they had already sailed from Capetown with large bodies of troops. They had called up fifty thousand fighting men of English and Dutch stock (the figures were: men of English descent 27 500; of Dutch descent 22 500) and for the first time in the history of South Africa, Boer commandos from the interior rode through the streets of Capetown to lead their horses into ships, and for the first time an armed expedition went by sea beyond our borders. By the time I was able to go, Botha had landed at Swakopmund with twelve thousand men, and Smuts had landed at Lüderitzbucht with an army of six thousand, while other columns were marching from the Orange River to make the issue doubly sure.

As soon as I could, I locked my office, and started to catch up with General Smuts. I travelled by rail to Capetown, my servant Ruiter with Bismarck and two other horses journeying in a cattle truck behind.

At Table Bay we embarked on a transport going up the west coast with reinforcements, and after a voyage of four days we reached Lüderitzbucht. There I learned that our troops had advanced, and now lay at the village of Aus, a hundred miles across the Namieb Desert. The railway had been repaired to within twenty miles of Aus, so we proceeded on a supply train through what is perhaps the most desolate tract on earth—leagues of shifting sand dunes as far as the eye could see—with no vegetation of any kind, and no water.

At Aus the worst of the desert lies behind and here I found General Smuts with his men, and joined his staff.

Until recently the Germans had had it all their own way. On account of the rebellion, only weak detachments could be sent against them, and several of these had met with disaster. In addition they had seduced Maritz from his allegiance, and he had handed over to them the troops under his command.

But now their time was come. Against our great display of force they had only eight thousand soldiers in the field, and Botha and Smuts were leaving nothing to chance. In the north, General Botha was marching from the coast towards Windhoek, the German capital, and here in the south Smuts was preparing to get astride the main railway line, so as to cut their forces in two, while at the same time overland columns were converging from the Orange River and from the Kalahari.

Nonetheless, the odds were not so unequal as they seemed, for the Germans were standing on interior lines, and in any case their chief defence lay in the difficult nature of the country. For German West is a very large territory. It stretches from the Orange River to the Cunene, nine hundred miles north, and from west to east it lies between the Atlantic Ocean and the Kalahari Desert, a width of four hundred miles. Much of this vast space is arid, so the moving of troops was by no means an easy matter, and if the Germans took to guerrilla warfare, as we had done against the British long ago, they might easily involve us in a long and inconclusive campaign.

Both Smuts and Botha were alive to this danger, and they were determined to prevent it.

As a preliminary, General Smuts had sent Sir Duncan McKenzie with eight hundred horsemen towards Gibeon, to cut off the retreat of the German forces operating in the south, and he was making ready to march the rest of his army into the hinterland.

To that end we busied ourselves with preparations. In our immediate vicinity the enemy had withdrawn shortly before, but they had left many unpleasant tokens of their occupation, for we discovered that they had mined the roads and the railway track, and had planted mines at random in the open veld, and in dwelling-houses, stables, and kraals, and they had poisoned the wells. As far as the wells were concerned we could not complain, for warning notices had been left, but to bury infernal machines in a place they had given up was new to us.

I made early acquaintance with one of these mines, and it cost me the life of my horse Bismarck. I was coming from the railhead one morning, and overtook an infantry company plodding along. I rode chatting to the officer at their head when suddenly there was a roar in the midst of the soldiers and a column of smoke and dust shot a mile high, whilst fragments of metal went whizzing in all directions. When the air cleared, two men lay dead and a dozen wounded, and many others were temporarily blinded by the spurting sand. My horse, stung by flying grit and pebbles, reared and plunged, and when I dismounted to help the injured, he gave a snort of terror, and wrenching free, headed straight for the waterless desert that lay westward for a hundred miles and more.

By the time we had made the wounded men comfortable and I had procured another horse, Bismarck was a mere speck on the distant horizon, and he was steadily making deeper into the sandy waste. I followed him for hours, for I hoped to save him from the certain death from thirst that awaited him, but in the end the animal I was riding gave in, and I was obliged to retrace my steps on foot, leading him behind me, and when last I saw my poor misguided horse, he was still going to his doom.

When I reached camp, and Ruiter heard of Bismarck's fate, tears ran down his ugly wizened countenance, for he loved the horse even more than I did.

Two days later, I witnessed another explosion. I was standing in the street at Aus when again there came the report of a mine. The roof of a neighbouring stable lifted bodily into the air, followed by the carcase of a mule, and an officer fell wounded to the ground. The mine had been set beneath the stable floor, and the mule had touched it off. Similar occurrences were comparatively frequent. One of our men turned the handle of a door in a dwelling-house, and was blown to pieces. Another, who lit the wick of a lamp suspended from the ceiling of a room, met with instant death, and in the north General Botha's troops had many losses of the same kind.

One evening, riding down a gorge near Kanus, we came on a grisly sight. Swaying from a branch of a tree were the mummified bodies of three Hottentots. They had been hanged here by the Germans some time before, to judge by their condition, but for what offence I never heard.

By this time General Smuts was anxious for news of Sir Duncan McKenzie's column that had disappeared into the void, and he ordered James Leisk and me to ride after them. Leisk in civil life was a highly placed government official, and we were old acquaintances.

I had two horses left, one for myself and one for Ruiter, and Leisk was also well mounted. We set out at once, our road running through wild country, sparsely inhabited by nomad Hottentot tribes. Occasionally we found a dead horse or mule to show that McKenzie had gone by, but we travelled nearly a hundred miles before we came on a few of his men, left behind at Bethany Mission to look after the weaker animals. They had no news and we pushed on. Game was not plentiful, but there was an occasional antelope to be shot, and we had no difficulty in finding water. We went by Wasserfall and Besondermaid to the Great Fish River, and thence up past Bukaross Peak, through the Berseba Reserve. On our fourth day, at Deutsches Erde, we struck an outpost. They said they had heard the sound of distant gunfire during the night, so we hurried forward and towards noon came up with McKenzie and his men in possession of Gibeon Town. He had got astride the Northern railway line just too late to cut off the German retreat, but he had fought a sharp rearguard action, in which he had captured some guns and a hundred and fifty prisoners, as well as several trains and large quantities of war material. He lost twenty-six men killed and fifty or sixty wounded, and the German casualties were about the same.

We stayed here for a few days. Food was scarce, and the men lived on what they could forage in the way of sheep and goats in the neighbouring hills, though gradually Dutch farmers from the surrounding district began to bring in supplies. They were mostly men who had settled here after the Boer War, to escape British rule, and now British rule had overtaken them once more. They said the Germans had treated them well enough, but there were too many irksome restrictions and too many officials to suit their taste. I had a look at the German prisoners. They were regulars, but not as spick and span as I had expected. Each of the captured guns bore an inscription, '*Ultima ratio regis*'.

After some days Leisk and I, and a Colonel Muller, were assigned two motor cars that had accompanied the expedition, and were instructed to go north towards Windhoek, to establish contact with General Botha's troops, who, if they had not already taken the capital, must be nearing it by now.

We reached Marienthal by the end of the first day, and here we found a picket of McKenzie's men that had pushed forward. They warned us to go carefully. Somewhere ahead, they said, the German force that had escaped was slowly falling back, blowing up the railway as it went. We started at dawn. From Marienthal the railway runs through the Reoboth Reserve, a huge area inhabited by a race of halfbreeds. It is a sterile, barren tract, across which probably no motor cars had ever ventured, and we had a trying time. We ploughed all day through heavy sand and blazing heat, until, by evening, we had used up every drop of water in quenching our thirst, and in providing for the radiators. We moved parallel to the railway line, and at every station the boreholes, wells and tanks were dynamited. Therefore, when at last we were brought to a halt for lack of water, we were in a serious predicament. There was no open water that we knew of within eighty miles of us; the cars were dry, and so were we, and we spent an anxious, thirsty night. At daybreak, after trying in vain to extract some water from a destroyed borehole, we were lucky enough to find a patch of Tsama melon growing in the veld. In these parts the game and the natives rely almost entire on this species of cucumber during the dry season. Liquid is extracted by gently heating the melons, and we were able to distil enough water for ourselves and for both radiators. We moved on, but saw no more Tsama that day, and by noon, owing to the intense heat and the heavy going, the cars gave out for the second time. We calculated that we were within walking distance of Reoboth Station, which by our map lay somewhere ahead, so we abandoned the cars and went on foot. The sun beat down; our drinking water was finished, and this knowledge made us the more thirsty. In our heart of hearts we felt that our chances of finding any water at the station were remote, seeing how thoroughly the Germans had destroyed the wells and boreholes which we had discovered up to now, and we tramped along the railway track in gloomy silence. At one spot we passed two lonely graves. On each headstone was the name of a German soldier with an inscription '*hier erdürstet*', to show that they had perished of thirst on some bygone patrol, and this did not raise our spirits.

After three hours, our tongues swollen with thirst, we came to a place where the railway line had spanned one of those waterless river beds that intersect the country at frequent intervals. The bridge had been dynamited, and on the sandy course below were two engines piled one upon the other, a mass of twisted wreckage. The Germans had mined the bridge, and then run the engines over. As we stood gazing at them, I caught a shimmer through the torn side of one of the boilers. We scrambled hurriedly down, and found a supply of water, providentially unspilt, in a corner of an engine tank. There was enough and to spare, and in a moment we were ladling out long satisfying draughts. When we had finished drinking we were new men, and still further in luck, for climbing a rise, I saw the buildings of Reoboth Station a mile or two beyond. Cheerfully we filled our bottles and an old bucket picked up near by, and walked back with sufficient water for the cars. By 10 o'clock that night we had reached the station with both machines. We slept till morning, and then inspected our surroundings. Here again the water supply had been completely demolished, but again we were fortunate. The tanks and boreholes were destroyed, and the rolling-stock standing on the line had been set on fire, but a little square-bellied engine, in a shed by itself, had been overlooked, and its boiler was filled to the brim with clear, cool water. This freed us from further care, for we knew that we would be running out of the desert beyond this point. From the trampled spoor around the station buildings, and from the general appearance of things, we concluded that the Germans had now abandoned the railway line, and were continuing their withdrawal by road. And on looking north-east, along the way they had gone, we could see a tall pillar of dust where their column was trekking fifteen or twenty miles away. They must have left in a hurry, for considerable quantities of stores and military kit were strewn about, and although the wells and water-towers were destroyed, the burning of the rolling material was incomplete.

As the railway line runs straight form here to Windhoek, sixty miles off, we argued (correctly as it proved) that General Botha must have occupied the capital, and that these troops, having got wind of his arrival, had swung east to avoid capture.

After we had satisfied ourselves of this, we continued our journey, through improved country, which enabled us to make better progress, though the going was still heavy. Far away to our right moved the dust cloud of the retreating Germans. We could make out a convoy of wagons escorted by infantry, and about two hundred horsemen, and this as the nearest sight I got of the enemy in South-West.

Towards evening we ran into the mountains around Windhoek, and before long we met a picket of General Botha's men. They said the town had surrendered, but the bulk of the German forces had retreated north into the wilds. We entered after dark to find the streets swarming with South Africans, some riding about, others on the sidewalks around their camp fires. We slept in a vacant yard for the night, and reported next morning to General Botha, whom we found in the citadel, where he had taken up his headquarters. I had not met him since the end of the rebellion on the day of the surrender at Reitz, and he looked a different man. To him the rebellion had been a deep tragedy of his race, but fighting for a territory which he regarded as part of his own country was another matter, and he was far more cheerful, as he sat in Governor Seitz's office telling us of the hardships encountered on his way up from the sea.

He had defeated the Germans in two important engagements, and he had brought his troops through the terrible desert belt by a series of brilliant marches that completely demoralised the defence. I was told that when Hauptmann Francke, the German Commander-in-Chief, saw the Boer horsemen appearing out of the bush in all directions, with no semblance of order or discipline, but relentlessly hustling his soldiers, he exclaimed bitterly: 'This is not a war, it's a hippodrome!' At all events General Botha's unconventional tactics were so successful that he was now in possession of the enemy capital with insignificant losses.

For the moment, the German forces had withdrawn north, along the Otavi railway line, and it was rumoured that they intended to resort to guerrilla warfare in the unknown country that lies towards the Cunene River. General Botha told us that he viewed this contingency with apprehension, as he feared the result of a long-drawn campaign on public opinion in the Union, where the Nationalists were conducting unceasing propaganda against the expedition. He told us further that Italy had come into the war on the side of the Allies, and he told us of the sinking of the *Lusitania*, and of great battles in France. He ordered me to report for duty to Coen Brits, pending instructions from General Smuts, so Ruiter and I went to find him at Karibib, where the old man greeted me with the usual cut of his sjambok by way of welcome. During the next week or two I visited Windhoek several times. The town is built against a hill, and it has many fine buildings and shops. Some of the dwelling-houses and hotels have hot water laid on from a thermal spring flowing out of a rock crevice in the public gardens, and on the plain outside stands an enormous wireless plant, the second largest in the world, it was said.

The German civilian population were polite but aloof, and I never met one who was not serenely confident that they were going to win the war. It was always the same. They said we might temporarily overrun South-West, but in the end we would pay dearly for having challenged the might of Germany.

I found a local German newspaper dated some days prior to the entry of our troops. The leading article ran:

> 'The early occupation of Windhoek by the South African forces is unavoidable. We must bear the inevitable with dignity. General Botha's troops are neither Russian barbarians nor undisciplined French, but they are men of the same Teutonic extraction as ourselves, whose commander would never countenance improper conduct by his men. The occupation can at most continue for a week or two as dire calamity has overtaken the Allies in Europe.
>
> Calais is practically in our hands, and with Calais we hold the key to England. British statesmen are not going to wait until we invade their prosperous land, and they will make peace to save their country from invasion. It goes without saying that the Fatherland will not conclude a peace which leaves German South-West under foreign yoke, and we may say with confidence that the enemy's banner will not long float over us.'

A later article of May 10th, 1915, was to the same effect:

> 'The last German squadrons left Windhoek to-day. We who were obliged to remain looked on in sorrow as our men rode through the streets in the chill autumn wind; we gazed at our departing troops with grief, and yet with envy. For sad it is to stay behind, knowing that the flag of the enemy will soon be hoisted, even if we have the certainty it will fly but for a brief season. We may rest assured that the Emperor will exact stern retribution from these South Africans for their attack on us. Therefore we await their arrival with dignity and calm. They are neither Belgians nor Frenchmen, whose civilians have committed so many offences against the law of nations. With unbroken spirit we shall bear the temporary yoke. That is our duty to our hero-Emperor [*Helden-Kaiser*], to our fellow citizens and to the Fatherland.'

Reading this, one realised that they were trying to keep up their courage, and I remembered the Boer War, when we had hoped against hope, knowing in our hearts how little hope there was.

Coen Brits was stationed Karibib, the village on the Otavi railway, and the German troops were now standing at Omaruru, forty miles up the line. We spent some weeks here, while General Botha was preparing for the death stroke. Supplies had to be brought up from the coast, animals had to be rested, and the damaged bridges and railway track had to be repaired, all of which took time. Old Coen was as genial and entertaining as ever. He provided me with a horse, and I rode to and fro on long journeys, carrying orders to outlying posts. Once there came a telegram for him from a Union citizen of bibulous habits, offering his services. Coen wired back: 'Don't come; all the liquor there is in South-West Africa I can drink myself.'

I was told that on the march from the coast his supply of alcohol had given out, and the only available bottle in his brigade was found to belong to a soldier. Coen was told that, as a brigadier, he was not supposed to drink with a private, but he easily overcame this difficulty, for he promoted the owner to second-lieutenant, and after the two of them had emptied the bottle, he reverted the man back to the ranks, satisfied that the military conventions had been properly observed.

I missed the closing scene of the campaign, for I belonged to the Southern Army and received orders to return, just as General Botha was making ready for his final thrust. Not long after we embarked on the transport at Walvis Bay, he loosed his forces on the enemy. They consisted mostly of Boer commandos, and their rapid advance was too much for the stereotyped military training of the Germans. In a few days the commandos rode hundreds of miles through wild uncharted country. If Hauptmann Francke was still planning to adopt guerrilla tactics, Botha was too quick for him and he was forced to surrender with all his men, guns and ammunition; and for the first time in the Great War, a German commander in the field had laid down his arms.

The campaign was over, and by August 1915 all our men had sailed back to Capetown, their task accomplished.

In spite of the rebellion, and in the teeth of violent opposition from the powerful Nationalist Party, General Botha and General Smuts had added to the Union a territory larger than Germany, and they had done it with fewer casualties than the cost of an average trench raid in France.

Chapter 6

To German East

The moment we returned home from the South-West expedition, the political situation in the Union claimed us. The five-yearly elections were on hand, and we forgot all else. We are a race of politicians, and the struggle that now followed made our previous quarrels almost tame in comparison. The Nationalists were smarting from the result of the rebellion, and we were angered because they had refused to assist us in the German West campaign, so feeling ran high, and at times it looked as if we were on the verge of another civil war.

General Botha asked me to take the field in the Free State, where the Nationalists regarded everyone as a renegade who supported the South African Party. Every meeting I addressed became a battlefield, and more than one village hall still bears the scars and bloodstains of those days. I also undertook to contest the Heilbron seat. I had been under arms shortly before against those whose votes I was seeking, and they had not forgotten it. After a turbulent offensive I was beaten by a huge majority, and what was worse, every constituency in the Free State was captured by our opponents. Luckily, the rest of South Africa showed sounder judgment, and General Botha remained in power. The clamour now died down, and freed from the danger of domestic troubles, Botha and Smuts turned their attention to the conquest of German East Africa.

Up there, the Germans had a strong garrison of regular troops, and an army of eight or ten thousand well-trained Askari, and there too the climate and the difficult nature of the country were their chief defence.

Von Lettow was in command. He was an able leader, who did what Francke should have done in the west, for he took to guerrilla warfare. Hitherto the British

Government had been unable to send out reinforcements, for they were hard pressed in France, and their small local army had found great difficulty in holding its own. But now the authorities had begun to consider the position, and had decided to take the matter in hand. South Africa was asked to supply an expeditionary force for the reduction of the colony, and General Smith Dorrien was sent form France to take command.

Once again General Botha called for volunteers, and within a few weeks drafts were being despatched by sea up the east coast to Mombasa, fifteen hundred miles away, from which they went to base camps in the interior. Before Smith Dorrien could take over he fell ill, whereupon General Smuts assumed command of the campaign, and he left South Africa in December 1915. I decided to go too. I had no *animus* against the German people, but I thought then, as I think now, that a victorious Germany would have been a disaster to human liberty. Also, my chief was going and, further, I could not hang back while so many of my countrymen were moving forward to an adventure in the wilds of Africa. I had to settle my affairs, for I foresaw a long absence, so I could not get away until two months later, and it was only in February 1916 that I sailed from Durban in a troopship with my native boy Ruiter.

After an uneventful voyage we reached Mombasa, and in company with other troops going inland we entrained for Voi, a camp on the railway line that runs to Nairobi. Our route took us at first through low-lying jungle, steaming with heat, and then across dreary scrub country devoid of man and beast. The line ran parallel to the German frontier, forty miles south, and it was occasionally attacked by small enemy forces that made their way on foot through the thorn to derail an engine or blow up a culvert; but we were not molested, though the line continued to be interfered with during the next month or two.

At Voi we lay over for several days. Here we learned that our troops had fought several important engagements. Von Lettow had held a formidable position on the Taveta Hills, from which General Smuts had ejected him after heavy fighting. As a result, the South African troops had advanced over the border, and were lying below Mount Kilimanjaro, well within German territory.

From Voi we travelled to an advance supply camp at Mbuyuni, near the German boundary, where I spent an interesting time.

The region from the Serengetti Plains on British territory, round by Kilimanjaro to Mount Meru, a hundred miles away, and then back to the Paré Hills, is probably the most fascinating part of the African continent. Within this charmed circle lie game-covered plains, and swamps and jungles and impenetrable forests. There lie the snow-capped peaks of Kibu and Mawenzi with their base in the tropics and their summits wrapped in eternal ice and snow. There is Mount Meru like a basalt pyramid to the east, and there are lakes and craters, and a network of great rivers, with strange tribes and beautiful scenery, such as no other country in the world that I know of can show within so small a compass.

I rode to Lake Chala, lying high in an extinct volcano, and I explored Lake Jipe, a curious sheet of water, half in British and half in German territory, and each of these journeys led through vast herds of big game. I saw giraffe and eland, wildebeest and zebra, and of an evening I used to sit on the banks of the Lumi River watching the thousands of animals coming down to drink.

It was all so beautiful that I forgot I was on my way to a war, until one evening we received orders to march next day. With our instructions came a change in the weather, for the rainy season was on hand. The water fell in torrents, and the camp underfoot was like a lake. Looking down towards the German border, we could see black clouds towering miles high into the sky and hear the incessant growl and mutter of thunder.

I saw now that campaigning in a country like this was going to be far more difficult than in German West. In that territory there were open plains, and above all there was no fever, no horse sickness, and no tsetse fly. Here lay before us a thousand miles of dense forest and bush, and a deadly climate, and with the lowered spirits that come on most South Africans when there is no sunshine, I did not envy General Smuts the task upon which he was embarked.

Next morning we marched out with the rain coming down in sheets. We plodded along to Taveta where we spent a night, and then crossed the German border. We passed over the Himu River and several other streams, and then made our way gradually through the forest to Neu Moschi at the foot of Mount Kilimanjaro, where the South African troops were camped in the rain. Here I was told that General Smuts was at Alt Moschi, a German fort lying on the slopes of the mountain, so Ruiter and I climbed the slippery road in a deluge, and by nightfall I was once more on his staff.

Military operations had come to a standstill on account of the weather. Our forces were mudbound at Neu Moschi and Kahé, a point on the German railway line that runs along the Pangani River to the coast. I do not know where von Lettow and his men were at this time, but they seemed to be scattered all over the country.

From such information as I could gather, General Smuts intended, as soon as the rains were over, to march down the Pangani, and then strike south towards the Central Railway that descends from the great lakes to Dâr-es-Salaam.

As a preliminary he had sent Jacobus van Deventer, our old Boer war commandant, with a column of mounted men and infantry, nearly five thousand strong, to make for the Central Railway via Mount Meru and Arusha. This expedition had vanished into the bush some time before my arrival. It was at present hung up by the rains two hundred miles away, and word had come back that our men were suffering great hardships from the weather, and from the ravages of malaria. For a while I remained at Headquarters. I climbed the slopes of Kilimanjaro and explored the wonderful forest, in company with my friend Krige. He and I had both belonged to Isaac Malherbe's corporalship in the old days of the Boer War. He was so dangerously wounded at the Battle of Spion Kop that he was left for dead, but he recovered and even accompanied our raid into the Cape Colony in 1901.[1]

There were many elephants in the forest, but although we came frequently on their tracks we never saw any. Once we almost reached the snow line, thousands of feet up. On General Smuts's staff were several British officers who had remained after Smith Dorrien fell ill, and as they were the first men from the trenches in France whom I had met, I listened eagerly to their accounts of the great battles overseas. One of them was McCalmont, the millionaire owner of Isinglass, a famous racehorse. Another was Venables. He wore an artificial hand, in lieu of one that had been shot away, and he

---

[1] See *Commando* (pages 44 and 112 of this trilogy—ed).

could release it by pressing a clip at the wrist. One evening, at the fort, a Swahili mess-waiter brought in a tray of refreshments. Venables pretended to reach for a glass, and without drawing his arm, left his dummy hand lying on the salver. The Swahili stared wide-eyed at the object for a moment, then he dashed tray and contents to the ground, and with a howl of terror rushed out into the night and we never saw him again. Another morning Venables came laughing into the office with a story that a party of Germans had approached the railway at Tsavo. He said the Babu stationmaster had telegraphed to Headquarters:

> 'One hundred Germans advancing on station, please send one rifle and one hundred rounds of ammunition.'

It was pleasant living at Moschi, with Kilimanjaro towering overhead. The snow-crowned peaks glittering at night under a full moon is the most majestic sight I have ever seen.

But I grew restless, and when I heard that three officers and a contingent of eighty men were going forward to join van Deventer I obtained permission to accompany them. I had not brought any horses from the Union. I had taken three of my own horses to German West, and had lost them all, so I had learned wisdom, and now General Smuts allowed me to choose what I wanted from amongst the staff animals. I took a brown and a chestnut for myself, and a wiry Basuto pony for Ruiter, and thus well equipped we set off with the reinforcements. For the first two days we rode through dense forest as far as the Sabok River, crossing numerous other streams flowing down from Kilimanjaro, all swollen from the rains that were still coming down.

To our right lay Mount Meru, with Arusha beyond. In the open spaces of the forest were great quantities of big game, and once I saw a herd of elephant beneath tall trees by a river bank. Beyond Meru the weather lifted, and we emerged from the gloom of rain and forest into the sunshine of the Masai Plains. The Masai are a fighting tribe always at war with their neighbours. They wear short pigtails like the old-fashioned British jack tars, and they carry long-bladed stabbing spears, and sword and shield. On one occasion while we were halted in a clearing, a raiding party of them came by in single file, and although their path ran within a few feet of where we sat beside our saddles, they looked neither to right nor left, but marched straight on, as if we were not there. They are a strange race. Their plains are alive with game, but they will not touch venison, and their food consists chiefly of milk and blood from the veins of their cattle. They draw what blood they require, and then close up the artery with a thorn pushed through the animal's skin. Counting cattle as money, they are said to be the wealthiest people in the world.

Far out on the plains we reached Lol Kissale, a lonely hill standing like an island above the bush, and here we came on a number of van Deventer's sick and wounded. They told us he had surrounded the 27th Field Company of Askari on this hill, and after a sharp fight had captured them all. There were four or five German officers and NCO's and about a hundred and fifty Askari, well-built, soldierly men in khaki tunics and shorts. From Lol Kissale we rode on through wonderful game country, with troops of giraffe and herds of zebra, eland and wildebeest.

The first night out from Lol Kissale we camped at Masaiwellen, and lions were roaring about us till dawn. Early next morning, as we rode along, we saw a lion and a lioness tearing at a dead horse beside the road (for van Deventer's passage had left many animals behind). One of the men fired and hit the lion, but he gave a grunt and sprang into the bush with his mate. We passed little Masai villages with their queer flat-roofed huts of mud, the inhabitants gazing at us as incuriously as if our presence in their domains did not concern them.

As on previous days, our road still ran through dense bush with numberless antelopes of all kinds grazing in the open spaces, but except for those which we had to shoot for food, we left them alone.

In two days we reached Ufiome, a little village in the hills on the far border of the Masai country. This place had been an administrative post of the Germans, and there was a substantial boma (fort) and various official buildings and dwelling-houses. We found a number of Boer families here. They had left South Africa to avoid living under British rule, and now it was overtaking them once more, just as it had overtaken their compatriots in German South-West, and as it had overtaken their ancestors who had moved north into the wilds during the Great Trek of 1835.

Near Ufiome, I saw three lions trotting in the distance across a millet field. They were so plentiful in these parts that some Boers to whom I happened to be speaking at the time scarcely troubled to glance at them, though to me they were an ever interesting sight.

We learned that van Deventer was thirty miles ahead at Kondoa Irangi, so next day, in heavy rain, we rode on. That afternoon we came on a small camp in charge of Major Hilgaard de Jager. He had not only fought against the British during the last Boer War, but he had fought against them in the war of 1880 as well, and he had taken part in the Battle of Amajuba where, so he told me, he had seen General Colley lying dead on the hilltop. He was a small wrinkled old fellow, with a fund of anecdote and dry humour that kept one in roars of laughter. With him I found my friend Jack Borrius of the Ryk Section. In spite of having lost an eye and a hand during our expedition in the Boer War, that I have elsewhere described,[1] he was serving here as a scout. He was one of the men who, with my brother Joubert and many others, had been handed over to the Germans by Maritz, and he told me the news that my brother was also in East Africa.

From de Jager's camp the country fell away to a long plain stretching to Kondoa Irangi, and by next afternoon we came in sight of the native town on the near side of the river, with the fort and European quarters beyond.

We reached there after dark and camped for the night in the open space before the Boma. We had no knowledge of the local military situation, so we were considerably surprised at being wakened at dawn next morning by the boom of guns, followed by a succession of heavy shells exploding around us on the square. Luckily the river bank was near, and we were able to hustle our men and horses under cover without suffering any loss, but it was surprising to be bombarded by sixty-pound shells in the heart of the wilds. The shell-fire continued intermittently for half an hour, when it ceased, and we emerged from the river bed to look around us. Some distance away stood a large church surrounded by tents, and there we found Colonel Fairweather of the Cyclist Corps, with his men. A shell had exploded inside the church, killing two

---

[1] See *Commando* (page 136 of this trilogy—ed).

men whose bodies were being extricated from the fallen masonry as we came up. We got directions for finding van Deventer's headquarters, and recrossing the river, discovered him and his staff installed in one of the houses facing the square. He explained things to me. Owing to the heavy rains and lack of supplies his advance was held up. Nearly eleven hundred of his men were down with fever, and the Germans, taking advantage of his immobilised condition, had brought up a strong force from the Central Railway, and were at this moment holding the line of hills overlooking the town. They had many field and machine guns, as well as several sixty-pounder naval guns that had been removed from the *Königsberg*, one of their cruisers that had taken shelter in the Rufiji River. It was with shells from these guns that we had made acquaintance that morning.

Von Lettow himself was said to be here, and a few nights before he had launched an attack on our lines that had only been beaten off by fierce hand-to-hand fighting in the dark. The enemy lay in an entrenched position across our front, and with so many of our men out of action from malaria, and with the rest on half rations, van Deventer was unable to continue his attempt to reach the Central Railway, his objective since leaving Mount Kilimanjaro. All this was disappointing, and I for one look back with no pleasure upon the long period of enforced inactivity that followed. Our men were strung out for miles to right and left, facing the German positions, and for the next two months there was stalemate. I was posted to the First Mounted Brigade, holding the left flank of our line in very rugged hills. Food was scarce and sometimes lacking altogether, and cold biting rains, varied by oppressive heat, prevailed much of the time. The Germans were before us in the ravines and gorges, but in such rough country it was difficult to know exactly where their front line ran. Often bullets whipped about our ears from some unexpected quarter, and it was but rarely that we caught more than a fleeting glimpse of the enemy. It was well for us that the Askari, like all natives, were remarkably poor shots, while the German soldiers were not particularly good either, so that our losses were not heavy, and we probably caused more damage then we received during our frequent brushes.

There was a little six-pounder German gun in our vicinity, daringly handled by an officer whom we learned to know by sight, so often did he appear from behind boulder or thicket, with his field-piece carried on a wooden frame by its Askari crew. In a moment, half a dozen rounds would come screeching at us, after which the gun was taken off to reappear at some other spot. Beyond wounding a few horses once, she did no harm that I know of, and the men laughed at 'Big Bertha' as they called her. One morning three of us tried to stalk the gun, but when we closed in on the patch of scrub where we had last seen her, all we found for our pains was a piece of paper bearing a derisive message: '15 Rupees for the bluddy Englisch', a joke at which we were not amused, after our long crawl in the heat.

On another occasion we were ordered to reconnoitre down a rocky gorge giving access to the open country beyond. The Germans, with great speed, rushed up two companies of Askari, who came at us as eagerly as hounds on the scent. Young Lieut Bowden stood on a rock to get a better view, and almost immediately fell back dead, and we had four other men killed and a number wounded, before the attack was staved off. Desultory fighting of this kind went on most of the time, while we were waiting for the fever season to pass, and for the roads to dry. I do not know how many men died of fever, but I think we left over three hundred of our countrymen in the graveyard at Kondoa Irangi.

During all this time the enemy forces confronting us must have been having their own troubles. In some Morogoro newspapers, that were brought in, were many obituary notices of officers and men *'gefallen auf die Höhe von Kondoa Irangi'* (fallen on the heights of Kondoa Irangi), and the names of many others who had died of fever. Moreover, like ourselves, they had their supply difficulties, for this region is inhabited by a poverty-stricken native tribe, who wander about with clubs and bows and arrows, so there was little to be had by foraging, and there was no big game within transport distance. In one of these captured newspapers there was a paragraph blacked out by the German Censor, so I set to work with a magnifying glass, and after a lot of trouble succeeded in deciphering most of the suppressed item. It had nothing to do with the military situation. It was an account of a revolver duel between a German officer and a planter.

The planter had killed his opponent and he was tried by court martial and hanged (*mit dem Tode durch den Strang bestrafft*). Apparently a great deal of feeling had been aroused, for not only had the reference to the affair in the paper been rendered illegible, but there was a command from von Lettow which said: 'Justice has been done and this unhappy affair is now relegated to oblivion (*die Sache gehört jetzt der Vergessenheit*). I call upon all citizens for the common good to refrain from further discussion.'

Suddenly, towards the middle of July 1916, the Germans evacuated their positions, and we awoke one morning to find them gone. Mounted patrols were pushed forward, and we came on many well-built hospital and other bandas in the valley behind their trenches. The numerous graves showed that they too had suffered severely. We then rode through the hills into the scrub-covered plains. Once I saw a single Askari running across a glade, but he was out of sight before I could fire, and a little later, hearing shots to our left, we made thither to find two of our men lying dead, but no sight of the enemy.

After a long and difficult march through the bush, we cut into the road along which the main German force was retiring. I was with our advance party, and as we rode on to the bank of the Barei, a broad sandy river bed with occasional water-holes, we saw twenty or thirty Askari squatted around their fires. They grabbed their rifles, and opened so hot a fire that we were glad to retreat up the road, to await the rest of our party. After a while they arrived and we advanced. The Askari had withdrawn to the opposite bank of the river, from which a vicious splutter of bullets whizzed about us. I dismounted and walked forward with some others, and as we went there was a thud, and one of our men pitched forward dead. So we remounted and galloped across the river bed under an ill-aimed fire from the Askari rearguard, whom we could just see making off into the dense thicket on either side of the road. We spent the night by the river, listening to the lions, and next morning van Deventer arrived. He said his whole force was coming on behind, making for the Chamballa water-holes, fifteen miles down the road. He ordered me to lead a small patrol by a detour through the bush, to scout the country to the east. We rode along the Barei River for the first day, camping on its banks that night, during which we spent most of our time pacifying our frightened horses, who threatened to stampede every time a lion roared. From there, next day, with a native guide, we threaded our way along game paths, to find out at the various native villages whether there were Germans or Askari about. From the fact that the natives were quietly at their kraals I knew the Askari were gone, for whenever there are any about the local inhabitants take to flight. The Germans recruit their Askari from the savage tribes beyond the lakes, and they are much dreaded by the unwarlike people who live in this area. In the course of the morning I saw a lioness squatting on her haunches close to a millet field in which native women, their infants on their backs, were unconcernedly hoeing the ground, and they merely laughed when I pointed out the lioness to them, so little fear have they in the daytime of these brutes. For safety's sake, however, I fired a shot, and drove her away.

Next day we made for Chamballa, a series of waterholes among some hills. The place was crowded with troops, horses and wagons, that had come up, and van Deventer was there. He told me that General Smuts was also on the move. He had marched down the Pangani River, and was now striking south for the Central Railway on a course parallel to our own, some hundred and fifty miles to our left. His force and ours were ultimately to join hands, but in the meanwhile each was independently groping its way through unknown bush country.

As far as we were concerned, the Central Railway was still ninety miles away, and whereas in the past we had been hampered by too much water, we were now entering a region that looked as if no rain ever fell on it.

I was ordered next morning to take out a patrol and search for a pan of water, reported by local natives as lying some distance off the main road. It was an interesting ride. We were in game country once more, and herds of eland, wildebeest and sassaby were grazing in all directions, and several times we saw giraffe. I never tired of looking at the strange and beautiful creatures of Africa, and I learned in these days the pity of killing them without need.

By midday our native guide brought us to the pan. As we approached we heard the trumpeting of elephant, and when we reached the water it was all muddy and churned where they had been drinking a few minutes before, but the animals themselves were crashing out of sight among the trees. I sent a man back to report the water, while we went on. We spent the night around big camp fires, for the lions were again holding a concert, and next day we reached Hanetti, a desolate spot with a few muddy waterholes and a small native village. The natives told us that the German forces had passed through the previous day, and that a strong rearguard was holding the next water at Chenene, twelve miles on, so we halted until our troops arrived.

Towards evening a weary horseman rode in from the left to say that the 1st and 3rd Mounted Regiments were held up at Tissu-Kwamedu, thirty miles east. They had made a flank march, and nearing there, after men and horses had gone for twenty-four hours without water, had found the place strongly occupied by the enemy. Our men were reported to be in a serious plight, as their animals were too exhausted to be ridden back to other water, and the enemy were holding a fortified position before the wells. Van Deventer was requested to send reinforcements, but our troops that were arriving at Hanetti were too fatigued to undertake a forced march. He therefore ordered a patrol to ride hard for Tissu-Kwamedu, with a message that the two regiments were to take the wells at all costs.

We set out with a native guide, and trekked steadily all through the tropical night, seeing the dim forms of many animals silently moving in the dark. Soon after daybreak we heard the crackle of rifle-fire, and pushing forward, were just in time to see our mounted men gallop across a wide clearing at the far end of which lay the enemy around the wells. Desperate with thirst, they had anticipated van Deventer's instructions, and were riding full tilt upon the rifle pits. The enemy had opened a ragged fire, but as we hurried up we saw several hundred Askari rise to their feet, and make for the bush behind. Their German officers seemed to be trying to stop them, then they followed their men and the fight was over. It was now a pleasure to see horses and men drinking their fill from the cool, clear water, for these are famous wells, known for their excellent and abundant supply. They lie on the old caravan route to the coast, and I have read that for a thousand years and more the great slave convoys from the interior were halted there, before being driven to Dâr-es-Salaam.

Three or four of our men were wounded, and there were a dozen dead and wounded Askari, and after a while a German officer came limping out of the bush to surrender. Going about among the men, I came on my brother Joubert, whom I had not seen for nearly ten years. He was a sergeant with the 3rd, and he told me he had only returned from hospital on the day that our advance started from Kondoa, which was the reason why we had not met before. He had much to say of how he fared in the past, of Maritz's treachery, and of his long months in a German prison camp in South-West. Here too, I met another acquaintance of mine, young Piet Swart, a Boer farm hand from Heilbron district. He had served under me during the rebellion, and was now a rifleman in my brother's regiment. He was haggard from fever, he had starved and suffered and he was in rags, but he held an original view of the campaign, for when I asked him whether he regretted having come, he said No: he had travelled in a ship, he had seen aeroplanes and Kilimanjaro and elephants, and if his parents wanted to see all this it would cost them over fifty pounds.

Next day our patrol started back for Hanetti. There was plenty of game on the way, and when a wild sow ran by with a string of youngsters squealing at her heels, I shot one, and we had baked sucking pig for supper that night.

At Hanetti, van Deventer was preparing to deal with the enemy at the Chenene water-holes. The 11th SA Infantry had come up, and the morning after my return they were ordered to advance.

Hilgaard de Jager rode ahead with his scouts, and I accompanied him. Our course lay through dense bush, so we were compelled to keep to the road, a pretty dangerous business, for the enemy custom was to lie in wait at a bend, fire a volley, and then decamp along some pathway, to repeat the process further on. That was what happened here. After we had gone some miles, the road entered a kloof flanked on either side by rugged hills, and as we approached the intake, half a dozen Askari and one German ran out, fired a single volley at us, and dived back into the scrub. No one was hit, and we caught a glimpse of a considerable number of Askari running up the wooded slopes to take position above. We waited for the infantry, and Col Burne at once pushed them into the bush. The enemy opened rifle and machine-gun fire on our men and a fierce little battle began. Then there came from the rear two engines of war that were new to me, although I had read of them. They were Rolls-Royce armoured cars, just arrived from base, and immediately sent into action. It was the first and last time, I believe, that they were used in this country, as they were found unsuitable for rough work, but on this occasion, at any rate, they justified themselves.

Capt Goldberg, a Jewish officer, was in charge, and he took his machines straight at the enemy barricade across the road. As he neared the work, machine-gun bullets rattled like hail on the steel plates, but he continued on his way, hosing the enemy with his fire as he went. Old Hilgaard's face was a picture when he saw the Askari running for all they were worth, before the armoured cars. He clapped me on the back and cried in Dutch (he knew no English): 'By God, man, those things look for all the world like two rhino bulls charging up-wind!' and he chuckled with glee at a sight that had thus far lain beyond his military ken.

The forward thrust of the cars had cut across the enemy position, and the rest of the Askari on either side of the road vanished into the bush, leaving us to reach the waterholes without further opposition. We had three men killed in this affair, and I saw a few dead Askari lying on the road, while there were probably more dead among the trees.

Next day the advance was continued to Mei-Mei, another water-hole, where de Jager captured a detachment of the 9th Field Company, all Europeans, mounted on little Somali mules. I did not see this fight, but I arrived in time to find the old Major distributing the loot among his followers. Of the thirty-odd prisoners, two were young Transvaal Boers. When spoken to, they stood stiffly to attention, and on being dismissed, they goose-stepped back to their companions, came to a halt with a stamp of feet, and fell out in best Prussian style, which made de Jager and his irregulars roar with laughter. This was the last effort the Germans made to hold us up. When we continued our advance we found them gone, and by next afternoon, scouting through the bush, we saw the gleam of white buildings and the Fort of Dodoma out on the plain, and also the station and metalled track, to show that one stage of the campaign was over, for we were astride the Central Railway at last.

Chapter 7

The Toll of Fly and Fever

We were met at the gateway of the Dodoma Fort by an enormously corpulent German official, who handed over the keys and a medical certificate as to himself.

General van Deventer decided to postpone his entry until next day, so he placed sentries at every entrance to the Fort, and ordered me, with an officer of his staff, to take up quarters inside for the night. My companion and I at once set about making an inventory of the war material and stores that had been left behind. By the aid of a lantern we went through room after room, and gallery after gallery, opening boxes and cases with a bayonet, and when van Deventer arrived in the morning we had an imposing array of loot awaiting his inspection in the courtyard.

Now that we were on the Central Railway, a turning point in the operations had been reached. Sooner or later the whole line must fall into our hands, and with that we would have driven von Lettow from the northern half of the colony, leaving him the alternative of surrender or of taking to the savage country lying towards the Rufiji, where he and his men would be little better than bushrangers.

We knew that General Smuts was advancing on Morogoro, the administrative capital, about a hundred and fifty miles down, and by all accounts the entire German forces were concentrated in the area between our two converging armies. So far as the railway was concerned, the sector between Dodoma and Morogoro was still in possession of the enemy, and during the next week or two von Lettow skilfully ran his troops up and down from one threatened point to another, in a manner that was to cause us a great deal of trouble before we finally shouldered him off.

Our task now was to work eastwards along the railway, to join hands with General Smuts across the terribly difficult country that still separated the two forces. Van Deventer made immediate preparation. The 1st and 3rd Mounted Regiments, that had been marching on our left flank during the advance on Dodoma, were lying at Njangalo, thirty miles east, having reached there after their fight for the wells at Tissu-Kwamedu. I was ordered to join them, so with my servant Ruiter I rode across the plains.

At Njangalo I found our men camped around the waterholes in picturesque country. There had been the usual skirmish for the water, in the course of which Major de Jager was shot below the heart. He was lying in a precarious condition under a grass shelter, and I nearly caused his death, for sitting by him one morning, I sought to while away the time by repairing the seat of my riding-breeches with a cutting from the sleeve of my tunic. My sartorial efforts were too much for him and he burst into fits of laughter, bringing on a flow of blood from which he barely recovered.

We remained at Njangalo for several days. I went out with the hunting parties to get meat, and we brought in twelve to fifteen huge eland on the wagons. Before leaving the Fort at Dodoma I had come on a dozen cases of Ersatz whisky. Not without difficulty I had smuggled one case on board a supply wagon that was following me to Njangalo. When the wagon arrived I satisfied myself that the box of contraband was still there, then I informed my friends that tonight was the night. After sunset an expectant circle stood round my fire, while I prized off the lid with a hatchet. When the contents were exposed there lay, not row upon row of straw-covered bottles as in the crates I had opened in the Fort, but layer upon layer of counterfoil receipt blocks, that had been packed away by some over-zealous German official, and the gathering dispersed in gloom.

General van Deventer now began his advance down the railway line. Owing to the difficult country, he did not follow the metals, but struck away for Mpapwa, an important German centre lying thirty-five miles eastwards among rugged hills showing in the distance. We started on a long march through waterless bush, and before dark we reached Chunyo Neck, the enemy holding the crest in force, and the only available water on the far side. Our infantry were up, and as the slopes were too steep and the scrub too dense for mounted work, we all climbed up on foot. Soon came the rattle of machine-guns, as the Germans searched the jungle, and as we neared the top I caught a glimpse of our old Kondoa friend, the little six-pounder, handled by the same white-coated gunner whom we had learned to know there. He loosed a few rounds, but when our QF battery came up from the rear and opened fire, the opposing force disappeared over the ridge into the bush behind, where it was impossible to follow as it was nearly dark. Of our men we lost four killed and eleven wounded, so the waterhole was an expensive one, as were most of them in these days.

Next morning we crossed the hills into a thickly populated area. All along the road stood native women with baskets of beans and poultry to greet us.

Mpapwa Town lay twelve miles away across dense bush, and we worked forward carefully, for the natives told us the enemy was waiting there. After a time we could see a well-built fort surrounded by other buildings and by a native town. As we came within range of the Boma, machine-guns opened fire, whereupon we scattered into the bush, until the rest of our troops came up. While we were halted, the Kondoa six-pounder improved the shining hour by shelling us, and four of our men were wounded, but this was the last we ever saw or heard of her.

Presently our battery arrived, and as soon as the guns began to shell the town, we saw the enemy move out. I was ordered to ride in with an escort to take possession of the Fort, and the mounted men were sent on a wide circle to get athwart the road beyond, and cut off the retreat. We found the gateway of the Boma standing wide open and the place was deserted. In the streets of the town lay a few dead Askari, and two or three wounded sat nursing their hurts, but the main force had doubled across the sandy river bed, and in a few minutes rifles were cracking at us from the slope beyond. Mounting a stairway to the parapets of the Fort, I saw our horsemen appearing and disappearing through the bush on their way to get behind the enemy. Some distance up the road on the other side of the river were several field companies of Askari, with a knot of European officers walking up and down in an undecided manner. I thought they were meditating surrender, but in this I was mistaken, for as soon as our guns got their range the whole lot vanished in the twinkling of an eye. Our mounted men were in their rear, and they were practically surrounded, but in bush fighting ordinary rules do not apply, and when our cordon tightened, they had filtered away like water through a sieve. Not only were they gone, but before long they were firing at us from a bush-covered rise to the left. The infantry under Col Molyneux were ordered to attack, and I went with them. It was hot work, with two or three hundred Askari blazing away at us. But their shooting was bad, and we went steadily to the top, until we saw the Askari running for it. We lost three men killed, but we killed a considerable number of them, and the ground was littered with abandoned rifles and equipment. I then returned to where I had left my horse, and rode back to the Boma. The mounted men had brought in ten German prisoners and twenty or thirty Askari, but the rest of the enemy got away. I spent the night camped in a garden beside the stream. Next morning I found a dead Askari not far behind the tree under which I had slept, and several more were lying dead in the vegetable plots fringing the stream. We lay over at Mpapwa for three days, as the grazing was good, and again I went out with the hunting parties to shoot eland. They were so fat and unwieldy that we rode up to the herds, and singling out the animals we wanted, shot them down like so many bullocks. It was an unsporting business, but we needed food.

From Mpapwa we continued east, and when we neared Kidete next day we were brought to a standstill. We had marched twenty-six miles without water, and again, on a line of rugged hills, lay the enemy barring us from the river behind. We were close to the railway line once more, and in addition to being strongly posted, the Germans had a 4.1 naval gun on a truck pulled by an engine, which steamed up and down shelling us as it went. Our infantry attacked at once, while the mounted men rode to turn the flanks. Under the heavy fire directed on them, the infantry made little headway. By dark they had suffered over fifty casualties, and were hung up halfway along the slopes. Once more we were in a serious predicament, for the nearest water behind was many miles away, and the only other water was in the hands of the enemy. I spent a thirsty night with the right flanking party, and by morning we found ourselves involved in such impenetrable country that we had to return the way we had come. When at last we got back to the main road we found that the left flank had been turned, and that the enemy had retired overnight, leaving us free to reach Kidete Station, where our whole army was lining the river bank, drinking their fill from the swift flowing stream.

We were now come, in the course of a single march, to totally different country. Instead of monotonous waterless scrub and bush, we had reached tropical conditions. We were suddenly in a land of waving palms and bamboo thickets, beautiful mountain scenery, and steaming heat. The mounted regiments rode down a long valley through which the railway wound, and far below we halted in the shade of great trees, and cooked a meal and bathed in the river, enjoying the wonderful landscape around us.

After midday I accompanied an advance patrol. Our course lay through picturesque groves of bottle palm and clumps of bamboo forest, and on rounding a bend we were brought up by the sight of a German troop train lying on its side, halfway down a high embankment. Part of the train was on fire, and a more complete smash I have never seen. I never heard how the accident happened, but under the wreckage we found nine dead Askari, and many more must have been injured, for there was an improvised dressing-station under a tree, with bloodstained bandages and uniforms scattered about. From here we worked our way down towards Karessa, where the valley narrows to a gorge not more than two hundred yards wide. As we neared the entrance to this ugly gateway, we were fired on by a few sentries posted overhead. Leaving our horses under cover, we climbed the side of the valley to where we could see into the gorge. There was barely room for the road, the railway, and the river to pass out into the country beyond. On the railway track was a party of Askari, laying land mines, as we afterwards found, and we caught them so unawares that we dropped five, the rest running wildly to the rear. As a hot fire was opened in return, we made for our animals, and galloped up the road to rejoin our main body.

When General van Deventer heard that the entrance was held, he halted until next morning, and then pushed his infantry up the heights on either side of the valley. After many hours of hard climbing through the dense growth we saw our men dotting the crest, and without firing a shot they outflanked the enemy rearguard from a position that would have cost many lives in a frontal attack.

The way into the poort was now clear. While we were riding through, some of our men crossed the river to look at the dead Askari lying beside the railway track. As we watched them, there came a loud explosion, and a cloud of dust and smoke, and a soldier was blown to pieces before our eyes by a mine upon which he had trodden. And another disaster befell us in this poort. In passing a timber thicket, our horses began to kick and lash. Halting to ascertain the cause we found what we took to be gadflies swiftly darting in and out, but one of the men identified the insects as the dreaded tsetse fly, a baleful omen for the future of a mounted force. The tsetse is somewhat larger than the common house-fly, with wings that fold scissorwise. It has a mysterious habit of adhering to well-defined belts, which for some unexplained reason it will not leave. One may take a horse close to a fly belt without seeing a tsetse, but the moment the invisible border is passed, they emerge viciously from the shade. Their presence seems to be unconnected with game, and probably some species of vegetation, not yet discovered, is necessary to their existence. The man who solves the enigma will deserve well of Africa. Fortunately, a fly-bitten horse will last for weeks in the absence of rain, so for the time being no immediate ill effects were to be seen.

All our men had marched through the gorge by dark, and that night we camped by the river at Muni-Sagara. A mounted patrol brought in a few German soldiers who had lost their way in the bush. They said Hauptmann Lincke was in command of the troops in front of us, and that von Lettow had gone to oppose General Smuts, who was nearing Morogoro.

Next morning we went on, the road and railway entering rough hill country densely grown with jungle. I was riding with a patrol beside the railway line when a single German officer leaped out of the tall grass and emptied his Mauser pistol at us from about thirty paces, after which he vanished. His aim was wild and no damage was done, but his appearance was a prelude to trouble, for it was followed by the roar of heavy guns and the howling of shells, coming towards and exploding around us. The Germans had several *Königsberg* naval guns, probably mounted on a train, and they had the range to such a nicety that we made haste to find shelter behind a bank that overhung the road. Here I had a narrow escape. My native boy Ruiter was close behind, so I handed him the reins of my chestnut, and he dismounted and sat with his back to the earthen bank, holding both our horses by the reins while he placidly puffed away at his pipe. As always during a halt in hot weather, I removed the saddle to ease my animal's back, and just as I had done this, a shell burst on us like a thunderclap. When the smoke cleared there lay my poor chestnut dead. I looked to see whether Ruiter was safe, and he was still holding the dead horse and his own by the reins and he was still imperturbably smoking. We were sad at losing the chestnut, but now that we were in fly country, he had met with an easier death than was awaiting all our other horses, although we scarcely realised it as yet.

General van Deventer came up and ordered us forward to reconnoitre. I sent for my spare brown horse, and we rode to a point from which we could see the Germans holding a transverse ridge lower down the wide valley. As our troops moved into view, they started to shell the road with very accurate fire, and our advance came to a standstill. In the course of the day, young Allen of the 9th went with me to pluck millet in a field. A ricochet that came skimming over the crest burst upon us, killing him on the spot, and I helped to bury the boy under a tree.

For a long time we were held up, while our QF Battery shelled the enemy position. We had about twenty casualties that day. Towards evening the 1st and 3rd Horse proceeded up the sides of the hills, and by next morning they had out-flanked the enemy to such good effect that when we advanced down the valley, we found them gone.

We now rode out of the hills. Beyond lay an unhealthy-looking plain, shimmering in the heat, and before us was the town of Kilossa. Here was the usual fort and the usual official buildings, and a large native quarter. There were railway workshops, a rum distillery, and for miles around great rubber plantations, their storehouses and sheds standing like islands above the trees. German rearguards were lurking in the vicinity, for later in the morning, while I was with a patrol, we heard shots in the bush, and met a party carrying back two dead and two wounded. They had run into an ambush, and had suffered these casualties without so much as a glimpse of the enemy.

We rested for two days at Kilossa. During this time an aeroplane came over. It was only the second one I had ever seen in my life, and it dropped a message to say that General Smuts had reached Morogoro, so our two forces were about fifty miles apart.

Van Deventer now marched south to Kidodi with the 1st Horse and the infantry, and the rest of us were ordered to move east along the railway line. Our first day took us as far as the Makata River, across a wide plain covered with game and tsetse fly, and we camped that night beside the water. Next morning I rode out with a hunting party. We killed four giraffe by galloping alongside them and firing shot after shot, until the poor brutes rolled over dead. Still, the men and the native carriers required food, and thus they were supplied. As I was returning to camp that evening, I heard angry words, and then the report of firearms, and presently I came on the body of a native belonging to our forces. His chest was ripped open by a heavy-calibre bullet, and, strangely enough, the face of the dead man bore a placid smile.

Ruiter, who had private channels of information among the porters, told me soon after we got back that the native had been killed by an Indian of the mountain battery. He said the two men had fought a revolver duel, and the victor, having killed his opponent, decamped with both weapons. The native and Indian spectators who had assembled to watch the combat disappeared too. It was apparently a fair fight, so I kept my own counsel.

From the Makata River, in a two days' ride, with the atmosphere like a Turkish bath, we reached M'lali, a native village at the foot of the Uluguru Mountains. Here, for the first time, we came in touch with patrols from General Smuts's force. They told us that Smuts himself was at the enemy capital, fourteen miles away, and that Coen Brits, my old crony, was on the road in our direction with his mounted brigade. They told us of their experiences since leaving the Pangani River near Mount Kilimanjaro, and of their long trek to Morogoro. They had to fight hard at times, but, as with ourselves, the real enemy had been the jungle, fever, tsetse and the lack of supplies.

Next morning we heard gun and rifle fire among the foothills where Brits was skirmishing, and when we got up we found that the Germans had retired into the mountains, abandoning one of the *Königsberg* naval guns, which we came upon in a clearing, surrounded by many empty shell-cases.

We had now finally pushed von Lettow off the Central railway line, and our information was that he and his army had retired into the Uluguru Mountains lying before us, a magnificent sweep of forest-clad heights, running sixty miles east by west, and forty or fifty miles deep. Our next task was to drive him out of this great fastness.

As van Deventer was still away, Coen Brits was in local command. I had not seen him since the German West days, so I rode over to pay my respects. He greeted me with a slash of the sjambok and a 'Good day you——, I'm glad to see you'.

He held the rank of Brigadier-General. Around the gilt oak-leaves on each gorget tab there twined sprigs of forget-me-nots, embroidered in vivid purple. Thinking this was some new insignia of office I asked him what it meant. Looking down affectionately at the adornments, the old man said that his wife had worked the flowers upon his uniform to remind him of her while he was at the war. We could not help smiling, but we liked him the more for his naive simplicity.

General Smuts came to see us at M'lali. He was thin and ill from malaria, but he spoke cheerfully. He told me that Roumania had joined the Allies, and he gave us the latest news from France. We had been in the wilds for so long that we had almost forgotten that there was another war, so remote did things in Europe seem to us. He had come to make arrangements for an advance, and as soon as he returned to Morogoro the 1st Mounted Brigade was ordered to move into the Uluguru Mountains, while Coen Brits with his 2nd Brigade was to make a wide turning movement round the western flank of the range.

Accordingly he and his men vanished into the bush, and we began to climb the slopes before us. We left our horses below, and as we neared the crest of the first parallel ridge, German outposts fired at us and then fell back. From the top we looked down into a great bowl-like valley, in the centre of which lay the white buildings of a mission station. We found a number of sick and wounded Germans there, and some nursing sisters.

Von Lettow had slept at the mission the night before, and he was still in the neighbourhood, for a native came trotting down a mountain path carrying a message in a cleft stick, and I relieved him of it. It was a note signed by von Lettow ordering the '*Bahnschutz*' (Railway) Field Company to retire southwards through the mountains to Kissaki.

We spent the night at the station, rain coming down heavily, and the next day we returned to fetch our horses, after which, skirting along the base of the mountains for twelve or fifteen miles, we once more entered the Uluguru range.

For two days we ascended and descended endless parallel heights, dragging our weary animals behind us. A great many of them were beginning to show the effects of tsetse bite. They grew thin and sluggish, for the poison acts slowly, and it was hard to watch the suffering the poor animals endured. My own surviving horse was still fit, but my servant's was sadly emaciated, and it was easy to see from the general appearance of the Brigade that our existence as a mounted force was drawing to a close. By the evening of the third day we were on the great watershed from which the mountain valleys and streams now drained southwards. Far below, we saw the native village of Kikeo in a deep valley, with several enemy field companies halted on the square. In the clear mountain atmosphere it looked as if one could drop a bullet among them, but in point of fact they lay two thousand feet beneath, and nearly four miles away. When we topped the skyline, there was great activity, and field company after field company marched down the valley into the darkness that quickly fell.

When it grew light next morning, a native came out of the forest with a letter in a stick addressed to the '*Truppen Kommando*' at Kikeo. It was written by a Hauptmann Schultz, and it contained a full report of our numbers, horses, etc. Schultz stated that these particulars had been obtained by Askari Ali Hassan, who entered our lines as a spy. According to the letter, Hassan had divested himself of his uniform and arms, and he had boldly come among us. He helped to cut grass for the horses, carried water and fuel, and took such careful stock of everything that he had us down almost to a man. We promised Ali Hassan a warm reception should he come again, but in the meanwhile we admitted his courage and resource.

When at last, after a frightful scramble, we reached Kikeo, several large storehouses were fiercely alight, and the air reeked with the smell of burning salt and oil. The Germans had collected great quantities of these articles here for the use of their troops, and on our approach they had fired their supplies.

From Kikeo the road taken by the retreating force was in good condition. The rivers and brooks were bridged, and the swamps adequately corduroyed, so we made fair progress although we did not catch up with the enemy, for our horses were growing weaker by the hour.

As we approached Sonkomero that night, still among the mountains but nearer the last foothills, we came on two more storehouses ablaze, and there was the crackle of thousands of exploding rifle cartridges, and the roar of bursting shells, for both buildings were crammed with ammunition that had been carried here by von Lettow's orders, in preparation for a stand in the mountains.

We estimated the destruction at a million rounds, and the men began to say the campaign was over. We were soon to be disillusioned on this head. Sonkomero lies in the foothills. During the day we had left the streams and valleys of the Uluguru Mountains, and here at Sonkomero we were practically on the edge of the southern plains that lie towards the Rufiji River. The natives told us the nearest water from here was the Mgeta River at Kissaki, so we marched out next morning. After a while the road crossed a low neck, from which we could make out Kissaki lying in the distance. The white Boma lay deserted, and the only sign of life was the flutter of Red Cross flags over a hospital building, so we reckoned to be there within the hour. But between us and Kissaki was five miles of jungle, in which, unknown to us, von Lettow was lying in wait.

As soon as we were clear of the foothills, the road entered a forest, then it passed through a wide open space that had been a cotton field, and beyond that it ran into a dense tangle of trees and elephant grass standing many feet high. The 3rd SA Horse led the way. As we neared the far end of the cotton field, we spied a German seated on a platform in the fork of a tree. He fired a single shot which killed a horse, and scrambling down the ladder, vanished to the rear. A few minutes later, as we rode into the jungle beyond the clearing, heavy fire broke out. We could see nothing, but from the volume of sound the enemy was in force, though so thickly matted was the grass that only spent bullets whirred by. Colonel Nussey had recently been appointed in command of our Brigade, and after a rapid survey of the position, he ordered the men to leave their horses and deploy on foot on either side of the road.

Once off the road, we were immediately swallowed in the rank jungle. Even the sky overhead was invisible, and one could not see one's next-door neighbour three feet away. So far from evacuating Kissaki, the enemy had dug rifle-pits and trenches, and from the noise of their fire there were thousands of Askari shooting at us. Our first task was to trample a pathway through the elephant grass to form a fighting front, so that the men could maintain contact, and then they scrabbled some sort of cover with their bayonets. We were committed to an unpleasant day. The heat was stifling; we had no water, and casualties began to mount.

At this very time, Coen Brits with his men lay only seven or eight miles away. He had marched round the western base of the Uluguru Mountains, and had tried to enter Kissaki the day before, when he ran into much the same kind of ambush that we were now involved in, and after losing sixty men, had been forced to retire. He was now camped on the Mgeta River some miles above Kissaki, but he was unaware of our predicament, for in forest country the sound of rifle-fire does not carry far. The Germans, earlier in the morning, had kept half their men opposing him, but when they found, as the hours passed, that he remained inactive, they moved all their forces to our front, with the result that their fire grew increasingly severe and they began to press us hard. They made several ugly rushes, and for the first time in the campaign I saw the Askari in action at close quarters, and I even heard them shouting their '*piga, piga*' as they came. It was confused fighting, for the jungle was so thick that one never saw more than twenty or thirty of the enemy at the same time, and only here and there could we make out their earthworks and barricades. We hung on. With repeated attacks threatening us we could not advance against the enemy works, and to retire under these conditions was impracticable, so we fought in the steaming heat. As darkness approached at last, the firing died down and the encounter came to an end. We had lost four officers and twenty-three men killed and many wounded, and we had to withdraw. Thirsty and hungry, our men lay on their arms beyond the cotton clearing, but I was ordered to ride back to Sonkomero to hurry on the native carriers with water.

I rode away in the dusk with the ugly memory of some of our men whom I had seen lying dead, their skulls smashed by the Askari, and as a climax to an unhappy day, I committed a murder that night. Shortly after I got to Sonkomero, while I was superintending the enlargement of the waterholes in the moonlight, the local village *jumbi* (headman) rushed up in a state of great alarm, followed by his wives and children. He said there was a German Askari hiding in the reeds, and as he evinced the liveliest terror, I took with me one of the details who had been left behind in the morning, and we went to investigate.

About a week before, a young Boer soldier named Cloete had been shot down by a wounded Askari to whose assistance he had gone. All ranks had been advised of the incident, and with this warning in my mind I cautiously approached the bed of reeds in which the Askari was said to be. The headman, frightened and trembling, took my arm, and pointed to a dark figure crouched in a tunnel of rushes. I knew enough of the Swahili language by now to ask him whether he was certain it was an Askari. He emphatically replied '*Ndio, ndio, Bwana, Askari Germani*,' and he showed such trepidation that I could not doubt him, for these 'tame' natives look on the Askari with dread. To make sure, I called out several times to the hiding man to come forward, but he paid no heed, and then the soldier who was with me clutched my shoulder and cried: 'Take care, he is going to fire.' At this I loosed two rapid shots from my revolver, and running in, found a native lying dead. He was clad only in a loin cloth, and he was unarmed. I shall never forget the feeling of shame and regret with which I looked at my handiwork. I spent a tormented sleepless night, and at daybreak a messenger having come to say that the Brigade was moving, I saddled my horse, only too glad to get away from this ill-omened spot. I picked up the trail easily. Our men had marched from the cotton field through the forest along elephant paths, and after a long ride I found them camped on the banks of the Mgeta River some miles above Kissaki. Not only were they here, but Coen Brits was here too with his horsemen, and with an infantry regiment that had come up in his wake.

The old fellow was as surly as a bear over the setback he had received, and his men and ours were able to sympathise with each other, for we had both taken an unpleasant buffet. Next day I was ordered to ride into Kissaki under flag of truce, with a letter of protest against the mutilation of our dead, and asking information as to some of our men who were missing since the fight. I cut a bamboo pole to which I tied a piece of cloth, and with an orderly as standard-bearer I rode away. I hoped to meet the redoubtable von Lettow himself, but this was not to be. As we trotted across the cotton field, two German officers stepped out on to the road and halted us. We were told to dismount, and, at a shout, half a dozen Askari came running from the trees to guard us, while the senior officer went in to Kissaki with the message I handed him. The Askari looked bloodthirsty ruffians who handled their bayonets as if they would have liked to spit us, but the officer was a decent young fellow. He proudly showed me his Mauser pistol, which he said was one of a number sent out in a blockade runner by the people of Germany, as gifts for the stand they were making. Afterwards another officer shouted gruffly from the forest that he was not to speak to the '*Engländer*', and then we stood in embarrassed silence.

An hour later the original officer returned with a reply to the despatch, and my orderly and I rode back the way we had come.

In the forest beyond the cotton clearing I saw movement in the grass beside the road, and stopping to investigate, we found a native lying mortally wounded. He said he had been working in his millet field the day before, when an Askari had shot him down. I gave him my water bottle. He clutched it with trembling hands and emptied its contents at a gulp, then with a low moan he fell back dead, so we left him there. The letter I brought from Kissaki denied the murder of our wounded, but gave news of several of our men lying in hospital, and it said they were being well treated.

That evening Coen Brits walked over to where I sat by my fire. He clapped me on the back and told me to cheer up. He said two of his men had passed on their way from Sonkomero to Kilossa, and they had left word that a uniform and a rifle had been found hidden in the grass close to where I had shot the native, who had been an Askari spying on us. I only hope the story was true, but I have a suspicion that he concocted the tale for my benefit, knowing that I was fretting over the incident, for with all his gruff exterior he was kindhearted and understanding.

Meanwhile we were living under famine conditions. There was little or no game in the forest, nor any cattle in this tsetse-haunted region, and the millet fields lay mostly reaped. We had about twelve hundred men congregated here. Supplies had to be carried by native porters over the mountains form Morogoro, sixty miles away, and for the next few weeks we lived on very spare diet.

It was now decided to manoeuvre the enemy out of Kissaki instead of making another costly attack, so Brits moved round west, and our Brigade headed east. For two days we fought our way through dense forest, mostly along elephant paths, though these sagacious creatures had disappeared, leaving the jungle to mankind and his follies.

At Dakawa, a native town, we learned that von Lettow had ridden through the night before on one of our captured horses, and that the Germans had vacated Kissaki. I went with the advance guard into the place. Except for the Fort and the Hospital, where lay a dozen of our wounded and a number of German officers, there was not much to see. Though the enemy had given up the town, they had not gone far. I was with a patrol of the 9th on the Tulo Road next morning. A scout named Carlyon had gone ahead and as we rounded a corner we came on him sitting his horse engaged in a heated altercation with a German officer, four Askari standing to attention beside him on the road. They were out of sight almost at once, but we fired a volley into the grass, and riding up, we found the officer with a bullet through his leg, and an Askari rolling in agony. Carlyon said that on finding himself held up, he began to tell the officer that the war in Europe was over, and that Germany was beaten, hoping to delay the picket until our arrival. His captor had heatedly denied defeat, and had lent himself so successfully to Carlyon's ruse, that he was now our prisoner instead. He had a diary which I took possession of. On perusing it later on, I was astonished to find that the British Navy early in the war had occupied Dâr-es-Salaam, and had voluntarily given it up again. It must surely have enormously simplified the campaign had they retained the port, for it would have enabled us to use it as a base from which to work into the interior along the central railway line, instead of having to fight our way through hundreds of miles of bush to reach it, as we had been doing.

The diary described the occupation of Dâr-es-Salaam as follows:

'August 6th, 1914. Alarm signals again! This time followed by live shell screeching overhead! Two English cruisers, *Pegasus* and *Astraea*, were firing at our wireless mast. We made our way to the railway station where all troops, as well as the crews from the *Möwe* and from the two passenger steamers, boarded the train standing ready to take us inland as soon as the English came. At the last moment I was detailed to watch the movements of the enemy ships cruising up and down before the harbour.

At 10.20 as I was passing the rooms of Staff-Surgeon (*Stabsarzt*) Gastlach, I heard a shot, and rushing in, found he had blown his brains out with a revolver. First test of my war nerves!

10.40. I reported the approach of an English pinnace (*pinaz*) with a cutter in tow, whereupon the trains steamed off into the *pori* (bush). I saw a naval officer and 18 men land. I went up and found the Englishman speaking to Councillor Methner at the customs office. While this was going on the sailors were lolling about and some of them occupied their time with carving their names—Thos Cann, Wm Smith— on the government jetty as if already the harbour belonged to them!

The upshot was that Dâr-es-Salaam is declared a neutral port and all inhabitants are bound to take no hostile action against Great Britain. The landing party afterwards returned to their ships and by evening the cruisers were out of sight.

August 7th. Presented to Herr von Lettow in the officers' mess tent. Helped to sink the *Möwe* in the creek.'

Why the British gave up Dâr-es-Salaam, when they had it, is a mystery to me, and why they did not at any rate carry off the *Möwe* sloop and the two passenger steamers, is equally had to understand, but most wars seem to start with muddle and blunder.

Soon after our encounter with the wounded diarist and his picket, Coen Brits came up with his men, and we moved slowly through the forest in order to strike the Mgeta River some miles below Kissaki. As we neared the river we came to a narrow lagoon, into which it spills during the rainy season, and in this lagoon swam a school of eleven hippo. Food being scarce we could not afford to be squeamish, and in less than fifteen minutes they were all killed. Trapped as they were, the wretched animals stood no chance against the shots that were fired whenever they came up to breathe, and they were ruthlessly slaughtered.

Leaving the hippo to be dragged ashore, we rode along the river, and after a while we saw a considerable number of Askari running on the far bank. We opened fire, and meeting with no opposition, crossed to the other side, where we picked up nine dead of the 1st Field Company, all neatly dressed in Khaki tunics and shorts. We went on through the matted grass until we cut into the Rufiji Road, and here we found the enemy strongly posted. They had log stockades at intervals across the road, from which came machine-gun and rifle fire, and from what we could make out, their front extended a long way on either side. Capt Haldane Murray, a South African member of Parliament, was killed while dragging a wounded man from the road, and several others were killed and wounded, though we did not realise it at the time owing to the dense vegetation.

Young Piet Swart, who had seen aeroplanes and elephants and had travelled on a ship, here saw the biggest thing of all, for I came on him lying dead by the river with a bullet between his eyes, his dead horse beside him. Lieut Winer of the 3rd was also dead, and there were several wounded men, shot down by a single volley poured into them at close quarters.

Coen Brits was now in command of both brigades. He ordered us to take up a line facing the Germans, so we dug rifle-pits and trenches and for the next three weeks we lay in the jungle with the enemy about four hundred yards away, though we saw little enough of them in the high grass and dense forest. We could hear them felling trees, and sometimes, after dark, they sang '*Deutschland über Alles*' and other songs, which the men declared was on 'rum nights', for they were enviously convinced that the Germans received a rum ration twice a week.

The weather now changed and torrential rains came down. When it did not rain the heat was terrific, and day and night the mosquitoes buzzed. This lowland is one of the unhealthiest parts of Africa, and soon malaria and dysentery were rife. The forest swarmed with tsetse fly and our horses began to die at such a rate that, weakened as we were, we could not muster enough hands to bury the rotting carcases, so the stench of hundreds of dead animals was added to the miasma of the swamps. Further, there was the food problem. With the heavy rains, the carriers failed, and where we had been on short commons before, we went on shorter now. A road had been opened from Morogoro east of the Uluguru Mountains, for the transport of supplies, but the Tulo River and other streams were up, and all the country was inches deep in black mud.

During this dismal time we lay on the south bank of the Mgeta with rifle and machine-gun bullets swishing through the rain. A battery had arrived but it could do little in such thick country, although one morning two of our men were killed by a 'short', within a few yards of me.

More than half of the men were down with fever, and I doubt if there were a dozen horses left, all told. My brown horse was still alive but my servant's was dead, and he himself suffered from frequent bouts of fever, although I remained fit and well.

In spite of the sickness and discomfort which we were enduring, the fact remained that we had driven the Germans into the wilderness. The railways and towns were in our hands, and only the remote southern half of their territory was left to them. In view of this, and of the many deaths from fever, General Smuts now decided to withdraw most of the white troops from the country, in order to replace them by Indian soldiers.

In pursuance of this policy, Indian battalions under General Hannington began to arrive on our front, and instructions came from the mounted brigades to return to Morogoro, as soon as the newcomers had taken over our line. They were smart-looking men under British officers, and as they were inured to malaria, they were more suited to campaigning in this deadly climate. With them came a unit of Frontiersmen. One of their officers was Selous, the famous big-game hunter, whose books I had read and whose exploits I had envied ever since my boyhood. I came on him in the forest one morning, when he was hunting nothing more dangerous than butterflies, with a net and a specimen box. He was killed in action near here, and he himself would have wished for no more fitting death after his long adventures in the heart of Africa.

As soon as the relief was complete, we left the dreary positions that we had been holding. It was pitiful to see the fever-racked men dragging themselves along on foot, for their animals were dead, and we had ceased to be a mounted army. The mortality amongst the horses was one of the saddest features of the Eastern African expedition. More than thirty thousand of these dumb gentle brutes died here, and that part of me which loved and understood horses somewhat died too.

The road to Morogoro did not head through the mountains along the way we had come, but round by the eastern base of the Uluguru. As I still had a horse, I was ordered to ride ahead to prepare for the reception of our men, and leaving my boy Ruiter behind I pushed on, with another mounted officer, Capt Fossbury. One night we camped at a broad river, where the tsetse hung in clusters on the flanks of our animals, a thing I had never seen before, and next morning each of them had an air bubble as large as a walnut running up and down its jugular vein, a sure sign of the end.

We had another eighty miles to go, and we toiled along. At a supply camp, we came on a number of sick men beneath the trees. From amongst them a gaunt figure staggered to his feet, and addressed me. Disease had so emaciated him, that I did not recognise my own cousin, Will Schreiner from Capetown, although we had practically grown up together, and his condition was similar to hundreds of others.

We went on, leading our stricken horses, for they at any rate served to carry such kit as we still possessed, and after several more days through swamps and forests, we came at length to Morogoro.

My brown horse had carried me faithfully since I left Mount Kilimanjaro, and now I stood before him, rifle in hand, and put him out of his misery.

At Morogoro I built a grass hut and with the help of the supply staff, made preparations for those coming on behind. We collected natives to build hospital bandas and living-huts, and as the railway to Dâr-es-Salaam was now open, we had everything in readiness for our men when they began to dribble in.

By the middle of October (1916) what was left of the mounted brigades had arrived, and another phase of the campaign was over.

Chapter 8

Last Safari

The work of reorganising the war on a fresh basis was taken in hand. As many troops as could be spared were ordered to return to South Africa and those of us who had not yet been notified were in hourly expectation of instructions to leave.

I was nominally a member of General Smuts's staff, but in reality I had all along been a free lance, roaming as I listed, so I was almost certain to be marked for departure. Jacobus van Deventer sent for me one morning. I walked over to his tent feeling sure that I was about to receive my orders with the rest. I was the more surprised, therefore, when he told me that a composite brigade was to remain in the country and that I was to take command of one of its four regiments, the 4th SA Horse. Further, I was to start for Kilossa at once. Fresh horses had arrived from South Africa, and on paper I was given a fully mounted regiment, but I knew that every one of these poor exiled animals was doomed, and that we would soon be on foot once more.

I made ready. I rode into Morogoro to say goodbye to General Smuts, who was proceeding to England, and I went to take farewell of many other friends who were returning home. Old Coen Brits gave me a final slash of his sjambok by way of benediction, and we moved off.

I left Morogoro with my new regiment after sunset to avoid the fly belt of the Makata River, but it was of little use, for both horses and men were freely bitten, in spite of the dark. Whenever we passed a patch of bush, out darted the fly, the horses kicking and lashing, and the men cursing and swearing, for the sting of a tsetse is as painful as the sudden thrust of a needle.

By the time we reached Kilossa, the tragedy of dead and dying horses was being enacted afresh, and as we moved from each camp site, there came the merciful fusillade of a firing party left behind to put an end to animals that could travel no more.

At Kilossa I received orders to make for Iringa, one hundred and seventy miles away. We trekked across the great plains to Uleia, and thence westwards, every mile of our road marked by dead horses. The 3rd and 9th Regiments had preceded me, and our course lay in their wake, through picturesque forest and hill country, abounding with big game. But the beauty of the landscape was marred by the sight of dead animals, left by those in front, and by the knowledge that our own were strewing the track behind.

We crossed the Rubeho Mountain by the Elton Pass, fit only for a goat to climb, and then descended to the great Ruaha, a broad river, flowing towards endless swamps and jungle, and elephant country.

On the bank of the Ruaha, near the ford, I found my elder brother, Joubert, in a dying condition. I had last seen him on the Mgeta and I had noted then how ill and haggard he looked. Now he lay here under a rude shelter of grass, unable to go on. He was pitifully weak from malaria, but his mind was clear. He spoke a little of the days when we were boys, and of the mighty changes the war would bring.

Poor fellow, he had never had much luck in life.

As a boy of eighteen during the Boer War he was captured by the British and sent to Burmuda for three years. On his release, he made his way to Madagascar, where, for a further long period, he had suffered great hardship and poverty. When at length he returned to South Africa, misfortune still dogged him. He was a poet and a dreamer by nature, so he did not prosper, and the outbreak of the war in 1914 found him serving as a private soldier under Maritz on the Orange River. He was among those treacherously handed over to the Germans, and he emerged form nine months of captivity in South-West with his constitution undermined by privation and hunger. He had nevertheless volunteered for the present campaign, and now he lay broken.

He was taken back to the Union and died there, so I never saw him again.

From the Ruaha we marched on, still losing dozens of horses every day. The saddles from the dead animals were stacked in native villages, as we passed, and for all I know they are lying there still. By the time we approached Iringa there were ten horses left of those we started with. These we used to carry the sick, for there were always men going down with fever, and for the rest, the entire regiment marched on foot.

At one point, a body of the enemy tried to ambush my advanced squadron after dark. They opened fire, wounding one man, but Capt Mullins got into action so quickly with a machine-gun, that they scattered and disappeared. When at last we got to Iringa, it was a small town situated high up on a rocky hill, with the usual boma for its chief feature.

We had now reached country lying five thousand feet above sea level, with a cool temperate climate, a welcome relief after the tropical heat of past months. The Germans had evacuated the town shortly before, but they had several field companies of Askari under Hauptmann Lincke and other European officers in the district, and so far as I understood the operations, we had come to clear these healthy uplands of the enemy, and to join hands with General Northey's troops, who were working in our direction from Nyasaland.

We lay camped for some days in a valley near Iringa. More troops arrived from the rear until we were quite a respectable force, and General van Deventer himself came by car from Dodoma, to direct affairs. My regiment was ordered south where Hauptmann Lincke was holding an entrenched camp near Mount Erica, in dense forest country thirty miles away, while other units were sent to various spots in the same vicinity.

My instructions were to find a suitable place from which to patrol the area east of Lincke's camp, and to keep his movements under observation, so we set out at once. In this fine climate walking was a pleasure, and even the men who had been down with fever stepped it with a will. Our transport consisted of two hundred native carriers, for by now there was not a single horse left, and we had oxen on the hoof. We went through beautiful country, rounded grassy hills with patches of forest, like a succession of English parks. In the open spaces grazed herds of eland and other game, and native villages dotted the slopes.

Beyond Boma Himbu, it grew more rugged and more beautiful. The hills were steeper, with deep gorges and swift torrents, and the forest was closing in.

Near Likinindas, after three days' marching, I took up a position on a spur of the escarpment commanding a magnificent view over the country that lay in the direction of the Mahenge Plains. The air was like wine, and after our long months in torrid jungles we enjoyed the life. I allowed the men sufficient latitude, and permitted them to shoot game when returning from patrol work, so that we had food in plenty.

We remained here for over a fortnight, and time passed lightly enough, for the Germans lay inactive in their camp, and until van Deventer was ready to move, our task was an easy one. I was a Big White Chief. The native headmen came in with gifts of poultry and matama, and I dispensed justice in a grass-covered courthouse which I had constructed for the purpose. I dealt with only one important case. One of my patrols, returning from an inspection of the German stockade, killed a local jumbi (petty chief) by mistake. He had been watching the Germans on his own account, and as he carried a rifle, my men, in the thick timber, thought that he was an Askari, and shot him down. Next morning the dead man's wives appeared, with the rest of the village at their heels. Long before they emerged from the forest I heard weeping and wailing, and as the procession came into view, the lamentations increased. After going into the matter, I awarded the bereaved widows two oxen in full settlement, and when last I saw them and their retainers, they were driving the animals along the hillside, singing and dancing joyously as they went.

On December 16th, 1916, I received a message from van Deventer that I was to come to Iringa, to attend a conference. I left camp at daybreak with an orderly, and we tramped the thirty miles by sunset. Officers commanding the other regiments had come in, and that night, in a large room in the Fort, he explained to us how he proposed to capture Lincke, or at any rate drive him into the low country.

The capture looked easy enough on paper, and before the meeting was over, van Deventer had the enemy surrounded on the map, within a ring of indelible pencil. But having seen the forest, the deep gorges, and the size of the country in which we were to operate, I was not so sure, and I told him so. However, next day I walked back to camp, and a few days after that I started off with my regiment to carry out the orders I had received, which were to get across the enemy's rear at the Muhanga Mission Station.

For the next three days we marched through a beautiful but difficult region. As we progressed, the forest grew denser and the climbing more steep. We had generally to go in single file along game paths, led by natives, and it rained much of the time. I was under strict injunction to reach my point in the drive by a given date, and as the distance proved to be nearly twice that shown on the map, I had to push the men unmercifully. They responded with such eagerness that we outmarched our carriers, and Christmas Day found us still plodding through primæval forest, without a morsel of food. Hungry and tired, we pushed on in the rain, and by dint of continuing all night, we got astride the Muhanga Road next morning. Here we discovered a herd of goats which eased the supply problem, for we had gone without food for thirty-six hours.

Van Deventer was now to move upon Lincke's entrenched camp from the north, with troops kept in hand for the purpose, while the rest of our forces closed in, on the flanks and rear. These measures were carried out according to plan, and on paper our opponents were encircled. In practice, it worked out differently, for the cordon we had established was full of loopholes, and each unit was in fact separated from the next by wide stretches of forest and kloofs, leaving many gaps through which men with knowledge of woodcraft could escape. We spent another night in heavy rain on the wooded ridge behind the Mission, and next morning we saw Lincke's force strung out on the shoulder of a distant hill. They had evacuated their camp at van Deventer's approach, and were seeking an avenue of retreat.

They were eight or nine miles away, with several deep gorges in between, and we only caught an occasional glimpse of them in the misty weather, as they came and went through the clearings. We placed them at about five hundred Askari with hundreds of porters, and as the 9th Regiment lay across their road in the direction in which they were going, we hoped that they would run into our men. Lincke was too clever for that. He slipped down some valley, and by nightfall had got clean away.

At all events we had now cleared these uplands, for the enemy was forced down the escarpment into the unhealthy swamps of Mahenge. The drive being over, the South African troops that had taken part were ordered to return to the Central railway line at Dodoma, two hundred miles away, leaving Indian soldiers to garrison the district.

We marched to Boma Himbu in three days. On the top of Mount Kyalu we passed Lincke's fortified camp, with trenches and dug-outs that would have cost us many men in a frontal attack.

Near the breastworks lay a dead Askari. Suspended from a leather thong around his neck was a metal disc with a design of raised bosses in parallel columns. The finder brought it to me and he said it was a Mohammedan talisman. That night around my fire we held learned council regarding the interpretation of the charm. Afterwards a trooper standing near said: 'Beg pardon, sir, that there article comes from a sewing machine, and them knobs is for regulating the stitches.' This closed the debate.

We saw the old year out, camped by a river at the bottom of a rugged gorge, and on January 1st 1917, we were back at Iringa once more. From Iringa we walked to Dodoma in six days, across level bush country that carried more giraffe and other big game than I had seen in the rest of East Africa put together.

The Fort at Dodoma, in which I had spent so agreeable a night, five months before, had been turned into a hospital, and most of the other buildings were soon full to overflowing with fever patients, for the long marches and the rains had laid low a great many of our men. We camped here for some days, and then came orders that we were to return to South Africa.

We were glad to go. The campaign had degenerated into something like searching for a needle in a haystack, with a handful of Germans hidden in thousands of square miles of bush. They had made a splendid stand, but they were not the real enemy. The real enemy were the deadly climate, the wild regions, and the swamps and forests, and scrub.

It is arguable that the expedition should never have been undertaken at all, seeing that the fate of German East depended upon the outcome in France. But I need not discuss the point, for this is not a history of the campaign, but merely a personal record.

From Dodoma we went by rail to the coast. We trundled past Kidete Station, down the long valley through which we had fought our way in August, the wrecked German train and its skeletons still lying there, thence by Kilossa and Morogoro to Dâr-es-Salaam, where long years before I had watched the poor little German parted from his friend, after the murder on board ship.

At Dâr-es-Salaam we marched over the causeway of the lagoon to a lovely palm-fringed beach and lay camped for a week or two, awaiting transport to South Africa. We boated on the landlocked estuary, fished, swam, and visited the scuttled German passenger steamers and the *Möwe* sloop, the very ships that were to be had for the taking when the British landed here in 1914.

One morning I had an unpleasant experience. Six hundred yards out in the bay swung a yacht at anchor that had belonged to Herr Schnee, the German Governor, and I decided to swim to it. When I was halfway across I was horrified to see an enormous shark approaching me, his rows of teeth and his white belly showing as he turned on his side. The brute came up with a grunting noise, and actually sniffed at me like a dog. Then I remembered to churn and lash the water with arms and legs, for I had heard that sharks might be driven off in this manner. My efforts did not seem to perturb the creature unduly, but perhaps he was not hungry, for he went leisurely on his way, while I struck madly for the beach, more frightened than I have ever been in my life.

Early in February 1917 we embarked on the *Aragon*, a luxurious steamer that had been Sir Ian Hamilton's headquarters at Gallipoli, and five days later we landed in South Africa.

Chapter 9

Overseas

With the greatest war in the history of the world going on in Europe, I did not feel that I could return to a quiet village life, so I decided to go overseas.

My boy Ruiter said he was coming too. He was, however, suffering from malaria, and, as I intended travelling to England by mail steamer, as an ordinary civilian passenger, I foresaw complications, if I arrived in London with a native on my hands. Accordingly I made arrangements for him to be sent on later with a draft of the Cape Coloured Corps, hoping that he would be able to join me.

I never saw this brave faithful servant again. True to his word, he enlisted for France, but when he got there he was lost in the confusion of millions of men, and the only news that ever reached me was a letter from the War Office, long after, to say that Driver Ruiter Makana of the 196th Battery was dead.

At Capetown I went to tell my father of my intentions. He said he did not understand why I wished to get myself killed in France for the sake of the British. But I had thought the matter out and I replied that I was going to fight not for the British, but *with* the British and the other allied nations. He said: 'Well, my son, if those are your views, I cannot stop you,' and he gave me his blessing, and his hopes for a safe return.

A few days later I sailed from Table Bay in the *Norman*, a fast ship of the Union Castle Company. We went via St Helena and Ascension Rock to Sierra Leone, which place we made in seventeen days. We anchored inside a great boom of floating logs, chained together as a protection against submarines. There were many other ships collected here, for this was the most difficult period of the whole war as regards the U-boat menace.

I gathered that the tonnage question was extremely critical and that the Germans were sinking nine and ten merchantmen a day, around the British coast, so that all these vessels had run for shelter.

As the *Norman* could do nineteen knots, we received instructions to move off without the rest of the fleet, and one evening after dark we slipped through the boom for the open sea.

Next morning we began the zigzag course, which had been adopted by ships in the danger zones, for the enemy submarines were ranging ever further, and we were told that they had even been sighted off the coast of America. We would steam ahead for a mile or two, then swerve to right or left for an equal distance, and so we continued in order to make it as difficult as possible for a submarine to fire its torpedoes. Looking back at our erratic wake that showed the drunken fashion in which we staggered about, one could well imagine that a U-boat commander would have had considerable trouble in laying his aim.

During the day, we received news by wireless that the United States had entered the war, on the side of the Allies, and this gave me particular joy, for America was the biggest republic in the world, and her action more than justified me with my father.

After a few days we began to approach the English coast, and our last day at sea was an interesting one.

This week, as we heard later, was the worst of the war. Over seventy British ships had been sunk, besides many French, Italian, and neutrals. A number of them must have been torpedoed in this very zone, because, from daybreak onward, we were continually passing wreckage. We saw dead cattle, a great deal of floating timber, a waterlogged lifeboat, and once I saw the body of a dead man, enormously distended, sliding down the oily swell of the sea only fifteen or sixteen yards away.

At about 8 am a message was received from a cargo steamer ahead, calling for help. She reported that she was being shelled by a submarine, and was in urgent need of assistance, so we went to the rescue at full speed. After an hour we came in sight of her. She was on fire, dense volumes of smoke pouring from her sides. She had been abandoned by her crew whom we saw rowing off in their boats. A mile away stood a rusty old tram steadily firing her aft gun, but although we could see the shells throwing great spurts of water where they struck, we failed to catch sight of periscope or U-boat.

It was clear, however, that an enemy submarine was about, and as the collier signalled that she was picking up the orphaned crew, the captain of the *Norman* sailed on. He was carrying the mails and millions of bar gold from South Africa, and he was under orders to take no unnecessary risks. When we looked back we saw the stern of the burning ship lift clear, and amid a cloud of smoke and steam she disappeared beneath the waves, leaving only the lifeboats making towards the tramp.

The wind now freshened to gale, and it grew bitterly cold. I watched a sailor throw a bucket overboard tied to a rope, and when he drew it up I dipped my hand in the water. It was like ice, and it made me realise the terror of being thrown into these wintry seas.

During the rest of the day we took turns at watching for periscopes, as we twisted and turned through the shark-infested waters, but no further trace of an enemy was seen.

By three in the afternoon came two destroyers to meet us, racing at full speed around our ship, like terriers, and every time that they dashed by we cheered the young naval officers perched on the rail of their bridge. Shortly after dark an airship approached and circled overhead. This was the first time that I had seen so queer a craft, and I looked on it with as much wonder as old Hilgaard de Jager had shown at the armoured cars at Chenene, for I was entering a new world, wherein many things were strange to me.

We now fell in with the minesweepers—small tugs of all kinds—dragging the sea with nets and cables. They stretched from horizon to horizon, and in the falling dark the sight of these cockleshells patiently at work on the stormy waters told me more of the doggedness of the British people than anything else which I saw in the war.

By midnight we were in the Channel. We heard the distant boom of guns, and there came fitful gleams, like sheet lightning, from below the skyline. Next morning we saw from the papers that we had just escaped a German destroyer raid. The firing had come from the Dover patrol which had intercepted the enemy ships and sunk several of them. We reached Plymouth before daylight.

After a lengthy examination we were passed ashore by noon, straight on to a train for London. Snow lay on the ground and it was biting weather, a great change from the tropical climate of East Africa, but I kept my eyes glued to the carriage windows, and I forgot about the cold.

As we approached the capital, we began to pass munition factories and training camps, and high above the smoke bank of London swung a number of observation balloons, glistening against the setting sun.

We reached Victoria Station at 8 o'clock. I had not been here since 1894, as a boy of twelve, and after all those years I could still remember the blaze of light on the streets at night.

But now all was wrapped in darkness. Owing to the Zeppelin raids the city was blacked out. The platforms looked ghostly and the streets outside were invisible. Only at long intervals was there a shaded lantern, while lampless taxis crawled slowly through the streets, hooting like ships in a fog.

All the houses were shuttered, and when we reached our hotel in Russell Square it seemed like a catacomb. Instinctively one spoke in a whisper, and trod softly down the corridors, so weird and abnormal was everything.

Next day I made my plans. I had come to take part in the war, but having lived in a small place for most of my life, I decided to see London first, so for ten days I roamed about. I visited museums, picture galleries, and theatres, and rode in trams, buses, and tubes, mixing with as many people as I could.

A Dutch South African feels at home at once in England, for the two races in our country have lived together for so long that although we quarrel at times, we understand each other's ways, and I felt no more of a stranger in London than in Capetown or Johannesburg, and had little difficulty in making friends.

It was a critical time. Russia had collapsed; the military position in France was stagnant, and the shadow of starvation lay across England, for the submarine danger was at its height. But in spite of enormous losses during the past three years, and in spite of present dangers, the people were confident. They appeared to take it for granted that Great Britain would win the war, and I heard no grumbling.

The London shops were well stocked with foodstuffs, but the papers said that one out of every three supply ships was being sunk. Everywhere, on walls and hoardings, were huge official pictures, twenty feet long, of a sharklike submarine seizing a ship between its jaws, with the words 'Eat less bread; let the menu beat the U-men,' all designed to urge the population to greater thrift.

I was taken by a man whose acquaintance I had made to a reception given for Dr Walter Page, the American Ambassador, who was presented with a Shakespearian folio, in honour of the entry of the United States into the war. The platform was crowded with notabilities, but he was the man with the strongest personality there. When he rose to speak, his ugly face lit up, and he stated the case for democracy with such depth of feeling, and put so clearly into words what one had long felt, but had been unable to express, that I left the hall with a lump in my throat.

Once, when I was walking in Pall Mall a man near me said: 'Here comes the great little Welshman.' I looked round and saw Mr Lloyd George, the British Prime Minister, whom I recognised from his photographs. With him was his secretary, and Lloyd George was slapping him on the back and laughing gaily at some story that he was telling him. The sight of his good humour inspired confidence, and I felt that if the Prime Minister could walk down the street in this breezy fashion, the situation could not be as serious as the papers made out.

Having seen what I could of London, I enlisted in the British Army. But before doing so I had learned several important things. Firstly, that barbed-wire entanglements and machine-guns had rendered mounted men almost useless in France, and that most of the British cavalry were in Ireland. This was a great disappointment to me, for I had been bred in a tradition of horsemanship, and had hoped to join a cavalry regiment. But as I had no desire to help police that unhappy country, I reluctantly decided for the infantry.

I learned further that I would have to undergo a long course of training before being sent to the front in France. Up to now my idea of a soldier was a man with a rifle and a supply of ammunition in his cartridge belts, but modern fighting had grown so complicated and there were so many things one had to learn, that I realised there was no help for it, and I would have to go through the treadmill.

Never having been in a training camp before, the prospect of being drilled and dragooned was distasteful, but I went to a recruiting office at Chelsea and handed in my name. I spent most of the day in a queue, waiting to be examined. At last I was led into a room, thumped and sounded, and made to run up and down a test staircase, for they said I had a malarial heart. After I had replied to many questions, I was given a batch of papers, and ordered to report to a camp near the Crystal Palace within three days.

I enlisted in the ranks because I had lately come to hold the view that it was one's duty to share the dangers of the greatest crisis in human history with the common run of men. My convictions on this head did not last. They vanished the very next day, for, having burnt my boats, as I believed, I went to call upon an uncle and aunt of mine in Cadogan Square. My uncle, Mr Schreiner, was the High Commissioner for South Africa in London, and father of that cousin whom I had found so ill on the Tulo Road the year before.

When he heard that I had joined the Army as a private he took me to Wellington Barracks, and introduced me to Col Mellish of the Coldstream Guards, who offered me a commission as second lieutenant in his regiment. My sentiments on the brotherhood of man quickly evaporated, and I accepted at once.

The Coldstream depot was at Bushey Park near Windsor, but I never got there. I was ordered to attend a preliminary course of drill on Wellington Square, and for several days, in company with other candidates for a commission, was barked at by a drill sergeant, as we wheeled and marched and halted strenuously.

I hated it. Inquisitive onlookers grinned at us through the railings. I was awkward on my feet, and disliked making a public exhibition of myself. Here again relief was at hand. General Smuts had arrived from East Africa in January. He was now a member of the Imperial War Cabinet, a strange turn of the wheel since the days when we had raided British camps and convoys together during the South African War.

I had purposely omitted to communicate with him, as I wished to follow my own bent, and complete my own arrangements. Now my uncle told him that I was in London, and he sent for me to the Savoy Hotel where he was staying. I found him with Jonkheer van Swinteren, the Netherlands Ambassador, and Miss Emily Hobhouse.

When I told him that I was qualifying for a commission in the Guards he made no comment, but I was to find next day that he had made a mental note of the information. We talked about various matters, and presently Mr Winston Churchill came in. I had seen him only once before, when he was a prisoner in Pretoria, in 1899, and now he was First Lord of the Admiralty. He and General Smuts had a discussion with the Dutch Ambassador, who said that if Herr von Kuhlmann became the next German Chancellor, there would be an early peace. They spoke of the internal troubles of Austria, and the effect on Germany of the British blockade. Mr Churchill said that the German military leaders were staking their all upon the present intensive U-boat campaign. They had even braved American intervention in the belief that they could bring Great Britain to her knees before the United States could send an army across, and the German people were being buoyed up by extravagant reports of the result of the submarine war. He said the submarine menace was an exceedingly grave one but that it would be overcome somehow or other. I listened eagerly to all this, for it made me feel that for a while at any rate I was near the heart of things. Presently the gathering broke up, and General Smuts and Mr Churchill went to a Cabinet meeting.

Next morning, while on parade at Wellington Square, I received a telegram from the War Office, ordering me to report for duty to the Senior Officers' School at Aldershot, with the rank of Major. This was General Smuts's doing. I was getting used to rapid promotion. During the South African War I rose from batman to Chief of Staff in twenty minutes. During the rebellion I jumped overnight from village lawyer to Commandant of a district, and in East Africa I unexpectedly found myself a colonel. Now I had graduated from Private to Second Lieutenant, to Major, in the course of a week.

I packed my kit and proceeded to Aldershot, where I presented myself to General Kentish, who allocated me to Lille Barracks, and my education began in real earnest. We started as privates, gradually working our way through the ranks, from section commander to corporal, thence to sergeant, platoon and company commander, and ultimately to OC Battalion, in order to acquaint ourselves in tabloid form with the whole field of infantry work.

In the beginning, many of the things we had to do were irksome and irritating to one unaccustomed to discipline, but as time went on I settled down to the strange life. The work was hard, for in three months we had to assimilate what would normally have taken as many years to learn. We were drilled and manoeuvred on Queen's Parade, and attended lectures upon a multitude of subjects. We were put through Stoke's mortars, Lewis guns, bombing, mapping, air photography, night scouting, trench-making, gas, smoke screens, and more other things 'twixt heaven and earth than had thus far entered my philosophy.

Most of the officers attending the school came from France. Others came from Egypt, Mesopotamia, Salonika, and even from the Russian front, and their experiences were an inexhaustible source of interest to me. From them I gained a pretty accurate view of conditions in the trenches, and of the ebb and flow of the war since 1914. We got week-end leave to London where I made many friends, and received great kindness and hospitality.

In June 1917 there was a vacation of ten days, which I spent at Chelsea Barracks, doing extra drill, to expedite my studies. I went on parade every morning with the Grenadier Guards. Among other evolutions they practised a species of kick-step, like a ballet dancer's, which I tried hard to imitate. It led the old sergeant instructor to say 'Sirr, ye make me weep tearrs of blood,' so I gave up trying to acquire that particular accomplishment.

During this time I had my first experience of war in the air. It was the first daylight raid on London. On a Saturday morning I was near the Mansion House, on my way to the Bank of Africa. I had my field glasses with me for repairs, and was strolling along, looking at the shop windows and the passers-by. Suddenly guns started booming. As everyone was gazing upwards, I did so too, and saw to my astonishment, at a great altitude, twenty-five to thirty large German aeroplanes, streaming along the sky like a flight of cranes. Puffs of shrapnel burst amongst them, but they continued undeterred, until they were directly over the city, and then with one accord they changed direction and, wheeling round and round, began to drop their bombs. These fell mostly near the Bank of England and the General Post Office, and from far and near came a succession of appalling bangs, mingled with the shrieks of women, and the noise of shattered glass and falling masonry. I took refuge in a doorway from which I had a good view of the enemy machines. They were twin-engined Gothas (so the newspapers said) and through my glasses I could distinctly see the men and the machine-guns in each, while the black and white crosses on the wings were also clearly visible.

A number of British planes now joined the fray. They were all flying at an enormous height, and although the shells seemed to be bursting among the German machines, the evening papers angrily declared that the guns had failed to reach anywhere near them. The enemy squadron having delivered its cargo now went speeding back, with the English airmen following hotfoot behind. Far away, I saw one machine crumple up and drop like a stone, but I heard later that it was a British plane manned by a French pilot on leave in London, who had volunteered to go up.

The raiders got away scot-free from over the capital, but they were intercepted on the coast and two of them were shot down. I saw photographs of the wreckage in the press next day. The whole affair had not lasted fifteen minutes, but it was an expensive quarter of an hour, for sixty-two people were killed and one hundred and fifty wounded, and a great deal of damage was done to buildings.

As soon as the bombing was over, I went to look around. I saw some of the dead. I saw workmen lift something from the spikes of an area railing, which turned out to be the remains of a well-dressed lady and a child, and I saw dead horses, smashed buses and motor cars, and tumbled walls. I helped a stretcher party to take a case to Scotland Yard, whither the dead and wounded were being carried, and there were more unpleasant sights in the rooms and passages.

At the end of my leave, I returned to Aldershot for the finishing round, and once more we drilled and skirmished and paraded. On one occasion, while we were doing a route-march, we saw German prisoners of war loading timber on to a railway truck. Across the road, in a porch, stood an old lady in a mantle, gazing intently at them. Our adjutant told me that she was the Empress Eugénie, widow of Napoleon III. My father saw her in her prime, at the Second Paris Exhibition in 1867, and he said that she was then a very beautiful woman. Now she was frail and shrivelled, and I wondered what her thoughts might be as she watched her captured enemies at work.

Another time Lord French inspected us, the same squat short-tempered man whom we had met on our way to the Peace Convention of Vereeniging in 1902. King George V also reviewed us. He rode up in a field-marshal's uniform, dismounted, and walked down the ranks. Here and there he stopped to speak to an officer, and, when he came to me, he halted again, shook hands, and asked where last I had served. I told him 'East Africa', and he knew all about the campaign. He enquired whether I had suffered from malaria; I said 'No, I was "salted",' an expression that seemed to amuse him, for he burst into hearty laughter.

At length, in August 1917, I passed out as a qualified infantry officer, and was ordered to report to the depot of the Middlesex Regiment at Chatham. I was only too pleased to escape from the great parade ground where I had passed so many weary hours.

During the few days I spent at Chatham, drilling recruits, we had a disastrous air raid. We were awakened at midnight by alarm signals, and hurried to our stations in accordance with standing instructions. Then we heard the drone of German machines, but although it was a moonlit night, we could not see them. A series of deafening crashes followed, and great spurts of flame shot up as the airmen dotted their bombs at random. The majority fell harmless on the slope beyond our camp, but two bombs struck the glass-covered drill hall in the town below. The building happened to be crowded with naval ratings from ships in the port, and the havoc was tremendous. A hundred and thirty-two men were killed outright, and ninety wounded. A cordon was formed around the hall, and there were terrible scenes amongst the wreckage, while crowds of women and children stood weeping in the streets. It looked to me, from the state of the roof, as if the two bombs had been released from either side of the same aeroplane.

I was told that this was the first real military damage done in England by air raids, for up to now only civilians had been killed. We got back to camp after daylight from the grim scene in the town below, and there was a telegram from the War Office, ordering me to France. This was exciting news, and also it carried three days' leave, which I spent in London completing my outfit, and saying goodbye to friends. On the second evening I was at the Savoy with some of them, and we sat talking till after midnight. The moon was at the full, and as I stood by the window overlooking the Thames Embankment, I heard a woman on the next balcony remark that it was 'fine bombing weather', a current phrase for a clear sky. Scarcely had she spoken, when a bomb went off at Charring Cross, and a second later another dropped on the Embankment below with a blinding flash and a roar. The projectile fell on the tramline, a few yards from Cleopatra's Needle. It struck a tramcar, killing the driver and three women passengers. The papers next morning praised the driver's heroism, for his tram was going at full speed and although he was disembowelled, he stuck to his post, and jammed on the brake in order to save a head-on collision before he fell dead.

So great a crowd collected that we did not go down to see, but when I passed there the following day there was a cavity in the street big enough to hold a motor car. Forty bombs were dropped during this raid, though the casualties amounted to only sixteen killed and fifty-six wounded, because of the better 'take cover' regulations, the papers said.

I had now experienced two night raids in succession, and, had I stayed longer, I suppose I would have got as accustomed to them as were the people of London, who seemed to accept these visitations philosophically. The evening before my leave was up, I went to a theatre, and here again air raids were taken as part of the normal routine, for there was a notice on the programme that the electroliers would be turned up for a minute when a raid was impending, to give naval and military officers the opportunity of leaving for their posts, and there was a reassuring statement that the roof of the theatre had a concrete layer two feet thick. Fortunately we were not disturbed, and the play ended without a hitch.

Chapter 10

A Taste of the Trenches

Next morning I started for France. There was no pomp or panoply. I caught a taxicab from my hotel to Victoria Station, handed my kit to a porter, and as soon as the train moved off, went to the dining-saloon for breakfast. We reached Folkestone in three hours, and at 2 o'clock officers and men returning from leave boarded the steam packet that crossed to Boulogne every day. Escorted by a destroyer and an airship, we made the Channel in safety, and by five that afternoon I stood on the soil of France at last.

After a night at an hotel I reported to the Railway Transport Officer in terms of the written instructions which I had received. I had no idea for what part of the front I was bound nor to what battalion I was posted. So far as I could make out, any unit in the fighting line that was short of officers applied to base, and unattached officers arriving at Boulogne were appointed to whichever battalions needed them. It was like taking a ticket in a sweep. When my turn came, I handed my papers to the RTO, who ran his eye down a list of names pinned to the wall, then gave me a card, which bore the name of the 7th Royal Irish Rifles, the battalion I had drawn. I enquired where they were stationed, but was told that no information was permitted, and was ordered to entrain for my unknown address at 11 am.

Punctually to time we drew out of Boulogne. All along our route were camps and depots, and mountains of war material were stacked beside the line. At halts and stations were soldiers from almost every land under the sun: Australians, South Africans, Canadians, New Zealanders, and there were Chinese, Indians and Malays at work piling up stores. In the fields we saw gangs of German prisoners harvesting the crops, well-built fellows, very like Englishmen. We crawled on. Towards afternoon, far ahead, I saw a shining object suspended in the sky. It was an observation balloon, and soon I made out many more to right and left. The officers in my compartment told me that they indicated the firing line, for they were strung out behind the trenches to keep watch on the German movements. As we got nearer, I could see that beyond the first line of balloons was a similar row, and these were German balloons behind the enemy front.

They were the first signs of the battle zone, in which for three years the nations of Europe had been slaughtering each other, and from now onward every town, village and farm that we passed was a shapeless ruin. On all sides were roofless walls, old trenches, and countless graves, and we saw the shattered cathedral towers of Saint-Eloi, upon a hill.

The front line at this time lay beyond the town of Arras, which we were approaching, and as the place came into view, great mushrooms of smoke and dust stood up amongst the ruins, and we heard the boom of guns and the bursting of heavy shells.

It was my first sight of gunfire in France, so I gazed at the explosions with respect, although we were in no particular danger, for our train came to a halt some distance away from the station. My companions said the Germans shelled Arras so punctually every evening that the railway time-table allowed for it, and our delay outside was included in the daily schedule. While we were standing here, I saw through the carriage window a number of British aeroplanes, returning from over the enemy lines. Black puffs of shrapnel burst around the machines, but they kept straight on for their roosting places in the rear.

As soon as the Germans ceased their attentions, we steamed into the gutted station from which they shunted us to another line running further south. After ten or twelve miles, we reached a mound of rubble that had been the village of Boisleux-au-Mont, and in the dark I heard a military policeman call out the number of my division, and knew that I had to disembark. A limber had been sent for me from my new battalion. I loaded my belongings, and climbed up beside the driver, who beguiled the way with a racy Irish account of the doings along this part of the line. We went by Boiry Bequerelle, Boiry St Marc and Mercatel, all in utter ruin. Our road ran parallel to the front line four or five miles away, and from that direction came the rumble of guns, and there hung a suffused glow in the sky, which my driver said was caused by Very lights over no-man's land.

The 7th Irish Rifles were not in the trenches. They were in rest billets at Ervillers, and at length we arrived. I reported at a hutment that did duty for headquarters. The Commanding Officer, Colonel Francis, and three others, were playing cards. They bade me welcome, and the Colonel explained that his second in command, Major Brigg, had been recalled for service in Ireland, so he had applied to base for a substitute. He seemed not a little surprised to find that they had sent him a South African Dutchman instead.

After some little conversation, an orderly was directed to lead me to my sleeping quarters in one of the camp huts. As we stumbled through the dark, there broke out from the front line, several miles away, a bombardment exceeding in violence anything I had ever heard before, even in Natal in the old days, which up to now had constituted my high-water mark in gunfire. The sky in that direction was illumined by the flash of many guns, and the air shook and swayed from the concussions. Making sure that a great battle was being joined, I hurried back for orders. To my astonishment, they were still calmly playing bridge, and when I enquired what was afoot, Col Francis, without looking up from his cards, said: 'Only some bloody raid or other,' and continued his game. I turned into my bunk that night uneasily speculating on what a real battle in France would be like if this were merely a casual affair.

Next morning I took over second in command. We were in Belfast Camp, as it was called. It stood on a plain. All around were hundreds of wooden crosses, where lay the German and French dead who had fallen in the autumn of 1914, during the first great crash of the conflict, which after three years was still raging only a few miles away. Many of the German graves were marked '*Unbekannter Deutscher Held. Fur Kaiser U Reich*', and most of the French crosses had been erected by the Germans. They had treated their fallen enemies with respect. Each cross bore the name, where known, of the dead soldier, and the legend '*Soldat Français. Tombé pour la Patrie. Erigé par les Camarades Allemandes*'. Their own dead they had treated with equal reverence, and the large German graveyards scattered about had finely sculptured monuments and tall memorial columns. There was one to the dead of the 121st Reserve Artillery, with bas-reliefs of Zeppelins, U-boats, and other scenes, finely carved.

They had honoured the dead, but they had treated the occupied territory in a ferocious manner, and had converted this once flourishing province into a wilderness. The only things that lay in the abandoned fields were ugly growths of entanglements, and blackened tree stumps, and there must have been enough barbed wire within sight of Belfast Camp to fence half the farms in the Orange Free State.

The day after my arrival we were ordered into the front line, to take over from a battalion that was coming into billets. At two in the afternoon we marched out, each platoon at intervals of six hundred yards, to minimise the risk from long-range shell-fire. After a six-mile tramp past the ruins of Croisilles, Judas Farm, and Saint-Léger, we reached the entrance of a communication trench at a place called Stayley Bridge.

The regiment we were relieving was Irish too, and the first thing I saw by way of introduction to trench life was the body of a dead man wrapped in a blanket to which was pinned a note: 'Pray for the soul of poor Mickey O'Neill.'

We now followed down the duckboarded CT [communication trench] for nearly a mile, and at length stood in the firing line, with only two hundred yards of shell-torn no-man's land dividing us from the enemy. This sector was part of the famous Hindenburg Line. The British, a month or two before, after furious fighting, had broken into and captured several miles of it, including a similar length of the extraordinary tunnel that ran below, and it was in this captured salient that we found ourselves.

When we had completed the formalities of taking over from the outgoing battalion, I started off to make myself acquainted with the portion of the line for which we were responsible. To our left was a continuation of the captured portion of the Hindenburg Line, which for a considerable distance on that side was held by the British. On our right the position was more complicated, for here British occupation of the Hindenburg Line ended, and the original German owners were still in possession beyond. There was only a block of sandbags fifteen yards wide separating us from them, and in the tunnel below an equal length of roofing was blown in.

When I visited the block in the trench, we were so near the enemy, that there was sacking laid down on the duckboards, to deaden the sound, and one had to tread on tiptoe, and speak in whispers, as the slightest noise brought over a stick grenade or a pineapple bomb. The Germans on the other side of the bank no doubt found their tenancy equally delicate, for whenever our men wished to make trouble, they lobbed across a Mills or two.

The struggle in which this segment of the Hindenburg Line had been captured must have been a desperate one. On every side lay relics of the recent battle; broken rifles, machine-guns and mortars, bloodstained tatters of clothing, and out in no-man's land were withered corpses that could not be fetched in, and several derelict tanks. In some places there were notice boards stuck on the parapet: 'Don't dig here; dead bodies,' 'Dead Germans; no digging,' 'Unknown British dead,' etc.

Occasionally the rampart for yards on end was constructed of dead men, British and Germans, hastily piled into the breaches during the fight, and subsequently walled in by sandbags. I spent some hours examining our sector. It was an involved task, for apart from the actual front line trench, there was a labyrinth of lanes and communications to the rear, with which it was necessary to acquaint oneself. And there was the Hindenburg Tunnel. This was an amazing work. Fifty feet below the bed of our trench ran the great passage, with many stairways leading down. From the main tunnel subterranean chambers, offices, and sleeping rooms branched off, and the whole was provided with electric light. The Germans must have spent many months and millions of money upon its construction, although I heard that it had been made by Russian prisoners of war. The British held three or four miles of it, but I believe the portion still held by the Germans stretched for twenty or thirty miles, to far below Bullecourt.

Having seen as much as I could before dark, I returned to battalion headquarters in a large cavern running off the tunnel. During my round of inspection a few shells had come over, and now and then a German machine-gun rattled away, but we were in what was called a quiet sector, and there was relative peace. We had dinner in the bowels of the earth, comfortably seated around a table, the mess-waiter bringing in the courses from a kitchen excavated next door. Having eaten in these unusual surroundings, I set out to visit our night posts, this being my especial duty.

I chose a soldier named Freeney to be my runner, a cheerful good-humoured fellow, who became my constant attendant. Inspecting trenches in the dark takes a long time, and it was midnight before we reached the spot where the Sensée River, a mere trickle of a stream, crossed our trenches into no-man's-land and then into the German line beyond. As we came to the river, a heavy shell brought down a section of the parados. A piece of timber fell on my head with sufficient force to dent my steel helmet and to make me see stars for a moment or two. When I looked up, I saw in the breach which the shell had made the partially exposed body of a British officer. Owing to the nature of the soil, the body was well preserved. The dead man was standing erect against the bank, one leg forward and his right arm poised as if in the act of flinging a bomb or hurling defiance, and it looked as if even in death his fighting lust was still unquenched. We left him there, and next morning, after a night in the tunnel below, I went to see whether he could be identified, but when I reached the spot he had already been walled up with sandbags once more. The sergeant in charge of the working party said that if once we started uncovering the dead for identification purposes, the whole trench would have to come down.

My first spell in the trenches was uneventful, as things went in France, but to a novice like me all was of interest. When not on duty, we lived in the Hindenburg Tunnel, where the reverberations of the guns came down the shafts like the pulsations of a giant piston. No-man's-land averaged two hundred yards, a wilderness of shell craters, dead men, barbed wire and wrecked tanks. If one peered over the edge of the parapet there was not a living thing to be seen, for both sides lived underground, but there was seldom a moment when a gun was not firing, or a shell coming over. The German batteries stood far back in concealed pits, and never once did I see their flash—very different from the days of the South African War, when the British guns were galloped up in full view, and fired at us across the open veld.

The tunnel and the trenches were full of rats, and sometimes we organised drives, in which the men joined with zest. On account of this plague, both British and Germans had introduced cats into the trenches, and the cats showed more sense than we did. One night, in going the rounds, I heard the mewing of kittens out in no-man's-land. I climbed over and groped my way towards the sound, until I came to an abandoned British tank. Crawling into the torn hull, I flashed my electric torch, and there lay a tabby comfortably installed with a litter of six. When I got back I told a neighbouring sentry what I had seen. He knew all about it, for he said: 'Sorr, the father of them kittens is a Boche cat from across the way, and we looks after them.' I found that the men took every care of mother and offspring, and that they were treated as 'trench stores' by every incoming battalion.

In spite of the shelter of the tunnel we had casualties among the working parties and sentries. I saw one of our bombers struck by a high-velocity shell that reduced the top of his head to pulp, and another time a shell fell into a Lewis-gun emplacement, killing three men outright, and wounding several more. I was passing down the trench when I heard the explosion and the groans. I had the wounded lowered by the winch into the sick-bay of the tunnel, and when I followed down, our medical officer, Dr Nicholls, and two assistants were holding one man down by force. He was shockingly injured, great gashes over his thigh and stomach, and he shrieked and writhed in delirium. It was a very painful scene; then his cries ceased, and he lay dead.

A few mornings later, when Freeney and I were coming up the trench, a fatigue party was repairing a section that had been blown in, and as we approached I heard the usual 'Make way there, men,' in order to let us pass. Then came a swish through the air and a pineapple bomb exploded in the middle of them. When the smoke and dust had cleared, there lay four men dead and five wounded, all piled in a blood-spattered heap. I attended the burial at one of the cemeteries behind the line. After the interment the bearers and the firing party tramped back along the communication trench quite cheerfully, but next morning the whole battalion sat around in gloomy silence. The Irish are a temperamental race, and the incident of the bomb had thrown them into a state of melancholy that an outsider like myself found hard to understand. However, by the following day the psychic wave had passed, and everyone was in good spirits once more.

We held this portion of the Hindenburg Line for the next eight weeks. Every ten days we were relieved from the front line to go into support, a few hundred yards back, after which we moved into rest billets, thence back to the front line. All this part of the line, from Arras to beyond Bapaume, was one of the quietest sectors in France. The storm centre in these days (September-October 1917) was north, in the Ypres salient, but down here no battles took place, and there were only the usual amenities of shell-fire, machine-guns and pineapples. British and German aeroplanes were frequently overhead, but the calm extended even to the sky, for I never saw anything that resembled an air fight.

At length we were withdrawn from the line, and received orders to pack up and march south. We went first to Belfast Camp, from which, one fine morning, we were played down the road by the band of an adjoining battalion, and started off along the Route Nationale of Picardy. We did an average of thirteen miles a day for five days, heading south as a rule, but we counter-marched a good deal, and as there were many other battalions travelling up and down the turnpike, we gathered that all these bodies of men were being moved backward and forward to mislead the enemy airmen, and that a big push was in preparation somewhere or other.

The secret was so well kept that it was only in hospital later on that I heard of the great tank attack on Bourlon Wood and Cambrai. We covered far more country than was represented by the distance as the crow flies, but it enabled me to see a large extent of the devastated area. Common ruin had overtaken this region. Every town, village and farm was reduced to dust. The woods were blackened stumps, and the very streams and canals had altered their courses and lapsed into bogs and marshes, their banks and dykes obliterated by shellfire.

Towards the end of our tramp we were back near our starting point. We passed the Somme battlefields and marched through Albert, where the famous Virgin and Child still jutted at right angles from the shattered cathedral tower. The men said the French soldiers believed the war would end when the statue fell, and not before. We went by the remains of Sailly-Saillisel, the Butte de Warlincourt with its great mine craters, and the remains of Delville Wood where I saw the graves of many South Africans. We marched through Bapaume, and the only thing I saw intact in the place was the monument in the cemetery to Faidherbe's troops who fell here in 1870. For the rest, the town was a heap of rubble. Where the Hotel de Ville had stood, was now a gaping crater nearly a hundred yards wide, for the building had been blown up by a delayed-action mine after the German evacuation some months before. All that was left of the Cathedral was the crypts and vaults, where lay many human skeletons blown from their ancient tombs.

From here we went to le Transloi, and thence by the ruins of Rocquiny, Bus, and Neuville, to a camp between Gouzeaucourt and Metz-au-Cour, and here we came to a halt. This part of the country was somewhat less devastated than that through which we had come. The woods were standing, and the Canal du Nord was more or less intact.

There was a large concentration of troops concealed in the neighbouring woods, and our own quarters nestled comfortably in a copse near the Neuville quarries. There were many rumours about the coming attack, but nothing certain, although our Brigade Major told me that we had been brought here to be 'fattened up', as he ominously put it.

On the first night of our arrival in camp I had another sample of the strange ways of the Irish. Colonel Francis had gone on leave, and I was in command of the battalion during his absence. Our men were mostly South Irish from Dublin and Cork. The Ulster Division under General Nugent had arrived a few days before us, and their headquarters were close by. In the course of the evening I sent a fatigue party to fetch supplies for our canteen from the Ulster depot. Soon after their return I heard a violent commotion in the marquee tent where we kept our stores. There was the sound of breaking crockery, mingled with oaths and shouts and, rushing up to enquire, I found that the men were busy wrecking the place. When I demanded the reason, several of them angrily flourished bottles in my face, to the accompaniment of threats and curses against the bloody Orangemen. To me the bottles seemed harmless, for they contained only soda-water; but, when I asked for enlightenment, it appeared that the root of the trouble was the labels, which bore the title 'Boyne Water'. The men started off in a body for the Ulster Division, to avenge what they considered a mortal insult. I had heard of the Battle of the Boyne, but it conveyed no political implications, and I thought the men had gone crazy. Fortunately I was able to telephone through to the Ulster headquarters, who hastily turned out several hundred men to surround the malcontents; and with the tactful assistance of our Adjutant, young Hartery, who understood Irish politics, we managed to get our men back to camp without bloodshed. Next day they were playing football with the Ulsterites as if nothing had happened.

I had another curious matter to handle while I was in command at this camp. I presided at orderly room every morning to try the daily batch of defaulters on minor charges of crown-and-anchor, loss of kit, etc. On this occasion, however, a soldier named Williams, a mere boy, was brought before me charged with desertion in the face of the enemy, the most serious offence in the military code. My duty was to hold a preliminary investigation and, if there was sufficient evidence, the papers had to go to Brigade, and the accused would stand trial for his life before a field general court martial. Williams was ushered in between two armed sentries, and Capt Hartery produced witnesses to show that the prisoner had deserted from our trenches in the

Hindenburg Line a month before.

I asked Williams what he had to say for himself. He replied that he had been shell-shocked at Ypres, and since then, whenever he heard a shell explode, his legs ran away with him.

I realised that if this went before a court martial he would be shot, so I said: 'My boy, can't you think of something better to say than that?' but he sullenly adhered to his statement and I had no option but to prepare the record for transmission to Brigade. That afternoon two soldiers from an English battalion in the neighbourhood asked to see me. They came into the orderly hut, saluted, and one of them, stepping forward, said they wished to speak to me about Private Williams. He said that he and his companion had recently been patients at a casualty clearing station near Bapaume, and Williams had been in hospital with them, delirious most of the time.

I had the prisoner fetched from the guard tent, and asked him whether he knew these two men, and whether he had been in hospital. He said he did not know them, and remembered nothing about a hospital. I asked him where he had been during the past month, and he said he supposed he had 'just hung around'. The two soldiers were positive of Williams's identity, and one of them said to me: 'Sir, the boy's mind is a blank; it will be murder if they shoot him, and him a volunteer.' I thanked and dismissed them, and sent an officer to Bapaume, to make enquiries. He returned next day with a certificate that Williams had been found wandering behind the front line a month before in a demented condition. It was decided to send him home to Ireland, but on his way to railhead he escaped, and after having lain delirious at Bapaume Hospital for some weeks, disappeared for the second time, and nothing more was seen of him until he was arrested under some sheets of corrugated iron close to the front line. This threw so much light on the case, that I tore up the court-martial papers, and Williams was sent to a mental home in England for treatment. Thus, thanks to the two soldiers, a grave miscarriage of justice was averted.

At Bray, beyond Gouzeaucourt, the troops were put through a course of training in co-operation with tanks. There were over thirty of these monsters ploughing their way across the fields with the men in artillery formation behind. All this, unknown to us, was for the Cambrai break-through. In the meanwhile there came an important change so far as our battalion was concerned.

I do not know whether it was one more ramification of Irish politics, but Colonel Francis was transferred to the command of a brigade, and the 7th Irish Rifles were broken up. I heard it said that there were too many Sinn Feiners among us. The men certainly talked a lot of politics, and even my friend Freeney waxed hot on occasion, but, coming as I did from a country where everyone talks politics, I paid little attention to their frequent wranglings. Whatever the cause, we were disbanded. I regretted it, for I had made many friends amongst these happy-go-lucky Irishmen, and I was sorry to part from them.

I received orders to transfer to the 6/7th Royal Scots Fusiliers near Arras, so I gave Freeney something for remembrance, and said goodbye to all my friends, none of whom I ever saw again. I travelled on the light line to Bapaume, and from there north to Arras.

Arras must have been a fine old town before the war, to judge by what was left of it, which was not much; and it was being pounded into still further nothingness, for the

Germans were throwing heavy shells into it every day, and throughout the twenty-four hours which I spent there, trying to get word of the Scots Fusiliers, 5.9's and howitzer shells dropped among the ruined houses at regular intervals. Most of the civilian population was gone, but here and there an old market woman sold cigarettes and tobacco, and there were many British troops quartered underground in vaults and cellars.

By next afternoon I had got into touch with my new battalion, and a limber came to fetch me. We reached the battalion transport lines at a ruined village or suburb, and obtaining a guide from the Quartermaster, set out on horseback for the front line.

We rode along for three or four miles over ground that had been captured from the Germans. Multitudes of wooden crosses standing over filled-in shell craters showed where the dead had been buried, and here again lay broken rifles, fragments of bloodstained clothing and all the litter of a recent battlefield. We passed a damaged German howitzer on caterpillar wheels, still standing in its emplacement. On the barrel was a chalked notice: 'This gun captured and claimed by the West Lancs'.

The system of thus marking captured guns and other trophies was a common practice, and during my march with the 7th Irish I had seen a broken-down *fiacre* twenty miles behind the fighting front. Some wag had inscribed on it: 'Captured and claimed by the 2nd Labour Battalion'—a gibe at the employment companies that did the road-making far in the rear.

During all the time that we were going forward there was a cannonade from the German side, and a liberal sprinkling of 5.9 shells, which were fired on the off chance of hitting something on the road, a busy thoroughfare that followed the right bank of the River Scarpe.

There was a continuous stream of supply parties moving to and from the front line, but as no one seemed to bother about the gunfire, I pretended not to notice it either. We passed beneath the arch of the famous railway triangle, the taking of which had cost so many lives, and a little beyond that we halted at a Scottish Church army hut on the bank of the river. These Church huts served as resthouses and reading-rooms for the troops, and we went in for a cup of tea.

There was an old sergeant in charge, and as he handed me my cup a heavy shell burst outside with a tremendous racket. He merely remarked 'Yon was a heavy yin,' and he did not so much as glance through the window to see where it had fallen. I resumed acquaintance with him some time later under less equable circumstances, but for the present I paid for the tea, and my guide and I resumed our journey until we came to the entrance of the communication trench leading to the front line. Here I sent him back with the horses, and entered the CT. I continued down the duckboarded alleyway for half a mile, and reached the headquarters of the 6/7th Scots Fusiliers in an immense dug-out in the front line, where I reported for duty. I was agreeably surprised to find that the Commanding Officer was a South African, Col de Haviland, Sergeant-at-Arms of the Union Parliament in Capetown.

I found another young South African with the battalion, Lieut Wilkinson, also from Capetown, so I felt at home.

Col de Haviland instructed me as to the state of the front line and such matters as affected us locally, and then we sat down to a meal, thirty feet underground. After dark I went to inspect the line under the guidance of a runner. He was a humorous fellow. When I asked him whether he was well acquainted with the sector, he spat in his hands, and holding up his calloused palms, grinned and said he reckoned he should know it, as he had dug most of these here trenches himself. He was as good as his word, for he picked his way to every nook and corner in spite of a black night and in spite of the twisted labyrinth of trenches and saps. Our left battalion front rested on the River Scarpe, and it was a damp, muddy business visiting the posts, for the ground was swampy and we had to find a path through reeds and brakes, to where the riflemen and bombers were stationed in forward pits and holes.

Once again I was in a quiet sector of the line. Up north the holocaust of Passchendaele was in full swing. There the British were engaged in disastrous attempts to break through to Ostende; attempts that were almost as bloody a failure as the German attacks on Verdun had been.

The result as far as we were concerned was that our sector was in a comparative backwater, and although desultory shell-fire went on most of the day, the knowledge that the storm centre was far off lent an atmosphere of peace and calm to our doings. There were one or two interesting incidents, however: interesting at any rate to me. Once, while I was inspecting some work in the front line, the enemy suddenly put down a heavy barrage, and we stood-to, expecting an attack. While we were manning the firestep, a British aeroplane came over to investigate. As the machine was flying unusually low we watched its course with anxiety, for numerous anti-aircraft shells were bursting around it. To confirm our fears, the plane began to sway from side to side and then it came down in a nose dive at great speed. A groan went up from the men, for it looked as if nothing could save the machine, but just as it was about to crash, it flattened out, and though still violently wobbling, the pilot landed her on an even keel behind us, a feat of no mean skill considering the pitted surface, the old trenches and the wire entanglements amid which he came down.

The aeroplane had landed in full view of the Germans, and their batteries began to shell it almost at once. The pilot lost no time. The moment his craft came to a standstill he leapt out and ran towards us. He was a cheery individual, for dropping into our trench he said: 'Do you fellows mind if I stay here a bit; the jolly old Hun is smashing up my kite'; and for the next few minutes we watched the demolition of his machine. The German gunners expended about a hundred shells on it, which led him to say in a contended voice that it must be costing them more than the bus was worth.

There was not much aerial activity except for the usual patrolling squadrons of both sides and the night bombers, but sometimes a formation of German machines, painted in all the colours of the rainbow, came tearing down our line. The men called them 'Von Richthofen's Circus', for they were said to be commanded by Baron Von Richthofen, the famous German ace. They were an extraordinary sight, some of the planes were a bright scarlet, others green or yellow or dazzle-painted like the sides of a ship, for what reason I do not know.

One afternoon three low-flying German aeroplanes came over, and as they passed there dropped from each a ballonet which slowly descended to earth behind our line. We retrieved them, and they contained bundles of the *Gazette des Ardennes*, a Flemish newspaper printed under German auspices. The airmen had made a mistake. They thought we were Belgian troops, for the papers were full of propaganda designed to create dissension between the Flemings and the Walloons. The articles were written in heavy style, and the efforts to foment race hatred between the two sections of the Belgian people were so ill-tempered that young Wilkinson said they would make even a South African Nationalist blush.

At this time, a fleet of seven or eight Zeppelins had set out to bomb London. They were caught in a blizzard and drifted helpless towards France where they successively came to grief, the last of them reaching as far as the Mediterranean, where it sank with all hands. The English and French newspapers were jubilant at this final proof of the failure of a weapon upon which the Germans had built such high hopes. One morning Brigade HQ sent down a number of handbills printed in German, setting out the fate of the Zeppelins, and we were ordered to attach them to rifle grenades, and fire them across to the enemy trenches. We did so, and next day came the German reply, similarly transmitted by rifle grenades. It said they knew all about the Zeppelins, but did we know that they had just captured a hundred and twenty thousand Italians at Caporetto? And what was more, they had, and this was our first word of it.

Our spell in the front line came to an end in due course, and we went through the customary routine of going into support, then into rest billets, and thence back to the front line once more. By this time I was quite at home in France. I had grown used to living among thousands of men in dugouts and tunnels and billets. Trench life was becoming my normal existence to such an extent that South Africa and old associations were imperceptibly fading into the background, and I seldom gave a thought to past or future.

But now I was suddenly projected into entirely different surroundings. We had moved from front line into support, where the whole battalion lived in a single great cavern hewn into the side of a deep railway cutting. One morning I was instructed to report to brigade headquarters to preside at a court martial on a self-inflicted wound case. At half past nine an orderly brought me a horse and we started off, following the road along the River Scarpe, by which I had originally come. There were a few 5.9 shells dropping about, and I remember seeing Von Richthofen's Circus streaming down the line in the distance, but to this day I do not know what happened next, nor do I know what became of the orderly and the horses. All I know is that I found myself coming to on a stretcher in the reading room of the Church army hut where I had been before, and the same friendly Scotch sergeant was bending over me with a mug of tea. A doctor was cutting away my riding breeches with a pair of scissors, and I have a dim recollection of handing over the court martial papers to someone. Then I was lifted into a motor ambulance, and lapsed into unconsciousness once more. I found myself, I do not know how long after, in a large hall in the Hospice de St Jean, in Arras. Through the shattered walls I could see French nuns in starched coifs, walking up and down in a cloistered quadrangle and, looking upward, I could see the sky through the rents in roof and ceiling for the place had suffered at the hands of the German gunners, and even now I heard the crash of heavy shells, exploding near enough to bring down flakes of plaster on my head.

My stretcher stood on the flagstones with a number of others, and a white-aproned surgeon with rubber gloves was probing my wounds, which consisted of several deep gashes in the leg and injuries to arms and head. He injected me with a serum and when I asked him whether I was badly damaged, he said it would be a long time before I was on my 'pins' again. A medical orderly came up with a book to take particulars of my name, country, next-of-kin, etc. When he reached the question of my religion and I told him 'Dutch Reformed', he nearly dropped the book, and said in a startled voice: 'What the hell is that?' Afterwards I saw him take another orderly into the corner, and there was a whispered conversation and curious glances at me as they examined the entry in the ledger.

The Germans were dropping more shells than usual into Arras, for an officer hurried in with instructions that the wounded were to be evacuated. We were carried to motor ambulances, and to the accompaniment of the distant boom of guns and of shells bursting near at hand, we rolled out of the battered courtyard. We were driven down the Frévent Road for six or seven miles to a casualty clearing station (CCS) out of range of the enemy guns, and here I lay for several days in a large marquee tent, with many others. Then I was taken by hospital train to Rouen. All I saw of Rouen was what was visible through the rear of the hood, but I remember that English military police were on point duty in the streets, and that the pavement was thronged with British troops.

I was lucky enough to get into No 2 British Red Cross Hospital, famous throughout the Army for its comfort and efficiency. I enjoyed being there. The nurses were good to us and every morning French newsboys came round with papers, fruit and cigarettes for sale, and we were allowed to buy wine. Most of the patients in my ward came from the Passchendaele offensive, still raging in the Salient, and from them I heard that things were going badly notwithstanding the glowing accounts in the press. There was a little Canadian lieutenant in the next bed who had been shot through the chest at Passchendaele, and before they got him away he was hit five more times, so heavy was the enemy fire.

It was while lying here that I first heard of the mutiny amongst the British troops at Étaples. It was kept secret, but from what I was told by a wounded officer it was a very ugly affair, in which a number of officers and men were killed and injured, before the rioting was quelled. The mutiny, so far as I could make out, was directed not against the war, or against the higher command, but against the so-called 'red-caps', the base police whose overbearing methods were resented by the fighting men.

The bed I was in was endowed by the English citizens of Sao Thomas, somewhere in South America. I was in Rouen for a fortnight and was then taken aboard the hospital ship *St Patrick*, for removal to England. We sailed down the River Seine, past beautiful country which I could see through the portholes, and reached Havre before dark. That night we stood out to sea, with all lights extinguished and everything screened, to prevent the electric torches of the nurses from betraying our presence to the submarines. I lay wondering what would happen to us, helpless between decks, if we were torpedoed, as the vessel threshed her way through the heavy seas, for the night was a stormy one. But we reached port in safety (Southampton, I think). We were carried ashore, and our stretchers placed in long rows on the station platform, where ladies distributed cigarettes, oranges, and even telegraph forms, offering to write out wires for those who wished to communicate with their relations. Then we were lifted into a Red Cross train for London. In London we were again laid on the platform, and officials came round to pin a card on each man's stretcher, with the name of the hospital to which he was to be taken. I drew Queen Alexandra's Hospital, Highgate. The driver of the ambulance was a stout pleasant woman, evidently a social figure, for she had her lady's maid on the seat beside her, and wore heavy furs. She rolled up the side-flaps to let us see the people on the streets, many of whom called out greetings, and the policemen stood to attention and saluted as we passed. We went through Hyde Park all crowded with fashionable folk, who waved their handkerchiefs. At Highgate I was carried upstairs and given a room to myself. It was a pleasant time. Friends and relatives came to see me and many of the patients used to hobble in on their crutches for a chat.

There was a young half-brother of mine studying medicine at Guy's Hospital. He came to visit me one afternoon, and while we talked away in Dutch, an old caretaker was cleaning my windows. He pretended to be scrubbing, but I could see he was all ears, and when my brother rose to go, he ran off in great agitation to tell Mr Patterson, the surgeon, that we were German spies.

There were many sparrows in the grounds, and they used to hop right into my room to squabble and fight over the crumbs which I threw to them. We became so friendly that I was able to recognise some of them as they sat on the trees outside. By the middle of December 1917 I was well enough to go to a convalescent home, and once again I was lucky, for I was sent, with several other wounded, to Melchet Court, a magnificent country estate near Salisbury, belonging to Sir Alfred Mond, Commissioner of Public Works. He and Lord Reading travelled down on the same train with us. Lord Reading (Rufus Isaacs) had just returned from America where he had been instrumental in securing the American entry into the war. I believe he received an earldom for his services on this very day, for I heard people on the train congratulate him upon his new honour. His son was married to Mond's daughter.

One wing of Melchet Court had been turned into a hospital with Lady Mond as Commandant, and here we were treated in princely fashion. We were not so much inmates of a hospital as guests at a country house. Every morning a butler in livery brought me my tea, and all night long a wood fire burned in my room. There was a beautiful carpet on the floor and a fine Madonna and Child on the wall. After I was able to walk, I had the run of the library, where I spent many pleasant hours, and we were taken for long drives to Stonehenge, Salisbury, the New Forest, and even to Portsmouth.

Once I was shown round Salisbury Cathedral by a young lady who lived in the Close, a sort of clerical compound, inhabited by churchmen and their families. To them the cathedral is the hub of the universe, and after I had been led through the aisles and chapels and had learnt from my guide the inner purpose of its builders, she said suddenly: 'Doesn't it make your blood boil to think that Cromwell's soldiers, the brutes, stabled their horses in the nave?' To her it was still a present living grievance.

At night I played bridge with Sir Alfred Mond and his family, and sometimes Lord Reading was of the party. He played even better bridge than General Botha, as I found to my cost. He told me he had run away to sea as a boy, and at one time had been a stockbroker, and there were many interesting anecdotes of his early years at the Bar. He said a furious litigant had once referred to him as a 'lineal descendant of the Thief on the Cross'.

One night the news came through that General Allenby had captured Jerusalem. Sir Alfred Mond and Lord Reading were both Jews, and both ardent Zionists. Lord Reading was visibly moved by the historic event, and in a voice quivering with emotion, he said to Mond: 'Alfred, at last the time has come for the rebuilding of King Solomon's temple.' Sir Alfred, with a wink at me, replied: 'Yes, Rufus, and what's more, you and I will get the contract and run it up for them in reinforced concrete, and beat old Solomon's building record into a cocked hat.'

In the library at Melchet Court was a framed letter written by Abraham Lincoln. It was couched in such beautiful language that I copied it into my notebook:

> *'Executive Mansion,*
> *Washington, Nov 21, 1866*
>
> To Mrs Bixby
> Boston, Mass.
>
> Dear Madam,
> I have been shown in the files of the War Department a statement of the Adjutant-General of Massachusetts that you are the mother of five sons who have died gloriously on the field of battle. I feel how weak and fruitless must be any word of mine which should attempt to beguile you from the grief of a loss so overwhelming, but I cannot refrain from tendering you the consolation that may be found in the thanks of the Republic they died to save.
> I pray that our Heavenly Father may assuage the anguish of your bereavement and leave you only the cherished memory of the loved and lost, and the solemn pride that must be yours to have laid so costly a sacrifice upon the alter of Freedom.
> Yours very sincerely and respectfully,
> A Lincoln'

In January 1918, thanks to good treatment, I was passed out for light duty, and was ordered to report at Fort Matilda on the Clyde, the depot of the Royal Scots Fusiliers.

Chapter 11

The Great March Offensive

I was at Fort Matilda for three weeks, during which time I never once saw the sun, and not once was the far bank of the Clyde visible through the mists forever swirling up from the sea.

We put new recruits through their drill, standing all day in the sodden fields, with six inches of snow underfoot, and a cold drizzle of rain that never ceased. Truly an awful climate to a South African accustomed to eternal sunshine.

I was sent to Edinburgh for a gas course. It snowed all the time and there was a blizzard such as I never wish to see again.

One morning I went with two naval officers to Rosyth, above the Forth Bridge, to view the Grand Fleet that had come in. The river was crowded with warships of all descriptions, from dreadnoughts like the *Warspite* and the *Queen Elizabeth*, down to flatbottomed monitors and scouting launches. I asked an officer from the *Warspite* what the truth was about the Jutland battle, and he said 'Oh, you can call it a draw,' though he insisted that another hour of daylight would have given the British decisive victory.

During the storm of a few nights before, two destroyers had been wrecked on the Orkneys and with the exception of a solitary seaman, the crews, totalling two hundred and seven men, had been drowned. The sole survivor had been picked up by the islanders, nearly dead from exposure, and he had been brought to Queensferry, where he was housed for the moment at an inn. He was 'on show' so to speak, and as my naval friends had access, we went to see him. His wife was with him, and she had strange views on the workings of Providence, for she said to us: 'Sirs, is not the mercy of God most wonderful? Blessed be His name for saving my man alone out of all his mates.'

I now returned to Greenock, and the weather was such that I was glad when I received instructions at the beginning of February 1918, to return to France. I left Glasgow by the evening express, and by five o'clock next afternoon was in Boulogne. As I was now definitely attached to the Royal Scots Fusiliers, I found, on drawing my card at the RTO's the following morning, that I was to entrain at 10.30 am, for the 1st Battalion, as second in command.

I clambered on board, and once more we journeyed through the countryside, now however not green and smiling, but all covered with snow, and bleak and sombre in the harsh winter weather. Towards evening we crawled by the ruined steeples on Saint-Eloi Hill, and then to Arras, where we again halted for the daily German bombardment to pass. While waiting outside the station I had an amusing experience. In South Africa we look on springbok biltong as a great delicacy. It is made by curing the venison in strips, until it looks rather like sticks of plug tobacco.

I had taken care to have a regular supply sent me from home, and now, being hungry, I sat whittling off chunks of biltong with my pocket knife and eating away with relish, to the unfeigned interest of the three young officers in my compartment. Having satisfied my hunger I climbed out to warm my feet during the halt and, as I tramped up and down in the snow, I heard one of the officers, who thought I was out of earshot, exclaim: 'My God, that fellow can hog tobacco!' On returning within I kept my own counsel, and must have remained for them the world's champion in this art.

From Arras we went further, and as no lights were permitted in the carriages after sunset, for fear of attracting night bombers, we sat shivering in the gloom, until at length I heard military policeman at a siding shout that all men for the IIIrd Division were to detrain. As the Scots Fusiliers were in the IIIrd, I disembarked with my kit and groped my way to the RTO's hut through a slough of mud and snow.

To my surprise I found that I was back at Boisleux-au-Mont, where I had alighted the year before for the Irish Rifles. The RTO informed me that the 1st Royal Scots Fusiliers were in the front line, and that I was to make for the battalion transport camp at Boyelles, some six or seven miles down the Arras-Bapaume Road. I stopped the first ammunition lorry going in that direction, and soon reached my destination, going via St Marc and Boiry-Bequerelle, looking more like disused brickfields than ever. At Boyelles I found the transport lines of the Scots Fusiliers, and Capt Hester, the quartermaster, gave me a Nissen hut for the night.

By a curious coincidence, the battalion was holding the identical sector in the Hindenburg Line that we had held when I was with the Irish. As I was well acquainted with these parts I set off on foot next morning, carrying the few essentials for life in the trenches in my haversack. The day was fine and sunny, and the snow was firm, so I enjoyed my tramp over the long slopes.

In due course I reached the intake to the communication trench at Stayley Bridge, and soon I had the old familiar feel of the duckboards under my feet again. When I got to the front line, Battalion HQ were in the same chamber down the Hindenburg Tunnel where I had lived before, and I reported to the Adjutant, Capt George Bissett, with whom I was long to be associated, and at whose death I was to be present in the end.

The officer in command of the 1st RSF was Colonel E I D Gordon. He was to all intents and purposes a South African, for he had served at the Cape station for many years, and had married a Capetown lady. He owned a farm in the Western Province, and he said he was going to live there if he survived the war.

I soon settled down to the routine of the trenches, and my duties, as of old, consisted chiefly in prowling around the line all night to inspect the posts and generally supervising our sector from end to end, and then returning to my berth in the tunnel at dawn for a few hours' sleep. Colonel Gordon frequently accompanied me on these expeditions. He was well versed in South African political conditions, and although he had been on active service since 1914, had closely followed events in the Union.

One dark night at 3 am he and I were splashing down the line, ankle deep in melting snow. Machine-guns were splattering, an occasional shell came howling over us, and my thoughts were anywhere but in South Africa. Colonel Gordon, however, plodding ahead, was considering our affairs, for suddenly he stopped, and turning to me, named a well-known politician in the Union, and said: 'Do you know what I would do with that fellow if I had him here tonight? I would send him into no-man's land to inspect the German wires.'

An order to examine the enemy wire entanglements was looked upon as almost tantamount to a death sentence, so the intensity of his convictions may be gauged, and I thought it a strange chance that had brought me under a Scotch commander, who talked South African politics at dawn in the mud of the front line of France.

The Scots Fusiliers had previously been commanded in this very area by Mr Winston Churchill. Bissett told me that on one occasion Mr Churchill tried to dam up the Cojeul River, a mile or two north of this, with sandbags stripped from the parapets. His intention was to create a head of water with which to flood the German front line, but he flooded the British front line instead, as well as many of the rear communication trenches, and there was a considerable flutter in the dovecotes of the higher command in consequence.

At this time, February 1918, the air was thick with rumours of a coming offensive by the Germans, and we were inundated with circulars and messages from Divisional and Army Headquarters, warning us of the imminence of a great attack, and prescribing the counter measures to be taken to parry the blow. The front line troops had to do a prodigious amount of extra digging and wiring during the next few weeks, and whole new systems of defence works were springing up far behind, upon which we were to fall back in case of need.

What certainly pointed to a big-scale offensive was the fact that the Germans were raiding intensively along the line, from the River Scarpe to beyond Cambrai. Scarcely a night passed, but somewhere along the line there would come the tremendous roar of a barrage, followed by a lull, during which we knew that the final rush was taking place, and that, away there in the dark, men were bombing and killing each other.

On the second day after my arrival, the Germans began to trenchmortar the King's Liverpools adjoining us. This went on for hours, and by sunset they had blasted a wide gap in the wire, clearly indicating their intention to raid. I walked over in the evening to enquire of the Colonel of the Liverpools whether he wanted any assistance, but he said he preferred handling the coming attack himself. Next morning at the first flush of dawn a violent German barrage came down. Then the shell-fire ceased as suddenly as it began, and clear on the frosty air there came the shrill call of a bugle, followed by the rattle of machine-guns, confused shouting and the bursting of hand grenades. Again the bugle sounded and the dim figures of the raiders went pouring back across no-man's land and silence reigned once more. The Liverpools lay in a hollow, so our Lewis guns could not be brought to bear, and in any event the raid went with such a swing that hardly five minutes elapsed between the first bugle note sounding the assault, and the recall. I went down the trench to see how they had fared. About fifty yards of their parapet was blown in and they were at work, busy as ants, repairing the damage. Most of their men had been withdrawn from the threatened point during the night, so the casualties amounted to only three men killed and a few wounded, but seven were missing, presumably dragged into the German lines. On the other hand, the Germans had left seven of their dead behind, and there were doubtless more lying in no-man's land. They were accordingly in possession of the fact that the King's Liverpools held this part of the line, and they had left behind them the information that the 29th Westphalians lay opposite, which I ascertained from a paysheet on one of the dead men.

I doubt whether this kind of knowledge was worth so much bloodshed, and the total death-toll from raids in France must have run into huge figures.

The Germans tried to raid us one night, but it was such a poor attempt that I am not even sure that it was meant to be a raid, although they got near enough to fling a few stick grenades into our trench, and a mortar dropped a round into one of our bombing posts, that killed two men and wounded five.

In the past, it had been the custom for a battalion to remain in the front line from six to eight days, after which it would be withdrawn to support, and then into rest billets out of range, far behind. Now, owing to the extra precautions being taken against the suspected offensive, we were kept in the front line all the time, so that when the storm ultimately burst on us we had not been out of shell and rifle fire for nearly two months.

However, things might have been worse, for the weather, though bitterly cold, remained clear and fine and the sun shone all day long throughout the last of February and most of March.

Colonel Gordon went on leave early in March and I commanded the battalion during his absence. I spent much of my spare time looking for troublesome German machine-guns. I had a friend, an artillery officer named Capt Mann, in charge of a battery behind us, and with his assistance we disposed of several guns cleverly concealed behind tree stumps. Captain Mann was killed at Boisleux St Marc soon after. He was one of the best friends I had in France.

One morning I saw my first air fight. I was standing in a gas post enjoying the sunshine when the sentry called out, 'Sir, there's two aeroplanes having a scrap,' and looking up, I saw the machines wheeling for position straight above us. Through my glasses I made out that the lower plane was a German two-seater with a British single-seater sitting over him. There came the faint popping of machine-guns, and presently the German began to sway. Then it came down, not rapidly at first, but in oblique dives as a coin sinks through water. Suddenly, when it was at about three thousand feet, it fell at a sickening rate. As the machine started on its final plunge, a man jumped or fell out, and he gathered such momentum that I could not long follow his descent. As for the plane, it crashed in no-man's land about fifty yards away in a cloud of dust and lay a tangled heap of twisted stays and broken wings, while the victorious British pilot circled round one or twice to make sure of his victim, and then sped away.

After dark that night, a patrol went out. They brought back the body of a young Bavarian airman and the remains of a parabellum automatic gun, but the other man was never found. The dead officer belonged to Flug 57 stationed beyond Lens. He had been to a theatre on the last night of his life, for there was a programme in his pocket showing that he had attended a play at Valenciennes the evening before.

On instructions from Divisional HQ I now began to send out patrols every night to inspect the German wire. These patrols consisted of an officer and three men, and I sometimes accompanied them. Wire inspections were looked on as next door to suicide, but with care they are not as dangerous as all that.

As a rule, we started at 1 am, crawling over the parapet on hands and knees and then through the narrow opening left in the wire for the purpose. We groped along in the dark, falling flat on our faces whenever a Very light soared up, to continue when it died down. We would creep up to the German wire and then along it, to see whether gates had been cut for their infantry to advance.

These patrols, though risky, proved uneventful, and we never lost a man at it. Once or twice we saw dark figures scuttling away which were no doubt similar German patrols. One night I came on a German bombing post, a regular little fortress sunk into the ground. There were rows of potato-mashers (stick grenades) neatly stacked, and half a dozen sets of steel body armour such as were used by German sentries in exposed posts for protection against Mills grenades and shell splinters. We carried them back, and they are now in the Imperial War Museum in London.

On another patrol, as we were crawling forward, a chance flare from a Very light disclosed five or six dead bodies lying close together, with some more dead beyond. One of my men phlegmatically remarked: 'Them here is Gordons, and them there is Boche,' and I remembered having heard that the Gordon Highlanders had had a midnight clash with the enemy in no-man's land a month or two before.

In the first week of March our Brigade (8th) was instructed to withdraw form the sector we had been holding, in order to take over another portion somewhat more to the left. The night we moved out, a heavy snowstorm set in and the cold was intense. Through this bitter weather we went up by Croisilles, past multitudes of wooden crosses, then by the York lines at Mercatel, into our fresh position near the ruins of

Wancourt Tower.

By this time, information of the impending German attack had grown more definite, and the atmosphere became one of tense expectancy. The front line was reorganised in depth. That is, all three battalions of our Brigade were in the front line system at the same time, one battalion holding the foremost trench, the next holding a line about two hundred yards back and the third a line five hundred yards behind the second. These three trenches, all lying close together, comprised what was called the front line system. Behind this, lay a second, third and fourth line of defence, a long way to the rear, marked on our maps as the brown, red and purple systems respectively.

These rear zones however were still incomplete and later, when we were forced to retire, we found them useless, and had to rely on old trenches left over from the fighting of former years.

The three battalions that formed our 8th Brigade were the 1st Royal Scots Fusiliers, the 2nd Royal Scots, and the 7th Shropshires (KSLI); and the three brigades making up our IIIrd Division of the 3rd Army were the 8th, 9th and 76th infantry.

Our Brigadier was General Tanner, a South African from Natal. Our Divisional Commander was General Deverell. Our Corps Commander was Lord Haldane and our Army Commander was General Byng. These three I had not yet set eyes on, for it is one of the evils of modern warfare that the higher command of necessity live far behind, keeping touch with their units by wire, phone or written instructions, and the men in the front line seldom or never see them.

When first we took over our new sector, the 2nd Royal Scots went into the front line, the 1st Royal Scots Fusiliers into the second trench and the 7th Shrops into the third. Our brigade front was about eight hundred yards wide and the German trenches were sixty yards away, with the ruins of Chérisy in the distance. Far away to our left was Monchy, in British occupation, and opposite it, behind the German lines, lay the Bois de Vert, overlooking all our front, and a thorn in the side of the British for long past. On the hill behind us were the remains of Wancourt Tower and in our rear lay what was left of the villages of Henin, Heninel and Wancourt. The valley of the Cojeul River behind us bristled with British guns of every description in readiness for the coming battle.

Every third day we changed over; the battalion in front shifting back third, the second battalion going first and the rear battalion moving into the second line. This kind of Washington Post made it a matter of considerable uncertainty which unit would eventually be in the front trench when the day came, and many bets were laid on the event.

Towards the middle of the month two deserters came over into the British lines, a Pole and an Alsation. They said the main German thrust was to be made between Monchy and Cambrai, with subsidiary attacks in the Ypres Salient and in Champagne. Great numbers of trench mortars and vast piles of gas shells stood ready along the German front line, and on the night before the assault, shock troops were to creep forward into no-man's land. Further, a heavy gas barrage would be placed on us, followed by a long bombardment, after which the troops lying out in the shell holes were to overwhelm us. According to them, dawn on the 16th March was to be the time. All this, as it proved, was substantially correct except that they were five days out in their reckoning.

The higher command was so impressed by the men's statement that they decided to put down a heavy bombardment on the German line during the night of the 15th. The 1st RSF happened to be in the front line that night and as no-man's land was only sixty yards wide, we were ordered to keep the men well down to avoid 'shorts', and at 3 am the firing started.

This shoot was, I believe, the biggest of its kind ever carried out in France. It was magnificent, but we were not appreciative, for we had a solid wall of shells howling within a few feet of our heads, and the noise was appalling. The bed of the trench was strewn next morning with shell fragments that had been blown back on us, but as we kept the men low we had only a few casualties. I never heard whether the Germans had really intended to attack that morning, but it was said that they suffered heavy losses, especially in the back areas, where they had concentrated large forces. Their reply to the bombardment was feeble, as they were probably reserving their ammunition. They dropped a few dozen shells into our trench and some gas. At daybreak we had another man killed, the sentry at the water tank. I saw him duck for a gas shell and then a whizz bang went through the tank, scattering our water supply and at its exit it caught and scattered him.

One of our Lewis gunners, examining the damage to the water tank, said to me: 'Sir, it's an anti-tank gun what done it,' and I was surprised to find that this mild witticism enjoyed great popularity in the battalion, for I heard the men repeating the joke amid roars of laughter during the next few days. Poor fellows, it was the last pleasantry most of them were to have.

On the 17th of March we completed our turn in the front line, and moved to the rear position seven hundred yards back, where we lay quietly until the 19th. I was watching German shells bursting around a British plane one afternoon, when there came a sibilant rush through the air and a loud report. One of the men, a few yards away, pitched down dead and another gave a yell and started to run, holding his hand to his side and dragging a leg. The dead man was caught full in the back as he was stooping to clean his rifle and he was eviscerated by what must have been one of the German anti-aircraft shells that had failed to explode aloft, and had gone off on hitting the unfortunate soldier. The other man died too.

I also watched a combat between about twenty aeroplanes. It was rather cloudy, and they were a long way off, so we could not distinguish friend from foe. I saw five machines crash to earth, one of them burning fiercely, with a long trail of smoke in its wake, but whether they were British or German we could not tell.

On the evening of March 19th, Colonel Gordon returned from leave, and the same night we moved into the second trench of the front line. Battalion headquarters were in a roomy dug-out thirty feet below the surface of the ground. In this dug-out we established the adjutant, signallers and runners, and Colonel Gordon and I lived down an old German shaft, with one of their concrete pillboxes still standing above.

The 2nd Royal Scots were in the front trench, two hundred yards ahead of us, and the Shrops in the third line, five hundred yards back.

The 20th of March was a cloudless sunny day. Things were so quiet that scarcely a shot was heard, and the brooding stillness was almost uncanny. George Bissett and I spent most of the day lying out in a grass-grown shell crater, reading and talking, and revelling in the sunshine, and the singing of the larks, which is such a feature of this part of France.

It was the calm before the storm. Towards evening I walked to the Cojeul Valley to see the guns, and on my return took out a fatigue party to Wancourt Tower; for our brigadier, General Tanner, looked in on his way down the line and suggested that as I was best acquainted with the locality, I should point out the dead bodies still lying there from previous fighting and have them buried.

I supervised this ghoulish work for some hours, and when I considered that the men had done enough, I dismissed them, and retired to our pillbox dug-out for the night.

At exactly 4.30 am next morning a tremendous roll of fire brought us to our feet, and even in the depths of the shaft we could distinguish the thunder of gas projectors being fired in enormous quantities.

I hurried up the staircase to see what was happening and immediately ran into a cloud of gas that sent me choking and gasping below, for my box-respirator.

At first only projectors were being fired, and we still thought that it might merely betoken a big-scale raid. Then our uncertainty was dispelled by the instantaneous crash, the like of which was never heard before on sea or land, from thousands upon thousands of guns roaring on a front of thirty miles, and we knew that the hurricane had broken on us at last. The noise transcended anything I had ever conceived, but it would be hopeless to attempt a description of the monstrous din. Hastily throwing on our equipment, Col Gordon and I climbed the stairs and made for battalion head-quarters a hundred yards up the trench, in order to get in touch with our companies and platoons.

As we ran, we were stunned by the concussion of literally thousands of bursting shells, and although the light was uncertain, for there hung a mist, we could see that all our front stood wrapped in a sea of smoke and flame, and the earth heaved and twisted under our feet. Amid this pandemonium we heard the guns booming for many miles along the line, to tell us that the great battle was joined. We reached headquarters dug-out in safety to find that already all the telephone lines had been smashed by the bombardment.

We ordered up three signallers with an electric flashlamp to communicate with brigade HQ in the rear, but they were blown to pieces within ten minutes, and for the rest of the time we held the front we were isolated, except for some runners that got through.

The battle now starting was the biggest and bloodiest of the war. It was to rage for weeks, and it cost over a million men, but our view of it was limited to a few hundred yards of tossing earth, obscured by columns of dust and smoke shooting heavenward.

We were never at any moment able to see how the tide ebbed and flowed beyond our own immediate neighbourhood, and the people in England knew more of its progress from day to day than we did.

When the attack opened, the 2nd Royal Scots were in the forward line, we were in the second trench two hundred yards back and the Shrops were behind us. To our left lay the 79th and 9th Infantry Brigades of the IIIrd Division and to our right were other units of the 3rd Army, with General Gough's 5th Army hinging on us.

We had a good field of fire over the heads of the Royal Scots but visibility was poor, and when at nine o'clock the German troops advanced, we caught but dim glimpses of their oncoming waves. We were nevertheless able to bring a heavy rifle and Lewis-gun fire to bear on them to swell that of the Royal Scots, and the Shrops in turn were able to fire into the enemy from the rear and in no single instance did a German soldier get nearer than bombing distance from our front line, in spite of all their courage.

All through March 21st and 22nd repeated attacks were made and every one of them broke down. We were drenched with gas for thirty hours on end, and they pounded and battered our trenches until we hardly recognised them, but the men who were left clung doggedly to their shattered ramparts and fought on. With the trench in ruins, it was wonderful that anyone survived at all, and our casualties were heavy. The Royal Scots, who bore the brunt of the attack, had fewer men killed than we, and we had less than the Shrops behind us, for the German bombardment was more intense the further it worked to the rear, and was lightest on the front line, for fear of hitting their own men. I was twice gassed, for it was impossible to wear one's respirator continuously. The Blue Cross mixture that the Germans were putting over caused eyes and throat to smart and burn and made one violently sick, but did not otherwise incapacitate me.

During the two days that we held the line, the enemy had the mastery of the air, in our quarter at any rate, and they were extraordinarily active, swooping over us at a low altitude in flights of fifteen to twenty machines at a time, machine-gunning as they came, and hovering over the British batteries in the rear, dropping flares to guide their artillery.

At midday on the 22nd a runner got through to us with a report that I still have:

'*Secret to 1st RSF,*
2nd R Scots,
7th KSLI.

IIIrd Division. GB 50 begins. Germans have broken into right Corps sector. We still hold front line of 3rd (purple) system roughly from right Corps boundary to St Leger wood, thence along Factory Avenue to Swift Support.
IIIrd Division will readjust its line along Croisilles Switch to Sensée River, thence to Brown Line. Aeroplane has dropped message to say enemy infantry visible on wide front long way through British positions from Croisilles southwards.'

This was disastrous news. It meant that the 5th Army on our right had given way, and it meant that we were outflanked and in grave danger of being surrounded. Col Gordon decided to form a defensive flank along 1st Avenue, a communication trench running back from the front line, and preparations were made to move into it after dark.

We spent an anxious afternoon under heavy fire, knowing that only about fifteen hundred yards away the enemy were well in behind us on the slopes of Henin Hill, and we could see for ourselves that to our left they had taken Monchy.

In the evening Capt Gosling, our brigade major, and another young staff officer, managed to reach us through the barrage. They carried instructions that the entire front zone was to be evacuated and that we were to withdraw to Henin, three miles back, before daylight. He told us that the Germans were in possession of the hill looking down on Henin, practically in our rear.

Supplies were to be destroyed, excepting shovels, which were to be brought along to dig a fresh defensive line; and the withdrawal was to be completed before sunrise.

It was a sore blow to surrender what the men had held so bravely. We burnt all papers and maps, and dumped our stock of Mills grenades down a disused shaft. The question of removing our reserve of small-arms ammunition had been solved long before, for the whole lot had been set alight by a shell, and the boxes of cartridges were blazing and crackling fiercely in the concrete pillbox in which they had been stored.

Col Gordon ordered me to lead a party of runners to Henin to reconnoitre the new ground we were to take up between Boiry-Bequerelle and Boyelles. I sprinted down to the remains of our sleeping dug-out to see that nothing had been overlooked. When I got there I found my servant, McColl, setting a match to letters and papers, having come on his own initiative to see to this. I noticed that the German concrete redoubt that had stood over the entrance had been completely blown away since Col Gordon and I had left the place on the morning of the opening attack.

On my return I assembled my runners and we set off down Foster Avenue to the rear. Foster Avenue was considered to be the finest communication trench in France. It had a double track of duckboards, and was revetted throughout its length. Bissett used to say he would undertake to ride a motor cycle up it, and there was a standing rule that any incoming battalion was to maintain the trench in the same good order as received, so we had taken especial care of its upkeep.

But now, as we picked our way along, I could scarcely recognise it, after the two days' bombardment, for our favourite CT had been reduced to a series of shell craters, with fragments of duckboard and wire entangling our feet.

It was full moon, so we were able to make fair speed over the tumbled surface, and we wasted no time, for the shellfire, though slackened, was still heavy, and great projectiles crashed around us as we went.

Soon we reached the exit, where Foster Avenue abutted on the Cojeul Valley, which we had to cross to reach the plank road leading to Henin. The shelling in the valley, too, was considerably lessened, but the valley lay under a haze of gas, through which we made our way past broken guns, wrecked gunpits, and dead gunners, all looking weird and ghostly through the goggles of our masks. When we reached the plank road outside the ruins of Heninel, we found the gas so thin, that we could remove our respirators, and rest awhile beside the Cojeul, here more like a water-furrow than a river.

The plank road, though badly knocked about, and full of loose beam-ends and shell craters, was still practicable, and it was crowded with horse teams that had come up to fetch away the guns before dawn.

On the bank near by were stretched long rows of wounded for transport to the rear, and already, off the road, came the muffled tramp of men, and we could make out columns of infantry withdrawing to the next line of resistance.

After a short rest I went on with my little party, following the left bank of the Cojeul. As we walked, we passed four men of the 2nd Royal Scots carrying a dead officer on an improvised bier, made from a length of duckboarding. The moon shone full on the dead man's face, and I saw that it was Capt Newlands, whom I knew very well. He looked calm and restful, and he might have been asleep, so little was there of death in his countenance. I asked the men where they were carrying the body to, and one of them said they weren't going to allow no bl—dy Boche to bury the Skipper, so the worthy fellows had taken upon themselves the self-imposed task of carrying their company-commander back to the next line of defence, to ensure him against alien burial.

At length we reached the crossroad at Henin, and I set about making arrangements for the laying-out of a fresh position. It was still night, but away to our right the countryside was lit by columns of fire pouring from the shafts of the Hindenburg Tunnel. The great gallery was alight, and huge pillars of flame were shooting upward, for the heavily timbered interior had become like a blast furnace. The conflagration lent an added note of desolation to the scene.

By sunrise, what was left of our battalion arrived. The men were come from two days of hell, but we had to set them digging straight away at an old trench, to make it capable of defence. The remnant of a battalion of the Coldstream Guards was digging in to our right, and to our left the rest of the Royal Scots and Shropshires were doing likewise. Having completed these measures for putting the new line in a fit state, Bissett and I spread a couple of old sandbags on the grass and flung ourselves down to snatch some rest, for neither of us had slept for forty-eight hours; Colonel Gordon stayed to look after things, for he seemed to be made of whipcord, and he said he was not tired.

We counted on getting at least a day's respite, as we thought it would take the Germans quite that time to discover that we had vacated the forward zone, but by 9 o'clock we were awakened and told that the enemy were advancing against us.

Starting to our feet we saw masses of their infantry swarming over Henin Hill in our direction. Teams of their light guns were being galloped up, and groups of men, about two hundred at a time, came dribbling forward into the dead ground beside the Cojeul River. The British artillery had not yet had time to take up new stations, but a few guns began to fire over open sights at a target that could hardly be missed. They caused the enemy heavy loss, and the slope towards the Cojeul was soon plentifully strewn with fallen men.

One howitzer battery in particular in front of Neuville Vitasse, dropped its shells in the thick of the German infantry, taking toll with nearly every round. Once I saw what looked like two full companies coming down the sunken road by the graveyard. They were advancing at the double and as they reached the angle by the Henin crucifix, a howitzer shell dropped among them. When the air cleared I saw a pile of bodies heaped in the cutting, and further off, in a ragged circle, lay more dead and wounded that had been blown outwards, the survivors running wildly up the road. Through my glasses I saw some of the wounded shake themselves free of such dead as were lying across them, then they crawled away, and German stretcher-bearers came hurrying down to their assistance.

Towards 3 o'clock in the afternoon (March 23rd) the Germans launched an attack on us from the Cojeul Valley. Their gunfire, which had been growing in volume all the morning, now became violent, and shells were rained on us, mostly from light field guns and portable mortars, that were carried by hand.

Suddenly, before we quite grasped the fact that an attack was coming, we saw waves of field-grey infantry advancing towards us from this side of the Cojeul. Our men, earlier in the day, had collected a quantity of rusty wire entanglements which they found lying about, and had thrown these out before our trench.

The front wave of the enemy got as far as this obstruction, but no further, for they were met with so steady a fire that in a few minutes the assault withered away. The attackers went scurrying back for the shelter of the hollow ground behind, leaving before us a number of dead and wounded. Of these, some writhed in agony and others crept off on hands and knees. One young German who remained crouching near by, not daring to run, came in to us when called upon, and he was followed by several others, who had thrown themselves down to escape our fire.

They said the attack had been hastily organised and that their officers had assured them that they would meet with little resistance, as the British were too demoralised to fight. Simultaneously with the attack on our battalion, other attacks were made to right and left and these also broke down. Our opponents were 80th Württembergers. They had their own regimental postage stamps, which the prisoners distributed amongst us, by way of souvenirs. They were rather a poor lot physically, but good-natured country bumpkins, such as one might meet in any rural district.

Some of the wounded kept calling for help, but a platoon sergeant who crept out was shot through the head, so we had to leave them to their fate.

The Guards Brigade to our right were heavily attacked before sunset. They told me later that, on this and the following days, they accounted for ten thousand Germans, a pardonable exaggeration, considering the swathes of dead and dying whom I saw lying before their trenches. The night was quiet, except for the moans of the wounded lying out in the open. There were frequent cries of '*Hilfe, hilfe, um Gottes Wille, hilfe!*', but as were obliged to sweep the ground in front of us, most of them must have perished.

The 24th of March was another day of wrath. Our trench, though considerably strengthened during the hours of darkness, offered but little protection against the high-angle trench mortars, and by midday our sector was again full of dead and wounded men. It was heartbreaking to see how the poor fellows were blown to pieces.

Once, I saw two men hurled ten to fifteen feet in the air by a shell, to come down shapeless behind the trench. There was a young soldier manning the firestep by my side. He was haggard and worn from the strain of the past days, and he blenched as he looked at the gruesome sight. His lips were trembling when I glanced at him, but he drew himself up and said to me, 'Sir, the Boche may break through somewhere else, but they'll no get through here.'

I have never held a high opinion of the military tactics of the British in the Great War. I think they could have fought it at a fifth of the cost and a fifth of the casualties, but of their stubborn valour, no man who has seen them in days like these can have a doubt.

After midday on the 24th, the Germans repeatedly sent their infantry to the attack, not only against us, but on a width of about ten miles, and we were kept busy until late in the afternoon. None of their attacks succeeded on our divisional front, but elsewhere they broke through in places. The German losses must have run into large figures, for the ground before us was ghastly with dead men, and with the cries of the wounded.

Once, in the thick of an attack, I saw a low-flying German aeroplane come firing down our line. It was pounced upon right over our heads by a Bristol Fighter, and shot to earth before the enemy pilot, as it seemed to me, was aware that an English machine had made its appearance. The plane crashed three hundred yards in front of us, where it lay like a dead locust, one wing sticking up into the air. The occupants must have been killed, for there was no movement under the wreckage.

After 4 o'clock the attacks ceased, but the shell-fire remained heavy. We did not know how the rest of the battle had gone, but we heard the unceasing rumble of guns in the south. A telegram about our own share was delivered to Col Gordon that evening, and I have kept it:

> '6.15 pm. From military secretary to MZO.[1] Field Marshal Commander-in-Chief sends his congratulations on splendid defence to-day stop he relies upon your steadfastness and valour to crush this new attack which will be enemy's last hope of success.'

A similar message was received by other battalions of the IIIrd Division, and two days later we saw an outstanding reference in the London *Times* to the 'Iron Division', as the IIIrd came to be called, wherein it received especial praise for its share in the great battle.

At 5 o'clock we received orders to move out after dark to a fresh position to the left of Boiry-Bequerelle, and I was sent with two runners to reconnoitre the ground. It was a welcome relief to get out of that infernal trench, even though the back area through which I went was being liberally sprinkled with shell-fire.

We hurried up the Neuville Vitasse Road, for enemy rifles and machine-guns were active, and as soon as we were under cover behind the rise, we branched off towards Boiry.

As we reached the *pavé* road that leads to Bapaume, two soldiers belonging to the crew of a tank standing near by started walking towards us, when a long-range German shell burst on them. I saw one man fly through the air and come down stone dead on the cobbles. The other gave a shout and ran towards me. When he came abreast, he continued on his way and I saw that his right arm was in shreds and that he was blinded. He ran past, keeping the road for a short distance and then, losing direction, pitched headlong into the stormwater drain. When we went to him he too was dead.

Having located our new position I returned to the battalion, and we moved out after dark from the trench in which so many of our men had died. By 3 o'clock in the morning we had the remnants of our companies installed in some sort of a trench that we had found and deepened. I do not think any officer or soldier had enjoyed two hours' consecutive sleep for the past three days, and we looked forward to the prospect of a little rest at last.

But our signallers had linked us up by phone with brigade, and just as Bisset and I had lain down on the floor of a deserted Nissen hut, there came a message that I was to report to brigade headquarters at Boisleux-au-Mont at once, together with a junior officer. Col Gordon pointed out that we were shorthanded owing to our heavy casualties. The Brigade Major replied that the order had come from the Divisional

---

[1]MZO was the code index of the 1st Royal Scots Fusiliers.

General, and was most explicit. Col Gordon said there was no help for it, I had to go, and he told young Lieut White to accompany me, so, dazed with fatigue and lack of sleep, we shuffled off in the dark.

I knew the road, and at Boisleux-au-Mont we found brigade headquarters down a catacomb, where, in one of the caverns, sat Capt Gosling over his maps, and on the floor lay General Tanner fast asleep, his first real rest, so Gosling whispered, since the 21st.

We were told that a car was waiting to take us to divisional headquarters at Bretincourt, and, greatly mystified, we stumbled back along the galleries and up the staircase to find a roomy Napier ready for us. White and I promptly fell asleep, until wakened at daybreak by the driver, in Bretincourt. Here a staff officer came to find us, and led us to a hutment standing on the village green, in which was General Deverell, our Divisional Commander, whom I now saw for the first time.

General Deverell proceeded to tell us of the very serious state of affairs on our right. The 5th Army had retreated, and the Germans had overrun many miles of the British front. He said it was practically certain that the whole line would have to retire in order to conform with the 5th Army, and arrangements were being completed to withdraw the 3rd Army, during the coming night. He had sent for me to inspect the area near Ficheux and Blairville Wood, as far as Wailly, to fix a new line of resistance for our Division.

We did not listen very attentively, for our most insistent need was sleep and we stood blear-eyed and stupid, while the General was speaking. He noticed this. He said he knew we were pretty well tuckered up, but we must go and do our job first, after which he promised us a good rest.

Our hopes of repose vanished indefinitely, for my instructions included an order to return to our battalion first, to fetch a party of guides, whom I was to lead to Ficheux, in order to acquaint them with the ground. We saluted and went off, but I prevailed on one of the staff to commandeer the General's car, which took us as far as Boisleux, where we ran into a sprinkling gunfire, and the chauffeur refused to go further, as he said he had no right to risk the car.

From here it was not a long walk to where we had left the battalion some hours before. I explained the position to Col Gordon. He said he was not a religious man, but he believed there was a God, and he did not believe the Germans could take Amiens. He was right, but we did not know it at the time. As for Bissett, the news of the *débâcle* of the 5th Army left him unperturbed, and he went about whistling and joking as always.

Accompanied by eight runners, White and I started back, past the brick factory and the railway triangle. The Germans were shelling the track, and we saw fragments of rails, rolling-stock and water-tanks, go into the air amid the smoke and noise of 5.9's and howitzer shells.

It was a weary journey. The sun was hot, and we were burdened with our equipment, and with the knowledge of evil tidings. To add to our troubles, young White's nerves had given way. He was a brave boy, and had been awarded the Military Cross two or three months before, but now he was on the verge of collapse. Every time a shell howled over us, he flung himself to the ground and covered his head with his trench cloak. Then he would rise shamefaced and trembling. I knew that in a war like this, any man may become unstrung, and I pretended at first not to notice. But after a time he came to me and said miserably that he was obliged to confess his nerves had gone. I advised him to report sick. For a moment he stood silent, and I could see that he was fighting temptation; then he said he would see it through, for the sake of his people at home. None the less our passage was torture to him. He walked along quivering and quaking to every explosion, and the poor fellow kept harping upon the possibility of being taken out of the line to help train the American units that were beginning to arrive in France. Someone on the staff at Bretincourt had put this idea into his head, and he told me that if only he could do this for a few weeks he would soon recover himself.

I comforted him as best I could, for I was feeling the strain myself and understood his condition.

On breasting the rise at Boisleux-au-Mont we saw a sight that gladdened our eyes. The country beyond was black with troops—a great army of reinforcements marching south to stem the tide—and there came mile upon mile of steel-hatted infantry, the vastest concourse of human beings that I have ever seen, and the most welcome, for truth to say my spirits had been at a low ebb. Apart from the military situation, there were the terrible things seen of late. No man can bear the sight of torn human flesh, with thousands of dead and wounded, and the stress of prolonged gunfire, without being affected.

But this great force marching on the enemy put new heart into one, and even White looked more cheerful. For a long while we watched them going forward. The men laughed and sang, and they carried themselves with an air of confidence that did us good to see.

In the afternoon, White and I, with the runners, came to Blairville Wood and staked out a new line of defence amongst the network of old trenches to the right of Ficheux.

By sunset, drugged with fatigue, we reported our task complete to General Deverell at Bretincourt. He told us the position was somewhat easier and that, while the 3rd Army might still have to retire, the withdrawal had been postponed, and he said we could now sleep until we were blue in the face. Beneath a gruff exterior, the old fellow had a soft spot, for he ordered a Nissen hut to be cleared for our party, and he personally conducted us thither. He wished us all a good rest, and we slept at last.

Vaguely I heard the crash of bombs during the night, for the German planes were active, and White told me next morning that they had kept him awake most of the time. Many bombs were dropped on the village and there were a considerable number of casualties.

At 8 am the General sent for us once more. He gave us a good breakfast and told me that I was to return to Blairville Wood, to fix upon points for the placing of reserve ammunition supplies. He gave us a car, and we completed the work, and returned to Bretincourt by midday. After this, White and I were provided with horses, and we were ordered to take a convoy of ammunition limbers to the new trenches that were being dug above Wailly. In addition, I was to report on the trenches between Ficheux and the railway arch.

The Germans were dropping long-range shells on these back areas, and we saw an ammunition dump go up, a sheet of flame shooting straight into the sky, German aeroplanes were troublesome too. They came every ten minutes, firing on the men at work on the reserve trenches. A two-seater came flying low over the carts, as they stood strung out on the road near the arch. The pilot was a master-hand. He flew his machine, not so much in swerves, but rather jolting her from side to side in an amazing fashion.

He swooped down again and again, coming so close that I could see the gunner standing in the cockpit, slewing his gun from side to side as he straddled us. Luckily the bumping of the plane disturbed his aim, and although he sent a stream of bullets whizzing about our ears, neither men nor horses were hit. I ordered the drivers and runners to open rifle-fire and this may have had some effect, for the plane now headed back for its own lines.

We watched its course for a few minutes and then, far away above Monchy, we saw three British machines dive down from a great height upon the German, and it fell in flames, leaving one half-regretful at the fate of its occupants, for they must have been gallant men.

Soon after, another German plane came over, again flying low to rake the working parties. An anti-aircraft gun mounted on a motor lorry had just come up, and it opened fire. I saw a shell explode against the fuselage. The aeroplane swayed unevenly, and then descended in an easy glide, landing not far from where we stood. To my surprise the pilot clambered out, and running forward, threw himself on the grass, and opened fire with a Mauser pistol at two soldiers, who were walking towards him with their shovels over their shoulders. They bolted for cover, and now from all sides came dozens of angry men from the working parties, brandishing spades and pickaxes as they ran.

They surrounded the airman and I hastened across, fearing that they might kill him, for an aviator with a crashed plane has no more right to fire on those coming to help him than has a shipwrecked sailor on a raft the right to fire upon his rescuers.

However, when I got there the men had merely disarmed the offender, who was standing in their midst clenching and unclenching his fists, his face twitching and his eyes glaring, like one under uncontrollable emotion. In the rear cockpit of the machine lay the machine-gunner, crumpled and dead.

Towards evening, our work accomplished, I sent the runners back to Col Gordon, and White and I returned to Bretincourt to report.

During the day White had again repeatedly spoken of his hopes of being transferred to an American training camp. Now, at the conclusion of our interview with General Deverell, we were ordered to return next day to duty in the firing line. I watched White's face at this, and the poor fellow looked as if he had received his death sentence, as indeed he had.

That night, the civilians in Bretincourt were greatly agitated. French political officers came riding through the village on bicycles ordering all non-combatants to leave the place in view of the threatened withdrawal. I thought the order very drastic. Most of the people were women and children, and old men, and it meant that they had to flee on foot, carrying their belongings on their backs.

In the streets I passed knots of them loudly protesting, for the French are like cats in the way they cling to their homes, whatever the danger may be. But the political officers were obdurate and we could not interfere in a matter between the French

Government and its citizens. It was a pitiful exodus, and, as it turned out, an unnecessary one, for the 3rd Army never retired at all.

We spent another night in our Nissen hut, once again to the sound of many air bombs, which did serious damage in the artillery lines close by. This helped still further to jangle White's nerves, and he looked a wreck next morning.

We then started back on foot to rejoin our battalion. Our transport limbers were standing at Wailly in charge of Capt Hester, and we touched there on the way. We found that a long-range shell had killed two men and thirteen horses just before we arrived. My horse, 'Major', was among the killed, and also Col Gordon's little pony which he had meant to take back with him to South Africa.

Capt Hester gave me a batch of London newspapers, from which I learnt far more of the battle than we knew locally.

According to the papers, the Germans were dangerously near Amiens, and in the north they were attacking on a wide front from Arras towards Meteren. The position of the British Army was reported to be critical, and things were looking very black.

In the news columns were several German wireless telegrams intercepted by the Admiralty. They were bulletins from the front, in the shape of telegrams sent from the battlefield by the Kaiser to his wife. The fighting was represented as a sort of family affair of the Hohenzollerns, after the manner of Frederick the Great.

One message ran: 'Wilhelm to Augusta: Our son Eitel Fritz gloriously advanced this day and our son Wilhelm attacked and drove the English in headlong rout—he has taken more booty than at Caporetto,' and it wound up with a boastful '*Morgen geht's weiter*,' as if the Kaiser and his son were only waiting for daylight to finish off the British Army.

White and I now walked from the transport camp to the front line, passing to the north of Ficheux, and then along the Mercatel Road. As we approached Mercatel, the German bombardment flared up afresh after the comparative lull of the last two days. Mercatel itself, and the Bapaume Road, were under heavy shrapnel and howitzer fire, and White's nerves were in a terrible state. I advised him to return to the transport lines, but he refused, and I let the matter drop.

We found our battalion holding a sector of the front line to the right of Henin, the village itself three hundred yards away being in the hands of the Germans. Battalion headquarters were in a sunken road behind the trench, a most uncomfortable place, for the cutting ran in the direction of the enemy, and their gunners kept dropping light and heavy shells around it until dark, so that everyone at headquarters was kept standing against the side of the bank, to present as small a mark as possible to the innumerable shell fragments that whizzed about our ears.

After dark, the bombardment subsided, and we were able to move up and down, to prepare for the next attack, which was sure to come at dawn. By the light of a candle-end in a cubbyhole I read the Kaiser's telegram to Bissett. It made him very angry. He said, 'When the Boche come on again we'll give the —— Kaiser something to wire to Augusta about,' and he kept muttering about it to himself all the evening.

Towards morning as I went the rounds, I saw Lieut White crouched down in the bottom of the trench. By the light of a candle shaded under his steel helmet he was trying to read a letter, and his hand shook and trembled as he held it. For the last time I advised him to go back, and told him there was time to leave before dawn. As before,

I could see him fighting the temptation to quit and, as before, he said he would stay.

When it grew light the German bombardment came down in earnest. Our casualties in officers and men mounted quickly, and by 7 o'clock we had only three company officers left. White was one of them, and, as the shell-fire lifted, we saw the waves of German infantry swarm towards us. Close to him stood a Lewis gun whose crew were all dead. He picked up the gun and carried it forward of the parapet for better vision, started to fire, sitting behind it out in the open, and there a bullet found him. He was one of the bravest men I ever knew.

The German attack did not reach further than the few coils of wire which we had been able to throw out, and it withered away before the fire of our men. Then came a lull, and shortly after eight a heavy bombardment was concentrated over the Shropshires to our left. The line there stood in smoke, and we knew that another attack was taking place.

After a few minutes a Shrops officer came running across from behind, and dropping among us, said that he had come to give us warning to guard our left flank and our rear, as the Germans had broken into their sector. This meant that, a little distance away, the enemy was in the same trench as our Battalion, and Col Gordon immediately sent word to the left company to form a bombing block, and ordered the runners and signallers to man the bank of the sunken road behind, as a protective flank.

I stood up to get a clearer view of the threatened point. There was a curtain of smoke and dust through which I saw men firing and throwing hand grenades. As I looked, I was struck with terrific force by what felt like an entire shell, but which later surgical operation established to be only a jagged fragment of one, the size and shape of half an orange skin, firmly embedded in my right thighbone. I staggered back to where Col Gordon and Bissett were. Our medical officer, Dr Flemming, was fetched, and he gave me first aid. His dressing-station had received a direct hit which had killed most of his orderlies, and such wounded as were there at the time, so there was nowhere else to go, and he advised that I be left where I was. Bissett's servant, Glossop, who also acted as mess-steward, had unearthed a brazier, on which he was calmly preparing breakfast, regardless of the battle around us, and he gave me a cup of tea which helped to revive me. In about twenty minutes came another attack, and there was a furious struggle with rifle-fire, and the bursting of German stick bombs. With this general uproar going on not many yards off, I lay remembering that if the enemy made even the slightest progress, I should be bombed or bayoneted, or become a prisoner of war, and so spent some crowded moments. But the attack was brought to a standstill, and, for a time, things simmered down in our immediate neighbourhood, although the guns still thundered away to right and left. At 10 o'clock Dr Flemming came to me. He said I should make an effort to get to the rear for proper medical attendance. All his stretcher-bearers were dead or wounded, and no ambulance could reach us through the heavy German shell-fire.

I was not at first anxious to go, for I was in great pain, and looking back from where I lay, I could see the Bapaume Road, which must be crossed in order to reach safety, and was being swept by heavy metal and by shrapnel, to prevent reinforcements from approaching our line. But as the shelling was just as severe where I was, and I knew that our line might be forced back at any moment (it was forced back five hundred yards soon after I left), I decided to risk it.

Col Gordon ordered Corporal Noble of the Guides and my servant, McColl, to hold me up on either side, and after I had said goodbye to those near me, we started off. I had noticed Glossop eyeing me appraisingly some time before, and now, when we had gone about a dozen yards, he came running after us with a slip of paper in his hand. He said, 'Sir, sir, you haven't paid your mess bill,' and handed me a hastily pencilled account for ninety francs.

I feebly protested at being dunned in these circumstances and promised to send him a cheque, but he returned to his brazier with a dubious look on his face, as much as to say he might as well write off the item as a dead loss. We started down the sunken road, and a heavy burst of shrapnel caught us. Two runners who were coming towards us were struck dead within twenty yards of us, so we decided to leave the road and go across the open.

We had chosen an evil time for our journey, for the shell-fire was momentarily increasing on the Arras-Bapaume *Pavé,* which we had to pass. Between us and the road heavy shells were throwing up columns of spouting earth, and overhead the air was flecked with shrapnel. We were covered with dust and half stunned by the noise. I had lost a great deal of blood and my wound was throbbing, so we made slow progress, resting every now and then in a shell crater to ease my leg, or to allow a particularly heavy gust of fire to quiet down. The barrage was so dense that it was like walking through a fog. In the sky we saw aeroplanes wheeling around, and everything pointed to the imminence of a fresh attack. Once, as we rested for a moment, an aeroplane detached itself from a number of others and crashed down at such speed that we could not distinguish its markings, and we heard a dull thud as it struck the earth some distance away.

As we approached Mercatel, we were obliged to make a detour to avoid a large ammunition dump that had been set on fire. Blazing fragments of Nissen huts and multi-coloured flames were shooting in all directions.

Our way now took us through ploughed land whose uneven surface caused me great agony, and we made still slower progress. As we crossed the field, a heavy shell burst ten yards beyond us and either the rush of its passage or the force of the explosion (we could not tell which) sent us sprawling over one another on the ground, with eyes and mouths full of grit, and a gush of blood from my wound.

In spite of everything our luck held, and at length we reached the Bapaume Road. What we had previously known as a cobbled highway was now a succession of shell craters, littered with dead men and horses, smashed motor lorries and limbers, for it was the main artery along which supplies came up, and the German gunners raked it night and day. Before crossing, we sheltered for a few minutes in a ditch, and when we detected a slight lull in the fire, the two young soldiers helped me up and dragged me over the battered road. We then continued until we found the high bank of a sunken lane, and were able to take a long breather in comparative sanctuary, for although stray shells were still dropping about, we were beyond the barraged zone at last.

I well remember the feeling of surprise with which I realised that the sun was shining brightly and that it was a beautiful day. Ever since dawn the atmosphere had been so obscured with dust and smoke up in the front line that it was strange to find one's eyes blinking in the unaccustomed glare of a clear sky.

After a long halt, we headed slowly for the Ficheux Arch. Another painful mile brought us in front of the British batteries by the railway embankment. They were firing at a tremendous rate, probably in answer to SOS signals from the front line, from which we could now hear the sound of heavy fighting.

German aeroplanes flew over the guns in the most audacious manner, dropping Very lights as target signals to their own side, a proceeding which intensely annoyed Corporal Noble, and he maintained a running fire of unflattering comment on the British Air Force, none of whose machines were in evidence.

We had to make another detour, as the forward blast from the batteries was so powerful that we could not face it, and were forced to branch away, until we found a clear space through which to go.

Beyond the railway arch, to my great relief, we came on an improvised dressing-station in a large Nissen hut beside the road.

I was now so exhausted, that I was unable to reach there, and sank down near the entrance. McColl spread my trench coat on the ground and he and Noble lifted me on to it. After a rest, they carried me into the hut, where I was given a mug of tea that tasted like nectar after our dolorous journey.

There was a considerable number of wounded lying in and around the hut, and the RAMC orderlies did what they could for us.

The Germans now began to shell the place, which stood conspicuously in the open. I do not think they knowingly bombarded a dressing-station, for it flew no red cross, but as the shells were dropping closer and closer, the walking wounded were ordered to make for some old trenches lying near by, and the stretcher cases were removed as fast as possible by the bearer parties.

I made an attempt to follow the walking wounded but found that I was too weak to go far, so I lay down beside the road, Noble and McColl squatting beside me. McColl had asked me to take him to South Africa after the war, and I gave him my address. Just then a Ford box car was driven up by a major of the RAMC. He had brought a load of bandages and medical supplies, and having delivered these at the old trenches where the wounded were being collected, had come on to see that no one had been overlooked in the hut. On his way back he noticed me lying on the ground, and stopped the car. Seeing the pool of blood in which I was lying, he got out and examined my wound, shook his head, and told my two companions to lift me into the back of his vehicle.

Then I said farewell to these brave boys who had stood by me so well. McColl was killed a fortnight later at Bailleul. Col Gordon sent me the papers found on his body, for he had no next-of-kin.

Our road ran up a long slope, and we were nearly hit once or twice by long-distance shells that were dropping about.

Looking backward, over the rear of the car in the direction from which I had come, there was a roll of gunfire along the front line four miles away, showing that the Germans had resumed their attacks.

That was the last I saw of the great battle. At this distance, the shell-fire lay soft and fleecy over the line, like a riband of mist, and it was hard to believe that under that delicate tracery men were killing and maiming each other.

Further along, the car stopped again, and I saw the major alight to examine a wounded man huddled near the road. He was a soldier from a London regiment, in great agony, for his right eye was destroyed, and his right arm hung in shreds. The major gave him an injection, and helped him in beside me. Before long the cockney grew quite talkative, as the opiate took effect, and when I asked him how he came by his injuries, he said, 'A blurry Boche frew a potato-masher straight at me gig-lamps,' meaning that he had been hit in the face by a stick grenade.

The car took us for some miles, and then the friendly major advised us to wait by the road until an ambulance could pick us up, as it was useless our going on with him and getting still further away from assistance.

He helped us out, and wishing us good luck, drove off. The Londoner and I lay down in the grass, and in about half an hour an empty lorry came up on its way back for gun ammunition. We signalled it to stop, and the driver and his assistant lifted us over the tailboard. An empty munition lorry is not an ideal conveyance for wounded men, and the jolting over the cobbles caused us both to bleed profusely, to say nothing of the pain of being shaken about like peas.

The lorry took us for five or six kilometres, until we reached a big casualty clearing station, where they unloaded us in a very limp condition. Bearers ran up, and, placing us on stretchers, carried us into a large tent and laid us on trestle tables for inspection. I did not see my friend of the potato-masher again, for a doctor gave me an injection, put a fresh dressing on my thigh, and within ten minutes of my arrival, I found myself in a comfortable motor ambulance, which already contained three other cases, and was starting for Doullens about thirteen miles away.

We reached there by two in the afternoon, and were taken from the car and placed in a courtyard, where lay many other wounded ranged side by side. Next to me was a tall young airman, still dressed in furs and leather headgear, like an arctic explorer. He turned his head and said to me, 'What have you got?' I answered, 'A shot in the thigh, and you?' 'Finished,' he replied, 'bullet through the stomach. I'll be dead tomorrow.' I never heard whether his unfavourable diagnosis proved correct, for he was taken off, and I did not see him again.

Later on they came for me, and I was carried into a large building, apparently the local Town Hall, for there was a raised stage at one end with painted scenery and wings, much like our village halls in South Africa.

On the stage, doctors were operating behind screens, and in a corner, only partially hidden by rubber ground-sheets, was an ominous pile of amputated arms and legs. Six or seven operations were going on at the same time, and the place reeked of chloroform and lysol. A surgeon undid my bandages. Then he said mine was a case for X-ray, and as there was no installation here, I was taken up a staircase, and my stretcher was placed on the floor of a large room already filled with wounded. The nurses were exceedingly kind. They belonged to a unit of the Canadian Red Cross, and as they had been driven from their permanent hospital near Bapaume to this temporary shelter, they had lost their equipment and had to leave most of us lying on our stretchers on the floor. I was very cold from loss of blood and one of the nurses said the action of my heart was weak, so she gave me an occasional dose of French brandy, which tingled new life into every vein of my body.

During the night, German aeroplanes dropped bombs on Doullens, but our hospital was not hit. The nurses said that Marshal Foch and Marshal Haig, with Mr Lloyd George and other prominent men, had been here two days before to attend a council of the allied armies, which accounted for the extra notice which Doullens was receiving from the air. By next day so many of the wounded had been evacuated to base hospitals that towards afternoon I was lifted on to a bed, a welcome relief after thirty hours on a stretcher. In the bed nearest me lay a young airman, with a gunshot wound through his lungs. He was very ill, but did not know it, for I heard him ask one of the nurses for a postcard, as he wished to let his mother know that he had a nice blighty, and would be home in a few days. She brought him a card, and, as he was too weak to write himself, she wrote at his dictation, but she shook her head at me, and I knew that he would never see his mother again. Before long I saw her place the screens around his bed, always an ominous sign in a hospital ward, for they are put around a patient *in extremis*, to spare the feelings of the other sufferers. I fell into a doze, from which I was awakened by one of the screens falling on me, and looked up to see the boy sitting upright in bed, his arms outstretched, then with a low moan he fell back dead.

Doullens was bombed again during the night, and once more we listened to the crash of the explosions. One bomb must have fallen in the street below, to judge by the roar and the trembling of the walls, but the hospital escaped injury.

We were glad to see the dawn, for after the long strain of the past week, it was an ordeal to lie helpless in the midst of the air raid. I have since heard that the hospital was hit a few nights later, and only hope that none of our little Canadian sisters were injured.

The morning after the raid I was carried downstairs to a motor ambulance which took three of us to the railway station. There were already many wounded waiting to be taken on board a hospital train, and I saw King George in service uniform walking up and down the platform, speaking to a wounded man here and there. I was told that he was on his way to the battle raging before Amiens, to find out for himself how things stood. Owing to the troop trains on the line, we were twenty-four hours in reaching Rouen, instead of seven, and it was a weary passage.

At Rouen, the wounded were transferred to ambulance cars, by German prisoners, and were then distributed to various hospitals. I found myself once more at No 2, where I had lain the year before. My wound had taken a turn for the worse during the journey, I was carried straight into the theatre, and was given an anaesthetic and operated upon at once.

I spent twenty days in No 2, and, after a second operation, was sent to Havre. From there we crossed the Channel at night in the *Guildford Castle*, a former South African mail boat now reconditioned for the Red Cross, and within an hour of reaching England, we were on a beautifully equipped train bound for London. At Waterloo Station, we lay once again on the platform, and a medical officer came among us with pasteboard slips printed with the name of the hospital to which each man was to be taken. I drew No 10 Cambridge Square, a small hospital in the private dwelling-house of Mrs Muirhead Campbell, a patriotic Scotch lady, and here I remained for the next three months.

In France the great battle still raged, but the 28th of March had been the turning-point. From then onwards, the German advance slowed down and was ultimately checked.

I have the Order of the Day addressed to our IIIrd Division:

'30th March. The General Officer commanding the 6th Corps is at a loss to find words adequate to express his intense admiration for the unconquerable valour which the IIIrd Division has displayed during the fierce fighting of the last nine days. The repeated efforts made in great force by a determined enemy to break through the left of the Corps where the soldiers of the IIIrd Division stood, were repulsed time after time, and where ground had to be yielded to maintain an unbroken line, every foot was contested. Had the IIIrd Division, much weakened and exhausted by several days of hard fighting and nights devoid of rest, not maintained an unbroken front, it is difficult to believe that the enemy could have failed to obtain his objective, the capture of Amiens and the driving of a wedge between the allied armies.'

I was glad to have witnessed so mighty a conflict in the company of such brave men.

And now, fallen out of the fight, I lay in the quiet refuge of the ward until the end of July, while my wounds were slowly mending.

Chapter 12

The Counterstroke

The months I passed in hospital at No 10, Cambridge Square, were uneventful. The only excitement we had apart from the newspaper reports of the fighting in France, was an air raid.

On the night of May 20th, 1918, forty German bombers came over. By now the air defences were much improved, and, as we lay in our beds, we heard the warning maroons, followed by the British anti-aircraft barrage. Through the open windows we saw the curtain of shell-fire hanging far up in the sky, and amidst the boom of the guns and the bursting of the shells, we could distinguish the crash of the bombs as they struck the ground. Mrs Muirhead Campbell and the nurses took it calmly, and they came among us with cups of tea and cheerful talk. Sixty people were killed and seven hundred and fifty were wounded, but it was the last aeroplane attack on London, for so effective was the artillery fire that seven bombers, each containing six men, were shot down, and the Germans never again repeated the attempt.

During July I was sometimes wheeled in a bath chair to Hyde Park, to see the American troops march by. They were landing at the rate of a hundred thousand a month. In these days there was nothing to prevent an American army from getting to France, for the German submarine menace had now been completely overcome. Instead of sinking sixty to seventy ships a week, as they were doing when first I came to England, they were unable to stop the Americans from crossing the Atlantic without loss, and it was but rarely that the destruction of a merchant vessel was reported, for the recently invented convoy system had practically made an end to the U-boat activities.

In the last week of July I was discharged from hospital with orders to proceed to

Fort Matilda. I was in Scotland for over five weeks on light duty in the training camps, for my wound was still unhealed. I was also sent to Grantham for a machine-gun course. On the way there, as we were travelling down the East Coast, the train was stopped midway between two stations, shortly after dark. All lights were extinguished, and we were told that a Zeppelin was approaching. I had never seen one, nor did I catch sight of one on this occasion, but presently, far out to sea, there was a great blaze in the sky, and this, we learned from the papers next day, was the L70, commanded by Strasser, the head of the German naval air service, who with a crew of forty men was brought down by a British airman, Major Cadbury, and all on board perished in the flames.

That distant ball of fire over the North Sea was the last Zeppelin to make an attack on England. So many of them had been destroyed that the Germans were finally convinced that these engines of war were death traps, and never again did a hostile Zeppelin cross the Channel.

Of late the submarines, the aeroplane raids, and the Zeppelins had all failed, and one after another these three great weapons which the Germans had forged, broke short in their hands.

On my return from Grantham I remained at Fort Matilda. I was several times examined in Glasgow by a medical board, but my leg had not yet healed and it was not until the 12th of September that I received orders to return to France. I went to Boulogne, and from there we travelled the old route via Arras the following day, and after dark reached railhead at a place called Achiet-le-Grand. Here I was speedily reintroduced to the war, for as the train drew in, a low-flying German machine swooped down and aimed two bombs at us. They fell a few yards in front of the engine, exploding with vast noise, but beyond throwing a shower of earth on the carriage roofs, they did no harm. We detrained, and were led to a reception camp nearby, where we spent the night. At about 10 o'clock a big enemy bomber came droning overhead. The British defence against them nowadays consisted of numerous searchlights, whose beams moved across the sky in all directions. Whenever a searchlight picked up a German plane it held him until other searchlights could converge, and they followed him as long as possible, on the chance of a British machine being aloft. On this occasion we saw the bomber caught in the beams. He looked like a great silver moth as he dived and swerved to escape the glare. Then a British two-seater darted into the broad pathway of light, his machine-gun spitting as it came. In a few seconds a vivid flame broke out, and the bomber began to drop in a sheet of fire which lit the countryside for miles around. As it fell, from far and near we heard the sound of cheering from the various camps in the neighbourhood, and the thought that in that fiery trail men were being horribly burned to death did not seem to occur to anyone. One man jumped out with a parachute, and in the light of the burning machine we saw him descending, but the plane and its remaining crew of seven fell a mile away amid a shower of sparks, followed by loud explosions, as if the cargo of bombs were going off. I passed there next morning, and the charred wreckage and fragments of human beings scattered about were a ghastly sight.

At Achiet-le-Grand, whilst awaiting orders, I was able to realise the tremendous change that had come over the scene in France during the five months of my absence. Then, the British were fighting with their backs to the wall, and from April to July, under the hammer blows of the enemy they barely staved off disaster. But in August the tide had turned, and in a number of desperate battles they had recovered every inch of lost ground, and were now back in their old positions, facing the Hindenburg Line once more. In the course of the mighty attacks and counter-attacks that had swept over this war zone, twelve hundred thousand soldiers, British, French and German, had been killed and wounded since March 21st, and now the stage was being set for the greatest battle of them all.

The Allies had decided to force an issue, by blasting a way through the Hindenburg Line, the most formidable defensive position in the history of war; and I had come in time to see it done.

On every side there was evidence of the impending attack. The slopes and hollows and ruined villages were crammed with troops, long convoys were bringing up ammunition and supplies, and hundreds of guns were moving into position. The exact date was a secret, but otherwise the event was freely discussed, and there was an atmosphere of confidence that augured well.

On every side, too, there was evidence of the fighting that had swayed backward and forward during the past months. Abandoned war material lay in all directions, damaged field guns, broken trench mortars, and other weapons; and there was not a tree intact or a building left standing, while tens of thousands of newly erected wooden crosses told what it had cost the Germans to take, and the allied soldiers to retake, a strip of blood-drenched earth scarcely twenty miles in width.

After considerable difficulty I traced the 1st Royal Scots Fusiliers to the ruins of Morchies Village, where I found them in billets five or six miles behind the front line. The Battalion had seen much hard fighting, and had suffered such cruel losses that there were few officers or men left who had been there in my time. Colonel Gordon had been transferred, and of the thirty HQ and company officers whom I had known, only Bissett and Lieuts Sleep and Gerstenberg, a young Jewish officer, were still with us. The others were dead or wounded, and Bissett now commanded the Battalion. In the ranks, pitifully few of the old hands remained, but Corporal Noble was there with his quiet smile of welcome. General Deverell was at the head of the IIIrd Division, but General Tanner had been promoted and our 8th Brigade was now under General Fisher.

On the night of my arrival, the Battalion received orders to return to the front line on the Canal du Nord, near Hermes. I did not accompany them, for there was a message from General Fisher that I was to remain until he had seen me next day, so I spent the night in the transport camp.

German bombing planes were active. The air was filled with the hum of their engines, and at short intervals came the crash of heavy bombs and sheets of fire where they dropped their loads. Again I saw a bomber shot down in flames. He was caught by the searchlights, and dodged and twisted in vain. A British pilot dived into the beams, and, with a single spurt of his machine-gun, set the plane alight. It started to fall, enveloped in fire, and as before, from the unseen camps came the sound of thousands of men cheering. Suddenly, as we watched, there was a thunderous detonation overhead, and great flames of green and red shot out, for the bombs on the burning machine had gone off, and the plane and its crew were scattered through the air. So fas as I know, not a fragment was ever picked up.

Next morning I rode over to see General Fisher at Brigade Headquarters behind Hermes. He was a sensitive highly strung man, and, as I was to find him, a splendid leader. He said he was troubled about Bissett and me. I was technically Bissett's senior, and he wanted to know whether I would serve under him. As I cared little for military precedence I told him that I would gladly serve under such a man as I knew Bissett to be, so it was settled that I should drop into my old place as second in command of the 1st Royal Scots Fusiliers.

I now joined them in the front line. HQ staff consisted of Bissett and myself, with Captains McInnes Shaw, Keegan the Adjutant (a South African), Pud Robertson (signalling officer), and Westmoreland, the doctor, all new men, with the exception of Bissett and me. The sector we held lay partly on the far bank of the Canal du Nord, with a few rifle posts forward of the main trench, and sixty yards beyond was the Hindenburg Line. The canal bed was dry, for it was still under construction when the war started. It ran here through a deep cutting, and in order to reach our positions on the other side, we had to clamber up and down tall scaling ladders, specially constructed for the purpose.

The day after my arrival there was a fierce battle, for the Germans had wind of the coming British offensive, and to parry the blow had planned to capture a substantial portion of our line and occupy the high ground on the Hermes-Beaumetz-Morchies ridge lying a mile or two behind us. They had therefore prepared a large-scale attack.

I had spent most of the morning and part of the afternoon examining our sector, and I suspected that trouble was brewing, for there was a continuous display of rifle grenades and gas and high-velocity shells along our parapets. Towards 3 o'clock, having completed my work, I was on my way to Morchies to make certain arrangements at the transport camp. I stopped to see Colonel Henderson of the 2nd Royal Scots, whom I had not met since the March fighting. His dug-out was close behind the front line, and we had scarcely settled ourselves below for a chat when a violent enemy bombardment came down. The air in the dug-out shook and quivered to such an extent, from the concussion of heavy shells striking above, that the candles were repeatedly extinguished, and, as almost always happens, the telephone lines to the companies were put out of action at once. From the intensity of the barrage we judged that the German infantry would soon be coming over behind it, so we climbed up the staircase, and stood in the mouth of the shaft to see what was happening. The shell-fire extended on a wide front. To the north it was flashing and smoking as far as Moeuvres, and southward it stretched to Havrincourt Village, a total distance of more than twelve miles. We debated an attempt to reach the line, but decided to wait until the barrage lifted, and remained for some time in the doorway, watching the low-flying German aeroplanes sweeping backward and forward machine-gunning the barraged zone. We pitied the poor fellows in the dust and fumes and spouting earth of the front trench.

At last the bombardment moved to the rear, and we knew that the critical moment of the assault had come. We ran across the top to make quicker progress, for the CT was badly smashed. The barrage was now standing like a wall behind us, and the shrieking overhead of the thousands of shells that went to its making was tremendous. When we reached the near bank of the Canal du Nord we saw that the enemy had followed close behind their barrage. They had overrun the forward rifle pits, and had broken into our front line, where we could make out hand bombing and much running and shouting.

It was the tail end of the fight so far as our sector was concerned, for the men of the 1st RSF, the 2nd Royal Scots, and the 7th Shrops, had stood their ground, and, as we climbed up the ladders, the German soldiers were hurrying back across no-man's land to their own lines. When we got into the trench we found many dead and wounded of both sides, and our men were guarding about thirty prisoners. The sector now quieted down, but to our left the battle still thundered away. The Germans had attacked on a twelve-mile front and it was, I believe, the last time in the war that they came over in the grand manner. They remained in possession of elements of the British front line, but nowhere succeeded in penetrating to any great depth, and nowhere reached the high ground at our backs. I took from a captured officer a beautifully drawn little sketch, only two inches square, with our trenches and rifle posts accurately marked, and indicating their final objective, which included the villages of Hermes and Demicourt. The British casualties in this battle were over six thousand men, and I suppose the Germans lost even more heavily as they were the attackers. The 1st RSF had ninety-nine men killed, wounded and missing. Among them was Lieut Gerstenberg, who was one of the three survivors since March. He had 'got one to himself', as the soldiers termed a direct hit from a shell, and he was blown to atoms. Poor boy, his pet joke used to be that he had joined a Scotch battalion as the next best thing to a Jewish unit. When I made for the RSF headquarters after the business was over, I found Bissett standing outside the dug-out, roaring with laughter at his two carrier pigeons. At the start of the bombardment he had ordered the signallers to release the birds, each with a message to brigade tied to its wing. But the pigeons had thought better of it, and instead of flying through the barrage had calmly remained on the roof, where they were pecking about for food.

Next day we buried our own and the German dead. These were mostly 78th Reserve Infantry. Afterwards General Fisher and Capt Gosling, the Brigade-Major, came down and I accompanied them to the slag-heap, a mound of detritus from the canal excavation, from which a view of the German line was obtainable. We took a wrong turning down one of the innumerable trenches criss-crossing in the rear, and it was a lucky mistake, for we came on a wounded lance-corporal of the RSF. He had been stationed in a forward rifle pit during the battle. A stick grenade had shattered both his ankles, and he had lain out there until dark. Then he started to make his way to the British front line by sitting on the ground and hitching himself backward on his hands, his broken legs trailing behind him. He had passed the front trench at a point where it had been blown in, and not recognising it, went on all night. When we found him he was far behind the line, but was still patiently heaving himself along. He was near the end of his tether from loss of blood, but he was a brave man, for the first thing he asked on seeing us was, 'Sir, did the enemy take our line?' and only after we reassured him on this point did he say: 'Then for the love of God give me some water!' A bearer party was requisitioned, and he was carried off on a stretcher, his steel helmet on his chest, and a cigarette between his lips, cheerfully waving us farewell.

We went on to the slag-heap and from there to the rise above Morchies, from which the British and German fronts lay unrolled for miles on either hand. We could follow the Hindenburg Line from Moeuvres to Havrincourt, and behind it we could see their rear defensive positions—great parallel trenches linked by an intricate network of CT's, and studded at short intervals with concrete emplacements. Far away, beyond the German lines, the spires of Cambrai were visible, and Bourlon Wood, a dark splotch on the horizon.

To me the system looked impregnable and General Fisher said Napoleon himself would have stood helpless before these works. He said that strategy and tactics were of no avail, and the only course was to hack a way through. As our battalion was to take part in the hacking process, I had a good look at the forbidding lines that for over two years had defied all attempts to carry them. I remembered that in all the years of trench fighting, neither side had ever achieved a complete break-through. Verdun, the Somme, Chemin-des-Dames, Passchendaele and the March offensive, had cost millions of men, and every one of them had failed. Now another attempt was to be made, and although we knew that the alternative would be to sit down and look at the Germans for another winter, yet the thought of the lives that would be lost kept us a silent party as we stood surveying the grim scene.

General Fisher and his Brigade-Major now returned to Hermes, and I went on to our transport camp, where I spent the next few days attending to our many requirements for the approaching battle. There were a hundred and one things to see to. We had air photographs and maps of the German line, and we brought the men out in batches from the front trenches to the camp, and there taught them the lie of every point, and post, and pillbox facing us across the way. We also made arrangements about ammunition, Mills grenades, Lewis guns, flares and signals, the removal of the wounded, and a host of other matters.

All through this time the enemy kept plugging away at the front line, and at the back areas, with light and heavy guns. Our battalion suffered no casualties, but much damage was done elsewhere, for so numerous were the camps, that it was hardly possible for a bomb or shell to drop without falling on troops or batteries or horse lines. This continued shell-fire was unpleasant, but it in no way interfered with the concentration that was being rapidly pushed forward, and the air throbbed with preparations for the great assault.

In addition to bombs, the German aeroplanes dropped leaflets intended to discourage the fighting men. These came fluttering down on us in shoals, each containing the same clumsy appeal:

'British Soldiers!
Do you know what's going on at home whilst you're fighting for your country? You probably don't know anything, and therefore we'll give you a little piece of information by reprinting a letter that was found a few days ago.
The letter is not very grammatical, but what does that matter? It's plain enough and she's a good girl who wrote it. She has brains all right and a good heart for the poor disabled soldier. Now just read the letter:
"London E. 28.8.1918.
I have been busy trying to bring our women out on strike, well I have succeeded in bring out 4 000. The reason why I am trying to do this is because us women are working side by side with the men but we are getting 12s 6d less a week."
Discharged soldiers are refused work because—Women do it cheaper!

Well, what do you think of that? They refuse to give work to your discharged pals for the beautiful reason that
            Women do it cheaper.
They let you die for the "Principles of Democracy" and at home they're sweating your womenfolk because
            Women do it cheaper.
At any rate now you know what
                  YOU
may expect if you are lucky enough to return to Blighty alive. You will get the benevolent reply:
      Thanks my good man,
            Women do it cheaper.
The employers will rub the palms of their hands, they don't need you any more, the longer the list of casualties the better their prospects for
      Women do it cheaper.'

This document showed an utter misunderstanding of the position in England, and the men roared with laughter at its string of absurdities. The British air propaganda was more effective. I picked up some of their leaflets, that the wind carried back from over the German lines. There was one telling statement headed '*Arithmetik*', with parallel columns giving the weekly decrease of the German Army through battle casualties, and the weekly increase in the allied armies through the arrival of American troops in France. Another leaflet contained an account of all German submarines that had been destroyed, with the names of their commanders and crews, and I picked up a circular which, to the beleaguered German people, must have sounded even more deadly, for it contained a price-list of meat and sausage and other foodstuffs to be had in any shop in England, and compared this with the lack of provisions on the other side. It wound up with the gibe that so far the net result of the submarine campaign had been to create a temporary shortage of marmalade.

While we were busy training parties of our men behind the line, I saw the Guards Brigade retake Moeuvres, from which they had been ousted during the recent attack. The Guards advanced behind a barrage a hundred yards deep, and through the smoke we saw the men enter the village. Within fifteen minutes from the start success flares went up, and the place was won. It was here that the Guards, on recovering the lost ground, came on a corporal and eight men of the Liverpools, among the ruins, where they had been holding out ever since the line was overrun days before.

I was sitting one afternoon on a fallen poplar above Demicourt, gazing once more at the Hindenburg Line through my glasses, when I saw a British two-seater taking photographs above Flesquières. A single-seater German plane came from the direction of Bourlon Wood straight for the slower flying British craft, which it quickly overhauled. A running fight ensued and the machines were at times so close together, that they seemed in danger of ramming one another. Then the dreaded point of light sprang up behind the engine of the British plane, and in a second or two the fire had run in a thin streak to the tail. The pilot banked to keep the flames from his observer and himself, and once the fire was almost extinguished, for I could see the man in the rear cockpit leaning back over the edge of his seat, apparently trying to beat out the last embers with his tunic or a cloth. But just when I was hoping that they were safe, the entire plane burst into flames and crashed to earth some distance away, amid a shower of sparks. The victorious German dived steeply to make sure that his prey was down and then sped off towards Cambrai, a something of exultation in his flight. I had the recollection of that German bomber and its crew too freshly in mind to care to inspect the wreckage, but I was told that the pilot and his companion were unrecognisably burned to death.

Another form of air activity was the shooting down of observation balloons. These 'blimps' were strung out behind both fronts, and I must have seen nearly a score of them set alight on the British, and perhaps a dozen on the German side, during the few days I was in camp. As soon as the fabric was ablaze, the 'balloonatics' as the observers were called, jumped for it and came swaying down to earth with their parachutes, always landing safely, as far as I could see.

On September 25th a batch of eight officers and a draft of two hundred men arrived from Scotland for the Regiment. Among them were Capt Freeman and young Lieut Bailey, both of whom I had met at Fort Matilda. I had to return to the front line after dark, so I took the new arrivals with me.

As we crossed the Cambrai Road, a German raider dropped its load of bombs near a searchlight. They went off with a tremendous noise and high flames, and young Bailey, who had not previously been in France, amused us by enquiring what all those fireworks were about.

Beyond Doignies, the Germans were shelling every road, for they probably knew that there was heavy traffic behind the front line and, indeed, it was clear to us as we went that matters were coming to a head. We found the highways crowded with columns of men and vehicles, and guns moving up, and it was with difficulty that we threaded our way. Shells repeatedly fell on the road we were travelling, and, from what I could make out in the dark, they did considerable damage. There were traffic police every two or three hundred yards, and in spite of the firing there was little confusion. Whenever a horse or a limber was struck, willing hands quickly shifted the obstacle from the road, and the bearer parties that were posted at intervals ran up to carry away the wounded.

As we were going through a sunken length, a shell killed several gunners, and their frightened team bolted right into us. A wheel crushed one of our men against the bank and had it not been for his steel helmet, he would have been killed. The rest of us got off with minor bruises. When we reached the front line, I reported to HQ dug-out, and introduced the new officers to Bissett, who speedily assigned them and the accompanying draft of men to such platoons as needed them. He was especially pleased with Freeman. He said Freeman would make good, for he had dropped down the stairs with a jaunty air of 'Here's Freeman, where the hell are the Huns?'—so he had sent him to the post of honour at the advanced rifle pits. The next time I saw Freeman he lay on his face with a bullet through his heart.

At eleven o'clock that night, Capt Gosling, the brigade-major, arrived. He brought with him the long-expected news that the Hindenburg Line was to be attacked on a fourteen-mile front at 5.20 am on the morning after next (27th September).

Bissett called a CO's conference, and before long all officers that could be spared from duty came trooping down the stairway of the dug-out. The meeting remains in my mind as a very solemn occasion. We sat round a rough deal table, and by the flickering light of candles stuck against the walls, Capt Gosling went over the operation order, explaining with the help of trench maps the portion of the enemy front that was to be carried by our battalion. I watched the faces of the young officers as they listened in silence to instructions that, humanly speaking, meant death to many of them.

After Capt Gosling had left, they remained quietly discussing the dispositions to be made. While we were at this, a runner brought a despatch from Divisional HQ, ordering the second in command (myself) and one officer from each company to be held in reserve during the attack, as a nucleus for reconstituting the battalion in case of heavy losses. The fact that the Divisional Commander envisaged such a contingency added to the gravity that had fallen upon us, and one could not but think wistfully of these fine young men about to face death.

There was shell-fire during the night, in the course of which we sustained casualties, and poor Bailey was smashed within a few hours of his first appearance in the front line.

Next morning the five of us, who were to remain out of the battle, walked back to our transport camp at Morchies. I procured a horse, and rode over to see General Fisher. He insisted on my obeying orders, but agreed to my request that I be allowed to take up some coign of vantage from which to witness the attack.

I placed a liberal interpretation upon his consent. I returned to camp, and after midnight set off on foot to the front line. It was comparatively quiet, save for the usual bomb-dropping, and once again there was a hum of activity on the roads, with infantry and tanks and guns moving up in the dark. When I got into the front line, every man of the RSF was on the firestep, from which they were to go over the top at dawn. I had no intention of breaking the letter of my instructions to remain in reserve, but I considered that the best spot for making use of the General's permission was from our parapet.

The battle, we knew, was to be one of the biggest and most decisive of the war. Its outstanding feature was the strictly limited objective allotted to each attacking unit. Every battalion was given a definite enemy trench sector, CT or redoubt which it was to capture, and beyond which it was not to go. As soon as each particular goal had been attained, other battalions from the rear were to leapfrog through to the next line of resistance, and, in this manner, the battle was to be pressed home, until the final limit set for the day had been reached.

The 1st RSF had to capture what was shown on the maps as Whitehall and Ryder sections of the Hindenburg Line, situated directly opposite us across no-man's land, so our share represented only an advance of sixty to eighty yards, on a front of three hundred yards.

The 7th Shrops were then to pass through us to attack the next trench, after which the 2nd Royal Scots in turn would pass through them to reach a trench behind that again, which would carry our 8th Brigade some eight hundred yards forward. From there, other brigades held in readiness, were to continue the thrust, until the Hindenburg Line was slashed in two.

It was an ambitious programme, but it was to be amply justified by the result.

However limited the advance of the Scots Fusiliers looked on the map, it was a most important one, for on them fell the task of rushing the front trench of the great fortressed line, which was bound to be defended with more vigour than the subsequent positions, and on their success depended that of the further attacks on the rear network of the enemy system.

I speak only of our own immediate task that covered little more than three hundred yards of the German front, but all along the fourteen miles on which the offensive was to be launched similar measures were ready, whereby the leading battalions were to break into the first trench, followed by successive waves of other assaulting troops coming on behind. The battle plan was on so huge a scale that the fortunes of a single battalion should be multiplied nearly six hundred times to obtain an adequate conception of its entirety.

It was 3 am by now. The men sat talking in undertones along the firestep, their bayoneted rifles in their hands and some lay asleep on the duckboards, while Bissett and Capts Shaw and Keegan went up and down, consulting with the company officers and making last-minute adjustments.

At 4 o'clock the enemy began to trenchmortar us heavily, and a few men were wounded. Then a stillness fell over the line. A million men were facing each other on this battlefront but there was scarcely a sound, save for a rare shot loosed by some nervous sentry, and the tension became almost unendurable.

As zero hour approached, whispered orders were passed and the men stood to, and then, punctually at 5.20, the British barrage came down upon the German line with one stupendous roar.

During the preliminary ten minutes the Fusiliers stood ready to vault the sandbags at the given word, and along the whole fourteen miles stood thousands upon thousands of other men ready to leap upon the enemy.

At zero plus ten minutes (5.30 am) the barrage moved forward, and the moment had come. Bissett dropped his arm as a signal, and the men swarmed over the parapet straight for the German line.

Almost at once the German SOS barrage came down upon them, as they scrambled and stumbled over the wires and screwstakes and shell craters that obstructed every yard of the way. I have a confused memory of shells spurting and flashing, of men going down in great numbers, and almost before there was time to think, I saw the German soldiers rise from behind their breastworks to meet the attackers, and then the Scots Fusiliers were clubbing and bayoneting among them.

The enemy gunners immediately drew in their fire to protect their next line of defence, and seeing that our men were on their objective, I rushed quickly across no-man's land and dropped down into the great Hindenburg Trench. Flushed with victory, the men were rounding up prisoners and shouting down the dug-out staircases for others to come up, a process which they expedited in places by flinging Mills grenades into the shaft openings.

The trench was six feet wide by eight feet deep. Every few yards along the parapet stood a machine-gun, and there were many trench mortars and anti-tank rifles.

The enemy soldiers had done their duty manfully, for on the floor of the trench their dead and wounded lay thick, and beside almost every machine-gun lay its crew, smitten down by the hurricane of the barrage.

By this time the British guns had lifted their range on to the next enemy trench, four hundred yards up the slope, and already the 7th Shrops were coming through us and deploying beyond. There was no excitement or hurry. They went forward at a walk behind the barrage, their rifles aslant, and we watched them reach and enter the area of the German counter-barrage. Many fell, but the rest went steadily on, almost hidden in the smoke and dust of the shell-fire. The German SOS drew still further back, and, when the air cleared, we saw the Shrops soldiers in possession of the next trench, and our men rose and cheered them.

Then the 2nd Royal Scots came past, and behind them other reserve battalions, streaming forward to further attacks, while to right and left the battle thundered on its way. It was a marvellous spectacle, but now that our battalion had accomplished its task, and the battle was surging over the rise in front of us, we turned to count the cost. Bissett and I walked back across the area over which the RSF had advanced. The wounded were being carried away, but, as was the custom, the dead, being past succour, were left for future transport.

We were sad to find how many of our men had fallen, for we counted over a hundred officers and men lying dead in the small space between London Support and Whitehall. The poor fellows, alive a few minutes before, now lay in all manner of attitudes, some still hugging their rifles, others horribly torn by shells, and others again in shell craters, as if they had crawled there to die.

At one place we came on a heap of flesh and clothing so mangled that, had it not been for two fieldbooted legs protruding from the awful mess, we could hardly have sworn that what lay here had been a human being. At first we could not determine whose remains they were, but seeing the rim of a steel hat beneath, I did some grisly work with a stick and got the helmet clear. I found the name of one of our young officers inside it. Bissett, at that moment, must have felt someone walking over his grave, for he shivered and said: 'My God, I'm getting sick of this awful war'; and for the first time since I had known him, he fell silent and moody.

In the meanwhile, the main battle raged unabated. Overhead wheeled squadrons of aeroplanes, and a steady flow of infantry battalions was hurrying past us to the further attacks beyond the long rise, from which came the sound of heavy rifle and machine-gun fire, and the bursting of many shells.

To our right, towards Flesquières, a dozen or more tanks were going into action. As we looked, one of them stopped and burst into flames, and one stood still with a rent in its side, but the others went on until we lost them in the curtain of smoke that hung over the village.

As Bissett and I were returning to our men holding the captured trench, British batteries from the rear began to come by, to take up fresh positions near the enemy. That they were able to cross the Canal du Nord so soon was due to the careful manner in which the battle had been thought out beforehand. A bridge had been built in sections, and the moment the German barrage lifted that morning, the RE's were seen coming down from Hermes with the bridge-lengths on wagons, and in a short time they had erected a trestle-way from bank to bank, over which guns and ammunition limbers and ambulances were now pouring on to ground which scarcely an hour before was held by the enemy.

By 8 o'clock practically every British battery had moved up, and along the lip of the Hindenburg Trench the guns stood in unbroken line, firing as fast as they could load. Being so near to us, the roar of all these pieces was magnificent. General Fisher stood eagerly watching the guns belching forth, and he turned to us and cried: 'Men, do you remember Lloyd George's speech: "We will put the guns wheel to wheel, and pound home the lessons of democracy"?' He said we were privileged in being there that day, and indeed we were witnessing a great event, for the mighty Hindenburg Line was going at last.

Shortly afterwards an artillery officer, with whom I had fallen into conversation while watching his battery in action, invited me to breakfast, and we feasted on bacon and eggs, cooked on a primus stove by his servant, within a few yards of where his guns were banging away.

As we sat down to our meal, we saw a German aeroplane dart into a flight of British observers, and in a moment one of them began to fall in flames. The rear occupant stood up, and spreading wide his arms deliberately leaped into the void. I could see him whirling round and round as he gathered momentum, and I stood thinking of the poor man's agony, but my host merely remarked, 'Hello, there's a little man jumped out,' and stolidly continued his breakfast. The conditions were ideal for air fighting as there was not a cloud in the sky, and a bright sun shone all day.

The air was alive with machines, and the casualties on both sides were heavy, for, as the morning wore on, I repeatedly saw planes shot down, and long before evening the number of wrecked machines scattered about was quite a feature of the landscape.

I now had time to look around. The RSF had taken over three hundred prisoners, and these were still standing about in batches, shaken and miserable, as well they might be after the terrible bombardment they had suffered. They belonged to the 97th Hanoverian Regiment, and strangely enough each man had the word 'Gibraltar' embroidered on his left sleeve. When I asked one of their officers the meaning of this, he said with a grin that it was a British battle honour conferred on their regiment for having assisted the English at the siege of Gibraltar in 1705.

By now many walking wounded were coming back from the forward battle line, and they told us things were going well. Large numbers of prisoners were coming back too, some under guard, others simply walking to the rear of their own accord, asking their way to the *'Englische Gefangenlager'*.

General Fisher had told us before he went that Bulgaria had just surrendered, and when I told a squad of captured officers this, one of them said *'Na! wenn dass so ist, ist's alles fertig,'* and I thought they seemed relieved at the prospect of an early peace.

Towards noon, Glossop, the same man who had so imperturbably made breakfast and had held me to ransom during the March battle, once more conjured up refreshments. He fetched table and chairs from a German dug-out, and saying it was a pity to miss the sunshine, served an excellent lunch in the open. In spite of the glorious weather it was a silent meal. Behind us the ground was strewn with our fallen, and along the parapet of the captured trench lay many German dead, so we sat with averted eyes. Presently Shaw drew our attention to the body of a dead man lying face downward close by. Bissett got up to see, and turned over the body. It was Captain Freeman, who two nights before had so buoyantly dropped down the stairs. He was shot through the heart.

Later on, hearing from wounded men coming back that the British advance was being held up before Graincourt, a village this side of Cambrai, I decided to go forward to see what was happening, for nominally I was off duty, and therefore a free agent.

First I climbed the slope across which the Shrops and the Royal Scots had attacked. They too had paid a heavy price, for numbers of their dead, and many dead German soldiers, lay stacked along the parapets of the trenches, from which they had been lifted. After a short halt to exchange views with Col Henderson, I bore away towards Flesquières by way of the numerous rear trenches of the Hindenburg system. These had all been taken by the successive assaulting columns and each trench was occupied by the men who had taken it. Everywhere lay hundreds of khaki-clad and field-grey dead, and everywhere improvised dressing-stations were dealing with the wounded.

When I reached what was left of Flesquières, the German gunners began to shell it so heavily that I made haste to get away to a rise, accompanied by a dozen soldiers who had been sheltering in the ruins.

From here the battle situation as far as Bourlon Wood stretched clear before our eyes. I could see the British firing line half a mile away, and German infantry four hundred yards beyond. Both sides were in open country, and for the first time in four years of war they faced each other from behind such natural cover as they could turn to account, without trenches or entanglements between.

The English were slowly advancing, and on the crest of a long grassy slope were German soldiers and machine-gun crews. The British shell-fire was no longer a barrage, but it was not negligible, and the shrapnel was taking heavy toll from among the exposed enemy troops on the rise. About four miles back stood Cambrai. Through my glasses I could even see a group of German officers standing on the round tower of the brewery, and tall pillars of smoke were rising from among the houses, as though the city was being given to the flames. On the outskirts of Cambrai were black masses of German infantry in reserve, while their thinly held line was fighting a desperate rearguard action, chiefly with machine-guns.

Away to the left was the real trouble, for there the British advance was hung up before the village of Graincourt. It was being stubbornly defended, and the German garrison was inflicting heavy punishment on the British troops, whose dead lay thick before the ruins. Strong reinforcements of the Guards Brigade, however, were coming up, and I watched them attack afresh. They were well handled. The fire of several batteries was directed on the village, and the men went forward in artillery formation, until they had established a fire line, when they rose to their feet and charged. Many fell, but the attack was pushed home, and soon the men disappeared among the wrecked houses, after which the enemy machine-guns fell silent, and batches of prisoners were marched out.

Graincourt being captured, I went to the right. On my way I passed the enemy gun positions, from which they had fired their barrage that morning, and I counted more than fifty abandoned field pieces standing in their emplacements. I went no nearer the firing line. The British had by now bitten three miles into the German defensive system since dawn, and they had reached the final objective of the battle plan at practically every point. Owing to the rapid advance, the gun fire was thinning, and ahead of me there was point-blank fighting between German soldiers, who were flinging stick grenades from shell craters, and isolated parties of British who were volleying at them from behind trees.

Great numbers of wounded were being carried back and, as rifle and machine-gun bullets were whistling too freely, I took a last look at Cambrai, now fiercely burning, and at Bourlon Wood, in the hands of the British at last, and started back in the falling dusk, passing on my way more dead men of both sides than I had yet seen in the war.

On this day the British took ten thousand prisoners and two hundred guns. On a fourteen-mile front, at a cost of eighty thousand men, they had blasted their way through the Hindenburg Line into the open country beyond, and from then onward the evil of the old trench warfare was a thing of the past, and a new phase had begun.

Chapter 13

Open Warfare in France

When I returned to where I had left our men in the captured Hindenburg Trench, a surprise awaited me. General Fisher was sitting his horse beside the parapet. He told me that the 7th Shrops had lost their Colonel, and I was to take command of the battalion.

I was sorry to leave the Scots Fusiliers after all we had gone through together, but in any case, we were brigaded together, so I was still in the same family circle. Indeed, all I needed to do, in order to transfer to my new command, was to shoulder my haversack and walk across to the trench which the Shrops were occupying two hundred yards away. I did this at once, Bissett accompanying me to see me settled in.

Next morning was quiet. I went round to make acquaintance with the companies, and the men lounged about the battlefield watching the dead being carried away for burial.

Later on Bissett visited my quarters and asked me to go through the German papers which I had collected in the dug-outs the day before, so I sorted them out. The most interesting document was a printed circular signed by Von Hindenburg, in which he warned the German soldiers against British propaganda. He said British airmen were dropping not only bombs that killed the body, but poisoned literature that killed the soul, and we gathered from letters from wives and relatives to the men at the front that a wave of pessimism was sweeping over the German people. This was borne out by a confidential report included among the papers I had found:

'From Supreme Command (*Oberst Heeresleitung*)
To Military Governor of Belgium
The officer commanding Namur area reports on 24.9.1918 that troops on leave are spreading alarmist rumours as to recent events at the front (*seitens der von der Front zurückkehrenden Truppen die letzten Vorgänge an der Front in den düstersten Farben geschildert werden*).
In order not to exercise an adverse influence on the situation, all armies are requested to take steps to counteract this spirit among the troops.
Copies to Crown Prince Rupprecht's Army, to 17th Army and to 20th and 40th Infantry Divisions.'

I also came on a curiously tactless instruction by Von Below, *Oberbefehls-haber der Infanterie*, which read:

'During the cremation of corpses brought from the front line it has several times happened of late that cartridges left in the pockets of the dead have exploded, whereby the furnaces were damaged and in one instance a stoker was nearly wounded (*Einer der Heizer ist beinahe verletzt worden*). In future all combustible matter must be removed from the clothing of the dead.'

Von Below seemed more concerned about his furnaces than about the soldiers in them, and when I translated this to Bissett, he said he would like to know what the German fighting men thought of his solicitude for the 'nearly wounded' stoker.

In the meanwhile the first battle was over. Word came that the Germans were hurrying entire Army Corps to the defence of Cambrai, and that the British were bringing up fresh troops in order to continue the attack. That same afternoon (September 28th) I received orders to march my battalion to a ridge lying north of Marcoing, ready to go into action if necessary at daybreak.

We went by Flesquières and Ribécourt across the complicated network of the trenches that had been the Hindenburg Line, past burial parties laying the fallen soldiers to rest, and past the dozens of hospital camps that had sprung up. On the way, we saw a German aeroplane swoop down upon a British two-seater. As we watched, the British machine burst into flames. It fell in a fiery trail, striking the earth close to the village of Masnières behind the German lines, where we found it next day.

We were now entering another chapter of the war, for dusk found us in open country, and we were faced with the novelty of having to bivouac on a bare hillside without trench or shelter. The men were new to this kind of thing. They were so accustomed to the routine of stationary warfare, with the enemy's position known to a yard, and with their every act regulated for them, that they were at a loss, and stood about helplessly.

I started all hands to break out timber baulks from some old gun pits that we found, and soon had everyone cheerfully sitting around blazing log fires, cooking their suppers. My attempt to teach the men how to make themselves comfortable was well rewarded, for in going the rounds after dark I heard a voice say: 'Lads, I would like to go big-game hunting in Africa with our new CO.'

As for the enemy, I had looked over the ground in front of us while it was light. Their troops lay two miles away along the slopes and woods from Cambrai southwards, and it was clear that they intended to fight.

British forces had been moving up all the afternoon, and behind us the guns were being wheeled into position for the next battle.

At 10 o'clock that night a runner brought a message to say that a CO's conference would be held at my camp by General Fisher, and after a while he and Bissett and Henderson arrived.

We sat around my fire and the General gave us our instructions. There was to be an attack on the Marcoing-Rumilly-Masnières line at daybreak by other troops. We were to hold our three battalions ready to take part when so ordered, but until we heard from him we were to stand fast.

After the conference was over and the others had gone, Bissett and I sat talking before the fire for a long time, and when he rose to go I walked a little distance with him before saying good night. When next we met, it was to see him struck down within a few yards of me.

I was up early to watch the first stage of the attack. We were able to look on in comfort, as our participation depended on what progress was made. As soon as it grew light, the British guns opened fire on the German line between Marcoing and Rumilly. The bombardment was somewhat ragged owing to the hurried manner in which barrages had to be improvised, since the vanished days of trench war of the day before yesterday. We could not follow what was happening at Marcoing, for the village lay in a hollow and all we saw was columns of smoke and brick-dust shooting upwards from the German shells, which showed that the British had entered it, and that the place was now suffering a counter bombardment. But we had a perfect view of the troops going up the slope to attack Rumilly, for we were on high ground, and looked straight down on the scene. The men advanced steadily, though a good many shorts from the British guns dropped among them, and the Germans broke salvos of shrapnel over their heads all the way.

Machine-guns and rifles were also crackling, and many fell, but the rest went on, and were soon in Rumilly with their flanks sweeping beyond the village. We saw the German defenders running wildly to the rear. Then dense bodies of German infantry came pouring form the Faubourg de Paris, a suburb of Cambrai, and from Niergnies. They rolled back the British line and re-entered Rumilly, whence came the sound of heavy rifle-fire and hand bombing, and of the soldiers who had captured it in the first instance very few escaped. Even the motor ambulances that had followed in the wake of the British attack were captured by the enemy. We saw the German soldiers running out of the village to surround the vehicles. They were recovered next day, still standing at the same spot, with their tyres slashed, but otherwise intact.

The operations were by no means confined to Rumilly and Marcoing, and it was in reality the first day of the extended battle for Cambrai, which was only to fall into the hands of the British after a week's hard fighting.

As we watched, we saw more troops thrown into the fight, and the British gunfire increased. Successive waves of infantry went forward once more, and, for the third time that morning, Rumilly changed hands. Towards 10 o'clock we heard that Marcoing, after repeated counter-attacks, was now firmly held by the New Zealanders, and that the 9th Brigade of our IIIrd Division was said to be in Masnières, two miles east of Marcoing.

During all this time, we had remained inactive. We of the Shrops were on the hill above Marcoing; Bissett, with the RSF, lay in a wood somewhere behind us, and the 2nd Royal Scots were to our left. But at midday a message came that I was to report to General Fisher with half a dozen runners, so I collected a party and, following the guide, found the General at the quarry outside Marcoing. Fierce fighting had taken place here during the morning and there were many British and German dead, while a large number of wounded were being attended to in the quarry. General Fisher told me that the battle was fluctuating, and that north of us the British attack had been checked, owing to the immense number of machine-guns which the Germans had brought into play. In our area, Marcoing was taken, and, he believed, Masnières too, but the situation was so obscure that my battalion was to march thither at once, to reinforce the 9th Brigade who were in difficulties. I was to go ahead with my runners to ascertain the position, and he would send back instructions to Major Robinson, my second in command, to follow on with the men. We started at once, and, making our way across an area littered with dead, entered Marcoing. It was being shelled with 8-inch howitzers, and roofs and walls were flying in every direction. In the lee of some of the buildings crouched the New Zealanders who were holding the village, and at a street crossing stood a traffic control, directing wounded and stragglers as calmly as a policeman on duty in London.

Hurriedly passing through, we emerged on an open plain, and skirting Marcoing Copse, saw Masnières in the distance. We met a few wounded men, but as usual they could give no coherent account of the situation. Next, we were brought up by the canal that ran between us and Masnières. All along the banks great columns of earth were shooting up, and high fountains of water spurted in the air, as the German shells fell in the canal. My instructions were to find out what the position was in Masnières, so the runners and I threaded our way among the pollards that stood along the bank, until we came to a spot where lay two half-submerged Rotterdam barges. By using these waterlogged craft, and by pushing out some loose planks towards the wreck of an old bridge, a portion of which still jutted into midstream, we managed to cross to the other side. We now followed the towpath until we reached a lock bridge from which we could see up the main street of Masnières. The place seemed deserted, but as I was preparing to enter, we came under rifle-fire from a party of Germans holding a big sugar factory, which showed above the other houses.

There was no sign of British troops, and except for the snipers in the factory, our small party seemed to have the neighbourhood to itself. After being accustomed to a war zone crowded with men it was strange to find ourselves in a sort of vacuum, and the isolation became oppressive, so with a few volleys at the building in which the Germans were posted, we moved on.

The lock bridge was still intact, and as it was the only passage left by which the battalion could cross the canal, when it arrived, I sent a runner back with a message to Major Robinson, asking him to bring the men to the bridge, and warning him that the enemy was still in the village. Then we moved along the bank, hoping that the bridge would still be there when our men came, although the German gunners were doing their best to destroy it. I went in the direction of Crèvecœur as far as the *estaminet* at the next lock, and there I found a few wounded men belonging to the King's Own. They said the King's Own and the Gordons had crossed the canal two hours before, but, after suffering heavy casualties, were hung up just over the rise. Following a trail of dead men we topped the slope, and immediately came under heavy fire from a sunken road six hundred yards ahead, which I could see was strongly held. No one was hit, and to our surprise we found before us a long trench length, to which we ran for shelter. Jumping into it we found the King's Own and the Gordons in occupation. The trench we were in was miscalled 'Mon Plaisir', and it had been constructed by the Germans as a reserve position during the tank battle the year before. It came in very useful now, for the shell-fire was increasing, and we could see swarms of German infantry along the Crèvecœur-les Épines sunken road. They had retaken Rumilly Village lying close by, and towards Cambrai the country was black with their troops.

I discussed matters with the two Colonels, both of whom were in very bad tempers owing to their heavy losses. While we were at it, a patrol came in to say that Masnières was evacuated, the small garrison in the sugar factory having doubled up the road to rejoin their main body at Rumilly. It was thereupon arranged between us

that, when my Battalion arrived, I would occupy Masnières, so I took my runners back
to the lock bridge. We came under lively fire as we hurried over the rise behind Mon
Plaisir, but again we had no one hit. When we reached the bridge I found it unhealthier
than ever, for the Germans seemed determined to smash it, so the runners and I
scrambled down the bank to the level of the water, where we squatted on some
wreckage that had accumulated against the concrete piers. This gave us shelter from
the heavy shells bursting around, and at the same time enabled us to keep a look-out
for the head of our Battalion, when it should appear on the opposite side. We spent the
next hour here watching the columns of water shoot up whenever a shell hit the canal,
and praying that the bridge would hold.

As the Germans had evacuated Masnières, they started to smash the place, and we
heard tremendous concussions in the village, and along the towpath over our heads.
Crouching below the canal bank, we got an occasional whiff of gas swirling over the
rampart, but as yet it was not heavy enough to inconvenience us, for most of it was
being thrown into the streets, and there we got the full benefit of it later on.

After a long wait, I saw Major Robinson and Capt Hetherington, the Adjutant,
come running up the Rue Vertes, so I signalled to them to cross the bridge to our side
of the canal. The head of the Battalion arrived on the opposite bank soon after, and we
began to get the men across, a few at a time. The German gunners were still trying to
hit the bridge, and unfortunately, as the last section of 'A' Company were coming
over, a shell burst on the concrete ramp on our side of the canal, and killed four men
on the bridge. The rest of the battalion crossed safely, and as Masnières was being
heavily shelled, I had the men ranged under such cover as was to be found at the
entrance of the main street, while Robinson, Hetherington and I entered the village to
investigate.

Shells were plunging around, and the crash of their deafening explosions
reverberated in the narrow streets, while shell splinters, bricks and tiles were flying
about. At the same time the Germans were firing phosgene gas, so we had to grope our
way through the dust-laden atmosphere in our box respirators, a difficult process, as
everyone knows who has tried it.

However, we succeeded in laying out a suitable position, and began getting the
men into line. The nearest German soldiers were only four hundred yards away behind
a barricade across the Rumilly Road, but I had little fear of them, as they were on the
defensive, and would be unlikely to attack us. Our trouble was the shell-fire and the
gas. To avoid unnecessary casualties, I ordered the company commanders to keep the
men in cellars, and to post a sentry at each stairway, to see that they did not go
wandering about, as they will do in a new village. The cellars were good protection,
and not a man was injured by the bombardment, but the gas hung so heavily that there
was the inevitable quota of loss, for it is almost impossible to wear a respirator
continuously.

Robinson and I took up battalion headquarters in a double-storeyed cellar below a
sort of chapel. We put the signallers in the top cellar, and the rest of us occupied the
basement. Here our medical officer, Dr Hubbard, joined us. He was an American, for
owing to the shortage of British doctors through war losses, many battalions were
provided with doctors loaned us from the American armies. Hubbard was an amusing
witty fellow, but on this occasion he dropped down into the cellar deathly pale, and

almost immediately he fell into a coma. He had been gassed while attending to some men who had been wounded beside the canal, for he had removed his mask the better to see what he was doing. He was carried away on a stretcher, still unconscious, but I never heard whether he recovered, for nowadays, in the war of movement, when a man was sent to the rear one generally lost sight of him for good.

Having made the needful dispositions to hold the village, I returned by a roundabout way to Mon Plaisir Trench, to see how the King's Own and the Gordons were getting on. In front of them the Crèvecœur sunken road was still strongly held by the enemy, and we could see many of their troops in and about Rumilly less than a mile away. As we did not know what was happening along the rest of the front, we arranged to hold our positions till further orders, and I took a short cut back to Masnières. Along the footpath I came on the remains of the British aeroplane that we had seen falling in flames the previous afternoon. Two airmen lay dead in the wreckage, horribly charred. From what I could see of their mummified faces, they were both mere boys. I found a silver identity disc bearing the name 'Lt Jacques, RSF' and later I had the bodies interred with the propeller blade for a tombstone.

I reached my own headquarters by dusk to find that the church had been shot away during my absence, but the chapel over our cellar was still more or less intact. Not long after I got below there was a thunderous detonation overhead, and the signallers and runners rushed down into the lower cellar, saying that a shell had come through the roof of the top storey. The force of the explosion had extinguished all our lights, and the clatter of the men stumbling down among us in the dark caused some confusion, until we lit up once more. At 9 o'clock that night I received a message from Brigade Headquarters to say that the King's Own and the Gordons had been withdrawn from Mon Plaisir owing to heavy losses earlier in the day, but that Bissett with his Scots Fusiliers were there, together with a battalion of New Zealanders.

Furthermore, the Scots Fusiliers, the Shrops, and the New Zealanders were to make an immediate attack on the Crèvecœur sunken road, in order to drive the Germans out of it. Bissett was to advance on les Épines, I was to take the sunken road from les Épines to about halfway to Crèvecœur, and the New Zealanders were to capture the rest of it.

All this was to be carried out in the dark, and the directions we had received left a good deal to the imagination, but I realised that the day of set battle plans was over, so I sent copies of the instructions by runner to Bissett and the New Zealand Colonel, and by the same means we arranged to start off at 10 o'clock for our respective destinations.

It was an inky night as the men silently fell in on the outskirts of the village, but I knew my direction from having seen the ground that afternoon, when I had also noticed how strongly the sunken road was held by the enemy.

At 10 o'clock we moved forward, slowly groping our way over the level plain that separated us from the road.

Soon furious fire broke out on my left against Bissett's men, and then came the clatter and flash of rifle and machine-gun fire, to show that the New Zealanders were likewise engaged. As it happened, the Germans were in the act of withdrawing from the sunken road, and when we of the Shrops reached the edge of the bank, and leaped into it, we found our portion deserted. In a short while runners from both Bissett and the New Zealanders came to say that they too were on their objectives, and we had successfully carried out our instructions with a loss of under fifty men between three battalions.

The signallers had linked up Masnières by telephone with brigade headquarters during the evening, so I was soon able to get word back to General Fisher. He sent orders that we were to hold the road, but that I personally was to return to the village, so as to be in direct touch with him. I left Major Robinson in charge, with instructions to report to me in our cellar below the chapel in the morning, and walked back with my runners. Close to Masnières we made out some dim figures marching along, and challenging them, found sixteen German soldiers under a *Vize-Feldwebel*, in charge of young Lieut Orchardson of the Shrops. He had come on them unexpectedly, and they had handed over their rifles without demur. The *Feldwebel* (sergeant) told me they were a ration party making for Rumilly, but had lost their way in the dark. Their presence here showed how fluid the front line had become, and how sudden had been the transition by which, in three days, we had passed from trench warfare, with its fixed battle front and its well-defined barricades and parapets, to a state wherein troops on both sides were wandering about in the open not knowing where their line ran. I sent the prisoners to Brigade Headquarters at Marcoing, and spent the night in our cellar.

Towards daylight General Fisher rang up. He said I was to find Bissett, and we were to make a joint reconnaissance of the position between les Épines and Crèvecœur. It would depend on our report whether the Divisional Commander, General Deverell, would order our two battalions and the New Zealanders to attack Serinvillers and la Targette, villages lying out on the plain beyond the sunken road.

Bissett had his headquarters under the old German *Kommandantur*, and, on receipt of my message, he came across with Capt Shaw and his runners. I had not seen him since the night of the CO's conference at my camp above Marcoing, and we hastily completed our arrangements. He was his old cheerful self, joking and chaffing, while we drank a hurried cup of tea down below. Then we collected our runners, and started in the dim light of dawn for the sunken road. Halfway across we met Major Robinson coming back. He told us things were getting pretty bad in front, for the enemy was shelling the road heavily, as indeed we could see for ourselves. I told him to continue to Masnières, to keep in touch with brigade during my absence. As he went off he said: 'Sir, I don't envy you your job; that road is going to be hell to-day.' I didn't like the look of it myself, for the shell-fire was increasing, and great mushrooms of earth were shooting up along its course. Major Robinson had not gone a hundred yards when, hearing a shout, we looked round in time to see him flung down in a cloud of smoke. We ran back and found him severely wounded about the face and chest, but still alive. He was carried off by our stretcher-bearers and Capt Hetherington took temporary second in command in his place. Bissett and I with our runners then continued on our way, more shrapnel breaking over our heads as we went.

When we reached the edge of the sunken road we could hardly make ourselves heard for the noise of heavy shells bursting along the bank, but we hastily agreed that he and Shaw would go towards les Épines, while I went down in the direction of the New Zealanders at Crèvecœur, after which we would meet to compare notes.

As I was about to jump into the sunken road, a number of whizz-bang shells struck the earth close by in quick succession. I looked round and saw Bissett clap his hand to his side and fall to the ground. He rose almost at once, and walked towards me, still clasping his side. Shaw and I helped him down the bank, and as the shell-fire was increasing, we took him to the entrance of a dug-out which the Germans had made in the side of the cutting. Supporting him down, we laid him on the floor. He made light of his wound, a jagged hole in his right side from which the blood poured in torrents, but his breathing became stertorous, and although we did not realise it, he was mortally injured. We had to leave him for the present, and complete our investigations for report to Division. Shaw and his runners proceeded to les Épines, where the RSF held the road, and I went with my party in the direction of the New Zealanders, lower down.

We crossed through the cutting of the road, and tried to walk out over the open to see the lie of the land towards Sirenvillers, but we were immediately fired on from a line of rifle pits about three hundred yards away. From the hasty view I had, I realised that the enemy stood in great strength all the way between Serinvillers, Niergnies, and Cambrai, and that although they had evacuated our sunken road overnight, they showed no signs of further retreat. As we went, whizz bangs and 5.9's were coming over in large numbers. Already some thirty or more Shropshire men lay dead and wounded, and I could foresee a heavy casualty list. I continued until I reached the New Zealanders. They were having an equally bad time. Many lay dead and the others were hugging the forward bank for shelter. Their CO had been killed, but the second in command was still alive. I asked him what he thought of our three battalions attacking Serinvillers, and he replied with some heat that he did not belong to a suicide club. We discussed the situation. The British were attacking further south, for we heard the roll of guns, but in this vicinity their batteries were silent, and, even in the air we saw only hostile machines, nor could we see any supporting troops in our rear. That being the case, we agreed that an attack with our weak forces across open ground against heavy shell-fire, rifles and machine-guns would only result in useless slaughter of our men. Having satisfied myself of this, I returned to look for Shaw. The German bombardment continued and the sunken road was not a pleasant sight, for in it lay many dead and mangled men, and the stretcher-bearers were busy carrying the wounded to Mon Plaisir. Shaw was back from his inspection, and I found him in the dug-out with Bissett. Bissett was conscious and took part in our counsel. Shaw had arrived at the same conclusion as the New Zealander officer and myself, so we drew up a report for General Fisher, giving him our views of the local position, and telling him that in our opinion an advance on Serinvillers with our weakened companies, unsupported by artillery, would be a bloody failure.

I sent the despatch back by runner and, pending further orders, we did what we could to get the men to dig better cover against the opposite bank of the road.

Some time later another runner brought orders that we were to attack Serinvillers after all with our three battalions. Guns had been brought up and at 11 o'clock we were to go forward. Shaw and I looked at each other in dismay, for we knew it meant the certain annihilation of our men. However, almost at once there followed a second runner with countermanding orders. It transpired that instructions to attack had been issued before our report reached Division, but this had since come to hand, and a stray aeroplane had also dropped a message to say that masses of German infantry were moving up from behind Niergnies. It was as well that the previous order was cancelled, for it subsequently took the whole of the 2nd and 4th Armies to dislodge the enemy form this line, and there would have been little left of the RSF, the Shrops and the New Zealanders had they been sent on so forlorn an errand.

In the meanwhile we were ordered to hold the sunken road, and for the next five hours we sat inactive under a pounding which worked great havoc, so that shattered men, broken rifles and bloodstained equipment lay about everywhere while the wounded sat huddled against the bank awaiting the bearers, or crowded into the dug-out where Bissett lay.

Shaw and I moved up and down the road, but except for telling each man to sink a sort of pothole for himself with his entrenching tool, there was nothing much that we could do.

At 4 o'clock that afternoon a runner arrived with a message that we were both to come to Mon Plaisir Trench to talk matters over with General Fisher. We said nothing at the time, but we afterwards confessed to each other how relieved we had been to get away from that beastly road after ten hours of shell-fire.

We decided to remove Bissett. Up to now we had left him in the dug-out, as it seemed best to keep him quiet for as long as possible. Shaw got a squad of bearers that had come up, and we carried him upstairs, and lifted him on to a stretcher. He was taken off, but when next we saw him we were standing by his deathbed.

Having seen Bissett on his way, we made the necessary arrangements with our company officers, and walked back across the plain to Mon Plaisir, where we found General Fisher waiting for us. We suggested to him that our men should be withdrawn from the sunken road after dark, as the place was a death-trap, and he agreed to this. During the night we fell them back about eighty yards, and here we made the men dig a system of rifle pits. By sunrise we were in occupation, and as the Germans never discovered the change they continued to shell the road for the next four days, thinking that we still held it.

A long pause now ensued for the bringing-up of fresh troops and guns, as the Germans were making desperate efforts to prevent the fall of Cambrai. During this lull they bombarded Masnières and Crèvecœur until both villages were destroyed. One morning I went to visit a forward post held by a Shrops platoon in a short trench length that had originally been dug by the Germans. At this point we were said to be the nearest British troops to Cambrai, which was clearly visible only three miles off. The town had been on fire for days, and all through our time here a pall of smoke hung over the place, while at night the glare in the sky served as a directing mark to our runners. The town had been set alight by the Germans, for the British guns never fired on it, by special request of the French Government, so it was said. While I was inspecting this trench length, the German gunners suddenly began to shell us. The men had fitted together a few sheets of corrugated iron as a cookhouse, and five or six of them were sitting there when the bombardment started. Most of the shells dropped short or over, but a 5.9 came straight down on the roofing, and exploded amongst the soldiers round the fire. I saw them blown in all directions, and, running up, we found three killed outright and two seriously injured. As we were attending to the wounded, a German plane came low overhead, probably spotting for the guns.

There was a squadron of British machines thousands of feet up, on its way across the lines. Two of these nose-dived at great speed, and started raking the German airmen at close range before they knew of their presence. In a moment their machine side-slipped, and came down with a thud not a hundred yards from us. Later on we climbed out of the trench to examine the wreckage. The plane was a Halberstadt and there were two dead men in it, still strapped to their seats. The German guns behind Niergnies reopened fire, so we bolted back, and the machine and its crew lay abandoned there for the rest of the time that we remained in this area.

That night, while going the rounds, we saw two figures approaching in the dark. A sentry challenged them, and we heard a shout: 'Don't fire, don't fire, we're British!' They proved to be Corporal Flood and Private Kane of the Manchesters. They had been captured during the March fighting and had now escaped from a prison camp at Caudry, where they had been at work loading trains, and 'helping the Boche to win the war', as Kane put it. They were in rags and very emaciated, but they were fair enough to say that the food they had received was at any rate as good as that which the Germans themselves got. They said that the fighting soldiers had treated them well, but that some of the *Landwehr* at the camp were brutes. I took them to Mon Plaisir Trench and gave them a good meal and a drink of rum in the dug-out, and then forwarded them to Brigade, with the assurance of getting long leave to England, which sent them happily on their way.

A few days after, Lt Wiles of the Shrops and I were sitting on the parapet of Mon Plaisir, chatting in the afternoon sunshine, when a two-seater British aeroplane came over from the direction of Cambrai, at about five hundred feet. As we idly watched it, the machine, for no apparent reason, literally flew into pieces before our eyes. Wood splinters, strips of fabric, and fragments of metal rained down on us, but that was all that was left, and the airmen must have been instantaneously killed. I think the only possible explanation is that a high-angle British shell, on its way to the German lines, had struck the plane head-on.

We had the usual narrow escapes while holding the line, and I was once ill for forty-eight hours from gas poisoning, followed by a headache that lasted for days. On another occasion, during an inspection of the cellars beneath the sugar factory in Masnières, a 5.9 crashed through the concrete flooring. Lt Sleep of the Scots Fusiliers, two New Zealand officers, and I, were very nearly buried under the avalanche of bricks and masonry that poured down. Sleep and I were the only two surviving RSF officers of all those who had been with the battalion at the time of the March offensive.

For a week we held the local sector with depleted strength, while the main armies were fighting elsewhere. Then troops began to move up, and the plain beyond the canal became crowded with men and guns of the 2nd and 4th Armies, to whom had been allotted the task of driving the enemy from Serinvillers and outflanking Cambrai.

Owing to the heavy losses which we had sustained, our Brigade was withdrawn at last from the firing line, and on October 8th we marched the remains of our battalions over the canal bridge that had defied all the efforts of the German gunners, and halted on the plain beyond, where we lay out of range, or at any rate free from shell-fire, for the first time for nearly a month.

Thus far Shaw and I had had our hands so full that we had found it impossible to enquire about Bissett. Under the system in vogue, once a man was carried from the front line he was lost sight of, and it became a difficult matter to trace him through the numerous clearing stations behind the line. But now we decided to look for him, and we rode to Beaumetz, the headquarters of the 8th Field Ambulance, and here, after considerable trouble, we ascertained that Bissett was at No 57 casualty clearing station at Crévillers. The Commanding Officer of the 8th lent us a car, and we started at once. Crévillers is (or was) a village just beyond Bapaume, and here stood a large hospital camp of marquee tents. We found the matron, who directed us to the ward where Bissett lay. At the entrance to the tent sat the faithful Glossop, on a roll of kit. Tears ran down his cheeks as he told us that his master was dying inside, and that it was only a question of minutes before the end.

In the tent were two rows of wounded men in cots. A nursing sister, hearing that we had come to see Bissett, whispered to us: 'Smile and tell him a few jokes and keep his spirit up; nothing else can save him.'

Shaw and I walked between the beds scrutinising the patients, but we failed to recognise Bissett, and even when the sister led us to his side, we scarcely knew him, so gaunt and altered was he. A smile and a few jokes were beyond me, and I could not speak for fear of breaking down. Shaw felt the same, so we stood silently looking down on what was but the shadow of our friend. His eyes were dimmed, and his face pale and shrunken and we could see that the end was very near. He tried feebly to speak, and muttered something about the Scots Fusiliers and the Arras Road, then he become unconscious, and we went sadly off, knowing that we had lost a brave and good companion.

We were back with our battalion that night, and next morning General Deverell sent for me and told me, because of Bissett's death, to hand the Shrops to Colonel Burne, and to take over command of the 1st RSF. I had been with the 7th Shropshires for less than two weeks, but I had made many friends. I have kept the only battalion order issued while I was in command:

BATTALION ORDERS
by Deneys Reitz
Commanding 7th Battalion, the King's Shropshire Light Infantry
In the field, Monday, 7th October, 1918

1. Command. Major D Reitz, 1st Royal Scots Fusiliers, took over command of the Battalion on 27.9.18.
2. Lights. Air reports point to an excessive amount of illumination at night in the forward area due to unscreened bivouacs.
3. Care of the dead. During recent operations several No 64 Army Books have been lost from dead bodies in the Corps area and in the case of Germans, identity discs have been removed. Care should be taken to prevent this.
4. Casaulties. The commanding officer regrets to announce the following casualties:—

Killed

Ellis	Monks	Pickard
Samuels	Sexton	Collins
Brown	Whettall	Parker
Donelly	White	Wood
Humphries	Gill	Jenkins
Davies	Jones	Clarke
James	Weedon	Evans
Gallagher	Payne	Fosker

Lewis	Jones	Bayley
Powell	Jones	Langslow
Bates	Booth	

Died of Wounds
| Cresswell | Williams |
| Trantor | Dorris |

Gassed
| Matthews | Healey |
| Jones | White |

Wounded and Missing
| Raynor | Jones |
| Taylor | Cotton |

Missing
Turner	Griffiths	Crellin
Johnson	Rawlings	Duckett
Oakley	Fitzsimmons	

Wounded
Corner	Hayward	Johnson
Smith	Layton	Lamond
Hudson	Parminter	Bailey
Asplury	Lowe	Sullivan
Brook	Chadwick	Holman
Thompson	Bevan	Davies
Meredith	Burgess	Legge
Nicholas	Broadbent	Walker
Davidson	Lee	Barker
Clay	Hanson	Yeomans
Wood	Hallard	Wenman
Alexandra	Phillips	Griffiths
Winterbottom	Wilson	Richardson
Cartwright	Jones	Powell
Brown	Munday	Durrant
Amplett	Moore	Anslow
Gough	Davies	Bright
Caine	Baker	Cooke
Winward	Turner	Birchall
Holton	Harris	Gallagher
Allmark	Plimmer	Jones
Hodges	Shaw	Cooper
Pople	White	Kingswell
Grayson	Law	Kendall
Jones	McGregor	Lowe
Tunnicliffe	Jones	Thwaite
Cholerton	Powell-Tuck	Mansell
Eaton	Perrins	Nicolas
Bradley	Cooke	Rumsey
Rhodes	Davies	Thraves

Jennings	Croft	Hollman
Jones	Whittington	Hillman
Coppack	Ryder	Bocock
Jones	Hitchin	Taylor
Robinson	Edwards	Ingram
Grainger	Vicars	Evans
George	Hinchcliffe	Moreton
Humphries	Bromley	Millward
Rostron	Bates	Orford
Pover	Madeley	Thelwell
Edmonson	Devine	Fleet

(Sgd) A C Hetherington, Capt and Adjutant 7th Batt. The King's Shropshire Light Infantry.

I have never been in Shropshire, but this order will serve to show how one of its battalions fared during a fortnight of the Great War.

Chapter 14

Nearing the End

The 2nd and 4th Armies now moved up. Our brigade was held in reserve, and my share in making ready for battle was confined to sending for two miles of white tape from Arras, with which I laid out a starting-line near the sunken road, upon which the troops were to assemble in the dark.

During the night of the 10th of October the attacking battalions silently filed through Masnières and Mon Plaisir, and from 2 am onwards the British guns began to fire. The Germans knew what was coming, for they replied in kind, and they caused heavy damage, as we realised at daybreak. The battle commenced before dawn, but except for the flashes of bursting shells there was nothing to be seen, although when sunrise came, the British had taken Serinvillers. It was being heavily bombarded by the enemy, and coming from the captured village was a steady flow of German and British wounded.

General Fisher was at Mon Plaisir Trench, and he ordered me to take my runners forward to gauge the position. We made for the sunken road and crossed it, then we found a trail of dead and dying Suffolks and King's Own to Serinvillers. On the way I came on a solitary German machine-gunner, sitting behind his weapon in a shell crater. Before him lay nearly a score of British soldiers that had fallen to his gun. The man himself was riddled with bayonet thrusts. I heard afterwards that he had refused to retire or to surrender, and here at his post he 'went down scornful before many spears'. When we reached Serinvillers, the place was going to pieces under heavy German shell-fire. I found that the British advance had been checked, and that the

Germans were still holding la Targette, a pistol shot beyond. After a hurried inspection, I walked in the direction of Niergnies, with a wide view of the firing line right up to Cambrai, where things were going none too well.

At Niergnies, close by, dense columns of German infantry were approaching, and in the middle distance were two tanks clanking towards us. Judging by their build, they had been captured from the British and were now being used against their former owners. Each had an iron cross painted on its sides. They were bearing straight on the King's Own, who were grouped in small parties across the plain, and the sight of the tanks and the heavy German reinforcements was taking effect, for some of the men were falling back, and it looked as if the whole line might give. Shells were bursting, and rifle and machine-gun bullets whizzing plentifully about. As I did not propose getting run over by tanks, I withdrew my party to a slight rise near les Épines from which we still had a good view. Batches of men came by, and when I questioned them they denied that they were retreating, but said that they could not stand against the tanks on open ground, and were making for the sunken road. A considerable number of them were 'coming back', as they called it, but the majority of the King's Own remained lying in the grass, awaiting the enemy counter-attack, and I could see detachments of Suffolks hurrying to their assistance. Soon there was a deafening rattle of Lewis-gun and rifle fire, but the advancing German waves did not seem to have much stomach, for they began to run behind a fold in the ground. I saw one of the tanks go ambling back to Niergnies, while the other stood close to the British line, firing its guns at short range. Then it burst into flames. The King's Own had found an abandoned German trench mortar and some ammunition, and after a few rounds they scored a direct hit, which put her out of action, while another shot fired the petrol tank. After a time, seeing that the fighting was stabilised, I returned to report to General Fisher. At the sunken road a column of about two hundred German prisoners was being marched to the rear in charge of British soldiers. The German guns were dropping random shells all over the place, and, as we approached, a projectile fell in the centre of the closely packed mass. I saw men, and pieces of men, fly into the air, the prisoners breaking in all directions. Running up, we counted nineteen Germans and five of the British guard lying dead, and there were many wounded. It was a dreadful sight. We did what we could until the arrival of the stretcher parties, after which we went on.

At Mon Plaisir, I reported to General Fisher, and that was all I saw of this day's battle.

So many fresh troops were moving forward, and the operation was now going so well, that next day our brigade was withdrawn for a week's rest.

We marched back past Havrincourt and Flesquières and the battlefield of the Hindenburg Line, and recrossing the Canal du Nord, went into camp near Hermes, now a deserted region, with the fighting so far ahead that even the gunfire was merely like distant thunder.

General Fisher knew how to handle us. Next morning a fine staff car drew up, and there was a message from him to say that the three Colonels of his Brigade— Henderson of the Royal Scots, Burne of the Shrops, and I—were granted four days' recuperative leave to Calais, and the car was at our disposal. It was a pleasant holiday. We went via Bapaume and the Somme battlefields and through Albert. When last I had been in Albert, eight months before, it still bore some semblance of a town, and the Virgin and Child still leaned from the cathedral tower. Since then the tide of the German March offensive and the British counter-offensive had swept over it. The Virgin and Child and the tower from which they had jutted were gone, and it was now the most completely devastated spot in France.

From Albert we went to Doullens, and I searched for the building in which I had lain wounded, but it was in ruins, and the rest of the village had been greatly damaged.

There was a section of the famous Spad *escadrille* of the Cicognes stationed here, with distinguished French aces walking the streets all a-glitter with decorations, the townspeople proudly pointing them out to us. We spent the night at the '*Trois Fils d'Aymon*', and next day we went on to Calais. We put up at the Officers' Mess, and had a good time. Henderson was a regular, who had been in the Mons retreat in 1914, and on active service ever since, a quiet undemonstrative man, who perhaps saw more fighting than any other officer in the Army. Burne was a South African. He had commanded the 11th Infantry in German East on the day on which old Hilgaard de Jager and I watched the armoured cars break the line at Kidete. Before that, in the Boer War, he was with the British convoy that we had sacked and burnt at Middlepoort in 1902, so we had many things in common.

There was a furious battle in progress south of Nieuport, where French and Belgian armies were attacking. We heard the rumble of gunfire, and we saw long convoys bringing in the wounded, while allied staff officers were rushing about the streets, so there was plenty of bustle and colour. The battle was going well, they told us, but we had had enough of battles, and motored to Zenninghem instead, through twenty miles of Dutch-looking country, with shady canals and windmills and stolid peasants trudging along. Here and there a French soldier on leave stood surrounded by admirers in his little village, and in spite of the far-off boom of guns, this was a quiet peaceful region, untouched by war.

On our way back to Calais we visited an aerodrome beside the road to see Capitaine Georges, the famous Belgian flying man, start off on one of his daily expeditions over the German lines. On some days he went up three times. The Belgians were very proud of their star performer, and a crowd of refugees always collected to see him go on his perilous journey. An onlooker told me that the month before Georges took two British officers joy-riding on successive days, and crashed his plane and killed his passenger on each occasion, so the British military authorities had stopped him from breaking the necks of any more of their people, and he was now limited to fighting the Germans.

In Calais we ordered the finest dinner that money could buy, for we knew that we were to go into action again, and as life was an uncertain lease, we feasted royally.

Next morning we started back, and stayed over a night at Amiens, which was in a battered condition. In the early days of the war the Germans had occupied the town for a short while, and during the fighting of this year they had very nearly retaken it, but Colonel Gordon's faith had been justified, although at the cost of great battles and many lives.

At an hotel I sat down to table with an old American colonel of engineers. His language was quaint, and among other things he asked me 'Was your boys badly bent in the last show?' and when I asked him why he was a Democrat he said that in the South one was born a Democrat. He showed me some Roman coins he had found in the Argonne, which looked as new and shining as if they had been minted the day before. They bore the head of the Emperor Hadrian and a woman's figure on the obverse side.

Early next morning we continued our journey, and by dusk we were with our battalions once more. The 1st RSF was at Ribécourt, where Shaw had fixed up Headquarters in a ruined nunnery. We remained at Ribécourt for several days, during which time the entire IIIrd Division was set to work salvaging the Hindenburg Line. We used our limber teams, and between us collected a hundred and thirty-three abandoned guns. They ran from monsters with barrels thirty feet long to little trench mortars. We also collected over three hundred machine-guns, and a great pile of Mauser rifles and other articles.

I rode across from Ribécourt to Masnières to have a look at the scene of our recent encounters. As a result of the last battle, the British line had gone forward quite eight miles, and Cambrai had been evacuated, so that the area around Masnières, Crèvecœur and Rumilly, which we had only known as steeped in shell-fire, now lay in peace and quiet. Even army headquarters had moved up to Masnières, and there were ASC and other base troops quartered where we had faced the enemy a week ago.

Beyond Mon Plaisir Trench the soldiers had marked out a football ground. They had filled in the shell-holes, and erected goal-posts, and as I rode by a match was in progress, the supporters of either side loudly cheering and shouting. A number of German dead had been moved out of the way. They were simply dumped beside the touch-line, where they formed a grim reminder of the sterner game that had been played here so short a time before.

On my way back to Ribécourt I came on a German dug-out, in a bank above Marcoing, and by the light of my electric torch I collected a bundle of journals and other papers that had been left behind. I looked through them that evening. One was a leaflet containing a sermon delivered by the Kaiser, and I remembered that in East Africa, in the fort at old Moschi we had found a speech of his to the naval cadets at Kiel telling them that they were privileged in having before them one who held the German sceptre by direct dispensation of the Almighty.

Now he said:

> 'He who takes up the sword without just cause will perish by the sword; but the sword I wield is as sacred as that carried by St Peter on the night of Gethsemane.'

This was accompanied by an article by one Dr Rosner of Berlin, reading:

> 'The Kaiser is with us. He remains from daybreak to sunset among his beloved troops in the battle zone. He has visited the trenches and positions they have captured from the enemy and he frequently expresses his astonishment at the glorious feats performed by German valour. From a battlepost (*Gefechtsstand*) he watches the progress of the fighting. Yesterday he was recognised and surrounded by a Division on its way to the firing line. The victorious (*siegesbewusst*) German soldiers cheered him enthusiastically as he briefly told them the news from the different fronts, and as he returned to his car the men crowded round him with heartfelt greetings before going joyously into battle for *Kaiser und Reich*.'

This bolstering-up of the Hohenzollerns seemed merely silly to me, but the German people, with all their fine qualities, have a sentimental streak which makes them susceptible to this kind of thing.

In one of the newspapers I had brought was an account of a recent interview between Ludendorff and a gathering of German pressmen whom he had summoned to Berlin to discuss the military situation. He complained of the pessimism spreading through the country and told them that Talaat Bey, an Ottoman official who had visited the capital shortly before, had returned to Constantinople smiling and hopeful, although Turkey was in a worse plight than theirs.

I translated this at dinner, and Corporal Noble who was in attendance, must have taken it in, for later on I heard him retailing the gist of what I had said to the runners and signallers in the lean-to that served as a cookhouse. Apparently Talaat Bey's optimism rankled, for after a long silence I heard a voice say: 'Well, boys, I guess we've wiped that smile off Talaat's mug by now,' and there came approving murmurs in the dark.

On October 20th we received our move order, and the whole brigade marched via Marcoing, Crèvecœur, Serinvillers and Wambaix to Catinières, over country that had been cleared of the enemy during the last fighting. We were now definitely out of the devastated area of France, for, from Serinvillers onward, the villages, though often damaged by shell-fire, were still villages. Most of the houses had sufficient roofing to provide cover, and, most pleasing of all to the men, there were often glass window panes and even beds and stoves left behind. Up to now, such places as they had been quartered in were heaps of rubble, and a watertight roof and unbroken window panes assured them more than anything else that the German Army was on the run.

We were in an area where for years past there had been enemy rest billets and training camps, and it looked as if they had intended to settle down for good. The names of the streets had been altered to Ludendorffstrasse and von Bülowstrasse, etc, and in every direction were large vegetable gardens sometimes extending for miles without a break, which must have formed an important addition to the German food supplies.

Now too for the first time we began to fall in with French civilians, who had been living in the occupied zone since 1914. Women and children and old men stood along the roads or in the village streets and gave us a feeble '*Vivient les alliés!*' as we went by. Most of them were haggard and starved, and from what they told us they had been living chiefly on cabbage soup and contributions from the American Relief Fund. The Germans had forced them to work in the military vegetable gardens at two paper marks a day. I gathered that their treatment had not been brutal, but pettily oppressive, with fines and penalties levied on an already impoverished population.

The day after our arrival at Catinières, there was a CO's conference at Brigade Headquarters, to which Henderson, Burne and I were summoned. General Fisher informed us that our 8th Brigade was to take part in an attack on the 23rd of October, and gave us detailed instructions as to our share in the battle.

The British front line ran beyond the town of Solesmes about four miles away, and the attack was designed to push the enemy back another few miles to within striking distance of the Valenciennes-le Quesnoy Railway, where they were said to be preparing a new line of resistance.

The attack was to be carried out by the 17th, 4th and 6th Corps. As far as our brigade was concerned, Henderson with the 2nd Royal Scots was to capture the village of Vertain, lying two miles beyond Solesmes. As soon as this objective was attained, the RSF were to leapfrog through and take the next village of Escarmain, after which the Shrops would go through to a brown line on our maps.

I still have the battle order:

'Secret.
Copy No 3.

8th Infantry Brigade.

Operation Order No 80.
22nd Oct, 1918.
1. The 3rd Army is to resume the advance on the 23rd October.
2. The attack on the 6th Corps front will be carried out by the IIIrd Division on the right.
3. The attack on the IIIrd Division front will be carried out by the 76th Inf Brig on the right and the 8th Inf Brigade on the left.
4. The 8th Inf Brigade will move to Solesmes under orders to be issued later.
5. The attack is to be carried out as a surprise, there will be no preliminary bombardment.
6. The attack will be carried out under a creeping barrage as follows:
   (a) The 2nd Royal Scots, Col Henderson, will take the first objective shown in red on Ref Map 51A.
   The initial barrage will come down for 6 minutes 200 yards beyond the road marked W.20.G by which time the 2nd Royal Scots will be in their assembly position immediately west of the road.
   The barrage will move at the rate of 100 yards in 6 minutes.
   The 1st Royal Scots Fusiliers, Col Reitz, will be formed up at zero hour on the slopes east of le Pigeon Blanc in rear of the 2nd Ryl Scots.
   The 1st Royal Scots Fusiliers will follow 1 500 yds behind the rear of the 2nd Ryl Scots and will be prepared to assist in the capture of Vertain should the latter be unable to carry out the task single-handed. The 7th KSLI (Shrops), Col Burne, will form in rear of the 1st Royal Scots Fusiliers.
   (b) At 08.40 hours the 1st Royal Scots Fusiliers will resume the advance from the red objective under a creeping barrage at 100 yards in 3 minutes up to the green dotted objective. The village of Escarmain will be included in the 2nd objective. The 7th KSLI will follow 1 500 yards behind the rear of the 1st RSF and will be prepared to assist if necessary in the capture and mopping up of Escarmain.
   The 7th KSLI will push on to the brown line.
   (c) OC 8th Trench Mortar Battery to move under orders of 1st Royal Scots Fusiliers.
7. After the capture of the final objectives, the 8th Brigade will organise in depth and will be prepared to continue the advance to the blue line.
8. Information from prisoners and civilians shows that the enemy are holding a rearguard position around the villages of Vertain and Escarmain. His artillery strength is unknown.
Issued at 11.15 hours.

B W Gosling, Capt and Brigade-Major 8th Inf Brigade.'

After the conference, Henderson, Burne and I rode off to look over the ground beyond Solesmes, across which we were to attack next day. When we reached the outskirts of the town we found that the bridge spanning the River Serre had been destroyed by gunfire, and that the Germans were steadily dropping heavy shells among the streets and houses, at the rate of about one every five minutes.

A traffic policeman at the broken bridge told us we could cross by a plank-way at St Python, lower down, so we followed the bank until we reached a sort of trestle bridge, leading over the stream into the courtyard of a large brewery, and thence under the archway and up the long street into Solesmes.

Solesmes was normally a town of about ten thousand inhabitants. It had prosperous-looking residences and a fine town hall. Most of the civilians were sheltering in cellars against the plunging shells, and only here and there did we see an anxious-faced woman or a child peering through window or doorway.

At the town hall were French political officers sent by their government to distribute gas masks, for here again the people obstinately refused to evacuate their homes, preferring to be gassed and shelled, when they could easily have gone away to some of the liberated villages in the rear until the enemy had been driven out of range. Fortunately all the houses had deep cellars and the casualties were light, although many suffered from the prolonged gassing.

We rode through the streets, with dead German soldiers still lying where they had fallen, and then up the road to the shrine this side of Pigeon Blanc Farm, where we left our horses and proceeded on foot. The Germans were briskly shelling all this area, and in the porchway of the farmhouse lay a number of British dead, who had been killed in the forward rifle pits. We hurried on to a rise beyond Pigeon Blanc, from where we could see the villages of Vertain and Romeries, two thousand yards away, with Escarmain lying further back. The Germans were in possession of these villages, and they had numerous machine-guns and rifle posts in the open country. As the shell-fire was heavy, and the air humming with bullets from the German rifle pits, we made a quick examination of the ground lying before us, and inspected the sunken road in which we were to assemble our companies during the night.

Having completed our reconnaissance, we fetched our horses and rode back through Solesmes and St Python to our battalions, in order to issue the necessary instructions for their march. By dark we had our men quartered underground in Solesmes, in various cellars previously marked down for the purpose.

We were to start for our assembly point at 2 am, and until then everyone was to remain below. We spent a disturbed night, for the Germans continued to shell the town and a heavy concentration of gas came over, so that sleep was impossible. Apart from frequent alarms and the noise of bursting shells and falling masonry, there were enemy planes droning overhead, and we heard the crash of heavy bombs at St Python, where they were trying to destroy the only bridge that was left.

Our Battalion Headquarters were in the cellar of a house situated in a street with the inappropriate name of Rue de la Gaieté. We had for fellow lodgers a number of women and children, half starved and fearful of the explosions, so that it was anything but gay.

At 2 am (23rd October) I fell-in my companies in the dark. A gas shell struck the pavement in front of C Company, and killed young Lieut Ferguson before my eyes. The 2nd Royal Scots, who were to lead the attack on Vertain, had already started, and as we moved up the inclined street, we came on several of their dead, and met their stretcher parties coming back with wounded, for the Germans seemed to know what was afoot, and shells were bursting in all directions.

The Royal Scots lost thirty men before they reached the sunken road beyond Pigeon Blanc, but we were luckier, for we had only seven hit, while the Shrops, coming on behind, lost over forty.

It was still night, and the blinding flashes of the shells and the crackle of machine-guns and rifles from the German line made it no easy task to carry out our preparations.

At 3.30 the British barrage came down. It was not the solid wall of flame of the old days, but it was heavy enough, and the Royal Scots went off behind it.

In the dark we could see the figures of the advancing men outlined against the barrage with the light playing upon their bayonets.

German machine-guns and rifles were spitting away, but they went on until they were swallowed up in the dark. As we were to follow fifteen hundred yards behind, we watched until we could no longer distinguish them, then when I judged that they would be nearing Vertain, I started my men off.

We advanced in open order across the level plain, passing many Royal Scots lying dead and wounded. They had caught the brunt of the enemy fire, which already was slackening down, and we lost only four men killed, and five or six wounded, even though shells dropped freely among us.

It was getting light by now, and we could see the dim shadow of Vertain before us. The Royal Scots were not in sight, but as the small-arm fire had ceased, I knew that they had entered the village.

To our immediate right, at Romeries, heavy fighting was in progress and further south too the battle was thundering away. We now came to a small stream, the Georges, through which we waded knee deep, and beyond that we were among the houses and gardens of Vertain.

As we were about to penetrate further, the German guns shortened range, and began to pound the village with 8-inch howitzers, accompanied by gas shells. This was additional proof that they had fallen back, for latterly it was their custom, whenever they gave up a town or village, to smash it with gunfire. They had done this to Marcoing, Masnières and Crèvecœur, and to all the other villages between Serinvillers and Solesmes, and now they were doing it to Vertain. I could not make out where the Royal Scots had gone, but I found afterwards that, having driven out the enemy, they had moved away to the left beyond the houses, to escape the counter bombardment. I collected my men behind a bank, until I had time to gauge the position. The tear gas was causing us great inconvenience. Owing to the cloud of brick-dust and smoke drifting from the village we were unable to use the eyepieces of our masks, so we contented ourselves with clipping the wire springs to our noses, and suffered in consequence from coughing and sneezing, and smarting eyes that gave us acute discomfort.

I ordered the men to remain under cover behind the bank, while I went forward with the runners to investigate.

Near by stood a large square of farm buildings on the road that linked Vertain to Romeries. In the entrance to the courtyard were two German machine-guns and a light trench mortar and several dead gunners, and as three or four shells dropped in the quadrangle in quick succession, we bolted into a doorway and down a cellar stair. We found the cellar well lit by candles stuck to the walls and in it were eleven German soldiers and two NCO's (*Vize-feldwebeln*). One of them stepped forward, and saluting at every few words, he said that they had been driven to take shelter by the British barrage and wished to surrender. I put a guard over them, and as I had to continue the attack to Escarmain at 8.40, I had the battalion brought to the farm. After sending scouts to look for the 2nd Royal Scots, Lieut Pud Robertson and I walked forward to reconnoitre the ground over which we had to go.

We found ourselves on an open grassy plain of considerable extent. It was clear that Vertain had been held by the enemy as an advanced post only, for now, six hundred yards distant, lay their real defensive line, in the shape of parallel rifle pits in front of Escarmain. The German guns were firing from the rear, but the infantry in the rifle pits loosed only an occasional round, not being anxious, I suppose, to attract the attention of the British batteries.

In the near foreground two kilted soldiers were digging away in a hollow, and Pud and I wormed forward to see what they were at. They were Gordon Highlanders who had pushed on in the dark during their attack on Romeries, until daylight found them out in the open all by themselves, so they had decided to dig in. As they were in the direct line of the barrage that was to come down, I took them back with me to the farm, after having satisfied myself of the lie of the land towards Escarmain. The Battalion was still at the farm, and contact had been established with the Royal Scots in the hedgerows and orchards on the far side of Vertain. To our right lay Romeries, also captured that morning, and there too troops were waiting to go forward.

At 8.30 the men were in the assembly line, ready for zero hour. It is always a trying time waiting for the final moment, but I had no fear of the outcome. From what I had seen of German army orders and newspapers, and of their infantry of late, I knew that their spirits were low, and that we were not so much fighting an army as hustling demoralised men.

At 8.40 to the second, the barrage came roaring down. A British 6-inch howitzer shell dropped between our front and rear waves, and killed three men, and all the way to Escarmain this infernal gun dropped shorts among us, causing eight or nine further casualties.

The rest of the barrage worked smoothly, and we followed behind it at a walk. The German infantry in the rifle pits opened fire on us, but they were rattled by the shells, and their firing was wild, whilst their batteries were too thin to do much damage. The moment the barrage reached their rifle pits the infantry crouched down while it swept over them, and as soon as they saw the curtain of bursting shells move on beyond, they came running towards us, hands in air, and our role was practically confined to following in the wake of the barrage and receiving the prisoners in batches as they came to meet us. Including the losses caused by the 6-inch howitzer, we had under fifty men hit in crossing from Vertain to Escarmain, and we took over two hundred prisoners on the way.

And now we reached and entered the village, the elated men rushing down the streets, and fetching out more prisoners from houses and cellars. They speedily cleaned up the place of such Germans as were still lurking about, and we then waded the stream that runs through Escarmain, and climbed the slope beyond to the Chapelle de la Rosaire, from which we had an extensive view across another open plain sloping down towards the Ecaillon, a small river two miles away. German infantry were streaming back, and we sped their passage with rifle-fire. Many gun teams too were galloping in the distance, and it was clear that the enemy was retiring on a wide front.

Our instructions were to reach the red line on the battle map, and no further, so we made no attempt to pursue, and I had the satisfaction of sending a runner back to brigade with a note to say that the 1st RSF had reached its objective according to orders.

We now had time to look about us. The German retreat was crossing the Ecaillon River far down on the plain, and on the bluffs beyond we could see them already hard at work digging new rifle pits. On a large field near the edge of the village was an aerodrome with a Halberstadt machine, and two abandoned guns with dead teams and dead gunners, struck down by the morning's barrage. The hangars were made of tarred felt on wooden frames, and one of them had served as an officers' mess. Painted on the wall inside was the usual coloured inscription about '*der Gott der Eisen wachsen liess*', which one found in almost every German billet and rest camp, and even on their notepaper, but in addition there was a scroll: '*Niemand fliegt ungestrafft zur Sonne*' (No man flies unscathed towards the sun): a fine motto for airmen.

After a while the enemy gunners, true to custom, began to bombard the village, so I made the men seek cover, while Shaw and Pud Robertson and I took up a forward observation post at the Rosary, where we had several narrow escapes from bursting shells. The runners brought in a German cavalry officer whom they had found in a copse close by, a Prussian, standing nearly six foot six, jack-booted and spurred like Bismarck. He was a Berlin lawyer, and he had no illusions about the result of the war. He admitted that Austria and Turkey were as good as done for, and that the German cause was a hopeless one.

After midday the British gunfire flared up again, and behind it the Shrops came through us, to the brown line of the Operation Order. They suffered only a few casualties, and had soon reached their objective, halfway down towards the Ecaillon.

As for Escarmain, a river flowed through it, spanned by an ancient bridge, and there was a large church, while on the slope above was a sort of public garden; otherwise it was only a small hamlet. There must have been a poet among the troops who succeeded us in this area, for in the November *Country Life* I found the following verses:

> How softly drop the patient trees
> In Romeries and Escarmain
> While on the uplands wild and brown
> Softly comes down the little rain!

> But we do chase the fleeting hare
> Across the bare lands of Vertain,
> Through sunken roads, o'er sodden plough,
> And hell for leather back again.

> *Chorus*
> Oh well she ran from horse and man
> Across the misty leas, Sir,
> Above Vertain and Escarmain
> And down to Romeries, Sir.

But when you gallop with loose rein
Above Vertain and Romeries,
Beware the shellholes in the mud!
Beware the dud i' th' turnips, please!
And keep eyes wide for rifle pits
Where lately Fritz crouched ill at ease
When the barrage fell in the pearl-grey light
On the day of the fight upon the leas.

Chapter 15

The Last Phase

Before daybreak next morning, October 24th, fresh troops continued the advance, and meeting with little opposition, pressed the Germans back towards the Valenciennes-le Quesnoy railway line, three or four miles on.

At 7 am I received instructions to march towards the Pont du Buat, by which the road to Ruesnes crosses the Ecaillon. I ordered up my horse, as I proposed riding into action for once, and we marched out. As we passed below the Rosary Chapel a shell struck an elm tree on the bank, bringing it down across the road a few yards in front of the column and holding us up for more than half an hour before we could clear the obstruction.

Beyond the station the road climbed a rise, and then descended to the Pont. We passed a number of German dead, and twice we had to manhandle abandoned guns and dead horses out of the way. Stray shells were falling, mostly in the open, so I strung the men out in artillery formation, to minimise the risk. Just as we had crossed the Buat Bridge, a high-velocity shell pitched on the road, right in the middle of 'C' Company section, instantaneously killing seven men. There were no wounded, every man that was hit was dead. The bodies were laid beside the road for subsequent burial, but the violent scene cast a gloom over us all, and the men now tramped along in silence, where they had been whistling and singing before.

Having crossed the stream, we took up a position behind the bluff where we had seen the German infantry digging in the day before. They had, however, fallen back again for some distance, and there was the sound of rifle-fire among the orchards and farmhouses lying on the plain beyond.

An orderly came up with a despatch from General Fisher, so I rode towards where a red pennant, on a lance stuck in the ground, denoted his presence. As I emerged into the open I came under fire from some buildings six hundred yards away, and when I broke into a gallop two machine-guns spluttered as well, but I reached the spot safely, where the General was posted in dead ground, out of sight of the enemy marksmen. From here we could see the village of Ruesnes due north of us about two miles away, and to our left, at an equal distance, another village named Beaudignies. A mile beyond that lay the fortified town of le Quesnoy, a mediaeval stronghold with walls, battlements and moats.

As well as the scattered rifle-firing among the farms and apple orchards dotting the landscape before us, the German guns were sprinkling the plain on which we stood with shrapnel. Not far off were several British batteries firing over open sights at parties of German infantry, appearing and disappearing among the trees, and wounded men were dribbling back. General Fisher said the Oxford and Bucks Yeomanry were pushing up towards the Valenciennes Railway, and I was to follow immediately to lend them support. As I rode back to where I had left the RSF beside the river, relays of German aeroplanes came swooping low over the guns, straddling them with bursts of fire, and I saw several artillery men fall dead and wounded in the battery positions.

Shaw, Pud Robertson and I climbed a high point on the bluff to look over our line of advance. There were a few dead German infantry lying about, so each of us picked up a Mauser rifle, and next time the planes came overhead we potted at them. One machine banked so steeply that Shaw called out 'My bird, I think, sir,' but the plane righted itself and sped away.

We now deployed the battalion and moved forward across the plain in the direction of Ruesnes, keeping among the orchards to avoid observation from the German machines. My orders were to advance as far as a line which looked on the map like a sunken road. An occasional shell fell near, and rifle and machine-gun bullets whizzed through the trees, but we saw neither Oxford and Bucks nor German troops, and when we came to what we had thought to be the sunken road we found a muddy ditch running through a wood, with the village of Ruesnes only a hundred yards away. As we could not take position in the knee-deep ooze, and as I could see that Ruesnes was not held by the enemy, I ordered the men forward to a row of houses along the road leading to le Quesnoy.

Le Quesnoy, with its forts and walls, lay straight down the highway, and as we hurried across the cobbles, there came a rapid succession of whizz bangs from its battlements, and a fusillade of bullets from the viaduct arch nearer by. Of the Oxfords and Bucks, whom we had been sent to support, there was still no sign, and as we were being enfiladed, I ordered the company commanders to get the men into cellars as quickly as possible. While I was talking to Capt Andrews of unlucky 'C' Company about his casualties, a shell came howling up the street, missing us by a foot or two, and striking the kerb, where it burst into the thick of his platoon sheltering against a house. It killed five men and wounded twelve, and the blood splattered pavement was as gruesome a sight as I saw in the war. The wounded were carried into a cellar, and with more shells coming, the men of their own accord found cover quickly among the buildings. Shaw, Robertson, Keegan and I found a good cellar beneath a double-storeyed house, where we fixed Battalion Headquarters, and I then sent a runner back to report to General Fisher.

In the meanwhile we climbed up to the attic, and through a rear window looked across the intervening orchards to Bellevue Farm, standing beside the Valenciennes Railway. This was the line upon which, it was said, the Germans intended to make a fresh stand, and it looked like it, for we could see many newly-dug rifle pits in the open ground beyond the track.

Owing to the intervening trees we could not estimate their strength, but a mile off the slopes above Villers Pol were black with German troops, and it was clear that we were in touch with a strong line of resistance. The German guns were hard at work breaking down the houses of Ruesnes and its suburb in which we were, so we descended the stairs and squatted in the cellar listening to the muffled detonations above. At 2 pm orders came for us to advance as far as a line marked on the map as the outer edge of some orchards lying three hundred yards on the other side of the Valenciennes Railway. The order stated that the Oxford and Bucks had already established themselves on the far side, but if so it was not in our vicinity, for there were no British troops between us and the enemy.

As we moved forward we came under fire from a half-hearted rearguard on the railway embankment, and, advancing through the trees, we saw them retire at the double. With a loss of seven men we crossed the metals, and settled ourselves behind hedges and other shelter.

And now only a few hundred yards in front lay the prepared German position, a deep network of rifle pits, with reserve troops swarming at la Folie Farm and Villers Pol. We were screened from observation and I set the men to dig themselves in, for we could advance no further. I sent a runner who found General Fisher in Ruesnes, and I received a message in reply to say that aeroplanes reported the Germans in great strength before us and, pending further instructions, we were to stand firm.

All through the night, and indeed for the next four days, the Germans continued to bombard our area. They concentrated specially on Ruesnes, and on the street running to le Quesnoy, and they treated the fields and orchards to gas throughout our stay. So heavy was their fire that we concluded they were deliberately shooting off their ammunition to save the trouble of removal in case of further retreat. Our men in the rifle pits were well hidden, so we did not have many casualties from direct hits, but as it was impossible to live in box respirators our losses from gassing rose at such an alarming rate that in the four days ending October 29th we had to send two hundred and seven men to hospital.

During the first night, our old friends the New Zealanders came into line with us on the right, and as the 2nd Royal Scots and the 7th Shrops were on our left, we were in familiar company once more.

The New Zealanders, at their nearest point, lay within five hundred yards of le Quesnoy, still held by the enemy, and even at Ruesnes we were under rifle-fire from its walls. In view of the next attack that was to be delivered, divisional headquarters were anxious to know whether la Folie was occupied. I was ordered to send out a night patrol to investigate, and General Fisher explained to me the importance of our knowing more of the enemy's dispositions. He said I was to send a reliable officer with ten good men. I chose Lieut Barnekow, a Swede who had recently joined us from the depot. During the attack on Escarmain he had behaved with great courage, singing and dancing ahead of the men, and as he hailed from the Malay States (he was a rubber planter) I thought he would make a useful scout. His favourite witticism was to say that he was the only Swede who had seen active service since the days of Gustavus Adolphus, so they would have to make him commander-in-chief of the Swedish Army after the war.

He entered into the scheme with zest and stole off at midnight with his men. We heard shots towards la Folie Farm an hour later, but when daybreak came the patrol was still missing. Both Division and Brigade were calling for information, so I went to look for Barnekow. I crawled out among the trees, intending to reach a spot from which I had previously reconnoitred la Folie. As I scrambled down the bank of a sunken lane I found the entire patrol lying in various stages of gas poisoning. Barnekow was able to tell me that on nearing the farm they were fired on. They beat a retreat, and on their way back ran into heavy gas accumulated in a hollow. They had struggled along until the last man who could see gave out and they were brought to a standstill. Fortunately this happened in the sunken path, where the German riflemen in the pits close by could not observe them. It was only with great difficulty that the stretcher-bearers reached and removed them to the rear, and I never saw Barnekow again, for he and his men all went to the base. I recommended him for a Military Cross for his work on this night and his conduct at the taking of Escarmain, and he got it.

That evening Division called for another patrol. Aeroplanes had reported that la Folie now seemed deserted, and the higher command wished to verify this news, so I was ordered to push out a patrol at dawn. During the night the Germans fired so many gas shells among the orchards that by daybreak there was scarcely an officer or man who would be of any use as a scout, owing to the state of their eyes. Most of them were sitting in the rifle pits with tears streaming down their cheeks from the smarting gas, and only a few could face the light with uncovered eyes. I therefore decided to do the patrol myself, for my eyes were practically untouched. I wormed my way towards the German rifle posts in the direction of la Folie. The pits were clearly defined by mounds of fresh earth, and after a while, when I raised my head I found myself within a few yards of one of them. All was silent, and I noticed mess-tins and other equipment lying near, which made me think the Germans had withdrawn their line. I decided to make sure, and crawled anxiously forward, expecting to look down the barrel of a Mauser rifle at any moment, but I found to my great relief that the pit was empty, and several others to which I made my way were also abandoned. I now went on to la Folie Farm which was unoccupied, though at Villers Pol, a thousand yards away, many German soldiers were walking about, and I saw two machine-guns and their crews among the willows by a stream, which enabled me to fix their new positions. I was away for over two hours, and on my return was able to hand in a useful report. For this patrol I was mentioned in despatches and received a bronze sprig, the nearest approach to military honours I attained during the war.

Although we did no fighting, this period was by no means an easy one, for the gassing and the shell-fire were abnormal, and we spent an unpleasant and perilous time at Ruesnes.

On October 28th I went to la Chapelle with Watson, my runner, and a French officer named Berthier, to interrogate two civilians who had escaped from le Quesnoy during the night. They had nothing of importance to tell us and on the return journey Watson and I branched off to see how the New Zealanders were getting on. As we came within three hundred yards of the railway embankment the Germans suddenly put down a very heavy trench-mortar bombardment on a sector of the track. At the same time they severely shelled the orchards through which we were approaching. We saw the New Zealanders break for the rear, and then amidst the smoke and dust came numbers of German infantrymen, yelling and brandishing their bayonets. As the New Zealanders were running, Watson and I bolted too, through shells dropping thick among the trees,

until we came on a machine-gun pit in the middle of the next field, and we fairly
tumbled down upon the two men below. From here we saw the Germans moving about
on the captured railway embankment, and just as our two hosts were preparing to train
their gun, the British batteries came down, followed by the New Zealanders rushing
pell-mell to the counter-attack. There was some rifle-fire and throwing of bombs, the
Germans in their turn scuttling to the rear, and the situation was restored.

This little episode was the last fight I witnessed in the Great War.

That evening General Fisher sent over a copy of a captured document that was a
revelation to us. We knew that there were peace rumours in the air, but we did not
know how desperate was the condition of Germany. It was an appeal issued by
Ludendorff, '*Erst General-quartier Meister*', to the German troops. It read as follows:

> 'Soldiers, stand fast or Germany will lie in the dust. Should the enemy discover that our
> morale (*Mannzucht*) is broken, all is lost, you will have fought and suffered in vain and
> the Homeland will hear the tramp of the invader.
>
> Have you heard? (*Habt Ihr gehört?*) The British declare that Germany has fallen. They
> say our armies are defeated; that Hamburg is to be annexed; that Alsace will be
> appropriated by France; Schleswig-Holstein by Denmark; East Prussia, Posen and
> Silesia by the Poles! Our Empire is to be disrupted!
>
> Is this to be? (*Wollt Ihr das?*) Was it for this that your fathers and brothers fell in battle;
> was it for this that your mothers and wives and children suffered? MEN, was it for this
> that you endured four long years of war?
>
> No, a thousand times No! (*Nein, und abermals nein!*) Still stands it in your power to
> stave off disaster. Hold but for a few weeks more and a peace such as you desire we
> shall wring from the enemy.
>
> Soldiers, grasp your weapons proudly; let every shot tell!
>
> Thus far they have seen only German faces, shall they now see only our backs?
>
> Stand, or the Fatherland is doomed, and you with her.'

This cry of despair from the highest German command brought home to us more
than anything else how fast the sands were running out.

As always in France, our outlook had been restricted. We had been so preoccupied
with our own narrow horizon that we had forgotten we were but a fraction of the great
allied hosts that for the past month had been sweeping forward from the coast of
Belgium to the Swiss frontier, raining blow after blow upon the weakened German
armies. We did not know that behind the scenes, Hindenburg and Ludendorff were
faced with mutiny and civil war. That Austria and Turkey and Bulgaria had collapsed;
that the Kaiser was about to abdicate and flee his country, and that already the German
leaders were negotiating for a surrender.

The paper before us did not tell us all this, but it told us enough to show that the
mighty drama was hastening to its close, and that at long last the end was in sight,
though we did not know that the Great War had less than a fortnight to run.

On the 29th of October our battalion was relieved by the Staffords. It was high
time, for we had a bare two hundred men left. I was ordered to proceed by Romeries
and Solesmes to Bévillers, where a camp had been erected for our gas patients. When
we marched through Solesmes we were, I think, the first troops back from the firing
line of those who had helped to drive the enemy out of range, and the civilian
population warmly welcomed us. Flags waved and people ran cheering beside us. Our

pipe band played, and I rode at the head of the column with my tin hat cocked, pretending I was used to ovations.

At Bévillers we went into camp with the Royal Scots and the Shrops, also withdrawn from the line.

I had swallowed a considerable quantity of gas in the orchards at Ruesnes, and was far from well.

Here again General Fisher did me a good turn. He knew that if I went to hospital I would miss the end of the war, now plainly in sight, so he lent me a car instead, and suggested that I should take fresh air by paying a visit to my South African friends at the Abbeville Field Ambulance.

I went through Cambrai, which I had hitherto viewed only at a distance, with German troops between, and from there to my destination by what had been Bapaume and Albert. Along the roads were thousands of German prisoners at work salving shells and other war material, and already French peasants were returning to the devastated area to look for the places where once their homes had stood.

I spent three days at the Field Ambulance, and thanks to the care of Dr Brebner, of Johannesburg, my throat and lungs improved so much that I could start back. I found the battalion quartered at Solesmes; fresh drafts had come up and we were almost at full strength once more.

During our rest period, the Guards Division had driven the Germans from where we had left them at le Quesnoy and Ruesnes, and the British line was now much advanced. On November 10th, we went to a village near le Quesnoy, with instructions to move at dawn to reinforce the Guards, who were fighting in the direction of Maubeuge and the Mormal Forest.

Capt Gosling, our Brigade-Major, in handing me my orders, said a German delegation was crossing into the French lines to ask for peace terms, but the attack was not to be stayed on that account.

At daybreak on the morning of November 11th we marched out. In front and behind us were thousands of other troops going forward, and one could feel the suppressed excitement in the air, for every man realised that this was the final thrust. By 11 o'clock we were in the battle zone, British and German guns were firing, and there came the crackle of rifles and machine-guns ahead.

Suddenly, far off, we heard the faint sound of cheering borne upon the wind. It gathered volume as it rolled towards us, and then we saw our Brigade-Major slowly making his way through the troops on the road. He carried good tidings, for around him the shouts grew deafening, and when at last he came up, he handed me a despatch which I have carefully preserved. It contained momentous news:

'To 1st Royal Scots Fusiliers.
M2. 11 Nov.
Corps wire aaa Hostilities will cease at 11.00 hours to-day 11th Nov aaa Troops will stand fast on line reached at that hour which will be reported to Corps HQ aaa There is to be no intercourse with the enemy and no Germans are to be allowed to enter our lines, any doing so will be taken prisoners.
From 8th Inf Brig
11.00 hours   GH Ewing, Capt and Actg
                                                                                   Brig-Major.'

Amid the demonstrations of the other troops, the Scots Fusiliers remained comparatively unmoved. A few cheers were raised, and there was solemn handshaking and slapping of backs, but otherwise they received the great event with calm. To me it was a supreme moment. I saw the beginnings of a new era for the world and for my country. Splendid visions raced through my brain which I felt an urge to communicate. I told Shaw to form the battalion in a hollow square beside the road and, sitting my horse, I prepared to address the men. When I faced them, however, I was overcome with stage fright; the inspired thoughts of a moment before had vanished completely and I could only stumble through a few halting phrases. The ceremony was a failure, but at any rate the guns were silent, the war was at an end, and one could once again make plans for the future.

I was instructed to march for a neighbouring village and remain there till further orders, the other troops going in different directions in search of cantonments.

As we came in, an old French *curé* was waiting for us, and when I dismounted, he flung his arms around my shoulders, and to my embarrassment gave me a resounding kiss on either cheek, before the whole Battalion. The men tittered, but dutifully restrained themselves. Captain Hester, our Quartermaster, tried to hide his smiles behind his hand, and the *curé*, releasing me, made a dash at him, and imprinted two more hearty smacks on his rubicund countenance. The men had been too polite to laugh at their Commanding Officer in trouble, but they made up for it by bursting into a roar of merriment at Hester's discomfited looks.

That night we celebrated the armistice by a rum ration to the men, and at the *curé's* house we toasted the occasion with a similar round or two before turning in.

Next day I rode to le Quesnoy, which thus far I had only seen from the outside. The town was a picturesque relic of the Middle Ages, enclosed by a moat and battlements, ravelins and counterscarps. The streets were crowded with civilians and refugees from the surrounding countryside, who were housed in the subterranean galleries beneath the ramparts.

There was plenty of news. Up to now I had scarcely had time to grasp the full import of recent happenings, but I got a London *Daily Express* of the day before, which I still have. The mere headlines were staggering enough:

> 'German Envoys pass into French Lines at Château de Francport.
> Foch's Historic Reception in a train.
> Kaiser Abdicates and Crown Prince goes with him. Reported to have fled to Holland.
> Red flag waves over Ruins of an Empire.
> Revolution in Germany.
> Socialists in complete command. They set up a central Republican People's Government.
> Liebknecht released. Minority Socialists in control of Hamburg and Bremen.
> Everywhere troops and sailors acclaim the Revolution.
> Fighting with officers proceeding in Berlin. Workmen's and Soldiers' Council control the City. Policed by Red Guards.
> Red Flag on Kaiser's Palace.
> Hanover, Cologne, Brunswick, Magdeburg, Frankfort and other important centres declare for the Revolution.
> Bavaria an Independent Republic.

The King and Prince Rupprecht have fled.
Schleswig-Holstein a Republic.
Famine Threatened.
Austria in the Throes of Anarchy.
Hungary an Independent State.
British Warships anchor at Constantinople.
Greatest day in History.
We are the Masters of the Starlit Roads.'

On a back page was a short paragraph giving the approximate cost of the War:

Killed	—	10 000 000
Wounded	—	15 000 000
Expenditure	—	£30 000 000 000

It was borne in on me that for one coming from a small village on the South African veld I was in the midst of great events and I rode back from le Quesnoy with my head in a whirl, for Europe seemed to be in the melting-pot.

Chapter 16

We Go Into Germany

Now we were to march to the Rhine. Each unit forming the Army of Occupation was selected on its fighting record, and our whole IIIrd Division was included.

We started on the 15th November, the villagers shouting *'Vivent nos libérateurs, vivent les Ecossais!'* and waving flags.

We trekked to Frasnoy the first day, skirting by le Quesnoy. At Frasnoy our mess was billeted on a pleasant family, one of whom was a pretty little schoolmistress. The Germans had made her work in the sawmills of the Mormal Forest, and she held up her hands for us to see how hardened they had grown. *Mademoiselle* and the rest of the family fiercely hated the Germans. She hissed through her clenched teeth that they were *'des brigands et des brutes'*, but she told me of a colonel of artillery who had been quartered on them. On the last day he kept telephoning to the rear for *'mehr Munition, mehr Munition'*, and finally, as the British advance approached, his car drove up and he bade them goodbye. He said *'Mademoiselle*, there come the English, you will soon be liberated, and happiness awaits you, but I go to sorrow and ruin.'

He drove off, accompanied by a young lieutenant, and as they were leaving the village a shell struck the car, killing them both. *Mademoiselle* said she regretted his death, for he had been kind to them.

From Frasnoy we marched to Maubeuge via Bavay. As soon as we got clear of the village we found the road thronged for miles with allied prisoners of war, who had walked out of their camps, their German guards having disappeared. There were men from almost every nation. We saw British, French, Americans, Italians, Serbs, Roumanians and Belgians streaming by, mostly in rags and half starved, but smiling cheerfully as they passed. Mingled with these, came thousands more of civilian refugees returning from Belgium (whither they had been removed). They trudged by with bundles or pushing barrows and handcarts, and so great was the congestion that at times we had difficulty in making headway at all.

I shall always remember this day's march, for it was like a triumphal progress. The sun shone brightly, our pipe band played merry tunes, and I rode at the head of a splendid battalion.

All along our course the prisoners and refugees cheered us, and often crowded round, nearly pulling me from my horse in their efforts to shake hands. The children clapped and crowded at the sound of the pipes, and their mothers held them up to see the soldiers go by, and in spite of their pinched faces, due to the trials which these poor people had endured, something of the courage of France still stood in their eyes.

Once, while we were halted on the road, a tattered figure stopped to look us over. He was dressed in an old French tunic, and he had wooden clogs on his feet. The men took him for a French prisoner of war, so they saluted him with the usual cries of '*Boche napoo, guerre fini, vive la France!*' during which the fellow quizzically surveyed them, then he said in broad Scotch: 'Ahm frae Glesgie maself—cheerio, lads,' and there was a roar of delighted laughter.

We reached Maubeuge by dark, going into billets in the Mon Plaisir suburb along the River Sambre.

Our method of finding billets was for an officer and a party of men to go ahead in the morning on bicycles to the place at which we were halting for the night. They called on the *Maire* and told him how many billets were required. As a rule the men were quartered in threes and fours on families, and whether in France, Belgium or Germany, the system worked satisfactorily. The men liked being with the civilians, who washed and cooked for them, and who in turn benefited by sharing their rations. Besides, it was the fixed custom for each billet to contribute a small sum of money on departure.

At Mon Plaisir we occupied a large house belonging to people named du Haut. The daughter, Solange, came to tea at our mess, and her artless prattle so captivated one officer's susceptible heart that for a long time after he carried on a correspondence with her, mostly dictated by me, for his French was limited.

Solange told me what I had not known before, that in August 1914, General Fournier had surrendered Maubeuge to the Germans with its garrison of forty-five thousand men and seven hundred guns. She said he was prevailed upon to do so by the wealthier classes, who wished to save their property from the perils of a siege, and the citizens were going to demand a court-martial on him.

From Mon Plaisir suburb we marched through Maubeuge, entering by the great archway. We went with the pipes skirling, and hundreds of citizens following us through the streets. We crossed the Sambre by a temporary bridge for the Germans had destroyed the other, and then left by the gateway at Malplaquet Barracks for Ferrier le Grand about four kilometres distant, where we halted for five days. This long delay was meant to give the German Army time to fall back in terms of the armistice conditions, and whenever we pressed too close upon their rear we had to lie over to give them more room.

At Ferrier le Grand, General Fisher borrowed a car from Division, and lent it to Henderson, Burne and me to drive to Brussels to see the King of Belgium make his entry. Crossing the Belgian frontier, we went first to Mons, now occupied by Canadian troops. Henderson had taken part in the Mons retreat in 1914, and he pointed out many places along the road where there had been fighting during the first weeks of the war.

The Belgian population in the towns and villages and at the farms, were decked in their Sunday best, and they cheered us at every turn as we sped by. The houses were gay with bunting, and across the streets and roads stood beflowered arches with inscriptions in French, Flemish and English. The English greetings read: 'You are the welcomes'; and there were large *médaillons*: '*De tous les Gaules, les plus braves sont les Belges. Julius Caesar.*'

Other placards on the walls and arches gibed at the unfortunate Kaiser:

> '*Guillaume II*
> *Roi des Barbares*
> *Chevalier des Bouffeurs de Choucroute*'

and there were caricatures of him, and of the Crown Prince, hotly pursued by Belgian soldiers.

When we reached Brussels the entire population was on the streets, wild with enthusiasm. Our car was boarded by pretty girls wearing their national colours, and Belgian Boy Scouts clung to steps and mudguards to show us the sights.

We arrived too late to see King Albert, but we spent an interesting day. Of all the troops, the French contingent made the bravest show. They were neater and marched better than the British battalions, whilst the Belgian soldiers looked slovenly and untrained.

General Leman, who had defended Liège, rode at their head, bowing to the populace, who gave him a frantic welcome. After the King, Burgomaster Max was the most popular figure, and then Cardinal Mercier.

We were astonished at the countless number of flags that draped the buildings, and the innumerable scrolls and mottoes on the walls, and we wondered where they had come from so suddenly. A waiter at Joseph's famous restaurant explained that a German firm at Mannheim had made the best of a bad job by manufacturing them, and the moment the last German soldier had left Brussels, they flooded the country with allied flags and inscriptions of welcome, making huge profits.

In the afternoon we went to Waterloo to see the battlefield. I had been here as a boy of twelve, and I showed my two companions where French students had pulled off the British lion's tale many years ago.

An old woman who sold postcards said that on the eleventh the German soldiers posted here had mutinied. They mobbed their officers, broke up their machine-guns, and went off with red cockades in their caps.

When we got back to Brussels, the newsboys were distributing leaflets containing a message from Burgomaster Max, of which I kept a copy:

> 'CITIZENS. On behalf of the Municipal Council I make known that Brussels, after having been occupied by the Germans since Aug 20th 1914, has at length been freed.
> Defeated by the victorious armies of civilisation, the enemy is now fleeing before the

bayonets of our soldiers.

Our victorious troops have entered the Capital.

Amid them, our King and Supreme Chief of the Army, the Queen and the Royal Family, pass saluted by our delirious acclamations.

Our flags are flying.

Our eyes are wet with tears; our hearts beat tumultuously in our bosoms.

Happiness beyond bearing; happiness unbounded!

Four years of misery beneath the invader's heel are effaced.

And let one united oath affirm our joy.

We have recovered our independence.

Let us swear to render our country great and true.

Vive la Belgique. Vive le Roi. Vive l'armée.'

That evening we returned to Ferrier le Grand via Nivelle and Manuge. We passed several abandoned German lorries, and at one point there was a large German bombing plane standing on its nose in the middle of the road, which caused us some difficulty.

From Ferrier, on the 25th November, we crossed the Belgian frontier and marched to Boussignies, an old-world hamlet lying in wooded hills. The château about which the village stood was fiercely burning. The inhabitants were looking on unperturbed, and when I enquired why they viewed the destruction of their chief building so calmly they told me that the retiring German soldiery had set it alight in the belief that it belonged to a Belgian landowner, whereas it really belonged to old Fraülein Weber, lately dead, whose three heirs were Prussian officers.

From Boussignies we went through the fortressed burgh of Thuin, perched on a height overlooking the Sambre, and thence to Cozee and Tarciennes. All along the way the road was strewn with the litter of the German Army ahead of us, and we passed dozens of Schutte Lanz motors, field guns, and other wreckage.

From Tarciennes, on November 28th, via Hanzinelle to Denée. At Hanzinelle stood a park of a hundred and fifty heavy guns, and a hundred and fifty machine-guns neatly aligned beside the road, in charge of German soldiers. Under the armistice agreement, surrendered war material was to be collected at stated intervals, and this was one of the places agreed upon.

I had not originally known the full text of the armistice conditions, but they had since appeared in the English newspapers that came up with our mail. The terms were almost as harsh as those of the Austrian ultimatum that started the war.

'Germany had to surrender:

Five thousand guns.

Three thousand aeroplanes.

Five thousand railway engines.

One hundred and thirty thousand railway trucks.

Their entire fleet except squadron flagships.

The whole of their merchant fleet to be at the disposal of the allies to revictual Europe.

Mainz, Coblenz and Cologne bridgeheads to be handed over.

Strasbourg and Metz to go to France.

All German troops withdrawn forty miles east of the Rhine.

Allied prisoners of war to be delivered at once.

War indemnity to be fixed by the Allies.

Poland to be an independent Republic.'

Hard terms for a proud nation.

At Oret we passed three hundred motor lorries and long lines of railway trucks laden with surrendered material. Close to Denée we found six Fokker aeroplanes standing in a row, and in the same field a number of Halberstadts, but these were burnt out.

At Denée I was billeted in a béautiful château. It belonged to a Belgian aristocrat, Frédéric de Montpellier, a relative of the King of Spain. He and his wife and their two fine boys gave us a hearty welcome. They were very religious and there was an altar on the main staircase at which there was generally one or other of the family kneeling in prayer. I saw a signed photograph of the Pope, and numerous crucifixes and other Catholic emblems. We dined in a magnificent baronial hall with good paintings and old panelling, and oaken beams.

On November 29th we crossed the River Meuse, at Yvoir, marching through very lovely country, like the scenery on the Thames. On our way along the river bank we again passed many derelict motor cars, and at Bioue were six Fokker planes and other damaged machines.

At Yvoir the Germans had thrown guns and limbers into the river below the lock, and we could see wheels and barrels protruding above the water. They had, besides, left machine-guns and trench mortars in the streets, and in the flower gardens in front of the houses. At the railway station stood a train loaded with 5.9 guns and two captured British tanks.

I was quartered in a neat little villa opposite the lock, whose owner told me that the Germans had executed a number of inhabitants of Yvoir in 1914, to keep the rest quiet, he said.

On November 30th we marched up the steep road leading from the river to the village of Spontin, passing searchlights, repair lorries, and other flotsam on the way. Spontin had been destroyed by the Germans in 1914. I had never believed all the German atrocities of which one read in the British newspapers during the war, but they had certainly acted with ruthless severity against this unfortunate little place. They had entered Spontin at daybreak on the 23rd of August 1914. Alleging that the villagers had fired on them, they burned down every house. Then they arrested the *Maire*, the *Curé*, and forty-eight other men, and executed them against a bank at the railway station. The gravestone of each dead man in the little cemetery above the village reads '*victime de la terrible journée du 23 Août 1914*', which was all that the survivors dared write on the tombs during the occupation of the enemy.

An old lady, in whose half-burned house I was lodging, showed me the spot in her back garden where her husband's brother and their servant were shot dead as they rushed out to escape the flames.

We stayed three days at Spontin to allow the German retreat to get on. Most of the men lived in a deserted manor house close by, for Spontin was in ruins.

I visited a château three miles away, belonging to an old man of eighty-two, lying bedridden upstairs. He told me he was the Belgian Minister of the Interior.

On December 2nd I rode to Dinant on the River Meuse. This town too had been destroyed in August 1914, and here over four hundred townspeople had been executed. At the various spots where the shootings had been carried out there were painted notices, put up since the Germans had left:

'Ici les hordes Saxonnes ont martyrisés nos Innocents.'

On December 4th we marched to Braibant, where I stayed in the house of a Belgian nobleman, Baron de Selys Longchamps. The Baron was a quiet unobtrusive man, but his wife was a keen politician. She waxed very fierce against the Flemish activists, whom she accused of treachery. She said that they put their race and their language before their country, and instead of standing by Belgium, their mother, in her need, they had divided the nation in time of war. It sounded to me like a very good description of some of our nationalist friends in South Africa.

Madame la Baronesse prided herself on having no class prejudices. She said *'Quoique nous sommes nobles, nous sommes libéraux,'* which she seemed to think was an unheard-of combination. When I asked her about the massacres at Dinant, Spontin, and elsewhere, the concentrated fury on her face made me realise the terrible legacy of hatred that the slaughter of so many civilians has left among the people of these territories, through which we were passing.

From Braibant we marched to Nettine via Ciney, again passing much war material—motor cars, aeroplanes and caterpillar tractors. Next day we reached Melreux, crossing the River Ourthe. At Melreux was a German supply dump, the biggest I ever saw. Rows of guns and limbers, great stacks of shells, harness, saddlery, cookers, uniforms, etc, worth millions of pounds. It was an extraordinary collection. The German soldiers had partially looted it, and had smashed valuable range-finders, field glasses and other articles, and around the goods trains lay the contents of boxes and crates, scattered with prodigal confusion for hundreds of yards.

7th December. To Soy, via Ny. Billeted in the post office. The postmistress said she had been allowed to carry on her duties unmolested all through the war. She told me the German soldiers that came through two days before had fought among themselves and there were shots fired in the village. The men put up red cockades and hooted their officers, derisively calling them *'Kamerad'*.

8th-9th. To Malempré in rain and snow.

10th. To Provedoux, close to the border of Germany. Slept at Salm Château, a rambling country seat, whose owner told me that he had assisted many French prisoners of war to escape through the woods to Maastricht in Holland.

On December 12th we crossed the German frontier at Beho. General Deverell stood by the boundary stone to take the salute as the men filed past. Most of the British battalions crossed into Germany on a wide front on this day.

We spent our first night on German soil at Espeler, a poverty-stricken village where the inhabitants stared dully at us.

The woman I was billeted with said her husband and three of her brothers were dead, and nineteen other men from here had been killed in the war. She favoured Germany becoming a republic.

From Espeler, on the 13th, to Braunlauf, an equally wretched little place.

14th. Long march to Schönberg via St Vith, a fairly large town. The people in the streets of St Vith raised their hats, but here and there I caught sight of better-class German women gazing through the windows at the invading troops, despair written on their faces.

I entered the post office to ask for a *Kölnische Zeitung*, as I wished to see how the revolution in Berlin was getting on. The clerk behind the counter said the newspapers belonged to subscribers and I could not have one.

He was a good specimen of officialdom. His country was tottering about his ears and through the open door he could see a hostile army marching through his town, but when I insisted on having a paper, he produced a set of postal regulations and pointed me out a clause that prohibited the handing-over of printed matter without written authority from the addressee. When I vaulted the counter and helped myself from one of the pigeon-holes, he looked as if the heavens were falling.

Many disbanded officers and soldiers stood about the streets and they punctiliously clicked their heels and saluted me, as I rode by with the Regiment.

15th December to Hahlschlag.

16th. To Blankenheim. This town was a centre of boar hunting, and most of the photographs on the walls of the hotel where I was quartered showed groups of sportsmen posed beside dead hogs.

17th. To Münstereifel, a walled town that looked in the snow like a Christmas card. In my bedroom at the Gasthof-an-der-Posten was an illuminated scroll painted on the wall to say that the 'Hochseelige' Kaiser Frederick had occupied the chamber in 1847 when he was a Corps Student at Bonn.

As we moved out of town the following morning, we passed a shop with a large sign over the door, '*Mathias Reitz, Schumacher*', and I heard one of my men in the ranks behind say in a stage whisper that he 'didn't know the Colonel was a Boche'. Later on, in the Cologne telephone directory, I found dozens of them, for my people originally came from these parts, four hundred years ago.

18th December. To Obergarten. In the dining room of the house I was billeted in was a book entitled *Deutschlands Seemacht*, with pictures of dreadnoughts and submarines. On the front page was an inscription to the effect that the work had been presented to 'Tertianer' Franz Muller by His Majesty the Kaiser, who had evidently been in the habit of presenting books of this kind as school prizes, to encourage the youth of Germany to take an interest in the navy he had built up, and which now, according to the newspapers, was in the process of being handed over to the British.

19th December. Marched to Disternich via Zülpich. Visited a fine old country mansion surrounded by a moat, where General Fisher was staying. The place, *Muddersheim*, belonged to Von Gehr, a German artillery officer just back from the war. He was very polite, and his wife, who spoke perfect English, came down the wide staircase beautifully gowned and smoking a cigarette.

On December the 20th we reached Merzenich, a small town on the outskirts of Cologne, and we now received instructions that we were to go into winter quarters here for an indefinite period.

We therefore settled down. The men were billeted on the people, and I requisitioned an hotel for the officers. I foisted myself on old Arnold Haase, the richest landowner in these parts. He was very friendly, and his wife looked after me like a mother.

Cologne and all the neighbouring towns and villages on the left bank of the Rhine were being occupied by British troops. Below us were Belgian forces, and upstream a French army of occupation was taking over the other bridgeheads.

In Berlin and elsewhere in Germany there was civil war and revolution, but owing to the presence of the allied soldiers there was peace along the river, although there had been riots and fighting in Cologne and Düren before our arrival.

Arnold Haase told me that when the retreating German troops came through they were a disorganised mob carrying red flags, and selling their arms and ammunition to the Bolshevist industrial workers at the factories. Marines from Bremershafen had terrorised the whole area, with the help of a band of riff-raff from the paper mills, and any officer who ventured to show himself on the streets was insulted and stripped of his insignia.

There was a Workers' and Soldiers' Council in Merzenich—*Arbeiter und Soldaten Rat*, as they called themselves; *Angst und Sorgen Rat* according to Haase. Their leader was a one-legged blacksmith who had been wounded at Verdun. He claimed that all landed estates should be divided among the people, greatly to my host's indignation, who declared that the fellow had stolen one of his pigs the other night.

There was an army order to arrest all Bolshevists, but these village orators seemed so harmless that I let them be, and sometimes attended their meetings, held in a large barn. On one occasion the blacksmith made a violent attack on Hindenburg and Ludendorff. He referred to them as *'diese verdammten Hetzbrüder, mit ihrem Siegesfrieden'* (those damned firebrands with their Victory Peace). He said anyone could have foretold last April that Germany could not hold out, for the people were starving, but these two sabre rattlers had pushed the country into a disastrous offensive by promises of a great victory, with peace to follow. There was something to be said for the ranter's opinion, as I had seen broadcasted photographs of Hindenburg bearing a signed message: *'Ohne Opfer kein Sieg' ohne Sieg kein Friede'* (Without sacrifice, no victory; without victory, no peace), and certainly he and Ludendorff had helped to lure the nation to its doom.

In a tobacconist's shop which I entered in Düren was a notice of a football match between the local *Verein* and some other team from a village close by. A revolutionary walked in, and tearing down the placard said angrily to the proprietor: 'Is this a time for sport? I suppose the shooting-down of the sailors was sport too!' He was referring to the killing of a number of marines in Berlin that morning, the news of which had just come through, and soon there were a number of other men shouting and gesticulating around the unfortunate shopkeeper.

My duties at Merzenich were light. I was responsible for the administration of the town and the area around it, with the *Burgermeister* and his councillors under me. The people addressed me as *'Herr Orst Kommandant'*, and respectfully doffed their hats when I passed.

As I had plenty of time on my hands, I often rode into Cologne. It is a fine city with its cathedral, and great iron bridge spanning the Rhine. At the entrance to the bridge is a statue of the Kaiser, after whom it was named.

I went across the river several times to see the wired strong-point on the far bank.

One morning every wall in Cologne was placarded with an appeal from the Moderates:

> 'Must a nation of whom 90 per cent desire peace and liberty and work bow to an armed minority of revolutionaries?

Is nothing to be spared us; have we to drain this cup of bitterness to the dregs?
STOP THE CIVIL WAR.
STOP THE STREET FIGHTING.
Let a National Assembly be constituted.'

Not that there was any fighting in the occupied area along the Rhine, but there was turmoil in the rest of Germany, and dozens of rival political parties were in the field. It was all very confusing, but the attitude of the British was to keep aloof and let the Germans fight out their domestic quarrels among themselves.

I met civilians and also ex-officers and soldiers and was able to listen to their experiences during the war, and to their opinions of Germany's present plight. Several times I heard the view expressed that submarining passenger steamers and bombing towns was no worse than the allied blockade, which also killed women and children and non-combatants.

Once I fell into conversation with a German cavalry officer newly returned from the Ukraine. He had crossed the Russian border only three days before and he said that on December 21st he had seen about forty Russian officers massacred at Kiev. They were hauled out of their camp by their men, and shot or clubbed to death at the railway station. He was obliged to sell his horse to a peasant to buy food, and when he ultimately reached the Russian frontier he was deprived of his arms and money, and the buttons and shoulder straps were slashed from his uniform. He had passed through Berlin on his way to Cologne, and when I enquired how things were going there, he shrugged his shoulders and said: '*Na, in Berlin revolutioniert man noch immer.*'

Old Haase sometimes took me the rounds of his estate in an antiquated motor car with steel springs round the wheels instead of rubber tyres, which had been unprocurable all through the war. He also invited me to a deer hunt on another property of his in the hills, but I was unable to go.

He had been a mighty Nimrod in his day, for the walls of his house were hung with antlers, boar heads, stuffed pointer dogs behind glass and other trophies of the chase. He looked on me with great respect because I told him of the big game I had seen in Africa and because I praised von Lettow. His one great fear in life was that the German war loans would never be repaid, and as he had sunk a vast sum in them his anxiety was justified. His wife was a homely body, and I ended by calling her 'Ma', a title which she smilingly accepted.

I was surprised at the attitude of our men towards the Germans. When we were marching through Berlin I used to hear snatches of their talk. They were angered by the stories they had heard at Spontin and other places of the German treatment of the civilian population, and they were going to do this and that to the —— Boche when they got to the Rhine. But now that they were here I had trouble in preventing them from giving away the entire contents of the battalion store-room to the local inhabitants, and there was the utmost good feeling among them.

We celebrated Hogmanay Nicht in the riotous fashion demanded by the regimental tradition of the Scots Fusiliers, and I was piped round next morning with a terrible headache, to toast the New Year at the messroom of each of the four companies.

I spent the first fortnight of 1919 attending to my duties, and riding about the country that lay all blanketed in snow.

The prospect, however, of spending the rest of the winter in these bleak surroundings was unattractive, and now that the excitement of war was gone, reaction had set in, and I was eager to return to South Africa. I applied for leave to proceed to London for the purpose of getting demobilised, and with the help of General Fisher my request was granted.

Then I rode over to the neighbouring villages where the 2nd Royal Scots and the 7th Shrops were quartered and there said goodbye to Henderson and Burne, and to the men of the two battalions with which I had been so intimately associated.

Next I parted from Shaw and Robertson, Keegan, Sleep and Hester and Corporal Noble, and many other good friends, and from the men of the 1st Royal Scots Fusiliers, and I was done with the Great War.

To me it had been terrible but not degrading, and I came away with a higher, not a lower opinion of my fellow men. My chief memory is of great friendships and of millions of men on both sides, who did what they thought they had to do without becoming the brutes that some writers say they were.

After visiting Düren to take farewell of General Fisher and General Deverell I travelled by train via Charleroi and Liège to Boulogne, and crossing by the channel leave-boat for the last time, arrived in London in due course. I soon found that it was easier to get into the British Army than to get out of it, and I spent several weeks frequenting the corridors of the War Office with hundreds of others, all vainly trying to get their demobilisation papers.

During the intervals of importuning the higher powers, I made several visits to General Botha and General Smuts, who were making ready to attend the Peace Conference at Versailles. General Botha had just arrived from the Union for the purpose. He looked ill and worn, for the long strain had told upon him, and the knowledge that so many of his own race misunderstood his actions and looked upon him as an enemy was breaking his heart.

He said to me that remembering how we had tasted the bitterness of defeat in days gone by and how the sting had been softened by magnanimous peace terms, he and General Smuts were opposed to a treaty that would leave the Germans a broken people.

Of the position in South Africa he spoke sadly. He said narrow men were still conducting a relentless racial campaign that was dividing the people, and a united nation was far off.

He died soon after his return to the Union, and I did not see him again. He was the most honourable and most lovable man I ever knew. From that night of the Spion Kop battle, eighteen years before, I had been his follower, and in South Africa we who hold his faith are still treading the road upon which he set us.

I grew weary of official delays, and as I was informed that it would be months before my turn came on the roster, I manœuvred three months' leave of absence and went to America, a country I had always wanted to see. I left on a troopship carrying the famous Sunrise Division, and I made many friends among the officers and men.

On my return to England in June 1919 my demobilisation papers were ready, and I was free to go home.

The *Guildford Castle* was sailing for Capetown with seven hundred South Africans returning from the war, and I was OC Ship.

There was the usual battle at Madeira with the Portuguese *gendarmes*, in which some of our men came off second best, but otherwise the voyage was pleasant and uneventful, and at length we saw Table Mountain rise out of the sea, with all Africa and a new life stretching away behind it.

NO OUTSPAN

by

DENEYS REITZ

With a preface by

GENERAL THE RIGHT HONOURABLE

J C SMUTS

Foreword

During the Boer War of forty years ago the writer of this book joined the republican army at the age of seventeen as a private guerrilla soldier and he remained under arms throughout that struggle. For much of that time he served under me and he and I had many exciting adventures and narrow escapes.

At the conclusion of hostilities he went into self-imposed exile to Madagascar rather than submit to British rule. There he endured great hardships and ultimately a letter from my wife found him to say that if South Africa, even under the Union Jack, was good enough for her husband, it was good enough for him.

The shot went home. Young Reitz made his way back to the Transvaal.

He was so racked with fever that my wife and I kept him for three years until at last he was restored to health and able to strike out for himself.

In the years that followed he came to see that for South Africa the only solution was co-operation between the English and Dutch sections of the community and he believed that this could only be effected inside the British Commonwealth.

Therefore when the last great war broke out in 1914 he threw himself wholeheartedly into the conflict.

He served under me once more in the campaigns in West Africa and East Africa after which he went to France where he ended up in command of a famous Scotch Battalion.

He was severely wounded but he returned to lead his battalion to the Rhine after the Armistice in 1918.

Of all these events Deneys Reitz has given a vivid account in two previous volumes. Now he has rounded off his further experiences in this book which is the story of his share, and to some extent my own share, in the public life of this country during the past twenty-five years.

It covers a period in which he and I were closely associated in a long-drawn struggle against political forces which we considered it our duty to oppose.

But of set purpose he passes lightly over these troubles and he has given us instead an entertaining narrative of his activities by sea and land and air in the course of which he has succeeded in proving, as he puts it, that in spite of our quarrels, South Africa is a country of good temper and good will, with the hope of a united nation to come.

J C Smuts

Pretoria
South Africa
December 1942

Contents

Chapter 1

After the Armistice

I

On the morning of 11th November 1918 British troops went into action in France near le Quesnoy and the Mormal forest. It was a stirring scene. Infantry marched to the attack; guns roared; rifles and machine-guns crackled; and the stage was set for another of those bloody battles that had been so frequent during the past months.

But there had been rumours of peace in the air of late and it was said that German envoys had crossed into the French lines with proposals for an armistice; so each man knew that he might be taking part in the final stroke of this particular Armageddon.

And as we were coming under fire from a village ahead, after several hours of orders and counter orders, we heard from afar the sound of cheering borne upon the breeze. It gathered volume as it came towards us; then we saw our Brigade Major riding through the press. The news he carried was obviously good for the shouts grew deafening as he made his way, and when at last he was near enough, he leaned from his saddle and handed me a dramatic message.

It was a hastily-pencilled note from Headquarters, and it said that as from 11 am hostilities would cease. Battalions were to stand firm on the ground held at that hour and there was to be no fraternising with the enemy. (I have since framed this document and it now hangs at our regimental mess in Ayr.)

Something like a hush fell upon the entire front as we realised that the Great War was over at last. Other battalion commanders received similar instructions and precisely at eleven the advance slowed down and then came to a halt. It was a supreme moment and, feeling an urge to communicate the splendid thoughts that raced through my brain, I swung my men into a hollow square, intending to address them on the mighty significance of the day. But as I sat my horse facing them, I was seized with stage fright, and after stumbling through some halting phrases I gave it up. If the ceremony was a failure, at any rate the fighting was over, the guns were stilled, and we had survived the war, an eventuality many of us had long ceased to believe in, so great had been the butchery.

On every hand we could now see troops pitching camp or marching to the deserted villages dotted around, in search of billets, and from what we could make out, the German soldiers across the way were doing the same. We made for a little French hamlet named Romeries where the *curé*, to my embarrassment, rushed out as I alighted and gave me a resounding kiss on both cheeks, while the men tittered at my discomfiture.

That night we celebrated the end of the war with a rum issue to all ranks. Afterwards, as I lay in my sleeping bag pondering the future, I made up my mind to return to South Africa at once. I did not anticipate any difficulty, because in former campaigns as soon as the business was ended we had proceeded home without further ado, each man going off on horseback, train, or ship, as suited his convenience; and I thought it would be the same now.

I discovered my mistake the very next morning, for instead of packing my kit, I received orders to lead my battalion into Germany as part of the Army of Occupation that was to hold the bridgeheads of the Rhine pending a settlement of the peace terms. In the upshot it took me eight months to get demobilised. For the moment, however, I was not unduly damped as the prospect of seeing fresh countries at the head of my regiment was pleasant enough.

In about a week we were ready. The Army of Victory, as it was called, 60 000 strong, was assembled, and we started away in parallel columns on a wide front, banners waving, bands playing, and the troops in high fettle. After some days we entered the liberated zone beyond Maubeuge where the French inhabitants had lived under German military rule for several years. We were greeted with frenzied delight. The people crowded around us with shouts of '*Vivent les Alliés; vivent les Ecossais*' and the women and girls embraced the soldiers, who received these demonstrations with sheepish grins. Riding in advance, I might have come in for a lion's share, but fortunately we had a kilted pipe band in the van, and the drum major with his embroidered facings, his Scotch tunic and the magnificent swing of his baton, was taken to be the commanding officer and drew most of the fire.

The population had fared harshly under martial law; they looked pinched and starved, and their joy at being freed from bondage was a touching thing to see.

Leaving France behind us, we entered Belgian territory where much the same conditions prevailed. We went by Thuin and the river Sambre, through the Ardennes, then across the Meuse by Spontin, Dinant and Salm Château, and we listened to many a sad tale of the indiscriminate shooting of civilians during the first weeks of the war. At the village of Bého we passed across the frontier into Germany. Our Divisional Commander, General Deverell, took the salute as we marched by and from now onward we travelled in sullen hostile country. Nonetheless, to lead a fine regiment through invaded territory with the pipes askirl and the colours floating in the sunshine was not without its thrill; and to sit one's horse looking down upon the populace came as near to 'riding in triumph through Persepolis' as is given to the average mortal.

At length, in a fortnight or so, we reached the outskirts of Cologne and we went into winter-quarters, with all the world blanketed in snow (a sight which never fails to surprise a South African, even after long experience of it).

I was billeted on a local magnate named Haase at Merzenich. He and his wife treated me well and the townsfolk called me '*Herr Kommandant*' and doffed their hats when I rode by. I frequently went into Cologne to see the Cathedral and other places of interest and I visited the British outposts and wired strong-points on the far bank of the Rhine.

Thus December passed, and we celebrated Hogmanay Nicht in the riotous fashion of the Scots Fusiliers. Next morning I remained in bed with a fevered brow, praying to be left in peace. Towards midday however I heard our pipe band beneath my window and looking out, saw my second-in-command, Major Shaw, gingerly dismounting from his horse; soon he was climbing the stairs and knocking at my door. If possible, he looked worse than I did and to my horror he informed me that custom ordained us to be piped round the four units to toast a New Year bumper with each of them. I groaned, Shaw said he felt like hell too, but we could not fail the Battalion on a point of national honour such as this; so I dressed and got on my horse and we rode the round and drank four stiff rum toddies in succession, the eyes of the men fastened upon us.

Shaw and I carried grimly through and I believe we emerged creditably enough from a frightful ordeal. I went teetotal after that for two years.

As the weeks passed, I tired of the bleak winter conditions and the monotony of garrison life; and our Brigadier, General Fisher, a man of understanding, granted me furlough on the basis that when I reached London I was to apply for my discharge. So on a given day I took my leave of the 1st Royal Scots Fusiliers. With them I had witnessed great events. In their company I had lived in the trenches and withstood the German spring offensive of March 1918 in which I was severely wounded. After long months in hospital I had returned to the Battalion in time to see the Hindenburg Line, the strongest military system in history, battered down by British troops, and thereafter I had commanded the Fusiliers in the concluding battles of the war.

I had lost many friends and now I was bidding farewell to those who remained and, looking back across the years, I remember with pride my service with this fine Scottish regiment.

I travelled by rail via Charleroi, Liége and Boulogne and thence by leave-boat to England. I arrived in London at night to find all the streets ablaze. I had been there only in wartime when everything was in darkness after sunset, so it took me some time to readjust myself to peace conditions. I called at the War Office the very next morning, thinking in my innocence that I would be given my papers, after which I proposed catching an outgoing mail steamer to Capetown. A preliminary brush with the clerical staff inside disabused me as to this and I began to realise that it was much easier to get into the British army than to get out of it.

On my first arrival in England, long ago, I had presented myself at a recruiting office, signed some papers, and was enlisted at once as a private. Now I found that there were many thousands of applicants before me and that I was to await my time. I was told that it would probably be a question of months, for the government could not loose millions of men upon the country as the process of reabsorbing them into civil life must necessarily be a gradual one. This was reasonable enough but it made my vision of an early return to South Africa fade into the distance. I decided to make the best of a bad job, so I roamed the streets of London, visiting museums and theatres and art galleries and dropping in at the War Office every other day to see how I stood.

One morning when I was queuing up at Whitehall on the off-chance of having word of my affairs, a band of angry ASC men rushed through the archway into the quadrangle, shouting protests at demobilisation delays. To me their outburst savoured of mutiny, but a young guardee subaltern of nineteen or so with three wound stripes on his arm came out and faced them. He ordered them to fall-in; to stand to attention and to tell-off by numbers, and so ingrained had become their sense of discipline through years of war that they instinctively obeyed him. He told them what he thought of their conduct, right-about-turned them, and they went away without a murmur. Then with a bored expression on his face he disappeared inside.

During these weeks I went to Hyde Park to a memorial service for the dead. It was a dignified ceremony 'with pomp and rolling music like a king'. There was a tall mound of wreaths, each bearing a message. Some were:

In memory of my dearest sweetheart killed in France 10 November 1918.
In memory of my dear son, torpedoed on the *Aragon*.
To the memory of Private J—G—killed in action 1917. I loved you in life, I love you
still. Your dearest friend J—M—
Torpedoed on the *Hawke*.
Killed in East Africa.
Killed in Palestine.
Killed in Salonika.
Killed in Suvla.
To the honoured memory of my five sons killed in France. The flowers of the forest are
a' wede awa'.

On 6 March 1919 I motored out to beyond Winchester with General Dawson of the
South African Brigade and we saw at a distance the rioting of the Canadian troops
owing to more demobilisation grievances. Five men were killed and thirty-five
wounded and hutments and buildings were fiercely ablaze.

While I was thus at large, General Botha, our Prime Minister, arrived from South
Africa on his way to the conference at Versailles, and I received a message asking me
to call on him at the Savoy. I went at once and found him discussing the peace
negotiations with General Smuts. They were perturbed at the trend of things. General
Botha said that we in South Africa had experienced the benefit of generous treatment
of the vanquished by the victor, and he and General Smuts agreed that it was a
mistaken policy to impose humiliating conditions on a beaten enemy.

I listened to them with absorbed attention for these two men and had counted much
in my life. General Botha I had first seen on the night of the Spion Kop battle more
than eighteen years ago, when he appeared among our shaken discouraged men to
wrest victory from defeat. In the long travail of the Boer War he was our commander-
in-chief and he was steadfast and unwavering to the end. In later years I learned from
him the faith I still hold: that for South Africa the only path is one of friendship
between the English and the Dutch, and eventual fusion into common nationhood.

As for General Smuts, I had served under him in the old guerrilla days as a boy,
and we had experienced many dangers and adventures together. Afterwards I stood
with him in German West and German East; and no shadow has ever fallen upon our
long friendship.

They said they had need of me when I returned to South Africa and on this note
we parted. I did not realise it at the time, but this meeting was a turning point in my
life.

II

My demobilisation still hung fire so I went to Ireland. Dublin was dirty and
neglected owing to the unsettled times, and Sackville Street lay in the ruins left by the
Easter rebellion. On the day I arrived, the Countess Marcowitz was welcomed home;
she had just been released from an English gaol for her share in the rising, and was a
local heroine. There was an enormous crowd to meet her. Wooden platforms had been
erected from which Sinn Fein leaders addressed the multitude. The Irish are natural

orators, and for the moment I was thrilled by their eloquence, but turning it over in bed at my hotel that night, it seemed to me that the talk had mostly been of 'The Harp that Once', of Ireland's former glories and of ancient grudges. So far as I could remember, no speaker came within a century of her present-day troubles and problems.

During one stage of the war, I had served with the 7th Irish Rifles in France and it struck me then as it struck me now, that the Irish politically resemble our Dutch-speaking element in South Africa. We too are more concerned with sentimentalisms of the past than with the practical questions of to-day and to-morrow.

I remember how the Irish soldiers sitting around their braziers in the trenches had talked politics whilst German shells howled overhead; and I remember that one night, as I was going the rounds with my batman, Private Freeney, I asked him what it was all about. He summed it up by saying: 'Sorr, it's the prastes and the politicians is at the bottom of all our troubles in the ould counthry.' *Mutatis mutandis* the same can be said of us in South Africa.

There was danger brewing in Dublin. Tanks patrolled the streets, bombing planes droned overhead and the people were in a surly mood. One morning while I was there, the English papers featured concessions the British Government intended giving to Ireland, but the Sinn Fein leaders would have none of them. They placarded Dublin with huge notices 'Damn your concessions, we want our country' and the press fiercely denounced Great Britain and all her works.

I was wearing then the cutaway tunic and the tartan breeks of the Scots Fusiliers. This evoked unfriendly comment as I walked about, and one morning at breakfast, several hardfaced men came in and sat themselves at my table. They demanded to know who I was, where I hailed from, and why I had mingled in the crowds last night.

I told them I was a South African, that I had fought against the British in the old days, and that I had served in France. One of them truculently said that by wearing an English uniform I was wearing the garb of a slave. I replied that in South Africa there were neither conquered nor conquerors and that we were a freer nation within the British Commonwealth than we had been under our own Republics, but they glowered at me and refused to be persuaded. They were, I suppose, a kind of vigilance committee sent to interrogate me and after somewhat threatening advice they left me in peace.

At night, errand boys ran selling broadsheets with patriotic ballads. Most of them were strongly anti-British, others reflected the brooding melancholy of the Irish temperament. Of this type I kept a few:

Irish Warriors

They went forth to battle and always they fell;
Their eyes were fixed above their sullen shields
They were not weak as one who vainly yields
A futile weapon; yet the sad scroll tells
How on the hardfought fields always they fell.

The O'Rahilly 1769

Now may we turn aside and dry our tears,
And comfort us and lay aside our fears.
For all is gone—all comely quality
All gentleness and hospitality
All courtesy and merriment is gone;
Our virtues all are withered every one
Our music vanished and our skill to sing,
Now may we quiet us and quit our moan,
Nothing is whole that could be broke, nothing
Remains to us of all that was our own.

On the Irishmen Executed in Dublin, May 1916

Pray every man in his abode
And let the church bells toll,
For those who did not know the road
But only knew the goal.

Let there be weeping in the land
And charity of mind
For those who did not understand
Because their love was blind.

Let no harsh voice applaud their fate
Or their clean names decry—
The men who had not strength to wait
But only strength to die.

Their errant scheme that we condemn
All perished at a touch:
But much should be forgiven them
Because they lovéd much.

Come all ye to their requiem
Who gave all men can give
And be ye slow to follow them
And hasty to forgive.

And let each man in his abode
Pray for each dead man's soul
Of those who did not know the road
But only saw the goal.

From Dublin I went to Belfast to stay with a friend I had met in the war and I spent a week there. In the course of it I came to the conclusion that the South Irish have a more passionate love of country, but it is coupled with an unbalanced emotionalism, while the Northerners are practical and levelheaded. If I were an Irishman, my strongest desire would be for an undivided country and an undivided nation but it seems to me that the way of the South is the way of that woman in King Solomon's judgment who preferred the child to be sawn in two rather than compromise with the other claimant.

On returning to London my discharge still hung in the wind, so I took a voyage to the States. Many troopships were conveying American troops back from the war and I secured a passage on one of them.

I embarked at Plymouth and we made, first of all, for the French port of Brest, to take on board 1 500 troops of the Californian Sunrise Division.

At Brest lay a fleet of German merchantmen surrendered under the armistice. Among them were the Cunarders *Kaiserin Augusta, Viktoria, Graf Waldersee, Mannheim*, and *Kribi*, all fine big vessels.

As soon as the soldiers arrived we set sail. I was surprised to find that President Wilson was unpopular with these men. They said he was at Versailles without a mandate from the American people and a young officer described him to me as a visionary without vision. During the voyage the men gave a concert one night and their comic man told us that France had fought for Glory, Britain for More Land, and America for Souvenirs, a statement that was borne out by the many German helmets, meerschaum pipes and other trophies the buddies carried with them.

After a pleasant crossing we reached New York. Strange and new to me were the tall buildings, the perpetual noise of trains and trams and the clanging of bells throughout the night. I watched the American Grand Fleet come in from the war and I wandered about New York, Boston and Washington for a fortnight. I had always longed to visit the country but now I fell into a mood that was probably a nervous reaction after four years in the field. I became homesick and caught a returning troopship to England.

We had a delegation of Japanese military officers with us, on their way to Versailles. They were cultured, well-educated men who outwardly conformed to Western standards, but I witnessed an amusing lapse. Their chief invited me to join them at tea next morning. At the appointed hour the following day, when I was ushered into their state cabin by an orderly, my host had apparently forgotten about me; for when I entered I found him and his fellow officers squatted on the floor and they were eating strange little cubes of what looked like dried fish from a newspaper spread between them on the carpet. My appearance put them out of countenance for a moment, then they rose and smilingly bade me welcome. They said they were so tired of European food that they were having a blow-out on Japanese army rations for a change. Later we headed into a terrible gale and were glad to make Liverpool alive, although in a raging blizzard.

At the War Office in London long queues were still patiently lined up, but South African demobilisation affairs had been transferred to Winchester; there, in June 1919, I obtained my papers at last and was free to return to my country. I was ordered to embark on the *Guildford Castle*, a ship I knew, for she had brought me from le Havre to England after I had been wounded the year before. She was carrying six hundred South African officers and men back to Capetown and I was appointed OC troops. Soon after we sailed it dawned on me that I was invested with a delicate task. In commanding soldiers on active service one has the legal sanction of the King's

Regulations to fall back on but with hundreds of discharged men unattached to any unit there was no machinery to enforce discipline and I had to rely on moral suasion alone. Luckily for me, officers and men behaved splendidly and my only trouble was a battle at Madeira.

When we cast anchor at Funchal I allowed everyone to go ashore to see the sights. I went too, but after a while I hired a rowboat and returned to where the *Guildford* was lying out in the roadstead and throwing off my clothes I dived overboard and swam about in the warm sea. After a spell there came angry shouts from the direction of the land, so I trod water to see what was amiss. I saw a crowd of our men engaged in an affray with Portuguese soldiers and *gendarmes*, swords and bayonets were flashing in the sun, and there was a great deal of noise; so I swam to the ship, dressed hastily, and was preparing to take a boat to the jetty, when a tug came alongside bringing all our men. Some of them were cut and slashed and most of them were in a bad temper, for having been unarmed, they had come off second best.

The heady *vinho tinto* of the taverns was at the bottom of the trouble. Flushed with this potent liquid a few of the South Africans had started a brawl. Others joined in and when the Portuguese intervened there was a heated *mêlée* at the pierhead which might have ended more seriously than it did had not the harbour tug opportunely come up. This enabled our men to beat a retreat and they returned to the ship with a dozen casualties and ruffled feathers. So ruffled, indeed, that a number of them, still under the influence, demanded from me the keys of the magazine as they intended to arm themselves and to clean up the island. I conferred with the ship's captain who immediately got under weigh, and only then did the tumult cease.

Next morning the delinquents came to apologise. In doing so, one of them said: 'All the same sir, it's the first time I have ever come aboard from a foreign port without a policeman's helmet.' He had a bayonet wound across his forehead but he regarded this as nothing compared to his failure to carry out a time-honoured custom.

From Madeira was a clear run to the Bay, and with Table Mountain rising from the sea and all Africa and a new life stretching beyond, I make a digression.

Chapter 2

Family Affairs

I

In the year 1791 my great-grandfather, Jan Frederick Reitz, emigrated to the Cape. He was a naval officer in the employ of Holland and he had taken part in the battle of Doggerbank and other actions against the British.

He must have had friends at court for he came out with papers (which I still possess) signed by the Prince of Orange himself, the then *Stadtholder*, which probably explains why he secured a lucrative post at Table Bay. In addition to such patronage as he may have enjoyed, he had more business acumen than any of his descendants have since possessed for he grew to be a considerable landowner and he prospered exceedingly.

When the British captured Capetown in 1806 he was relieved of his perquisites but he cherished no rancour for, having raised a family, he sent his sons to be educated in Edinburgh.

One of these was my grandfather, Francis William Reitz, born in 1806. It was intended that he should be christened François Guillaume but the English Chaplain of the fleet, the only divine who was on hand, being unable to spell the French appellation, took it upon himself to compromise on an English rendering—so runs the story in our family.

My grandfather inherited a large estate and many slaves. He became a member of the Legislature and a Justice of the Peace and like other grandees in those spacious times he kept open house; the result being that when he died at a ripe old age most of his acres were gone. He left little land but many children. One was my father, Francis William Reitz the second, born in 1845 in the Cape Colony. By the date of his birth, great events had been shaping the future of South Africa.

Soon after the capture of the Cape by the British, discontent began to spread among the Dutch colonists, or Boers, as they were called. There was an unsuccessful rising in 1815 and the execution of the ringleaders coupled with long native wars and the emancipation of the slaves resulted in that strange exodus known as the Great Trek. Thousands of Boers abandoned their farms, loaded their wagons, and with their wives and families, their flocks and their herds, they shook the dust of British governance from their feet and headed for the uncharted wilds of the North.

Knowing my countrymen as I do, I think the cause of their leaving was not so much hatred of British rule as a dislike of any rule. For nearly two centuries they had been pioneers in wild country, each man a law unto himself. They had to rely upon their own resources against savage tribes and savage beasts, and they had become a race of individualists acknowledging no authority save that of their flintlocks. They had chafed at the tyranny of the Dutch East India Company and they were equally resentful of British domination, so they moved into the unknown. It was an epic wandering. During the years that followed, lost to view, they trekked across the plains that lie north of the Orange River and, making their way over the ranges of the Drakensbergen, they descended into what is now the province of Natal. There they fought and eventually conquered the powerful Zulus, the bravest and most warlike nation in Africa.

The battles, massacres and hardships they endured have become matter of history and in the end they established the Transvaal Republic in 1852 and the Orange Free State in 1854. During all these years my grandfather remained quietly on his land like most of his neighbours, for the Great Trek was the work of the more nomadic Boers further inland. He raised his large family and when his sons, including my father, were old enough they in turn were sent to Scotland to be educated.

My father returned to the Cape in 1870 having qualified as a barrister. Before settling down he became a diamond digger, entered the Cape Parliament, and married a beautiful Norwegian girl. Then he practised at the bar and in 1875, the infant Free State Republic having set up a Supreme Court of its own, he was offered and accepted the position of its first Chief Justice.

He and my Norwegian mother started by ox-wagon for their new home, a journey that took them nearly three months, and thus it came about that my brothers and I were born and bred in Bloemfontein, the Free State Capital. There were five of us, two older and two younger than myself, and we led a carefree, Tom Sawyer-like existence. There was no piped water, no railways, telephones, or electric lights, and motor-cars and aeroplanes and wireless were still undreamed of. We had a string of Basuto ponies in the stables and the wide uplands teemed with game; so we hunted, fished and rode to our heart's content.

Sir John Brand was President of the Republic; when he died in 1889, my father was elected in his stead and to us boys life became even more interesting.

The country was run on simple lines. When my father wished to summon his Executive he sent my brothers and myself on horseback to collect the members of his Cabinet from their distant farms, and on arrival they lived with us until the deliberations were over, after which they went as they had come.

Sometimes my father had to go on long tours through the country districts and we accompanied him, riding our ponies beside his state coach. He was invariably escorted by a squad of mounted artillerymen. We proudly fell-in with the gunners and we looked at the ancient Krupp muzzle-loader they took along with them as part of the family plate, so to speak.

In the back blocks, commandos would assemble to greet my father and we sat on the roof of his coach to watch the shaggy horsemen galloping by, firing blank charges from their Martinis as they came. At the conclusion of these parades the men dismounted and the President had to walk down the line to shake hands with all of them. On one such occasion there was a family joke that we never forgot.

It was my father's custom to say to each burgher as he went down the line 'good day, good day, how are you?' To which would come the stereotyped reply, 'Very well thank you, Mr President,' whereupon his said, 'I'm glad, I'm glad,' and passed on to the next man. But once when he asked a greybeard how he did, the old man answered, 'Sir, my wife died last night,' and my father automatically said, 'I'm glad, I'm glad,' and moved on unconscious of the brick he had dropped.

In such manner life flowed easily enough, and we spent a happy childhood. But this idyllic condition was too good to last. Unknown to us, storm clouds were gathering. Up North in the Transvaal, there was increasing friction between the older Boer population and the newcomers who had flocked into the country on the discovery of the gold fields. In the Free State we had hitherto lived on a friendly footing with the British but in 1896 Dr Jameson's ill-starred Raid changed everything overnight and where goodwill had reigned, now came suspicion and distrust. My brothers and I were too young to realise it but the Jameson Raid was a harbinger of war in which we were to be deeply involved and which was to shatter our little universe entire.

II

The chief result of the raid was to convince the Transvaal and Free State governments that the British meant to conquer us. A mutual treaty was made, arms and ammunitions were imported in large quantities from Germany and France, and defensive preparations were made.

While these ominous events were shaping, our family affairs underwent a change.

My mother died, and in 1896 my father resigned the Presidency of the Free State owing to ill-health. When he recovered we moved to the Transvaal. He was appointed Secretary of State, the second highest position in the country and my brothers and I were put to school at Pretoria.

For the next two years diplomatic relations with Great Britain ran downhill and even in our classrooms we talked of little else than the approaching conflict.

My father naturally took an active part in the negotiations and in the drafting of despatches to the British authorities. I frequently accompanied him to President Kruger's house, where they discussed the situation and I sat an interested listener. At length in October 1899 the storm burst. War was declared and the two republics entered upon their long death struggle. As for myself I was seventeen and I went straight from my classroom into the thick of the fighting, and so did my brothers. The war lasted for nearly three years. The Boers put up a heroic resistance but our leaders, in their blind love of liberty, had pitted us against overwhelming odds. We scored a few spectacular successes in the earlier stages but the weight of men and guns and the power of the whole British Empire were too much for us and at length we were beaten to our knees. In June 1902 peace was made. I went through an exciting time, fraught with dangers and hardships, and had many adventures and many narrow escapes of which I have written elsewhere.[1]

The declaration of peace found us a scattered family. My father had remarried years before and my stepmother and her young children were refugees in Holland, as was my youngest brother Jack who had gone to the war at the age of twelve. My two older brothers were prisoners of war in Ceylon and Bermuda and my father and I and my next younger brother were the only ones still under arms when the end came. We refused to accept the peace terms and Lord Kitchener ordered us to be put over the border into Portuguese territory. From there my father went to the United States and my brother and I to Madagascar, under the French flag.

I eked out a precarious existence for some years, riding transport by ox-cart from Tamatave to Antananarivo, and my brother went to Mauritius. Ultimately I received a letter from Mrs Smuts, wife of General Smuts, in which she said that her husband, together with Generals Botha and Hertzog and the other Boer leaders, were at work rebuilding our country from the ruins of the war and if South Africa under British rule was good enough for them, it was good enough for me.

This turned my thoughts strongly homeward, though I could not at first reconcile myself to submission. I attempted to work my passage to America on a tramp steamer as I wanted to find and consult my father. I got as far as a port in the Red Sea but I was wretchedly ill from long-continued bouts of malaria; and after having been knocked about in a brawl with some of the crew, I gave in. I obtained work on a southbound cargo boat and with considerable difficulty managed to make my way back to the Transvaal.

I was a physical wreck and had not General Smuts received word of my condition it would have gone hard with me. For the next three years he and Mrs Smuts kept me in their own home and for their help and understanding in those dark days I have not sufficient words of gratitude.

---

[1] *Commando* by Deneys Reitz.

In the years that followed, my father learned that the British were treating us generously and he too returned, and one by one my brothers drifted back. Slowly we picked up the threads of life, and our family began to retrieve itself from the tragedy that had overtaken us.

Meanwhile South Africa was marching onward. In 1910 the Act of Union merged the two British colonies and the two former republics into a single state, and with General Botha as our first Prime Minister it looked as if there was to be peace and unity at last. But the Dutch are an intensely race-conscious people, as determined to maintain their separate identity as are any of those fierce little Balkan communities that have given the world so much trouble. Before long there came rumours that General Botha's policy was too pro-British and that it would lead to our being swamped by the English-speaking section of the population.

The differences increased and opposition against General Botha and General Smuts became widespread. General Hertzog, who had also taken a prominent part in the war, seceded and formed a separate group to combat the South African Party which general Botha had created. These quarrels rent South Africa for many years.

I passed my law examinations and I settled down to practise in the village of Heilbron in the Northern Free State, and before long I was dragged into the political vortex. Tempers ran so high that it was almost impossible to keep out of the ring; I supported Botha and Smuts while the Free Staters went over to General Hertzog almost to a man so I found myself wellnigh alone.

I endured stormy days in the years that followed and at many an angry meeting I was howled down and roughly handled. I made a host of enemies and lost many friends in the course of this senseless feud. Then came the outbreak of the Great War and with it our bigotries came to a head in the shape of a rebellion.

The insurrection started with the capture of the village in which I lived. I escaped under cover of dark, and collecting a band of adherents I made my way to the Transvaal where I joined the government forces under General Botha. It took us several months to quell the rising and there were heavy casualties on both sides. General Botha and General Smuts treated the captured rebels with leniency and thus ended this unpleasant affair. Thereafter I served in the campaigns in German West and German East and then I was in France until the armistice.

Now I have come full circle, and I return to the *Guildford Castle* approaching Table Bay.

Chapter 3

Capetown Politics and Zululand Travels

I

During the years of the Great War, our political quarrels had come to look so petty and so narrow that I scarcely gave them a thought and, as I stood on deck, I told myself that nothing would induce me to take part in them again.

But politics, South African politics at any rate, are a habit-forming drug, like alcohol. Even as the ship was berthed, two Cabinet Ministers and a dozen Members of Parliament came aboard, all talking at the same time of the elections and of the iniquities of our opponents. In a few minutes old ties reasserted themselves and before I walked down the gangway I was committed to the fray.

The troops were landed and we marched through the streets of Capetown amid cheering throngs to the city hall where the Mayor addressed us. Then each man set out for his near or distant home and I returned to my quiet village of Heilbron. I led a settled life for some months, but towards the end of 1919 a General Election was on hand. I was summoned to Pretoria by General Botha and he and General Smuts reminded me of our discussion at the Savoy. The result was that I undertook to stand for Parliament, a decision that was to alter the current of my life for many years.

The political outlook was not reassuring. General Botha had founded the South African Party at the time of Union in 1910 and it had been in power ever since. His followers comprised the moderate Dutch and practically all the English-speaking citizens.

On the other side stood the Nationalist Party led by General Hertzog, a formidable antagonist. He was supported by a large percentage of the Dutch whom we accused of intolerance and racialism but who knew their purpose, and their strong racial sentiment carried further than our humdrum appeal to common sense.

The Great War with its nationalistic revival among the smaller nations had given our opponents a tremendous leverage. They had gone from strength to strength and it was disturbingly clear that the South African Party was on the down grade. To counter this, delegates came from all over the Union to attend a gathering at Bloemfontein at which General Botha was to preside.

On the appointed day a vast crowd was assembled in the hall and when he entered we rose as one man to cheer him. He looked ill and worn. In Paris he had fruitlessly striven against the peace terms and the strain of this, following the tension of the war, had undermined his health; as he spoke we realised that he was a stricken man.

General Botha told us in homely words of his desire for peace and for unity. We listened to him with rapt attention but we were hearing him for the last time. A week later he died. In the sorrow of this great loss we were fortunate in having General Smuts to step into the breach, and he became Prime Minister.

The elections now began. Rural orators thundered from every platform; newspapers conducted heated propaganda, and we of the South African Party expounded the gospel of peace and goodwill in language as violent as that of our enemies whom we accused of disseminating hatred and discord; the country was in a turmoil. It was almost worse than the trenches. I held scores of rowdy meetings, fought three strenuous (and expensive) contests within a year, and when the shouting and the tumult died I found myself a Member of Parliament. General Smuts offered me the Portfolio of Crown Lands and Irrigation.

The campaign had been a furious one and the South African Party emerged in a weakened condition, but with a small majority that still enabled it to carry on.

At this long distance it hardly matters, but the new government was made up as follows:

General Smuts, Sir Thomas Smartt, Colonel Mentz, Mr Patrick Duncan, Nicolas de

Wet, Sir Thomas Watt, F S Malan, H Burton, and myself.

So now I was a Cabinet Minister, with dominion over palm and pine, as it were, for I was given charge of all the public domains of South Africa. These lie chiefly in the remoter regions; there are jungles and deserts and swamps; there are forests and high mountain ranges and little-known tracts inhabited by wild beasts and wild men. It was a fascinating task, but there was a fly in the ointment. With our party daily losing strength and with our Nationalist opponents coming strongly up behind there was insecurity of tenure and my new kingdom was a precarious one. However, I was sworn in by the Governor-General Lord Buxton and before him, in April 1921, I promised allegiance to His Majesty King George V and I took my seat in Parliament.

Years afterwards some legal pundit discovered an Act which imposed a fine of so much *per diem* on any man who sat in Parliament or in Cabinet without being a British subject and it was charged against me that having refused the terms of the treaty of Vereeniging in 1902 I was neither a British subject nor a Union national.

The penalties were cumulative and by the time my offence was unearthed I had incurred a debt approximating to the German reparations, and a special Bill was hurried through the House to absolve me.

But all this was still in the future, and meanwhile I sat through my first Parliamentary Session at Capetown, rather bored by the monotonous debates. As soon as the Session ended I decided to go off on a tour of inspection by way of introduction to my work. From now onward, during the years I was a Cabinet Minister, across other years when I was a private Member of Parliament, and when I held office once more, I was able to see and hear many things; and in the following pages I am recording such of them as seem of interest. It is of these I wish to speak rather than of racial and political differences which mar the happiness of our country; and I intend to leave aside as far as I can the trivialities of party strife. I decided to go to Zululand first of all for I had heard much of the territory but had never visited it before. Accompanied by a few departmental officials I travelled by rail to Durban from where our journey proper was to start.

This was my first ministerial essay and I was new to public honours. On the way from Capetown to Durban I was met by delegations on the platform of nearly every wayside halt and by mayors and magistrates and party leaders. I sat back and pretended I was accustomed to this sort of thing.

From Durban the road took us north through the lovely coastlands of Natal and at the village of Stanger, after some days, we reached the southern border of Zululand.

II

Zululand is a delectable duchy. South to north it runs from the Tugela River to Portuguese territory and west to east it lies between Swaziland and the Indian Ocean. It is the home of the Zulus, the finest and bravest and fiercest aboriginals in Africa.

Up to not many years ago there were scarcely any Europeans here and its northern parts are still almost unknown.

Due to recent development of the sugar industry there are now large coastal tracts under cane between the Tugela and the Umfolosi rivers and here a number of white planters have settled; but beyond the Umfolosi there were as yet no Europeans except officials and a few traders and missionaries.

The history of Zululand has been a long record of intertribal wars and of wars against the Boers and the British, but to-day there is peace.

My first introduction to the Zulu past was at the village of Stanger. Walking about one morning outside the village I was shown the grave of Chaka, the savage monster under whom the Zulus first rose to power. The grave was an unkempt hollow within a rusted fence put up by a settler to keep his cattle from trampling upon it. The graves of the other Zulu kings are piously tended and they are always marked by thickets of euphorbia trees, yet the body of Chaka, the greatest of them all, lies in an empty corn pit where it was thrown when he was murdered nearly a century before.

I was interested and I have collected information about Chaka. He was born in 1785, son of Senzanagakoma, a petty chief, and Nandi was his mother, so the missionaries say. At the age of sixteen he took service in the army of Dingiswayo, the then Zulu king, and incidentally their first king I have been able to obtain any knowledge of. Chaka showed such courage that he rose high. There is a legend that he owed his subsequent career to an Englishman, Dr Cowan, who in 1809 was sent by Lord Caledon, Governor of the Cape, to seek an overland trade route to Delagoa Bay. Cowan, it is said, reached Port Natal, where Durban now stands, by ship and from there he made his way to Dingiswayo's kraal. He was hospitably received and remained there for six months. The Zulus say he told Chaka that British troops conquered by the use of the bayonet and Chaka remembered his words.

Ultimately, so runs the tale, Dr Cowan went towards Portuguese East and he was murdered by the Quabe clan on the Maputo river. He was charged with sorcery. The witch doctors accused him of having crossed the ocean in a shell and of having demanded elephants' tusks for food, so he was put to death.

When Dingiswayo died in 1816 Chaka, though not of the royal blood, murdered the heirs and seized the vacant kingship and he made good his title by effecting a change in their fighting methods that revolutionised native warfare in South Africa. Before his time each warrior was armed with a bundle of throwing spears which he hurled at the enemy from a distance, and if these failed their purpose, he decamped. Chaka, bethinking him of the British bayonet, did away with all this. In place of the lighter weapons he introduced the dreaded *iklwa*, a single broad-bladed stabbing spear to be used only at close quarters, and he insisted on stern discipline.

With his new-model army he took the field and his soldiers swept all before them. The javelin-throwing tribes could not stand against his *impis* wielding the weapon he had devised, and his name was a terror in the land. He conquered such subordinate Zulu forces as ventured to oppose him and enlisted the survivors in his ranks. When he had sixty thousand fighting men under his command he started upon a bloodstained course beyond his own borders and his regiments harried far and wide. They raided deep into the Eastern Cape Colony and on the plateaux where the Transvaal and Free State provinces subsequently arose, they destroyed the native inhabitants to such an extent that even into our times the scanty population of the high-veld bears witness to their ferocity.

Chaka gave no quarter. In six years, so it is said, more than three millions fell victims to his stabbing spears; and having eliminated his foes, his blood lust turned upon his own people and he killed for the sake of killing. If a warrior dropped his shield on parade, Chaka ordered him to be cut down. If Chaka fell ill, twenty were strangled to ease his pain. When his mother Nandi died, six thousand men and women were clubbed to death. If a European trader ventured to the royal kraal two hundred were executed to impress the visitor with his omnipotence.

Accounts are extant by men like Isaacs and Fynn and Captain Gardiner of the Royal Navy, who witnessed many of his atrocities, and they calculate that he put to death more than eighty thousand of his subjects before Nemesis overtook him. He went so long unscathed because by Zulu tradition a commoner may not lay hands upon a king, no matter how heinous his conduct.

But in 1826 his two brothers Dingaan and Mahlangaga took courage. One evening as Chaka sat gloating over a fresh pile of slain they crept up on him from behind and drove home the stabbing spears he had himself invented. The Zulus have it that on receiving the mortal thrusts he stood up, and seeing who his assassins were he exclaimed 'Sons of our father, what is this ye do,' and like Caesar, he bowed him to his fate. His corpse was wrapped in a green ox-hide and contemptuously thrown into the corn pit where it still lies.

I asked an old Zulu headman why they do not honour his grave and he said: 'The other kings slew to maintain law and order, but he killed out of wantonness, so he alone lies unhonoured.'

Chaka was succeeded by Dingaan, a man scarcely less cruel than the man he had murdered. He made the mistake of attempting to match himself against the Boer pioneers who from 1836 onwards began to cross the Drakensbergen into Natal. He lured their leader and sixty of his men into his kraal at Umgunghlovu and brutally massacred them, and his *impis* killed hundreds of their women and children. But the remaining Boers exacted stern retribution. They mustered only eight hundred men and this small force defeated his armies and burnt his capital in 1838.

Dingaan fled north and after wandering destitute for months he was murdered on the Pongola river by the natives living there.

He was followed by Panda; Panda by Cetewayo, Cetewayo by Dinizulu and Dinizulu by Solomon the present king.

III

At Stanger I was delayed for nearly a week, discussing local problems of which, as I was to learn during my term of office, a fertile crops springs up whenever news gets round that there is a Cabinet Minister in the neighbourhood. After that we forded the Tugela and we went via N'Gunghlove (the place of elephants) to Eshowe. We rode across grassy savannahs and, further inland, the green hills of Zululand rose tier upon tier towards the western mountains. Kraals dotted the slopes and herds of sleek cattle grazed on all sides. Frequently we saw parties of Zulu on the road, both men and women splendidly built. The young bloods carried shields and the short-handled spears that Chaka had bequeathed them, and they wore ostrich feathers in their hair.

From Eshowe we rode to the Nkwalini river, through good cattle country, but at present unoccupied, and then to Ntambanana, crossing two more rivers where we had trouble with our horses, for the streams ran broad and strong.

From here we turned east to the ocean, making for Richard's Bay to examine its possibilities as a port. Our course ran by several rivers and by palm-fringed lagoons where hippo and crocodile lay basking on the sandbanks. We decided that Richard's Bay was not suitable for a harbour, but we feasted royally from an oyster bed we came upon.

Some distance out, the remains of a ship lay in the surf and George Higgs, a planter who had ridden down with us, told me the following story:

The wreck was that of the *Newark Castle*, a passenger steamer that had gone ashore during a storm in 1906. Of five hundred passengers and crew only three reached land. They were the first mate, a Major Boyd, and a French lady he had dragged to safety, thinking she was his wife. No European lived along this coast, but a party of Zulus appeared, headed by an old *induna* who by signs ordered them along. Finding themselves in custody of beplumed savages with shields and assegais, the unhappy castaways made sure they were for the cooking pot. Higgs on his distant estate was informed of the wreck by his natives, for news travels unaccountably among them, and he went on horseback to see. After a long ride he came on the procession; the woman in tears and the two men plodding along, gloomily resigned to their fate. When they saw him galloping towards them, rifle in hand, they knew they were saved and their relief was unbounded. The French lady in her joy bestowed on the *induna* a gem-studded watch she had found in her pocket after the rescue.

The old Zulu chieftain accepted the trinket and turned it over carefully in his hand. Then he squatted down and with the point of his spear he prised open the cover and scooped out the works, after which he emptied the contents of his snuff horn into the receptacle and put the jewelled case to that use ever afterwards.

Higgs said further that among the flotsam thrown on the beach was a watertight chest filled with wads of French bank notes with a face value of fifty thousand pounds. He retrieved this booty and thought he was made for life. He tried to cash in on the Banque de France but that institution refused to pay up and when he went to the Courts he was worsted. He still thinks he was given a raw deal.

From Richard's Bay we turned inland and then north to the Umfolosi river. This stream approaches the Indian Ocean through a vast papyrus swamp stretching as far as the eye can see. A portion of the delta has been reclaimed and here is a settlement of planters who grow sugar cane for the mills.

I had been advised at Capetown that heavy rains up country were threatening mischief in the Umfolosi area and word now came that the floods had reached the plantations. It seemed that the river had brought down a multitude of logs and uprooted trees which had formed a jam in the recesses of the swamp, threatening to submerge the canefields and ruin the settlers.

Hurrying forward we found everyone away. Men, women and children had gone off to the danger point and as a guide and a boat awaited us, we set out. We were rowed through a network of winding channels and creeks shut in by walls of dense papyrus. Now and then we emerged into open water where hippo splashed; and once, as we went beneath a high bank, a dozen or more crocodiles that had been lying asleep above plunged over the side within a few yards of us, dangerously rocking our boat and sending a cloud of spray over our heads.

By four in the afternoon we arrived at the scene of action. We have a saying in South Africa that a 'practical' farmer is one who expects practically everything to be done for him by government. But the Umfolosi men had not waited for government assistance. They had tackled the job themselves. They cut and hewed a way through the swamp until they reached the obstruction, and finding that neither fire nor explosives could shift the barrage they set to work to dig a canal round the north flank to release the imprisoned waters.

When we got there the canal was nearly completed and shortly after, the last men were withdrawn to allow the remaining few yards to be blown away with dynamite. There was great excitement. The planters and their families stood out of range as the charges were touched off. With a roar these did their work. A tall column of mud spouted skyward and now the pent-up flood came racing through, with driftwood swirling by and crocodiles turning cartwheels in the current that swept them along. We even saw a hippo battling against the stream, a comic look of dismay on his ugly countenance as if he could not make out what was amiss.

We watched the widening gap for a long hour. Then we rowed back and as we went, we could see by the tidal marks on the papyrus stems that already the waters were receding and that the settlement was saved.

Next day, after much rejoicing, we crossed the Umfolosi at a point above the swamps. We travelled north, passing the Duku-Duku forest, and from there to Somkele and the Hlu-hluwe plains.

We saw plenty of big game; large herds of blue wildebeest, zebra and other antelopes; also a black rhino and lion spoor, but no lion. Beyond the plains we halted on the banks of the M'Kuzi river at the mouth of the Ubombo gorge. I went after birds with a shotgun when we had pitched camp and below the krantz I came on a number of human skulls and bones scattered about; when I made inquiry on my return I was told that this was the battlefield of Itshana where in 1884 Dinizulu, with the help of Boer auxiliaries, had defeated Usibepu. I remembered that many years ago, seated around a fire one night during the South African War, General Botha had told us of this battle in which he had taken part.

IV

Usibepu was a minor chief who in his youth had commanded a regiment in Cetewayo's army.

Cetewayo was born in 1829 and he became King of the Zulus in 1873, having succeeded Panda who in turn succeeded Dingaan who murdered Chaka. In 1878 Cetewayo declared war on the British and his *impis* invaded Natal. In this war Usibepu played a conspicuous part and he led the attack at Isandhlwana where he inflicted a sanguinary reverse on Lord Chelmsford's troops. He also led the van at the battle of Ulundi, a year later, when the British forces broke the power of the Zulu nation.

As a result of this defeat Cetewayo was taken prisoner and exiled to St Helena. During his absence, Usibepu ruled in his stead but in 1882 the Imperial Government restored Cetewayo and Usibepu was relegated to comparative obscurity once more. Having tasted power he was dissatisfied with the new order of things. He picked a quarrel with Cetewayo and soon he and his tribe were raiding into the King's territory, lifting his cattle, killing his subjects and taking their wives.

In March 1883 Cetewayo sent against him an army thrice outnumbering his own but Usibepu led his men with such skill that in the Umsembe valley he defeated the King and killed thousands of his warriors. Not content with this he moved against Cetewayo's kraal at Ulundi, leaving his head kraal fifteen miles from Nongoma and with twelve thousand men started on what must constitute a world's record for a non-stop infantry march.

Mr Finney, the magistrate at Nongoma, whom I met later, has lived in Zululand all his life. He told me that as a boy he had stood beside the road at sunset watching Usibepu's warriors go by. Usibepu, a short, broad-shouldered man of fifty, rode at their head on a pony and behind him silently came his *impi* on foot. After the fighting men trotted the mat boys, few more than ten or twelve years old, carrying food and sleeping mats for their masters. Mr Finney said these boys were an invariable adjunct of Zulu warfare, a sort of primitive army service corps following in the wake of their forces. They passed him at dusk at a steady lope and continuing all night, they fell upon Cetewayo at Ulundi by daybreak fifty-six miles from their starting point.

At Ulundi, Cetewayo had assembled his army, his councillors and the old men of the nation to give advice. They were taken completely by surprise. Usibepu's weary men fell upon them and routed them in a single fierce onslaught. Cetewayo himself was wounded and with the remnant of his people he escaped to the Nkandhla forest, his capital going up in flames behind him.

Usibepu was now lord of all Zululand and he held his own until Cetewayo died in 1884. His successor, Dinizulu, decided to call in the help of the Transvaal Boers and by a promise of land and cattle he secured the adherence of three hundred mounted men. Among them was Louis Botha, my chief of later years.

Around that camp fire he told us how they had ridden down the mountains to join Dinizulu at Magut on the Pongola river. Dinizulu had with him 15 000 of Cetewayo's best warriors but they were so terrified of Usibepu that only the presence of the Boer commando persuaded them to go forward at all.

Usibepu knew of their coming and he knew that a strong body of Europeans armed with rifles was with them so he stood on the defensive at Itshana (where we were camped) with the M'Kuzi gorge at his back to secure his retreat. Louis Botha said that when first they came in sight of Usibepu's men they were lined up below the cliff, shaking their assegais, striking their shields and chanting defiant war songs to the stamp of their feet. This so unnerved Dinizulu's oft-defeated ranks that a movement to the rear set in and it was only when the Boer horsemen entered the line that they moved to the attack.

Instantly Usibepu led a charge at the head of his men and Dinizulu's army once more turned tail; then the Boers came into action, each man standing before his horse, and they poured a stream of bullets into the oncoming warriors. Under their close-range volleys Usibepu's men faltered and broke. They fled down the gorge and to this day the sunbleached bones of the dead are strewn where I saw them. General Botha told us he was sorry for Usibepu; he had received hard measure. But for the Boers, he would have held his own.

This stout-hearted old *condottiere* lived to fight many another battle and he died at Nkonjani in 1902, game to the last.

V

From Itshana we moved on. A road leads up the Ubombo mountains to the magistracy above. At the top stands a stone courthouse and a trading post. From here one overlooks the coastal plains and, south-east, the great lagoons of St Lucia are visible, while below, the Mkuzi and Pongola rivers wind glistening in the sun. To the north, almost the whole of Swaziland lies in sight.

At the courthouse a deputation of half-breeds awaited me. They were the offspring of John Dunn, an Englishman who had entered Zululand in 1853. He served in Cetewayo's army and he led an adventurous life. He fought in the native wars of those days and Cetewayo made him a chief and allotted him a tribe. To-day, his numerous dun-coloured progeny are still on the lands Cetewayo gave them and they had come to urge that the eldest direct descendant should be recognised by the Union Government as a chieftain, with legal status and emoluments.

I listened to their arguments but I knew, from local talk, that in later years John Dunn had lost favour with the Zulus. At the battle of Ginginhlovu in 1879 he had sat on a chair on an ox-wagon within a British square, for he was ill at the time, and from this coign of vantage he had picked off some thirty of Cetewayo's soldiers with his rifle as they charged.

The Zulus never forgave him this and his heirs carry no influence, so I advised against the petitioners. Old Natal residents who knew John Dunn say that he built himself a comfortable home on the Tugela river. European visitors would find English quarterlies and magazines on his study table and though he still ruled his tribe, his establishment was run on the lines of an English manor house. He attended the races at Durban in a top-hat, morning coat and spats, but he would not enter a house in which there was a white woman. He died in 1892.

Having disposed of the Dunn claim, we descended the far side of the Ubombo and made for the Pongola across which we were ferried by Tonga piccanins to the accompaniment of their rabelaisian boating songs, and we rested at Otobotini for the night.

Purchasing supplies at the trading store next morning, I asked the Goanese clerk behind the counter what was that euphorbia grove on the shoulder of the mountain above Pongolapoort.

He looked uneasily to see that no native was about then he whispered, 'Sir, that very sacred place; no can say more.' I was intrigued, so I asked the local trader. He took me aside, for the matter was taboo and he feared for his custom. He told me that the thicket in question held Dingaan's grave.[1]

After his defeat by the Boers in 1898 the king had fled north attended only by some of his wives and a few mat boys. Wives? Concubines perhaps? I believe that neither Chaka nor Dingaan ever married and neither of them had any known off-spring—if this be so, it is a curious fact in view of the uxorious habits of the average Zulu Kings and Chiefs. Wandering for many months, the fugitives reached the top entrance of the Pongola gorge and making their way down the canyon they had come into the open country beyond. Here, at a spot pointed out to me, the N'Gawo tribe, not recognising him, killed the whole party.

Among the Zulu, royalty is sacrosanct and for a commoner to lay hands upon a king is an unforgivable offence. Therefore, when the N'Gawos learned that they had put the king to death, there was consternation. So strong is the law that to this day, nearly a century after the event, the N'Gawo tribe is still in coventry. The other Zulus

---

[1]The following further details with regard to Dingaan's burial place were supplied by the Chief Native Commissioner for Zululand:

Pietermaritzburg
14 August 1942

When collecting taxes at the Kwayiweni forest (also known as the Hlatikulu forest) in 1921, I paid an informal visit to Chief Mtshakela's kraal not far from the fringe of the forest. This forest is about 18 miles south of the Ingwavuma Magistracy and is the one in which Dingaan took refuge and where he was subsequently killed by the Swazis after his defeat at Blood River in 1838.

Being aware of this I asked Mtshakela if he knew where Dingaan had been buried, and to my surprise he replied in the affirmative and stated that he would point out the grave to me when a favourable opportunity offered. We were alone at the time.

Shortly afterwards I was transferred back to Natal and it was not until I became Chief Native Commissioner in 1933 that I again had an opportunity of meeting Mtshakela at his kraal. I was with a number of other officials at the time. I reminded him of our conversation and asked him whether he was now in a position to show me the grave but he replied in the negative and expressed his ignorance of the previous conversation. From his manner I could see that he had been embarrassed by the presence of my friends so I discreetly dropped the matter. He died not long afterwards.

Mtshakela was the son of the late Chief Sambana who died in or about 1914 well over 100 years of age. Sambana was therefore a grown up man at the time of Dingaan's death and probably knew him.

The Nyawo tribe, of which he and Mtshakela were chiefs, have lived on the Ubombo range from early times in an area that was at one time a part of Swaziland.

The reluctance on the part of Mtshakela to show me Dingaan's grave is probably due to a desire not to revive the existence of Dingaan's grave in their midst, a fact which had practically been forgotten, and which might lead to estrangement with the Zulu house. This is my opinion and it is shared by responsible natives.

I am told, although I have forgotten the source of my information, that the late Sir Charles Saunders once saw the grave so that of its existence there can be little doubt.

Inquiries into matters of this kind must be made discreetly as it concerns the resting place of the spirit of a great Zulu King which is always treated with awe and veneration. A number of early Zulu chiefs are buried in the neighbourhood of Umgungundlovu (Dingaan's *stad*) and the area is hallowed ground for the same reason.

(Sgd) H C Lugg

Mr Lugg is Chief Native Commissioner for Zululand with an unsurpassed knowledge of the Zulu, their language and their history.

do not associate with them nor is inter-marriage permitted.

I tested this myself for I asked an old *induna* and he growled 'Our daughters are not for the dogs that murdered the king'.

According to the Zulu way of thinking, it is permissible to levy war on their sovereign but to a commoner his person is inviolable—none but a member of the royal house may lay hands upon him. When, for example, Usibepu fell upon Cetewayo at Ulundi in 1883, one of the attacking chiefs named Ralijana stabbed the king in the thigh, not recognising him in the heat of battle. Though the wound had been given to a king against whom they were in arms and whose capital they had set alight, yet so grave was the fault that Usibepu deposed Ralijana and exiled him to a distant kraal.

Similarly, Chaka escaped the penalty of his crimes as long as he did because no man dared transgress this inflexible rule and it was only when his own brothers took action that the end came.

The N'Gawo tribe, to save face, do not admit that they killed Dingaan. It is considered bad form to raise the subject and when I asked one of them about it he answered hesitantly, 'It is true that the king came among us, but he died of dropsy.'

Leaving Otobotini, we followed down along the left bank of the Pongola river through bush-covered plains teeming with game, and in the broad stream we saw many hippo. Here, too, we saw *Inyala*, a rare and beautiful antelope believed to be found in no other part of Africa. Selous the famous hunter once came all the way from England to secure a single specimen for the British museum.

This area is sparsely populated by Tonga natives, poorer in physique than the real Zulus from the healthier uplands. Occasionally we came on a trading post occupied by some lonely white man but otherwise no Europeans are settled in these parts.

After those years of war it was pleasant to journey through wild country and it was pleasant to sit at night around a camp fire listening to the hippo snorting in the river below and to the distant grunt of lion.

At a native village I touched at there was a trader with only one eye and he told me this with a show of pride. A neighbouring chief came with his headmen one morning. They were fully armed and in a truculent mood. The chief said his daughter was about to become a mother and he accused the trader of being the culprit. The thing looked serious, but the trader said, 'See, I have only one eye. My father and my grandfather before me had only one eye. No member of my family has ever had two eyes. Let us then await the event. If the child be born with a single eye, condemn me if you will, but otherwise I must be acquitted of the charge.'

The Zulus are a fair-minded race and they regarded this as a reasonable proposition. In due course a coffee-coloured infant made its appearance, but as it had the normal complement of eyes, the chief and his adherents turned up in a body to beg his pardon!

At length we reached Indumu, a trading station near the Portuguese border. Beyond Indumu was a series of lakes or lagoons, the largest of which is Inyameti, a sheet of open water several miles long. The post was in charge of two brothers named Rutherford who had served in France. They had constructed a sort of boat built up out of petrol cases and soap boxes and as I had a retinue of native porters to feed I decided on a cruise to shoot a hippo. Theirs was a frail vessel and it shipped so much water that we provided our two native paddlers with an empty tin apiece for baling purposes. But they had a clearance system of their own. Disdaining the tins, the laid themselves flat on their bellies in the bottom of the punt and as the water filtered through the seams they sucked it into their mouths along with cigarette ends and other jetsam and they squirted the liquid overboard; thus these human bilge pumps kept us afloat.

We came on a school of hippo asleep on a mud bank. Silently we manoeuvred our barge to within range. As I was trying to take aim from the prow of my unsteady perch, an old bull lifted his head and saw us. Instantly he bellowed an alarm and the whole herd came rushing by for deeper water, nearly swamping us with the wash they raised. A baby hippo that had been asleep on its mother's back missed us by inches in its frantic haste to rejoin its parent.

It was a long time before I had another chance. We had beached our ship to prepare a meal in a small clearing in the surrounding jungle. As I watched the kettle, an enormous bull broke surface sixty or seventy yards out. My rifle lay beside me on the ground and quietly reaching for it I hit him squarely between the eyes from where I sat. He disappeared in a flurry of spray and in less than an hour he rose, feet upward, and floated on the surface.

It was nearing sunset by now and other hippo were closing in, blowing angrily. They are generally more vicious towards dark and we knew the risk of venturing among them at this time of day; so we lassoed the carcass and anchored it to a tree for the night.

The following morning, with the help of a crowd of natives who appeared from the bush, having had news of the kill, we dragged the animal ashore. The sight of fresh meat goes to the natives' heads like wine and there was so much excitement at the cutting up that we had difficulty in rescuing enough of the spoil to satisfy the needs of my own camp.

During the process of dissection, one of the natives held out an old-fashioned leaded bullet of unusual shape which he had prised from the dead hippo's shoulder blade. From the look of it, it must have lain imbedded for many years. An ancient Tonga hunter standing near took the bullet and holding it on his open palm, declared that it had been fired by Sjali, the *Umlungu umkulu* who alone in former days carried a weapon of this calibre. He was speaking of Charles du Pont of whom on our way up I had heard frequent mention as well as of his fellow venturer Robert MacNab. Since then I have met others who knew them both and I have pieced together their story.

VI

In the 'eighties of last century, Northern Zululand was a sort of Alsatia where the Queen's writ did not run. It was a refuge for lawless characters who lived by the chase and by levying tribute of corn and cattle from the natives. Chief among them were Charles du Pont and Robert MacNab.

Du Pont was a Frenchman from Mauritius of whose antecedents I was unable to glean particulars; but Mr David Forbes, a friend of mine who lives in the eastern

Transvaal and who knew MacNab intimately, told me about him.

MacNab's people were prosperous ironfounders in Paisley. His parents died when he was seventeen and he and his brothers inherited the plant. He suffered from an ungovernable temper, and quarrelling with his brothers, he abandoned his patrimony and he shipped before the mast on a sailing vessel bound for the East.

During the voyage he fell foul of the master who clapped him in irons. At Bombay, though still under arrest, he was allowed on shore to stretch his legs. While crossing a bridge he saw the captain fishing in the river below. He loosened a heavy coping stone and dropped it on his head from a considerable height. The captain fell like a log and MacNab fled inland.

He made his way on foot across the breadth of India. He was several times chased and severely thrashed with bamboo rods by natives from whose fields he had stolen rice and at times he was taken before the rajahs of the districts through which he passed. One of these threw him in prison but others helped him along with a few rupees at a time.

At length he reached Calcutta and the first thing he saw was the vessel whose captain he had probably murdered, so he fled once more and ultimately shipped on board a packet bound for South Africa. At Durban he deserted and made his way to Zululand where he joined hands with du Pont, who was already on the spot, and before long they ruled the country between them. They were in the direct line of Drake and Frobisher and the old freebooters.

They gained sway over half a million Zulus. Far from civilisation, they upheld a system of their own. They raised levies and warred on surrounding tribes; they exacted toll from natives, they collected ivory and they made and unmade Zulu chiefs.

MacNab once entered a native kraal and finding several inmates down with smallpox he shot the rest to prevent the disease from spreading; and I was told by an eyewitness that on one occasion he shot his Tonga servant whom he had sent to the river to fill a bucket of water and who refused to hurry when ordered. Another time he severed a native's arm at the wrist with the blow of an axe for attempting to steal his trek riems.

At one stage MacNab was captured by the Portuguese while he was raiding into their country and was lodged in gaol at Delagoa Bay. David Forbes went to see him. The gaol consisted of a single large room into which all prisoners were herded irrespective of race or colour or offence. MacNab was the only European and there were forty or fifty natives and half-breeds locked up with him. He had drawn a chalk line half-way across the floor, dividing the prison in two. On his side he sat in solitary state in an armchair beside a fire and he made all the others keep to their own portion of the room.

Du Pont was an equally reckless character. At this very spot where I was camped at Inyameti lake he had started a dispute with a young trader named Sussens as to the ownership of a dead hippo that was floating on the water. Each claimed to have killed the animal and to settle the argument they agreed to a shooting match. A mark was set in a distant tree and Sussens was the first to fire. As he walked forward to observe the effect of his bullet du Pont shot him in the back, killing him instantly.

MacNab and du Pont continued thus for a number of years until they quarrelled over cattle. MacNab, accompanied by a man named Constable, decided to retake them from du Pont. They approached du Pont's wattle and daub house after dark and summoned him forth. Du Pont opened the door and seizing MacNab's right hand as if in greeting shot him through the chest with a revolver held in his left. Then he leaped within and bolted the door. Constable battered it down and entering, he emptied his revolver at random.

Du Pont was standing on a table in the middle of the room and he was brought to the ground with a shattered ankle. From where he lay, aided by a timely flash of lightning, he shot Constable dead. Then he crawled outside and put another bullet into MacNab for full measure.

Strangely enough MacNab survived, but the two men now divided their kingdom. Du Pont shifted across the Portuguese border and he lives there to this day. MacNab moved over to Swaziland and both of them long remained powerful figures in their respective spheres.

I saw du Pont some years later, a frail, slightly-built man with silver hair and fluted voice, more like a music master than the fierce desperado he has been. MacNab is dead long since. He lies buried on Inhaca Island near Lourenço Marques.

I remained at Inyameti for a few days and then began the homeward journey. The hippo I shot is the last that has been killed there, for I had the lake and the adjacent land proclaimed a sanctuary and since then they have lived in peace and they are increasing in number.

From Inyameti we recrossed the plains, following up along the banks of the Pongola by the way we had come, once again camping at night by lagoons where lion roared and fish splashed and hippo snorted; and so we came to Otobotini, thence over the Ubombo mountain and down the other side past the Itshani battlefield. From here we swung west up the right bank of the Mkuzi through country inhabited by brave old Usibepu's tribe. After two days we reached Nongoma, the chief magistracy of Zululand, a charming little spot more like an English hamlet than the control centre of half a million savages.

The road that goes through Nongoma forms the boundary line separating Usibepu's people from the main Zulu nation now ruled by Solomon. Usibepu's successor is Chief M'Bogo, whom I did not meet, for he had word that Solomon was to visit me at Nongoma and they are hereditary enemies.

Solomon lives at his royal kraal a few miles from Nongoma. He came attended by a retinue clad in leopard skins and ostrich feathers but he himself was incongruously arrayed in a frock coat and a top hat, so he lacked the unspoilt dignity of his followers. He complained that Cetewayo, his grandfather, had never received the *lobola* (dowry) from the various *indunas* upon whom he had fobbed off his discarded wives; and he asked that the Union Government should assist him in collecting arrears from the defaulting tribes. *Lobola* is paid with cattle and as cattle disputes are the most fruitful cause of fighting among the Zulu the prosecution of this claim would have involved the country in civil war, so I discouraged the request.

From Nongoma we travelled to Melmoth, listening to pleas brought forward by chiefs and headmen, then we returned to Stanger, our original point of entry and our Zululand journey was at an end.

I determined, however, to come again and again to this attractive country, our Nationalist opponents and the political situation permitting.

Chapter 4

Freedom on the Orange and Pretorian Bondage

I

At Pretoria, our Administrative Capital, I attended to official business and for the next few weeks I was in bondage. Then I broke loose, to the far west, to the lower reaches of the Orange River.

This great stream rises in Basutoland and runs thence across the breadth of South Africa to empty itself into the Atlantic, eight hundred miles away. It drains the entire Free State and much of the Transvaal and Cape Provinces so that in the summer nearly half the waters of the Union roll between its banks.

On the islands towards the coast are European settlements and there was something like civil war among the irrigators owing to quarrels in respect of distribution of water in the canals and furrows. I found them nursing shotguns and rifles across their knees as they fiercely eyed each other from opposite sides of the sluice gates, and it cost me long days of difficult negotiation before the factions came to some kind of agreement.

The most important centre along here was a place called Kakamas. I had operated in these parts as a Boer guerrilla nearly twenty years before. At that time it was a mere outpost with a few reed huts; now it was a thriving hamlet with power-driven mills, electric lights and other signs of progress, including the doubtful blessing of hostile political parties whom I had to address amid the cheers and boos that are an invariable feature at similar gatherings in our rural districts.

From Kakamas we travelled slowly down the left bank of the river and so came to the Aughrabies falls. These are little known on account of the remote desert country in which they lie, but they are among the highest in the world.

Close to the edge of the falls, the river narrows down to a granite portal not more than fifteen yards wide and through this restricted gateway the accumulated waters of half a continent plunge down five hundred feet sheer into a mighty gorge not unlike that below the Victoria Falls at Livingstone. A lonely farmer lives in the vicinity and one of his sons guided us to a point from where we could watch not only the immense column leaping over the rim, but could see the foaming cauldron far below.

The young fellow had grown up beside the river and he said he knew a way to the bottom of the gorge. The rest of my party hung back, and they were sound judges, for it was a fearsome descent. We had to go by a crevice in the face of the cliff and we slowly made our way, testing each foothold before trying the next until at last we got to a spot where a jutting ledge gave us standing room just above the heaving cataract. We were now some four hundred yards below the falls, and looking up the gorge, we could see the water coming over with a roar of thunder and there stood a cloud of mist and spray. From the falls the torrent came racing down towards us in angry flood throwing up great waves and eddying wildly.

But I watched the driftwood and I noticed that some of the logs slowed down at a certain point and even started to float upstream again. From this I concluded that the water, probably due to submerged rocks, was taking a rotary movement and that for all its frightening aspect, the gorge was not as dangerous as it seemed; and I decided to make a test.

I stripped and dived in and it was as I thought, for there was something of an upstream current and I was able to make headway. I was tossed and buffeted a good deal and at times there was a sensation of remoteness from the outside world; for on either side the walls of the mighty canyon stood so high that but a strip of blue sky showed, making one feel a mere speck in the waste of waters.

I am a good swimmer and I covered the four hundred yards by dint of battling and I was even able to get into a vast cavern behind the fall. The water came over with such force that it set up a downward current of air like a giant ventilator in a mineshaft. It was a vivid experience.

After cruising around in the calm backwater in the rear of the falls I returned the way I had come and rejoined my guide who had been watching my escapade with some alarm. We now climbed up the cliff and after another terrible scramble we reached the top in safety. At the Boer homestead the old farmer held up his hands on being told what I had done but when I asked him whether the gorge had been swum before he bluntly said that no one had ever been such a damn fool as to try. All the same my record stands.

Our host propounded the theory that the great cleft up which I had swum was full of diamonds and he may have been right for since then at a desolate spot near the mouth of the Orange has been discovered the fabulously wealthy diamond deposits of Alexander Bay; and experts hold that the gems have been washed down the river.

So rich is the occurrence and the diamonds are strewn in such profusion that the government has enclosed the area with wire entanglements and men armed with machine-guns stand guard night and day. Picked searchers under close supervision collect the glittering spoil and war planes are used to convey the treasure across the intervening desert. Much later, I was to make further contact with the Orange River islands, the falls, and Alexander Bay, but for the present we moved into Namaqualand.

This vast tract lies south of the lower Orange. Much of it is barren and rainless but it is inhabited by Boer farmers ever on the rove in search of grazing and water. They are a fine hardy type and I renewed acquaintance with many of them who had been under arms with us against the British in the old days. They are devoted to Namaqualand and to them it is fair and beautiful, though not many others would think so.

Nevertheless, there is a fascination here that grows on one and I had learned to respect its hardbitten people during the days of fighting and adventure I had spent among them.

We journeyed as far south as Vanrhynsdorp, the little village that had served as our headquarters in 1902. I saw the graves of comrades who had been killed and I saw the place where I had helped to execute the spy Colaine.

At every town and village I had to deliver a speech, for politics is the ruling passion. For our farmers it takes the place of theatres, cinemas, and sport. It is the national pastime, like bull-fighting in Spain.

When at last we struck the railway line there was a heavy batch of correspondence awaiting me. Among the letters was a request from General Christian de Wet asking that I should visit him. I had fought against him in the 1914 rebellion, but I liked and respected the old warhorse so I started out to see him.

When I was a boy he was a member of the Free State Volksraad in the republican time. He entered Bloemfontein once at the head of an armed force to protest against the building of a railway line from the coast; for he held the view, not altogether without subsequent justification, that this dangerous innovation would facilitate an invasion by the British.

In 1899, in the first month of the Boer War, he made a name for himself by surrounding and capturing a large force of British troops near Ladysmith in Natal. I was in that battle and we took over a thousand prisoners. This exploit brought him into prominence and when, before long, disasters fell thick upon us, he was appointed Commandant General of the Free State.

By that time we had been driven from Natal, Bloemfontein was occupied, and all seemed lost. Christian de Wet rose superior to misfortune. Aided by President Steyn, my father's successor, he rallied our disheartened commandos and when the tide of invasion rolled north, he remained in the rear and conducted a brilliant guerrilla campaign. He held out against tremendous odds and his raids and forays and escapes, his feats of endurance and courage won him an international reputation, generously endorsed by the British themselves.

In 1912 there sprang up the feud between the supporters of General Botha and General Hertzog and de Wet supported the latter. At the beginning of the Great War he went into revolt. Because I was a Free Stater and because my father had been President of the Free State he expected me to join his movement and he was bitter because I took up arms on the side of the Botha government. We defeated him at Mushroom Valley and he was captured after a long chase. He was imprisoned, but General Botha sent him back to his farm on parole and there I now found him.

I was shocked at his appearance. Instead of the square virile figure I had known, there stood before me a haggard, shrunken man. His beard was ungroomed, his laces dragged on the ground and his clothes hung loosely on an emaciated body. His hands were swollen with some disease and he tottered in his gait as he came to greet me. I placed him in a chair and asked why he had summoned me, but he was unable to say. He sat with his hands pressed against his forehead trying vainly to remember and I had to go off with the question unsolved.

I like to think that knowing his end to be near, in his darkened mind had come the wish to say a last word for remembrance and friendship before he trod the common road. He died shortly after and we decreed him a State funeral. He is buried at the foot of the National Monument at Bloemfontein.

II

Now I had to return to Pretoria to official servitude for long months, interrupted only by excursions into the country districts to hold political meetings. These were very rowdy at times for our opponents were increasingly aggressive and it was plain to see that our sands were running out. For the rest, I attended to my task and I was called upon to handle more insoluble problems twixt heaven and earth than I had dreamed to lie within the scope of a South African portfolio.

These were so many and so varied that my colleagues and I sometimes ruefully asked ourselves whether Cabinet Ministers in other countries with much larger populations suffered a corresponding increase in burden and if so, how they managed to survive at all.

I learned the joys of helping to run a democracy. Deputations of farmers crowded in demanding higher agricultural prices and they were followed by deputations from the urban centres demanding lower costs of living. Divergent interests of mine-owners and mine-workers had somehow or other to be reconciled. Railwaymen clamoured for better wages and the general public clamoured for decreased fares, the granting of the one making the other a financial impossibility and in either case alienating the political support of the unsuccessful side.

When we promoted an official with an English name we were accused of pandering to the British; if a civil servant bearing a Dutch name was advanced we were accused of racial favouritism. If we taxed the gold mines, Johannesburg and the Reef towns were in an uproar. If we failed to tax them, rural politicians declared that we were in the pay of Hoggenheimer and the capitalists. Stretching a hand to assist one industry brought a flood of demands for equal treatment from a score of other enterprises.

At every meeting in the country districts we were denounced for spending too much money on the towns and at every urban meeting we were assailed for spending too much on the farmers. Swarms of locusts came from beyond our borders and when we spent a million pounds in exterminating them we were met with legal actions for sums almost equalling that amount in respect of cattle that had died from locust poison.

Then we had to contend with the vagaries of the South African climate. If we budgeted for a heavy maize crop and a shortage of wheat, as like as not, we found ourselves with a shortage of maize and a surplus of wheat by the end of the year.

There came a severe drought in the midlands. We introduced a Bill to assist the victims and while we were debating the matter in Parliament the same people were washed out by torrential rains and a Bill having started life as a drought relief measure was hurriedly changed into a flood relief Act.

And there were the rain-makers, inventors of perpetual motion pumps, infallible water diviners and droves of job hunters. However, we did our best in a sea of troubles and, after all, it was an interesting, eventful life.

Apart from less important difficulties we were faced with a more serious problem before the end of the year. A religious fanatic of the Fingo tribe named Enoch collected a large following from among the natives in the Transkei territory. He predicted the speedy end of the world and advocated defiance of all authority. They called themselves 'Israelites' and they built a fortified camp below Ntabalangu near Queenstown.

We sent a military force to disperse them and when the officer in command called upon Enoch to surrender he led his men to battle. Armed with crude swords and battleaxes the deluded zealots charged down upon the soldiers who opened fire and killed more than two hundred of them.

There was an outcry. The press and the public said, and I rather agreed, that our troops had exceeded the bounds of necessity, as these ignorant savages could have been starved into submission without the shedding of blood. Fortunately the Israelites were distrusted by the other natives and no unrest was caused among the tribes, but the incident served to weaken us still further politically.

I may add that we received many indignant letters from Europe protesting against the massacre of the 'Israelites'. It was thought that we had been conducting a large-scale pogrom of our Jewish citizens.

Soon after this, in January 1922, there arose the most serious crisis of our term of office: for we had to face an armed revolt on the gold mines.

It began with a dispute on a colliery, the workers of which laid down their tools. The strike spread to the Reef and the position became aggravated, as the original leaders were superseded by extremists who called a general strike and they resorted to violence.

At the head of the disturbance were Fisher and Spendiff, two Australian communists, and the outbreak assumed alarming proportions. The rank and file of the workers were mainly young Dutchmen from the country districts, brave and reckless and traditionally prepared to settle their quarrels with a rifle.

Revolutionary commandos sprang up overnight and as many of the insurgents had relatives and friends in the rural areas there was the danger that the conflagration might bring about a nationwide civil war.

In Johannesburg and along the Reef, anarchy reigned. A workers' republic was declared; dissident rebel forces captured the outlying suburbs and townships; police were shot at sight and their barracks and stations were besieged and bombed while incendiarism and street fighting were the order of the day. Johannesburg was completely surrounded and our government troops with difficulty held the inner ring of the city.

As the youngest member of the Cabinet I bore less responsibility than the others, but it was a trying time.

With Johannesburg and the gold mines practically in the hands of the insurgents, General Smuts proclaimed martial law. Fifty thousand mounted burghers were called up and he made a dramatic dash through the rebel lines into Johannesburg. He was fired on at close range, but he got safely through and took command in person.

He attacked them next day with infantry and guns and he surrounded their stronghold at Fordsburg with his horsemen. After causing leaflets to be dropped from aeroplanes warning the women and children to evacuate the town, the government commandos closed in under cover of gunfire and Fordsburg was taken. As our men entered, Fisher and Spendiff shot themselves and the rising collapsed.

It had been an expensive affair. More than seven hundred people were killed and there was heavy material damage. Politically, the effects were disastrous. Our opponents blamed us for having acted too harshly and our supporters blamed us for not having acted quickly enough, so we were ground between the upper and the nether millstone.

Then, to add to our troubles came the trial of a number of the ringleaders. They were not prosecuted for high treason but for coldblooded murders of civilians and for the shooting down of natives.

As always, a reaction set in. Thousands may lie unremembered on the field of battle but the public blenches at executions. When five of the worst offenders were sentenced to death, mass meetings were called, petitions were signed, and reprieves were demanded. But we decided to hang these men. They had committed atrocious murders, not in the heat of action, but by deliberately killing non-combatants.

I think we did the right thing in the circumstances, but we paid the penalty that befalls those who do the right thing in a democracy. The revolution cost us heavily in prestige and the executions in the Pretoria gaol cost us even more.

The hanging of a man named Taffy Long did us most harm. He was a soldier with a good war record. He had served at Gallippoli and had been decorated for courage. Every returned soldier in the Union clamoured for his release and Prince Arthur of Connaught (our Governor-General) at first refused to sign the death warrant. Still, he had been found guilty of a brutal murder and we felt that the better soldier he had been the less justification was there for his conduct.

I regretted his fate though in Cabinet I voted for his death. He was a brave man. The evening before he was to die he asked for something to read and he was given a Bible. He looked at the sacred volume, read its title, and sent it spinning through the open door of his cell into the passage beyond. He said: 'Bible! Bible be damned, bring me one of Nat Gould's novels.' He went to his doom next morning singing the Red Flag.

III

In June, Senhor Brito Commacho, the Governor of Portuguese East, invited me to visit him and he indicated that he would arrange an elephant hunt for me in the interior. I did not particularly want to shoot an elephant for I had learned during the East African campaign in 1916 the pity of uselessly slaughtering wild animals; but I did want to see that part of the world and I was glad to get away to calmer surroundings after the excitements of the Rand upheaval.

My last visit to Delagoa Bay had been made under less propitious circumstances. Returning from exile in Madagascar, whither I had gone to escape British rule, many years before, I had worked my passage on a tramp steamer to Lourenço Marques, hoping to reach the Transvaal from there. But the Portuguese immigration laws prohibited a stranger from landing unless he had promise of fixed employment or could make a cash deposit of twenty-five pounds.

I had neither, so I was classed as an undesirable alien and forbidden to leave the ship. The timely intervention of a fellow exile who lent me the requisite amount saved me and I was allowed ashore.

Now it was different. I was a State guest and I was received by the Governor and his staff and a squadron of cavalry escorted me to the Residency.

I spent a few days with Senhor Brito Commacho in friendly discussion of various matters affecting our two countries, then he and I travelled down to the Swaziland border to look into the railway position at Namahacha.

On the bank of the Maputo river we came on a young Englishman standing by a dead elephant he had just shot, and he showed us the body of a hippo floating on the water below. He told us that as he fired at the elephant the hippo broke surface and he bagged it with a second shot. It was wanton butchery for I hold that one is entitled to hunt only for food; but he was so proud of his unique right and left, and I was so newly come from the killing and hanging of human beings, that I refrained from comment.

On our return to the Bay the Governor sent me on the promised expedition up north. I was accompanied by several Portuguese officers and we made for wild country beyond the Limpopo river. Big game was plentiful: zebras and wildebeest, giraffe, koodoo and impala.

At the administrative centre at Magude there was a stockade, garrisoned with soldiers, and the *Commandante* ordered a war dance in my honour. Five thousand Tonga warriors took part, brandishing shields and spears and chanting battle songs.

Then came the elephant hunt. We followed the spoor of a large troop through dense bush for many hours. After a long trail we came up with them and the native guides skilfully brought me near an immense bull carrying what looked like ninety-pound tusks, but as I was about to fire the wind veered and the herd scented us. There was a mighty stampede. Bulls trumpeted, cows rushed about angrily in search of their calves whose squealing added to the din and the whole lot went crashing off into the jungle. That was the last we saw of them. It was a wonderful sight and I trudged contentedly back for fifteen miles to our camp.

The Tonga natives prefer zebra meat to anything else so I went out to shoot one for our servants next morning. A Portuguese medical officer came with me and it did not take us long to come up with a dozen of them. I fired and dropped a big fellow dead in his tracks. Simultaneously the medico loosed off with a diminutive automatic and as the animal fell he flourished his tiny weapon and called out '*o pistole, o pistole*' meaning that he had killed the zebra with the Browning.

He was so pleased that I said nothing and when he told his wife about his exploit on our return to camp, she threw her arms around him in fervent embrace. To this day he believes he shot that zebra but I watched the natives cutting it up and I extracted my soft-nosed bullet in a flattened condition from the carcass.

One morning an *askari* brought in a Muscat donkey stallion that had escaped into the scrub more than a year ago. The natives had sometimes caught a glimpse of him running wild with a troop of zebra, but whenever they attempted to catch him he scampered off with his new associates and it was not until now that they had succeeded in cutting him from the herd.

He was a sorry spectacle. His coat was caked with mud and dust and burrs and grass seeds. He looked like a musk-ox with his matted hair and he was covered with scars and bruises where the gentlemen zebras had kicked him, but he had an unquenched impenitent gleam in his eye as if to say that he had had the time of his life and was going again at the first opportunity. The old Portuguese Commandante slapped him under the belly and wished him luck.

Now I had to return home. I had enjoyed a fine holiday and the Portuguese officers and officials had been so hospitable that I was sorry to leave them. I travelled back to the railway line at Xinavene and thence to ministerial drudgery at Pretoria.

IV

In August of 1922 I had to go up to Secocoeni's country to look into land questions. It is a wild mountainous region inhabited by an offshoot of the Bapedi tribe and therefore of Basuto origin. The country is called after Secocoeni who was a powerful chief in the days prior to the first Boer war in 1881.

He was the indirect cause of that war which in turn brought about the second Boer war and its incalculable effects on the history of South Africa, so here again I collected such data as I was able to find.

When the Transvaal republic was established in 1852 the Bapedi refused to accept its jurisdiction and when Secocoeni in 1875 became their paramount chief he began to raid and harass the European settlers.

Thomas Burgers was President at the time. He owed his position to the fact that he had been a clergyman of the Dutch Reformed Church in the Cape Colony and the Boers thought it would be a sort of fire insurance to have as head of the state one who stood under Divine guidance.

On assuming office he found that he had acquired an uneasy inheritance. The Boers of those days were rugged unbending Calvinists and when they found that instead of the stern sectarian they had applied for they had saddled themselves with a President who held a broad interpretation on religious subjects, there was trouble. He was a Freemason, he travelled on the Sabbath and he even attended dances when any were given in Pretoria.

His conduct was regarded with such horror that a large party of Boers from the Western Transvaal abandoned their farms and trekked away across the Kalahari desert rather than submit to so impious a ruler.

What was still worse, Secocoeni was marauding and looting from his stronghold at Tjadi and to crown it all, the British Resident at Pretoria intimated that this defiance was causing unrest among the Zulus in Natal and that unless he was brought to book Her Majesty's Government would be forced to annex the Transvaal.

Poor Thomas Burgers did not know which way to turn. He had found no favour in the eyes of the people, his coffers were empty, discontent was rife and he had no option but to take the field against the recalcitrant chieftain. He could raise only eight or nine hundred men for most of the Boers refused to serve under one whose dogma was suspect. Even Paul Kruger made it known that he would not be answerable for an expedition led by one of the ungodly and he stayed at home, so Burgers took command in person and he led his half-hearted army against Secocoeni. He found him down the Steelpoort valley and ordered an attack. The men were lukewarm and the attack failed. Other attempts were made, but Secocoeni held his own and after eight months of desultory fighting the campaign was abandoned.

With difficulty the President extricated his force. The enterprise had cost him dear, for the British government carried out its threat, and using the unsuccessful issue as an excuse, troops entered Pretoria, the Queen's sovereignty over the Transvaal was proclaimed, and the republic for the time being ceased to exist.

Secocoeni, having defied the Boers and having helped to bring about their downfall, now defied the British. Two punitive expeditions were sent against him without success and it was not until 1879 that Sir Garnett Wolseley marched in with a strong force of infantry and guns and aided by five thousand Swazi levies he stormed Tjadi and captured Secocoeni.

Now followed the Boer war of 1881. Under the leadership of Paul Kruger and Piet Joubert, the Transvaalers rose in arms against Great Britain. They inflicted a succession of reverses on the troops sent against them and after the disaster of Amajuba, peace was made and the Transvaal regained its independence.

Paul Kruger was made President. He respected Secocoeni for his courage, and finding him still a prisoner he released and placed him at the head of his tribe once more.

But Secocoeni's star had set. A kinsman named Mampoer felt aggrieved at being deprived of the authority he had wielded during the absence of the chief. He stole into Secocoeni's hut one night and stabbed him to death. President Kruger ordered his arrest, but he took refuge with Njabel, a petty chief, who refused to surrender him. A commando was sent and after considerable fighting both were captured.

Mampoer was hanged for murder, but Njabel was set at liberty, for he had acted in keeping with tribal usage in refusing to give up one who had taken sanctuary with him.

The President was determined to avoid further trouble and he parcelled out much of Mapoch's country to his burghers to form a permanent garrison. Their descendants still occupy the ground and it was in this very connection I had come.

The old surveys were faulty, beacons had been wrongly placed or removed, water-rights overlapped and numerous difficulties had arisen all of which I was expected to settle out of hand. In the shade of a mimosa tree beside a river I took evidence and listened to claims and counterclaims that had grown ever more complicated during the past forty years. When Parliament met again I put through a Bill which evoked some sort of order of out chaos.

As for Secocoeni's tribe, though dispossessed of most of their land, a portion has been reserved to them. They have remained a fine courageous people, easily distinguishable by their proud bearing and physique from the lesser breeds that surround them.

The member of Parliament for this area had accompanied me. He was an old man who had served in the abortive attacks on Tjadi and he told me the following story:

After President Burgers' unsuccessful attempts, he and his men withdrew up the Steelpoort valley. Their sole transport consisted of a wagon carrying reserve ammunition. It was in charge of a white man who had proved himself such a coward that he had been assigned the servile task of driving the mule team.

At the head of the column rode the President with his officers and about half-way down was the wagon with the discredited driver on the box seat. At one point they passed a boulder-strewn kopje close to the road and as the wagon came abreast, a shot rang out and the driver fell dead. The bullet had been fired by a native warrior who was now seen running off and he was brought to earth mortally wounded.

He was asked why he had selected the man on the wagon for his victim and the brave fellow replied that he had decided to sacrifice his life in order to kill the Boer leader. He had lain in wait and from his hiding-place he had watched the approaching commando. Looking down the ranks he concluded that the only man who had been given place of honour on the only vehicle must necessarily be the Boer commander and he stayed his hand while the President and the others went by and he fired at and killed the poltroon who mattered least of all. The burghers were generous enough to let the poor wretch die in ignorance of the fact that he had immolated himself in vain.

Having disposed of local troubles, I moved on, for other questions were calling. I went northward over the Drakensberg escarpment and we descended into the Low Country by Kowyn's pass, then a mere track and terribly steep.

From the foot of forest-clad mountains we travelled on through the bush. We saw little game but the natives complained that lion were causing heavy losses among their stock. At one village we came to they had killed a big male the night before and the carcass lay by the headman's kraal. The skin was in ribbons and the skull was battered in with knobkerries. When I asked why the teeth had all been broken he said, 'the teeth were knocked out because these are the teeth that took our cattle'.

We continued, still bearing north, through scrub country to the junction of the great and little Letaba rivers. Here again the natives complained of lion. At one *stad* four men had been seized within the last two months and I saw an old man who had been terribly injured. A lion had dragged him off and then released him; his right eye and nearly half his face was torn away and he was in a dying condition. At night we heard the roaring and there were many tracks, but we saw no lion as the bush was too thick.

We went up along the Sami river to Sibasa's country and then to the chief of the knob-nose kaffirs. Thence over the Zoutpansbergen into the fever-stricken plains that lie towards the Limpopo, our northernmost boundary. I joined a hunting party. Sable antelope, wildebeest, zebra, and koodoo were plentiful but I shot for food only.

Now we turned East of the Wanetsi river, semi-desert thickly covered with mopani trees that always denote a lack of water, and thereafter south on the long homeward trek.

Chapter 5

With General Smuts in Natal

I

In the winter of 1923, after we had toiled through a long parliamentary session, General Smuts and I stumped Natal in connection with the proposal for closer union between South Africa and Rhodesia. We held that in the common interest the two countries should draw nearer. On our side of the boundary line, however, the cattle farmers were hostile to the project. They said the Rhodesians with cheap land and cheap native labour would swamp their markets.

Across the way was even more active opposition. The people of Rhodesia were unwilling to be dragged into our race and language squabbles and our ideal of a greater South Africa found little support. We spoke in many towns and villages, but it all came to nothing in the end. A plebiscite was taken in Rhodesia and the result was overwhelmingly against us.

Having said our say, we proceeded to Zululand, for General Smuts wished to examine the prospects of building a harbour on the coast. He had enlisted the services of Sir George Buchanan, a famous marine engineer, and we took with us an escort of mounted police.

I was glad to be in Zululand once more. We travelled by very much the same road I had previously gone. We touched at the Place of Elephants, then across the Umfolosi delta, now rapidly being planted up with sugar cane and then across the Hluhluwe, still swarming with big game. We passed Etshani battlefield with its bleaching skulls and over the Ubombo mountains. From here we turned east, making for the Indian Ocean. We went on horseback for there were no roads. All this expanse was uninhabited by Europeans and the native population consisted of Tongas who seemed to spend most of their time in getting drunk on the juice of the *umlala* palm from which they distil a potent wine.

Herds of zebra and wildebeest grazed on every side and we saw many *inyala*. Unfortunately we also saw many tsetse flies and as we rode, these insects darted viciously at our horses and at the mule teams of our two supply wagons and we knew that all our animals would die, although we ourselves were in no danger as the Zululand tsetse fly is a sub-species of the *Pallidipes* and does not carry the germs of sleeping sickness to human beings.

The harm was done, so we continued on our way, for a fly-bitten horse will live for weeks before the poison takes effect; there is even a current belief that not until rain falls does it operate at all.

Near the coast we reached Sibaya, the largest fresh water lake south of the great equatorial lakes of Africa. We followed its western shore, with schools of hippo watching us knee-deep in the water as we passed; then we branched through the Boswani swamp, a tangle of forest and crocodile-infested lagoons, and so came to Sordwana bay where a river empties itself into the sea.

This was one of our objectives, as we hoped that the estuary might be converted into a safe anchorage for ships; and Sir George Buchanan commenced to survey its possibilities while we fished from the rocks with improvised tackle, and explored the surrounding country, and hunted for the pot.

Once we came on a small lake lying dark and still in a gloomy patch of forest. The natives said it was haunted because here, in the old days, those condemned to death by the chiefs were thrown to the crocodiles. So much do they dread the place that they will not allow their children to look upon it and no man is allowed to drink of its water. Indeed there was something so eerie and sinister about the spot that we were glad to ride out into the sunshine again.

George Higgs, my planter friend, was with us. He told me that beneath one of the sand dunes at the river mouth lies buried a hoard of ivory. Many years ago a trader named Bishop established himself here. He amassed thousand of tusks which he hid in the sand. He fell ill and his Zulu gunbearer carried him to a longboat and single handed navigated his master down the coast to Durban. Bishop died after landing and the ivory, so says Higgs, still awaits the lucky discoverer.

Sir George Buchanan completed his survey and his report lies buried deep in its pigeonhole at Pretoria. He went down with fever and we had to send him back for medical treatment. The balance of our expedition struck camp and we slowly journeyed north, keeping well inland to avoid the heavy going nearer the coastline.

Our way ran over pleasant open country dotted with parklike groves. Game was abundant and in the trees monkeys chattered and swung from the branches. This was the first real holiday General Smuts had enjoyed for many years. He threw off the cares of State and we agreed to forget our political troubles for the time being, so we rode along gaily and he told us many interesting things about his work in the British War Cabinet, in Palestine, and in Italy, and of the peace negotiations at Versailles.

Although we were travelling through fly country, the natives had plenty of cattle. For some unexplained reason this insect is found in belts and is not uniformly distributed as one might expect. The natives can tell the tsetse zones within a hundred yards and they are able to raise stock, despite the scourge. I hold the view, an unpopular one in Zululand, that the fly is not entirely dependent on game and that some form of vegetation, as yet undiscovered, is necessary for its existence.

As we passed the grazing and hunting grounds of the various Tonga chiefs, we were met with ceremonial and the driving up of cattle. News of our approach was bush-telegraphed in advance and they and their warriors appeared with tom-toms and the paraphernalia of the war dance, and brought us the usual gifts. They employ the honorific style of speech like the Orientals. I have a working knowledge of the Bantu dialects so I was able to follow what they said. A chief would step forward to welcome General Smuts in flowery language. If he were a lesser light who could not afford an ox, he would say, 'I bring you my humble tribute of a mangy fowl', whereupon a fat goat would be produced.

If on the other hand, he owned many cattle, the chief said, 'I am a poor man, I bring you a miserable goat'; and a sleek ox would be driven before us to be killed.

Apparently, however, this procedure is sometimes reversed, for David Livingstone in his *Journeys in South Africa* says: 'November 1853. The Bechuanas presented me with a miserable goat, pompously exclaiming "behold an ox".'

Etiquette demands that the gift be accepted but it is considered the height of ill-breeding if the beneficiary keeps for himself more than a few tit-bits. The rest of the meat is to be handed to the chief's retinue to gorge upon.

In this manner we rode along, and at night we chatted around great camp fires and we slept beneath the stars. Once more we skirted lake Sibaya and, still going north, we reached Kosi lake out of which a river of the same name discharges into the sea.

The broad estuary was covered for miles with fish traps, long wooden palisades that criss-cross from bank to bank. At Kosi Bay was a small mission station in charge of an American preacher. He had an uphill task for the local natives seemed as little anxious to achieve salvation as the rest of our South African tribes. He told us that the inhabitants of the peninsula on the other side of the river had never seen a white man.

This peninsula consists of a tongue of wooded hills twelve or fifteen miles long lying between Kosi lake and the sea. It is densely populated though the missionary could give us no details as he had never been there. On our upward journey we had noticed from a rise near Mungusi that the peninsula was notched at one point and it looked as if there might be an outlet from the lake into the sea; so after we had spent a few days examining our immediate surroundings, General Smuts said he was going to investigate.

Early one morning therefore we forded the river at low tide and rode into the peninsula. At our appearance the natives took to the bush and there was wild alarm. Through glades and clearings we saw them fleeing, the women holding their children and setting up the usual long-drawn wail they produce when they think there is trouble.

General Smuts ordered Lieutenant Hedges of our police patrol to gallop forward and shout greetings. He did so, and before long we heard his stentorian voice echoing among the trees. He called to say that we were friends and after a while several of them began timidly to approach. We told them to overtake the others and reassure them of our intentions. In a few minutes we heard their messages being relayed from rise to rise in the native manner of transmitting news and within the hour confidence was restored.

Men and women came trickling back and some of the bolder spirits were even proffering snuff to Lieutenant Hedges whom they took to be the leader of our party owing to his vocal efforts, his fluent command of the vernacular, and his uniform.

He told us the natives had bolted not so much because of the white men but because in this fly-infested country none of them had ever seen a horse; and from the way they stood excitedly round our animals he may have been right.

Our march, begun in consternation, now assumed the appearance of a royal progress. From every direction, men and women and children flocked in to see us ride by. It was rough going, over steep hills with heavy sand underfoot and thick jungle overhead.

At length we came to a hill so steep that it seemed to bar all further advance. To our right, far below, was Kosi Lake and on our left the Indian Ocean. In the lake there were hippo on the mudsills and some were moving beneath the water like submarines. On the other side there were sharks lazily swimming in the surf.

It was an interesting sight, but as our horses could not negotiate the vertical rise before us we were hung up for a long time until the natives hacked a path which enabled us to reach the brim of an appalling slope down which, somehow or other, we managed to scramble to the beach and we now rode along until we came to the gap we had seen from Mungusi.

There was no outlet to the sea, but we found that a mere ridge of sand was all that separated the lake from the ocean. We reckoned that a steam shovel could dig a passage in a few weeks for ships to sail into the land-locked waters behind and we thought we had discovered a harbour for Zululand at last.

Since then, owing to political and financial considerations, nothing further has been done and that low sand dune still awaits the theodolite and the plumb-line to prove its value.

We rode back to camp, making along the firmer waterline to spare our horses and we reached home long after dark.

Two days later we broke up and journeyed parallel with the Portuguese border until we got to Indumu and Inyameti lake where I had previously shot the hippo. We rested our animals here. They fed and showed no outward sign, but with my experience of the tsetse fly in East Africa I knew that all was not well. They dragged their feet and from their pulsing flanks it was clear that the venom was doing its deadly work. In the end, of the horses and mules we took to Kosi Bay not one survived and several of our coloured teamsters succumbed to malarial fever.

At Indumu we were on a rough but practicable road and a car awaited General Smuts and myself. Leaving the rest of the expedition to work southward on their weakened horses, we forged ahead, following the track up the left bank of the Pongola as far as Otobotini, then over the Umbombo range and down the other side; from here we travelled along the Mkuzi river and thus to Nongoma.

We passed a little native *stad* called Baganoma. It was from here that Usibepu started on his record-breaking march to Ulundi and it is here that he lies buried. His grave is surrounded by the customary euphorbia thicket and is carefully tended by his tribe.

At Nongoma ten thousand warriors were assembled to meet us. The Zulu nation is divided into two main sections, the Usutu and the Mahlagazi, and there has been a feud between them since the time of Chaka and Dingaan. To this day faction fights are common, with the killing of men, burning of huts, and the hurried despatch of police contingents to separate them. Each tribe has its own territory and at Nongoma, the road which runs through the village is the dividing line.

Of the ten thousand men gathered in our honour, approximately half were Usutu under King Solomon and the other half were Mahlagazi under their chief M'Bogo, son of Usibepu. In order to prevent trouble, Mr Finney the head magistrate had given instructions that each clan was to marshal on its own side of the road. He was uneasy, for even at a distance we could hear them hurling taunts and challenges to each other and it was obvious that things might easily get out of hand; especially as we found on approaching that many of them were indulging in the provocative custom of *giya* whereby a man would break rank and rush forward, leaping and stamping, his shield and stabbing spear held threateningly aloft, while he boasted of his prowess in battle and of his victories over the other side. Under this mutual irritant there seemed every chance of a bloody tribal combat; but the Zulu, for all his fierce qualities, is an overgrown child and at the sight of our cavalcade, the Prime Minister riding at our head, King Solomon in top hat and morning coat beside him, and the prospect of speeches (they love oratory as the Irish do), their attention was distracted.

General Smuts mounted a wagon that had been drawn up by way of a rostrum and Mr Finney called for the royal salute. At a sign from him they gave the '*Bayete, Bayete*' in full-throated roar and for the moment the danger was past. M'Bogo strode out, and turning to his men he commanded them to sit down. They obeyed, and Solomon from the wagon gave a similar order, and both sides settled on their haunches. Mr Finney, who had grown up among them, spoke first. Then Solomon and M'Bogo made us welcome and now Mankulumane stood up to speak.

Mankulumane was a magnificent savage of over ninety years, tall and erect, and every line of his heavy jowl spoke of strength and character. He had been chief counsellor to Cetewayo and Dinizulu as he was now to Solomon, and the Zulus look on him as the greatest orator of all time.

He spoke in court Zulu, a more involved language than is in everyday use but with some knowledge of their tongue and with the help of an interpreter I was able to follow him.

He played upon his audience in masterly fashion. One moment he worked them into a rage and whole batches of warriors sprang to their feet to glower at their hereditary foes across the common border; then by a dexterous turn he sent them rocking with laughter at some witty tale of cattle or the chase.

Next, in lowered tones, he spoke of the former glories of the Zulu people, of the spirits of the dead and of great battles of the past, and when he chided them for their quarrels they sank their heads between their knees and rocked and moaned in unison.

What struck me most in his peroration was his reference to Dinizulu, his former lord.

Dinizulu was sentenced to prison in 1906 by the Natal Courts for alleged complicity in the Bambata rising. Many people at the time doubted the justice of the verdict and a barrister uncle of mine, Mr W P Schreiner, went to great personal expense to defend him, free of charge, in a trial that lasted for months. In 1910, when General Botha became Prime Minister of the Union, he released Dinizulu who died soon after. His conviction and imprisonment are still deeply resented by the tribes.

Mankulumane was at Dinizulu's burial and in referring to it in his speech he said: 'I am not a Usutu. I belong to the M'Gangkwe tribe; we were conquered by Panda. But the Usutus, once we submitted, gave us their trust. Although we had fought against them, I rose to high honour, even to being chief counsellor of their kings. Throughout many wars that confidence, once given, was never withdrawn.

'But see how the white man treated Dinizulu! He submitted to them and they pretended to accept his word but it was make-believe. When Bambata rose at Nkandhla forest they, whilst lulling the king with soft words, surrounded him. He lies dead of a broken heart.'

Mankulumane ended in slow measured tones and there was dead silence as he finished. All of us were impressed by what he had said, and some of us perhaps a little ashamed.

Then came a war dance, each tribe in its own territory. It was magnificent, but we were relieved when it was over without a breach of the peace. We returned on horseback to Nongoma and the great *impis* marched off in clouds of dust.

Next morning we continued the homeward journey, passing several European villages on the way. At one of these the people told us that a white rhino had recently paid them a visit. There are two kinds in Zululand, the white and the black. The black rhino is smaller and more vicious than the square-lipped variety. Both are shortsighted and inclined to charge at anything they scent but cannot clearly see. On this occasion the white rhino walked through several garden lots, coming away with a tangle of fencing wire around his head. Then he entered the village and lumbered down the street. Seeing the open door of a cottage he put his head inside and dislodged the electric bell and battery, both of which hung on the horn of his nose when he backed out. Unperturbed by this, he ambled into a yard and collected a clothes line and the family washing with all of which he disappeared into the forest beyond. As he went the electric bell made contact and it started to ring while the fencing wires still trailed behind and the multicoloured garments fluttered along his flanks like a battle-ship on gala day.

A Zululand game ranger told me he was walking along a path once with a native piccanin behind him when they saw a white rhino lying asleep in a clearing. The piccanin ran up and kicked him in the ribs. He started angrily to his feet, but on seeing his tiny aggressor he gave a snort of disgust and moved off.

We went via Eshowe and Melmoth and we passed the spot where Dingaan's capital had stood. Under a rude cairn lie the bones of Piet Retief and his men who were murdered here in 1836.

Further on we went by the place where the Prince Imperial, son of that upstart

Napoleon III, was killed by the Zulus. I saw his mother, the Empress Eugénie, in 1917 at Aldershot. She was old and shrunken, but my father had seen her in the heyday of her youth at the Paris Exhibition, and he told me she was then a very beautiful woman.

When we reached the Natal railway line a special train was ready for us and we returned to Pretoria in July 1923.

II

I worked in office and I went on numerous political and departmental journeys. *Inter alia* I sailed round from Durban to Port Elizabeth and from there I went to the Sundays River valley where Sir Percy FitzPatrick, who wrote *Jock of the Bushveld*, had established a settlement.

Close by, in what is known as the Addo forest, there still exists a small herd of elephant. Up to 1920 there had been over a hundred but the fruitgrowers in the valley complained of the damage they were doing and a noted hunter was sent to thin them out.

He shot ninety and there now remained only about a dozen whose execution was also being demanded, but I resisted the pressure and I proclaimed the forest a sanctuary. To-day the herd is breeding up well and buffalo and other game are likewise increasing.

A friend of mine, Nat Harvey, who lives close by, said he saw the elephants in his dam one hot morning. They were drawing up water with their trunks, sluicing their bodies with obvious enjoyment. He swears that an old bull started to squirt the sloping wall of the dam until he had a mud slide. Then he clambered out and went along the crest until he reached the top of the chute he had made and sitting on his hams he slid down. He hit the water below with a tremendous splash and he was so pleased with his performance that he began afresh and before long the other elephants followed his example, each making a slide and tobogganing into the dam. They continued at their game for more than an hour; then they marched off into the bush, flapping their ears, waving their trunks and pushing and jostling each other in high good humour.

Nat Harvey treated me to a wonderful stew which he said was veal, but I knew it was buffalo calf he had poached; for I had noticed the skin pegged down behind his stable. As an accessory after the fact, and as the dish was beyond praise, I kept my own counsel.

In former years the Sundays River valley was a prosperous centre of the ostrich feather industry. With the advent of the motor-car, however, the fashion changed and women ceased wearing plumes. Most of the ostrich farmers were ruined and the great birds have largely disappeared. None the less one still occasionally sees a few of them in the paddocks as there is some demand for the feathers to be made into mops and dusters.

And I learned of another use for ostriches. Nat Harvey and I were standing before his house one evening when a native boy brought him a letter from a neighbour asking for the loan of two of his birds.

I inquired what on earth the man wanted to borrow ostriches for and I was told they were needed to weed his lawn. It appears that round here a troublesome growth of spiked thorn (*dubbeltjies*) springs up, which if left undisturbed kills off the grass, and as ostriches eagerly graze the thorn they are used as animated weeding machines.

On my return to Pretoria I stayed at home for a week, after which I set off on an expedition to the Sabie and Komati low country of the Eastern Transvaal. I wanted to look into the possibilities of establishing a permanent reserve in order to prevent the extermination of the big game.

The Sabie river area was already a game sanctuary in the sense that hunting was forbidden, but it had no legal standing. President Kruger constituted it in 1898, but no safeguarding law had ever been passed, and as things stood there was the ever-present danger that under political pressure it might be abolished.

This was no idle fear because the sheep farmers of the high-veld had long been conducting an agitation to shoot out the game to enable them to put these parts to winter grazing. They were a powerful group and already, under duress, the government had at various times been forced to excise portions of the reserve on the same principle as the Russian sleigh-driver who threw some of his passengers to the wolves to save the rest. It seemed to me that if a stand was not made now it would soon be too late.

Another difficulty was that more than a third of the ground was privately held and the owners, not unnaturally, complained that their land was useless to them if they were not allowed to shoot the game.

I conceived the idea of striking a bargain by giving them crown land outside the reserve in exchange for their farms, and the purpose of my journey was to explore the situation from this angle.

I took with me several officials and expert land valuers and we travelled first of all by rail to Komatipoort on the Portuguese border. Along the Komati river as far as Swaziland the land is all state property and I proposed compensating farm owners in the game reserve with some of this ground.

The country consisted of a bush-covered plain wedged between the Komati river on the one side and the Lebombo mountains on the other and there was a concentration of wildebeest running here such as I have not seen in Africa. We reckoned once that in the course of a single morning we passed fifteen thousand of them and at times we actually had to 'shoo' them from the road, so tame and so plentiful were they. In addition, troops of zebra galloped by and we saw koodoo and sable antelope, and in the river schools of hippo swam undisturbed. No Europeans lived in this country and we encountered only wandering Swazi cattlemen. Having seen the ground, we turned back towards the Sabie river.

I had been in this part of the world as a boy. In the year 1900 we had fought a three days' battle against Lord Roberts's army on the heights above Machadodorp. Under a merciless pounding we ultimately broke and our commandos fled down the valleys, to outward semblance a disorganised mob, but General Botha rallied us at Hectorspruit and he led us by Ship mountain and through the Sabie country to begin the long guerrilla campaign that followed.

Now I was here on a more peaceful errand. We struck in somewhat east of our former trail and progressing slowly, for the bush was dense and there were no roads of any description, we made for a point on the lower Sabie river which we crossed, and after three days we reached a place called Tshokwane, on the Massintonto.

We saw great quantity and variety of game. At one pan on which we emerged, I made special note in my pocketbook of over two hundred wildebeest, many zebra, nineteen sable, two giraffe, several reed buck and a herd of *impala*. As we watched, four stately koodoo bulls trotted into the clearing and behind them ran a couple of warthog, tails in air, with a string of squealing youngsters in their wake—an indelible picture of wild life and wild scenery. After sunset lion roared about our skerm, and Major Scott, of the Land Board, whom I had sent on ahead, had an exciting adventure when two lion stampeded his mules one night.

His native cook-boy jabbed them off with his assegai as no one could shoot for fear of killing porters and mules in the dark.

We pitched a base camp at Tshokwane and from here we made journeys in all directions to assess the position. Having completed a preliminary survey we worked our way out via Sabie bridge, Pretorius Kop and Mtimba to White River from where it was but a short distance to the railway line and civilisation.

To-day all that area has been opened up; roads have been built and thousands of tourists pass comfortably by motor-car through what is now the famous Kruger National Park, but we had to do the journey with mules and pack donkeys.

At Mtimba I met ranger Wolhuter. A lion had pulled him from his horse and as he was being dragged away he managed to unsheathe his knife and he plunged it into the animal's heart.

David Livingstone, who was also mauled by a lion, says in his book that he experienced neither pain nor fear. He propounds the theory that this was due to a merciful dispensation of Providence by virtue of which a mouse in the jaws of a cat or any other creature seized by a beast of prey undergoes a numbing of the senses and a deadening of pain.

Why Providence should permit the major tragedy and only intervene when the damage has been done is a question for theologians, but I asked Wolhuter as to his sensations at the time. He said that so far from feeling no pain he suffered excruciating agony and as for his senses being numbed, every nerve in his body was tense with horror.

Before leaving White River, I attended a meeting of irate sheep farmers. They said they had word that I was down here to set aside the Sabie country as a game reserve and they threatened me with those pains and penalties which, according to them, will befall a Cabinet Minister who pays no need to those who have a vote to cast.

But I realised that action was necessary if Paul Kruger's dream was to come true and I opposed their demands. When I returned to Pretoria I set about exchanging land and drafting a Bill designed to turn the Sabie reserve into a nature sanctuary for all time.

It was not given me to complete this task and the Kruger National Park is the work of my successor in office, but I like to think that I helped to prepare its foundations. Also, I came back from that expedition with an abiding love of the Low Country and its inhabitants that was considerably to influence me in later years.

Chapter 6

A Stormy Year in the South

I

It was the end of 1923 by now and at the various Cabinet meetings I attended after my return to Pretoria I found that General Smuts and the other Ministers were perturbed at the political situation. We had lost a number of by-elections, our parliamentary majority had dwindled to vanishing point, and from towns and country came the rumble of discontent.

The South African Party had been in office since 1910. It had guided the Union through the Botha-Hertzog troubles, through the 1914 rebellion, the Great War and the 1922 insurrection, and its enemies had multiplied as time rolled on.

To fill our cup, came the world depression and a calamitous drought, and our political fortune was at low ebb. So it was clear that the end was in sight.

Parliament assembled at Capetown early in 1924. The opening weeks ran heavily against us and after a stormy course, General Smuts summoned a Cabinet meeting in April to discuss a dissolution. We were sick and tired of the indignities that are forced upon a government with a small majority and we unanimously agreed to go to the country for better or for worse.

There was a dramatic scene in the House that afternoon when the decision was announced. Our own supporters sat glum and lowering for they knew it meant defeat, while there was tremendous shouting and cheering from the opposition benches. General Hertzog and his followers knew that the fight they had waged for so long was won at last.

In this manner a disorderly session ran to an end and now both sides girded their loins for the coming general election. We took the field and for the next six or eight weeks the heavens rang with the din of the hustings and with the mutual recriminations of rival candidates.

Onlookers think the narrow bigotry of South African politics is due to hatred between Dutch and English, but this is not entirely correct. It is true that there are always zealots who stir up trouble over questions of race or language but in ordinary life there is comparatively little ill-feeling between the two sections. They intermingle and intermarry freely and they get on well together when left alone by the priests and the politicians.

Since the peace of Vereeniging in 1902 not a blow has been struck, not a shot has been fired, as between one race and the other. The 1914 rebellion was an inner feud between us Dutch and the 1922 upheaval on the Rand was a labour dispute with no racial complexion of any kind.

What in reality lies at the root of our troubles is not hostility between the two peoples, but the difficult psychology of our Afrikaans-speaking community. For nearly three centuries they have been individualists, roving the interior far from constituted authority, every man a law unto himself, and to this day they resent discipline and ordered rule.

No sooner have they set up a leader or a government but they start undermining their own handiwork and all our history has been one of hiving off into bickering factions and of internal quarrels among ourselves.

Even during the Great Trek, the *épopée* of our race, there were petty divisions and sordid jealousies, and under the two republics there was constant civil strife, with opposing commandos chasing each other about the countryside. We are like the Irish; when we have no external enemy we turn upon ourselves.

I was as bad as the rest. I regarded General Hertzog and his supporters with the same unreasoning dislike that a Scottish clansman would look upon a neighbouring faction: and I plunged into the fray with a fierce loyalty to General Smuts, my feudal chief.

I have forgotten the issues of that election, but I kept a record of my share of it. The place-names will be meaningless to anyone not closely acquainted with the geography of our country, but reaching the towns and villages and districts mentioned, involved journeys of many hundreds of miles, sometimes in torrid heat, then again in piercing cold or blinding dust storms.

It involved bad roads and discomfort and hectic meetings, long hours of speechmaking, day after day, for weeks in succession, under crossfire of shouts and abuse and questions, and it required a sound constitution.

I give my election itinerary to show how seriously we take our politics in South Africa:

From Capetown to Johannesburg with General Smuts, addressing meeting in Town Hall. Shouted down.

To Rustenburg district holding five meetings in two days. Very hot; very dry.

On tour to Northern, Eastern and Central Transvaal speaking at two and three meetings a day for nearly a fortnight. Then to Krugersdorp, Klerksdorp, Bethal and Heidelberg towns—twelve gatherings.

To the Western Transvaal, five meetings with several banquets and after-dinner speeches thrown in.

To Ermelo and Carolina districts; ten meetings in four days. From there to Kimberley, first vote of confidence of the campaign.

Addressed series of rowdy meetings along the Vaal river alluvial diamond diggings.

(The miners did not allow me to forget our hanging of Taffy Long and the others. Invariably rough house.)

To Port Elizabeth and Somerset East. Six meetings. Back to the Transvaal recombing Heidelberg, Standerton and Rustenburg districts. Two and three meetings a day.

To Northern Transvaal beyond the Olifants river; temperature 105 degrees in the shade and the temperature at some of the meetings still higher.

Doubled back by rail to the Cape Province to hold meetings in the north-western district of Namaqualand.

To Wellington, second vote of confidence; elsewhere only votes of no-confidence.

To Sundays river valley and then up through the Midlands into the Kalahari desert to try the sparsely populated cattle areas.

I had to finish this portion of my tour at a town called Kuruman and I was told that a warm reception awaited me there. It was worse than that. A *wapinshaw* was being held on the commonage and a record crowd had assembled, for apart from the military display and the lure of a political meeting, the first aeroplane to visit these parts was to give a demonstration of machine gunning and bomb dropping.

As the village hove in sight I realised that something was amiss. Horsemen were galloping wildly and people ran in all directions. Arriving on the scene I found that the air force pilot had dropped a 20 lb Cooper bomb among the spectators by mistake, killing six and wounding forty.

It was a grim sight. Three men, a woman, a young girl and a boy were dead and the wounded lay scattered around. For a moment it looked as if there was to be a lynching. Defence officers were being mobbed and there were threats of shooting them out of hand and there came angry shouts that General Smuts and his government had done it on purpose.

Then old Coen Brits, under whom I had served in German East, rode up. In his powerful voice he told them that it was true a bomb had been dropped yet it might just as easily have been a thunderbolt from heaven in which case they would have had to blame the Almighty instead of General Smuts. Strangely enough, his crude logic impressed his hearers and the storm died down though up to midnight knots of men stood muttering at street corners.

Incidentally that bomb blew our election prospects in the quarter sky high.

'From Kuruman to Olifantshoek, Postmasburg and Griquatown; more meetings in the heat of the desert, holding forth from town hall platforms or from a wagon or a wool bale or whatever else could serve as a platform. Then to my own constituency at Port Elizabeth for the final round of speeches before polling day.'

If it be considered that the rest of my colleagues in the Cabinet were equally busy and that in addition there were about 200 candidates in the field, all vocal and all active, some idea will be gained of the fervour that attends a general election in South Africa.

And as usual, the hatred and the bitterness, the charges and counter-charges, the broken meetings and the free fights were almost exclusively confined to our Dutch-speaking voters. The English citizens stood aloof from our tribal follies.

The result of the election was disastrous. The Nationalist Party were returned with a large majority and we had to resign from office and hand over the reins of government to General Hertzog and his victorious legions.

I thought the country was doomed, but I had managed to hold my seat and I attended the first session of the new Parliament fearing the worst. We found, however, as time went on that a party making violent propaganda while in opposition settles down more soberly when invested with the responsibilities of power; and I had to admit to myself grudgingly that the advent of the Nationalist Party brought no revolutionary changes.

II

In June 1924, towards the end of the session, I had a pleasant surprise.

There is an institution known as the Empire Parliamentary Association which all Members of Parliament in Great Britain and the Dominions are entitled to join.

Periodically the Association sends a group on visits of goodwill to different countries of the Empire and this year South Africa had been chosen as their venue. Some forty or fifty Members of Parliament arrived at Capetown on an extended tour of the Union and Rhodesia and I was elected by ballot as one of the local delegates to accompany them. They were led by Mr J H Thomas, the Dominion Secretary, and a number of us went to a civic function at the town hall to welcome them.

The Mayor delivered an address to which Mr Thomas replied. He thanked us for the reception, spoke of the object of their journey, of the Empire and the Dominions and then he went on to discuss the workings of the British Constitution. He wound up by saying, 'Ladies and gentlemen, in me you have a splendid example of the beauties of a democracy, for I who was recently an engine driver am now one of His Majesty's Cabinet Ministers.'

There was loud applause and I was called upon to say a few words. I pointed out that in me they had an even finer illustration of the joys of a democracy, for I, who was recently one of His Majesty's Cabinet Ministers, would now be glad of a job as good as an engine driver's.

A few days later the Parliamentarians started off. I found that my father was to accompany us. He was a Member of the Union Senate who had elected him as their representative.

I was the more delighted at this for we had seen but little of each other for a great many years. As children, my brothers and I had been his inseparable companions by coach and on horseback in the days when he was President of the Orange Free State Republic, but after he became State Secretary to Paul Kruger we saw less and less of him. Then came the vicissitudes of the Boer War and subsequent exile, he in Texas and I in Madagascar. On our return to South Africa, he became President of the Upper House and I was a struggling lawyer in a small village a thousand miles away, so we met only at rare intervals. The Great War and the post-war activities that followed kept us apart and now, after almost a lifetime, we were to travel together for the next few months.

He soon became the central figure of the expedition for he was a polished raconteur and a mine of information to our overseas guests, and I noted with pleasure how they deferred to him and his wide learning. He was a scholar in the best sense of the term. He had a mastery of Latin and Greek and he spoke French, German, High Dutch, and Afrikaans with equal facility; his command of English and his knowledge of English literature were probably unsurpassed by any in this company of savants, authors, public men, and men of the world that made up our group of Parliamentarians.

My father was a poet too. Not a great poet, but a true poet, for he wrote poetry for the love of it. I have watched him on occasion. His lips would move silently; then he would take an envelope or an odd scrap of paper, and there appeared a ditty, a couplet, or a song.

In the Boer War his Afrikaans poems went far to hearten our sorely tried men in the field, and they are still remembered.

He wrote as easily in English as in Dutch, and I have been told that his parodies of the *Recessional*, the *Wearin' of the Green*, and other jingoisms had moved even humourless men like Lord Milner and Lord Kitchener to unwilling laughter.

At Bloemfontein is the grave of an infant sister of mine who died long ago. On her headstone is an inscription which he composed:

> Her tiny feet that never trod
> This thorny world of ours,
> Are standing by the Throne of God
> Amid his fairest flowers.

When the British ordered us out of the Transvaal in 1902 I saw him, as our train crossed the Portuguese border, sitting motionless for a while, then he took a pad upon his knees and wrote a few lines which he handed me. I have them yet.

> *South Africa*

> Though foreign shores my feet may tread,
> My hopes for thee are not yet dead.
> Thy freedom's sun may for a while be set,
> But not forever; God does not forget.

His Afrikaans translations from Robert Burns are known to every schoolboy in South Africa, and I even remember a time when I was about seven when I thought my father had originally written these poems in Dutch and that a fellow named Burns had translated them into very indifferent English.

On Dickens and Thackeray and Lord Macaulay and the earlier giants he was an authority but Sir Walter Scott and Robert Burns were his heroes. He had been educated in Edinburgh and the British Members of Parliament paid homage to and must have wondered at this gaunt old Boer who talked of *The Heart of Midlothian* and *Rob Roy* and of *Tam O'Shanter* and *The Cottar's Saturday Nicht*, and who loved Scotland so dearly.

III

The first item on our itinerary was a visit to Basutoland. This territory is the Switzerland of South Africa, a small but mountainous region lying in the middle of the Union but still administered from London after approved mid-Victorian style.

We had been invited to the annual '*Pitso*' or Grand Council, held by the paramount chief and his subordinates, and for the benefit of our guests, twenty thousand mounted Basuto natives were assembled, they alone of all our tribes excepting the Transkei being a race of horsemen.

They breed a sturdy little mountain pony and the sight of the long columns winding down the slopes was of absorbing interest.

The Basutos have never been conquered. From 1848 to 1880 the British and Boers in succession tried to capture their fastness at Thaba Bosigo, but without success; and after the Free State Republic under my father's predecessor Sir John Brand had conducted several wars against them, they appealed to Queen Victoria to take them under her wing; and thus Basutoland has remained an independent protectorate to this day.

They are a fine race, second only to the Zulus in courage and physique.

When I was a boy, our grooms and stablemen were always Basutos. Many of them had served in the border forays and I used to listen to their tales of shields and assegais and battleaxes with which they had ridden into action against the white man's firearms.

The founder of the Basuto nation was the famous chief Moshesh who in the 1840's collected the refugees, fleeing to the safety of the mountains before the impis of Chaka and Dingaan, and welded them into a separate nation.

We spent several days attending the *Pitso* and making journeys to outlying kraals and mission schools to give the Parliamentarians an opportunity of studying this phase of our native problem at first hand.

The Basuto wards were somewhat before my time, but when I was five or six years old, Sir John Brand was President of the Free State and we children had the run of his home. He had been in command against the Basutos and one morning he was telling us about the fighting, when his wife entered the room. After listening a while she unhooked a cutlass from the wall and drawing the blade, she pointed to deep notches along the edge which she said were caused by the skulls of the warriors her husband had slain in battle. Sir John, who stood in awe of his consort, heard her out in silence but presently, when she left us, he looked round to make sure she was not within earshot, then he whispered to us, 'My boys, I never killed a Basuto in my life. Those dents were made by hacking maize stalks for horse fodder.'

I have another memory connected with Basutoland.

After Sir John's death, my father was elected president of the republic in his stead, and we often accompanied him on his official tours. Once, as we were riding across the southern plains that stretch towards the Basuto frontier, we saw three figures showing against the skyline, and galloping thither, we came upon an aged Basuto couple, husband and wife, together with their daughter, a strongly built girl of twenty or so.

Her two parents were so old and decrepit that neither of them could walk and she told us a moving tale. She said that in their youth her father and mother had migrated to what is now Northern Rhodesia, twelve hundred miles away, and she was born there.

At length, feeling the end of their days to be approaching, the old people were seized with a consuming desire to return to their native land. They were too poor to hire ox or horse and they set out upon their long journey in this wise.

The girl carried her mother forward for twenty or thirty yards, set her down, and returned to fetch her father, whom she similarly carried and placed before his wife. Then she made two more journeys for the sleeping mats, cooking pots and other belongings.

In such manner they had progressed through both Rhodesias, through the length of the Transvaal and Free State and now their odyssey was nearing its end for already the mountains of Basutoland were showing on the horizon.

She said the tribes on the way had given them food as they passed and she thought they had been three years on the road.

My father was so affected by this brave girl's filial devotion that he sent for a wagon to take them to their destination.

Our Basutoland visit being concluded, we made for the native territories of the Transkei in the Eastern Cape Province.

Most of the British delegates were anxious to study native life and customs on the spot and some of them gave me the impression that they had come to South Africa with a preconceived opinion that our administration was harsh and repressive. Just as during the Great War there were people in England who considered that German soldiers by preference walked about with Belgian babies spitted on their bayonets, so there are people across the water who think the average Dutchman in South Africa walks around like Simone Legree, slashing at every native within reach of his rawhide sjambok. They do not know that our small European community successfully governs eight million natives, including the Zulus, the most warlike savages in Africa, and that there has been unbroken peace for over a generation.

All through our expedition, members of Parliament gave talks on problems of common interest to the Empire and when my round came I spoke on the native question.

I began by saying that when the Boer War broke out, every male adult citizen in the two republics was called to arms. They went off leaving their wives and families, their flocks and their herds and their crops in charge of their native servants and in no single instance that I knew of had that trust been betrayed. Since then the same system holds good. If a farmer goes on business or pleasure, he has no hesitation in putting his natives in command during his absence.

In my own case, I said, my wife and I were away for five months every year at the Cape and we always entrusted our two small sons and all our worldly goods to our Zulu houseboys, secure in the knowledge that no harm would befall the infants and that not a teaspoon would be missing on our return.

I pointed out that scores of thousands of natives from Rhodesia and the Protectorates and from as far away as Nyasaland flocked into the Union every year in search of work, a condition that would scarcely obtain if they were badly treated.

One of the English Labour Members rose and said that was all very well, but we refused the native the vote and we refused him social equality. I replied that even civilised nations like the Germans, Italians, Russians and others seemed incapable of making a proper use of the franchise and that being the case, what would be the good of conferring it on aboriginals who, in the nature of things, understood its value still less.

I told him furthermore that in none of their territories had the British given them the vote or social equality.

In how far the dissidents were satisfied with my homily I cannot say, but several of them told me they now saw the question from another angle.

The Transkei was in the grip of a terrible drought, reported to be the worst in sixty years, and the government was hurrying trainload after trainload of foodstuffs into the affected area for free distribution to the natives, a matter that did not escape the notice of our travelling companions.

We made an extensive journey through the reserves and we were present at meetings of the different tribes—Gaikas, Kosas, Galekas, Pondos, Tembus and Fingos, all hereditary enemies but now living amicably side by side under European laws save for an occasional faction fight due to the kaffir beer they indulge in at births or deaths or weddings or any other event affording an excuse.

Not only was the drought creating havoc in the native territories but the economic slump in the outside world was also hitting them hard and as to this a local magistrate told us an amusing story:

A native brought a bale of wool to a European trader for despatch to the coast. The trader forwarded the wool but when accounts were made up it was found that owing to the depression, low prices, high railway rates and other causes, the transaction had resulted in a net loss of eighteenpence.

Accordingly, when the unfortunate owner of the bale came to inquire, the store-keeper said, 'Jim, I'm sorry but I had to pay in 1s 6d on your behalf which you must refund me.' Jim replied, 'Baas, me no got any money to give you.' The trader, wishing to ease things, said, 'All right, you bring me a chicken to-morrow and we'll call it square.' Next day Jim turned up with two chickens, one under each arm. The kindhearted trader said, 'But Jim, you old fool, I told you to bring only one chicken, why do you bring two?' 'Well, you see Baas, I've got another bale of wool outside for you to send away.'

From the Transkei we made for East London, Port Elizabeth, and other coastal towns, and then north through the Free State, Natal and the Transvaal. We covered a great deal of ground, but we kept to the railways and the beaten track so our journey missed the attraction it might have had if we could have gone among the wild animals and the remoter parts.

It became a rushing from one place to another, led by robed mayors and councillors to inspect halls and swimming baths and abattoirs and we attended municipal banquets and civic functions and listened to long speeches to which we retaliated in kind.

Nevertheless we had interesting companions and the long hours spent on board our official train passed quickly enough with discussions and debates and lectures.

My father excelled at these. No matter how widely the talk ranged he always held his own and embellished the subject of each conversation from his inexhaustible store of general knowledge. And as for South Africa, he spoke with authority on every phase of its history and its economic conditions. From the way his hearers kept jotting down notes I should think the bulk of the information they took back was furnished by him during the course of our travels.

Also, he possessed a keen sense of humour and often he would round off his observations with some witty tale to illustrate his meaning. At Pretoria, after a day spent in showing our guests round the Union Buildings and other places, including President Kruger's old home, the discussions that evening naturally enough ran upon the days prior to the Boer War when my father was Secretary of State of the Transvaal. He gave us a vivid account of Paul Kruger and his times; of his giant physical strength, his rugged personality, and the simplicity of his ways.

To demonstrate this last, he said that shortly before the outbreak of hostilities in 1899 they were holding an important Cabinet meeting to discuss the approaching crisis. In the midst of their deliberations the door suddenly flew open and a breathless native servant girl burst unannounced into the council chamber and cried out to the President, 'Baas, baas, the old missus says you must come at once, someone has stolen all the biltong (dried meat) from the clotheslines in the back yard.' On hearing this, Paul Kruger sprang to his feet, jammed on his stovepipe hat, and without a word to his colleagues, rushed off to look into the domestic tragedy; and that was the last they saw of him until next morning.

In speaking of those times, the name of Mr Joseph Chamberlain inevitably cropped up. He it was who penned the despatches from the British Government to the Transvaal that led to the war. My father had to reply and their correspondence became increasingly acrimonious.

I remember how he used to return home from office fuming against Mr Chamberlain and all his works until my brothers and I regarded him as a sort of Corsican ogre and in both republics he was held in execration as the man who was responsible for the disasters that overtook us.

My father enlarged on Chamberlain's iniquities until some of the British delegates began to take up the cudgels on the other side and a rather uncomfortable argument was started, so he created a diversion. He said, 'Gentlemen, I must tell you of the other Mr Chamberlain' and he went on to relate that in addition to the Colonial Secretary there had been a man of the same name who manufactured a popular remedy known as Chamberlain's cough mixture. The Boers were under the impression that the vendor of the patent medicine and the writer of the peremptory despatches were identical and he said he heard an old burgher say to President Kruger, 'Chamberlain's politics are damned rotten, but we must admit that his cough mixture (*hoes druppels*) is very good.' There was hearty laughter at this joke and the talk drifted into calmer waters.

I heard my father tell them about his library. He had possessed a valuable collection of Roman Dutch law books, ponderous tomes, bound in parchment, printed in heavy black-letter type and couched in archaic Netherlands almost as difficult to read as Chaucer. When we evacuated Pretoria in 1900 on the approach of the British army, our home was left to look after itself, and one morning, soon after Lord Roberts had occupied the city, a fatigue party turned up with a Scotch cart into which they began to load my father's books.

A lady living next door asked the sergeant in charge why they were taking them, and he replied, 'Reading for the troops, mum.' The thought of Tommy Atkins being served out with ten-pound volumes of Grotius and Bijnkershoek by way of light literature moved the Parliamentarians to such mirth that all through the rest of our excursion they broke into smiles at intervals as they repeated the tale among themselves.

I may add that someone in authority must have realised the rarity of these works for long after the peace many of them were discovered in the public library and returned to us. In this manner with good fellowship and good cheer, comfortably housed in a luxury train, we 'did' the Union pretty thoroughly. We inspected towns and villages and hamlets, as well as beauty spots, experimental farms and irrigation schemes, and not even Messrs Thomas Cook & Sons could have made a more thorough job of it.

Then, by invitation of the government of Southern Rhodesia, we headed for Bulawayo and Salisbury.

Before doing so, we lost Mr Thomas, for he had to hurry back to England to face some political impasse or other. We regretted his departure. By the time he left us everyone called him, 'Jimmy, my boy,' and slapped him on the back in the course of their talks. Earlier on, I saw him address a meeting of Free State farmers for nearly an hour without once taking his pipe from his mouth, a feat that aroused considerable admiration among that hard-smoking community.

He was uncertain in the use of his aspirates. One of the British members assured us that shortly before they sailed, Mr Thomas took part in a debate in the House of Commons with regard to the Kenya Highlands; and that next morning the London papers reported him in all good faith as having spoken on the *Islands* of Kenya.

At all events he was a jovial man of the people and we liked his free and easy ways.

While we were looking at President Kruger's statue in Pretoria I told the Parliamentarians the story of Jacob Epstein at work on a statue of one of his amorphous females with the usual distorted limbs and bosom. As he carved, the figure showed signs of coming to life and Epstein, unlike Pygmalion, took no chances for, dropping chisel and mallet, he ran for his life.

My father said this reminded him of another tale, about Mr Samuel Marks and the *Venus de Milo*.

Mr Marks was a Jewish citizen who had come to South Africa many years ago. He started as a rag and bone merchant but in the end, by shrewdness and foresight and by undeviating honesty he amassed a great fortune. He was a personal friend of Paul Kruger and he was ultimately elected to the Union Senate.

He decided to acquire a marble replica of the *Venus de Milo* which happened to be for sale at Capetown. When the statue arrived in Pretoria and it was unpacked from the crate Mr Marks was indignant to find that the figure was armless. He blamed the South African railways for careless handling and he lodged a claim for damages, and what is more, said my father, 'the railways paid up'.

In Bulawayo I met a pioneer who had traded and hunted in Rhodesia when Lobengula was King of the Matabele. He told me that Lobengula kept tame crocodiles in a waterhole near his kraal. Offenders were bound hand and foot and placed beside the pool while the king sat watching the reptiles drag their victims under the surface. He also said that the first time Lobengula was presented with a rifle he amused himself by taking potshots at any of his subjects that happened to be passing and woe betide the unfortunate who attempted to evade the royal amenities by running too fast.

The present town of Bulawayo is built on the site of Lobengula's former capital, which was burned down by the Chartered Company's troops in 1893.

Lobengula fled across the Shangani river and was never seen gain. It is said he died of dropsy, but I think this is a euphemism, as with Dingaan, and he too was probably murdered by some local tribe.

The Matabele are an offshoot of the Zulu nation. In about 1835 they broke away from Dingaan and under their chief Moselekatze (or M'Siligaas), they settled on the Pongola for two or three years. Here the circular foundations of their huts can still be seen. Tsetse fly having appeared among their cattle, they moved up and overran the Transvaal, where they settled until driven out by the emigrant Boers. They then moved north into Rhodesia and quickly subjugated the local tribes.

Moselekatze was one of the few Zulu kings of those days to die in peace. I have seen his burial place in a cave at Fort Usher, near Cecil Rhodes's tomb. He was succeeded by Lobengula who reigned until he found his unknown grave in the bush.

The Rhodesian government treated us like princes of the blood and we visited the

Zimbabwe ruins, the Matoppos, the Mazoë valley and other places of interest, after
which we took train to the Victoria Falls, one of the sights of the world, though a
description of its wonders is beyond my power.

We lived in the sumptuous hotel built by the administration and the 5th of October
was my father's eightieth birthday. The event was celebrated by a dinner given him by
the entire party and I was touched by the high regard in which he stood. Speeches
were made and an address was handed him drafted by Mr Ramsay Muir, the
distinguished publicist, signed by all the delegates. I am entitled to set it out in full:

> *Victoria Falls,*
> *Southern Rhodesia.*
> *5th October 1924.*

Dear President Reitz,

We, who have been your travelling companions, thrown together in the most intimate
way for over six weeks, desire to seize the occasion of your eightieth birthday not only
to congratulate you upon passing another milestone in your long, full, and public-
spirited life, but to assure you of the affectionate regard we have learned to hold for you.
One and all, we account it the greatest privilege of our memorable tour that we have had
the opportunity of knowing you in your ripe and vigorous old age. You have helped us
in many ways of which you are unaware, to appreciate the manliness, courage and
generosity of the great people in whose history you have played so large a part.

Your life has covered almost the whole of the distressing period of discord between the
two races upon whose friendship and co-operation the well-being of South Africa depends,
and in all these troubles you have played a manful and an honourable part. We like to
regard it as a happy augury for the future that you should be spending your eightieth
birthday in companionship with public men drawn from the four quarters of the globe—
men of five nations and at least three languages, all now united in peace, and in the earnest
desire that the comradeship of the peoples whom they represent shall never be broken.

What is more, you celebrate this notable anniversary at one of the remoter outposts of
the white man in the dark continent which you and yours have done so much to win for
civilisation. It is our sincere wish that you may be long spared in the enjoyment of your
great powers of public service, and that you may see unbroken peace, a harmony of
peoples, and a healthy and just prosperity established beyond the risk of disturbance in
the land to which you have devoted your life.'

Our pilgrimage to the Falls was the turning point of the Empire expedition and from
here began the homeward journey. My father and I accompanied the delegation back to
Capetown, and as their ship steamed out we waved farewell to many new friends.

Chapter 7

Journeys from Johannesburg

I

I now settled down in Johannesburg to earn a living at law and journalism. I joined
a partnership which left me free to move about, and during the years that followed

until I again held a South African portfolio I did not vegetate. Almost at once I was employed on an investigation which took me to Swaziland.

This little protectorate lies wedged between the Transvaal on the one side and Zululand and Portuguese East on the other. It owes its present position to the fact that in the early days, when President Kruger tried to obtain access to the Indian Ocean, the British annexed Swaziland as an interposing barrier. Like Basutoland and Bechuanaland, it is administered from Downing Street.

The Swazis are a branch of the Zulu nation that hived off many years ago. From about 1878 to 1891 Umbandine was king of Swaziland and it was to look into a land grant made by him that my services were enlisted.

Before starting off, I spent some days in the Deeds Office at Pretoria looking up the Swaziland records filed there. I found that Umbandine, untutored savage that he was, had worked an ingenious racket. He discovered that in exchange for a written document promising a grant of land or a grant of anything else, he could obtain cash and cattle and unlimited gin. It was easy money and he made an industry of it. He issued enough 'scrip' to paper most of Swaziland. He gave titles to twice as much ground as there was in the whole protectorate and he sold to optimistic purchasers a wide range of superimposed monopolies. He conferred on dozens of licencees the sole right to erect breweries, distilleries, power plants, sawmills, railways, tramlines, schools, hospitals, glassworks, soda water factories and a host of other fantastic privileges.

I even came upon one agreement in which he handed over, for valuable consideration, the non-existent law courts, police force and Orphan Chamber of Swaziland and as a final clean-up I lighted on a concession in which he ceded all remaining rights not granted in previous concessions.

It is hard to believe that white men in their senses could have thought they were fooling the king instead of his befooling them, and Lord Milner had made short work of these claims by cancelling the bulk of them. However, he confirmed some of the land deals that had been reported on as genuine.

Among these was a cattle ranch concerning which a dispute had arisen and it was about this that I went down. I travelled in heavy rains to Mbabane, the administrative centre of Swaziland, in search of information, and here I collected such evidence as was available. Then I rode along the mountain slopes to see N'dhlovokazi, the Queen Mother. Her name means 'Great She-Elephant' and she did not belie the title, for she was a huge woman of about seventy, an imperious-looking old lady who governed her son Sibozo, the present king, with a rod of iron.

Sibozo is a son of Bunu, grandson of Umbandine and great-grandson of Umswaas, and these four are the successive kings of Swaziland that I know of.

I failed to extract anything useful from the queen-mother or from the king, and beyond the fact that I was told she had forty thousand golden sovereigns with President Kruger's effigy stamped on every one of them buried under the floor of her hut, I left no wiser than I came.

From the royal kraal I descended to the plains, beautiful park-like country, the young grass soft and green underfoot as an English lawn.

I was making for the home of my friend, Mr David Forbes, on the black Umbuluzi river. He had intimately known Umbandine and I wished to consult him. I passed quantities of big game on the way, sable, koodoo, roan antelope, etc, and for the first time in my life I saw a pack of wild dogs on the hunt. They were chasing an *impala* doe and the manner in which these savage brutes tore alongside their victim, snatching living flesh from its body as it ran, was a sickening spectacle which I could do nothing to prevent as they were too far off.

Travelling through the bush next day, I came on a novel procession. Several Swazi headmen with their wives and a sprinkling of armed attendants were driving before them a flock of about three hundred goats which they were taking up to N'dhlovokazi. It appeared that in addition to being queen-mother, she was also rain-maker in chief, the only woman, so I am told, who has ever held that post among the Bantu; and the natives come from as far north as the Zambezi river to invoke her pluvial powers.

During the recent drought the headmen had clubbed together and they had propitiated her with a substantial gift of livestock in order that rain might fall. Soon after, the heavens broke and for weeks on end South Africa was inundated by the worst floods we had suffered for many years. There had been heavy losses of crops and animals all over the country, especially in Swaziland, and as there were ominous signs of more dirty weather to come, the headmen had concluded that N'dhlovokazi was overdoing the rain-making business and they were now going up with treble the value of their previous donation to beg her to call it off.

I heard a story in Zululand once of a missionary who owned a mackintosh that the natives held to be strong medicine. They said, 'The white man has a magic coat for making rain—whenever he is seen to wear it, lo, the weather is overcast, and rains fall.'

Mr Forbes received me hospitably and I spent a pleasant week riding with him and watching the herds of game on his ranch. One night there was the grunt of lion round the house and next morning the natives reported that they had killed nine heifers not far from the homestead. A shoot was organised, but we did not come up with the marauders.

Mr Forbes had many interesting things to tell of Umbandine. He also spoke of the days when he served in the Secocoeni war under President Burgers, and of the days of du Point and MacNab. He said MacNab was at heart a kindly man, but liable to fits of ungovernable rage, and these were the cause of his many acts of violence rather than inherent brutality. MacNab always travelled on foot, no matter how distant the journey, and he dropped dead one morning at an Indian trading store in Portuguese territory where he had halted for a drink of water. He was on his way to Lourenço Marques and he lies buried on Inhaca Island.

Mr Forbes moves into Swaziland every year for the winter grazing but his real home is on his estate of Atholl near the village of Amsterdam in the Eastern Transvaal. He gave me an amusing account of how this little hamlet received its name.

In 1882 or so, a number of Scotchmen settled in that area which is still known as New Scotland. As time went on, the newcomers decided to establish a township and Robert Burns being their patron saint, they agreed to call it 'Roburnia'. Under the law of the land they had to obtain the consent of the head of the state before building lots could be surveyed. Accordingly, a deputation waited upon President Kruger in Pretoria. He gave them a courteous hearing, looked at the blue-prints and charts they laid before him, and agreed to their project.

But as he was about to sign his consent, he looked up for a moment to ask what the village was to be called. '"Roburnia", your honour,' said the chairman. Hereupon the President flew into a rage and thumping his desk he exclaimed, 'Roburnia, Roburnia, I tell you I won't have any kaffir names in this country,' and turning to his young Hollander secretary he asked him where he was born. 'Amsterdam, sir,' replied the secretary, and the President growled, 'Amsterdam you will call your village and not otherwise.' The discomfited representatives had to submit, and 'Amsterdam' it has remained ever since.

I tried this story on a Scotch audience in Johannesburg at a Burns' nicht gathering later on, but it met with a frigid reception.

I now said good-bye to Mr Forbes and started back for home, going via Bremersdorp where I saw Charles du Pont at his sister's house. He had come from Portuguese territory to see her and he looked harmless enough, but they say his word is still law on the Maputo river where he lives. No man is allowed to hunt elephant there even if he has a government visa, unless he also has du Pont's permission.

Should this preliminary be omitted, du Pont sends bands of natives to scare away the elephant until the delinquent pays up.

When I reached home the difficulties of Umbandine's concession were settled by arbitration and thus ended a pleasant outing.

II

Early in 1925 I went on a business trip into German South West, the territory we had invaded and captured in 1915.

It is a large and barren country. It stretches from the Orange river in the south to the Cunene, eight hundred or a thousand miles to the north, and from west to east it lies between the Atlantic Ocean and the Kalahari desert, a width of four hundred miles.

I travelled first of all by rail to Windhoek, the capital, where I discussed various matters with the officials at the 'Tinten Palast' (government buildings) and then I returned down the line to Rehoboth to report on an alleged gold strike.

I had been here nine years before under different circumstances. Some companions and I had been following in the wake of the retreating German troops during the 1915 campaign. We clung to the railway track hoping to find water at the stations and sidings but everywhere they had dynamited the wells and boreholes and tanks.

By the afternoon of the second day we were in a serious plight. Our flasks were empty; we had come too far to return for we would have been dead of thirst before we could reach the nearest water to the rear, and ahead of us almost certainly we would find none, so thorough was the work of demolition we had encountered.

We stumbled along in the heat, our tongues parched and swollen, and the knowledge that the prospect of water was remote increased our sufferings.

Towards evening, when we were approaching the limit of endurance, we came upon a railway engine lying in a dry riverbed where the Germans had wrecked it; and in a corner of the boiler we found a few gallons of water providentially unspilt. This saved our lives and continuing forward we came to Rehoboth where next morning we discovered more water in a little engine that had been overlooked in a shed.

Now I sat on the hotel stoep with a tall glass of iced beer in front of me remembering my previous drouth. The place is the chief town of a race of half-breeds which migrated hither from the Cape Colony about sixty years ago. Their language is a variant of Afrikaans which in turn is a variant of high Dutch, so it requires expert knowledge to understand their talk. They are proud of their near-white origin and their efforts at copying European customs are rather pathetic. They have set up a sort of parliament and a small standing army with muzzle-loaders and flintlocks and they run a law court of their own.

One of them to whom I spoke had original ideas on class distinctions. He had been defeated in one of their periodic elections and he said to me in a disgusted tone what would amount to this, 'Can you believe it; they rejected me, who was born in a bed and in a room, for my opponent who was born on the ground behind a bush.'

I have modified this, for the original was rather more naturalistic. His outlook was that of a Vere de Vere who had been beaten by a coal heaver.

The Rehoboth half-breeds assisted us in the war and the Germans took heavy toll of them. The mummified corpses I had seen dangling from a tree in 1915 were part of the price they paid for adhering to our cause.

I was unfavourably impressed with the gold occurrence and I now went south to Kalkfontein, a village established by the Germans in olden days, and from here I travelled by car, a ramshackle Ford whose owner, Carl Weidner, was awaiting me. Weidner was a well-known character along the Orange river. He lived at a place called Goodhouse on its banks, where he managed a large citrus estate for an English Company that had commissioned me to report on the property.

Goodhouse[1] lies ninety miles from Kalkfontein through ninety miles of desert. Whenever we met with heavy sand, which was every mile or two, we had to deflate the tyres to half strength to obtain a gripping surface, and as soon as we reached firmer soil we had to get out and pump them back to their original size under a broiling sun, a gruelling task which we performed a dozen times during the day, and it took us sixteen hours to reach our destination.

The area we passed through is inhabited by the Bondelswart tribe of Hottentots and it is hard to understand how any human beings are able to exist in this sterile region. Not long ago they had broken into rebellion and they were bombed into submission by aeroplanes sent from the Union. I met their chief Jacobus Christian at Goodhouse and he gave me his version of the business.

He said there was a dispute with the magistrate with regard to taxes on hunting dogs when suddenly Abraham Morris, the half-breed outlaw, returned from across the Orange and before he knew what was doing there was an armed rising and they were being bombed from the air.

Abraham Morris and his brother Edward were two half-castes, grandsons, it is said, of a Scotch missionary by a Hottentot wife. These two men with their strain of coloured blood were looked down on by the Europeans, and they conceived a violent hatred of all white men in consequence.

---

[1]Goodhouse '*Ga Daus*', meaning 'Ford of the Sheep' in the Hottentot language.

From 1906 onwards they assisted the Bondelswart chief Marengo against the Germans until Edward was killed and Abraham was driven into the Cape Colony and exiled. He remained there until the recent mutiny in which he was pursued into the desert and killed by Carl Weidner's son-in-law.

The Bondelswarts, from having been hardy freebooters, are now a fear-haunted people, so terrible was the reckoning by our machines; and I could not but feel sorry for this primitive community overwhelmed by civilisation. The impression they left on me was that they were more sinned against than sinning and I doubt whether to this day they know what it was all about.

I enjoyed Carl Weidner's hospitality at Goodhouse for a week and as the temperature stood at 108 degrees in the shade from seven am to five pm daily, I spent most of my time swimming in the tepid waters of the Orange river and only after dark by lamplight did we drag forth the ledgers and account books.

Having completed our labours, old Weidner and I worked our passage back to Kalkfontein, once more deflating and inflating the tyres on the way. We reached the village after midnight and found that during hot weather the entire population move their beds into the middle of the main street. So we had to drive with care in order to avoid ramming the sleeping inhabitants.

Next morning, at the court house I saw three bushmen in charge of a European policeman. They were under arrest for murder and this was only the second time in my life that I had seen pure-blooded specimens such as these.

They are a yellow-skinned pygmy race standing about four-foot six, and they have tremendously developed hindquarters which serve them like the camel's hump from which to draw on in lean periods.

The policeman told me that shortly before, while out on patrol, he had come on a bushwoman lying in a small hollow she had scooped in the ground, and she was in the very act of parturition. As he approached, the child made its appearance and the mother, seeing him ride up, hastily scrabbled the new-born infant in the sand to dry it, and holding it close to her body she fled into the bush like any wild animal.

He said he had been present when Mr Van Ryneveld, the magistrate, was killed the year before. They saw a bushman running through the trees and Mr Van Ryneveld, wishing to interrogate him, galloped forward to head him off.

When brought to bay he pulled out one of the tiny bows they carry and shot his captor with a poisoned dart at a range of a few feet. The magistrate died in great agony in less than an hour and by next morning the body was so decomposed that it fell to pieces when they tried to handle it.

These little bows are about two inches long, beautifully fashioned from what appears to be rhino horn. The arrows are the size of a safety match, of heavy wood, the points covered with a deadly poison brewed from some vegetable toxin or from putrid caterpillars (no one seems to know which). The arrows are carried in a tiny leathern quiver and each has its point sheathed in grass to prevent accidental contact. The bushman also carries his ordinary hunting bow and he uses the smaller weapon in the same way as a gangster might carry an automatic pistol in addition to a larger gun.

On the other hand some people think that bushmen carry these miniature bows and arrows for shooting at the evil spirits with which they believe themselves to be surrounded on all sides.

The fact remains however that in the German time the carrying of these little weapons was strictly forbidden by law on account of shortrange ambushes committed with them on soldiers and police.

From Kalkfontein I travelled back to Windhoek and then to Walvis Bay. Up to now, the only drinking water to be had at this forbidding spot was by distillation from the sea but word had come that a spring had been discovered in the dunes some distance inland and I accompanied a party of inspection. We found a strong supply of fresh water surrounded by reeds and bulrushes and there were many birds. This fountain has since been piped to Walvis Bay and as a result a well-equipped port is arising there.

While we were ploughing along in the sand I heard a police officer ahead of me telling someone how he had been in a blockhouse at Springbokfontein towards the end of the South African War in 1902 and how a Boer sniper had crawled up and shot two of their men through the loopholes.

I pricked up my ears at this and when he had finished I told him I was the sniper in question. He was a jovial Irishman named Drew and he bore no malice for he slapped me on the back and said, 'So it was you, was it, you Dutchman, we must have a drink on it'; and a drink we had when we reached the bay.

From Walvis I returned to Windhoek to interview officials and others, and I met a shaggy old Boer hunter whose talk was to send me on a long journey. He hailed from Angola but he had spent some years in a region known as the Kaokoveld which with a wide sweep of his arm, he vaguely described as lying far to the north.

He told me of big game and strange tribes and of many adventures and he told me one story in particular of how, when he was stalking an antelope towards dusk he suddenly saw a goods train crossing the rise.

For a moment he thought he had lost his senses, then he realised that what he was looking at was not a goods train but hundreds of elephant marching head by tail in single file across a hill.

His stories made a strong appeal, and the thought that there was in that distant corner a remnant of the old savage Africa unspoilt as yet by the white man so fired my imagination that I decided that I would go and have a look at it for myself.

III

I could not start out of hand for I had to return to Capetown to attend Parliament, and there were business and financial arrangements to be made to allow of a long absence; but as a preliminary I went to the Tinten Palast to make inquiries.

The officials were uncertain about the Kaokoveld. They said it was a practically unexplored tract lying below the Kunene river, between the Etosha pan and the sea. The natives were warlike and under the old régime the Germans had not attempted to occupy it for fear of precipitating a war in such inaccessible country. The Union mandatory administration had left the Kaokoveld alone for the same reason. I was told there was not a single European up there; neither settlers, traders nor missionaries, that the territory was wholly unpoliced and that any white man entering there would do so at his peril and on his own responsibility.

All this made me the more determined to go. Fierce and warlike natives as often as not turn out to be decent fellows when properly handled, and I had no qualms on that score.

I travelled back to Capetown and sat through a long and dreary session, but while members droned and debates dragged, I dreamed of a far-off country and I saw elephant like goods trains passing over the hills. I also made practical research and I found that if the Kaokoveld is unknown to the world in general and even South Africans have scarcely heard of it, yet it has occasionally been traversed by Europeans. Green and Ericson, two famous hunters, had frequented it in the 'seventies of last century, and the German explorers Volkmann and Hartmann and a few others had been there. In our own time Major Manning and Lieutenant Hahn had made journeys and submitted official reports, deeply pigeonholed and forgotten.

In the course of my inquiry I found too that the Kaokoveld was the scene of a curious episode in our South African history that has gone almost unrecorded.

The great northward trek from the Cape Colony which started in 1835, came to a standstill in the 'fifties, for most of the Voortrekkers had settled down in the Free State and the Transvaal to a less roving life. But the old spirit, the desire to be ever on the move which is so strong a characteristic of the Boers, was still alive and in 1874, for no apparent reason, a large number of them once more inspanned their wagons and trekked off into the western desert with their families and their stock. The migration was the more inexplicable in that they had succeeded in establishing a republic of their own and for the first time were able to enjoy peace and quiet, free from British rule which, like the Irish, they had always declared to be at the root of all their troubles.

They issued a statement that they were leaving the Transvaal because they looked on President Burgers as the anti-Christ; he was a freemason, he had been seen at dances, and he travelled on the Sabbath; but the real propelling power was the old unconquered fever, the wanderlust that had started them on their fateful path so many years before.

About three hundred families shook the dust of the Transvaal republic from their feet and in May 1874 set out on what was practically a continuation of the Great Trek. The survivors and their descendants are still to this day trekking somewhere in the interior of Africa.

After four years of dangers and hardships they had crossed the Kalahari desert and the intervening wastes and what was left of them reached the Kaokoveld in desperate condition. They had lost more than half of their number from thirst and disease, and word of their awful plight ultimately filtered through to the Cape. I unearthed a report in the *Cape Times*, dated 3rd September 1879, which described their sufferings somewhat luridly as follows:

> 'On Thursday last the hopeless condition of the migratory Boers who four years ago quitted the Transvaal in order to seek a new Canaan somewhere towards the West coast of this continent was brought to the notice of the House of Assembly. The story was harrowing in its delineation of human endurance, so harrowing that it is surprising to most people that the distress of these unfortunates has not previously been urged upon the government. The Statement made in the House yesterday reads thus: In 1874, three hundred Boers, discontented with the existing régime, and perhaps also impelled by the spirit of emigration, left the Transvaal with their families. Travelling west through the

Kalahari, they suffered great privations and died in scores from thirst and fever.

Only seventy men and three hundred women and children of nearly nine hundred that started are alive. The main body is now halted in a region named the Kaokoveld, close to the Atlantic seaboard, but hundreds, mostly women and children, have succumbed so that the survivors are chiefly widows and orphans. Many have not so much as a dog or a fowl left. They are indeed in a miserable plight.

Here a child is being carried to its grave; there an old man is dying, yonder five or six of both sexes are given up as past hope; there a mother, or perchance a father, watches the death throes of his children.

All this makes such a picture of horror as, may God grant, we shall seldom have to witness and still less to be in the midst of.'

As a result of parliamentary action and public subscriptions, a sum was raised and a shipload of food and clothing was sent from Capetown to Walvis Bay in charge of one Richard Haybittle, who succeeded in getting into touch with the remaining trekkers and was able to alleviate their distress to some extent.

Those who were left decided to settle in the Kaokoveld which they found healthy for man and beast, and they built permanent homes and dug irrigation canals; they even erected a church at a place they called 'Rustplaats', imaging that they had found rest at last.

Here they lived for some years, tilling the soil and hunting elephant, but in the end the old spring-fret was upon them once more, and they trekked north through the Kunene into Angola and beyond, where they or their children or grandchildren are still trekking about nowadays.

After they had left, the Kaokoveld lapsed back into its primordial state and save for a few explorers who entered at long intervals, it has remained unvisited and undisturbed by white men.

This was the country I intended to see and the moment Parliament rose I made ready to go.

Chapter 8

Kaokoveld Adventures

I

Knowing little of the conditions I was to meet, I intended to travel light. I laid in a side of good bacon, a bag of potatoes and onions, a pocket of wheatmeal and a store of salt, coffee, tea and sugar.

These plus my rifle and a sleeping bag and some spare clothing formed my equipment. For the rest I was going to live on the land. I took a motor-car, thinking I would at any rate be able to push in some distance with it, after which I proposed to wait upon circumstances.

With the car in a truck behind and my impedimenta in a railway coach I left

Capetown for the long journey to Windhoek and from there I went by narrow gauge to a place called Outjo, a small desert outpost from which my journey proper was to begin.

The road from Outjo runs due west roughly parallel to the southern boundary of the Kaokoveld, and for the first hundred miles it bore some resemblance to a highway; so I was able to make slow but steady going as far as Otyitambi, a lonely spot occupied by a German pioneer. By this time I began to doubt the wisdom of having brought a motor-car. I had several rolls of netting wire by means of which I hoped to negotiate the heavier patches of sand by laying the wire in front of the car. It did not work, for the wheels simply chewed up the coils, and when next day I left Otyitambi it took me eight hours to do twenty miles up what is locally termed a *schlucht*, or dry river bed. I came to the conclusion that the petrol era had not yet dawned in these parts.

I was at my wits' end, for I could persuade the car neither forward nor backward and my only alternative seemed to be to return on foot to my German acquaintance at Otyitambi and there make other plans.

As I sat cogitating on the front seat I saw smoke rising about a mile ahead and walked thither to find out what it meant. Fortune had unexpectedly smiled on me. Camped by a waterhole I found an old man named van der Merwe who, with his wife and son, were halted here with their sheep and cattle.

This was a lucky encounter without which I would never have succeeded in entering the Kaokoveld. Van der Merwe senior had actually been a member of the Thirstland Trek of 1874. He was a youth of fourteen at the time and he gave me an absorbing account of the trials and dangers they had endured in the Kalahari desert, the 'Great Thirst' (*Groot Dors*) as he called it. He witnessed many terrible sights of men, women, and children dying of thirst and of cattle licking the wagon tyres because they gleamed like water. He had settled in the Kaokoveld with the other survivors and then trekked with them into Angola.

Later on he moved back into the Kaokoveld where for a long time he and his family surreptitiously lived, for the Administration at Windhoek, fearing trouble with the Natives, had forbidden any European to remain. He and his son hunted and raised sheep and cattle and lived an existence that must have been monotonous with adventure. Now the old man had come south as he wished to take up land nearer to civilisation and to legalise his position which was in constant jeopardy owing to his unlawful presence in the forbidden land.

I stayed for nearly a week at the waterhole during which I picked up much useful information from him and his son Daniel, a young man of about thirty who likewise knew the Kaokoveld and spoke several of its dialects.

It was clearly impossible to make any further attempt by car and it was clear too that I would find great difficult in securing guides, for the local natives look on the Kaokoveld with dread. They have heard so many tales about the savagery of the tribes within its borders and the fierce animals and the evil spirits that dwell in the bush that they will not enter what to them is a land of terror. All the way from Outjo I had offered high wages to anyone who would accompany me: but in vain.

Now all my difficulties were solved, for Daniel van der Merwe junior offered to join me, and not only that but his father produced a light cart and a team of donkeys. They had talked the matter over and decided that they could not allow an amateur like me to go off by himself. Of the many flukes I have enjoyed, this was the greatest of all, for without the assistance of the van der Merwes I would still have gone in, but I question whether I would ever have returned.

We completed our arrangements. We took back a party of natives and we pushed my car under a tree where I found it unharmed months later. Then we said good-bye to the old couple, and Daniel and I started away. The transition from motor transport to donkey conveyance was abrupt, but I soon got used to it; and by dint of travelling at night to save our animals from the heat of day, we reached the police post of Kamanjab on the afternoon of 1 August 1925. This was our final contact with the world outside, and from here we were headed for the blue.

We rested for two days and I had further inkling as to the value of Daniel as an ally; for he disappeared into the bush on foot on the morning after our arrival and returned after four or five hours bringing with him four trek oxen with gear complete, together with a native piccanin who, he informed me, was coming along as our driver.

The oxen he had cajoled or commandeered from a half-breed in the neighbourhood and the piccanin he had shanghaied. The urchin was being fairly dragged along, so reluctant was he to accompany what he seemed to look on as a forlorn hope, for he shared the fear of the outside natives about the Kaokoveld.

Daniel was reticent as to how he had procured the oxen, and when I asked him about our whining helpmeet he said, 'Oh, I just ordered him to come; they've got to do what I tell them round here.'

This held good throughout our journey. His word was law in the Kaokoveld and his orders were invariably obeyed.

Daniel press-ganged another native to take the now unneeded donkeys back to his father, and at sunset next day we said goodbye to the two policemen, the last white faces we saw until our return. Then we set out.

We travelled most of the night and by dawn were well inside the limits of the Kaokoveld. We outspanned near a rugged kopje where Daniel knew of water under a rock, and we rested for the day.

It was scarcely light when I saw a troop of elephant in a mopani thicket and in all directions grazed herds of gemsbok (oryx), their horns three and four feet long and straight as arrows. They stand as high as a pony and have chocolate-coloured markings. I shoot for food only, so I satisfied myself with watching the scene through my glasses, as the sight of big game never palls.

About midday a curious cavalcade rode up consisting of David, the chief of the Toppenaar Hottentots, and a following. This tribe lives at Zesfontein, to the west, which does not lie within the Kaokoveld, but they were taking a short cut through one corner of it on some expedition of their own. They were mounted on riding oxen and most of them carried firearms of sorts.

The Toppenaars were once a powerful and numerous clan, but they are dwindled to a mere handful and to-day they count only forty male adults. I was told that this is due to inbreeding, but my own opinion is that they are dying from a disease called civilisation. Like the Red Indians and the Australian black-fellow there is a virus in their blood that is intolerant of the presence of the white man, and in not many years from now they will have gone the way of other extinguished races.

In the late afternoon we went on. The country was flat but the bush was not thick and everywhere stood rugged kopjes. As the next waterhole was at a place called Khairos, a long distance off, we pushed the oxen and save for short rests, continued through the night. We generally avoided travelling by day, but went forward next morning, with intervals to breathe our cattle, until sunset, when we reached water.

Again we passed elephant and I saw a few giraffe, while there were many gemsbok in the long open glades or 'marambas' as they are called.

At Khairos waterhole live two Herero chiefs, Langman and Herman, both wealthy as wealth goes round here, for they possess hundreds of cattle and large flocks of sheep. All through the Kaokoveld the Hereros have become the ruling class, in spite of their small numbers and in spite of the fact that they are interlopers and usurpers who fled hither before the German troops during the Herero war of 1906.

The rightful occupants are the Mahimba, a race of good physique but lacking in the qualities that make for supremacy, and they have allowed a handful of Herero fugitives who came among them less than twenty years ago to drive them from the waterholes and grazing grounds. By a process of high-handed brigandage the Hereros own most of the livestock in the country and the Mahimba are virtually their slaves.

The Hereros seem to be a race with a strongly-developed instinct for domination. They are big, heavily-built men, inclined to swagger and bluster, but brave and resourceful, and it is not surprising that the Germans found them such a hard nut to crack. They originally inhabited the mountains around and south of Windhoek and I suppose they derive from the Bantu.

When we reached Khairos I had further proof of Daniel's way of doing things, for we had not long been outspanned when both Langman and Herman came to pay their respects to him and a fat sheep was dragged towards us as an offering of goodwill.

Early next morning I had another surprise. A tall Herero reported for duty, clad in a military tunic, riding breeches and putties, and Daniel introduced him as our new cook, Andreas by name, an ex-sergeant of the former German police whom he had conscripted by means best known to himself.

Andreas, unlike his fellow victim, was quite willing to join up for the duration, and he turned out a useful and efficient member of our staff. He spoke German reasonably well, stood smartly to attention and clicked his heels when spoken to, and replied to orders given him with a salute and a '*zum Befehlen*' in approved Potsdam style.

I asked Daniel what remuneration our two henchmen would expect, but he said it was bad policy to spoil the Kaokoveld natives by teaching them to require payment for services to a white man. I let it go at that.

On leaving Khairos next day, we followed a faint track which he optimistically called the Road of the Angola Boers. He said it was the route taken by the Thirstland Trekkers when they passed through forty-five years ago. They had no doubt cut a passage for their wagons at the time but it required a better eye than mine to see any trace of it, and we had great difficulty in getting our cart along in the thick bush. We travelled due north to Otyitundua, reaching there in five or six days.

At most of the waterholes we found well-to-do Hereros in command. They owned considerable herds with the usual Mahimba serfs looking after them. At several places the Mahimba complained of lion but we saw none. The country improved as we went. The trees were taller, the grass more plentiful and to elephant and giraffe and oryx were now added herds of zebra and koodoo and springbok.

At night we halted, as a rule, some distance from the waterholes, for the elephant came out after dark to drink and we watched them as they filed by. The bulls and cows never drink together but on alternate nights. The bulls pad along quietly and taking their fill, they splash and roll in the mud, then they go off as softly as they came, but the cows can be heard approaching from a distance and they objected to our presence, for whenever they scented us, they trumpeted angrily and the calves ran squealing about, between them creating a din that was pretty alarming at first.

However, they never attempted to molest us, and on moonlit nights we were able to see them clearly. When we passed elephant in the daytime they shuffled off, though once or twice a bull faced round, his ears outstretched and his trunk uplifted as if he meant to charge. Daniel and I stood ready with our rifles in case of need, but we never had occasion to fire.

On our way to Otyitundua at several spots there was running water, and at one of them we saw the first relic of the Thirstland Trek; for here, beside a well-trodden elephant path, lay the lonely grave of one of the trekkers, and from now onward we repeatedly came on similar milestones of these indomitable pioneers. The graves are covered with mounds of limestone and they are still in good condition. Daniel even knew the names of those who lay beneath.

At Otyitundua are the ruins of houses they built in 1878 and 1879 and the remains of their cattle kraals and walled gardens as well as the irrigation furrows they cut to lead water to the plains below. It is hard to understand why they left a place such as this where they could have enjoyed peace and plenty under what to them must have been ideal conditions after their wanderings in the desert, but the trek spirit drove them ever onward.

The evening we reached the hill at Otyitundua a troop of elephant coming to drink frightened a herd of cattle belonging to a local Herero and the terrified animals stampeded past our cart with the elephant on their heels; and but for the fact that Daniel had taken the precaution of double-tying our oxen with gemsbok riems to a big tree, they would have gone too, for they got wildly excited and tugged and strained at their bonds. Had they broken loose I doubt if we should ever have seen them again.

The cattle and the elephant streaming by in a cloud of dust amid bellowing and trumpeting was a sight to remember. It seemed to me that the elephant were as frightened as the cattle and that when the cattle started running they had become infected too, for they made no attempt to attack the herd. The last we saw of them, oxen and elephant were intermingled, each apparently bent on getting away from some fancied danger in the rear.

We travelled in two days to Ubombo, across picturesque game-covered plains, with quantities of gemsbok, zebra and giraffe, and more elephant. Once I saw several full-grown giraffe, with two calves. One calf was about eight feet high, but the other could not have been more than a few days old. It was so tiny that at first I only made out a head and a pair of ears above the long grass and I took it to be an antelope of some kind. Then they crossed an open glade and I was able to see what it was as it sprawled along, all legs and neck, beside its mother.

At Ubombo we were within the immediate sphere of Oorlog's power. He is the most forceful Herero chief in the Kaokoveld and the farther we went the more we heard of him. Several bands of Mahimba waited on us at Ubombo to complain of his depredations. They said he and his followers took their cattle and wives at will and certainly he has laid a heavy hand on them if all we heard between this and the Kunene river were true.

There were many springbok on the flats below the fountain and Daniel and I shot half a dozen to feed the Mahimba envoys. These buck have bigger horns than I have seen anywhere and some of the specimens would run Rowland Ward's records pretty close.

In addition to antelope there was plenty of guinea fowl, partridge, and pheasant, so we kept our larder well stocked. One morning a large flock of guinea fowl running into several hundred came up a game track in single file. I waited until the front of the line was twenty yards off and then I whistled. The birds looked up and I sliced seven of their heads off with one bullet. It was rank murder but it kept us in poultry for more than a week. We halted at Ubombo for several days then travelled for two days through increasingly thick bush to Gauko-Otawi, the 'Rustplaats' or resting place of the Trekkers. Here it was that in 1878 they had built a church, their trek-fever temporarily stilled; they thought they had at last reached the land of their dreams.

And here was a region that might have satisfied the most restless nomad of them all, for there was running water, and grazing and hunting grounds such as Nimrod himself would have envied. But they stayed for only two years—to the Boers Utopia always lies beyond the next horizon—and once more they abandoned the homes they had built and the fields and gardens they had laid out, and went on a trail, the end of which they are yet seeking.

At Gauko-Otawi, with its abundance of water and its wooded hills, the elephant concentrate in greater numbers than anywhere else. At dusk every evening Daniel and I stood inside the ruined church and watched them pass, almost brushing the walls as they crossed the clearing to drink at the pools.

As usual, a Herero refugee, one Thomas, had established his kingdom here. He was a great hectoring bully, standing well over six feet, and he had with him half a dozen compatriots with whose assistance he keeps the local Mahimba in subjection. He had turned the old irrigation furrows of the Boers to good account and he had fields of wheat and vegetable and maize below.

In order to drive away the birds by day and elephant and antelope at night he keeps a small army of Mahimba underlings continually shouting and beating tom-toms.

Our oxen were by now so footsore from the rough country we had come over that we considered it impossible to take them any further, especially as the country ahead was growing increasingly mountainous.

Up to now we had kept to comparatively open country, but to the north lay a sea of tumbled ranges which were negotiable only along narrow elephant paths where no vehicle could hope to go. Even the old Trek-Boers had swerved eastwards from here, but I was determined to see what lay beyond and to visit Oorlog's kraal, for I had heard so much of this old freebooter on the way up that I decided to abandon our cart for the time being and to push on by other means.

To that end we had to enlist the co-operation of Thomas, as even Daniel van der Merwe's knowledge of the Kaokoveld, extensive as it was, stopped short of the tract we were making for.

Thomas was generally half drunk from a beer they brew from honey and he was truculent at first. So Daniel exercised some sort of 'third degree' on him which produced a couple of trained riding oxen; and having ferreted out the information that another Herero chief named Cabrito, living at a fountain twelve miles away, owned two Portuguese ponies he insisted that these animals should be added to our transport.

After a day or two we set off for Cabrito's, each of us on a pack ox with a square of tanned sheepskin to serve as a saddle and a thong passed through its nose in lieu of a bridle.

We had ordered Thomas and his Herero followers to accompany us. They refused and turned up intoxicated at our camp armed with several Martini Henri rifles. Daniel took it quite calmly. He told them if they did not obey I, who was a big man in the South, would see to it that a police post would be established here in the near future. This thoroughly alarmed Thomas for he knew that once Europeans were stationed at Gauko-Otawi his power would be gone for ever. Daniel sent them back to put away their rifles and next morning we started. We were an ill-assorted crew for Thomas and his men did not relish their forced attendance, while the Mahimba serfs were delighted at their discomfiture and openly capered with glee as we filed off.

After a weary ride, for an ox makes uncomfortable seating, we reached Cabrito's village. He too had been a fugitive from German vengeance and he too had built up a little principality and possessed many cattle and sheep, although he had reached the Kaokoveld empty-handed not many years ago. He had wheatfields and much tobacco for there was running water and the furrows of the Trekkers to lead it to his crops.

Cabrito was a pleasanter fellow than Thomas. On hearing the object of our visit he let us have the horses plus saddles without demur: two well-knit ponies that he had bought from an Angola Boer who had come into the Kaokoveld the year before to poach elephant.

I chose the bigger pony of the two for I was the more heavily built. He had been clawed by a lion and he had not yet recovered his nerves, as I was to find, for though he had good staying powers he shied and plunged at every bush and at every sound, and was an uneasy animal to ride.

We spent two days at Cabrito's kraal looking for a troop of lion which he said had killed many of his cattle; but we did not find them. We saw several black rhino during our search, fierce ungainly beasts whom we left alone because I had no wish to kill them, or to be killed by them.

After this we rode back to Gauko-Otawi to make our preparations. We instructed Andreas and the piccanin to remain in charge of our cart and stores during our absence and after requisitioning the services of four Mahimba guides from Thomas, Daniel and I rode off two days later.

By nightfall we reached a village named Owatjana. The natives here were Mahimba, guarding cattle belonging to Thomas, and they said that lion were raiding almost nightly, so for safety's sake we double-thonged our horses and built our fires close to the thorn hedge surrounding the huts. It was as well. Shortly before dark we had prepared and eaten our supper and Daniel and I were lying on our blankets talking to each other. Our guides were squatting a few yards away by their own fire, when suddenly a tawny form leapt almost over our heads and there came the bloodcurdling bellow of an animal in mortal terror. A lion had seized an ox, only five or six yards away from us, and we could see him snarling and savaging his prey. We reached for our weapons, but rifles were useless for he was right up against a hut; from within came the frightened cries of native women and children, so it would have been almost impossible to fire without hitting one of them.

We were nonplussed for a moment, but our Mahimbas showed presence of mind. They grasped burning faggots and Daniel and I followed their example. Then we rushed up and thrust the brands in the lion's face. He gave an angry 'woof' and for a moment it looked as if he was going to claw at us; but then he leaped away and disappeared into the bush.

I doubt whether thirty seconds had elapsed between the time he had sprung upon the ox and the time we chased him off, yet in that brief interval he had killed his victim, snapped its hind leg above the elbow, leaving·the bone sticking out, and had broken off one of its horns; which gives some idea of the fierce dynamic energy of these brutes.

From his spoor the next morning it was clear that he had stalked us the previous afternoon for nearly five miles as we rode along; so it was just as well for us that at the last moment he preferred to take an ox instead of one of us.

From Owatjana we continued our journey, and now we entered the wildest country I have seen in Africa, with rugged mountains following upon each other in apparently endless succession. Through these we laboriously threaded our way, mostly by elephant paths, for they have an eye for gradient as good as that of a railway engineer.

Our progress was slow, but we made steady northing through a region that has probably never been visited by Europeans. We rode on for five or six days, barricading ourselves with thorn skerms at night as if against an enemy, but though we heard lion roaring we had no further trouble from them.

In these parts the natives had never seen white men and they flocked in to inspect their unusual visitors. Under Daniel's knowledgeable treatment I found the Mahimbas to be good-natured, intelligent children. The young men are slender and graceful, but after their thirties they quickly shrivel into old age.

Their staple food is a concoction named *omeira*, made from fermented milk, and they provided us with a calabash of it at every village we passed. It is a palatable nourishing dish which we enjoyed drinking.

The Mahimbas have no faith in the cleansing properties of water. Daniel said they never wash, but in lieu thereof they rub their bodies with fat. Each man wears around his neck a segment of sheep intestine filled with grease which exudes a gentle trickle over all his body as he gets heated; and by this system of automatic lubrication they keep themselves satisfactorily oiled.

I gathered that they are blissfully unconscious that they had once been citizens of the German Empire, and they are equally unaware that they are now nationals of the Union of South Africa. The only authority they know is Oorlog's and they stand in great awe of him. They had a lot to say about his drastic methods, but they seemed to accept the law of the strongest with resignation.

Money is meaningless to them. A Mahimba will run fifty miles on an errand if promised a few inches of tobacco twist where he won't go half a mile on a cash basis.

A young Mahimba lad accompanied us for nearly a week to get a baking-powder tin which Andreas had promised to give him as soon as it was empty; but when I presented him with a coin he spent several days drilling a hole into it with a nail and then he hung it round his neck by way of ornament.

In this manner, travelling slowly through jagged country we reached Gangisema, Oorlog's headquarters, towards the end of September.

II

Oorlog knew of our coming long before we rode into his *stad*, his scouts having watched our movements ever since we had left Gauko-Otawi, so he told us later.

He is still a fine figure of a man, tall and straight, though he must be nearing eighty. Strictly speaking he is not a Herero at all as his father was the one-time well-known 'Bechuana Tom' who acted as gunbearer to Green the famous elephant hunter. His mother, however, was a Herero and he looks on himself as one.

On our arrival Oorlog and about thirty followers, mostly his sons, were awaiting us. They were clad in European clothes, for the Herero makes a point of dressing like the white man as a mark of his superior status over the skin-clad tribes. He spares no pains to acquire suitable garb, whether by smuggling from Angola or by going nearly three hundred miles east to the missionaries in Ovamboland to make his purchases.

Oorlog's seat of government consisted of a collection of grass huts though he had a wattle and daub house himself, with glassless windows and a pitched roof. Close by was a hot spring and after having palavered for a while we offsaddled our horses under a tree near the water.

We remained here for ten days. I rode out occasionally for koodoo, which was the only game I could find in the vicinity. Oorlog and his men continuously importuned us for meat and though many of them had rifles they were short of ammunition and preferred to let me do the hunting. I did not much like the killing of these beautiful animals but in view of our situation Daniel thought it politic to fall in with Oorlog's demands.

For the rest, I spent an interesting time, studying old Oorlog and extracting from him something of his past history. It appeared that as a boy he had accompanied Green on elephant hunts in the interior. Then he joined the Thirstland Trekkers, as a guide, through the Kalahari and he too had witnessed the dreadful sights of that disastrous period and he had gone to Angola with the survivors. He served in several native campaigns and the Portuguese, recognising his courage and ability (so said Oorlog) gave him the chieftainship over two fighting tribes.

In command of these he was engaged for many years in various wars. He gained a great reputation but little else, he said, for in the end most of his warriors were killed and he fell into disfavour. His version was that in fighting against the Konyama tribe he was seriously wounded (he showed me the scars) and on his return, before his hurts were mended, he was ordered to march the remnant of his force to Mossamedes, there to be shipped up the coast on yet another campaign at Loando.

He says he refused to obey, whereupon the Portuguese put a price on his head and he escaped south into the Kaokoveld.

There is, however, another side to the story, for when I was in Angola during the following year the Portuguese told me that while it was quite true they were going to ship him up the coast, it was not to a war in Loanda, but to the Island of St Thomas where they proposed imprisoning him for life on account of the robberies and murders he had committed. Be that as it may, Oorlog is a picturesque old scoundrel and although he fled from Angola as recently as 1917 he has established himself as paramount chief of all this region. He has gathered around him a band of Hereros who pay him unswerving loyalty. Even Thomas at Gauko-Otawi and Langman and Herman as far south as Khairos accept him as their overlord, and they stand in fear of him.

He told me he has taken a wife from every tribe within reach on both sides of the Kunene. He said women are always jealous of each other and whenever a plot is hatched against him, he is sure to hear of it from one or other of them.

He told me he has about fifty sons alive plus fifty or sixty sons he does not know of and he thinks at least thirty more must have died. I asked him how many daughters he had and he scornfully said that no one ever bothered to count daughters.

Having spent much of his time with the Angola Boers, he speaks Dutch fluently as do several of his sons whom for this reason he refers to with pride as '*oorlams volk*', meaning 'enlightened people'.

Gangisema lies about six days' ride from Zwartbooi Drift, the nearest fordable point on the Kunene, but Daniel fished out that there was a direct path down the Mahango gorge which would take us there in two days. I chose this route as I wished to see the river of which I had heard and read.

Oorlog tried to dissuade us for he said no white man had ever been down the gorge and the going was terrible. We suspected that the wily old fox wanted to keep the path a secret as a backdoor into Angola and we insisted on attempting it. Oorlog with a shrug of his shoulders instructed four of his sons to take us through.

We started at daybreak one morning and after a long ride we began to enter the gorge, a mighty chasm by which the Mahango river has slashed its way to the Kunene.

We owed Oorlog an apology. I have never encountered a worse passage for man or beast, not even in the Boer War. For eight hours we toiled, leading our horses now on one side of the precipitous mountain wall, now on the other, along a boulder-strewn track that wellnigh broke our hearts. At length, towards sunset, we emerged from the lower end of the canyon where it abruptly debouches on to the foothills that run down to the Kunene river thirty miles away. On reaching the exit, we continued until we reached a Mahimba village after dark and camped there for the night. The natives were excited, for an hour or two before three lion had leaped among their stock in broad daylight, killing six oxen and five sheep among the reeds close to their huts.

Next morning they came to say that the lion were still there so Daniel and I took our rifles and went to see. We found the place a shambles but the lion had decamped into the jungle on hearing us approach and short of their coming to look for us there was little hope of our coming on them. One old bull must have died gamely. On his horns were bloodstained tufts of hair and from the trampled ground it was clear he had put up a spirited fight.

We stayed over that day and next morning as we were riding along we came on a party of Mahimba on the move with their families and cattle. They told us they had burned their kraal and were seeking safer quarters, for lion had broken into one of their huts the night before and had carried off three women and a babe in arms.

Daniel, who was a bit of a wag as well as guide, philosopher, and friend, said the lion served the same purpose in the Kaokoveld as doctors do in more civilised areas by thinning out the population. That night we camped far out on the plain and a lion and lioness and two cubs prowled round and round us as we saw by the spoor next morning.

Leaving the Mahango riverbed to the left we rode on and after a difficult trek through rough hills we reached the Kunene river by midday at a spot which I believe has never before been viewed by a white man.

We passed numbers of zebra and koodoo and once, when I had gone ahead of the others and was waiting on the edge of a ravine for them to come up, about forty zebra and ten or twelve koodoo walked below me. There were several foals and calves nuzzling in against their mothers and they were so near that I could easily have dropped a pebble on their backs.

We struck the Kunene at a point where the stream divided into a number of separate channels with wooded islands in between, some of them very large and on the far bank stretched Angola to the north. The scenery was magnificent. Giant trees, tall palms and thick tropical vegetation, combined with the flowing waters studded with crocodile, was like a picture from the story books of one's youth.

We made our camp under a huge Anna tree that looked like a drawing by Gustave Doré. Curiously enough there was no sign of elephant. One would have thought that the river belt with its unlimited waters and its luxurious growth would attract them, but the South African elephant, like most of our other big game, prefer the more arid parts and as long as they have a muddy pool to drink at and to wallow in they appear to be satisfied.

On the first evening of our stay I learned something new about lion. Up to now we had taken every precaution, building zarebas at night and carefully tying up the horses close to the fire. But now at sunset, when I suggested to Daniel that we should fetch in our steeds, I was surprised to hear him say we could leave them out till morning. When I protested he replied, 'Look at the ground at your feet and you will see.' I looked but saw nothing to justify our leaving the ponies to their fate.

Then he showed me that the river bank was covered with a species of small thorn, spiked on all sides like a medieval mace, and he said a lion had too much respect for his paws to venture into an area carpeted with them. And so it proved, for although we left the horses out every night we had no trouble on this score.

We camped by the river for more than a week. It was possible, by looking for narrow channels, to get from island to island, and we spent most of our time exploring. We had perforce travelled light and as our supplies consisted only of tea, sugar, salt and a little Boer-meal, we had to supplement our larder by hunting.

One evening I had a narrow escape. I had waded through to a large island where, after a long stalk, I shot a koodoo bull. By the time I had finished skinning and cutting him up into portions for fetching next morning, it was nearly dark so I covered the meat with branches and decided to return to the mainland through a channel of the river close by instead of fighting my way back through more than a mile of thick reeds to the shallow spot where I had forded the stream earlier in the afternoon.

The water was about fifteen yards wide and although I saw a crocodile floating a hundred yards upstream, only his eyes and snout showing, I risked a crossing.

Holding my rifle, camera and boots above my head I went in. When I was half-way over I was chest deep and looking towards where I had seen the crocodile I was startled to see that he had submerged and that an ominous forked ripple was rapidly moving towards me.

I hurled my boots into the reeds on the far bank, took the camera by its sling and catapulted it after the boots and retaining my rifle in hand I made a wild dash for the other side, dragging myself up in the nick of time; for as I scrambled clear the crocodile broke surface immediately below with a vicious snap of his jaws.

It was foolish to have chanced it for I knew from what I had seen in Madagascar and East Africa that crocodiles are clumsy brutes on land but in their own element they flash by like an arrow. It took me a long time to find my boots and camera and as I trudged back to camp in the dark I swore I would never again take risks of this kind.

This was my second escape. Many years ago I had an unpleasant experience with a crocodile in Madagascar and to spare them seems to me to be misplaced mercy.

Next morning we brought in the koodoo meat and I presented Oorlog's sons with the skin which they greatly prize for the making of sandals. We dallied in this lotus land and I clambered about the islands, and I shot every crocodile I could see for I loathe these brutes.

At last we had to bid this great river farewell and reluctantly we started south. Our unshod horses had not yet recovered from the effects of their passage down the Mahango gorge and both were lame. So Daniel and I walked every inch of the way back to Oorlog's capital leading them behind us. It took us four days, and after we reached Gangisema we rested for about a fortnight to give the ponies time to recuperate.

Then we said good-bye to Oorlog and his men-at-arms and we rode the way we had come.

In the course of nine or ten days we worked back to the comparative civilisation of our cart at Gauko-Otawi, living on game all the time. In the long run this palls as a staple article of diet.

We found on arriving that Andreas had taken the oxen to a place called Ombaka, three days distant, for better grazing, so we had to send a Mahimba runner to recall him. This caused a delay of over a week which I spent in hunting an occasional gemsbok to placate Thomas and his men.

As our boots were finished and Thomas, now in a more chastened mood, offered to make us each a pair of sandals if I got him a zebra, I executed one of these unoffending animals and he implemented his promise by turning out two serviceable pairs of dazzle-painted footgear.

In going out to hunt I frequently saw elephant and occasionally black rhino. One morning I watched a bull elephant through my glasses. He was rubbing the under part of his neck against one of those tall antheaps that stand over ten feet high. He was enjoying himself, for he kept twisting and turning his head to get the maximum amount of scratching surface.

Suddenly the antheap snapped at its base and toppled over in a cloud of dust. The bull nearly sat down on his haunches with fright and then, apparently realising what had happened, stood for quite a while swaying on one foreleg and then the other as if laughing at the joke against himself.

During much of the time I spend in the Kaokoveld we were pestered by a species of small black midge. They hover round in swarms and have an irritating way of settling on one's eyelids. Daniel says they are always to be found where there are elephant and they make for the eyes to seek moisture.

They were as big a nuisance to the elephant as they were to us for once, as I stood behind a tree looking at an elephant in a glade, I could see by the way he was impatiently flapping his ears and swinging his trunk that the gad-flies were troubling him.

But he knew how to deal with them for presently he walked forward to where there was a patch of loose soil and lowering the tip of his trunk to the ground he drew in a quantity of sand. Then he took aim and squirted the charge into the swarm. It was like firing a No 6 shot cartridge at a flock of finches and he made short work of his tormentors.

When I told Daniel this he said he had seen them do the same thing by spraying water at them.

Whilst waiting for the oxen at Gauko-Otavi I witnessed another surprising occurrence. Thomas and Cabrito were preparing to set out to visit Mahonna Katiti, a neighbouring Herero chief who lived somewhere east of this. Before starting, a sheep was killed and the entrails were carefully decanted on to the outstretched skin. Then Thomas and Cabrito and their followers squatted solemnly around and they pointed with sticks and assegais and rifle butts and discussed the convolutions of the intestines as carefully as ever did the Roman augurs. After a long debate they decided that the omens were unfavourable and postponed their departure to a more hopeful occasion.

At length Andreas and the piccanin arrived with the oxen and we started on the home trail. We jolted along with our cart, day after day, much as on the upward journey and once more we camped at waterholes or, when the weather was hot, trekked at night, the dark forms of elephant sometimes noiselessly moving by.

These final stages were without undue incident save that by now our clothes were in ribbons and our original supplies were long since exhausted, so we existed solely on game without bread, tea, coffee or sugar to vary the monotony. Towards sunset one evening we pulled up at the police station at Kamanjab in our zebra-skinned sandals, looking like scarecrows, so the two policemen said.

We now travelled to where Daniel's parents were still camped by the waterhole. I sent back the oxen in charge of Andreas and the piccanin with adequate gratuities to their original owner and I retrieved my car where I had left it under a tree long before. It was unharmed and the engine started up without difficulty, so I said good-bye to those who had befriended me so well and went by easy stages, encountering heavy going at times on account of the sand and the rough country. When I reached the railhead my car was a wreck. I sold it to a local trader for a song, and if I had failed to see elephant like goods trains coming over the hills, I had at any rate carried out my resolve to make close acquaintance with the Kaokoveld and its people.

I journeyed home by rail to Johannesburg. My family met me at the station. My small boy John, aged five, hugged me and said, 'Daddy, all the time you was gone I *thinked* of you a little bit every day.' Surely as warm a welcome as any man could wish for.

Chapter 9

Ranch Inspection in Southern Rhodesia

I

I had not been back for more than a fortnight when I was off again. Sir Abe Bailey, our multi-millionaire mine owner, commissioned me to report on his land holdings in Southern Rhodesia.

The fee was a goodly one, with everything found, so for a month or two I roamed about that country. I visited Matabeleland and Mashonaland and I did some shooting for the pot, but we had been sumptuously fitted out and I wanted for little. I made beyond Gatooma through a wild area teeming with eland, sable, and other game and I reached as far east as the Lou Block beyond the Lundi river.

South, I inspected Sir Abe's ranches in the Matoppos and to the north I got to Sinoia and the Mazoë, with an occasional return to Salisbury or Bulawayo to replenish my stores.

Compared with my Kaokoveld expedition it was a luxury trip. It was interesting, but the parts I visited are known, and I ran an uneventful course, though once while I was on the Ngesi river one of Sir Abe's men was seized with a serious ophthalmic complaint. He went blind and was in great agony. I tore him all through the night to Bulawayo and the doctors afterwards said that if he had been brought in a few hours later he would have permanently lost his eyesight.

At the Lundi I shot a good many crocodiles on the sandbanks. I dislike unnecessary killing of animals, but as I have already mentioned, I do not believe in showing these brutes any mercy.

After completing my work I drew up a report which I sent to Sir Abe with account annexed and received a gratifying cheque by return of post. I was now in funds and I went north by rail to Elizabethville in the Belgian Congo, intending to have a look at the place before returning to the Union. I spent a fortnight there, and then I met a Portuguese, Senhor Cabral, who told me he was going to the west coast of Angola by car.

He was an official of Robert Williams & Co, the British firm that was building a railway from Lobito Bay to Elizabethville. The Company had sent a Ford car and a lorry through Angola and the intervening Congo forests some weeks ago as an experiment and he said he proposed doing the return journey to the coast with these two vehicles. He offered to take me along and though we were warned on all sides that the rainy season was on hand and that we were fools to attempt a passage at this time of year I thought the opportunity too good to be missed and agreed to accompany him. The Ford was a museum piece and the lorry was not in much better shape, but we started off for a place called Chilongo on the main line north of Elizabethville from where we intended jumping off into the interior.

At Chilongo, Cabral went down with fever and we were held up for several days.

There was a sort of roadhouse here, run by a Monsieur Forthomme and his wife and pending Cabral's recovery we stayed here.

All over the Belgian Congo there were large notices posted up forbidding Europeans under heavy penalties from striking or otherwise laying hands upon a native. At Chilongo I had personal experience as to how this veto operated.

During my first night at the inn my valise was rifled and all the money I had with me, some eighty pounds in Bank of England notes, was stolen. This was a serious blow for it left me penniless and I immediately reported my loss to Forthomme. He was upset for he told me that other thefts had taken place of late and they reflected on his hostelry so he asked me to leave the matter in his hands.

I found next morning that he had done useful work during the night. His native servants lived in a compound at the back and he had wormed his way behind their huts to listen-in and he heard what he wanted to know. In one of the huts a group of natives were squatting round a fire and one of them was telling the rest that he and a companion had taken a number of bank notes from the stranger's bag. At first they thought it was merely the usual small denomination Belgian paper money, a fistful of which might be worth ten shillings, but on closer examination they found themselves possessed of what seemed to them a small fortune.

They were sophisticated enough to know the value of British notes and they said they had buried the money and were making for Elizabethville next day to obtain the Belgian equivalent at one of the banks.

Forthomme, having learned this, crept away and at about nine o'clock the following morning I saw him drag two natives into his office. He had previously interrogated them and they had denied all knowledge of the theft. Now he was taking sterner measures. For nearly an hour I heard the sound of lashes descending, followed by groans, and at last the two natives were carried out. They were unconscious and their backs were a mass of weals and blood. They were laid face down in the yard and Madame Forthomme called for a dish of warm water with which she bathed their wounds.

Presently they came to and there was Forthomme standing over them again with his sjambok as if to lay on once more. The two wretches had endured the previous flogging, determined not to disclose where they had hidden their wealth, but now their courage broke and they sullenly muttered a few words; whereupon Forthomme walked to the ashpit behind the kitchen and there, after some digging, he unearthed my money in a tin. When I asked him whether he was not afraid of breaking the law by flogging natives he said he *was* the law round here.

He and his wife and I nursed Cabral until he was better and though he was still weak and shaky we now set off. I drove the car and a Portuguese half-breed named Antonio drove the lorry. We also had two other natives who had come up with it from the coast.

We started in pouring rain which hardly ever ceased throughout our journey. Both car and lorry were heavily laden. Cabral had executed so many commissions at Elizabethville for friends on the railway construction staff that the back of the car was piled to the roof with articles of every description, while the lorry carried eight hundred kilos of piping together with our kit and still more parcels, chiefly whisky for the New Year, and drums of petrol.

Our road ran due west. It was a mere track through the forest and it was often two to four inches under water. The soil however was sandy, giving the tyres a firm grip, and the smaller streams were bridged with log structures that enabled us to cross without difficulty.

On the first day out, some thirty or forty kilometres from Chilongo we reached the Congo river which we navigated by means of a pontoon built of logs laid across dugout canoes. As far as Bukama the river is called the Lualaba, and after this it takes the better-known name. The country beyond the river is a high plateau, 5 000 feet above sea level, for the most part covered with forest in which considerable rivers rise at intervals.

After crossing the Congo we had to pass three more rivers and many smaller streams before dark and we camped for the night on the bank of one of them, having done about ninety miles that day; and this was good going in view of the rain that continued to pour on us and the delays in working the pontoons.

Next morning Cabral had fever again, as well as the two natives on the lorry, so I continued to drive the Ford with my patient pretty ill on the seat beside me. The road grew more difficult as there was mud in place of sand and repeatedly I had to walk considerable distances into the bush to collect natives from the villages to haul us out.

This involved unloading and reloading the cars to lighten them and as it rained torrentially all the while, I began to see that motoring in the Congo in the wet season was a diluted pleasure.

I came to Kayoyo towards evening with Cabral running a high temperature and with no sign of the lorry. The place is a Belgian military station on a biggish river draining towards the Congo basin.

The Administrator of the district lived here together with subordinate officials and a contingent of Askari. They hospitably received Cabral and after seeing him installed in comfortable quarters I drove back in inky darkness and heavy rains to find the missing lorry.

After nearly two hours I came on it standing in a quagmire with Antonio disconsolately shivering on the front seat and the two sick natives moaning under the tarpaulin. They had decided they could go no further, but I forced Antonio to start up the engine and made him go on ahead of me.

Before long, what with the blackness of the night and the downpour of the waters he overturned down a bank so I left him to spend the night as best he could to guard against looting and took the natives with me to Kayoyo for treatment, getting there long after midnight, drenched and weary.

In the morning, Cabral, ill as he was, took a band of prisoners from the lock-up to assist in righting the lorry which we managed after a long struggle. It was undamaged and able to proceed under its own power. We spent that night and the next day at Kayoyo to give the invalids a breather and the day after that we proceeded once more, reaching Setenga by dusk, the last Belgian post before the Angola border.

Still the rain continued, and the officer in charge told me it had so far been the wettest summer in thirty-one years. I could well believe it for it transcended anything I had ever experienced.

Tsetse fly were plentiful in the forest. They were so numerous that I saw them sticking to the radiators and at halts others would settle on the bonnet, evidently in search of warmth, for the days were chilly on account of the damp. I saw no vestige of game in these parts and yet many people hold that the tsetse cannot live without game to feed upon.

My own belief is that the fly feeds on animals when available, but that blood is not essential to its existence, so that its life cycle depends on some vegetable matter.

We passed a small native village called Dilolo. I had a copy of David Livingstone's book with me and I should say that this was the very spot he mentions when he halted on his way to the Kasai river in 1852.

At Setenga we were allotted a rest house and were able to fill up with petrol from a dump established here by Robert Williams & Co. Cabral and the natives were shown every attention by M Istaz, the officer in charge.

II

We rested here a day and the following morning we crossed into Angola (Portuguese West Africa). We found ourselves on the great divide or watershed which runs like a vertebral column athwart the country.

The rivers appeared to drain impartially due north into the Congo basin or due south into the Kunene and Zambezi catchment areas. One moment we would pass a stream that in the end disembogues into the Atlantic, and a mile or two further on we met with another heading for the Indian Ocean on the far side of the African continent.

The watershed is not mountainous in appearance. It seemed to be a wide open plain covered with tall grass and at the time I crossed, it stood mostly under several inches of water.

Soon after we passed into Angola we struck the headwaters of the Zambezi, a mere brook as yet, and not far away we fell in with the head of the Luashi river, likewise only a trickle, but soon to become a mighty torrent running west and north to the Atlantic.

Beyond the Luashi lay more great open plains. The heavens were still coming down upon us, the rain had scarcely stopped for a few minutes since we had left Chilongo, and we toiled mile after mile through flooded country. Whenever the contours left dry spaces there was plenty of big game, but I saw no tsetse. There were roan antelope, sable and what I took to be lechwe, also thousands of oribi.

Once, a herd of roan raced us for about two miles. They kept parallel to and just ahead of us, too frightened and too stupid to swerve away and at last they were so winded with splashing through the mud that they halted and I was able to walk up to within a few yards of the puffing, heaving animals. They faced me nervously, switching their tails and snorting, but they did not move away and I walked round to have a good look at the splendid creatures. After the eland, they are the largest antelope in Africa, with serrated horns curving back, but they are not so graceful as the sable.

In spite of the waters covering much of the ground, the going was not as bad as it might have been, for the plains were flat and sandy; terrain which, if anything, is rather improved by wet weather.

Our first day's run into Angola took us as far as a place called Mashiwa, a miserable native *stad* perched on a rise, and here we spent the night, my patients in a bad way.

Antonio had been stricken with malaria that morning and Cabral, ill as he was, had driven the lorry while I managed the other car. As a result he was so weak next morning that he could not stand on his legs; I had to carry him to his seat and I ordered Antonio back to the wheel of the lorry. I made him go on in advance to make sure of not having to return for him as I had had to do at Kayoyo. Whether in retaliation or whether he was half delirious he backed the lorry into the car and one of the metal pipe lengths pierced my radiator.

I repaired the damage with a compound of manioc with which I plastered the hole, but for the rest of the journey until we got to the railhead I had to stop on an average of every twenty minutes to plug the radiator with more manioc porridge, a supply of which I carried beside me in a bucket.

We got along after a fashion though at times I feared Cabral would die on my hands. He was a splendid fellow. In the Congo territory he was known as *le petit Portugais*, for he stood over six feet. He was so ill that at every stoppage to mend the radiator, I had to lift him out to permit of his lying down for a few minutes on such dry surface as I could find; but he never complained, and every now and then he wanted to take the wheel to ease my labours. We conversed in French, and when he felt well enough he recited French poetry and declaimed from Racine and Molière.

We now entered a sparsely populated region and it was lucky that the cars behaved, for had we suffered a breakdown or got mudbound there were no natives to help us out and we might have been marooned for weeks. In spite of fever among the crew and my troubles with the radiator, I enjoyed this part of the journey. Game abounded wherever it was dry, and picturesque islands of timber dotted the plains. The vast herds of antelope gave one some idea of what the Transvaal and Free State highveld must have been like when first the old pioneers gazed upon it, and it was such a hunter's paradise as I had dreamed of as a boy even though I no longer wished to hunt.

On this day I nearly ran down a roan bull. He was asleep in the grass beside the track when the roar of our engines woke him. He leaped up and crossed behind the lorry but in front of the Ford, and I missed him by inches as he cleared the mudguards.

It rained all the time; it had been raining ever since we had left Tshilongo and we had begun to look on it as a normal condition, but our clothes were beginning to rot and our boots were green with mould.

One evening Cabral was so ill that I ordered Antonio to drop behind and I raced all out to reach the next Portuguese military station. I got in after dark, the radiator spouting at every pore and the casing red-hot. The two Portuguese officers stationed here did all they could and they treated me with great hospitality.

This post stands on the upper waters of the Kasai, but I was too worried to remember the name. The Kasai ran only a small stream though further north it becomes one of the largest rivers in Africa and at Chikapa it becomes navigable into the Congo, so I was told.

Onward next day, everyone in better condition thanks to the kindness of our hosts. It still rained and we still crossed wide flats with plenty of wild animals. We reached the Luachi river that night, a wide stream that runs into the Luena which in turn empties into the Zambezi, and thus into the Indian Ocean; whereas during the day's run we had crossed the Kasai and the Lucano, both of which flow into the Congo and thus into the Atlantic.

Cabral was very ill that night, but next morning he insisted on our proceeding. We touched at a military post on the Luachi and then, some miles beyond, the lorry sat down on its haunches with a broken rear axle. It took us all day in drenching rain to fit a spare that luckily was on board. Cabral, weak and shivering as he was, worked like a Trojan and towards evening we had repaired the damage. We spent a miserable night beside our vehicles and at daybreak we were able to continue.

We were moving from the plains and getting into unflooded timber country, and though the rains still continued, the run-off was greater and the surface was mostly free of standing water. The few natives we met told us there were lion but we saw none, though other game was in evidence.

We spent another hard day, having to unload both car and lorry on three different occasions to climb out of sticky mud patches, but that night we were almost back to civilisation for we made a small village called Moxico that boasted about ten Portuguese traders and several officials, including the Governor of the Province who lived in a residence on a hill.

In the morning we took the road again, through alternate forests and swamps. The never-ending rain caused us the usual troubles out of which we were helped by natives. It was a trying day but my patients were on the mend, and despite the mud and the damaged radiator which still needed constant plugging, we reached a place called Munyango that night and came on the advance guard of the Lobito railway construction in the shape of three members of Robert Williams & Co, who were doing survey work. The actual railhead was at the Cuanza river eighty or ninety miles away and the engineers said they reckoned that the line would be completed as far as the Belgian frontier by the end of 1927.

We spent the night at Munyango and the following morning we went on, the rain coming down as always.

Just before entering the notorious Cuanza swamp I met with a party of Boers moving through the forest with their wagons and cattle. It was like coming on a continuation of the Great Trek. There were actually a few survivors among them of the original Thirstland episode, gnarled old men and women sitting under the tented hoods. The others were a younger generation, but still fevered with the eternal unrest that is the heritage of the Afrikaner people.

There were about seventy all told. They had come up from Humpata de Janiero down south and said they were on their way to the Congo because they were dissatisfied with Portuguese rule. Yet to my mind the driving impulse was the same 'spring-fret' that had started them from the Transvaal more than forty years ago and had kept them on the move ever since.

There appear to be about three thousand Trek Boers in Angola and when I asked what the others intended to do I was told that all of them would probably migrate into Belgian territory.

I asked them for concrete charges against the Portuguese and I thought their complaints lacked substance. They said they were not allowed to use the motor roads with their wagons, but this prohibition applies to every citizen of Angola; and as the roads were built for cars and their heavy wagons played havoc with the surface in wet weather, I sided with the Portuguese.

Then they objected that each man was allowed only twenty-five rifle cartridges per annum. This certainly pressed hard on them, but knowing the destructive qualities of my people with regard to killing game, and being a game protectionist myself, I was unable to sympathise.

These two matters constituted their main indictment and I must say that taking it all in all the Portuguese have been surprisingly patient with them. It must be remembered that the Trek Boers in Angola have consistently refused to accept Portuguese nationality and even those born there continue to look upon themselves as South African subjects. I wondered what we would have said if the case had been reversed; if for the past forty years several thousand Portuguese had been roving about our country shooting our game and refusing our citizenship.

Nonetheless one cannot but admire the unconquerable spirit of these nomads who have roamed the wilds of Africa for longer than did the Israelites in the desert, yet retaining their language and racial proclivities intact.

After spending several hours with them we toiled till dark through the mud and water of the Cuanza flats, pushed on occasion by a crowd of natives from the villages around who had been specially ordered by the local Administrator to help cars across the swampy sections; for with the railway construction close at hand there was a good deal of traffic.

The Cuanza is a wide river flowing north-west towards St Paul de Loanda. It teems with crocodile and it is said to be navigable lower down. I met a young Boer named Zeedyk crossing in a canoe to return to his wagons on the far bank. His parents had died of fever and he had not a relation in the world. He possessed three wagons and several teams of oxen, inherited from his father, and he was making for the Kasai in the Belgian Congo. He was alone save for his native drivers and though he knew of the other trekkers ahead he preferred being by himself. So this self-reliant youngster was moving into the void on his own.

The railway had reached the Cuanza and construction trains were already crossing by a temporary wooden bridge. There was a steel pontoon upon which our car and lorry were ferried over, a change from the dugout makeshifts we had used up to now, and on landing on the opposite side we found ourselves on a good hard road at last. For the first time since leaving Chilongo, eight hundred miles behind us, we were able to whizz along at something like a fair speed and it brought us by sundown to Gamacupa, a tidy little European camp that had sprung up as a result of the railway.

The members of the staff and their families were housed here and they received us with open arms for we were the bearers of gifts. All those parcels and packages and whisky we had brought from Elizabethville were consigned to recipients at Gamacupa. There were rubber balls and dolls and other presents for the children and it was good to see them unfolding the wrappings with laughter and cries of joy.

This was the end of our motor journey and Cabral and I thankfully handed in the two battered hulks to the storeman. The trip would not rank as a feat in dry weather but in the rains it had been a pretty difficult undertaking.

After a few days' halt to make sure that Cabral was on the mend I said good-bye to him and to Antonio and the natives and boarded the Benguella train for the coast. I new saw Cabral again. He was a very good fellow.

I travelled down through picturesque hill-country to Benguela, and from there to Lobito Bay. The bay is formed by a curious spit of sand a mile and a half long running out to sea like a breakwater. I was told by an engineer who was at work at a jetty on the foreshore that there is nothing quite like this arm of sand anywhere in the world. It never grows greater or less and though it is composed of loose sand, not the stormiest weather adds to or subtracts from its shape. It slopes into the water so steeply that in bathing I used to take running dives as from a springboard without fear of hitting bottom.

The British Consul kindly put me up during the four or five days I remained at Lobito. He told me that he was continually in difficulties about the Angola Boers. They were not Portuguese subjects and as they or their parents had left the Transvaal in 1875 they are not Union Nationals, so the Portuguese administration look on them as British subjects. The Portuguese say that the trekkers originally came from the Transvaal and as the Transvaal was annexed in 1902 they are considered to be British. Accordingly whenever an Angola Boer gets into trouble his case is remitted to the British Consul for disposal.

The Portuguese currency is of low value and he told me that a local bank having to receive a sum equal to about £1 200 sterling found three ox-wagons drawn up before the door carrying seven tons of coinage all of which had to be brought in and counted by the unfortunate tellers.

In less than a week I was lucky enough to catch a southbound ship. On the way down the coast we stopped for two days at Mossamedes and during the halt I met the Administrator who gave me the Portuguese version of Oorlog's activities in Angola, which I have already touched on. He said Oorlog was a brave and resourceful man but a constant breaker of the peace whose depredations were such that in the end it was decided to imprison him for life; and had he not escaped into the Kaokoveld, he would have spent the rest of his existence in captivity.

There were several Portuguese officials on board on their way to new appointments at Delagoa Bay and other Portuguese centres. From what I could gather there was a kind of 'Washington Post' continually going on. Owing to the speed with which Cabinets in Lisbon rose and fell, governors and administrators chased each other round the coast of Africa all the time, for as soon as one of them reached his destination a fresh incumbent sent out by a more recent Cabinet was already on the water to supersede him.

The voyage to Cape Town was pleasant but without incident, and by January 1926 I was home once more.

Chapter 10

The Quest of the Bontebok

I

During the next year or two I kept no consecutive record but jotted down such events as I thought to be of interest.

My notebook says that during the first few months of 1926 I attended Parliament at Capetown and that our Nationalist opponents accused us of being imperialists and traitors to the True Cause and we charged them with racialism and with exploiting Afrikaans sentiment for vote-catching purposes.

This sort of thing has gone on since 1912 and will no doubt continue for another generation or two until we realise the futility of it all.

In spite of our wrangles I was on terms of personal friendship with some of our enemies, chief of whom was my successor, the new Minister of Lands, Mr Piet Grobler. He was a relative of the late Paul Kruger and he was a gentleman of the old school, liked by everyone regardless of party cleavages.

I lost no opportunity of attacking his government and his party, but in spite of this he asked me one morning to undertake an investigation into the question of the 'bontebok', a rare antelope that was almost extinct.

Mr Grobler was interested in the protection of wild life in South Africa, and on the strength of my previous efforts in the Sabi country he wished me to look into the matter. I gladly accepted the task. I was furnished with a car and a couple of officials, so leaving Parliament to its talking we set out at once.

The bontebok (*Damaliscus Pygargus*) are large, white-faced, white-bellied antelopes with chocolate-coloured backs and flanks and they carry lyre-shaped horns. In former years they roamed the coastal belt of the Cape Province in countless thousands, but they were by now so reduced in number as to be very near vanishing point.

In the face of the wanton slaughter of our game that has gone on for more than two centuries it is fortunate that so far only the quagga (a species of zebra) has become extinct and neither money nor tears will bring him back to life again; now we were threatened with the loss of an even more interesting type.

This was largely due to indiscriminate hunting, but also to the fact that the bontebok die out if they have to share their grazing with domestic stock; and of late years sheep farmers had increasingly invaded their ancestral haunts.

With my two companions I made a survey of the position. We examined the long strip of country that lies between Cape Agulhas and Algoa Bay, for in this area alone were a few of them said still to survive. It was hard work over the hills and dales of the south and after careful search we found that, all told, there were less than seventy bontebok left in the Union and therefore in the world, so narrow had the margin of safety become. These were running in small groups mostly in the neighbourhood of Cape Agulhas (the southernmost point of Africa) and it was clear that if immediate steps were not taken they would soon join the quagga in oblivion.

In the end I was able to find a suitable tract of land in the district of Bredasdorp. We had it enclosed by an eight-foot wire fence and enlisting the help of neighbouring farmers, sixteen bontebok were with difficulty shepherded through a V-shaped approach and driven into the sanctuary. To-day the rest of the bontebok have gone, but from those sixteen animals a herd of over two hundred has been bred up and the continued existence of *Damaliscus Pygargus* is assured.

When I returned to Parliament I was glad to find that Mr Grobler had introduced a Bill to turn the Sabi into a statutory game reserve to be called the Kruger National Park. Under his Act a Board of Trustees was established and I was appointed one of their number.

This was a handsome gesture and while it in no way diminished my antipathy to the Nationalist government I was sincerely pleased, for it opened a new vista. From now onward I was enabled to journey to the Low Country at frequent intervals and more and more I was to come beneath its spell.

The moment Parliament rose the new Board of Trustees held its first meeting and we set to work with a will. There was much to do. In the Park there were as yet no roads, no bridges, no pontoons across the rivers and the sole means of access was on foot or by pack donkey.

The Low Country lies east by west from the Swaziland border along the Komati plains, thence over the Crocodile, the Sabie and the Olifant rivers up towards Tzaneen and the Zoutpansbergen, a distance of about three hundred miles. South to north it is held between the great escarpment of the Drakensberg and the Lebombo range, a breadth of a hundred miles. This great area was still little known and the larger portion of it lay inside what had now been proclaimed the National Park. Within its confines were elephant and lion, hippo and giraffe, roan and sable antelope; zebra, sassaby, koodoo, wildebeest, waterbuck and a great variety of other fauna such as probably no other portion of the world of equal size can show.

Our mandate as a Board was to create a refuge where hence-forward the royal families of all the mammals could live in peace; our mandate was to put a stop to hunting and poaching and to open up the Reserve so that the public could visit it and learn the beauty of the wild life of South Africa.

At the conclusion of the meeting it was decided that the Members of the Board (there were eight of us) should proceed in twos, each couple to take stock of a different portion of the Reserve to prepare the ground for the laying down of roads, the building of rest camps and, above all, to provide crossings over the rivers.

Paul Selby and I were deputed to the Crocodile River area along the eastern borderline of the Park. He was an American by birth and a mining engineer by profession and he had spent most of his vacations in the Low Country studying its animal life and taking photographs. For these reasons he had wisely been nominated to the Board. He was a man of resource. He had started ahead of me, for I was detained, and when, ten days later, I alighted at a railway siding nearest to my destination in the Reserve, I found that he had succeeded in towing his car through the Crocodile River, the first car that ever entered the Park, and he was at a spot known as 'Dead Man's Bush' so called after three poachers who had recently been shot here.

He had discovered a suitable spot at which to place a pontoon and already he had made blueprints for its construction and had mapped out a road to the Sabie River on which a gang of native boys were hewing down trees and blazing the trail. I enjoyed the life and we saw much game. Giraffe, sable, wildebeest and buffalo fed in sight of our camp, though lion were not as plentiful as they have since become. We spent many hours taking pictures. In those days game photography was in its infancy. Few people had realised how little attention wild animals pay to motor-cars, and it was a novel experience to us to find that we could drive up to a troop of waterbuck or a herd of wildebeest while they grazed unperturbed. We thought at first that our success was due to the pains we took to cover the ancient Ford from stem to stern with boughs and foliage under which we sat crouched behind an old-fashioned box-camera swivelled on a universal joint like a machine-gun. Since then we have learned that these precautions were unnecessary, for game seems to register no emotion on the appearance of a car; but at the time we went to great trouble to camouflage our vehicle, and as we rattled and jolted over antheaps and fallen logs we thought we were very clever when we manoeuvred ourselves near enough to take a shot. At present, every second tourist in the National Park takes photos of lion and other animals from his car with a pocket kodak, but Selby was the pioneer. His studies received wide notice and I basked vicariously for having helped him.

There was a troop of buffalo in Dead Man's Bush led by a bull whose horns we considered to be a world record. We spent much time trying to photograph him but he always hugged the deeper shadows.

For many years, poachers from the adjacent Portuguese territory had been raiding over the frontier to shoot game. They were generally half-breeds in command of gangs of Shangaan natives. Their practice was to come with pack donkeys and after shooting all they could they loaded the meat and decamped across the border. A sort of sporadic guerrilla warfare had been carried on against them with frequent casualties on both sides.

Selby and I planned the development of this section of the Park and I like to think that our labours have borne fruit. At all events, visitors now run in and out by car and they go to Lower Sabie and Skukuza in a few hours by the roads we laid down where it took us a month to hack our way through the jungle.

This was my first expedition as a Board Member but I was to go on many another similar journey. In time I learned the lore of the wilds, I learned to track game and I even became somewhat of a lion hunter; and increasingly I became a devotee of the Low Country.

II

Early in the year 1900 I was serving with the republican forces in Natal. I took part in the siege of Ladysmith and in the Tugela battles and when we were at last pushed back we stood on the defensive on the Biggarsbergen, licking our wounds.

During the lull, I obtained home leave for a few days and travelled up by rail to Pretoria.

Pretoria is only thirty-five miles from Johannesburg and as I had never been to the Golden City my father and I took train one morning and ran across. The place seemed deserted, the streets were empty and doors and windows were boarded.

We walked about for most of the day and then, towards evening, there came a diversion. Suddenly, just as the street lights came on, a terrific explosion rent the air and a huge column of smoke shot a mile high into the sky where it stood towering like a great mushroom. On all sides we heard the crash of falling masonry and broken glass and men and women, previously invisible, poured into the streets making for the scene of the catastrophe. From their shouts we gathered that the government ammunition plant had blown up and we followed in their wake. Soon we reached a large block of buildings fiercely ablaze; shells and cartridges were detonating, sending spurts of green and yellow flames in all directions.

Some thirty dead men lay in a row on the pavement and wounded were being carried off. It was a grim scene and it is still a vivid memory for I was a boy at the time, of an age when things make a lasting impression.

My father and I helped where we could, and late that night we returned to Pretoria. Next morning there was intense anger when an official bulletin was issued stating that the disaster was the work of a British spy who, it was said, had connected a live wire from the municipal power station in such a manner that when the town lights were turned on the factory was set off.

Up through the intervening years I had nursed a grievance over this for I thought it a dastardly trick.

Now I had fresh light shed on the subject. I had occasion to visit a town in the Eastern Transvaal on legal business and here I met a man named Begbie. In the course of the conversation he told me that in 1895 he had erected an iron foundry in Johannesburg and he had built up a flourishing concern.

When the Boer War broke out however, President Kruger requisitioned his foundry and with the help of Netherlands railway engineers the place was turned into a munition work. Begbie was allowed to remain in the Transvaal, but he was forbidden access to his property, so he managed to get his Zulu servant Tom engaged as a Bossboy with instructions to report to his master from time to time as to the treatment the machinery and buildings were receiving.

The Europeans employed in making munitions were mostly Italian artisans, many of whom had flocked to the Rand on the discovery of gold.

A few days before the explosion, Tom came to Begbie with a troubled look. He said, 'Baas, old Tom very much afraid. Dem Italian peoples smoke cigarettes all time, all time, and dey throw de stumps over de place. Baas, soontime everything go bang— me plenty afraid.' Begbie allayed his fears and told him to return to duty and Tom went off mumbling and shaking his head. The plant went up within the week and poor Tom went up too.

Begbie said he had not the slightest doubt that this is how the accident happened and I believe his explanation is correct.

III

In 1927 I once more attended Parliament. It was a fiery Session for the Nationalists introduced a Bill in which it was proposed to abolish the Union Jack and to substitute for it a purely local flag. We on our side of the House had no objection to a flag of our own, but we took the standpoint that the new flag should not outrage the sentiments of our English-speaking fellow-citizens and that it should contain a symbol of our membership with the British Commonwealth.

The Nationalists at first would have none of it and there was so much bitterness throughout the country that for a while we were on the verge of civil war. In the end, reason prevailed, and a compromise was arrived at in terms of which there was to be a distinctive South African flag flown alongside the Union Jack on our public buildings and on state occasions. Now we have two official capitals, two official languages, two official races, and two official flags, and somehow it works.

Later in the year the Prince of Wales arrived at Capetown on HMS *Hood* and there was a succession of receptions and banquets in his honour, some of which my wife and I attended; but the only detail I can remember is an incident at a dinner at

Government House.

The Prince stood on a dais to receive his guests, whose names were announced as they entered the hall by a loud-voiced herald.

Among the guests was one of our prominent financial magnates, Sir Jacob Graaff and his wife. When they came forward the herald in a stentorian tone proclaimed the arrival of 'Sir and Lady *Giraffe*'. There was a roar of merriment in which Sir Jacob and his spouse heartily joined.

I thought the Prince highly-strung and nervous and he seemed to hate the life of enforced publicity he had to lead.

Although the 'Flag Session' (as it was called) ended in a somewhat calmer atmosphere, feelings still ran high, especially in the rural districts, and both sides took the field—we to denounce the Nationalists for their racial bigotry during the flag debates, and they to cash in on the fact that we of the South African Party had insisted on and prevailed in keeping the Union Jack as an emblem of our country.

I had to address a number of meetings. These gatherings mostly ran true to form. There were the usual boos and heckling and votes of confidence and no confidence dear to the hearts of the farmers, and an occasional scuffle between hot-tempered zealots on both sides. But once I ran into more serious trouble. I was due to speak at three pm in a small village west of Pretoria. I arrived half an hour before my time and as we entered the single street I saw a commotion at the far end, with a crowd of people milling round. I thought it was a motor accident so I told my driver to hurry on. When I got there I found a free fight in progress in which a considerable number of combatants were knocking each other about. I pulled one of them from the fracas by the tail of his coat and he breathlessly explained that it was a political meeting. Thinking that some rival orator had forestalled me I asked whose meeting it was. He replied, 'Colonel Reitz's political meeting', and he returned to the Donnybrook.

The mere fact that I was to speak, coupled with the opening of a new bottle-store that morning, had inflamed local opinion and the result was one of the worst uproars I had experienced since our post-rebellion elections of 1915.

They tell me that the floors of some of the town halls in the Free State bear traces to this day of bloodstains dating from my election meetings of those times and I remember being called upon for a cheque of eighty-two pounds in respect of damages to one municipality for broken chairs and doors and windows. The present melee was as bad as any of them. I leaped on to an improvised platform that stood against a wood and iron tearoom, hoping to make myself heard and I was instantly seized by the legs and dragged down into the maelstrom below. Luckily the crowd was so densely packed that everyone was pinned by his neighbours and fists could scarcely be used; though once, as I glanced over my shoulder, I saw a frenzied partisan trying to bang a petrol box, subsequently found to be loaded with bricks, upon my devoted head.

By dint of the crowd swaying this way and that, the wall of the tearoom was stove in and I found myself precipitated, with others, right inside the building where we sprawled among the debris of cups and saucers and plates that cascaded from the broken shelves above.

When at length the hubbub subsided we had to telephone to Pretoria for motor ambulances to transport the more serious casualties and the mix-up resulted in a batch of lawsuits and much heartburning.

Needless to say the bad blood was all between Dutch-speaking Afrikaners and I don't suppose there was an Englishman present.

IV

Parliament met again towards the end of the year and it was during this Session that some wiseacre discovered that because I had refused to take the oath of allegiance after the peace treaty in 1902 I was not a British subject and I was not entitled to sit in Parliament. Furthermore I had incurred a cumulative penalty for every day I had illegally held my seat.

The lawyers declared that technically this was correct, so the Nationalist Government very decently introduced a Bill to validate my position. While the matter was under discussion I absented myself from the House in terms of a rule that a Member shall withdraw from a debate wherein his personal conduct is at issue, but *Hansard* has the following:

> 'The Minister of Justice (Mr Pirow): In introducing this Bill I need not go any further than to show what will happen to Colonel Reitz if it be not passed and if some enterprising Member were to take the matter to Court.
>
> He is not entitled to sit in this House and what is more, he has incurred forfeitures to an enormous sum.
>
> I have not permitted myself the pleasure of working out the exact amount at so many pounds a day for so many years, but I have been told that at a shrewd estimate it is in the vicinity of the German reparations.
>
> I understand that an Hon Member will move that the Bill be called the "Deneys Reitz Relief Act".
>
> An Hon Member (laughing): Mr Speaker, in view of the doleful finances of the country, it would be as well if the Hon Minister extracted from Colonel Reitz some of his illgotten gains. But, joking apart, I am glad that at long last he is to have his rights restored.'

In this cheery manner the Bill was passed.

Chapter 11

Northern Transvaal and Kruger National Park

I

Early in 1928 I set off on a journey to the Northern Transvaal with a prospecting party to investigate an ancient gold working. These workings are fairly common, though it has not yet been established when and by whom they were operated. Theories on the subject range from King Solomon and the Queen of Sheba to Arab miners in the sixteenth and seventeenth centuries.

The working we were bound for lay in rough mountain country and it involved a long and difficult tramp before we located the spot. There were traces of old shafts and trenches and I picked up a number of stone hammer heads, but our prospectors, after a thorough survey, reported that owing to lack of water and to transport difficulties the mine was unpayable; so we reloaded our pack donkeys and toiled back to where a motor lorry awaited us nearer to civilisation.

On our way south we stayed over at a small town and here I unexpectedly ran into my younger brother Rolf. He was a barrister and he told me he was defending a 'twin murder' case before the circuit court next morning.

Twin murders are practised among certain of our native tribes. They originate in the belief that whenever a child is born, another child is born in the jungle and this spirit-child is a banshee. When, therefore, twins appear the natives believe that one or other of them is an evil genius and as they cannot tell which is which, they take no chances and kill them both to be on the safe side.

So strong is the superstition and so great is the power of the medicine men that no woman dares to refuse their behest and she strangles her twins and faces a charge of murder rather than defy the tribal custom.

When I was a Cabinet Minister we frequently sat in appeal in these cases. Our custom was to commute the death sentence to imprisonment for a year or two as we knew that the accused had acted under duress but whenever there was evidence to incriminate a witch doctor we hanged him. This only happened twice in my time for as a rule a native is too frightened to testify against them.

When the court opened on the following day I strolled across to watch my brother handle his brief. The wretched mother stood weeping in the box and the body of the hall was filled with tribesmen who had come in for the occasion.

The first witness for the Crown was a policeman who stated that, on information received, he had visited the accused's village and behind a hut he had disinterred a calabash containing the dead bodies of two newly-born infants. The woman admitted that they were hers but said they had been stillborn.

My brother rose to cross-examine. He began by asking the policeman whether the calabash had been buried in dry ground or wet. At this the judge somewhat impatiently said, 'Surely, sir, the question is irrelevant?' I rather thought so myself and almost blushed at my brother's ineptitude, but he was unperturbed and with a shrug the judge allowed him to proceed. The policeman then replied that he had found the calabash in dry soil.

I was puzzled, for there was no sense in it and to make matters worse my brother now put an even more pointless request for he demanded to know whether the bodies of the two children had grass circlets around their necks or their wrists.

This was too much for the judge who irritably said, 'Tut, tut sir, you are trifling with the court; I must ask you not to waste my time.' Again I was inclined to agree with his lordship and again my brother seemed impervious to rebuke for he insisted that his questions had an important bearing on the case; so the judge with a pitying look told the witness he could answer the question.

The policeman thereupon replied that both twins had circlets of grass around their necks.

The witness was stood down and after some further evidence for the prosecution my brother called the local Native Commissioner. This official told the Court that he was well acquainted with the tribe the accused woman belonged to, having been stationed in the district for many years, and he said that it was their invariable custom when twins were stillborn to bury them in dry ground with plaited grass around their necks whereas if the twins had been strangled they were buried in swampy ground with grass about their wrists.

This collapsed the case for the Crown and I went off in the knowledge that my brother knew his job.

Since writing the above, I have come across the works of Miss Mary Kingsley, a niece of Charles Kingsley of *Westward Ho*. She appears to have travelled extensively in French Equatoria, Lagos and Sierra Leone and at all events she made a study of the fetishes and voodoos of the Gold Coast. She says about twin murders:

> 'Twin killing holds good for over 2 000 miles, both among the Negro and the Bantu. It amounts to this. Twins are everywhere among African Negroes held in horror. The natives always believe that their origin is scandalous. One of the functions of the process of initiation to the secret society of a tribe, both male and female, is the assignment to each initiated member of a spirit companion. A child of a man is also a child of his spirit companion. That is to say it is part human and part spirit. Now, if it turns up as twins, the human has been encroaching on the rights of the spirit companion—it is a sort of adultery, therefore they have to be killed.'

Allowing for tribal and other variations, there is a distinct family resemblance between the Gold Coast superstition and that current among our own natives.

II

A few weeks later I travelled down to the Low Country again to see how work was progressing in the Kruger Park. By now things were well advanced; roads were being built, camps were being erected and already the area between the Crocodile and the Olifants River was accessible to tourists. The Reserve was rapidly taking shape under the guidance of Colonel Hamilton the Head Warden and a number of other European rangers we had appointed.

The main object of my journey was to seek a crossing over the Olifants River, as the Board was anxious to open up the as yet unknown Shingwedzi country that lay beyond and I had been asked to take the matter in hand.

I passed Skukuza on my way and there I saw a curious sight. A threequarter-grown hippo had been attacked and mauled by a troop of lion ten miles down the river. He had managed to escape and, strangely enough, some instinct had moved him to seek the white man's protection, for when I saw him he was standing on a sandbank just below the head warden's house where he had been for over a fortnight.

His sides were lacerated and the poor brute must have suffered agonies; the fish tore at his wounds when he entered the water and when he climbed out, the tick-birds and the flies tortured him. He allowed us to approach within a few yards of him and eventually he made a complete recovery.

From Skukuza I continued by easy stages to the Olifants River accompanied by ranger McDonald. A fair number of visitors were coming and going and McDonald who was a good teller of tales, used to amuse them with animal yarns to which they eagerly listened. He always took with him his native police-boy and one evening, sitting by a camp fire with several tourists, this gentleman furnished a comic interlude. Knowing how successfully his master was able to interest his hearers, the police-boy decided to try his own hand at it. He spoke good English and he began to spin an adventure which he said had befallen him.

He told of how he had been chased by a lion and how he had run for his life, the lion gaining on him until with a roar it leaped on him at last. At this point his powers of invention failed and he stopped dead. His audience had been following him with bated breath and one of them asked what happened next. He considered it his duty to round off his story satisfactorily and so answered with all simplicity, 'Baas, the lion ate me.'

I reached the Olifants River some miles above its junction with the Letaba and after a long search I found a suitable spot for a pontoon which in due course was built and launched by Paul Selby.

As I walked along the river-bank, the carcass of a dead hippo came drifting downstream and presently it grounded on a sandspit. Outwardly there was no sign of injury, but when the natives skinned it we found that the flesh underneath was pulped along the backbone and ribs. The boys said an elephant had pounded it to death and later they showed me a mudhole beside the river all trampled and pitted where the battle had taken place.

On my return journey I went via a trading station called Acornhoek lying just outside the Kruger Park. A friend of mine named Whittingstall lived here and when I looked in at his house I found that he had recently been mauled by a lion.

He was a skilled hunter but he made the same mistake that so many others have made; he wounded a lion and went after him in thick bush. Ninety per cent of lion casualties are due to following a wounded animal into high grass or scrub.

A lion, like any other game, runs away if wounded, or if very badly hit and unable to go far, hides under cover, but if brought to bay he will charge, and it is then the accidents happen.

Whittingstall in his anxiety to finish off the lion followed it with this two native trackers. He told me the next thing he saw was a ball of yellow hurtling through the air towards him. He fired but was thrown to the ground and seized by the shoulder. His natives saved him. One of them pulled the lion by the tail as it stood over him and the other drove his assegai into its heart.

Whittingstall in firing had smashed the lion's right foot which forced it to balance on the remaining three legs so that it could not claw him. This probably also helped to save his life for while a lion's bite is serious enough, his teeth are more or less aseptic; but to be clawed is certain death from blood poisoning for the sheaths are clotted with decayed flesh.

Whittingstall told me his sensation was that of a powerful steel vice crushing his shoulderblade and arm, and the pain was awful.

He was taken to hospital and he made a good recovery. When next I saw him he said with a twinkle in his eye, for his newly-wedded wife was sitting beside him, that the most serious after-effect of his accident was that he had married the nursing sister who had looked after him.

III

In this same year I undertook a flight over the Kruger National Park to study the reaction of game to low-flying aeroplanes. South Africa was becoming air-minded and private flying had increased to such an extent that complaints reached us of pilots who had taken to swooping down and stampeding the animals. The Board obtained Government consent to use Defence Force aeroplanes and I was asked to join in the venture. We obtained three single engined Wapitis, old-fashioned crates but with a long range and a cruising speed of about a hundred miles an hour.

Sir Pierre van Ryneveld, the head of our air force, piloted me and the passengers in the other two machines were General Tanner, under whom I had served in France, and another member of the Board.

We took off from Pretoria at dawn and crossed the Transvaal highveld in three hours, then down the Olifants River gorge banking round the corners of the cliffs and nearly skimming the water at times. Thence out over the Low Country still following the river. Here the plane carrying General Tanner made a forced landing in the bush and we only heard afterwards that no one was hurt. We continued on, criss-crossing over elephant, giraffe and other game, roaring close overhead to watch the effect. The animals seemed bewildered at the noise and they milled about wildly. Some herds stampeded so frantically that we judged they would not come to a halt until they reached Portuguese territory. Even the crocodiles on the sandbanks went somersaulting into the water for safety and we were able to collect useful data from which the Board subsequently framed its regulations as to flying over the Park.

We went as far as the Olifants junction from where we turned east over the Sabie country and crossing the Barberton hills we flew over Swaziland and sat down at last in a clearing beside the Pongola River in Northern Zululand after a non-stop run of eight hundred miles. Next morning hundreds of natives flocked in from the surrounding jungle to see the strange things that had appeared from the sky, and there was much chattering and excitement. The other plane refused to start owing to battery trouble and Sir Pierre and I took off without it. We headed for lake Sibaya and everywhere we saw the natives running for shelter as ours was the first plane that had passed here. Then out over the Indian Ocean and up along the little-known coastline as far as the mouth of the Kosi River.

Once, as we sped along, there was a Tonga woman on the beach. She was carrying a baby in her arms and the sudden appearance of our plane as we rounded the dunes so terrified her that she dropped the infant and ran into the scrub. The child lay where it had fallen and we saw a wave creeping towards it. Sir Pierre circled and tried to land in order to effect a rescue, but before he could do so the mother rushed back and rescued her offspring. From Kosi Bay we turned inland once more and after flying up the Usutu canyon we emerged on the high veld and reached Pretoria by sunset, having covered a great deal of ground. Thus we completed an interesting excursion.

A week later I took part in a hectic by-election in the Eastern Transvaal. There was serious rioting and feelings ran high, but our candidate got in by a narrow margin. For the rest, I opened an agricultural show or two, made many speeches in various constituencies, and then revisited the Kruger Park under somewhat unusual circumstances.

IV

The Board of Trustees, wishing to secure the goodwill of the Prime Minister, had invited General Hertzog to visit the Park and I was one of the hosts.

General Hertzog and I had not been on speaking terms since the Botha-Hertzog feud of 1912, but we thawed somewhat during the journey and I had to admit that he made a charming and courteous guest. He was a strange man. Like General Smuts he was university-bred and a fine classical scholar but he was a fierce hater. I had originally met him during the Boer War when, under his command, I took part in a spirited encounter against the British near the Orange River.

After the peace of Vereeniging he became the leader of a *risorgimento* movement designed to champion the cause of the Afrikaans people, their language and their culture.

At the passing of the Act of Union in 1910, when General Botha became our first Prime Minister, he was included in the Cabinet but proved a difficult colleague. A split soon developed. He hived off and formed the Nationalist Party which we of the South African Party had been fighting ever since.

As I was the son of a former republican President and one who had served through the Boer War and gone into exile rather than submit to British rule, General Hertzog took it for granted I would support him, but by that time I had come to understand the evils of overdone race worship and I followed the policy of General Botha and of General Smuts. He never forgave me and I had consistently opposed him ever since. Now we were thrown together in a neutral zone so to speak. We had to be on good behaviour towards each other and I began dimly to see that in the fervour of our political wrangles I had perhaps judged him somewhat hardly.

I was a strong believer in the friendship of the British and I hoped that within the restraining influence of the Empire it would be possible to build up a nation out of the Dutch and English people in our country. I had always thought that General Hertzog was a narrow racialist with a deep-rooted hatred of our English fellow citizens but from the talks we now had I gathered that while he suffered from an exaggerated Afrikaner complex, he appeared to have a real desire for co-operation and racial peace in South Africa. I had always found him to be illogical and somewhat muddleheaded yet I glimpsed a side of his character that made me less hostile, a matter that was not without important results some years later.

We saw elephant, lion, giraffe and much other game and we so impressed General Hertzog that we never had any difficulty afterwards in obtaining adequate funds from the Nationalist Government for carrying on the affairs of the Park.

At the conclusion of the tour we all returned to Pretoria together and I spent the closing days of 1928 with General Smuts on his ranch. While he botanised I accompanied him on his rambles and we talked of old times and of things to come.

Chapter 12

General Election and Sandringham Relaxations

I

The Nationalist Government's five yearly term of office expired in March 1929 and another general election was due.

I had been Member of Parliament for Port Elizabeth since 1922 and in spite of my infrequent appearance among them my constituents had put up with me and they asked me to stand again. But now I received an offer I could not resist, for I was asked to fight the Low Country seat. At the time of Union the whole of the Low Country had been carved into a single parliamentary district (called Barberton) which the Nationalists had held in unbroken succession since 1915. They looked on it as one of their strongholds but my growing acquaintance with it and its people decided me that the time had come to wrest it from them, for I had long been hankering after so fascinating a constituency, more especially as the whole of the Kruger Park lay within its boundaries. Somewhat ungratefully I said good-bye to Port Elizabeth and prepared to invade new territory.

The long travail of a General Election now began. Our prospects were not good. It was true that the Nationalists were losing ground, for in a democracy it is almost axiomatic for any government to weaken from the first day it attains power, as disgruntled place-hunters and self-seekers who cannot get what they want turn and rend it.

But General Hertzog was still a formidable opponent and he still possessed a strong following among our Dutch-speaking element. I took an active share and I lent a hand all over South Africa, rushing about by rail and road and air and at intervals I returned to canvass my domain.

The Low Country with its mountains and rivers and jungle is beautiful and picturesque, but it makes for difficult electioneering. Nature has divided it into so many watertight compartments that I had to travel on horseback and on foot to secluded valleys, isolated mining camps, and distant forestry settlements. I ranged from the heights of Kamshlobaan overlooking the Swaziland plains to Komatipoort on the Portuguese border and up along the slopes of the Drakensberg to Tzaneen in the far north. I visited squatters and farmers on their ranches and small communities tucked away between the rivers. There were up-to-date fruit-growing centres and there were scattered groups hidden in folds of the Berg who still lived and thought in terms of the old republican days of thirty years ago. It was strenuous work carried out in addition to my activities in other parts of the country.

I found that my membership on the Park Board was a liability instead of an asset. Once, while I was addressing a gathering under a tree on the bank of the Crocodile River, an old Dutch farmer rose to complain that hippo from the Kruger Park had raided his farm the night before and consumed £200 worth of his tomatoes, and he said if I did not take better care of the animals in my charge, he and his neighbours would vote against me. On another occasion, just as I was getting into stride, a herdboy rushed up to say that a crocodile had pulled his master's bull into the water and here again the blame fell on my shoulders.

A few days later I was travelling along in a small open car with the secretary of our party. The road was a mere track with grass standing high between the ruts. Suddenly we bumped into a full-grown lion that must have been lying asleep in front of us. He leaped aside with an angry snarl and it looked as if he meant to come at us.

The engine had stalled and for a moment we faced an ugly situation for we carried no arms. Then my companion got the two-seater started and we moved off. I was due to address a meeting in Barberton town in the evening and I made use of that lion. I said: 'Ladies and gentlemen the election is going well but this morning we had the first setback.' The audience pricked up at this and I went on to tell of our collision. I said that as I knew the lion wasn't on the voters' roll we did not stop to argue with him.

The story went well and I got a motion of full confidence.

Up in the mountains are Boer colonies settled here for nearly a century. To them time stopped at the close of the war in 1902. The Great War had reached them but as a dim echo from the outside world and their politics still hinged on forgotten controversies of the past. A man who surrendered to the British columns in 1900 is an outcast and only those who fought to the end are held in respect. I clambered up to meet a number of these sturdy mountaineers, bigoted and primitive, but fine and brave and obstinate. As I began to speak, a weatherbeaten veteran rose and turning to the rest he said in Dutch, 'Before allowing the candidate to proceed we want to know where he was in the last war.' I was just about to reply that I had served in East Africa and in France when he supplemented his question by saying, 'What I mean is did he serve with General Botha or in the Free State with General de Wet?' I answered that I had served under them both right up to the end. I think I got most of their votes.

By the time polling day arrived I was a physical wreck but I was Member of Parliament for the Low Country.

In the rest of South Africa our Party fared badly and the Nationalists were returned to power by a large majority, so once more we were doomed to the outer regions. Indeed, my victory was the only bright spot, for it was the only seat we captured from our enemies in the whole of the Union, whereas they had taken a number of seats from us.

As I was sitting in my compartment at the railway station at Pretoria next morning I heard two porters discussing the election results. They spoke in Afrikaans and they were obviously Nationalist supporters. One of them said, 'Yes we have won the election, but the only pity is that '*daardie bogger*' Colonel Reitz is back in Parliament again.'

II

, Now that I was Member for the Low Country I took a step I have never regretted. With the growing lure of the wilds I purchased a tract of land known as Sandringham. It lay close to the Kruger Park and had big game of many kinds; roan and sable, zebra, koodoo, wildebeest, sassaby, waterbuck and lion; and to crown it all there was a section of the Shangaan tribe with a petty chief and witch doctor complete. They were elemental savages armed with spears and they owed me allegiance by virtue of my owning the grounds; so I was a sort of feudal baron with a tail of warriors at my call.

I made the purchase not only for myself but for my two boys. John was eight and Michael was five and I wished them to know the beauty of the Low Country, to learn its woodcraft and to learn self-reliance and how to handle firearms.

From then onward we have been down every year. We pitch camp on the bank of the Umbabat, a watercourse that runs on a frontage of nearly ten miles across the property, and to guard against lion we build a zareba of thorn branches inside which we erect our tents and many are the interesting things we have seen and done on Sandringham.

Almost at once we had what the boys thought was a great adventure. On the morning after our first arrival we came on a kill in the shape of a dead wildebeest and it was clear that he had been pulled down overnight by a lion; so we returned to consult Mafanela the witch doctor. He was a villainous old scoundrel but noted for his ability to track lion. He cleared a space on the ground with his foot, threw the bones and muttered the usual incantations. Then he declared the omens to be propitious and he agreed to accompany us to where the carcass of the wildebeest lay.

My wife and boys came along too for it was their first lion hunt.

When we reached the spot, Mafanela carefully examined the spoor and he said four lion were close at hand. I ordered him to follow their tracks which led towards a thicket about three hundred yards away.

Mafanela was carrying a shotgun in case we flushed a covey of partridges on the return journey, and I had a rifle. As we approached the thicket he grunted disapprovingly and said the lion would have made off as there were too many of us in the party. However, we continued, and despite his prophecy, four lion suddenly rose up and growled at us in unison. To my horror I saw Mafanela raise the shotgun and aim at the nearest animal. Knowing the probable effect of peppering a lion with a No 6 cartridge I rushed forward to stop him, but luckily he did not understand the mechanism of the gun and he had not pulled over the hammers. By the time I had knocked up the weapon the lion had disappeared in the bush, as they generally do after the initial roar which as often as not is a bluff intended to cover their retreat.

As a hunt the affair had not been a conspicuous success but John and Michael had a close-up view and they crowed with delight at having gone after real lion.

From the start we have adhered to the rule that there was to be no unnecessary shooting at Sandringham, and we hunted only for the pot. It was a day or two afterwards that I took John on his first attempt at big game. With a smelly native guide we tramped through the bush until we came on a herd of sable. I tried to manoeuvre John close enough to ensure a mortal hit but the sable were restive. As long as we continued to move they grazed quietly, but the moment we halted they were off, as is the manner of all antelopes. This happened a number of times and John's face grew tense with disappointment. At last I tried an old ruse. Animals cannot count, so we walked obliquely until we were within a hundred yards of our quarry and as we passed an antheap I whispered to him to drop down while the native and I walked on. He did so and the sable failed to notice the decrease in our number and seeing us still moving they remained standing long enough for John to drop a magnificent bull.

He was so overcome with excitement that he flung his arms round my neck in an impulsive embrace and not content with this he hugged the Shangaan and gave him a smacking kiss, greatly to that worthy's astonishment. I sent for an ox-drawn sled on which the sable was loaded and we made a triumphal return to camp, John riding proudly astride his victim.

That night I watched the little fellow. He stood with his hands clasped behind his back gazing into the log fire, evidently deep in a brown study. At last he heaved a sigh of content and turning to me he said, 'Daddy, I can't hardly believe it really happened to me.' He has since gone on many another adventure but I think his first sable will remain the greatest memory of them all.

I shot birds, for partridge, pheasant and guinea fowl are plentiful and on occasion I hunted lion.

Nowadays tourists in the Kruger Park see many lion. They loll in the shade and they look harmless enough from a motor-car, but walking them up in the scrub is another matter. This is not a hunting narrative but I give one instance of a lion hunt I took part in.

During the following year when we were once again at Sandringham Mr Whittingstall came to my camp one morning, long recovered from his hurts. He said a native youth had been mauled by a lion some hours before and he was in a kraal near by. It was unusual for a lion to attack a human being in broad daylight and as he thought it might be a maneater he suggested that we should go after it. We set out and proceeded to the kraal where the native lay to find out where the attack had taken place but we could get no information as he was unconscious and died that afternoon. We collected two men from the village to serve as trackers and started off. The grass stood breast-high and the going was heavy, but with marvellous skill they followed the course along which the wounded boy had come; and after four or five miles we found an axe and a bundle of poles and it was evident from the pools of blood and other signs that this was where the tragedy had occurred. The lion must have charged him while he was chopping wood and he had been carried for about thirty yards. Then for some reason the lion had released him. The poor fellow had vainly tried to defend himself, for the axehead was covered with tufts of hair. He had managed to drag himself to the village where we had seen him and one can imagine the untold agonies he suffered during that terrible journey.

Our natives now cast around and they returned to say that from the tracks they judged three lion to be close by.

Most people have the Biblical idea that lions raven abroad seeking whom they may devour. This is true of lions after dark, but in the daytime, as often as not, they lie low and one has almost to step on them before they break cover.

We decided to beat the scrub in which they were lying, Whittingstall taking the one side and I the other. The thicket was only about two hundred yards wide, but though we walked through it several times we found no lion. We were inclined to give it up, for the heat was stifling and we could scarcely believe that the lion were still there. The natives, however, were emphatic; the spoor led within and there were no outward tracks, they said, so we decided on a final attempt. We entered about fifty yards apart and as I came on a denser patch three lion rose at me from about six feet away and they emitted the most appalling noise I have ever heard. Had they charged me I would have been lost, but here again they were bluffing. I had time only to hit the nearest brute and before I could fire again the other two bolted in the jungle. It sounds safe and easy and I have done it a number of times since then, but it is not quite so safe and easy as it sounds.

The fact remains that lion will seldom molest a man in the daytime. During the years I have camped on Sandringham I often hunted them, and my trouble has been that they run for it before one can get in a shot. I once put up a huge male. He clawed at me and as I fired, no less than six other lion came tearing past from behind. They had crouched in the undergrowth and allowed me to pass them and only when they heard the sound of my shot did they come racing along, almost brushing me in their haste to get away.

Another time, Lady Mary Grosvenor, daughter of the Duke of Westminster, wished to enter the Kruger Park. As it was out of season I took her in by virtue of my membership on the Board. One evening we came on a troop of eight lion trotting towards the car. I could see they were merely inquisitive, but as I did not want them to frighten my guest I jumped out and waved my hat at them, knowing that they would clear off. They did so, but I had great trouble in convincing Lady Mary that I had not performed an act of derring-do.

This rule has its exceptions, for if a man comes on a lioness with cubs, or a lion at its kill, or in the mating season, there may be trouble.

Another erroneous idea, sponsored by the Book of Daniel, is the one about a lion's den.

In all Africa I have not known a lion to live in a cavern or a den, for he has no fixed abode, and he invariably lies-up under a tree or a bush to sleep or rest.

We had other interesting experiences on Sandringham. One winter my boys and I rode out at daybreak with only a saloon rifle, intending to try for a guinea fowl. Buffalo had never been known within a hundred miles of here and yet, on this particular morning, as we hitched our horses to a tree and walked forward into some bush where we had seen a flock of birds disappear, there stood two enormous buffalo bulls facing us. They were only a few yards from us and they were in a bad temper. Their eyes gleamed like living coals and they pawed the ground angrily, throwing dust over their shoulders the while and advancing slowly. It was a dangerous moment. I told John and Michael not to run but to back quietly from tree to tree. They kept their heads and obeyed and as soon as we were in the open once more the buffalo retired back into the shade whence they had come. The natives reported that they were two rogue bulls from Portuguese territory and their ill-temper was due to their having been shot at with muzzleloaders and blunderbusses.

What would have happened had they charged us does not bear thinking about for the popgun I carried would have been worse than useless. When I returned later in the day with a 9 mm rifle the animals had disappeared and we never saw them again.

Another time John and I were resting under a tree half-way down the sloping bank of the river when a cane rat shot past us, flying for his life. Behind him, from the bank overhead, followed the largest mamba I have ever seen. The snake was at least twelve feet long and it missed us by inches, its body straight as a lance, only its head raised out of alignment.

Rat and serpent vanished into the reeds but had it contacted either of us it would doubtless have buried its fangs, for a mamba is the fiercest and deadliest of all our reptiles. So swift are its movements that I have seen one dart across my path and rubbed my eyes, not quite certain that I had seen it at all.

I know of only one case where a man was bitten and lived to tell the tale. He was a friend of mine and as he crossed a footbridge in Zululand, a mamba reared up from the grass and struck him in the thigh. So great was the impact that he was thrown to the ground. Luckily he carried an anti-snakebite outfit and he injected the serum at once but he was at death's door for six months, and for two years thereafter he lay in hospital.

I have another friend in the Low Country who had a Shangaan servant possessed of a concoction which rendered him immune to snakebite, for the odour nauseated them. This native would walk up to a mamba and with his bare hands cuff it on both sides of its head as it reared. The mamba would hiss and make as if to strike but the stench of the *muti* was overpowering and it would draw back, whereupon the Shangaan would seize and drop it into a calabash held in readiness.

In course of time this native quarrelled with a Swazi headman in the neighbourhood. The Swazis look upon the Shangaan tribe as an inferior caste and the headman had made no secret of his contempt for the snake catcher. He took a strange revenge. My friend walked along at daybreak one morning to hunt and there rose before him a mamba swaying from side to side, neither advancing nor retreating.

He thought this curious so he shot the creature and on closer examination he found that it was leashed by the tail to a stake sunk in the middle of the pathway. Further on lay the dead body of the Swazi headman and on his chest were the mamba's imprints. The headman had been to a beer drink during the night and staggering to his kraal along the beaten track he had walked into the tethered snake and met his doom.

Late one night we were aroused on Sandringham by the sound of lion snarling and grunting around our camp. I reached for my electric torch and walking to the gate I flashed a light. In the beam there stood a tawny lioness on her hindlegs tearing at the wildebeest meat we had hung from the branches of a tree about fifteen yards away.

On the ground lay two more lion crunching a hindquarter they had already pulled down.

My wife and John and Michael peered over my shoulder at the strange scene. Then all three lion bounded away into the dark. Presently we heard them about the pots and pans in the smaller skerm where we did our cooking, then they came scratching at the thorn fence that surrounded our camp and showed every intention of breaking in.

I told John to fetch my rifle. To my alarm he said he had locked it in the car to prevent the dew from rusting the barrel. As the car was under the very tree where hung our meat and where first we had seen the animals I was in a quandary. The lion seemed determined to get into our camp and I realised that if they did there would be a tragedy which would be blamed on me, so in sheer desperation I decided to fetch the weapon. I walked outside and turned my torch on them where they were at the fence. They retired and I now saw all three of them crouch down close to the car. They lay motionless as lion will do in a beam of light, and with my heart in my mouth I walked forward slowly for I knew that at any sign of haste or irresolution they would pounce on me. The brutes watched me intently, their eyes gleaming like emeralds, but they made no move and at last, after a few seconds, though it seemed an age, I was near enough to leap at the door of the car, turn the handle, and I was safe inside. I found the rifle fully loaded and as it is almost impossible to hold a torch and aim at the same time I had to satisfy myself with loosing several shots in their direction and so drive them away. I shall not easily forget my passage across.

One year a young nephew was camping with us. He went out at dawn carrying only a shotgun, intending to shoot partridge. At breakfast time he had not yet returned. By noon we began to wonder, and his mother grew uneasy, and when at dusk he was still missing we realised that he had lost himself in the bush. We fired shots; we hoisted hurricane lamps up tall trees and we patrolled the road all night without a sign of him.

His mother aged ten years by morning for the lion had roared louder than ever and she was in terrible distress.

We knew that apart from wild beasts, the boy must be without water for there is none on Sandringham except in the river, and clearly he had missed his way in the jungle beyond, otherwise he could have returned by following its course.

It was not till noon next day that he was led in by a native who had found him wandering in a circle, half demented with thirst after a night spent at a burning log with lion and leopard going and coming within the glare of his fire.

Very few Europeans lived in the vast scrub country that lies around Sandringham and these were practically outlaws.

They generally subsisted by poaching game and they made rare visits to some trading station to exchange skins and dried meat for ammunition. Mostly they were Dutch for we Dutch are nomads, and we are difficult people. I came across some of them occasionally and once I had trouble. I found a bearded giant who had halted his ox-wagon beside the road on my ground. With him were his wife and daughter each weighing about two hundred pounds.

I did not mind his cattle grazing on my land nor the pile of firewood he had collected, but when I asked him whither he was going he pointed north and said he proposed cutting a road across-country as he was making for the Olifants River.

This would involve the making of a new highway right athwart my property for poachers to follow so I emphatically forbade him. Thereupon he jumped down from his wagon and he fetched his rifle threatening to kill any man who tried to prevent him.

I was unarmed; my son John was with me, and I could not afford to run any risks so I drove back to camp to fetch my rifle. When I returned to the wagon I repeated my orders about the road.

He was truculent, but I covered him and he then gave in. I told him if he cut that road I would shoot every one of his trek oxen and thereafter, if he persisted, I would shoot him. I commanded him to stay where he was for the night and next morning my boys and I turned up, each carrying a firearm, and we escorted him and his wagon to a point beyond Sandringham after which we let him go his way.

He uttered threats as to what he was going to do to me, and months later, when I was absent in Parliament, he defied my instructions and did actually cut the road.

On our next visit we dug a booby trap into which he fell. He was seriously injured and thereafter he left us alone and now the road he made has reverted to the jungle once more.

I went down alone one Christmas. It poured heavily and the ground was so sodden that I could go neither backward nor forward and I spent the better part of a week curled up in the back of my car.

It was too damp to light a fire and I lived on biscuits and tinned foods. As I gazed through the windows at the driving rain I felt like a frog in an aquarium and in the distance the lion roared dolefully at the filthy weather. I did not repeat the experiment in the wet season.

These are a few of the things we did on Sandringham. We travel thither every winter. We do little hunting and we pass our time studying the game and we make long expeditions on foot and on horseback.

I shoot birds and sometimes we go after lion. In this manner, during the years, the place has afforded my two sons much joy, and to me it has been such a refuge from our political troubles that we look on it as a terrestrial paradise.

Chapter 13

Lion Hunts and False Bay Fishing

I

In January 1930 the victorious Nationalists summoned Parliament and we of the South African Party belaboured them. I forget what it was all about, but I took part with zest and I delivered many speeches all deeply interred in *Hansard*.

The Prince of Wales paid us a second visit and he invited me to a private lunch at Government House. I had lately published a book named *Commando*, written in Madagascar nearly thirty years ago, in which I described my experiences during the Boer War. He had read it on the voyage out and he wished to discuss it with me. He was even more nervous and highly-strung than when last I had seen him.

Mr George Bernard Shaw came to South Africa too a little later and he likewise asked me to lunch as he had read my book.

I envied him his literary career and I admired his cheek, but unluckily I failed to remember his invitation and went for a swim instead. I heard afterwards that he was furious and he did not renew the offer. Nevertheless I achieved greater distinction as the man who forgot to lunch with 'GBS' than if I had kept the appointment.

For the rest, I attended to my private affairs, spoke at numerous political meetings in the country districts, made an occasional tour through my constituency and went into the Kruger Park as often as I could, for I loved the work we were doing there.

On one of these trips I was accompanied by Mr Oswald Pirow, the Nationalist Minister of Justice who had piloted my Relief Bill through the House. He was on the Board and we were sworn political enemies, but for our common interest in the Low Country we were personal friends.

The whole of the Kruger Park lies in my electoral division and once, as we stood watching a team of oxen pulling our car through a river, a troop of old-man baboons came barking towards us.

Pirow: Look, here are some of your constituents to welcome their Member of Parliament.

Myself: If those baboons voted for me, they showed a damn sight more intelligence that the people who voted for you.

Pirow: Shake hands: we're all square.

Pirow had visited Russia shortly before and as we travelled along he said that in Moscow he was taken over the Kremlin by a guide who spoke broken English and French.

In discussing the Soviet Government Pirow hazarded the view that it was a good thing to have a parliamentary opposition to keep things equal.

'*Opposition, M'sieu,*' said the guide, '*venez avec moi, and I weel show zem to you.*' Leading him to a window he pointed at a cemetery behind the fortress where lay some five hundred newly made graves. '*L'opposition, M'sieu, les voilà.*'

Pirow thought this was rather a neat way of dealing with oppositions but being in opposition myself I was not amused.

During the course of the same morning he watched an athletic display on the Red Square. There was running and jumping and hurdling, and he suggested that it was a pity the art of boxing had not been included in the curriculum.

The Soviet leaders, however, have their tenderer moments. They had disposed of their parliamentary foes by wholesale liquidation, but the guide answered, '*Le Boxe M'sieu, ze government 'ave prohibit le Boxe, zey tink il est trop brutale.*'

We reached Sabie Bridge that night and Colonel Stevenson Hamilton, the famous warden, hospitably entertained us at his headquarters, for there was as yet no accommodation for travellers.[1]

Colonel Hamilton has probably shot more lion that anyone living. He kills them when it is necessary but he is also their arch protector and he has studied their habits for nearly a lifetime.

That evening, as we sat overlooking the river, he told us something of their ways. He said that as a rule lionesses cub down in June whereas the rest of the Low Country fauna litter in December of every year. His theory is that nature has thus ordained it so that the cubs are about six months old when the kids and calves and foals of the *impala*, wildebeest and zebra arrive and they can therefore start practising to hunt on the newly-born young and then gradually work up to the catching of larger prey as they grow stronger. If Hamilton is correct, it seems a fiendishly cruel system.

He told us further that a lioness occasionally reaches maturity without finding a mate. To satisfy her maternal instinct she will adopt her sister's cubs, and she turns herself into what he calls a 'maiden aunt'. While the parents are away hunting, she mothers and looks after them, petting and fondling them and she does this during the months of their babyhood after which she waits for the next litter and repeats the process.

As to this, I once shot two lionesses with a right and left and my native trackers told me that they were twin sisters, six years old, and that they had never been mated. There were cubs in the bush beyond.

From here I went to open a bridge across the Komati River on the Portuguese

[1] See Colonel Hamilton's book, *The Low Veld and its People.*

frontier. A number of their officials had been invited and we toasted them in lukewarm champagne, for the thermometer stood at 114 degrees in the shade.

For 1931, entries in my notebook are scanty. I took an active part in the political war which ran turbulent as ever, and I visited the Game Reserve several times to see how things were going.

I find that I accompanied an American oil king and his wife into the Park. They brought with them two secretaries, a valet and a chauffeur, cheery young fellows who were delighted at the prospect of spending several days among the game as had been planned. But I overdid my staff work, for in the course of the first morning, knowing where lion most frequented, I took the party down along the Sabie River and we came on twenty-one in a few hours. This was too much for the magnate's better half. She ordered us to return to camp and to pack up. She said she refused to remain another minute in this savage country and she had us all out of the Reserve by four o'clock that afternoon.

My diary says further that a few weeks later, also during the closed season, I took Sir James Reynolds MP, for Liverpool, to the Park; I showed him lion, giraffe and much other game; a lioness tried to charge us, and we encountered a terrific cyclone and torrential floods.

I see too that a meeting I held in the Northern Free State was wrecked through an ill-timed joke. My listeners were mostly Nationalist opponents and I held forth on their unreasonable attitude. I said that no matter how hard we tried to satisfy them they were always discontented and to illustrate this I told a story of the man who bought an Irish terrier: The first night he locked it in the kitchen and it scratched at the door and howled all night.

Next morning he said, 'As you don't want to stay inside you can sleep in the open,' and he locked him out.

That night the terrier scratched at the door and howled all night trying to get back.

The third evening the man said, 'If I lock you in you howl, if I lock you out you howl, so now you can do as you please,' and he left the door open for the terrier to stay in or out as he liked. That night the animal sat on the threshold howling all night. When I told the meeting that the Nationalists reminded me of that dog, they rushed my platform and we ended in free fights and a general uproar.

My family and I had a narrow escape about this time. There was a well-known pilot in Johannesburg. He had assembled a new Dragon plane and he invited my wife and boys and myself on a test flight. We sat on empty petrol boxes and as he had several thousand flying hours to his credit I felt no anxiety, though I did not like the careless manner in which he banked and turned, and when we landed I noticed that the plane keeled over until one wing tip was practically skimming the ground.

I think it was a case of familiarity breeding contempt as he did things a less experienced flyer would never have attempted. He shut off one engine to prove that he could fly on the other alone and he slowed down to almost stalling point before revving up again.

When we grounded I heard one of the mechanics say, 'We don't like that kind of flying here, it gives the Club a bad name.'

Next morning he went up with Sir Bernard Oppenheimer and he stalled the machine. It fell like a stone and when the two men were dragged out they were both dead.

II

Parliament sits at Capetown for five months per annum but on looking through my little pocket diaries such as one receives from business firms by way of advertisement every Christmas, references to the doings of the House are meagre. On the other hand there are many entries with regard to fishing, such as 'Out on Bay', 'Sailed *Lucky Jim*', 'Big haul at Cape Point', 'Spent night at sea', '68-pounder on 2.0 line', etc, etc.

The Bay in question is False Bay and John and Michael and I have derived almost as much pleasure from its waters as from Sandringham itself. I told them I was writing about Sandringham in a book and they demanded that I should write about False Bay too.

By the time this journal is published (if ever it be published), I shall have fished on False Bay off and on for twenty years, and during the latter half of this time my boys have fished with me, always during the Parliamentary Sessions.

False Bay is aptly named. Unlike Table Bay on the opposite side of the Cape Peninsula, it is a treacherous expanse. Dead calm one moment, and then fierce south-easters beat in from the Antarctic; the waves lash mountain-high, everything on board bangs and pitches from rail to rail, and one has to run for shelter without loss of time.

The mouth of the bay is thirty miles wide and from the Cape of Good Hope to Cape Hangklip it lies open to the great swells rolling in; and it requires good seamanship to navigate its stormy reaches in an open boat.

But the weather is not always rough, and the days I best remember are those when we sailed at dawn, the surface smooth as glass. As the fog slowly lifted, we saw vast flocks of malagasy duck and terns and seagull and cormorant diving into the shoals of sardine, the fall of the birds lashing and churning the sea like shellfire in France.

Amid this hurly-burly come schools of porpoise, a whale or two, and seals and penguins and sharks, the whole forming a spectacle probably unequalled anywhere in the world. Then we throw out our lines and pull in great fish—Cape Salmon, cabillaud, Steenbras and other kinds weighing from fifteen to thirty-five pounds and more—until our fingers are numbed and the boat is down by the head with the weight of our capture.

We used to go out on *Lucky Jim*, an eleven tonner belonging to our friend Mr Jim Taylor, the Grand Old Man of False Bay. He was possessed of great wealth and great kindness. He held broad tolerant views on South African affairs and his knowledge of the Bay and its moods was unrivalled. As often as wind and weather permitted he took us with him and many are the happy hours we spent in his company.

The False Bay fishermen are a breed unto themselves, mostly coloured people, with a dash of Malay blood in their veins, and the lives they lead are those of *Captains Courageous* and the *Newfoundland Banks*.

The howling storms often make communication by word of mouth impossible so they have evolved a sign language of their own. This is only for the elect and it is not until one has become a member of the lodge, so to speak, that they will initiate an outsider to its mysteries. Mr Taylor and John and Michael and I have by now been accepted as belonging to the craft and we know the cabala of the Bay. In passing other boats we put hand to forehead, touch our left cheek or right, or lip or chin; we make three cuts across our arm or dip our tackle high or low, bend a wrist as if to kill a mackerel, or describe a circle, and those across the water have been told what fish are running, how deep the nearest bank, and whether seal or shark have interfered with our lines, and the time of day.

The fishermen have grown so accustomed to their alphabet that even in port a man will ask for a match to light his pipe, tell of his thirst, or say he is turning in, by show of hand instead of by word of mouth.

Another matter they will not reveal to any but those who have graduated into their confidence is the lie of the banks. These are located by means of secret crossbearings on points along the shore, and in time we came to know them so well that we are able to cast anchor on the fishing grounds almost as expertly as the men themselves. From the colour of the water, the strength of the currents, and the behaviour of the birds we can forecast what fish are running, and we are acquainted with every headland and indentation along the seventy miles of coastline.

There are nearly a hundred varieties of edible fish in the Bay and there must be few places where finer sport is to be had on rod and line.

At all events my boys look on Sandringham and the Bay as the two most delectable spots on earth and they are proud of their accepted status on the banks.

We had trouble with the seals. They breed on an island and for years Mr Taylor and I have conducted a quarrel with the Union Fisheries about them, for whenever we complain of their depredations we are told that they live on crustacea alone and that they do not eat fish.

Having frequently been robbed of our catches, we wax indignant every time we receive this reply, but we have failed up to the present to convince the government officials that they are wrong.

A seal will come swimming around a boat and when a fish is hooked one feels a sharp tug and hauling in the line finds only the head dangling, the seal having taken the rest.

Once a seal starts on this it is useless shifting anchorage for he will follow the boat and repeat his tactics until we give up in despair and return to harbour.

It is illegal to shoot seals in False Bay but we carry a small rook rifle to frighten them.

An old bull seal, however, refused to scare. We knew him well from a white mark on his shoulder and he often worried us. One morning he took a dozen cape salmon from my hook and to add insult to injury he broke surface on each occasion derisively to wave his booty in my face. At long last he had eaten his fill and we saw him streaking towards the island.

Our coloured skipper cried, 'Tank de Lord, Master, de old ruffian he be gone, now we catchum fish again.'

But his joy was shortlived. The bull was back in less than half an hour and he brought his wife and two baby seals with him. He had apparently decided to let them in on a good thing. We started home in disgust, cursing the Union Fisheries Department as we went.

Another time, an eighty-foot whale cruised slowly by. My boy John fired at him with the rook rifle and we could hear the pellet plop against his side though he could hardly have noticed it as he moved along unhurried as before. Later I heard John boasting to his envious schoolfellows up north that he 'had shot a whale'.

This little rifle helped us to elucidate a problem. It is one of the mysteries of the African continent how quickly vultures flock to a kill. There may not be a bird in sight, but within a few minutes they appear out of the sky to gather round the carcass. They cannot scent fresh meat from miles away nor can they see a dead animal from the great distances they come, especially in dense bush, yet they congregate in a very brief time.

One afternoon we stumbled on what I think is the solution. A malagasy flew overhead. John fired at it and to my surprise he brought it down. The bird fell into the sea with a splash and almost at once a distant gull, seeing the malagasy drop, came to investigate. Other gulls from further away realised that one of their number had spotted something and they followed to see.

Then more gulls realised from the movements of their friends that something was afoot and they too closed in. Soon there were nearly a hundred of them screeching around the body of the floating goose.

None of them could have scented the dead bird and only one of them had seen it fall, but here they were, crowding around. I believe that the same explanation holds in the case of vultures. There are always a number of them soaring far apart, mere specks invisible to the human eye, and should one of them see a kill lying below, he drops steeply. The next nearest vulture, perhaps a mile away, notices the other dive and, his interest aroused, he follows. Then the next and the next vultures guess from the movements of their neighbours that there is to be a feast and they likewise proceed in the same direction. In this manner the ripple spreads in an ever widening circle and the vulture population over a large area gather on the ground. Here again none of them could have scented the kill, and only one of them had actually discovered the dead animal.

I saw another curious incident. A school of killer whales came ashore. Some were high and dry, others were flapping in the shallow surf frantically attempting to follow those that were already on land.

Two young Dutch farmers living in the neighbourhood waded in and slewing some of the smaller fish around, pushed them into deeper water and headed them out to sea. But they refused to be rescued. No sooner were they left to themselves than they turned back and insisted on beaching themselves again.

Mass suicide by killers is not infrequent along our coastline. The theory is that when they are pursued by shark or other enemies they strand themselves in a panic. But I hold a different view.

In the interior of Africa legions of ants and swarms of hopper locusts will set off in a given direction. Some primordial urge starts them upon their given way and having started, no obstacle diverts them. Should a river or a veld fire bar their passage, still they press forward, only to perish.

I believe a similar law applies to killers. From some distant point, propelled by nature, they make for their destined goal and it may well be that navigational errors, due to change of wind or tide, deflect them from their course and when, instead of the open sea they find land ahead of them, a blind impulse still drives them on and like the ants and the locusts, they go to their doom.

We witnessed an amusing event one morning. There hung a thick blanket of fog through which we cautiously felt our way. After a while we unexpectedly ran into a space of open water lying in brilliant sunshine. The surface was calm but as always, even in good weather, the ground swells rolled in at intervals, silent and smooth as glass, though they swing a boat twenty feet high as they come.

A few miles from the coast is a lagoon inhabited by duck and as we sailed across the clear patch, two of these suddenly appeared out of the surrounding wall of mist and sat down with a splash. None of us had ever known fresh-water duck to alight on the sea, so we watched them.

For a few moments they paddled about contentedly, and it was evident that they thought they were back on one of their quiet inland pools. Then came a towering ground swell that bore them swiftly on high. When they topped the crest they looked at each other with a wild surmise and as they tobogganed to the rear gave a squawk of dismay; and rising quickly, they disappeared into the gloom, leaving us helpless with laughter.

With such diversions, False Bay has been a haven of rest from the quarrels of Parliament and a great source of interest to my boys just as Sandringham has been a sanctuary and an infinite pleasure to us all.

Chapter 14

Depression in the Union and British Interlude

I

The year 1932 was a hard one in South Africa. Twelve months before, Great Britain had left the gold standard and the Nationalists obstinately refused to follow suit.

This gave rise to the most serious economic depression we have ever faced. Politically we made full use of the problem and launched a damaging attack against the Government from one end of the Union to the other.

Our public has been worked into a frenzy by so many forgotten causes in the past that I shall not linger over the Battle of the Gold Standard, but it lasted for nearly two years during which we conducted a relentless campaign. By the end of 1932 the rising tide of discontent had grown so strong that General Hertzog's government was tottering.

It had been an exciting time. I spoke at scores of meetings all over South Africa as did the rest of our Party.

Then, early in 1933, came the dramatic intervention of Mr Justice Roos. He is dead and gone and his name is scarcely remembered to-day, but in his time he played a considerable role. I knew him and had fought him, in Parliament and out, for many years. He was an able lawyer and a jovial cynic, but he was not very wise. He had been Minister of Justice under General Hertzog's administration until, some time previously, his health failed and he took to the Bench.

Without warning he now dropped a bombshell in the Nationalist ranks, a bombshell that was to have far-reaching effects and which, incidentally, brought about a great change in my own affairs.

Suddenly he resigned his judgeship and took the field against his former chief.

Mr Roos, though not in Parliament, controlled a *bloc* of about twenty Nationalist members in the House and if their votes were thrown against General Hertzog, they would inevitably bring about his downfall. And Mr Roos approached us with a curious proposal: he said that if we undertook to make him Prime Minister, he would break the Nationalist Party for us.

I met him several times during the discussions. He looked ill and worn. There was no trace of his old genial self and he told me he knew he had only a few more years to live. He added that before he died he meant to reorganise the economic and social fabric of the Union, and bring about a united nation.

I gained the impression that his illness had unbalanced his mind and I prefer to think that, sickening for death as he was, he failed to understand the implications of his somewhat dubious plan.

At this juncture General Hertzog dropped a counter bombshell, coming forward with the suggestion that we should call a halt to our racial warfare. The fight had been going on for over twenty years without either side gaining a final verdict, and all the time South Africa was suffering. He pleaded for an amalgamation into a new central Party of which he was to be the leader and in which our Dutch and English citizens were to be equally represented.

At first we thought this was merely a ruse to stave off defeat, as it was evident that at the next General Election we would drive him out of power. But General Smuts and I and others did not like the Roos overtures for they savoured of trickery and though we were confident of success at the coming polls, we felt that this would mean a continuation of the old racial dogfight which had done so much harm.

We therefore laid the Roos-Hertzog conditions before our Party and in caucus after caucus there was heated debate. Our supporters were so embittered at the pinpricks inflicted on them during the long Nationalist régime that they were prepared to go to almost any lengths to get rid of Hertzog and his government and there was a strong desire to make terms with Mr Roos.

We had a difficult task to dissuade them from what we saw would be a fatal course, and in the end we prevailed. What turned the day was the manner in which General Smuts rose superior to personal ambition. For the common good he was prepared to forgo the certainty of once more becoming the head of the state and his willingness to serve under Hertzog whom he had opposed for half a lifetime overcame their final difficulties. He asked the rest of us to agree to the lesser sacrifice of our own personal sentiments.

The negotiations, the quarrels and the arguments by no means went as smoothly or as quickly as might appear. There was tension throughout the country. The press raved and there was dissension and disunion in our Party, and I suppose the Nationalist counsels were equally divided. It was an uneasy, troublesome period, but a road was found and our 'Fusion' Party, as it was called, came into being.

A section of extremist Afrikaner opinion under Dr Malan hived off into a separate group and a section of extremist British opinion under Colonel Stallard did likewise; but the balance, representing the moderates, ranged themselves behind General

Hertzog and General Smuts.

The charge of opportunism was levelled at us but as for the South African Party, we stand absolved. By entering into a compact with the Nationalists we deliberately gave up certain victory for the sake of peace and co-operation between the two white races of South Africa.

Now came the question of constituting the new government. Under the Concordat, General Hertzog was to be Prime Minister with the right to nominate half the Cabinet and General Smuts was to be deputy Prime Minister with the right to nominate the other half.

Our final deliberations had shifted from Cape Town to Pretoria and one afternoon General Smuts phoned me to come to his farm. I motored out and found him in the wood and iron shack he has lived in for twenty-five years. He told me he was at his wits' end over the formation of his share of the new Cabinet. There were so many claimants and only five vacancies.

I saw at once how his mind was running and I said that he was not to consider me. I had followed him, man and boy, in peace and war, for over thirty years and I was content to serve under him as a private in the ranks.

He appeared relieved and after adding and deleting various possibles on a list he had before him he showed me his final Cabinet selection, which did not include my name. He seemed unhappy about it, but I gave him an assurance that my loyalty to him did not depend on Cabinet rank and that he could rely on my unswerving support.

On this note we said good-bye. As I climbed into my car I thought that he and Mrs Smuts gazed at me rather wistfully and I sensed that they felt I had, in a way, been dropped overboard. I was quite content, however, but as I started off he bade me promise that I would drive to Mr Patrick Duncan's office in Johannesburg to tell him what we had decided on.

As Mr Patrick Duncan had been a member of our Cabinet long ago, and as I knew what a high opinion General Smuts had of him, I did as he asked me. I saw Mr Duncan and explained the position to him. He later became Sir Patrick Duncan, the first South African Governor General of the Union, but I was never able to find out from him or from General Smuts what took place between them. Later in the evening my telephone rang and General Smuts was at the other end. He said he did not feel he could leave me out of the new Cabinet and that I was to be in Pretoria next day to be sworn in as a member of the Government.

I was not eager, for I had experience of the endless worries and uncertainties of a South African portfolio, but to me General Smuts was the law and I accepted office. That was more than eight years ago and I have not regretted the decision.

Fusion broke down at long last, but it has at any rate proved that with give and take on both sides, English and Dutch can work together in good fellowship in this country.

II

I took over the portfolio of Lands that I held nine years before and I had charge of Irrigation and Forestry, fascinating posts involving a maximum of travel.

As soon as the new Cabinet was formed, we held a General Election to test public opinion and we conducted a lightning campaign. For the first time in my life I appeared on the same platform with General Hertzog and I even stumped the Western Transvaal with General Kemp whom we had imprisoned in 1914.

South Africa overwhelmingly endorsed us and from now onward for more than six years the old South African Party and the Nationalists worked together and we began to think that unity was at length achieved.

I was returned unopposed for the Low Country and my wife, who is more politically-minded than I am, was returned for Parktown North, an important constituency of Johannesburg. She was the first woman Member of Parliament in South Africa. The elections being over and won, Parliament met at Capetown in a brief session and then, as when I first became a Minister, I set out to visit a portion of my kingdom as yet unvisited.

I had decided to inspect the Kalahari which lay under my control. This desert lies between German South-West on the one side and the Transvaal and Southern Rhodesia on the other, a breadth of four hundred miles or so, and lengthways it stretches from the Orange River in the south to the Okavango swamps six hundred miles northward.

Much of it is good cattle country, it contains plenty of game, and there are roving tribes of bushmen, the most primitive of all human beings.

Some officials who were to accompany me went on ahead to Kuruman, the mission centre where the Moffats and David Livingstone had laboured a somewhat unfruitful vineyard in years gone by, and I followed by air. At Kuruman I had cars and a lorry with petrol and water, and sending the plane back to Pretoria, we started off.

Using the dry bed of the Kuruman River, we travelled for two hundred miles to its confluence with the Molopo, another dead river that flows at rare intervals after heavy rains, perhaps twice in a century.

In this country of eternal sand we ploughed along at about ten miles an hour. After days of heavy going we reached a point where the Nosop and the Oup, two more fossil rivers, join together, and now we lumbered up the Oup to Mata-Mata on the south-west frontier.

Some time before, the Trustees of the Kruger Park had set aside a triangle of ground in this area, a million acres in extent, as a sanctuary for gemsbok (*Oryx Gazelli*) and the true hartebeest (*Bubalis Cama*). These varieties had been nearly exterminated by nomad poachers and by bushmen hunters.

We had selected the land by looking at the map, for none of us had ever visited this part of the world before; indeed, very few people in the Union had ever heard of it. Now I pushed cross-country from the Oup to inspect the Reserve and I was the first of the Board to see it—a waste of dunes which we navigated by compass. We developed a technique of our own for crossing the sandhills. The secret is to deflate one's tyres to half strength and never to attempt a dune on the slant; to accelerate and run straight ahead so that the impetus carries the car eight to ten feet upwards and the engine stalls; then to go back along the ruts the wheels have made and make another charge that carries us a short length beyond the first attempt. Continuing the process the rise is topped at last. It is a cruel strain on mechanism and chassis, but we crossed a long succession of dunes in this way, and went right through the Reserve in a few days at an all-over pace of about two miles per hour.

We saw gemsbok and hartebeest and an occasional bushman running at the sight of these strange monsters invading his ancestral hunting-grounds; and we put up several Kalahari lion, a smaller and less yellowed species than those of the Transvaal.

I had arranged for a camel patrol to await us and here again, I learned something new about lion. We emerged on the Nosop River one evening and as we pitched our tents I was surprised to see the camel drivers hobble their animals and turn them into the bush for the night. We had seen a lion slinking at dusk and to me it seemed wanton cruelty to send the camels thus helpless into the dark, but the drivers were easy. They said a lion will never attack a camel, hobbled or otherwise, that a lion only attacks from the rear, and as a camel always faces round, they are not molested. My own belief is that lion cannot bear their musty smell; but at all events our camels grazed unharmed. I rode a camel now and then but on the whole I prefer to walk.

Having inspected the Reserve, we continued, travelling up the bed of the Nosop River to a point shown on the map as Union's End. Here we found a tribe of half-breeds that had been marooned for over two years, a subsection of Simon Kooper's nation, about a hundred strong. They had come to Union's End to hunt, but a drought had cut them off and they had been obliged to remain at this spot ever since, for here was the only water within a hundred and twenty miles. Luckily for them the South African Government had put down a borehole for our troops during the 1915 campaign. The hole was a hundred and seventy feet deep and as there was no pump or windmill, the only way they could reach the water was by letting down a gallon paraffin tin at the end of a long line of gemsbok riems; it was a full-time job and they worked in relays night and day. Had the thong broken the tin would have fallen down and blocked the borehole, and all of them would have perished. They had never seen a motor-car. I offered to send back for lorries to evacuate them but they were too terrified of these strange vehicles so I left them there. I learned afterwards that they got out in safety with the next rains.

Animals in these parts do not drink, for there is no surface water. They obtain moisture from the Tsama melon and other herbage.

As for lion and other carnivora, they are said to drink the blood of their prey, but according to the bushmen they quench their thirst from the liquid in the large intestine of the beasts they kill. I was told that hunters in the Kalahari find enough water in a gemsbok's paunch to have a drink and a wash and that once they become used to it, fresh water is insipid and tasteless to them.

As we returned down the river we came on two honey badgers. We have a Dutch saying, 'tough as a badger', and I would add 'brave as a badger', for as we passed them I saw a pair of cubs, the size of hedgehogs. I was on the driving seat of the water lorry at the time and the badgers thought we had designs on their offspring. To them the lorry must have looked about twenty times the size a mastodon did to a palaeolithic hunter, yet they were unafraid. They charged forward in defence of their brood and the valorous creatures actually bit and hacked into our tyres, squealing with rage the while. I ordered my driver not to injure them and the brave creatures trotted off in triumph to collect their young.

We now made for Upington, a village on the north bank of the Orange. A prolonged drought was working havoc on both sides of the river and I went to investigate. In order to reach Upington we ploughed over two hundred miles of barren country. We went by Rietfontein, the most desolate outpost of Southern Africa, and we went by Haksteen Pan, thirty miles long with a floor so smooth and hard that at sixty miles an hour our cars raised no dust and left no visible tracks. The effects of the drought were terrible. The Hottentots who inhabit this area exist at the best of times on a mere fringe of life for this is one of the toughest lands on earth. We found them living on locusts and roots and digging for ants. I asked one of them how they were faring and he said in Dutch, 'Sir, we Hottentots can live on wind and sun, but the whites are getting hell.'

The Orange River was a row of stagnant pools. Hundreds of European farmers had moved to the river in search of water and in search of such little grazing as was left on its banks.

We crossed to the south side and hurried along via Goodhouse, Pella-Pella, and other places unmarked on maps, and by a wide sweep we struck the river again at Vioolsdrift. All along our route dead cattle and sheep and horses met our eyes and our nostrils; it was a sad journey.

At Vioolsdrift a number of families had sought refuge. They had come from their stricken farms, for here at any rate was water to drink, and such of their animals as were left to them could gain sustenance of a kind by feeding on the willows and reeds.

When we came among them down a narrow gorge debouching on the river, they were nearing starvation. Wherever a tree was left, a whole family was camped for shelter and like the Hottentots we had passed, they too were digging for ants and snaring jackals for food. They were a brave hardy people among whom I had lived in the days of the guerrilla war, and I knew their fine qualities.

The menfolk had pathetically begun to dig a canal to bring what little water there was on to flat ground, where they hoped to sow wheat and maize, but their levels were wrong, and a jutting crag had defeated their labours. Ruin was staring them in the face.

I despatched one of my cars to civilisation and in less than a fortnight engineers arrived and within a month three hundred men were at work building a dam across the river and constructing a canal. To-day, where I had found a hopeless starving community there are ten thousand acres of fields and gardens under irrigation, and scores of comfortable homesteads and smiling families. It cost the taxpayer of the Union ninety thousand pounds but this settlement, conjured from the desert, is a tangible thing I have achieved.

Later I received an artless address. It read:

> 'Hon Sir. We the undersigned render our thanks. You promised to help us and we doubted. But the marks of your car were still in the sand when your workmen arrived to build this dam, and now we are saved.'

Then followed the signatures of many people.

I was criticised in Parliament during the next session, but I had helped a brave community whom I learned to respect in days gone by, and I have no regrets.

From here we went further south to Springbokfontein, the place I had helped to capture in 1902. In the village cemetery I found the graves of Stewart and van Couvorden, the two young soldiers I had killed. From the inscription on their headstones they had fallen on the 1st of April and not on my birthday as I state in my book *Commando*; but it was easy to lose count in those times.

It must be unusual for a man to look upon the graves of those fallen by his hand. I had experienced this once before, at the grave of the spy whose execution I have elsewhere described.

I now travelled west to pick up the railway line and so returned to Pretoria; from there I flew to Windhoek to discuss the Vioolsdrift scheme with the authorities, as some of the land I was putting under water lay on their side of the Orange River. I was escorted by two other machines, for our route was across uninhabited desert and it was advisable to have accompanying planes to report forced landings or other mishaps. At Windhoek I entered into an agreement with the Administration and then we flew back. We had come on a roundabout course via Upington and Keetmanshoop but on the return journey I decided to take the direct way. This had only been attempted once before, by Sir Pierre van Ryneveld, our flying ace who commanded the Union Air Force.

We purchased hand mirrors to flash our position to a rescue party should we come down in the desert. However, all went well. For nine hours we winged it over the most forbidding expanse I had ever seen and so we flew the 'Great Thirst'.

III

Having been in the grip of a terrible drought for two years, South Africa now suffered from equally disastrous floods. With us it is always feast or famine. The land is parched and thirst-stricken or the heavens are loosed upon us.

I have spoken of the Drought Relief Bill which we had to turn into a flood assistance measure, and my father once told me of how he rode through a forest at Knysna when he came on an old Boer lady standing disconsolate by the road. Halting to inquire what was amiss she replied, 'Oh, sir, the elephants and the grubs got into my fields last night.' The largest of quadrupeds and the smallest of insects had combined to ravage her crops, and this is typical of how extremes meet out here.

Thus it was now. From lands lately parched, with flocks and herds lying dead for want of water, reports came in from every direction of heavy rains and losses of human beings and livestock.

This was early in 1934. I had gone to the Cape with my family to await the approaching session of Parliament and on reaching home one evening after a long day's fishing on the Bay with my two boys, there were telegrams to say that the Orange River was in spate and that the people on the islands below Upington were in grave peril.

When I was formerly Minister of Lands I had had a survey of these islands made and I had placed the settlers there. Now they were in jeopardy, so I went to see things for myself. Our Air Force had an old Wapiti two-seater stationed at Capetown and I requisitioned it. The pilot was Lieutenant Viljoen, and I took off at daybreak next day. In six hours we were approaching the Orange.

I had known this sector of the river for more than thirty years but what I saw now was different. Instead of narrow streams and channels meandering among the islands, a mighty torrent more than three miles wide was flowing down with only the tops of the larger islands above water. The smaller ones were drowned out.

I landed at Upington and collected what information I could. Bridges were under water, the railway line had gone and telegraph and telephone communications were broken. No one had news of the islanders. There was a dilapidated motor launch that had served as a ferry and I asked for volunteers to man it. Of the six men who offered themselves, four were local Jewish traders. Each of us took an inflated inner tube of a motor tyre as lifebelt and we discarded most of our clothing, for the water ran rough and turbulent.

After a dangerous passage we made Cannon Island. The inhabitants cheered as we came up. Their homes and crops were gone but they were in no immediate danger as the floods could not reach the higher levels. Then we visited the other islands that were not submerged. On one of these, a few square yards alone still showed above the waters. On this the two occupants had drawn a wagon; on the wagon was a kitchen table, and on the table stood two chairs upon which they sat philosophically smoking their pipes. Neither of them could swim and when I asked them what would happen if there was a further rise, they shrugged their shoulders and one of them said in Dutch 'then we'll go down with the others'.

I invited them on board, but after inspecting our craft they refused. They were wise, for shortly after leaving them we got into rapids and our ship sank.

Fortunately we were close to a bank and with difficulty and good luck we managed to wade ashore. It was nearly dark, we were drenched to the skin and most of our clothes and other belongings had gone down. So, cold and hungry we cowered together for warmth on the sand spit. The nearest mainland was a mile and a half away and in between raged a torrent on which it seemed no boat could live.

But word must have gone forth of our plight, for towards the small hours of the morning the headlights of motor-cars began to appear and it was obvious that they were trying to locate us. The roar of the waters prevented our shouts from reaching them, but now we had experience of the strange system of log-swimming that is practised by the Hottentots along the river. They take a six foot log. At the upper end they drive in a stout wooden peg to serve as a handle and with this crude raft they fearlessly enter the water no matter how strong the current. Sprawled across, one hand grasping the peg and one leg encircling the log, with their free leg and free arm they propel themselves.

As we sat shivering in the dark we heard a shout, and a dripping figure appeared among us. It was a Hottentot sent by the District Magistrate. Hearing that we had not returned he collected as many log-swimmers as he could and he ordered them into the river to search the islands.

Before dusk I had looked across the heaving waters and I did not like what I had seen. Submerged reefs broke the current into great waves from ten to fifteen feet high and to plunge into this in broad daylight requires a stout heart; but the Hottentot swimmers precariously astride their logs, did not hesitate to make the passage in the dark.

The man who reached us made light of his feat and when we had told him what we had to tell, he re-entered the stream and was swallowed into the night. He made the return journey in safety for not long after daybreak we saw a large boat navigated by more Hottentots approaching us from above. We watched them anxiously, but as the boat was coming downstream and not across the current it had an easier passage and ultimately they were able to take us off.

The home journey was difficult, but after a struggle we got in amid enthusiastic plaudits from the crowd that had collected to watch the rescue operations.

I was told that these swimming logs are passed from father to son like family heirlooms and I heard of a European who tried to chop one for firewood being half murdered before he was extricated.

A car owner raced me back to Upington and I planned to drop supplies on the islands. We manufactured parachutes from sheets and tablecloths and we attached tins with food of various kinds. Loaded with these I made several journeys over the stricken area and in every case I was able to drop the bombs with accuracy and saw men and women and children rushing to retrieve them, waving their arms in greeting as we flew by.

Having provisioned them as well as I could, I went down the river next day to see what had happened to the construction works at Viooolsdrift.

We passed Cannon Island and the other islands as before, then down to Keimoes and Kakamas where I could see immense damage. Soon after crossing Kakamas we saw a great pillar of smoke in the sky. It was spray rising from the Aughrabies Falls. We circled round. Above the Falls the flooded river was three or four miles broad, then the water entered the ravine and leaped into the canyon, five hundred feet below.

It was a stupendous sight and I believe that my pilot and I were the first men to see the Aughrabies in flood, for normally it is impossible to get near during the rains. My record for swimming up the gorge years ago also holds.

We continued down the river and after a while we were over Goodhouse. I had been at this place not long before and on that occasion old Carl Weidner had subjected me to a lecture on his favourite topic—that South Africa was drying up.

As we passed overhead I could see his orchards and fields under water and only the roof of his homestead was visible. The poor old fellow was standing in his shirtsleeves surveying the havoc from a rise, so I dropped him a message: 'Terribly sorry, but you said South Africa was drying up.'

The note fell almost at his feet and I saw him pick it up. He read it and then he shook his fist at the plane; but when I met him long after, he chuckled and agreed that the joke was on him.

From here we continued to Vioolsdrift. The engineers had received timely warning and they had succeeded in dragging most of the tractors and machinery out of harm's way. Among the white tents on the hill I could see the workmen gazing at the progress of the floods and here again I left a greeting.

Beyond Vioolsdrift we flew over the most jagged country I have seen in my life— serrated mountains that stood up like shark's teeth and our engine selected this moment to do frightening things. There came a series of bangs and knocks which felt as if the machine were being torn to pieces. I was in communication with Lieut Viljoen by earphone and I heard him say, 'Beg pardon sir, engine trouble.' This was only too obvious and a moment later he said, 'Sir, I'm afraid we will have to jump for it.'

The parachutes we wore in those days were bulky cumbersome things and I had unbuckled and thrown mine into the narrow tunnel to the rear of the cockpit. It was not easy to crawl down that restricted passage but in a matter of seconds I went on hands and knees and fished it out. The knocking and shaking of the engine was unabated and I confess that the thought of leaping out on to the forbidding range below was uninviting. I had replaced my earphone askew so the pilot's voice was faint, but I heard him tell me not to go overboard until he held up his hand. In spite of the jolting cylinders, the propeller was still going and Lieut Viljoen was nosing upward. He climbed until the engine gave out and in the comparative silence that followed he telephoned to say that he thought we would make it. I did not know what he meant, but looking ahead I saw, far away, a glint of the Atlantic Ocean. He made skilful use of our height and he handled his machine in such a manner that after a tense half hour he glided her safely on to the coast.

We were lucky, for besides making a good landing, we found ourselves close to Alexander Bay, the State diamond diggings to which I made earlier reference. Soon the manager of the works and his staff were on the scene and instead of having to leap from an aeroplane on to a remote and barren desert we found a warm welcome and comfortable quarters.

The engine of our plane was so badly damaged through an oil leakage that it was abandoned and only the fuselage was taken back for salvage.

While awaiting the arrival of a relief machine I had time to inspect the diggings. They are enclosed in a double ring of wire fences, twelve feet high, lit by arc lamps at night and patrolled all day by armed men.

In this desolate area, diamonds to the value of sixteen million pounds have been unearthed and production at the same rate can go on for another century.

When finally a plane was sent to my rescue, I was flown to Capetown. John and Michael were at the aerodrome to meet me. They said it was unfair, I was always having adventures without them.

At this time I happened to visit the trout hatcheries near Capetown. I found that in addition to trout, a consignment of Black Bass had been imported from Canada and the fish were thriving. I was told that they breed in dams and stagnant waters, but when I suggested trying them up north the Curator said he had made several attempts to send fingerlings by rail but in each case they had died.

I procured a dozen bass, each some three inches long, and putting them into a carboy I flew them up to Johannesburg next day in a Wapiti. They were all alive and well when we landed and I had them placed in one of the municipal ponds. They have increased so prolifically since then that I have caused every government irrigation work in the Transvaal and Free State to be stocked with their progeny.

IV

The 1934 session of Parliament was dull. From my notes I gather that there were long debates over some recondite constitutional issue as to whether the Crown of England was divisible or indivisible. The jingo element raved, but to me it was as divorced from reality as the medieval disputes about the number of angels that could stand on the point of a needle or the abstractions of the Holy Trinity; so I fished on the Bay.

On 27th March of this year my father, Francis William Reitz, aged ninety, died, full of years and of honour. He was decreed a state funeral and General Smuts and General Hertzog were among his pall bearers. A mighty throng stood bowed in the streets of Capetown as his cortège went by.

At the conclusion of the session we returned to Pretoria and between spells of departmental duties I went on various journeys.

I paid another visit to Zululand, taking my younger brother Jack with me. At the age of twelve he had been at the siege of Ladysmith during the Boer War in 1899. Now he was Mayor of Bloemfontein and a Member of the Free State Provincial Council.

After a long journey, meeting deputations and listening to grievances, we reached the Umfolosi River and here I had a Waco plane awaiting me as I intended flying over the papyrus delta I had first inspected when the sugar planters dynamited the barrier in 1921.

My brother had never flown before and when I asked him to join me he refused. He said, 'I promised Billy (his wife) I would not fly without her consent, and I must keep my word.'

These were still the days when to go aloft was looked on as a perilous undertaking and before starting friends shook hands and said good-bye in mournful voices, hoping for the best. But I could see that Jack was eager so I coaxed him inside the machine and before he could change his mind we were up.

We circled the swamp, then we turned inland over the Umfolosi reserve, seeing buffalo and white rhino and other game. Then we made for the coast and as a Waco can sit down on a tablecloth, we looked for a clear patch near the beach and came safely to earth.

That evening I met a young cub reporter and prevailed on him to send a press telegram to Bloemfontein to say that 'Mr Jack Reitz, our Mayor and Provincial Councillor, has been assisting his brother the Minister of Lands, in an aerial survey of the Umfolosi delta.'

He entered into the spirit of the thing, and in three or four days a copy of the *Bloemfontein Friend* was in my post. There was a headlined account of our trip, with prominent mention of Jack's doings, so I left the journal on a table in our tent. Presently he walked in and seeing his favourite paper he began to read the hometown news.

I watched him. As he reached the item about himself he sat up with a jerk and a broad smile illuminated his countenance. He slapped his thigh and looking at me he exclaimed, 'By God, I don't know what Billy will do about this, but I would like to hear what those fellows at the Coffee House will say when they hear of it.'

At Bloemfontein, he and his cronies met every morning to gossip and he knew that they would regard his exploit as a seven days' wonder; for flying had not yet reached that peaceful township and anyone who had been in the air was looked on with respect.

I spent the balance of my trip to Zululand flying to various places. I went to St Lucia Bay, Sordwana, Sibaya, and to my old haunt at Indumu where I found the hippo largely increased since I had turned their lake into a sanctuary fourteen years ago.

Then, leaving my brother and the rest of my party to work their way back by road,

I flew to Pretoria. In the next three months I twice flew over the wild country that lies towards the Limpopo and over the river system of the Njeleli and Pafuri, a region South Africans had scarcely heard of at that time. I saw elephant and much other game. I looked down on the fastness of the Zoutpansbergen and on the lake of Fundudzi which the Bavenda natives consider to be sacred.

I now took up a project I had long considered. When first I was a member of the Union Cabinet, I was shown documents in the Irrigation Department with regard to a scheme originally mooted by Mr Cecil Rhodes. He wanted to build a dam across the Vaal River at Warrenton, near Kimberley, by means of which its waters could be diverted to the lower-lying area of the Harts.

In 1922 I sent out survey parties to investigate the possibilities, but the ensuing change of Government brought the scheme to nothing. Now that I was in power again I took it up afresh. I had lived in the Northern Free State before the Great War and I was intimately acquainted with the upper course of the Vaal River. It seemed to me that instead of damming the Vaal at Warrenton, as Mr Rhodes intended, we should build a mighty weir four hundred miles above to impound ten times the water he had dreamed of. By running this down the bed of the river to Warrenton and thence to the Harts we could irrigate a hundred and twenty thousand acres of soil now lying useless in the Kalahari desert.

Much of this ground belonged to the Batlapins, a tribe of Sechuana under the para-mount Chief Mankorane, and I had to obtain their consent. So I travelled west and met the Chief and his counsellors. As I appeared before them they stood respectfully, each man holding up his arm in salute crying 'Poola-poola' which in their language means 'rain-rain'. In a drought-stricken country rain is like God to them so 'Poola' is their cry.

I addressed the headman and when I pointed to the baking sands and undertook to bring them running water they laughed, for no man had in his lifetime seen running water here.

Nevertheless I made a treaty under which they granted me the land and I journeyed back. On the second day east, there rolled towards us a wall of brick-red dust, a thousand feet high. Nature stood still: the birds fell silent and there came a hush. The headlights of our cars penetrated only a few feet and for twenty minutes we fought for breath.

Then the curtain passed and in its wake followed a cloudburst which in a few seconds turned every runnel into a torrent. We were delayed for many hours and as I watched the tide recede I saw a curious thing. Rain had not fallen in these parts for six years but now on the edge of the water there sat dozens of frogs, so tenuous as to be almost transparent, and they croaked away vigorously. How they had survived, and whence they came, were matters beyond me.

On my return to Pretoria I persuaded my reluctant colleagues that the work had to be constructed, and in due course I piloted an enabling Bill through Parliament. I was hotly attacked and the press said I was squandering the nation's money on a whim of my own; but to-day there stands an inland sea, ninety miles long, with a coastline of four hundred miles, and down on the Harts are thousands of settlers making a living where before was only a waste of desert.

Also I made good my promise to the Batlapins, for water now flows where no water had run in the memory of man.

The Vaal-Harts project has cost the Union six million pounds. It is the largest irrigation scheme in the Southern hemisphere, and here, too, I have no regrets.

I made other flights on official business. On one of these General Smuts was a fellow passenger. We landed at a small village in the Karroo where the Mayor and Town Councillors invited us to an *al fresco* breakfast on the aerodrome.

The General was in good humour and he told delightful stories of the days when he and I had raided these parts during the Boer War. I thought I would spin them a yarn of those times too, so I recounted the tale of the ambush in 1901 when General Smuts had his horse shot under him during the first weeks of our invasion of the Cape Colony. I said that a young British officer had examined the General's wallets and found a Greek Testament among its contents. Scanning the book he was heard to exclaim, 'I wonder why this Boer officer is learning Pitman's shorthand?' I sat back for applause, but I drew a blank and it was borne in on me that neither the Mayor nor his Councillors had ever seen Greek script or Pitman's shorthand.

I found time to take my boys to Sandringham for our annual camping and we went into the Kruger National Park to see the progress of the Letaba causeway. We met two enormous bull elephants beside the road and I pulled up within a few yards of them. Immediately beyond was one of our Board posters nailed to a tree, with the notice, 'Beware of the elephant.' Michael leaned across and in a hoarse whisper inquired, 'Daddy, *how* does one beware of elephant?' As the use of firearms is not allowed in the Park I didn't know then and I don't know now. Fortunately the great beasts shuffled off into the bush and we were free to continue our journey.

V

In August 1934 the Government of Southern Rhodesia invited my wife and myself to Salisbury. We travelled via the Limpopo River and the Zimbabwe ruins and thence east to the Melsetter escarpment from where we turned through Umtali and so reached the Rhodesian capital after an interesting journey. We were guests of the State and we were royally entertained with banquets and balls and their traditional hospitality.

I opened an agricultural show, made speeches at many functions, then we started for the Victoria Falls.

After a long run we came to Bulawayo by midnight. We had left at five am that morning and looked forward gratefully to rest. As we were having a final cup of tea at an hotel, a policeman brought me a pencilled note telephoned by the Rhodesian Governor from Salisbury.

It said that our son Michael was lying in hospital at Johannesburg desperately injured as the result of an accident.

The news had been wired from Pretoria, but as we had already left Salisbury when it arrived and no one knew exactly where we could be found, they had communicated with every telephone centre and every police station along our route. Outlying towns and villages were asked to watch for us and practically the whole of Rhodesia was on the lookout. I can never adequately express my gratitude for the trouble they went to.

We started south at once. We travelled all through the night and as we tore along, policemen and officials at telephone booths and post offices flagged us with news of Michael's condition. What they told us was not reassuring: 'Unconscious, but there is hope.'

We made West Nicholson and we passed Beit Bridge on the Limpopo towards sunrise. Stopping only to refuel we hurried on. The Union Government too was kind. At intervals men stood beside the road to say our boy was still alive as we raced across Northern and Central Transvaal and when we reached the outskirts of Johannesburg that evening, after a record run, Colonel Baston, of the police, stopped us. Our hearts sank for we thought he bore evil tidings, but he had come to show his sympathy and he said he had visited the hospital and that Michael was still alive.

Jaded and weary we pulled up at the children's hospital after dark. Michael was in a critical condition. His skull was fractured and his face was battered to pulp and he had been unconscious for two days. Next morning he came to. His eyes slowly opened and he stared bewilderedly around. Gradually he recognized his mother and myself. Then he said, 'Will you give me a watch if I recover?'

I am thankful to say he got that watch. He made slow progress but in a month he was out of danger.

My eldest brother Hjalmar came to see him. He stared at the boy's mangled face, all swathed in plaster and lint, then he looked at me and said, 'As Michael resembled you before the accident, any alteration must be an improvement.' I was so happy about Mike's progress that I swallowed the insult.

VI

Before the end of the year I made journeys by land and sea and plane, fighting by-elections, attending social functions, and dealing with many problems.

I had one amusing trip. The leader of our political opposition was Dr Malan, a tight-lipped Covenanter with no sense of humour. I heard that he was to speak at an election meeting at Heilbron in the Northern Free State where I had lived for many years, so I collected a bundle of leaflets containing unfavourable reference to him and his followers and got into an aeroplane. I timed my visit to a nicety, for as I circled overhead he was addressing his supporters on the show ground. Taking careful aim I dropped the literature in such a manner that the pamphlets fluttered straight down on his audience. They thought these were from their own party and there was a scramble to pick them up.

I saw them reading the bulletins and then flinging them away in disgust and I crowed at the old bigot's discomfiture. It was an undignified trick but we carried the seat by a large majority.

Towards the end of 1934 I changed portfolios. Thus far I had been Minister of Lands, and General Kemp had been Minister of Agriculture. Owing to the exacting nature of the task his health broke down and I lightheartedly agreed to take over from him. As Minister of Lands I had occupied an interesting and difficult post but I soon discovered how much more troublesome an inheritance I had now assumed.

Everything was rotten in the State of Denmark. Maize prices stood at zero, wheat had slumped to below production cost, fruit and citrus industries were in the doldrums, co-operative societies clamoured for help and tobacco-planters, cattle-breeders, and dairy farmers demanded the impossible. It was like a lawsuit in hell and the unfortunate Minister of Agriculture was expected to work miracles. I began to realise why my colleague had cracked up and the task nearly undid me too; but this was not yet.

The 1935 Parliamentary Session opened in January. I introduced a Bill that I count unto myself for righteousness. I had long been watching the export of our smaller wild birds to Japan and the East. They were mostly snared in the Transvaal Low Country and I found that nearly eighty per cent of them died from terror or heartbreak before they reached the ships. Even the railway porters cried out at the shame of it.

I brought in a Bill to end this cruel traffic. The farmers opposed me. They said the birds would increase under the protection of my Bill and endanger their crops, but I fought it through the House and to-day the whole of South Africa is a sanctuary in which no wild bird may be captured or caged; a matter wherein we stand ahead of the rest of the world.

Then I went on stump to East London where the ultra-British section howled me down. They had an association called the 'New Guard' whose purpose was to champion British interests in the Union. Though I had served in the Great War and had shed my blood in France I was roundly told that I was a Dutchman and they would have none of me. When the meeting broke up I called out, 'Gentlemen, you will apologise to me for this some day' and there came the answering shout, 'Never, never, you are a traitor.' Time has brought its revenge.

I ran down to Sandringham with John and Michael for our yearly camping, and I satisfied them at last, for I took them on a hunt and we shot two big lion after an exciting chase.

Also, we climbed up the slopes of the Drakensberg escarpment and there I selected a piece of land more beautiful, in my eyes, than anything in the country. It has a crystal clear mountain torrent of its own, it has flower-carpeted forests and from the rim one looks down a mighty gorge and almost the whole of the Low Country lies stretched beyond.

I purchased the ground and I had it surveyed and registered in my name. If ever dreams come true, I hope to spend the evening of my days on 'Forest Glade', as I have called it.

Here are extracts from my notebook for the next two months:

> Flew to Capetown and thence by car to inspect irrigation scheme in the North-West. Back by air through heavy storms and thunderclouds.
> To Warrenton, Kimberly and Douglas on official business.
> To Upington, Griquatown and other centres in the Kalahari addressing political meetings.
> By air to Uitenhage, near the south coast, to take part in a by-election. Our candidate successful.
> Flew over the Addo Forest to see the elephant. Back to Pretoria in 4 hours and 45 minutes. Met deputations plus job hunters and people with insoluble conundrums and grievances.
> To the NW Transvaal. Travelled up along the Matlabas River to its junction with the Limpopo.

Along the Magol River into the Waterbergen. For nearly a hundred miles we passed swarms of locusts whose ravages will be blamed on me as locust extermination is part of my job.

To Durban; to the Western Transvaal; to Bloemfontein to attend a Party Congress.

And so it went on, with the opening of a few agricultural meetings and other functions thrown in for good measure.

VII

This year I had another pleasant surprise.

The Empire Parliamentary Association is a body which every Member of Parliament in the Commonwealth is entitled to join. It sponsors journeys of goodwill to different parts of the Empire and for 1935, Great Britain was the venue. All the Dominions and India were asked to send delegates. Each Parliament elected its own representatives and our House nominated six. I was to accompany them as leader and I was nothing loath, for I had not been overseas since the Great War.

I travelled to England by air. With my private secretary, Mr Cooper, who accompanied me on most journeys, we started off. We went via Broken Hill in Northern Rhodesia, thence by Mpika and Mbeya across the African jungle and so, via Iringa, Dodoma and Moshi, where I had campaigned of old. We flew by the peaks of Kilimanjaro to Nairobi, seeing much big game below.

From Nairobi we went to the Great Lakes and down the Nile. At Bor we circled a large herd of elephant. Some of them were swimming or wading the river, only their trunks showing above the water. We landed at Khartoum, and at Luxor, and we viewed tombs and temples and vanished pomps of yesterday.

In Cairo, museums and Coptic churches and the El Ashras University took several days of our time. At the University the students learn thousands of *surahs* from the Koran and nothing else. We 'did' the Pyramids where an Egyptian youth offered me beads and scarabs for sale. I asked him whether they came from Birmingham, but he smilingly said, 'No sir, dey is from Czechoslovakia.'

We were invited to the Palace where Prince Hassanein received us. He had accompanied Rosita Forbes to the Kufra oasis out in the western desert.

The 1st Royal Scots Fusiliers, the Battalion I had commanded in France, lay in garrison on the Suez Canal and I was invited to inspect them at Ismailia. I went by fast military plane with a fighter escort and we flew the Delta in less than an hour. I was met on the aerodrome by what I took to be a second lieutenant from the stars on his shoulders. He was a cheery little fellow and as we drove along in his car we cracked jokes and I dug him in the ribs at a particularly good story he told. When we reached barracks a guard of honour turned out to salute him and I found that he was Brigadier-General Sir Frederick Pile, Commander-in-Chief of the Near East.

I had slipped up on the new insignia of rank, for crossed swords to denote a brigadier had been abolished since my time. However, Sir Frederick and I got along like a house on fire.

The Scots Fusiliers treated me regally, with parades and a march-past and a regimental banquet. It was midsummer north of the Equator and I spent hours every day swimming in the Canal; and as I swam, Italian troopships glided by, for Mussolini had started on his Abyssinian adventure.

At the conclusion of my visit I was flown back to Cairo and Mr Cooper and I resumed our journey. We stopped at Alexandria for a night. Sitting at a club overlooking the harbour with some friends, we were shown King Fuad's yacht at anchor in the roadway.

They told us that some months previously the King had decided to sail for Malta. Ten days later the yacht came back. They had been unable to raise the island and the commander of the yacht said, 'Malta *mafish*, there is no such place.'

From Alexandria we went by flying boat across the Mediterranean via Crete where we landed; to Athens; then to Brindisi on the Italian coast and by rail, skirting the Adriatic Sea to Turin. Everywhere walls and houses were placarded with fascist slogans about a greater Italy, and soldiers were marching and counter-marching, but I thought the people were apathetic.

We saw the beautiful lakes of northern Italy, then crossed the Alps to Switzerland. Mr Cooper was in the seventh heaven. He had never left Africa but he had been nurtured on Byron and Keats and Shelley and Browning and to him Italy and Switzerland and the snow-covered peaks of the Matterhorn and the Jungfrau were sheer romance. He quoted poetry all the way and I am afraid I somewhat damped his ardour by telling him of the *nil admirari* American who, when asked after his return from a tour though Switzerland what he thought of the Alps said he 'remembered having seen risin' ground on the left'.

A night-run to Paris, then by air to Croydon through fog and rain, flying blind without so much as a glimpse of the country below or of the English Channel.

In London I found myself sumptuously installed at Grosvenor House as a guest of the State. I occupied a luxurious suite with the Union Coat-of-Arms in colours on a shield over my door.

One of my first callers was a grizzled soldierly man who turned out to be Lord Vivian whom I had last seen in our fight against the 17th Lancers in 1901 when he lay wounded among the rocks. On the strength of this he put me down as an honorary Member at Brooks, the oldest club in London, and he often dropped in for a talk.

A week later the rest of the South African and Dominion members arrived and now began a round of sightseeing and speeches and functions in the course of which we were nearly killed with kindness. Ancient Guilds entertained us in their halls and we supped from gold and silver plate that had survived the Cromwellian wars.

We attended the House of Commons and we were taken to a hundred and one places of interest. I was twice summoned to Buckingham Palace and twice I donned a top hat and a morning coat, in which unaccustomed garb I had audience of His Majesty King George V.

He told me he kept both my books at his bedside in Windsor Castle and he offered to confer on me the Distinguished Service Order. I was unable to accept this owing to a law the Nationalist Government had passed in 1926 prohibiting Union subjects from receiving decorations. I saw the Prince of Wales at St James's Palace once or twice. He seemed more highly-strung than ever and I little dreamed that, in a measure, I was to sit in judgment on him in time to come.

There was a South African cricket team in England and already they had won two test matches. At a luncheon at Claridge's I responded to a toast and I said that I had seen a newspaper placard in the street that morning, 'Britain faces disaster'. Relations with Mussolini were strained over the Abyssinian adventure and an excited Frenchman cried out, 'My God, this means war with Italy'; but it was only the state of the cricket score!

On another occasion some thirty of us were standing about in front of Grosvenor House waiting for cars to fetch us to various points. A number of boys and girls stood around, each carrying an autograph book and a fountain pen.

We thought the children had realised that the Elder Statesmen of the Empire were in town and we waited self-consciously for the young folk to screw up their courage to ask us for our signatures. The moments passed and still the autograph hunters kept aloof until at last a beauteous damosel emerged from the hotel. She was a film star and she was immediately surrounded by her admirers bearing books and pens on high. We climbed sheepishly into our cars.

We toured many parts of England and Scotland. In Glasgow the fruit distributing industry gave me a banquet by virtue of my being Minister of Agriculture in charge of export from South Africa. I made the usual speech, and having touched on refrigeration, marketing, packing and kindred topics I went on to tell how my father had spent his youth in Scotland and of his great love for Robert Burns. I said that he had translated many of Burns' poems into Afrikaans and I repeated my former tale that there was a time when, as a small boy, I thought they had been written in Afrikaans and that a fellow named Burns had translated them into indifferent English.

The story was well received. On the strength of it I was motored up to Ayr to see the Burns Cottage and the Burns Museum that afternoon. The first thing I saw as we entered was a faded manuscript under glass; I rubbed my eyes for the document was in my father's handwriting! It was his Afrikaans rendering of *Tam O'Shanter*. The Curator was unable to explain how it had got here beyond the fact that a Capetown lady had sent it in some years ago.

I turned to the friend who had brought me from Glasgow and I said, 'Didn't I tell you that my father wrote these verses in Afrikaans? and here you are.' It was a tremendous success.

During a visit to Cardiff in charabancs we played a trick on the rest of the Empire Parliamentarians. I had noticed that the bus-conductors spoke Welsh so I arranged with them and with the other South African delegates that they should speak Welsh to us and we would reply in Afrikaans. They played up—they jabbered meaningless words at us and we jabbered meaningless words at them. The Parliamentarians were completely taken in for they were unable to distinguish between the two vernaculars, and at the end of the journey one of the Australian representatives said, 'You South Africans are a wonderful lot—how on earth came you all to know Welsh?'—and his surprise was echoed by the others.

I trust it will not be thought that I did nothing in Britain but play the fool, for indeed I transacted a great deal of government business. I had an office at South Africa House on Trafalgar Square and there I handled important trade and agricultural matters.

I saw endless deputations, called on Cabinet Ministers, inspected pre-cooling plants, made arrangements for shipping space, and attended to many affairs. At night I went to dinners and made speeches and broadcasts, visited docks and industrial areas and generally I was kept very busy. I interviewed among others the Prime Minister, Mr Stanley Baldwin, at 10 Downing Street and my old acquaintance Mr Jimmy Thomas at the Colonial Office.

Mr Thomas was breezy as ever. I waited on him one morning to discuss meat problems. As it neared eleven o'clock I suggested an adjournment for tea. He exclaimed, 'Who the hell drinks tea at this hour of the day?' I told him I did, and that with us it was a ritual. He would not hear of it at first, but in the end an indignant Under-Secretary was sent to a restaurant to order the cup that cheers.

I enjoyed every moment of my visit, but now there fell a blow which spoiled my stay. I was standing on the balcony of South Africa House watching the traffic in Trafalgar Square. A diminutive telegraph boy came through the doorway and saluting, he handed me a cable from my wife. It said that our boy John had lost his right eye and his right hand in an explosive accident, and was in hospital critically injured.

This was sad news. I gazed out unseeing for some minutes then, suddenly, I looked up, and there stood Nelson on his column with one hand and one eye. It was a strange coincidence. Nowhere else in the world could a man have received such woeful tidings and have received such instant solace.

I rushed within and despatched a message to John: 'Terribly sorry, but through my office window stands Lord Nelson who climbed very high with one hand and one eye.'

I learned afterwards that he never looked back. He showed great fortitude and General Smuts cabled me some days later that he was out of danger and now that an examination of his left eye had become possible it was found to be intact.

An equerry from the King and Queen brought their Majesties' sympathy and many other friends showed their kindness, for word had appeared in the press.

When ultimately I received full details it appeared that the boy had been experimenting with chemicals. He rammed a product made to his own formula down the barrel of a horse pistol that hung on my study wall. In doing so the charge went off. It wrecked the room and it wrecked him too.

He made a wonderful recovery.

A professor who had listened to one of my lectures at Oxford and to whom I had confided the spiritual strength I had gained from Nelson's statue, sent me the following lines by the Poet Laureate:[1]

TRAFALGAR SQUARE, SEPTEMBER 1917

Fool that I was: my heart was sore,
Yea sick for the myriad wounded men,
The maim'd in the war: I had grief for each one:
And I came in the gay September sun
To the open smile of Trafalgar Square;
Where many a lad with a limb fordone
Loll'd by the lion-guarded column
That holdeth Nelson statued thereon
Upright in the air.

[1] From *The Poetical Works of Robert Bridges* (Oxford University Press) by permission of Mrs Bridges and the publishers.

The Parliament towers and the Abbey towers,
The white Horseguards and grey Whitehall,
He looketh on all,
Past Somerset House and the river's bend
To the pillar'd dome of St Paul,
That slumbers confessing God's solemn blessing.
On England's glory, to keep it ours—
While children true her prowess renew
And throng from the ends of the earth to defend
Freedom and honour—till Earth shall end.

The gentle unjealous Shakespeare, I trow,
In his country tomb of peaceful fame,
Must feel exiled from life and glow
If he think of this man with his warrior claim,
Who looketh o'er London as if 'twere his own,
And he standeth in stone, aloft and alone,
Sailing the sky with one arm and one eye.

I finished the remainder of my programme with a heavy heart. There was still much to do. I visited Edinburgh, Liverpool, Manchester and other centres in pursuit of information that might be of interest to my work in South Africa and when at last all was completed Mr Cooper and I made ready to return.

The Parliamentarians were staying on for some weeks longer so we said farewell to the many friends we had made and, no aeroplane being available, we returned by sea.

It was a peaceful quiet voyage after the overwhelming hospitality we had partaken of. We looked in at Madeira with its memories of the 'battle' on my way from the Great War, and beyond that we sailed uneventfully to Table Bay.

I travelled up by rail to Johannesburg and my family was at the station to welcome me. John was there, tall and erect, wearing a glass eye, his right arm in a sling. I remembered with a pang the little fellow who, years ago, had met me at this station with his, 'Daddy, all the time you was gone, I *thinked* of you a little bit every day.' Now it was I who had *thinked* of him while I was gone.

Chapter 15

Ministerial Work Continues

I

I plunged into the official maelstrom at once.

Having left London on the 2nd of August, by the 23rd of that month I was back in South Africa and I was inspecting the site of the great Vaal River dam where many hundreds of workmen were feverishly pitting themselves against time to get the foundations in before the rains.

By the 27th I was holding political meetings in my constituency, and on the 30th Mr Cooper and I were at Lourenço Marques in Portuguese territory on departmental business.

From there we travelled down through the bush, intending to cross the Maputo River and make south for Durban. It was wild tropical country with elephant, buffalo, and other big game, but on reaching the banks we found the ferry had sunk; so we turned north by a mere track and by nightfall we made the little hamlet of Stegi on the border of Swaziland.

On 1st October we left Stegi, under considerable difficulties owing to car trouble; traversed Swaziland, Zululand and Northern Natal to Durban. I opened an Empire Forestry Congress, with speeches, public dinners, etc, then went back by road to the Transvaal to grapple with Beef and Butter and other agricultural problems that sprang hydra-headed at my throat.

I travelled about holding political meetings and discussing the grievances of wheat farmers and maize farmers and cattle breeders and dairy owners and others demanding compensation for damage by hail and locusts and drought.

It was strenuous, but at all events there was no stagnation. In proof of this my diary says:

> Left for Capetown by air to open Quality Wine Exhibition.
> Fished on Bay.
> Back to the Transvaal to address meetings along eastern Reef towns.
> To Bloemfontein by air to open Agricultural Conference; fifteen speeches.
> To Northern Transvaal by car in heavy rain.
> Investigated upper reaches of the Letaba River with view to building an irrigation scheme.
> Angry deputations of timber growers.
> Through Low Country by new road via Gravelotte to Sandringham, teeming with game.
> Back to Pretoria; fortnight of departmental work.
> Journeyed via Eastern Transvaal and via south coast of Natal to Griqualand to hold meetings.
> On return to Pretoria flew to Bulawayo in record time of 2 hours 35 minutes to St Andrews banquet.
> Back to Pretoria next day in 2 hours 40 minutes in Hart Fury Defence Force machine.
> To Southern Free State addressing meetings for a by-election. In spite of my eloquence, our man lost by over three hundred votes.

And so it went on till the end of the year; and this is a fair average sample of ministerial work in South Africa.

II

Sometimes questions cropped up which gave one an opportunity for more interesting things.

North of the Kalahari Desert lie the Okavango and Chobe swamps. They owe their existence to the fact that at a certain stage the Okavango and the Kwando Rivers spread over the surrounding country and ultimately their waters are lost in the sands.

This region is little known and such maps as I have seen are faulty and meagre. Now, by a lucky fluke, there rose a controversy.

A South African scientist, Professor Schwarz, had written a book in which he put forward the theory that the Okavango, the Kwando, and the Zambezi rivers originally ran due south through what is now the Kalahari, and that in some comparatively recent geological cataclysm the Zambezi had been diverted to the Indian Ocean.

As for the Okavango and the Kwando, he was of opinion that within less than a century they had become choked by a growth of reeds which forced the water into the swamps.

According to him, the rainfall in South Africa had been abundant prior to these events but now that the lifegiving streams no longer flowed in their ancient channels, the country was slowly but surely drying up. He said the Kalahari was a direct result of this process and that the rest of the Union would likewise become a desert in course of time. He suggested that the calamity could be stayed by dredging the Okavango and the Kwando and emptying the swamps into the Great Makarikari Depression and into Lake Ngami lying about a hundred miles south of the swamps so as to form a vast inland sea. The increased evaporation of moisture that was sure to follow would bring increased precipitation of rain to South Africa.

His views attracted widespread attention. Next to politics, droughts are our chief preoccupation and the thought of achieving a standing rainfall fired the public imagination.

Schwarz died, but so great was the interest he had evoked that a body was instituted known as the 'Thirstland Redemption Association'. Its membership rapidly expanded and in time the Association came to be a political factor of some magnitude. It brought pressure to bear on the Government, urging that the swamps be drained into the Kalahari Desert as Schwarz had planned.

This would have involved the expenditure of millions with no certainty of results so the demand had thus far been resisted, though by way of compromise a survey party had been sent up a few years previously to take contours and levels. The report was unfavourable but the protagonists were unsilenced. They said the inspection had been hasty and the officials who made it were jealous of the Professor and his work.

Dissatisfaction grew apace. Heated charges were levelled by the press and at public meetings and as I was Minister of Irrigation, the brunt of all this pother fell upon my shoulders. And so I decided to have a look at it myself.

Much of that area is remote desert country so I commandeered three machines, to be on the safe side. They were single-engined Wapitis, old-fashioned, but reliable. They were in charge of seasoned pilots and mechanics of the Union Air Force and I took with me the Director of Irrigation, Mr Lewis, an expert of international repute.

We left Pretoria at dawn, flying across the northern Transvaal and southern Rhodesia and we reached Livingstone near the Victoria Falls that night.

We had some difficulty in convincing the local citizens that we were not on our way to the Abyssinian campaign and the arrival of our war planes created much excitement. Next day we took off, flying due west.

We made up along the Zambezi as far as Katima Molilo, then, leaving the great river on our right, we sped along the Caprivi Gipfel across the Linyanti swamps. We passed the Kwando (Chobe), then over hundreds of miles of curious transverse dunes until at last we struck the Okavango at Andaras on the Angola frontier—unmapped, unflown country. We landed in a clearing at a place called Kupembe, forty miles below Andaras, on the river bank.

At this point the Okavango begins to open into the broad swamps in which it ultimately loses itself and it is from here downward, according to Professor Schwarz, that the natives in the past used to come on rafts made of bundles of reeds and rushes. At the end of their voyage they abandoned their frail ships which floated down and sooner or later struck against a tree or a sandbank and took root. This process multiplied *ad infinitum* caused a block in the river which in turn caused the swamps.

Schwarz held that by digging a canal through the reeds for hundreds of miles the Okavango and Kwando Rivers would resume their ancient course to the south and thus redeem the Thirstland of the Kalahari.

While Mr Lewis made his readings I had time to look around. The river ran about forty yards wide, swift and clear, but I could see that some miles below it began to divide itself up in a number of smaller streams with wooded islands.

This area must be thickly inhabited for in a surprisingly short time after our arrival nearly three hundred river-bushmen appeared on the scene, chattering with excitement at the giant birds that had come among them.

They are called bushmen but facially they struck me as more akin to the Congo pygmies. They are black-skinned where the real bushman is as yellow as a Mongolian, and though they are short in stature they are squat and ungainly where the South African bushman for all his simian features is delicately moulded in limbs and hands and feet.

I noticed their curious build. They had remarkably broad shoulders and powerful torsos but their legs were thin and spindle-shanked and they walked in an ungainly waddle. They spend most of their lives sitting in their dugouts to paddle along the waterways, with the result that their arms and chests and shoulders develop out of all proportion to the rest of their bodies.

When Mr Lewis had finished his survey we drove the river-bushmen from the clearing by signs, for none of us knew the language, and we took the air again. One of the machines smashed an aileron against a tree but it rose unharmed and now we followed south, photographing the swamps, seeing herds of buffalo and lechwe and occasionally a few elephant. We passed over the Selinda spillway, a narrow ribbon of greenery running east by west for about a hundred and fifty miles, from the Okavango to the Chobe River. The natives say that some years the water in the spillway discharges into the Chobe and at other times the current is reversed and it flows from the Chobe into the Okavango.

This will require closer investigation but at any rate we satisfied ourselves that the swamps were caused by the configuration of the plains and not by Schwarz's theory of piled-up rafts.

We flew about eighty miles southward then east by the Linyanti and Chobe swamps and so back to Livingstone where we stopped a few days to overhaul the planes.

Mr Jalland, the District Commissioner, had kindly invited me to stay with him. He was on the aerodrome to meet us. His old Barotse gunbearer, Sigaswe, accompanied him and as he looked round-eyed at the Wapitis, his master asked him what he thought of them.

Sigaswe answered, 'Bwana, I have seen the white man's magic; his railway trains, motor-cars, gramophones and other wonders, but they die just like the Barotse.'

I was taken to a cinema show for the local natives that evening. It had been filmed by the Chamber of Mines in Johannesburg in pursuance of a 'Safety First' campaign to teach the native miners how to avoid accidents and rockfalls underground.

The fool of the piece was called Jim Fish. His role was to do everything in the wrong way in order to teach the others how to do it correctly. All through the picture Jim Fish got blown up by careless handling of dynamite or he would tumble down a shaft and break a limb or derail a tram or drill into a misfire. At regular intervals he was carried off on a stretcher.

The Livingstone natives reacted somewhat differently to what the promoters of the picture had intended. Every time poor Jim blew up or fell down there were roars of delighted laughter and when the reel ended with a final tragedy in which through gross carelessness he brought death and destruction on himself and his fellows, the applause fairly lifted the roof.

When our planes were ready we set out to check up on the Professor's suggestion to empty the swamps into Lake Ngami and the Makarikari and thereby increase our rainfall. We flew along the Zambezi and thence across the Chobe swamps to Maun at the lower end of the Okavango swamps. Elephant, hippo, buffalo and lechwe were down below. At Maun there is a police station and European officials of the Bechuanaland Protectorate who hospitably entertained us.

Next day we set a course north-west up the Santandibe channel to map that part, seeing herds of buffalo, elephant, hippo and so on. These swamps are uninhabited owing to the prevalence of tsetse fly, though there are cattle-owning natives on the outer fringes.

We flew as far as the Selinda spillway once more (also known as Makawegana), after which we turned south along the western marches, shown on the maps as Taokhe, then over dry barren country to Lake Ngami.

From Livingstone's book and other works of travel I had gained the impression that Ngami was a real lake with palms, and picturesque savages rowing their canoes on its waters. But whatever it may have been centuries ago, we found it to be merely a shallow wind-swept pan surrounded by a treeless desert. It contained not a drop of water and so little is it of a lake that from the air we could see the natives had dug wells all over its surface from which they were hauling up water for their animals.

Then we went back to Maun up the dry bed of the Nghabe. There were pools in the Botletle from Maun downwards but beyond, towards Rakops, there were none. The Botletle is the river or rather the dry water-course running from the Okavango swamps at Maun to the Makarikari a hundred miles south, and it was along this that Professor Schwarz had proposed filling Ngami and the depression.

On the following day we started from Maun at nine am. We did another wide sweep over the swamps to take more photographs; then we turned south down the Botletle River to the Makarikari.

I doubt whether Schwarz could ever have visited the depression before writing his book! As we approached it we saw a strange phenomenon. The Makarikari pan (it is nothing more) is eighty to a hundred miles wide and over it stood a murky haze towering four thousand feet in the air. Although a stiff wind was blowing the pall did not sway or billow but remained stationary, its outer circumference following the rim of the depression. Mr Lewis considers the haze to consist of finely powdered salt drawn up by the heat, for when we flew low the entire bed of the pan was covered with ten to twelve inches of it.

It seems clear that to divert the fresh waters of the Okavango into the Makarikari will merely produce another Dead Sea. It lies but a hundred miles south of the swamps so if the Schwarz theory be correct then it is curious that the presence of the swamps so close by, with a much larger superficies of open water, does not have the same effect as he says would be achieved by draining the swamps into the Makarikari.

The flight over the Makarikari completed the objects of our expedition and we now headed across the Kalahari Desert arriving at Pretoria without further incident. The flying time of the whole trip was 26 hours 50 minutes. The distance covered was 2 670 miles.

I published an account of our observations and it killed the Thirstland Redemption Association. At all events I have never heard of them again. Early in 1936 I returned to Capetown for the approaching session of Parliament.

It proved a dullish year. Parliament droned on until the middle of June and but for an occasional sortie into the country districts to hold party meetings and to open an agricultural show or two I remained in the House listening to the dreary debates.

I was under constant fire from the opposition benches. The farmers attacked me because food prices were low and urban members shot at me because the cost of living was too high. I was Public Enemy No 1 and there were numerous complaints against me and my Department.

However, any Minister of Agriculture in South Africa is a scapegoat and as I look on Parliament and politics dispassionately, I was not unduly perturbed.

The session petered out at last and by the end of June I was addressing meetings along the coast of Natal in an endeavour to persuade our ultra-British friends that our only salvation lay in both races working together. I was not very successful.

In Durban and in the villages dotting the littoral most of the voters were as jingoistic and racial on their side as were the extreme Afrikaners on the other side.

Between these ultimates, English and Dutch moderates have been striving for many years to build up a united nation in this country, and the road is long and stony.

Having stated my creed, I journeyed through Pondoland to Port St John's by lovely country. Thereafter the Swaziland Administration invited me to pay their Protectorate an official visit and I spent some interesting weeks travelling about being lavishly entertained. In the meanwhile my family were camped on Sandringham and I returned down along the Komati River and through the National Park to join them.

My boys and I went after lion, but though we flushed several, they were too quick for us in the bush and we failed to get one.

On our return from Sandringham I worked in office at Pretoria, attended Cabinet Meetings and I helped at by-elections, spoke at agricultural congresses, and met irate deputations in the countryside.

I went mostly by air. I might be in Port Elizabeth on the south coast of the Cape one week and in Natal or the northern Transvaal the next, for the old leisurely pace of the ox with which I had grown up as a boy has gone for ever and now I hurtled through space like a madman.

And the numberless speeches I delivered! I once saw a picture of a deceased politician in Hades. Bound to a chair with ropes, his punishment was to be compelled to endure recitals of gramophone records of the speeches he had inflicted during his lifetime. There was a look of excruciating agony on his face—I only hope I shall be spared similar torture in the hereafter.

I had three flying incidents during this year; two nearly ended in tragedy, the other was humorous.

I was proceeding from Capetown to the Orange River in a recently acquired twin-screw machine belonging to the Defence Force. As we approached the river after four hours' flying, there came an ominous knock in the port engine. I noticed the pilot and his mechanic uneasily watching through the window, and I could see that the propeller was revolving erratically.

Searching out a patch of level ground we landed safely. Pilot and mechanic descended and walked forward to investigate. Then the pilot called to me, 'Sir, come and see what a picnic we have escaped.'

We found that the split pins of the propeller boss had not been wired, with the result that all the nuts had worked forward. Several had already disappeared into space and others were on the verge of following suit. The pilot said another few minutes and the propeller would have broken away. Since then I have listened to many arguments by the Air Force as to what would have happened if the 'prop' had gone. Some hold that it would have shot straight forward but others say that with the nuts falling off at different moments the chances are that the propeller would have sheared sideways into the forward cockpit killing its occupants and leaving the passenger (myself) and the plane to nosedive into the earth.

The second incident arose out of my irrigation activities.

The Department of Irrigation was in my charge and of late years I had become increasingly interested in the subject. I had persuaded the Government to build the Vaal-Harts scheme at a cost of six million pounds and I was dotting the Union with other irrigation dams.

At the beginning of the session just ended I was hotly assailed for spending twenty thousand pounds on a certain irrigation survey without parliamentary sanction and the opposition devoted several days to castigating me. I had some time before inspected a place called Loskop, in the Transvaal, where I was determined to build a large dam. I let the Nationalists rave about the £20 000 and towards the end of the session when everyone was tired and jaded I slipped a million and a half on to the Estimates for the Loskop project and it was passed without a word of comment.

I put a thousand Europeans at work and as often as I could I motored out to see how things were doing. After a while I instructed them to clear the bush for an aerodrome and as soon as this was ready, Mr Lewis and I flew from Pretoria to test its qualities.

After a long journey we reckoned we were on the mark and we climbed lower to what looked to us to be our destination. Smoke fires had been lit to indicate the wind but we were puzzled by a large bucksail stretched on the ground bearing in six foot letters the word 'Poksol'. I could not understand the meaning of this banner with a strange device and my pilot, pointing down, shook his head and he passed back a scribbled note to say that we must have missed our bearings. I was doubtful myself, but as our fuel was running low I ordered him to land. We did so without mishap and a number of workmen came forward to meet us. When I asked them what place this was they said it was Loskop, so we had reached the right address after all. When I asked what the inscription on the canvas stood for they explained that, looking from an aeroplane in the sky, all words must necessarily read back to front as in a mirror, so they had inverted Loskop into Poksol for our benefit.

I tried to persuade them of their error, but they were only half convinced and some of them went off shaking their heads, as if to say I didn't know what I was talking about.

The third incident took place soon after. Mr Lewis had repeatedly urged me to have a proper map of the Union compiled but I had refused, partly on account of the cost and partly because in my ignorance I thought the existing maps were good enough.

I was soon converted to his viewpoint for shortly after the Loskop trip I had to fly down to northern Zululand to visit a survey camp.

Just as we were about to take off my pilot, Captain John Daniel, came to me. He said he was rather troubled for the only map he carried was one he had torn from a schoolboy's atlas. He said it was pretty inaccurate but it was the best he could lay his hands on. I told him to proceed and after a flight of some hours we were over Zululand. With a faulty map we lost our bearings and presently, while we were flying low over St Lucia lake, our engine developed a popping and knocking that reminded me unpleasantly of a similar occurrence on the Orange River during the floods. But now there was a difference; on the former occasion we might at any rate have baled out by parachute with some assurance of a safe landing. Baling out over St Lucia was a tougher proposition.

When the engine trouble started we were almost skimming the water so there was no hope of doing a long glide to the nearest shore which on either hand was about ten miles away.

St Lucia lake, which is tidal, teems with both shark and crocodile and I doubt whether anyone could swim fifty yards without being seized.

Even as the Wapiti engine knocked and spluttered I remembered the grisly story I had heard of a young Norwegian missionary who tried to wade a shallow inlet of the lake to visit his fiancée and her parents awaiting him on the far side. Although the water was only knee-deep he was attacked by a school of man-eaters and he was torn to shreds under the eyes of the horrified onlookers.

However, to the immense relief of Captain John and myself the engine defect suddenly rectified itself and we were able to continue our journey and after a longish search we located the survey camp. Having completed the business I had come on I flew back to Pretoria.

I had had enough of faulty maps by now. The crocs and sharks of St Lucia converted me and the first thing I did on my return was to tell Mr Lewis to go ahead. We enlisted the co-operation of nearly every land surveyor in the Union and they responded with enthusiasm. Thanks to their field notes the Irrigation Department built up the present topographical sheets without which no airman goes aloft. It cost £85 000, but to-day, with British air training centres all over the country, flying by day and night, I like to think that Mr Lewis and I between us, with our map, have prevented many a crash and that we have saved many lives. Had it not been for his representations and for those uneasy moments over St Lucia lake, our airmen and the British pilots would still be flying by charts torn out of a schoolboy's atlas.

In December an Empire Exhibition was opened in Johannesburg which cost a million of money and drew hundreds of thousands of people. My chief recollection of the event was a dinner in the Exhibition grounds at which Jim Mollison, the famous flying-man, was the guest of honour. He and a Frenchman had tried to break the London-to-Capetown record and had just missed doing so.

On 12th December I attended a Cabinet Meeting in Pretoria at which we discussed the situation that had arisen with regard to King Edward VIII and Mrs Simpson. After a long debate we drafted a cable to the British Government in which we stated our opinion that if he insisted on marrying her he should resign the Throne, and having thus in some degree sat in judgment on the King of England I took my family down to the cottage we have built at False Bay and my boys and I and Mr Taylor fished from *Lucky Jim*, making good catches.

Chapter 16

Touring by Land- and Air-ways

I

January 1937. Parliament opened early this year and I was kept busy piloting a complicated Marketing Act through the House and through the Senate—a business that required more patience than Job was ever called upon to exercise.

In May, General Kemp and I toured the Free State Province for three weeks. Each of us made four speeches *per diem* plus bazaars, banquets, receptions and travelling from *dorp* to *dorp*. Whether we did any good I cannot say, but it was a monstrous programme and a severe physical strain on both of us. After that we returned to Parliament and I flew to Pretoria to attend a Coronation Service on Church Square to the new King, for Edward VIII had abdicated and George VI reigned in his stead.

During a journey to Port Elizabeth I took advantage of being near the Addo Forest to have a look at the elephant for whom I had decreed this sanctuary long ago. The neighbouring citrus farmers occasionally send up a load of oranges by wagon. Whenever the elephant hear the rattle of wheels they know there will be a pile of fruit near the Ranger's house and they silently pad in after dark to feed. Turning on the headlamps of a car does not disturb them so they can be watched from near at hand.

I was interviewed by many deputations and private individuals at Port Elizabeth who discussed a wide range of subjects. Then I embarked for Capetown on the mail boat. From here I had to travel up north to the country lying between the confluence of the Orange and the Vaal Rivers, the area where once the Griquas held sway.

The Griquas were a yellow-skinned race, a cross between the bushmen and the Hottentots and originally they lived along the coastal belt of Malmesbury in the Western Province of the Cape. As European penetration extended, they were forced inland and after many tribulations the bulk of them ultimately moved to this territory. They had acquired a slight infusion of European blood which seems to have made of them a happy-go-lucky carefree tribe, proverbial for their love of horses and strong drink.

They speak a jargon of pidgin Dutch and their good humour, their queer speech and queer ways are often quoted at convivial meetings and often some wag will give a rendering of a Griqua preacher exhorting his flock, a Griqua orator addressing his political supporters, or a Griqua in his cups. These stories take the place among us of *Uncle Remus* and *Brer Rabbit*. They have a tang of their own not easy to reproduce except in the Griqua vernacular.

A local resident told us a story at a dinner given me at Kimberley on my way through, to illustrate their way of looking at things. He said that in the old days the Griquas constantly quarrelled among themselves, splitting up into hostile factions, each under a different leader. They carried fire-arms and they marched out against each other. They were not, however, cast in the heroic mould and their style of warfare involved nothing more serious than long distance powder-play after which the opposing armies drew off, the side that had expended the most ammunition, and made the most noise, claiming the victory.

There came a time when a more mettlesome leader arose at the head of one of the bands. He disciplined his men and taught them to take aim instead of blindly firing into the air, and they shot to kill. This was in flagrant abuse of the prevailing rules of war, but his opposite number was equal to the occasion.

Calling his followers together at dusk as the new leader was approaching with his force he pointed to the enemy and he said: 'Brave men of the Griqua clan; there comes the foe! To-morrow fierce battle will be joined and many of us will be killed and wounded. If we knew to-night which of us will be killed and wounded to-morrow we could send them out of harm's way this evening, but as we do not know, I think it best for us all to get out.' This fitted so perfectly with the views of the rank and file that the proposal was carried *nem con* and they decamped in a body, satisfied that they had brilliantly outmanoeuvred their opponents.

There was hearty laughter at this specimen of Griqua logic. An officer sitting beside me who had served in France told me he had felt like that himself at times before going over the top and, on consideration, I rather agreed with him.

I followed with another story of a Griqua band who were in peril of being surrounded by a rival force. They called upon their leader to invoke the assistance of the Almighty which he did. He prayed: 'O Lord, we are in grave danger, please send Thy Son to help us.'

But his men protested. They said, 'This isn't child's play, tell the Old Man ("*die Ou Baas*") to come himself.'

To-day the Griquas are practically extinct, drink and the devil having done for the rest.

Back I went to Pretoria to attend to office duties and Cabinet Meetings and I moved about by land and air, hurrying to and from political meetings, conferences and congresses.

I grew to be case-hardened and whether I was called at three am in wind or rain to start on a long journey or set off at midnight in a jolting goods train for some distant village, was all one to me and I liked the change and bustle.

II

Now came another diversion. Sir Robert Brooke-Popham, Governor of Kenya, invited me to pay him an official visit and I welcomed the opening. Arrangements were soon completed and Mr Cooper and I left in a Defence Force Speed Envoy machine. We reached Broken Hill, northern Rhodesia, the first day in seven hours fifty-five minutes flying time, and went on the next day via Mpika and Mbeya. At the latter place we circled over Mount Wessel Hickmann and looked down upon the waterfilled crater, lying dark and sinister beneath. Next day to Dodoma, in Tanganyika, six hours flying time. This was the place I had helped to capture from the Germans in 1916 and I still have the German flag I took from the Boma. We flew by Kondoa Irangi with its unpleasant memories of the old campaign and then across the Masai flats, with lion, giraffe, eland and other game far below. We climbed to 14 000 feet to escape the clouds. As we emerged above the ceiling there stood the ice-covered cone of Kilimanjaro, a truly magnificent sight.

We landed at Moshi, where I had sojourned of yore, then over Lake Challa and the Soda lake to Nairobi, once again seeing lion and giraffe and rhino. When we halted at Moshi to refuel I inquired after the local District Commissioner on whom I felt I should pay a duty call. I was told he had left that morning on safari. In my time, to go on safari meant a string of porters and weeks of absence in the bush. I asked how long he would be away and his subordinate replied, 'Oh, he went off at seven in his Ford car and he ought to be back this afternoon.' Which shows how things are deteriorating in Darkest Africa!

At Nairobi, Sir Robert and Lady Brooke-Popham hospitably entertained me. I occupied a suite in Government House and there were dinners and banquets. When I had sampled the festivities of Nairobi I went to see the rest of Kenya.

The Speed Envoy machine we had come by was too fast for the smaller aerodromes up here so I chartered a Rapide from a local company and with Colonel Turner, our South African Trade Commissioner, and Mr Cooper, I set out. For its size Kenya is perhaps the most remarkable country in the world. Within its restricted area lie great mountain peaks, extinct volcanoes, wide rivers, swamps and forests and strange tribes and big game and fertile uplands. There are lakes with flamingos in unbelievable numbers, and there is a vigorous European community, mostly British, but with a strong dilution of South African Dutch, who are building what will perhaps become a sturdy nation in years to come.

We flew from Nairobi over lakes Naivasha and Nakuru. We saw the vast crater of Menengai and we crossed the Uasin Gishu plateau to Eldoret where many Afrikaners from the south are doing well. I was entertained at ranches where one can sit on the stoep looking up at Mount Kenya on the one side and at elephant browsing in clearings in the forest on the other.

At the village of Kitale I was on the aerodrome one morning. Mount Elgon, a forest clad peak, stood 16 500 feet into the sky.

General Smuts is a great mountaineer and much of his spare time is devoted to climbing inaccessible peaks in the Union. Once, when I looked him up at Capetown, I found him in bed with two doctors in attendance for he had overstrained himself during one of his weekend assaults on Table Mountain. I condoled with him but I said the Japanese had a wisecrack. 'He who hasn't climbed Fusi Yama once is a fool and he who climbs it twice is a damned fool.' The General said I had a perverted sense of humour.

Now there stood before me a mountain worthy of my steel and I asked a bystander how long it would take to reach the top. He said ten or twelve days to collect sufficient native porters and another ten days for the safari. I turned to the pilot of the Rapide and asked him how long it would take us to get there. He inspected the sky, wetted and held up a finger for the wind and said, 'About an hour, sir.' This was more like my idea of mountaineering and we took off at once. We rose steeply and in less than the stipulated time we were looking spellbound into the mighty cauldron, feeling as if we had reached the moon.

Long afterwards, at a Parliamentary luncheon in Capetown at which General Smuts was present, I steered the conversation towards mountaineering and soon he was telling us of his recent ascents.

I awaited an opening and then I said, 'Sir, I know you often climb our mountains at the Cape, but after all none of them are higher than six thousand feet whereas I have been to the top of Mount Elgon, a matter of nearly 17 000!'

General Smuts exclaimed, 'What's this, what's this, do you mean to say you climbed Mount Elgon and you never told me about it?'

I then began to describe the difficulties of obtaining porters, of the dense forests to be penetrated, of the eternal fogs and rains that shroud the slopes and of the troubles of gear and supplies. General Smuts listened with obvious interest and the others too hung on my words as I brought my story to the pitch of being about to start off on the expedition. Then I sprang on them the anticlimax of my aerial prank. There were roars of laughter and General Smuts thumped me on the back and called me a ruffian and a scalliwag.

The Administration of Uganda invited me to an elephant hunt. I have never had any desire to shoot an elephant but like the Portuguese Administration on a former occasion, they had pitched a camp and had gone to a great deal of trouble and I felt it would be discourteous not to go.

The Rapide took us via Jinja and the Ripon Falls to Entebbe on Lake Victoria Nyanza, and leaving Colonel Turner and Mr Cooper here, I flew to Mbarara where I was met by Captain Pittmann, the game warden. We travelled by car to the Njamagesani River on the Belgian frontier, crossing the strange waterway that links Lake George and Lake Edward. In this channel were more hippo than I have seen together. Captain Pittmann thought there were two thousand of them in view.

Beyond our camp lay Mount Ruwenzori, one of the marvels of the universe. I gathered from what Captain Pittmann told me and from what I had read in Stanley's *Travels* that the summit is rarely visible owing to eternal mist and clouds; but I was lucky, for the jagged mass stood clear for several minutes once and we had a complete if hurried view of the entire massif before the curtain of mist and rain enveloped it once more.

With Captain Pittmann was his ranger, Jock Jardine. I was anxious to know something of Uganda history so I asked him whether there had been much fighting in the country. 'Only among the missionaries,' said Jock, and I could well believe it, for on every second hill stood a mission station belonging to some denomination or other, and they were all at loggerheads.

On a Sunday morning I was lying in my tent when I heard the sound of a tom-tom and the tramp of many feet. Opening the flap of my tent I saw about two hundred native warriors armed with spears and shields. They marched along stamping and singing on what I took to be a tribal raid, but when I rushed over to inquire, Captain Pittmann said there was a church close by and so far from being on the warpath they were going to morning service; the tom-tom was in lieu of a bell to summon the faithful.

Then came the elephant hunt. Natives had been sent far and wide, and in a few days they reported the presence of a herd. We set out and after a long tramp we saw five splendid tuskers standing in a glade.

On the way from Mbarara I was struck by the large numbers of bicycles one passed. Uganda must have the largest bicycle population in Africa, for every native seemed to possess one. Jock Jardine told me he once stopped a native lad with a long package wrapped in banana leaves across his handlebars. The boy said it was his father's body he was taking to his village for burial. Jock said too that he had met another native carrying an American harmonium balanced on his machine. And now our elephant hunt was ruined by a cyclist. This is how. I carefully stalked the bulls until I was within thirty yards. As I was choosing the largest of them and was lifting my rifle to the aim, a native youth on a bicycle emerged into the clearing from a forest path. He was bent forward pedalling furiously and as he came, from sheer *joie de vivre*, he was ringing his bell for all he was worth. The effect was ludicrous. The great brutes whipped around with a snort of dismay and off they went in the wildest alarm. We never saw them again.

We started at sunrise the following day to have another try. On the broad plain where the Njamagesani enters Lake Edward we saw many elephant, but failed to get near enough for a shot as the ground was too open. We walked all day. It was an interesting experience, watching them feeding or standing in the river sluicing themselves. Captain Pittmann and Jardine seemed to know every individual elephant by sight.

In the afternoon as we were resting on the edge of a deep valley a mixed herd of fifty or sixty passed below us. One was a huge bull with tusks quite six feet long. Captain Pittmann said, 'Jock, where does that fellow come from; I've never seen him before?' Jock replied, 'I dinna ken yon felly either, but d'ye note the colour of his teeth, he must be from thae forests on the ither side o' the Congo.'

I scrambled down the side of the gorge and I got within ten yards of where I could see his trunk raised above the surrounding undergrowth as he pulled at the palm leaves overhead, but he never exposed himself and after a while he crossed the river into Belgian territory where he was safe and where in a clearing I had a good view of him—the biggest elephant I have ever seen, his tusks an umber brown which according to Jock denoted his forest origin.

As we trudged back to camp that night Captain Pittmann and Jardine were dejected because they had failed to get me a kill, but I assured them that the pleasure of seeing elephant at close quarters was all I wished for, and they cheered up.

Next day I returned to Mbarara. The Rapide awaited me and I flew back to Entebbe to pick up Colonel Turner and Mr Cooper. After this by air to Thompson's Falls, Rumuruti, Nanyuki and other places and in the fullness of time we sat down at Nairobi once more.

Farewell festivities awaited me, and I had to attend numerous parties given me at the Muthaiga Club where everyone forgathers towards evening. Once, in refusing another 'sundowner' I said, 'Gentlemen, if this goes on I shall end up in an inebriates' home.'

The Governor of Uganda who was present replied, 'That's all right, Nairobi is an inebriates' home.'

My visit coming to an end, Mr Cooper and I resumed our Air Speed Envoy and after a last hectic affair at the Club we started back. A squadron of British fighters was stationed at Nairobi because of the Abyssinian war and they escorted us for a while by way of compliment.

We made Lusaka, the capital of northern Rhodesia, at sunset, and Sir Hubert Young, the Governor, received us. Next day, landing at Livingstone and Bulawayo for petrol, we reached Pretoria before dark, one's every idea of time and space set at naught.

Chapter 17

The Kalahari Irrigation Scheme

About ten days after my return from Nairobi I happened to fall into conversation with General Smuts about the Okavango swamps and the Schwarz theory. I told him there was nothing in it as far as increasing our rainfall was concerned, but that it might be possible, by cutting a channel through the swamps, to run water south into the Kalahari down the at present dead river for a hundred miles and more, and so develop a considerable portion of the Kalahari lying uninhabited and useless.

He was interested and he suggested that I should go up again to explore the situation. I needed no encouragement for office life has never appealed to me. I took the preparations in hand without delay, sending a motor lorry ahead to establish dumps of water and petrol, and a week later I followed. Mr Cooper was with me once again as well as my trusty friend Waldeck who has driven me for years and I decided to take John and Michael to see the Africa that lay beyond our borders.

Our outfit consisted of a Ford car and a lorry. The first leg of our journey was plain sailing; north-west through the Transvaal by reasonably good roads, and in two days we entered British Bechuanaland. From here our troubles started. We had to plough through heavy sand to Palapye and then to Serowe, the headquarters of Tshekedi, who had succeeded the famous Chief Khama.

Serowe is the largest native town I have seen in Africa, its orderly stockades neatly laid out. Beyond Serowe we entered a waterless desert. The track was so heavy that we never averaged more than ten miles an hour through dull scrub-covered plains with occasional herds of hartebeest and gemsbok and a jackal or two.

Our petrol consumption was terrific and the radiators required frequent replenishment, but we were able to fill up from the caches and we had no difficulty on this head. We pushed on for some days, camping where we found an open space in the bush at night. After that we got into a country of huge circular pans encrusted with soda or ash so finely powdered that our cars raised a cloud of what looked like a smoke screen belching from a destroyer; and as there was no wind to drive the cloud away, the rear vehicle had to keep miles behind to obtain visibility.

On these pans springbok were plentiful and John and Michael, both dead shots thanks to their training on Sandringham, provided for the larder.

The first waterhole we reached was at a place called Rakops on the dry course that leads from Ngami. Once every twenty years or so the waters from the Okavango swamps push down as far as this but I believe the stream has never flowed beyond here in human memory.

From Rakops we bumped our way across the most atrocious surface I have ever taken a car over and at length we reached Maun which I had previously visited by aeroplane.

Maun is the administrative centre for these parts. There is a District Commissioner and other officials as well as a trading post and everyone was kind to us.

I pitched camp on the other side of the water so as not to be cut off, for earlier in the year the Okavango had come down in flood and now, after more than three months, the effect of the heavy rains up-country was becoming evident. Having taken all that time to seep through the swamps, the normally dry river bed was a running torrent and the head of the water was already twenty-five miles below Maun.

We spent a week exploring our surroundings. Bird life was plentiful—duck, pygmy geese, and others. As for guinea fowl, partridge and pheasant, in no place in Africa have I seen such quantities. Sometimes we had to stop the car and sound our hooter to drive them from under our wheels.

Then I decided on a voyage of exploration into the swamps.

I obtained two 'Makoro' (dugout canoes) with a dozen paddlers and at Maun I saw a rusted iron boat lying on its side where it had been abandoned by some trader.

It was full of holes, but my two drivers tackled the job with blowlamps and solder and they produced a seaworthy craft by next day. To propel this, eight more paddlers were requisitioned and our flotilla set out, accompanied by a native policeman to keep the crews in order.

The swamps are of such vast extent that we could penetrate only a fractional area, but what we were able to see was interesting enough.

Our way ran up narrow channels between palm-fringed islands. The endurance of the rowers was astonishing. All day they stood in the dugouts and in the iron boat, wielding their paddles and singing in chorus.

Big game abounded. On the first evening of our journey we dragged the boats ashore and while we were busy preparing to camp a column of dust rose from the bush on a large island a mile or two away. It was a herd of wildebeest, some three hundred strong, come down to drink.

John and I were paddled across to shoot one, but it was too dark by the time we got there and we returned empty-handed, to the disgust of our native following.

Next morning we were on the move by sunrise and we continued all day with only an occasional halt to land on some foreshore to prepare a meal.

The paddlemen clamoured for meat so, towards sunset, we pitched camp and I went off by canoe to hunt. I carried a .416 Rigby, a weapon recently presented to me by Mr Taylor, and this was the first opportunity I had had to try it out.

I saw bush pig and there came troops of lechwe splashing through the shallows, but I failed to get a shot from the rocking dugout; so I tied up and walked across one of the islands. I had not gone far when a lechwe ram jumped up and I brought him headlong down. Returning to the canoe I was taken back to camp and I sent a party of natives to cut up and bring in the meat.

That night there was contentment. My little army sat around their fires chanting and chattering for hour after hour, eating their fill.

In this manner we sailed on. My two boys were thrilled at everything they saw and to them it was a great adventure.

With twenty-five mouths to feed the meat supply I had provided did not last long and one afternoon, having prepared camp on a large island, I took my Rigby and started inland accompanied by the native policeman and a young river bushman who had appeared among us.

We had not gone a mile when four magnificent buffalo bulls walked in single file from among the trees. I have often heard it said that a buffalo is the most dangerous of all wild animals; more ferocious than a lion and craftier than an elephant. But a fig for buffaloes! I stalked to within fifty yards of them and shot the largest bull out of hand. It was not sport, it was an execution, it was like shooting a tame ox in the backyard, and were it not that we needed food I could have regretted the deed.

When I looked round, the diminutive bushman was still with me, but the policeman had dropped so far to the rear that he was a mere speck in the distance.

At a further stage up the swamps we came on a branch of the Bukerhu or Bakuba tribe who for generations have been noted smiths and metal workers. The daggers and other weapons they make are in great demand. In former years they had mined and smelted ore under primitive conditions but now the guild has modernised the plant, so to speak.

One of them had been to Windhoek, the capital of German West, four hundred miles away. Here he obtained work on a railway line in course of construction and seeing a stack of rails in the goods yard, he had an idea. He hurried back to the swamps and since then, whenever supplies of metal run low a dozen of them make their way across the intervening desert to Windhoek and awaiting the cloak of a dark night, they pilfer a rail-length or two, returning in triumph carrying on their shoulders enough raw material for the next financial year. This, at any rate, is what the native policeman told us.

After a glorious holiday, we turned at last and when we were back at Maun I found that the water level had risen so high that there was but a strip of herbage three yards wide between the edge of the current and the forest lining its banks; and it was only along this strip that our cars could travel. Further delay would end in our being trapped, so we bade farewell to Maun and the good friends we had made.

It was touch and go, but we managed to extricate ourselves. The ground was already squelching and sodden underfoot and if the water had risen another few inches we would have been marooned. However, we found more solid going after ten miles or so and then we travelled day after day along the eastward track that goes to Livingstone.

We made a detour to the M'Babe plains, then via Kutchikau and Kissane to the junction of the Chobe and Zambezi Rivers, sleeping in patches of mopani at night and passing through endless forest by day with giraffe and other big game on all sides.

We were such a ragged crew by the time we reached Livingstone that we dared not show ourselves at the fashionable government hotel; so we halted our caravan in the bush.

From Livingstone we felt our way back to the Union in leisurely stages and on crossing the Limpopo into the Transvaal John and Michael insisted on our rounding off the expedition by making for Sandringham where we camped a while before starting the homeward run.

One of my Zulu houseboys had accompanied us on the journey as cook and general factotum. After our return I heard him telling the other native servants in my kitchen of his adventures and when they asked him what country he had visited he said he had been to England, and I think he believes it to this day.

As for the swamps, our visit strengthened my conviction that they can be drained and led down into the Kalahari desert and a large area now waterless and uninhabited could be redeemed. But the area is so remote from railways and markets that it will probably be many years before the matter is seriously taken up.

Chapter 18

Agricultural Problems: A Trip to Rio

I

For the next six months I attended to my office in Pretoria and agricultural problems accumulated on my devoted head. Locusts ravaged the sub-continent. I was blamed for not having killed them off; milk and wheat and maize prices slumped and there was a drought which brought in a procession of rural deputations demanding financial assistance from the State.

Our political opponents exploited our difficulties. I give a few samples of messages I received.

> A disaffected co-operative society in the Free State wired me:
> 'Grubs are destroying our crops, what are you going to do about it?'

From a drought-stricken area: 'Thanks for your broken promises. Our sheep are dead and we live on the sale of their skins.'

And again: 'Labour shortage in this area. We demand you send us three hundred native workers immediately.'

My replies were not always conciliatory. To crown everything there was an outbreak of foot and mouth disease among the herds in my own electorate of Barberton and, to prevent the epidemic from spreading to the rest of the Union, I was faced with the dread decision of ordering the destruction of nearly ten thousand head of cattle belonging to my constituents. In addition, I quarantined the entire district with the result that large supplies of fruit and vegetables could not be marketed and they were of necessity left to rot.

These drastic measures did not conduce to popularity, but the people of the Low Country are reasonable and after the disease was stamped out they agreed that I had acted for the best and in the long run I was forgiven.

I flew some three thousand miles on departmental affairs, then I took my family to the coast for Christmas and the boys and I fished and found sanctuary on the waters of the Bay.

II

1938. A brief session of Parliament at Capetown in February, and our five yearly term of office being ended, a general election was required by law. It was the old story of a flushed and hectic campaign about issues now forgotten. Rival orators thundered at each other; charges and counter charges were levelled and, again, the ill will and the friction was between the Dutch, while the English-speaking voters stood aloof but supported the less intolerant side.

I was absent for two months addressing meetings in almost every constituency in the country. I went by train and car and air, and I blush to think that I delivered upwards of seventy speeches in support of our candidates. Then I attended to my own district for a week or two, inflicting another thirty speeches on my supporters.

When the dust of conflict died down we found that we had been returned with the largest parliamentary majority ever accorded to any government in South Africa. We assembled the House in triumph and looked forward to another five years of internal peace. It was well that the future lay hidden from us!

The new Parliament was still sitting when there came the news that Hitler's troops had marched into Austria. We felt that a majority of Austrians desired the *Anschluss* so we were not unduly perturbed, and with the agricultural worries that beset me on all sides I had no time to give this turn of events much thought; and when the session was over, feeling in need of a rest I took my car and started from Johannesburg intending to go to Sandringham after lion.

I went alone for I felt the need of seclusion. On the second day, travelling at sixty miles an hour, my car skidded from the road, came round in a swerve, and dashed sickeningly across a heap of stones into a grove where overhanging branches tore most of the roof off. After a further wild career the car came to a standstill against a tree. I was shaken but uninjured.

I found that two of my tyres were burst from the various impacts and it took me several hours in a broiling sun to repair the damage. Then, with my front axle out of alignment and a wrecked superstructure, I crawled along. By nightfall I was near the homestead of Captain McBride, an old friend whom I had known in the 1914 rebellion, and I managed to reach his door. That night I went down with pneumonia.

It was distant country, but McBride looked after me for ten days like a mother. Mrs Whittingstall from Acornhoek, who had nursed her husband when he was mauled by a lion, heard of my plight and she brought hot-water bottles and other medicaments for she was hospital trained. And an uncertificated but highly qualified American lady missionary from a station nearby sent kettles with which they steamed my lungs and later the district surgeon looked in by chance on his way to vaccinate a local tribe against smallpox.

On his return up the escarpment he sent a telegram which brought Mr Cooper and my driver hurrying by car and then the matter was caught by radio and my wife and two boys raced down. Thanks to the care I received I was already lying on a blanket in the sunshine when they arrived. After a few days I was well enough to be taken to Sandringham and here we camped, and before long I was somewhat groggily on my feet.

For once, I was restless on Sandringham, and having heard that natives were burning down valuable forests in northern Zululand we went thither, travelling via the Kruger Game Reserve and then up the Komati.

Towards sunset on the first day the sky grew overcast. We were in thick bush country near the Swaziland frontier and as we halted to discuss our plans there arose a curious soughing noise like that of a distant waterfall; and then a terrific hailstorm burst upon us with a roar. We got the cars under cover of trees but this did not suffice. Stones the size of hens' eggs drummed down on us like shrapnel and we spent a miserable night. Next day we slithered along the muddy track to Stegi, a little village on the Ubombo range from where, after a good night, we travelled along the crest of the Berg by a newly-constructed route that led to the gorge of the Usutu River. Here, after much delay, we worked our cars across the pontoon and swung east by a path that had been cut by the Johannesburg Chamber of Mines for the recruiting of natives. By dark we reached N'Indumu close to Inyameti Lake where I had shot a hippo years before.

Times had changed in northern Zululand. When first I came up here in 1922 we rode fly-bitten horses through unknown country. Now it was possible to take a car up to Kosi Bay and Lake Sibaya and at N'Indumu there was a police station with a sergeant in command. He made us comfortable and the following morning I went to see how the hippo had fared since I had turned their lake and the surrounding country into a sanctuary. More than sixty of them were disporting themselves in peace and safety and the sergeant told me many troops of Nyala antelope were to be seen at dawn as they returned from grazing. Previously they had been nearly exterminated.

From Inyameti we went to Kosi Lake. The route was sandy in places and mud-bound in others, but all went well and towards sunset we pulled up on the high bluff overlooking the water. On the far side stretched the forested peninsula across which General Smuts and I had ridden in search of a harbour. I have told how, at that time, the natives took to the jungle at the sight of our cavalcade, for they had never seen white men or horses.

To-day the Chamber of Mines had not only constructed a road of sorts to Kosi Bay but they were recruiting in these parts and the natives, so far from running in terror, looked on the arrival of motor-cars with equanimity.

The Agency had gone further. They had a boat with an outboard engine on the lake and we were scarcely arrived before a headman appeared to say that word had come from the 'big baas' in Johannesburg that it was to be at our disposal. Captain Colin Bain-Marais and his wife and son met us here by pre-arrangment. They were old friends and in less than half an hour my two boys and young Colin and the headman were chugging far out on the darkening surface. We were anxious about them, but towards midnight they returned talking as if they had cruised the Spanish Main.

We camped on the bluff for a happy week and explored the coastline of the lake. We navigated to Mananda point where General Smuts had thought to dredge a passage, and we sailed through the narrow channels that connect the main body with the two smaller lakes towards the estuary. The boys fished and hunted and had a wonderful time.

Once, on a calm windless morning we cranked up the recalcitrant engine and set off to take soundings, for the natives said the lower lakes were fathomless. With a reel of twine and a lead we established the average depth of the lakes to be from forty to sixty feet and having done this we set out for the top end of Kosi. At midday we landed to build a fire and cook a meal and then we cruised along the southern shore. Presently we came to an inlet. To our surprise this broadened out and we found ourselves on another lake, smaller than the others, but still of wide extent.

Schools of savage-looking hippo were disporting themselves and they were not content to lie with their eyes above water as they generally do, but the bulls came diving towards our boat, their bodies half way out of the water, setting up an alarming swirl. We made for the channel by which we had come and then the engine stalled and Mr Jackson, an official of the Irrigation Department whom I had bidden to meet me, stood by with a Lee Metford rifle to repel boarders. He was the man I have spoken of who had been struck by a mamba and survived to tell the tale.

Luckily the hippos satisfied themselves with rushing towards us and slewing away at the last moment while we spent an exciting time trying to start the engine. An outboard is cranked on the principle of a humming top. A length of cord is twisted round the flywheel and given a sharp pull which, with luck, sets it in motion. But my driver and the boys pulled frantically with no result and my wife and Mrs Bain-Marais, as the mothers of children whose lives they considered I had jeopardised, left me in no doubt as to what they thought of my conduct in bringing them here.

At last by joint efforts the engine spluttered into action, and running the gauntlet we left the plunging snorting animals behind us. To this day I cannot understand what went wrong with them. Perhaps it was their first experience of internal combustion.

As we emerged from the channel into the main lake more sorrow awaited me. A strong wind had blown up and the surface was in a tumult. Waves raced at us, threatening to swamp our boat and, of course, the outboard went on strike for the second time. We lost distance and were fast drifting on to a leeshore with the prospect of shipwreck and the spending of a night on the narrow beach that separates the waters of the lake from the surrounding animal infested jungle. Here again I was subjected to withering comment as the author of the expedition, but in the gathering darkness, Waldeck, who had taken out and cleaned the carburettor and had blown into tubes and pipes, succeeded in starting up the engine just as we were stranding. The waves had subsided a little by now and by dint of using our oars to eke out the waning powers of the accursed invention, we made camp long after nightfall. During the next few days the joint maternal *animus* against me began to fade; now Time, the healer, has softened the incident to such an extent that I have on occasion heard my wife and Mrs Bain-Marais recite the epic of Kosi Lake to admiring guests at five o'clock tea in the course of which, to my surprise, I receive a meed of praise for valorous conduct in the great adventure.

To make up for the fright I had given everyone and to recover my good name I took the party to Sibaya, the largest fresh water lake south of the Great Lakes and I took them to the mouth of the Kosi River as my boys wished to inspect the place where General Smuts and I had ridden our horses through in former years.

Then we went to Mungusi to see the damage done to the forests by natives burning the trees to procure land for their crops. I drafted a report which attracted official attention and now a European ranger and staff have been appointed to save what is left of the timber in northern Zululand.

On completion of this work we journeyed southward across the plains, the boys and I taking pot shots at my 'favourite' crocodiles on sandbanks and lagoons and we made over the Pongola at Otobotini where I had listened to the ribald boating songs in years gone by and so to Hluhluwe, now a game reserve. We watched rhino lumbering in the undergrowth and wild dogs and other game, and I visited the tsetse traps for which I had placed large sums on my departmental vote and which bid fair to rid us of this pest.

Then we returned home. A session of Parliament followed, I forget for what reason, but I do remember standing up one afternoon to answer questions and suddenly the hall went round, and everything was blacked out.

When I came to, I found myself lying in my office with several doctors in attendance. I was thumped and punched and they declared I had sustained a nervous breakdown. They were unsympathetic and one of them said, 'If you think you can rush through life at high pressure like this for forty years you must pay for it.' General Smuts came in and looked down at me where I was lying on a couch. He told me the trouble was I took too little exercise. I was dazed and giddy, but I collected myself enough to answer that Chauncey Depew in reply to a similar charge had said the only exercise he ever got was acting as pall bearer to his friends who *did* take exercise. This time General Smuts said I had a *macabre* sense of humour.

Be that as it may, I was ordered a complete rest so I decided on a voyage; and with Mr Cooper to assist me I sailed on a Japanese cargo boat for Rio de Janeiro.

III

It was pleasant but hardly restful. After a comfortable voyage we steamed into Rio with a background the most beautiful in the world and as we reached the quayside, Brazilian officials and representatives from the British Embassy came on board to meet me as did also our Union Consul-General for the Argentine who had come up from Buenos Aires for the same purpose.

I was given free passes over every railway system in the country and now began a round of sightseeing and festivities and generous hospitality almost surpassing that of Britain.

We were taken for hundreds of miles into the interior to visit *fazendas* and citrus estates. We were flown from Rio to São Paulo, the industrial centre of Brazil, where the population was revolutionary and discontented with President Vargas who, with the support of a strong army was running the republic on the lines of a benevolent autocracy.

I did not meet him in person, but I had a sneaking admiration for his methods of which I took careful note for future reference.

I had intended merely to run across to Brazil and back, but now the Union Government cabled to ask whether I would proceed to Uruguay and the Argentine on a courtesy visit. I agreed and together with our Consul-General and Mr Cooper I embarked at Santos for Montevideo where we did more sightseeing and then up the mighty Plata River to Buenos Aires.

Here again we received princely hospitality. Once more free railway passes were showered on us with state coaches and special dining saloons. We did long journeys to inspect cattle ranches and stud farms and we sailed three hundred miles up the Parana to the refrigerating and canning works in the province of Entre Rios and were taken to Mar del Plata, the fashionable watering place where the citizens of Buenos Aires spend their holidays.

I had a long interview with President Ortiz. *Inter alia* I inquired whether diplomatic relations between the Argentine and Brazil were good. He said they *were* good until the Argentine started sending over football teams to Rio.

The President kindly detailed several officials to attend on me wherever I went and they conducted us on long tours.

The Governor of Mendoza, at the foot of the Andes, invited my party and myself to be his guests. We travelled by rail for six or seven hundred miles across the vast pampas, luxuriously installed in a special coach, and were sumptuously housed and entertained on arrival. The people of Mendoza, like those of São Paulo, are not enamoured of the Central Government and here too the germs of discontent and future rebellion were in evidence.

From Mendoza we took the air and flew over the Andes to Santiago the capital of Chile. It was a wonderful experience. The route took us up a mighty gorge and we looked down on the statue of Christ on the international frontier and on the landslide which had buried a long sector of the railway some years before, since when communication across the Andes has been made by mules and air.

We skirted Aconcagua, the highest peak in South America, and on landing at Santiago we found ourselves in the middle of a Presidential inauguration, the streets crammed with troops and guns; but here too I sensed an undercurrent of hostility. We motored to Valparaiso on the Pacific Coast and then we returned across the Andes to Mendoza. Thence we returned in our state coach, by rail to Buenos Aires.

Throughout our journeyings in South America we carried diplomatic passports which ensured that we and our baggage were expedited without trouble or delay at the customs barriers, and ports of entry and exit. There was one exception however.

I had brought with me a morning coat and top hat for official occasions, though I found use for neither as the Latin Republics don't believe in ceremonial. My topper travelled in one of those cylindrical mid-Victorian affairs long out of date. Wherever we went in Brazil and Uruguay and the Argentine the rest of our luggage was always checked through without trouble, but this unusual article was an object of suspicion. They seemed to think the hatbox contained an infernal machine and it became an infernal nuisance. We encountered no difficulty with our other kit but there was a constant hold-up while customs officials and soldiers gathered round to examine and discuss this incriminating exhibit and it was only on my being fetched back on each occasion to unlock and bring to light my silken headgear that *exequator* was given.

The box had caused us so much trouble and loss of time that when we re-embarked at Buenos Aires at the end of our visit and I found more people examining the offender, I seized it with an oath and pressing it into the arms of our Consul-General demanded that he take it home with him, as I never wished to set eyes on it again. He looked sheepish and embarrassed as he went off with the ill-omened package.

We sailed down the la Plata and up the coast for Rio on a German passenger ship. In press interviews I had made no secret of my dislike of Hitler and the Nazi terror and the South American papers had given prominence to my remarks. Therefore, the Germans boycotted us on the voyage. Stewards refused to answer the bell, baths were never available, we were pushed into a dark corner of the dining saloon, and the food they gave us was execrable.

By this time Hitler had invaded the Sudetenland and as he had vowed after his annexation of Austria that he had no further territorial ambitions in Europe it was clear that his promises were piecrust.

At any rate, my experience of their bad manners on the ship and my talks with German passengers and crew gave me an insight into their mentality and outlook which served to strengthen my dislike of Nazi methods; and I determined that so far as in me lay I would help to keep my country free of their doctrines.

At Santos I refused further contact with them and we transhipped to a British liner to Rio where we spent a week of entertainment and then started homeward bound on another Japanese cargo boat, Mr Cooper and I being the only passengers.

The Japs are a suave and crafty race, but they are polite, which is more than I can say of the Germans, and though our quarters were rough they did their best to make us comfortable.

After an uneventful voyage we reached Capetown in January 1939 with my family at the pierhead to meet me.

Chapter 19

In the Ministry of Mines

After my breakdown in Parliament three months ago, General Hertzog, with understanding sympathy, had decided that the portfolio of Agriculture would kill any man, so early in 1939 he made me take over the Ministry of Mines. This was a quiet haven and for the ensuing Session and some months thereafter I had a comparatively easy time.

The Gold Mining Industry of the Witwatersrand is so efficiently run that my post was almost a sinecure; but as Irrigation and Forestry were still under me I was not altogether idle. I took part in the debates in the House and once I travelled by car through Namaqualand to Port Nolloth, the dreary little harbour where General Smuts and I had been taken aboard a troopship in 1902 on our way to the Peace conference at Vereeniging at the close of the Boer War. I was pressed to spend half a million pounds to turn the place into safe anchorage for big ships, but after a careful inspection of the rocky coast, and knowing the poverty of the hinterland, I turned down the project.

Later, I flew from Capetown to inspect the diamond diggings at Alexander Bay where I had made a forced landing during the Orange River floods. The whim took me to fly upstream to view the rugged mountains over which the engine at that time had broken down. The pilot had no maps and a heavy mist lay over the land, but I directed him from the cockpit and what we saw confirmed my former impression that the country below was the most jagged, frightening region a single engined machine could negotiate in the African continent.

I told General Smuts about it on my return and he flew up some weeks later. He came back and he said it was the worst he had ever seen.

In March, while Parliament was in progress, Hitler invaded Czechoslovakia, and now we realised that Europe was heading for war.

We are a small people in South Africa and we play an infinitesimal part in the affairs of the Empire, yet it was only natural that we should ask ourselves how this was to affect us. General Smuts and I agreed that it vitally touched our country. We felt that only within the British Empire was there security and if we contracted ourselves out we should not long retain our freedom as we would be seized by one of the great predatory powers for the sake of our strategic base at the Cape and our mineral wealth, and because of our internal political weakness.

In Cabinet and in Parliament those Ministers and Members who had been supporters of the old South African Party prior to fusion in 1933 stood by us, but we were unable to obtain the views of General Hertzog and his wing on the all important question as to whether South Africa would remain neutral in case of war with Germany or whether we would stand by Great Britain. Every time General Smuts sounded the Prime Minister he was told that it would serve no useful purpose to discuss the matter as Hitler did not intend war, his reputation having been built up on bloodless victories. The other ex-Nationalist Ministers and Members of Parliament were equally reticent, so that with a crisis approaching we were unable to formulate a policy.

Early in July my family and I camped on Sandringham. My boys and I went on several lion hunts with our old friend Mr Whittingstall, who shot one right in front of John and Michael to their great excitement. The morning after we returned home General Smuts came to me. He said Sir Ernest Oppenheimer and his son were flying north to view a volcanic eruption in the Belgian Congo and they had invited us to accompany them. He said he felt that war between Germany and Britain was not a certainty and we might as well have a final holiday.

I did not wait for a second asking and on the seventeenth, piloted by Captain Halse, we started from Johannesburg. As the weather was bad we did not get beyond Pietersburg the first day, then in two days' flying to Zomba, the capital of Nyasaland, where we stayed with the Governor. We flew over Mount Mlanje, a stupendous mass of rock, probably an extinct volcano, about thirty miles from Zomba. General Smuts thought this would prove to be the highlight of our journey, but I told him the highlight was the Wessel Hickman crater near Mbeya. He said he had been to Mbeya several times and he had never heard of either crater or mountain there. Next day we flew for three hundred miles along Lake Nyasa and as we neared Mbeya I pointed out Mount Wessel Hickman to the pilot and asked him to climb over it, which he did, and we looked down into the dark water-filled depths of the crater as I had done once before. When we landed, General Smuts made me the *amende honorable* and he said that this indeed was the highlight of our journey. But we were both wrong for the real highlight was still to come.

On 20th July from Mbeya over Lake Rukwa and skirting the entire length of Lake Tanganyika we landed at Usambara, in Belgian territory, to refuel. Lake Tanganyika, especially the eastern side, is a magnificent example of one aspect of the Great Rift Valley that lies longitudinally across Africa. The coast stands up a stark wall of naked rock like the Mountains of the Moon and it is probably the most characteristic area of the depressed sector of the Rift as opposed to the great peaks and volcanoes that were thrown skyward.

Now came the climax. From Usambara we flew to lake Kivu, a stretch of water surrounded by hills and dotted with green islands forming almost as beautiful a sight as the northern Italian lakes. As we sped onward we saw in the distance a tall column of steam and as we drew nearer we found that it was caused by molten lava flowing into the lake on a front of about five miles.

Inland was a fiery river of lava pouring down from a 10 000 foot volcano, Mount Nyamlagira, fifteen miles away, and to the right stood another volcano sending forth a cloud of dense smoke.

This was the highlight of our expedition. We flew along the blazing torrent. It had made its way down the slopes, destroying everything in its path and for long distances on either side the trees stood scorched and withered from the heat, and the acrid smell of sulphur reached us even on high. At intervals bubbles of lava, thirty or forty yards across, slowly welled and heaved like simmering porridge. When they broke, flaming spurts shot upward in all directions.

Lifting the nose of his machine, Captain Halse climbed up the contour of the volcano and soon we were over the source of the eruption. The lava was not ejected from the crater itself, but from a number of huge vents blown in the flank of the mountain. Round the vents were tall cones of yellow sulphur from the bowels of the earth.

Climbing to 11 000 feet to escape the effects of atmospheric disturbance we circled over the crater, one and a half miles in diameter, a seething cauldron of fire and brimstone, a wonderful sight indeed.

In the floor of the deep crater, on the far side, was a smaller crater of immeasurable depth and we learned afterwards that the Belgian Government was unaware of its existence, so perhaps we had made a discovery. I have witnessed strange and interesting things in my life, but nothing to equal this daemonic spectacle.

General Smuts too must have felt the grandeur of the scene. I noticed his hands showed taut as he grasped the rails of his seat and his features were tense as he gazed at the fiery tumult below. He told me that evening that to him it was a culminating experience.

Now we made east, and skirting round the other volcano, we landed at Kisenyi, on the northern end of Lake Kivu. A Russian woman had established a guesthouse here. She did not claim to be a daughter of the Tsars like the refugees in China, but she was obviously well bred and we speculated on her history and how she came to be in this remote spot. She made us comfortable and we spent several hours watching the lurid flare of the volcanoes pulsing across the dark background of the night.

On the following day we sailed for twenty miles to where the lava was reaching the water. Our glimpse from the air had been so transient that we wished to have a closer view. It was an amazing sight. On a front of several miles, a viscid mass of burning lava was flowing into the lake at about a yard a minute, and as it met the water great clouds of steam rose hundreds of feet into the air.

We navigated cautiously. As we approached we dipped our hands and the water was lukewarm; then it grew hotter and from ten yards away we were nearly at boiling point and the skipper of our craft grew anxious.

In Great Britain I had visited iron foundries where steel was poured from crucibles and we were given coloured glasses to protect our eyes; but the incandescence of molten lava at close quarters was beyond belief. I think our early progenitors must have evolved their ideas of hell fire from volcanic upheavals.

The Bay of Saki into which the flow was discharging seemed to be gradually altering its coastline and if the eruption continues for a year or two it will probably be obliterated.

We returned to Kisenyi by sunset to learn that a party of South African students had met with an accident. Some of them had gone into the Parc Albert, to see the big game. While they were watching a herd of elephant, a large bull rushed at their car, ripped up the roof with his tusks, and after smashing radiator and bonnet and mudguards he flung the vehicle on its side and then disappeared into the bush. Of the six occupants, five sustained only minor bruises but the sixth, Professor Gevers of Johannesburg, had both his legs broken. He was brought in that afternoon and arrangements were made to fly him to the hospital at Nairobi where he ultimately recovered.

In the meanwhile, General Smuts and I and Sir Ernest and his son decided to visit the Parc Albert the next day. Our road took us through a beautiful country of high volcanoes and magnificent scenery. A few miles after we had entered the Parc Albert we saw the battered car lying some distance from the road and we went to have a look at it. To our surprise we came on the elephant that had done the damage lying stone dead about two hundred yards away, an immense bull with eighty pound tusks. The cause of his death has remained a mystery.

I think, however, he died of anthrax. While I was in Uganda two years before, my camp on the Niamagesani River overlooked the waters of Lake Edward. A mile or two out was a small island of perhaps fifteen acres. Captain Pittmann told me that some time previously he gazed across one morning and to his astonishment he saw four elephant there. They must have swum thither, for the intervening stretch was twenty fathoms deep. The elephant remained on the island for a long time and he saw them daily. Then he noticed that only one elephant was left and he rowed over to see what had happened. He found the other three animals lying on their flanks, their trunks and limbs distorted as if they had died in mortal agony. He came to the conclusion that the symptoms were those of anthrax. Every square yard of the island was pitted and trampled, the trees were torn down and there were great holes the elephant had scooped with their tusks. He had seen them do this before when smitten with the fell disease.

One of the students I met when visiting the wounded professor at Kisenyi told me that in entering the Parc Albert they had followed the usual custom of posting a native guide on their front mudguard to warn the driver against tree stumps and antheaps. As the elephant charged the native leaped to earth and fled into the scrub. He hid himself for several days before he reappeared. He explained his absence. He said he had seen that the elephant was dying by the way it drove aimlessly at trees and dug its tusks into the soil. He knew from his medicine man that when elephant acted thus they were bewitched and misfortune was on hand. Therefore he had thought it best to make himself scarce. We didn't blame him; the medicine man had been right for once.

Our party spent some days in the Parc, with Ruanda as our headquarters. There were buffalo, more elephant, lion, and literally thousands of hippo and much smaller game.

Back to Kisenyi and from there by plane across Lake Kivu to Costermansville, an administrative centre at the southern end. The Belgian authorities staged a war dance for us by the Watussi, a tribe of long-limbed, slender, hamitic warriors, hardly one of them standing less than six feet six. They looked over-bred and their angular cheekbones and hawklike noses reminded me of the royal mummies I had seen in the museum at Cairo. By contrast, there was a dance by a tribe of pygmies who looked more like baboons than baboons look like baboons.

As I sat between General Smuts and the local Governor I caught snatches of talk from behind me coming from Belgian officials and their wives. They were discussing the probability of a European war. I heard one man sum up the situation. He said: '*Peuh, les Anglais ne se battront pas, ils sont une nation de négociants.*'

From Costermansville we flew down the Ruzizi gorge, an arresting sight, and then to Lake Tanganyika and to Albertville, then down the river that strangely breaks at a right angle from Tanganyika to the Congo.

We landed at Kabalo and from there up the Congo. North of Bukama grazed the biggest herds of game I have seen in Africa. Countless thousands of lechwe and other species; troops of elephant and buffalo.

We stopped at Elizabethville to fill our tank and then flew to the N'Kana copper mines in northern Rhodesia. Total flying time for the day seven hours thirty five minutes.

For the next few days we toured the mining centres and were amazed at the development in the heart of the African jungle brought about through Sir Ernest Oppenheimer's foresight. Townships had sprung up, factories and furnaces were in full blast, the European workers were comfortably housed and the native quarters and hospitals were as good as those on the Rand.

All through our expedition, General Smuts was like a schoolboy on a holiday as he had been on that faraway trip he and I had made into Zululand years ago. With the Rhodesians he was in his element and at dinner every night he had many interesting things to say, a few of which I noted down.

Once he spoke of his journey to Palestine across the submarine-infested Mediterranean after General Murray's setback at Gaza in 1917 and he told us of how he and Mr Lloyd George went to Italy after the Caporetto débâcle. He said the Italian General Staff and the politicians were in a state of panic and they spoke of a separate peace with Germany. Signor Orlando and the rest of the Cabinet had completely lost their heads. They shouted and gesticulated at one another over the conference table and behaved like madmen. Orlando at one stage cried out, '*Je suis Sicilien, je suis Sicilien, je me retirerai à mon île et là je mourrai dans la dernière tranchée.*' Mr Lloyd George acidly remarked that dying in the last ditch in Sicily was hardly a contribution to the problem of stemming the tide on the Isonzo.

The French delegates were openly scornful, and General Smuts told us it was only Mr Lloyd George's tact (and, I have no doubt, his own) that smoothed over a dangerous impasse and kept Italy in the war. He said King Victor was the only Italian who shewed a glimmer of statesmanship.

Another evening, speaking of the Peace Conference of Versailles, he said only Clémenceau and Lloyd George carried heavy guns; the rest were small men. He said that President Wilson was doctrinaire and didactic though he had the most comprehensive vocabulary of idealism he had ever heard.

In lighter vein General Smuts said he once had a Basuto named John Sapetla working for him on his farm whose correspondence was always addressed to the 'Rt Hon Mr John Sapetla, Esq, care of JC Smuts.'

He summed up his opinion of the Nationalist Party by telling us that during the last elections an inmate of the Pretoria asylum had rung up their leader Dr Malan and said, 'Doctor, doctor, I just want to let you know all we lunatics over here are Nationalists.'

I slipped in a couple of yarns too. One I had from my grandfather. In his youth he owned a number of slaves he had inherited from my great grandfather. Two of them, Samuel and George, had quarrelled in their youth and they remained bad friends for the rest of their lives.

At length, Samuel lay dying of old age in his hut, and my grandfather told the other offender to make his peace. Accordingly George, an old man too by now, went to where Samuel lay on his deathbed and he opened negotiations. He said, 'Samuel, I'se come to tell you how sorry I is about that thrashing I gave you long ago.'

On hearing this, Samuel raised himself on his elbows and replied, 'You black scum, you says you gived me a thrashing; you is a damn liar—I whipped the hide off you by the cattlekraal that day and you knows it.' Having delivered himself of this parting thrust he fell back and contentedly breathed his last.

I told another story apropos of the fact that in the Union we are inclined to look on manual labour by Europeans as *infra dig*. An old Boer was invited to spend a few days with an English friend in Johannesburg, a noted tennis player. He was taken to see a match in which his host took part.

After a strenuous game the latter returned from the courts exhausted and streaming with perspiration. The farmer looked him up and down and said, 'Man, why don't you let your nigger do that for you?'

These quiet Rhodesian memories constitute what were, perhaps, the last carefree hours General Smuts and I are destined to enjoy for, our visit ending, we flew back to Pretoria where grave issues awaited us.

Chapter 20

The End of the 1930's

It was August 1939. War clouds were gathering in Europe, but we found that General Hertzog, our Prime Minister, had withdrawn to the seclusion of his farm and we could get no information from him. Obviously, if war broke out between Germany and Britain, the Government of South Africa would have to state its policy; we would have to say whether we intended standing by the rest of the Commonwealth or not.

I have refrained from stressing our Cabinet difficulties during the six years I served under General Hertzog. He was a man of culture and a gentleman, but he was possessed of an uneasy temperament and there had been frequent trouble and several acute crises which had led to resignations of some of our colleagues. General Hertzog never seemed to realise that he and his wing of the United Party were in the minority and that he was being kept in power by General Smuts and our side of the coalition. He seldom consulted us and on various occasions unpleasant incidents and unpalatable measures had been forced on us.

General Smuts throughout showed real statesmanship. He knew that many of his followers thought he was weakly submitting to affronts, but time after time he counselled patience. He said we were engaged in a vital attempt to persuade Dutch and English to work together and if at last there came a time to break it should be on a question of national importance instead of these minor quarrels.

That time was on hand. From the start the United Party had been united only in name. The old Nationalist stalwarts who had joined the new party under General Hertzog in 1933 had done so with mental reservations and we on our side had entered the pact with misgivings.

Nevertheless, both sections had done their best, and we had struggled along and somehow or other we had managed to keep the ship afloat. Now came the crucial test.

Earlier in the year when all could see that Europe would soon be plunged in conflict, General Hertzog had repeatedly promised that he would summon Parliament before he decided on war. But he never undertook to consult Parliament should he decide *not* to go to war, and it had never struck anyone to question him on the point.

I have every reason to believe that he and his wing in the Cabinet had agreed to remain neutral and that they intended doing so without calling Parliament together.

This would have placed General Smuts and his supporters in a terrible predicament for there would have been no constitutional means of reversing a neutrality decision.

A unique coincidence saved us from this dilemma. Under the South African Constitution, all laws have to be passed by the House of Assembly and the Senate combined. It so happened that towards the middle of August the government Law

Advisers discovered that the life of the Senate would expire in a few weeks and unless both Houses met to pass a law extending the period no legislation passed by the Assembly alone would be valid.

Hereupon General Hertzog reluctantly summoned Parliament for a brief three-day Session in order to cure this technical defect.

The last thing he desired or expected was for war to burst upon him while the House was sitting. But this is precisely what happened. As our special parliamentary train pulled into the station at Capetown on the morning of Friday, September the 1st, we were met with the news that Hitler had invaded Poland and that Britain and France would soon be at war with Germany. General Hertzog's luck was out; he was caught in a mesh. With Parliament met together he could not now prevent the House from taking a vote on the question of peace or war and his plan to remain neutral without Parliamentary consent had been frustrated.

Parliament was to open next morning (Saturday) and throughout Friday there was suppressed excitement. Members stood in knots in the Lobby eagerly discussing the position, but no one knew what the Prime Minister was going to do, for he preserved a sphinx-like silence.

At ten-thirty am on Saturday everyone was in his place when the Speaker stood up and the moment prayers were over a score of Members were on their feet demanding to know what the Government intended to do. It was an extraordinary situation. The Cabinet consisted of thirteen Ministers of whom General Smuts and six others of us were old South African Party men, so that we were in majority of one, but thus far General Hertzog had given us no inkling of his views though we were co-responsible for whatever line was to be adopted.

Now General Hertzog could no longer evade the issue and, pale and tense, he stood up to say that as the only business of the House on opening day was to give formal notice of a Bill to prolong the life of the Senate he would make a pronouncement on Monday morning. We adjourned, no wiser than before.

That afternoon we received notice of a Cabinet meeting on Saturday at three pm at Groote Schuur, the historic residence bequeathed to the nation by Mr Cecil Rhodes as the home of future Prime Ministers of the Union. He did this at a time in the Boer war, when the likelihood of there ever being a Union of South Africa seemed remotely improbable.

I can remember how in 1902, as a youth, I was serving in the field under General Smuts. Word came through that Mr Rhodes was dead and of that strange proviso in his testament. We received the news with scornful laughter; it seemed to us a bitter mockery that this Englishman should speak of a United South Africa and of a Prime Minister while we were still at each others' throats. If anyone in those far-off days had ventured to tell me that I was to enter that very building as a Union Cabinet Minister to speak on behalf of taking arms at England's side I would have thought him insane.

But so it was. I had climbed up through the intervening years with General Smuts as my leader. He and I and scores of thousands of South Africans of Dutch descent had come to see that the British had treated us fairly. They took our country but they gave it back to us with Natal and the Cape thrown in for good measure. We enjoyed greater liberty and security than we had under our own republics and we saw that our only hope of survival as a free nation was inside the Commonwealth.

Therefore we attended this gathering at Groote Schuur determined that South Africa should once more play its rightful part against German aggression.

It was a momentous occasion. I was the first to arrive and I watched the other Ministers as they drove up in their cars, each vehicle bearing the embroidered pennant of the Union. We were ushered into a reception chamber hung with priceless tapestries, and containing Chinese vases and lacquered furniture. General Hertzog awaited us. It was evident from the start that he had sent for us not in order that we might consult with him but so that we might receive his orders.

He strode backward and forward across the carpeted floor and spoke for nearly three hours without a halt, raking up the bitterness of the South African war and speaking in exalted tones of the humiliations we had undergone at the hands of the British and of the mighty work of reconstruction that Hitler was carrying out. The burden of his theme was that South Africa should remain neutral. If Hitler won the war he would not molest us and if the British were victorious we would be safe anyhow.

It was growing dark before he ended and it was decided to adjourn until next afternoon when we were to meet again.

General Smuts and I and the other five Ministers who stood with us decided that night that if General Hertzog insisted on neutrality we would carry it against him and take a vote in the House.

Next afternoon the Cabinet Meeting was a repetition of the previous one. Again General Hertzog harangued us interminably and it was a long time before General Smuts was allowed an opportunity to state his views.

He began by saying that the decision he had come to was the most serious he had been called upon to take in all his life—then he went on to say why South Africa should stand by the Empire and declare war on Germany. There was an occasional interruption by General Hertzog, but all felt the heavy responsibility that lay on our shoulders and throughout the discussions ran with decorum. When at length General Smuts declared it to be his intention to test the matter in the House, a hush fell on the room for we knew it meant the break-up of the government and it meant many other things still lying shrouded in the future. It was I who finally brought the conference to a close. I expressed my opinion as to our entry into the war; then I stood up and said to General Hertzog, 'Sir, it is quite evident that we have reached the parting of the ways. Those of us who are opposed to neutrality cannot remain in office with you; therefore this meeting is our last as fellow colleagues. I wish to thank you for the courtesy you have invariably shown us during the time we served under you and I hope the personal friendships we made will not be affected by what has happened.' Hereupon everyone rose, a butler brought in liquid refreshment which all partook of; we shook hands and what was perhaps the most critical Cabinet Meeting ever held in South Africa was over.

General Hertzog in the course of his lengthy speech had indicated that on Monday, September 4th, he was going to move a Resolution in Parliament declaring South Africa to be neutral in the war.

He was such an autocrat by nature that I verily believe he had never paused to consider whether he could carry his motion through the House. In the past, his method had been to walk into our Caucus and lay down the law with a slap of his fist on the table. He brooked no opposition and at any hint of criticism he would threaten to resign and appeal to the country.

This generally sufficed to bring his own immediate followers to heel, and on our side Members had more or less let him have his way for the reason I have already indicated—they had accepted General Smuts' advice not to precipitate a break on minor differences.

I am convinced that he thought he could walk into Parliament in the same way on Monday morning and force his neutrality motion on us by sheer domination of his personal prestige. Relying on this ascendancy he had never troubled to count heads and he had no idea how Members were likely to vote on a fundamental issue such as this. Had he done so an interesting but not reassuring problem would have faced him.

The South African House of Assembly consisted of 153 Members of parliament of whom all but six were now in Capetown. Of those present, 147 in all, 104 belonged to the United Party, 29 were Nationalists forming the official opposition under Dr Malan, a dour old Calvinist, 7 were Dominionites (the British equivalent of Malan's Afrikaans extremists) under Colonel Stallard, a Tory of the mid-Victorian school, 4 were Labour Members, 3 were Native Representatives.

On paper therefore, General Hertzog had a large majority against all comers but his snag was that of the 104 United Party Members serving under him, 66 were supporters of General Smuts and he could only rely on a personal following of 38, a fact he had never seemed to realise during the six years of his reign.

On the other hand, the 29 Nationalists, all violently anti-British, would vote for anything anti-British and they would support a neutrality motion. With his own tail of 38, and with the 29 Nationalist recalcitrants, he commanded 67 votes against our 66, but we knew that the 7 Dominionites, the 4 Labour Members, and the 3 Native Representatives were with us, giving us a majority of thirteen.

We had made a preliminary canvass, and we were sure of our ground, but General Hertzog in his blind arrogance thought he had a majority in the House and that he could carry his neutrality motion. Indeed, he told both the Governor-General and General Smuts so and now he had blundered into a pit for his own undoing.

That evening, General Smuts and I and the five Cabinet Ministers who had supported us at Groote Schuur met in the Civil Service Club in Capetown and drafted a counter-resolution which General Smuts was to move next day.

By Monday morning, dame rumour had been busy. The House was to open at ten-thirty, but from nine o'clock onwards Members were thronging the Lobby and we were eagerly questioned: Was it true that Cabinet had broken up? Was it true that General Hertzog was to introduce a Neutrality Motion? Why hadn't he summoned the Party Caucus? What right had we to decide without consulting the Party? and so on, and so on. They were understandably indignant, for General Hertzog should at any rate have consulted his wing of the Party; but that was his affair, and we left him to explain things to his own people while we hastily ranged for battle.

Mr Speaker droned the stereotyped prayer and the Bill to extend the life of the Senate was passed. Now came the real business before us. The public galleries were crowded and there was breathless silence when General Hertzog rose to put his motion for neutrality. He spoke for a long time and he repeated the arguments he had used to us at Groote Schuur—Hitler was justified; the British connection would always drag us into wars, and we in South Africa should remain out of the conflict.

Then General Smuts put his counter-resolution. He briefly stated our case for participation in the war. A long debate followed which lasted until nine pm that evening and then the bells rang for the most dramatic division I have ever attended. The tellers took a long time to check their lists but it did not need them to inform us that we had won the day. I watched General Hertzog where he sat across the floor of the House.

His face was ashen and it seemed to me that only now had it dawned on him that he was staring at defeat. The other five Cabinet Ministers who voted with him looked angry and perturbed and I gained the impression that they were furious at the way their leader had bungled himself into an impasse.

But it was too late. The tellers completed the tale of votes and handed the lists to Mr Speaker. He stood up to announce the result:

> 'Ayes in favour of the Hon the Prime Minister's Neutrality Motion—67.
> Noes, in favour of the motion to enter the war—80.
> The noes have it.'

We had won by a majority of thirteen.

It is possible that General Hertzog might have secured a small majority had it not been for his blundering tactics in eulogising Hitler and had it not been for the forceful and powerful speech by General Smuts in reply which brought round many waverers.

The decision was quietly received for during the count we had sent a whispered message to our side, 'Men, don't rub it in—let there be no gloating.' We felt it was too grave a crisis for noisy demonstrations and now all the Members filed out, most of them deep in thought, for the full significance of what had taken place had scarcely come home to them as yet. Firstly, it meant that we were at war with Germany and that we might soon be at war with the Italians.

It meant too that General Hertzog was beaten and that he would be obliged to hand over the government of the country to General Smuts.

Only that morning General Hertzog had called on the Governor-General, Sir Patrick Duncan, to tell him that he was introducing a neutrality motion and that he had a majority for it in the House. Now, a few hours later, he went to Government House to resign his office after having been Prime Minister of the Union for fifteen years. With all his faults, we were sorry for him, but we rejoiced that General Smuts was at the head of affairs once more and that South Africa would have his wisdom to guide us instead of our being at the whim of a man who, though possessed of great qualities, was too obstinate and too erratic and illogical to be relied on in times like these.

The Governor-General immediately called upon General Smuts to form a new Cabinet. From the voting in the House it was clear that we held a majority only by the grace of the Dominionites, the Labour Members and the Native Representatives, all of whom had sunk their party differences in the common cause. Therefore General Smuts decided to create a National Government.

By Wednesday, September 6th, his task was complete. The new Cabinet was constituted as follows:

1. Prime Minister and Minister of Defence—General Smuts.
2. Deputy Prime Minister and Minister of Native Affairs—myself.
3. Minister of Finance—Mr JH Hofmeyr, next to General Smuts the finest brain we have in the Union.
4. Minister of Agriculture—Colonel Collins. A Boer War veteran under the late General Botha.
5. Minister of Justice—Dr Colin Steyn, like myself, son of a former Republic President.
6. Minister of Railways—Mr Claude Sturrock, a canny Scotsman.
7. Minister of Lands—Senator Conroy, of Irish and Afrikaans descent.
8. Posts and Telegraphs—Mr Clarkson, from Natal.
9. Interior—Mr Harry Lawrence, a brilliant young English-speaking South African.
10. Commerce and Industries—Mr Stuttaford, English-born; merchant-prince from Capetown.
11. Minister of Mines—Colonel Stallard, leader of the Dominion Party.
12. Minister of Labour—Mr Walter Madeley, who has for many years headed the Labour Party in South Africa.
13. Minister without Portfolio—Major Piet van der Byl. Dutch South African with a fine record in the last war.

All this may sound small beer to the outside world but to South Africa it was a mighty event, as vital to us as were the stones to the frogs in the fable, and the country rocked on its foundations.

The Nationalists accused us of having lured them into a trap, huge demonstrations were organised and for a week or two there was danger of another rebellion such as we had coped with in 1914.

Nonetheless, though our political activities might seem insignificant to onlookers from a distance the fact remains that if the Union had stood aside it would have been a serious blow to the solidarity of the Commonwealth and to its morale.

On Wednesday, September 6th, the newly-constituted Cabinet waited on the Governor-General and we were sworn of office, after which we left for the Transvaal to take up our duties at Pretoria. Our first task was to build up an army, for during the years that General Hertzog was Prime Minister and Mr Pirow Minister of Defence, our forces had existed on paper only. General Smuts very soon put a different complexion on affairs and so eager was the response to his call for volunteers that in the months that now followed no less than 130 000 recruits flocked to the colours.

The nationalists who comprise nearly forty per cent of our European population stood sullenly aloof, otherwise the number would have been nearly doubled; but in spite of their abstention we have to-day the strongest army South Africa has ever put into the field and our men, including John and Michael, streamed north to the defence of Kenya and the other territories of Central Africa.

II

About a fortnight after our return to Pretoria, I was at work in my office one morning when the telephone bell rang. General Smuts's private secretary was at the other end; he said the Prime Minister wished to see me.

I strolled along the stone-flagged corridors of the Union Buildings, idly speculating as to why the General had sent for me and I told myself he wished, no doubt, to discuss some matter concerning my Department. I little knew that I was going off on the most interesting journey I have ever made. General Smuts was at his desk when I entered. He is a man of few words. He said, 'Take a chair and read this.' It was a cable from the Prime Minister of Britain, Mr Chamberlain, and it invited General Smuts, or his next in command, to attend a conference in London to discuss plans with delegates from all the Dominions for the joint conduct of the war.

Having read the document I looked up and asked, 'You wish me to go?' He nodded. That was all that passed between us and a few days later Mr Cooper and I took the air.

We flew to Durban and after inspecting the coastal defences we set out on the long flight to England. We travelled in a Sunderland flying-boat, reaching Delagoa Bay in two hours fifteen minutes. We made inland across Natal and Zululand. To the right we passed St Lucia lake and in the distance was Kosi Bay and all Maputoland that I knew so well. On our left was my hippo sanctuary of Inyameti.

At Lourenço Marques were several German ships that had run for shelter. After refuelling we went on, crossing the Pungwe River delta, vast swamps and winding channels and at Beira, our next halt, saw more German ships at anchor with British cruisers outside to watch their movements. German sailors shuffled through the streets looking bored and miserable.

We reached Mozambique by dusk and we spent the night on a houseboat moored off the island. There was a magnificent German liner, the *Watussi*, lying inshore. After we left she broke bounds, but near Cape Point she was sighted by a South African aeroplane and ordered to make for False Bay. She scuttled herself and now she lies on the bottom of the sea not far from our old fishing grounds where John and Michael and I used to cast our lines with Uncle Jim.

That evening as we sat in the saloon of the houseboat listening to the wireless, news came through that the *Royal Oak* had been torpedoed with the loss of eight hundred lives—it was like an echo of the first weeks in the last war.

On 15th October, we took off from Mozambique at four-fifteen am and flew to Lindi, to Dâr-es-Salaam, to Mombasa and thence cross-country to Kisumu. On our way we passed the Rufigi and other deltas—the German cruiser *Königsberg* was still lying on her side, in the mud since 1916.

The colour of the sea over the coral reefs was unbelievably beautiful. Flying over Zanzibar I descried the hulk of the Sultan's gunboat where she had been sunk and where I saw her in 1902. From Mombasa to Kisumu is about three hundred and fifty miles. We saw Voi and Taveta, known from the former campaign, but Kilimanjaro was invisible beneath a vast blanket of clouds.

On 16th October we journeyed from Kisumu via Lake Victoria Nyanza to Fort Bell, thence to Rejaf, crossing and recrossing the Nile above and below its entry and exit to and from Lake Albert. Great swamps and sudd country spread out below us.

From Rejaf, the Nile at times a long way to the right, were great plains, and then desert country. Then from Malakal to Khartoum. As a boy I had devoured Father Ohrwalder's account and Slatin Pasha's account and Churchill's *River War*, about the Mahdi and the Khalifate, so I was the more interested at what I saw.

On 17th October, we went from Khartoum to Wadi-Halfa and from there non-stop to Cairo. I was carrying important despatches for General Wavell, then Commander-in-Chief of the Near East, and we met on a houseboat on the river. He had with him a glittering staff and I travelled in flannels and Norfolk tweeds, so I must have looked somewhat incongruous; but we held a conference and he offered to send me on to England in a warship.

I thought, however, that the air was faster, and I promised to jettison any compromising documents into the Mediterranean should it become necessary. We flew from Alexandria to Crete on the eighteenth and from there to Athens and Corfu. The next day we travelled from Corfu to Rome in three hours sixteen minutes and from Rome to Marseilles in two hours fifty-nine minutes, seeing Elba and Corsica below.

In walking down the Cannabière and by the docks, I noticed an occasional swastika on the walls and there were posters with '*à bas la guerre*' and other anti-government slogans which did not look healthy. Later, in Paris, I was to see even more disturbing evidence of how France was riddled and divided by political enmities.

From Marseilles we flew up along the Spanish frontier, the Pyrenees well to our left. Civilian planes had to keep below 2 000 feet under a new war regulation so we had a wonderful view of the lovely country.

We passed over or within sight of Arles, Nîmes, Beziers, Toulouse, then along the course of the river Garonne to lac Biscaross, not far from Bordeaux. We landed on the surface of the lake for fuel and then took off on a non-stop flight across the Bay of Biscay, Cap Nazaire, Belle Ile, etc, across parts of Brittany and Normandy, Rennes and Brest, if possible even more beautiful country than the south of France, and so over the English Channel to sit down on Southampton water at last. Signs of war were on every hand, civilians carrying gas masks and the streets full of soldiers and sailors and marines.

We took train to London, arriving there in a complete black-out. On our way up, we had found that Alexandria and Marseilles were darkened during the night, but their efforts were child's play compared to the London black-outs, so opaque that one literally could not see an inch and it was necessary to walk with outstretched arms to avoid cannoning into posts and pillar boxes and people.

At the railway station I was met by the Duke of Devonshire, Mr Anthony Eden and Admiral Bromley, feeling their way across the platform with the help of electric torches which I found during my stay in England to be indispensable after nightfall. I had made acquaintance with the Duke of Devonshire when he was on a lion hunt near Sandringham six months before and throughout my visit he showed me a great deal of kindness.

In stygian darkness Mr Cooper and I were driven to Grosvenor House where I had lived on my previous sojourn and now there was an even more palatial suite at my disposal.

Next morning I looked out through my window on to Hyde Park and a clear sunny day. There were gun pits among the trees and scores of anchored balloons swung overhead like silver fish in the sky.

In spite of all these warlike preparations there was an air of unreality about the situation. The Germans had overwhelmed Poland in three weeks, but since then there was a strange calm. Everyone had expected that France would immediately be attacked and that from the very start heavy air raids would be launched on Great

Britain, more particularly on London. So certain was the government of this that nearly a million children had been evacuated to the country; elaborate arrangements had been prepared to remove all civil service departments to the Provinces; underground shelters had been excavated; churches, museums and art galleries had sent their treasures away and even the stained glass windows from cathedrals and guildhalls were taken down and stored in vaults, and every building in London was heavily sandbagged against bomb splinters. But, thus far, not a single German aeroplane had attempted to approach the capital and save for an occasional hostile machine over the Firth of Forth the war remained what the comic papers called a '*sitzkrieg*' instead of the '*blitzkrieg*' that was anticipated. So much was this the case that during the weeks I spent in London I gathered the impression that people were becoming bored and I even heard the view expressed that it would be rather a good thing if the Germans did bomb the place—it would liven things up.

There was little warning of the wrath that was yet to come, but during all the time I was in England and from what I saw in France I was puzzled and uneasy, though I could not say why.

To me the first session of the joint war council was an outstanding event.

Mr Chamberlain was in the chair. He was a son of that Mr Joseph Chamberlain whom my brothers and I had looked on as a Corsican Ogre in years gone by and I thought of the strange turn of the wheel that had brought me to sit with him in this council at the nerve-centre of the British Empire. Among the others who attended were Mr Winston Churchill, Sir John Simon, Chancellor of the Exchequer, General Ironside, Mr Anthony Eden, the Duke of Devonshire, Lord Halifax, Lord Chatfield and other notabilities.

The British are a phlegmatic race. Mr Chamberlain opened the proceedings with a few words of welcome, then passed straight to business. Decisions to build great armadas by sea and air, to raise huge military forces and to expend thousands of millions of money were arrived at with never a raised voice and with no sign of flurry or excitement. It might have been a meeting of some suburban country council discussing the rates.

I could not help comparing their quiet unperturbed demeanour with the account General Smuts had given us of the Italian War Council he had been present at in 1918 when everyone shouted and gibbered and gesticulated at everyone else like so many madmen.

During the time I was in England I sat at many another conference at No 10 Downing Street, though on some occasions our meetings were held at the War Office, the Admiralty, and elsewhere.

These gatherings of necessity occupied most of my attention but I had much other work to do, including negotiations for the purchase both here and in America of guns and munitions and aircraft for our army in South Africa.

In addition I gave broadcasts, interviewed press correspondents, went to banquets, kept innumerable appointment at South Africa House with people who wished to see me on innumerable subjects, visited naval ports and shipping, munition factories, arsenals and training camps and at weekends I was generally able to get away for a rest.

I spent a few days with the Duke of Devonshire and his family on his Chatsworth estate. The mansion is perhaps the finest in Britain, but it was now turned into a girls' school to house evacuee children from Manchester and we stayed in a small factor's cottage a mile or two away.

I spent another weekend with Admiral Tottenham and his wife at their home on the Isle of Wight. Other weekends I went to Cambridge, Windsor Castle, and Marlborough.

I kept a hurried diary of which I give a few condensed extracts. If anyone thinks there are too many earls and titles 'tis no fault of mine.

> To Harrow, Boxill, Eton.
>
> Met Lord Vivian whom we had wounded in the Boer war.
>
> United Services Club with General Ironside, and Lord Hankey. Long discussions at South Africa House and at Dominions Office with Anthony Eden and Duke of Devonshire re Swaziland and Bechuanaland Protectorates.
>
> Broadcast in English, German, French and Dutch at the BBC.
>
> Attended to hear Mr Chamberlain's weekly statement in the House of Commons.
>
> Mr Churchill took me round the bomb-proof vaults that have been constructed beneath the Admiralty against air raids.
>
> Lunched at Savoy with Mr Anthony Eden, Lord Halifax, etc.
>
> Lunch at 11 Downing Street with Sir John Simon and Mr Strakosch, the financier. Through the window saw Mr Chamberlain, feeding his birds at No 10 next door.
>
> Attended government luncheon at Savoy. Mr Chamberlain, Churchill and most of the British Cabinet.
>
> Lord Mayor's banquet at Mansion House.
>
> Zeesen broadcast attacks General Smuts and myself calling us flunkeys of the Empire. I reply over the BBC in German to say that in South Africa we are no one's lackeys for we are free to do and say what we please—the flunkeys are the Germans who have allowed Hitler and his gangsters to deprive them of their liberties.
>
> News of German pocket battleship *Deutschland* or *Graf Spee* at large in N Atlantic.
>
> Inspected Portsmouth naval base. Dined with Mr Churchill at Admiralty House.
>
> Dined with Sir Nevile Henderson. His hatred of von Ribbentrop so intense that when he started to tell us of his experiences as Ambassador in Germany, one of the guests quietly removed plates and glasses and cutlery out of reach for fear he would sweep them to the floor in his vehemence.
>
> Dined at Buckingham Palace with the King and Queen and later had several audiences with him.
>
> To Woolwich Arsenal; to Aldershot to see the training camps. To Air Command centre twenty miles from London. All underground, in bomb-proof chambers. Lunched at White's Club with Lord Weir (War Supplies) and Lord Harry McGowan (Imperial Chemicals).
>
> Gave a reception at South Africa House to more than five hundred guests with all of whom I had to shake hands and say a few words of welcome.
>
> New form of magnetic mine laid by Germans in Thames Estuary. Saw Mr Chamberlain about this. He was laid up with gout. He said he was in agony and as he had never drunk a glass of port in his life it was grossly unfair, but, with a faint smile, 'Don't worry about the shipping losses; we shall overcome this menace as we have overcome many another.'
>
> At Brooks Club with Lord Trenchard who asked me to support him in demanding an assault on the Siegfried line—'all nonsense this sitting still and waiting for the Germans to attack.'

Dined Carlton with Mr Attlee, the Parliamentary Labour Leader.
Conference with Hore-Belisha *re* guns and aeroplanes for South Africa.
To theatre with Mr Waterson, our High Commissioner.
At Australia House: meeting with Casey and Bruce.
Lunched at Inner Temple with Lord Roach and other judges.
With Sir Hanbury Williams at Windsor Castle.

I developed a huge mail and I spent hours every day dictating replies to the staff that was placed at my disposal at South Africa House. And I was called on by many old friends and called on them in turn. I met interesting men and women, and my sojourn in London, though it entailed hard work, was an absorbing experience.

Now came another outstanding interlude. It was arranged that the representatives on the War Council from India and the Dominions should visit the front line across the Channel. Mr Anthony Eden led our company; the others were Mr Casey, Australia; Mr Crerar, Canada; Mr Frazer, New Zealand; Sir Zafrulla Kahn, India; myself for South Africa, and some military attachés.

On 9th November we sailed from Newhaven to Dieppe at night on a zig-zag course; all was well. Next day we went by road from Dieppe to Paris where we lodged at the famous Hotel Crillon near the Arc de Triomphe, mostly covered with sandbags.

At the moment of writing, the Hotel Crillon is occupied by German officers, and France lies in the dust, but for the time being all seemed well and not one of us dreamed of the catastrophe, though again I felt uneasy.

Everyone seemed immersed in party politics and even the staff at the hotel would rush out to buy the latest newspapers on the streets; then they stood arguing in the dining-room while we patiently hoped for breakfast. The morning after our arrival we motored out to Vincennes, an ancient fortress, now the GHQ of the French armies: where General Gamelin, the Commander-in-Chief, met us—a cheerful stocky man of about sixty-five, fresh-complexioned as a schoolgirl.

He struck me as a highly-trained, intelligent man who, as with most French officers, had made a lifelong study of his profession at arms. I inquired about the Duc d'Enghien who was executed here in Napoleon's time and he took me to see the very spot in a moat where this judicial murder had taken place.

He spoke bitterly of the situation, saying that they had constructed the Maginot Line at vast expense, but the Belgian government had raised objections to a continuation along their frontier, so it was only half a bulwark. Yet now that they were threatened with invasion, the Belgians were so intimidated by German threats that they refused to indulge in staff talks and he prophesied that either British or French troops would have to move forward of their works to go to their assistance. His prophecy was only too true.

One evening we dined with French Cabinet Ministers and Party leaders at the British Embassy. Again I was puzzled. Reynaud, a little game-cock of a fellow, was the only one who inspired me with any confidence. Laval and the rest seemed to me mere intriguers and logrollers. I was buttonholed by them in turn and I was warned not to confide in the others. There was such an atmosphere of distrust and suspicion that they appeared to hate each other more than they feared the Germans.

I remember thinking to myself that if, in South Africa, a Cabinet were imaginable between General Smuts, General Hertzog, Dr Malan, Colonel Stallard, the wild young racialists of the Nationalist wing, plus a dash of communists and a few socialists there would be reproduced in miniature something of what was evident on a larger scale here to-night. It did not augur well, but I was insufficiently versed to draw conclusions, though I was bewildered by what I saw and heard.

We had two air raid alarms at the Crillon and were taken down the lift to a huge cellar stacked with many thousands of cobwebbed bottles of wine (all no doubt imbibed by the Germans since then).

From Paris we travelled north via Peronne across country I knew from the last war. We passed through Masnières which I had helped to recapture when I commanded the 7th Shrops, and we stayed a night at Arras where I had lain wounded in the Hospice de St Jean in 1917.

Next morning we proceeded to Habacque, an old château which housed Lord Gort, the British Commander-in-Chief and his GHQ and we spent a few days visiting the front line towards Lille.

Casey, the Australian Cabinet Minister, and I were driven in a car by the Duke of Gloucester, brother of the King. Casey, like myself, had served in these parts of old. We shook our heads at what we saw. The new line, under hurried construction, seemed an amateurish affair. The trenches were shallow, the concrete domes the French had built at intervals of eight hundred yards, contained only a single anti-tank rifle apiece and the loopholes faced sideways with no frontal view. We thought the psychological effect on troops unable to see ahead of them would shake their morale, and taking it all round we did not like the look of things.

We watched the soldiers at work in their new battledress and we listened to Lord Gort and General Montgomery and others as they told us of their plans to hold the enemy.

We were taken over Mont de Bouvines, an obsolete fortress dating from 1870, now held by British troops and we watched a maze of muddy trenches and tank traps being haphazardly scooped out by steam shovels.

Then we were entertained at Lille by the *Préfet* and the *Maire*. I saw a monument to French civilians executed in 1914, with the inscription, *A nos fusillés*.

A hostile machine came high overhead dropping pamphlets. One of them was brought to me. It showed two scenes. In the first a British and a French soldier stood with poised arms as if to dive together into a lurid pool of blood. In the next the French soldier had gone in with a splash while the British soldier had remained on the bank derisively sneering at his submerged companion.

We attended a military concert at Arras. Lord Gort and his staff were present. Watching the faces of the row upon row of soldiers in the dimly lit hall I wondered what the future held for them.

To Cambrai, St Quentin, Laon, Rheims and Verdun, replete with memories of the last war. Then we halted at Metz in Lorraine on the River Moselle.

There was a war-market at which patriotic Frenchwomen handed in their jewellery for sale and I purchased bracelets and brooches for the common cause. The newspapers were printed in German and the owner of a kiosk said to me, '*Unsere Sprache ist Deutsch, aber die Herzen sind französisch*'; and a young officer told me that round here they liked the Germans and got on well with them. It was rather confusing.

We visited several British air squadrons behind the French Army, their Spitfires cunningly hidden in copses and woods. The aerodromes from above must have been indistinguishable, as all the fields looked alike.

In their quarters I spoke to a young New Zealander who the previous day had shot down a Messerschmidt. I asked him what crew the German machines carried—he said he didn't know. I asked how was that, seeing that they could have counted them when the plane crashed. There was silence for a moment and he and his companions looked embarrassed; then he said, 'You see, when a machine hits the ground from 27 000 feet, there isn't much left.'

All they had salvaged was a bent propeller blade and half a machine-gun. The rest was marmalade, as one of them put it.

Another pilot told me that two or three days before he was right on a Messerschmidt's tail and about to kill it when a shell from a French anti-aircraft gun shot his propeller away. His cock-pit window was blinded with oil but he managed to land by peeping through a gash in the side.

These pilots told me with a grin that the French were 'one up on them'. The British anti-aircraft batteries had shot down only nine French machines whereas the French batteries had downed ten British planes in various dog fights against the German air-arm.

We entered the Maginot Line at Mont de Welshe. When first I read of its construction some years ago I thought it would soon become as obsolete as the Chinese wall, for tourists to gape at.

But having been within its entrails I changed my mind. If one can visualise a hundred and fifty miles of battleships buried bow to stern with only their turrets visible it will give some idea of this gigantic undertaking. It must have cost the French people as much as their Navy cost the British. The tragedy is that it did not run the entire length of the frontier.

As far as it was built it was impregnable to frontal assault and indeed it was never taken, for the Germans wisely made no attempt to carry it; but to-day the Great Maginot Line is useless and deserted, for tourists to gape at after all.

During the time we spent up and down it, we saw heavy guns moved from the bowels of the earth at the touch of a finger; we watched ghostly electric trains running silent along endless corridors, with men and munitions, and we were hospitably entertained in bastions and bays.

Yet there was an air of unreality. I remembered the last war, with never a moment without shells howling across or machine-guns rattling away. Now there was deathly quiet and I did not hear a single shot fired in France though powerful armies stood face to face.

We were allowed to lower and raise the guns by pressing levers and swivels much as a child would be allowed to switch on the lights or press the button of the hooter in a motor-car, but when I suggested that I should be permitted to pull a trigger and fire a shell or two at the German lines across the way the French officers gazed at me as if I had uttered a blasphemy.

It was uncanny. French officers told me if they sent six shells over the way, exactly six shells were returned and when they unloaded petrol supplies at night the Germans turned on their searchlights to assist the soldiers at their work. It didn't make sense to me, but I think Hitler was beguiling the French into security on the Maginot Line while he was preparing his thrust at the weaker defences up north.

Before we left, Mr Anthony Eden and I were made honorary members of the garrison of Mont de Welshe and we were invested with badges. We returned to England via Arras.

From a pock-marked tablet I remembered seeing in Arras in 1917 this city has been devastated a score of times in the past. There was little enough left when I was there then but it had been rebuilt. Now it is once more a heap of ruins from all accounts.

We stayed over at Boulogne, the port of entry for most of the British Army in the Great War. It was unchanged save for a majestic statue of Britannia on the sea-wall.

There were frequent air raid alarms which seemed to cause no alarm for everyone strolled unconcerned, and once I saw a number of Spitfires streak across the sky chasing a German machine out of sight. The *préfet* of Boulogne with whom I was conversing at the time gave them a perfunctory look and said *'les aviateurs allemands ont une série complète de photographies de notre ville'*.

I listened-in to Zeesen that night and curiously enough there was mention of Boulogne. It said that while the Germans did not intend to attack French cities and towns from the air, Boulogne was to be razed to the ground because it had become a British port where troops and supplies were being landed and it was to be mercilessly bombed. To-day it is the other way about for Boulogne has become a German base and the RAF are mercilessly pounding it.

We embarked for Dover by daylight escorted by Destroyer H30 frisking around like a fox terrier.

As soon as we arrived in London, Mr Casey and I asked for an interview with the Prime Minister.

Word must have reached the British Cabinet that we were dissatisfied with what we had seen for it came to our ears that the military side objected to our speaking to Mr Chamberlain and there was talk of 'interfering Colonials'. However, we insisted, and in the end we were called to 10 Downing Street.

Mr Chamberlain was seated alone at the great table in the historic room in which, I was told, war had been decided against Napoleon, against Russia, against our South African Republics and against Germany in 1914 and again in this struggle.

I opened by describing the Gort Line and its French equivalent and of our experiences in that area during the last war. I said, 'Sir, if you will pardon my saying so, the Germans will go through there like a knife through cheese.'

Casey followed and we expressed our conviction that the line without adequate protection during long-continued shellfire would be a shambles.

Mr Chamberlain was somewhat vague and aloof. He said, 'Gentlemen, my military advisers tell me we cannot construct shelters in muddy soil and shells bursting in damp ground don't do much harm.' We argued the matter, but we made no progress and the Germans did go through that line like a knife through cheese.

III

I resumed my activities at South Africa House in Trafalgar Square and attended many sittings of the War Council at Downing Street.

One morning, Lord Trenchard and Lord Vivian took me to lunch at White's, one of the oldest clubs in England. After they had gone I fell into conversation with Sir Hubert Gough and Mr Dulanty, the High Commissioner for the Irish Free State. Sir Hubert Gough had commanded the 5th Army in France when the Germans broke the British line in the spring of 1918 and as I was severely wounded during the withdrawal, I listened with keen interest to his account of the disaster. I am bound to say that I agree with him as to the shabbiness of the treatment he received at the hands of the War Office for what was not his fault but that of the Higher Command.

He is an Irishman who dearly loves his own country, but he realises that with all her legitimate grievances against the English she can only solve her problems by remaining within the British Empire. As I am a South African who dearly loves my own country and who realises that with all our legitimate grievances against the English we can only solve our problems by remaining inside the Empire, we met on common ground.

Dulanty was an Irishman of intermediate type. He possessed a wide range of general knowledge and a deep love of English literature and of English poetry. But he had been reared on tales of British atrocities from the days of Queen Elizabeth and Cromwell and the autobiography of Wolfe Tone and the hanging of Robert Emmet and other Irish patriots of varying calibre and he held forth to me of Dublin Castle, the Easter shootings and the Black and Tans.

I pointed out that a hundred years ago they hanged a dozen men a day at Tyburn Cross for minor offences, and added, 'You Irish blame on the British what you should blame on the barbarity of those times.' I told him I had seen a list of Courts Martial at the Cape in 1806 in which scores of British soldiers were condemned to be hanged for petty contraventions, but any Irishman who was executed on similar charges was canonised as a national martyr. He considered this for a moment, then he slapped his knee and exclaimed, 'By God, perhaps there may be something in that.'

In further talk I mentioned that the German radio from Zeesen had been vilifying General Smuts and myself as flunkeys and lackeys of the Empire. Dulanty said, 'You know, when I read General Smuts's speeches and heard your broadcasts I said to myself: those fellows have been nobbled by the British.'

I replied, 'Mr. Dulanty, no one can nobble us. We are free men in a free country and we stand by the British because we believe that with so many predatory powers seeking whom they may devour our safety lies within the Commonwealth; and we believe that a United South African people is only attainable within its shelter.'

I then went on to say, somewhat ponderously perhaps, that in my opinion Mr de Valera had fatally blundered. He should have realised that a united Ireland was more important than constitutional academics and that as with us in the South, a united Ireland could be achieved only inside the Empire. Had South Ireland stood by the North in the present crisis, partition would have fallen away and a united Irish nation would have come into being at last. Once this was accomplished there was time enough to sit down and consider whether they wished to secede and in all probability by that time they would not think it worth while.

Finally I asserted that Irish and South African problems were akin. Ireland was severed geographically, South Africa was divided racially. Along the line we were following was a reasonable chance of nationhood, but the road the Irish Free State was travelling would take them farther and farther from their goal. Dulanty heard me out and after sitting in thought he jumped up and cried, 'You've got to go and speak to "Dev".'

I protested that Mr de Valera might refuse to see me, but he said, 'You leave it to me, you leave it to me,' and we parted on this note.

Two days later, as I sat in my office in South Africa House, the telephone rang and a trunk call came through from Dublin with an invitation from Mr de Valera to come and see him. An aeroplane was provided and next morning Mr Cooper and I left Heston on a non-stop flight to Dublin, with Holyhead and Anglesey and St George's Channel below. This was the first time I had been here since 1919. The place looked shabbier than ever and it did not seem to me that Ireland was prospering.

We were put up at the famous Shelborne Hotel as state guests and that afternoon Mr de Valera and I met in his office. We talked for nearly three hours. It was agreed that our discussions were to be confidential, so I shall not touch upon the subject matter of the interview beyond saying that I put before him very much the same views I had expressed to Mr Dulanty and he on his side stated the case for Ireland as he saw it.

I judged him to be a man of high character, but professorial and doctrinaire. He reminded me of General Hertzog—both of them are gentlemen but very difficult gentlemen, and they are prone to sentimentalise on the glories of the past and the traditions of their race to the exclusion of more practical considerations.

During our interview we were closeted alone, but that evening I had an opportunity of meeting the other Ministers at a banquet that was given in a block of buildings which under the former régime had been known as the Castle. Mr de Valera presided. He was in a genial mood, though he lacks a sense of humour. He drank nothing but water and he ate sparingly.

The rest of the Cabinet was less austere. I hope I am not doing them an injustice, but from their talk, which grew livelier as we proceeded, I gathered that the chief qualification for an Irish portfolio has something to do with the number of men shot by the incumbent during the late troubles.

They had many tales of ambushes, the bombing of troops and police barracks, the killing of British officers, and burnings and executions and the sorry happenings of recent years. But with it all, I sensed an undercurrent of uneasiness. Like our own Nationalists in South Africa, they were sincere racial fanatics but I think they felt that the Irish Free State was not playing an heroic part in sheltering behind the British and refusing to help them in a struggle in which their own future was equally involved. However, I listened to much high-flown talk, for the Irishman is quite as voluble as we Afrikaners when we break loose on the virtues of our people and our past.

At one stage, I said to Mr de Valera, 'You know sir, we Dutch in South Africa are very like the Irish.' He asked what I meant. I told him that, like the Irish, we were always hiving off into separate factions and were eternally quarrelling among ourselves. 'Would you believe it, that with a war on our hands, we are split into three separate parties down South?' 'Three,' said Mr de Valera wryly. 'You are lucky; we are split into twenty-four.'

Mr de Valera and I had agreed beforehand that with our exhausting conference of that afternoon we would retire early, so at ten o'clock we broke up. He took his departure in a taxi-cab and I was glad to think I was going to bed. As I was about to leave, an official came up to say that one of the Cabinet Ministers who had been unable to attend the dinner would like a word with me to discuss mutual economic problems.

I was sleepy and fatigued, but as I thought he was awaiting me in an adjacent room and that it would be a matter of ten minutes or so, I heaved a sigh and went along. Instead of being in the next room, he was twelve miles away on a country estate, and poor Cooper and I were motored out, mostly by farm roads shut in by stone walls on either side.

At length we reached our destination and as we came up the drive there was a mansion lit up and at the entrance the Minister with an hilarious group of friends, welcomed us in. It was a night of wassail. Never a word was spoken of mutual economic problems, but there was singing of patriotic songs, poems about old Ireland and fierce amber-coloured whisky. There were ladies too, who warbled sweetly of bayonets gleaming at the rise of the moon; the *Harp that Once*; and the *Island of Sorrow*.

Dawn was on its way and the birds were twittering by the time the consortium ended and it was nearly breakfast time before we got back to Dublin.

I was awakened at ten feeling as I had felt after that Hogmanay nicht with the Scots Fusiliers twenty years ago, and again I kept a still upper lip as we were taken round museums and art galleries.

One of the collections we saw consisted of uniforms and other relics used during the Easter rising. Among these were some rifles that had been fished up from the *Aud*, the German ship that was to have landed arms for Sir Roger Casement's attempted invasion. These rifles were obsolete single-loading Mausers of 1870 such as they had armed their native levies with in East Africa and it threw some light on the sincerity of their help to the Irish cause that they should fob them off with these antiquated weapons.

Our visit ending, we flew back via Liverpool where we landed. From Liverpool to Heston I slept all the way. Mr Cooper said it was the roughest journey he had ever experienced, but I was oblivious.

IV

I now resumed work in London and I was kept busier than ever for the time was approaching to return to South Africa.

My diary says that I dined once more with the King and Queen at Buckingham Palace, and that I broadcast again at the BBC in English, French, Dutch and German, which one of the staff told me was a record for one speaker.

I attended a final series of War Councils, had interviews with Mr Churchill, General Carr, Mr Hore-Belisha and others, and then four or five days before I was due to start home the Portuguese Ambassador called on me with an official invitation from his Government to proceed to Lisbon to talk over matters affecting our joint interests in Southern Africa.

I cabled the offer to General Smuts who immediately approved of my acceptance, and needless to say I was delighted at the prospect. I have always liked the

Portuguese, and having received courtesy and kindness from them in their Colonial territories, I looked forward to seeing their home country.

I spent my final days in England bidding farewell to friends and acquaintances; I said good-bye to Mr Chamberlain and other members of the British Cabinet and on a given morning Mr Cooper and I were flown from Heston to Paris.

As we crossed the Channel there was a convoy steaming along, escorted by destroyers and protected from air attacks by Spitfires racing overhead—the most warlike scene of the war, thus far.

We stayed over in Paris to get our passports and, accompanied by one of our legation officials, we did such sightseeing as was possible under existing conditions.

I paid six francs to view Napoleon's tomb in the Invalides and when I got to the circular balustrade, the entire tomb was covered with sandbags and there was nothing to see except, in the distance, the concierge who had sold me the ticket. He had a broad grin on his face.

We motored out to Versailles, walked through Père Lachaise looking for the grave of Héloise and Abelard, and listened to Maurice Chevalier and Josephine Baker, the famous negro actress, in a fifth-rate comedy, at a fifth-rate theatre (the others were closed down).

In order to reach Lisbon one had to go by rail via Spain and therefore, when all was ready, we started off one evening from the Gare d'Austerlitz. Travelling through the night we found ourselves at Hendaye by dawn, a small coastal town not more than a few hundred yards from the Spanish border.

As the railway bridge across the river had been blown up during the civil war, we disembarked. We had no trouble on the French side. After replying to a few questions we were allowed to stow our baggage in an ancient taxi and we trundled down to where a temporary wooden bridge spanned the stream.

Half-way across was a barrier with scores of Spanish soldiers and officials, wearing glazed cocked hats and long cloaks. Whilst in Paris I had taken the precaution to obtain a document from the Spanish Embassy requesting all and sundry to facilitate my journey. The minute was an imposing one with large red seals and with General Franco's name in heavy lettering at the top. I thought all difficulties would vanish at its appearance, but things worked out differently. When I exhibited the parchment, it was carefully scrutinised and handed round by customs officers and soldiers for voluble discussion. Then it was taken away for half an hour to some military post during which time we were ordered not to leave the car, and to make sure, a number of soldiers with bayoneted rifles stood guard and several climbed into the car and sat themselves down beside us. At length we were taken to another bureau for further questioning, then to Irun, a town mostly in ruins, where we were handed, still closely guarded, from one official to another for interrogation. I had several times to produce the ambassadorial *exequatur* and I had to sign numberless forms specifying my origin, destination, and reasons for entering the country, etc, etc. My inquisition lasted from seven o'clock in the morning until long after midday by which time, I suppose, I was given up for a fool and a dolt and was at length released.

I succeeded in hiring a car which took us to San Sebastian from which town we managed that night to obtain accommodation on a south-bound train.

Next day every time there was a halt, the passengers were commanded to line up on the platform and once again we were questioned, our baggage opened for examination, and our money counted.

It was a humiliating business, and as we journeyed past cities famed in history— Salamanca, Alcantara, Valladolid—I felt like hating the Spaniards; but I remembered the ordeal they had been passing through and I said to myself they were probably living on their nerves and one should make allowances.

At all events, late that afternoon, at Valencia, as I was once more queued up for another interrogation, a train drew in from the opposite direction. It consisted of an engine, a dining car and a luxurious coach and it had been sent by the Portuguese Government to meet me. Highly placed officers were on board and after they had spoken to the minions on the platform a sudden change came over the scene. Now, as we walked along, the Spanish officials, from having been arrogant and hectoring, became obsequious, and they bowed and scraped and saluted as we climbed into our new quarters.

The train was backed, and in a few minutes we were speeding away to the Portuguese frontier under happier auspices. Instead of insults and lawless soldiery, we were in the company of gentlemen. Dr Saldanha, their leader, was a direct descendant of the Portuguese navigator who had been the first to climb Table Mountain at the Cape in 1572 and the others were men of equal standing.

I was glad of it—on our joint Portuguese border in Southern Africa there is not a fort or a soldier and we have never quarrelled, and I liked to think that I was to represent my country among them.

We reached Lisbon at seven o'clock that evening. A surprise awaited me. I was met by the British Ambassador and by several members of the Portuguese Cabinet; the square outside the station was lined with thousands of troops and a multitude of onlookers. As I alighted a salute of guns boomed forth, the first time in my life I had been thus honoured, and as we emerged, I was greeted with vociferous cheering, the battalions saluted, and massed military bands came into action.

I was put up at the Aviz Hotel, a marble palace originally built by some newspaper magnate—the most sumptuous place I have ever seen. I was assigned two reception rooms, study, bedroom, and a Roman bath almost big enough to swim in.

The days that followed were pleasant and active. I was fêted and banqueted; I was taken to Cintra, Rio Frio and other show places. I had dinner with President Carmona, a magnificent affair, and I had long conferences with Dr Salazar, the man who recreated Portugal from the chaos of ten years ago; I sat in council with Dr Machado and various Cabinet Ministers and with Sir Walford Selby, the British Ambassador; I saw the graves of Vasco da Gama, Bartholomew Diaz and Camoëns; I visited museums and art galleries and Moorish castles, the curious statue of Adamastor, the hall of coaches, historic buildings, cathedrals and many things of interest.

Everyone called me 'Your Excellency' or 'Votre Excéllence' a title I never got quite used to, but there was no escaping it, and etiquette demanded that as a state guest I was to walk on the right hand of any Minister or other dignitary who happened to be escorting me. Also, I was tipped that it was 'not done' to open the door of a motor-car myself—I had to wait until an attendant performed this office for me and only then was I free to step out.

During my stay in Lisbon, news came of stout-hearted defence by the Finns against

Russia. I could see that Portugal viewed the European situation uneasily, but here too I was on a confidential errand so I cannot say more about my visit than that I was royally entertained and I formed what I hope will be lasting friendships in this pleasant country.

When my task was finished I had to think of returning to South Africa. In wartime it was not so easy. I could have returned by sea to England and from there to Capetown, but sailings were uncertain and I might be delayed for weeks. An alternative was to make for Gibraltar in the hope of being taken to Alexandria in some British warship and then by air up the Nile. This too was an uncertain route and Mr Cooper worked out a more imaginative itinerary. He came to me with a suggestion, supported by maps and timetables, that by doubling back through Spain via Madrid and Barcelona to Marseilles, we could board an Air-France machine to Algiers and then go across the Sahara Desert to Brazzaville, the capital of French Equatorial Africa.

The idea appealed to me but I asked him how we were to get from Brazzaville to the Union. I thought he was stumped but he returned to the charge next day. He said our air mail plied from Windhoek in the south-west territory to Loanda in Portuguese West Africa and we could cable a request for a machine to fetch us. Acting on his advice a message was despatched to Pretoria and General Smuts wired to say that an aeroplane would be sent to meet me at the Congo river.

The Portuguese Government now very kindly placed a car at my disposal for the first leg of the journey to Marseilles and in order to avoid a repetition of the previous annoyance from Spanish soldiers and officious officials, Senhor Saldanha was deputed to accompany me. I invited Colonel Pienaar, our Minister Plenipotentiary, to join me and Mr Cooper and Miguel, our driver, a queer old character who in his day had been an all-in wrestler of considerable fame, made up the party.

I took formal leave of President Carmona, Dr Machado, the other Ministers, the British Ambassador (who was lying in bed with a broken jaw) and many other friends and at daybreak one morning we set out; we crossed the Tagus on a pontoon and travelling through the lovely Portuguese countryside reached the Spanish frontier by eleven am.

Thanks to Senhor Saldanha, the formalities of crossing into Spain took less than twenty minutes instead of eight hours as on the former occasion; and on behalf of the Union of South Africa I sent a long telegram to the President of Portugal thanking him and his administration for their kindness to me.

We went on. Soon we were passing through Badajoz with its famous breach where Sir George Grey's father was killed in 1806.

When this fortress was captured recently by Franco's troops there were, I was told, horrible scenes of massacre and executions.

Our road took us by Talavera and Merida, and we saw picturesque castles and towers dating from Moorish times and the ruins of Roman bridges and aqueducts. These parts were more or less unspoilt by the civil war, but everyone seemed poverty stricken and listless and I did not see a decently clad man, woman or child anywhere in Spain. Tea, coffee, sugar and bread were not to be had; shops were empty and the few cars we passed were incredibly dilapidated; as a rule their windows were broken and sacking was used instead of glass.

Once, as we were going through a town, one of these cars coming down a side street rammed us and smashed the rear mudguard of our Buick, to the despair of old Miguel. The driver of the offending museum-piece explained that he had no brakes at all so he had to descend any incline in low gear, a precaution he had omitted on this occasion.

At intervals were huge collections of derelict cars, buses and lorries, each about a thousand strong, and I was told that these had transported the local Red armies in their last stand near the frontier. They were too far gone for salvage.

Refugees were moving along the roads, pushing barrows and handcarts containing their belongings. They were Reds returning from Portugal where they had found sanctuary up to now. The weather was bitterly cold and I noticed that towards dark these unfortunate people halted in the lee of the stone walls round the fields for shelter from the wind and there they crouched and shivered through the night.

The country beyond Badajoz was more or less unscarred, but when we neared Madrid, the scene was changed. We crossed a snow-covered mountain chain and beyond that, towns and villages were in ruins; bridges had been destroyed and lines of trenches ran out of sight on either hand. The actual approaches to Madrid and the suburbs were heaps of rubble and we had to make frequent detours to avoid fallen masonry that blocked the road. The bridge over the Manzanes, the gateway to the capital, was lying in the water below, so we had to make a long turn with entire blocks burnt out; and there were deep craters where bombs had torn up the streets.

The people looked depressed and one sensed an undercurrent of hatred from their bitter looks as they eyed each other.

We spent a night at the Ritz, said once to have been the finest hotel in Europe, but now doors hung awry, there were no locks or latches, the carpets were worn and the whole place reeked of decay. Meals were served in a magnificently proportioned diningroom, but consisted chiefly of goats' meat—no bread, no sugar, milk, tea or coffee. Many of the guests were Moorish officers and there were Moorish troops on the streets.

A supporter of the Franco régime told me a grisly tale. He said during the first weeks of the troubles the Reds had seen red in Madrid. They killed every policeman they could find as these were considered to be hostile to the revolution. They were stripped and eviscerated and the naked corpses were hung on the flesh hooks of every butcher shop, exposed to public view beside the carcasses of cattle and sheep. He told me further that in the courtyard of the Cuartel de la Montagne (a military barracks) the Reds herded a hundred and twenty loyalist officers and machine-gunned the lot. Then they forced the city photographers to make pictures of the scene for distribution among the public.

In the evening paper was an account of the reburial that morning of one hundred and two Nationalist officers shot by the Reds at Almeida.

From Madrid we went to Saragossa. All along our route the villages were as completely ruined as those in the devastated zone in France during the Great War and shell-pitted trenches criss-crossed in every direction. These parts had been held by the Reds for three years and it looked as if the country was not yet pacified, for we met squadrons of cavalry on patrol and long convoys of mule carts driven by angry-looking peasants with soldiers in charge. We gathered that the troops were forcibly requisitioning supplies though they could not have been very successful as this area was largely derelict. Towards Saragossa we found the road crowded with military lorries, the drivers of which seemed to take a malignant pleasure in refusing our faster car the right of way. When we hooted for them to let us pass they would look back and seeing us, they deliberately started to zig-zag to prevent us from overtaking them, grinning at our furious shouts. So it is not surprising that we made slow progress.

We stopped at a military depot to replenish our petrol tank, and I watched the procedure. Lorry after lorry drew to the pumps and filled up, giving no chit or voucher, and so little supervision was exercised that each time the nozzle was withdrawn a gallon or two of petrol was squirted on the ground. A looker-on, probably an ex-Red, whispered to me that they were doing a roaring trade by filling and emptying and refilling their lorries and selling the petrol to civilians. When at last our turn came old Miguel took as many litres as the receptacle of his Buick would hold and when we paid and asked for a receipt the soldier at the handle glared angrily at us for trying to disturb the happy-go-lucky system in vogue.

From Saragossa to Barcelona we went through country heavily fought over. The bridges were down, towns and villages were destroyed, and we saw fresh graveyards with hosts of wooden crosses like those I remembered behind the lines in France. The inhabitants of the region were chiefly anti-Franco. They looked downtrodden and resentful, but at a few kind words they would break into laughter and jokes.

At one place we were held up at a river. The bridge had been damaged but some workmen were repairing it. A score of military lorries were likewise held up, for the overseer refused to let them pass while he was jacking a sunken girder into place. Dr Saldanha walked forward and explained to him that we were South Africans on our way to catch an aeroplane at Marseilles and if we were delayed we might miss the connection.

He was adamant at first, but after considering our predicament he gave way, though he said it might lose him his job. There came cat-calls and jeers from the military drivers who were not allowed to pass, but when I offered him five hundred francs as a *solatium* he refused with dignity, and I could only prevail on him to accept twenty francs for distribution among his workmen.

From Saragossa we continued to Barcelona on the Mediterranean coast. The place had been heavily battered during the disturbances and the sea front in especial was in ruins. From Barcelona, next day, we went north. At first the road runs almost on the beach for a number of miles and then it turns inland. All this country is strongly pro-Red and Franco was not taking any chances for everywhere troops were marching and counter-marching.

In most places the bridges had been dynamited by the Red armies during their final retreat to the French border and frequently we had to leave the main road to make our way along muddy *routes vicinales*, so we lost much time.

On every hand was evidence of the passage of the defeated Red armies. To them it must have been a *via dolorosa*. Dead cars and lorries and buses strewed the way and every town and village had been reduced to rubble.

Shortly before we came to the frontier there lay the world's biggest scrapheap. There must have been fifteen to twenty thousand motor vehicles of every description, all smashed or rendered useless by the Reds before they crossed over into France, and

I was told that nearly a hundred thousand refugees had gone by.

At a small post in the Pyrenees we had a last encounter with Spanish officialdom, but thanks to Saldanha and Colonel Pienaar we were not delayed above an hour. Then the Civil Guard gave us their salute by placing their hands over their hearts, and before long we were on French soil once more.

The first place we reached on the other side was Perpignan where again we saw a great pile of cars that had been abandoned by refugees flying before the nationalist troops. We ran short of petrol here and as rationing was strict, garage owners refused to sell us any without a permit. I went to see the local Prefect and when I told him who I was he surprised me by producing a telegram from Marshal Pétain, then French Ambassador at Madrid, requesting that I should receive every assistance and be given as much petrol as I wanted.

After we had left Madrid the old gentleman apparently sat down and worked out how far we would get under the existing petrol restrictions. He must have concluded that by the time we made Perpignan we would be running low and he probably anticipated that we would appeal to the Prefect, so had kindly wired him.

I was told in Madrid that Marshal Pétain was a defeatist in the sense that he thought France was rotten to the core on account of her political divisions and that she would be unable to put up a prolonged fight. He was not an admirer of Hitler and the Nazis, but he believed the Italian fascist system was suited to the temperament of his people.

We went by Arles and Nîmes and other old-world towns to Marseilles where we spent the night. I am a good linguist. I say it without boasting for I am aware that the faculty of picking up languages is a knack which some people have and others haven't. It certainly is not a sign of great intellect and a waiter in any continental restaurant will talk six or eight languages where a much abler man may speak only one or two.

However that may be, the morning after our arrival at Marseilles I walked down to a kiosk to get a supply of the latest newspapers as the Portuguese and Spanish journals I had brought with me were indefinite as to the Finnish war and the trend of recent events. I purchased several French and Italian papers as well as a London *Times* and a *Haagsche Post*, and armed with these I returned to the hotel. On a table in the lounge I spread out the papers to read up the news and to compare it with the contents of my Portuguese and Spanish issues.

Two English visitors who had been sitting there walked out after a while and as they went I heard one of them remark, 'By Jove, that fellow seems to know a lot of languages.' 'Yes,' said the other offhandedly, 'I suppose he's one of those Cook's guides who show the tourists around.'

V

Dr Saldanha and Colonel Pienaar and old Miguel now left us on their long return to Lisbon and Mr Cooper and I started on a much longer journey. We crossed the Mediterranean in a French aeroplane on a non-stop flight to Algiers. We saw the Balearic Isles below and only one small ship all the way.

At Algiers I was met by consuls and officials, including Lord and Lady Dillon who, as far as I could make out, seemed to be doing liaison work between the French African troops and the British Army. The place was crowded with soldiers; foreign legionaries, Turcos, Spahis, and members of other picturesque regiments, in baggy trousers and burnous. They spoke bravely and were in high spirits, but the subsequent collapse of France must have left them in a sad plight.

Lord Dillon brought me details of the naval action in which the German pocket battleship *Graf von Spee* was knocked about and had to seek refuge in Montevideo harbour.

From Algiers we flew straight across the Sahara Desert by Air-France in three days. In spite of having been taken for 'a man from Cook's' I shall not turn the journey into a Baedeker but I made note of our itinerary: On the first day our course went via El-Golea, Anolef and Aguel-Hog to Gao on the river Niger (eight hours fifty minutes flying time). These places are oases, each situated hundreds of miles from the next, and the surrounding country is an abomination of desolation; nothing to see, nothing grows, and there is no living thing. How human beings ever found those waters is a mystery.

Next day we flew to Zinder and Fort Lami on a broad river flowing into Lake Chad which we could see in the distance. Both these places looked as if they had stepped out of Ouida or out of PC Wren's novels. (Four hours forty-eight minutes flying time. Dreary country underfoot all the way.) The river at Fort Lami is wider than the Zambezi, yet I had never heard of its existence until now.

From Fort Lami via Fort Archimbault and Bangui to Brazzaville on the Congo. (Flying time six hours fifty-two minutes.) The Governor of the Province accompanied us from Bangui. He was a full-blooded negro from Martinique, and French officers and civilians showed him the utmost deference and guards of honour stood to the salute as he passed. He was accompanied by a field-marshal or something, a local aborigine, a dear old fellow, his face all tattooed with tribal marks but in close-fitting French uniform, képi, sword and many decorations.

Brazzaville is the capital of French Equatorial Africa and across the river is Leopoldville, the capital of the Belgian Congo with Stanley Pool, a wide island-dotted stretch in between.

General Smuts had cabled a promise to send an aeroplane to fetch me at Leopoldville so we chartered a motor boat and we were ferried across.

In Leopoldville I met the Governor General, the British Consul, *M le Maire* and other magnates. Our plane was not due for some days and in the meanwhile we were hospitably entertained. We were motored along the Stanley Rapids—an amazing sight, amazingly little known—two hundred miles of pitching, tossing river on which no ship or boat could survive for ten minutes. I was shown phases of native life and examples of what the Belgians are doing to uplift them.

Within short reach of Leopoldville there are cannibal tribes. I was told by a Belgian anthropologist who worked in a clinic I visited that no African eats human beings for food. He does so as a ritual, just as our own natives in the Union eat parts of a lion in order to gain strength and courage, and just as our witch doctors order the killing of people to enable them to distil medicine and charms from certain organs of the body. In the same way, so-called cannibals eat portions of a slain enemy to acquire strength and merit and as a sign of victory but, said he, the idea that anywhere in the world there was cannibalism in the accepted sense of the term is erroneous!

While I was at Leopoldville we received news that the *Graf von Spee* was scuttled and that her commander had shot himself in Buenos Aires.

I remember that during the last war I had seen a picture in a German paper of a tablet erected to Graf von Spee and his two sons who perished in the battle of the Falklands:

> *Im tiefsten atlantischen Ozean*
> *liegen drei Deutsche Helden;*
> *liegen drei Grafen von Spee.*

The end of this Graf von Spee was less heroic.

The Belgian administration placed a river steamer at my disposal in which I recrossed the Congo to Brazzaville to make a state call on the Governor General of French Equatoria. He was very deaf and one had to speak into a sort of battery standing on his deck. Everyone was very courteous and attentive.

I toyed with the plan of cancelling the aeroplane and going up the Congo instead but as this would have involved several weeks of delay I decided against it so we waited in patience. In the fullness of time we saw a speck in the sky, and a large Junker sent by General Smuts sat down on the aerodrome, piloted by Captain Madeley, a son of our Minister for Labour.

He flew me from Leopoldville to Loanda, the capital of Portuguese Angola. Here, again, I was met by the Governor General of the Province and for the second time in my life I was honoured with a salute of guns. I was sumptuously installed in the Governor's Residency and in the afternoon I was shown round Loanda with the old fort and interesting chapel.

There was an official dinner that night which started at nine pm and ended at midnight; a somewhat trying function after a long day. Next morning we took off early and flew down the coast to Mossamedes, thence to Lobito Bay. Ceremonial receptions were held at both places. At Lobito Bay were two German steamers that had run in for shelter when the war broke out. As far as I know they are still rotting there.

From Lobito Bay we continued, still hugging the beach until we reached the mouth of the Kunene River, and then we turned inland across the Kaokoveld which I explored seventeen years ago.

During that expedition I had struck the river far inland at a point where it was a mighty stream, flowing broad and strong among wooded islands teeming with big game and at night I heard the sound of a distant waterfall. I told myself at the time that some day I would navigate a longboat up the coast and I would do what no man had ever done before—sail across the bar and work my way up the Kunene, where elephant were standing on palm-fringed banks and hippo and crocodile splashing in undiscovered country.

Now my plan was being realised, but not as I had dreamed, for although I was crossing the bar of the river and was about to cruise up along its pathway I found that no one could take a longboat inside nor could he sail beside elephant on its palm-fringed banks and hippo and crocodile splashing in its waters, for the simple reason that the Kunene during its final sixty miles to the ocean loses itself in the 'Namib', the desert belt that stretches northward from the Orange River for a thousand miles; and thus it reaches the sea a mere trickle scarce six inches wide on which a child's toy ship could hardly keep afloat.

We went up the river for fifty or sixty miles. It was mostly dry except for an occasional waterhole, though there was probably an underground flow beneath the sand. Afterwards we branched away south-east over the Kaokoveld and I was able to pick up landmarks I still remembered. The Kaokoveld has largely retained its isolation. But our air service from Windhoek to Lobito Bay and Loanda necessitated an intermediate aerodrome which has been laid out within a mile or two of Cabrito's village where I obtained horses for my journey long ago. Once a week a machine flies over the country and the Mahimba serfs and their Herero overlords in the neighbourhood have grown so accustomed to these strange creatures that they barely look up when one passes overhead.

We landed at the drome to take in petrol—it was in charge of a ranger who, with his wife and small child, are the only Europeans in the whole of the Kaokoveld. He told me that there are many white rhinos and if this be true, it is a fact unknown to our scientists in the Union.

On taking off I asked the pilot to make a turn to bring us over the Etosha Pan for I was anxious to see it. The Etosha Pan is a shallow depression about eighty miles by eighty (I should say). In the winter it is dry, but in the rainy season it stands three to four inches under water. Whether there is some chemical substance in the soil or some type of vegetation that attracts the fauna I do not know, but thousands of wildebeest, gemsbok (oryx) and other antelopes are always teeming in and around the Pan.

It is said that game animals, being nimble and lightfooted, move on its surface wet or dry without getting bogged, but that no human being has ever successfully crossed it and one hears legends of hunters who tried to do so and were never heard of again. One tale runs of a party of Boer hunters who set out with a string of ox wagons to hunt far out on the Pan and they too disappeared from ken.

I had not seen the Pan before so I looked down on it with interest. We flew low; the entire area was under water and there were herds of game splashing their way through, or grazing in all directions round its margin. At one spot I noticed two gemsbok rams fighting. A gemsbok is said to possess the most formidable horns of any antelope. These are three to four feet long, sharp-pointed, and straight as a sword. There is a popular theory that even lion give the oryx a wide berth for fear of being impaled. Nevertheless, these two animals charged and butted, and, it seemed to me, tried to savage each other with their teeth, making no attempt to use their horns.

Perhaps it is out of place here to interpolate a theory of my own, but I believe that the horns of antelope, and of all the *bovidae*, are not weapons of defence or offence at all, but are evolved on some sexual basis. With the exception of the gemsbok, the sable and one or two other species that have straight stabbing horns (perhaps a biological fluke) the great majority of antelope have lyre-shaped horns or horns with their points corkscrewed or twisted in upon themselves. If Nature intended horns to be fighting implements I can hardly conceive of anything less suited to the purpose than those of buffalo, wildebeest, koodoo, waterbuck, *impala*, blesbok, springbok, sassaby, hartebeest and the rest, to say nothing of the absurd hat-racks adorning the heads of

European and American deer.

A buffalo will kill a foe by pounding him with the curved bosses of his horns and not with their points, and the lesser *capridae* depend on speed to elude their enemies. Their horns may be of use in clearing twigs and branches from their eyes as they flee through thorn and scrub, but in a fight they would be a let and a hindrance. Another consideration is that if Nature intended antelopes to defend themselves with their horns, it is at least curious that in so many cases the males are magnificently provided with spiralled and curved appendages while the females, upon whom devolves the duty of defending their young, are in this respect left defenceless.

However, this is a digression. Having circled over the Etosha Pan and having looked down at the old German fort at Namutoni, we touched in at Outjo, an outpost village, to fuel, and that evening we landed at Windhoek, the capital of the South-West Territory which we took in 1915. My unheralded arrival caused some local excitement and I was detained far into the night talking to eager listeners.

I think Mr Cooper and I are the only South Africans who have flown the Sahara Desert along the route we had taken. Moreover, I do not know of anyone who has travelled from England to South Africa as we had, for there was no air communication with the Belgian Congo and we had only been enabled to do it by the aid of the machine General Smuts had sent to bridge the gap between Leopoldville and Angola.

From Windhoek we started on the home run, flying down the south-west barrens to Upington and from there to Johannesburg, and so ended this entrancing journey.

VI

For several months after my return from England the war seemed to hang fire and then, in April 1940, the storm broke.

I remember that I had gone up to the Transvaal to open a new irrigation scheme among the Barberton mountains, and as I was about to perform the ceremony before a large audience, I heard a shout. I looked up and saw a runaway motor-car tearing down the slope straight into the crowd; it killed and wounded a number of people and I was hurled clean over a fence.

That night at the hospital I heard a woman's voice from out of the dark say that news had come on the wireless of German warships steaming up the coast to invade Norway and during the next few days came news of the fighting at Stavanger, Trondjhem, and elsewhere. Soon followed the rape of Belgium and Holland, the fall of France, the declaration of war by the Italians and the grave plight of the British army in Flanders.

We were kept advised of the position from London each day. The British Government cabled us at first that they hoped to evacuate 20 000 men to England. Next day they spoke of 40 000, and the day after that they even spoke of saving 80 000. Then came the epic of Dunkirk and the bringing away of almost the whole of the expeditionary force.

Out here in South Africa, we too were faced by what seemed to be a dangerous situation. Italy had 200 000 soldiers in Abyssinia and we expected an immediate move to invade Kenya, and in due course our own country, for at the time there was little to stop them. Kenya had a few battalions of Askari and as for a South African army it had existed largely on paper when the war began, though General Smuts was feverishly at work building up a new one, and volunteers were flocking to the colours.

In the meantime the Afrikaner racial extremists openly exulted at the British reverses. In Parliament and over the countryside they shouted that England was but a twitching corpse, that Hitler would dictate his peace terms in London within six weeks; the British Empire was crumbling and they were going to establish an Afrikaner dictatorship in which General Smuts and his followers were to be called to account on Gestapo lines.

And a strange movement had sprung up to implement these threats. It was known as the '*Ossewa Brandwag*' (the ox-wagon picket). Its members, which were said to number a quarter of a million, drilled secretly at night, and they indulged in bomb throwing, sabotage and other subversive acts quite foreign to the normal character of our Afrikaans people. Their avowed intention was to prepare an organisation modelled on the Nazi system which would take control the moment word came that Great Britain was crushed.

General Smuts and I and most of our colleagues took the view that in the long run our Afrikaans-speaking citizens were too level-headed to be permanently led astray by alien propaganda of this kind. From long experience we felt that in a country like the Union it would be a mistake to create cheap martyrs so we gave the '*Ossewa Brandwag*' and our other opponents plenty of rope. Their overdone racial fervour smacked to us of the Ju-ju and Voodooism of Lagos and the Gold Coast.

Not everyone on our side agreed with us, and there was a time when I could not show my face anywhere without some well-meaning but irate and jittery individual rushing at me to demand the shooting out-of-hand of every '*Ossewa Brandwag*' firebrand and the instant gaoling of all opposition Members of Parliament and political leaders!

General Smuts told me he suffered from similar importunities and that his invariable reply was, 'Leave it to us, leave it to us; we know what we are doing, please don't rock the boat.'

Time has amply justified us. Now (in 1943) the '*Ossewa Brandwag*' has practically fizzled out and the various republican groups that sprang up in the hope of an immediate German victory are at present so busy wrangling among themselves that we scarcely give them a thought.

All along, I have striven to avoid as far as possible overmuch reference to our inter-tribal stupidities, but I was forced to touch on them here and there for the sake of giving an idea of the South African political background. I have only this final word on the subject. Our white population is under three millions. Of these, roughly 55 per cent are of Dutch descent, and 40 to 45 per cent are of British extraction. Of the Dutch section about half are standing aloof from our war effort. They hold that the war is in the interest of Great Britain alone, that it is none of our business and that we had no right to drag them into the maelstrom.

And yet, in an army of volunteers, something like 35 per cent of our soldiers and 35 per cent of our casualties in Abyssinia and Libya have been Afrikaners.

And there is another list, which it may be lacking in good taste and subtlety to call a casualty list. It is the notices of engagements and marriages between Dutch and

English couples that appear in the newspapers every day. These show that they are intermingling and inter-marrying all the time in rising tempo and by 1960 or thereabouts even the racial politicians will not be able to tell them apart. So much for local politics as I see them.

All this time, General Smuts was hard at work, and in spite of our small population and our racial differences he produced the strongest army in our history, with more than 200 000 men in the field. They went first to Kenya for the expected Italian onslaught and when that did not materialise they went to Abyssinia.

In a short and brilliant campaign some 40 000 British and South African troops sent a vastly greater Italian army into headlong flight. As for our men: I was told that an Italian army document was picked up which read, 'The Italian troops are retreating in good order. The South African troops are advancing in the wildest confusion.' This was probably just what did take place.

In our campaign in German West in 1915 General Botha's shaggy horsemen came galloping through the bush with no semblance of discipline but relentlessly hustling their opponents. Hauptmann Francke, the German commander-in-chief, was so outraged by their breach of military decorum that he flung up his arms to heaven and exclaimed, 'This is not a war; it is a hippodrome!' But inside of a week he and all his men were prisoners.

It was like the story of the British soldier in the Crimean War. He lay in hospital with a sabre cut across his skull. A kindhearted old lady asked him how he had come by his hurts and he said, 'It was like this, Mum. The Roosians don't know about fighting. I rides at one of them there Cossacks with me sword and I gives him the thrust. Instead of giving me the parry, the bloody fool 'its me over the 'ead.'

Our soldiers in Abyssinia paraphrased Mr Churchill's famous speech by saying: 'Never before have so few done so much to so many,' and that, in short, is a good account of what happened. When the campaign was over, the South African troops went to Libya where they fought with unvarying fortitude.

John and Michael have been in the thick of it. They joined as private soldiers. How John got into the army with one hand and one eye I do not know.

I passed the Johannesburg drill hall one morning and in a long queue of volunteers I noticed him half-way up the line. I pretended not to see him and at lunch-time he told me that he had been accepted and that he was to report to a training camp next day. I have been told that when he was asked how he got into the army as a private he said it was 'through family influence.'

We have a coloured woman named Louisa who does the family washing. In camp John had to do his own laundry and he found it hard work. When he came home on his first leave he said to his mother, 'Mummy, I have come to the conclusion that we are scandalously underpaying old Louisa.' He went on to serve in Libya and escaped out of Tobruk just before its fall by a lucky chance. Michael is a fighter-pilot in the South African Air Force, and he too is in Libya.

As for myself, my age debars me from active service, but I have not been idle. As a sort of junior War Lord, with a seat on Councils and Committees dealing with munitions, supplies and other matters, I move about a great deal. Twice General Smuts sent me on confidential errands to the Portuguese Governor General of Mozambique, and he and I flew over his territory looking down on herds of elephant and big game, while we discussed matters of common interest.

And General Smuts and I and Sir Pierre van Ryneveld (who flew me to Zululand long ago) made a long reconnaissance flight to Ovampoland and to the mouth of the Kunene River in connection with our defences. Winging down the Kunene we saw the curiously striated Zebra Mountains and an immense canyon which disappears underground at one point to reappear nearer the river. It comes in on the left bank and I think an expedition to look into this would repay investigation. The canyon can easily be recognised by the curious serrated filigree of its edges. I doubt whether anyone except the occupants of our plane has ever seen this strange phenomenon.

I revisited the Okovango Swamps by air once more, on military observance, and I saw what has not been seen in human memory. This was the Botletle River in flood right down to the Makarikari, with the natives building fish traps far below Rakops. As for the Makarikari, it was a vast sheet of water, eighty to a hundred miles wide, where previously I had seen it only as a sunbaked pan of salt. Professor Schwarz's dream had come true at last and the great depression was full, but it has had no effect whatsoever on our rainfall.

The King of Greece who had escaped from the débâcle of Crete arrived in this country with some of his entourage and I took them into the Low Country. The two Greek Princesses Royal camped on Sandringham and they greatly enjoyed the experience of spending a few nights in the open among the lion.

After that I accompanied General de Bettencourt, the Portuguese Governor-General, also into the Low Country—it is a good place for quiet talks away from prying eyes. And I made another military journey to Ovampoland and the Kunene River, going overland this time. On the upward journey we followed the old route through the Kalahari Desert along the dry beds of the Kuruman and the Oop rivers seeing thousands of gemsbok (oryx). Thence we travelled up through Windhoek and via the Etosha Pan to Ondangua, the administrative centre of Ovampoland (three houses and a store).

On the return journey we followed the left bank of the Kunene River as far as Zwartbooi Drift, the port of entry into Angola (one hut), passing the Rua Cana falls on our way. From Zwartbooi Drift we travelled south through the Kaokoveld where I sojourned of old. Many hundreds of its Mahimba, naked savages in my time, have joined the army and are now in uniform, five thousand miles to the north.

When at length we returned to Windhoek I had much to do. I visited Swakopmund and Walvis Bay to see the coastal defences, and I met the Herero chiefs. Their home is in the mountains north of Windhoek and the Hereros remember the cruelty of the German regime when so many of them, men, women and children, were chased into the desert to perish. When they were told what was wanted of them their leader stood up and said, 'Is it the Germans you wish us to fight? Show us the road, show us the road.'

I recently inspected over three thousand of them in the Transvaal, all magnificently trained and proud of their bearing, and all straining at the leash.

I have been to Rhodesia on army matters, and was flown from centre to centre, from camp to camp, by Lord Douglas Hamilton.

Several times I camped on Sandringham and on such occasions as I was able to reach the Cape Peninsula I fished on the Bay. But, alas, without John and Michael, for the happy days when we were able to live among the game and sail on *Lucky Jim* lie far behind.

On one of these visits, I had an unpleasant encounter with a lion on Sandringham. Going after partridges one evening with my shotgun, I saw a small kingfisher caught in a native trap. It was fluttering in the air, one leg held by a piece of string attached to a reed. I stood my gun against the river bank and walked forward to release the bird. As it flew away I caught sight of an enormous lion crouching about five or six yards away, looking very much as if he meant to spring. I backed out slowly and by the time I reached the shotgun, the lion had backed out too.

During the many times General Smuts has gone to Egypt and Libya to visit his troops he has left me in charge of South Africa. Once, while he was absent, British naval craft brought in several Vichy ships intercepted on the Madagascar route, and I interned the ships and their crews and the six hundred troops they contained. The local French plenipotentiary made furious protest and he told me that if I held these ships his government would see to it that all French vessels would in future be escorted by warships. But I smiled and put the whole lot on Robben Island in Table Bay, for no one cared a rap about Marshal Pétain and his government.

Many of the troops were Hovas from the Imerina. When I visited them I was able to speak to them in their own language, of which I still had a smattering from the days I lived among them nearly forty years back; and they grinned delightedly.

Having quarrelled over the seizure of the ships I placated the French Minister to some extent by lifting 70 000 bottles of wine out of one of their vessels for the use of the internees. So I had an ovation when next I visited them. General Smuts, on his return, endorsed everything I had done in this matter of internment.

In the course of my journeyings it has been a matter of quiet satisfaction to me to find that the irrigation schemes I had built are producing immense quantities of wheat and other foodstuffs, which go far towards the provisioning of the great British convoys that are sailing our coasts on their way to Egypt and India.

And now, with Russia grinding up the flower of Hitler's brave young Nazi soldiers, with America and Australia holding Japan in the Far East and with American and British troops landing in North Africa I come to a close. I realise that in comparison with the mighty events shaking the world, my narrative has small significance.

But I wrote this book because I like setting down things seen and experienced and also because I wished to prove that in spite of our racial and political squabbles, South Africa is a country of good will and good temper, and has the hope and prospect of unity into a single nation in years to come.

Consolidated Index

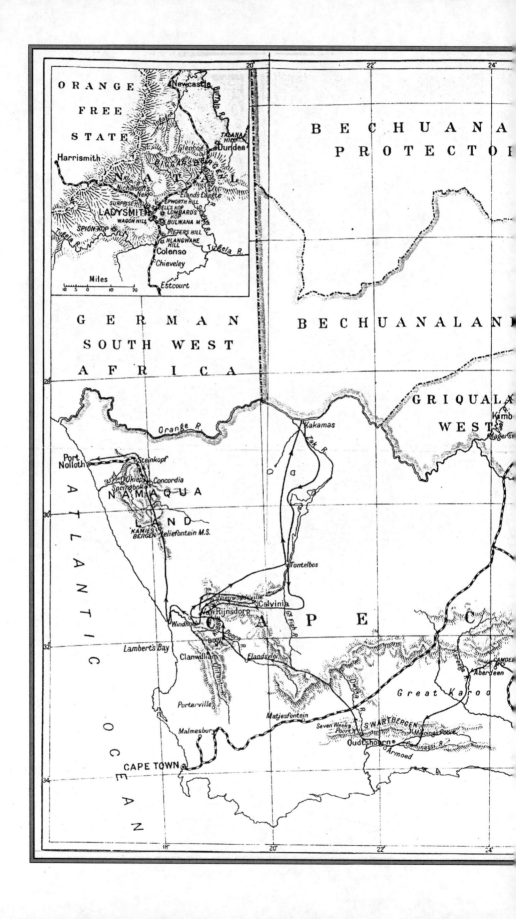

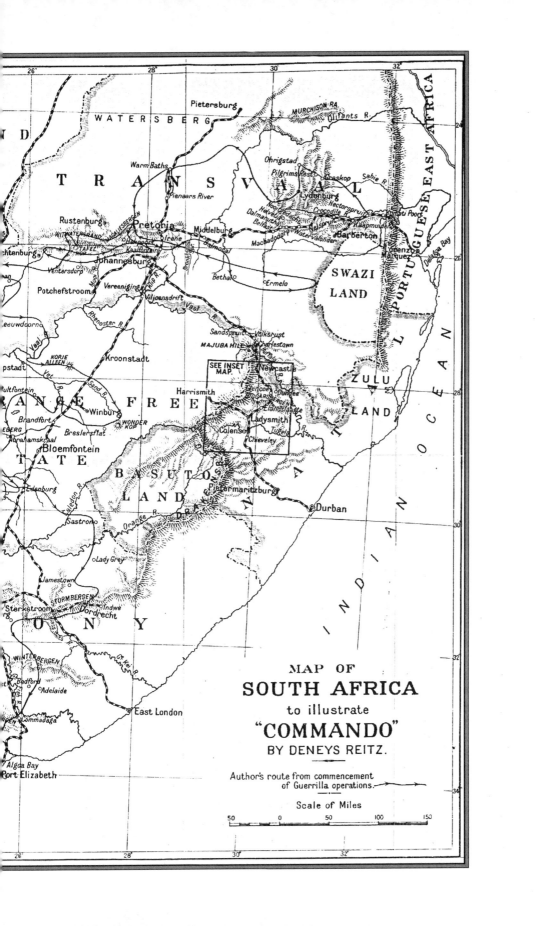

MAP OF
SOUTH AFRICA
to illustrate
"COMMANDO"
BY DENEYS REITZ.

Author's route from commencement
of Guerrilla operations.

Scale of Miles

50   0   50   100   150